ESSENTIALS OF
BUSINESS LAW

ESSENTIALS OF
BUSINESS LAW

Eighth Edition

Anthony L. Liuzzo, J.D., Ph.D.

Wilkes University
Wilkes-Barre, Pennsylvania

Connect
Learn
Succeed™

ESSENTIALS OF BUSINESS LAW

Published by McGraw-Hill, a business unit of The McGraw-Hill Companies, Inc., 1221 Avenue of the Americas, New York, NY, 10020. Copyright © 2013 by The McGraw-Hill Companies, Inc. All rights reserved. Previous editions © 1990, 2003, 2007, and 2010. Printed in the United States of America. No part of this publication may be reproduced or distributed in any form or by any means, or stored in a database or retrieval system, without the prior written consent of The McGraw-Hill Companies, Inc., including, but not limited to, in any network or other electronic storage or transmission, or broadcast for distance learning.

Some ancillaries, including electronic and print components, may not be available to customers outside the United States.

This book is printed on acid-free paper.

Printed in China

2 3 4 5 6 7 8 9 0 CTP/CTP 1 0 9 8 7 6 5 4 3

ISBN 978-0-07-351185-6
MHID 0-07-351185-4

Vice president/Director of marketing: *Alice Harra*
Publisher: *Scott Davidson*
Sponsoring editor: *Sarah Wood*
Director, digital products: *Crystal Szewczyk*
Development editor: *Vincent Bradshaw*
Marketing manager: *Kelly Curran*
Digital development editor: *Kevin White*
Director, Editing/Design/Production: *Jess Ann Kosic*
Project manager: *Jean R. Starr*
Buyer: *Susan Culbertson*
Senior designer: *Srdjan Savanovic*
Senior photo research coordinator: *Jeremy Cheshareck*
Photo researcher: *Ira Roberts*
Manager, digital production: *Janean A. Utley*
Media project manager: *Cathy L. Tepper*
Cover design: *Nathan Kirkman*
Interior design: *Gino Cieslik*
Typeface: *10/12 Times Roman*
Compositor: *Aptara®, Inc.*
Printer: *CTPS*
Cover credit: *©Robin MacDougall, Getty Images*

Credits: The credits section for this book begins on page 667 and is considered an extension of the copyright page.

Library of Congress Cataloging-in-Publication Data

Liuzzo, Anthony.
    Essentials of business law/Anthony L. Liuzzo.—8th ed.
    p. cm.
    Includes index.
    ISBN-13: 978-0-07-351185-6 (alk. paper)
    ISBN-10: 0-07-351185-4 (alk. paper)
    1. Business law—United States. 2. Commercial law—United States. I. Title.
  KF889.85.L58 2013
  346.7307—dc23

                                2011034232

The Internet addresses listed in the text were accurate at the time of publication. The inclusion of a Web site does not indicate an endorsement by the authors or McGraw-Hill, and McGraw-Hill does not guarantee the accuracy of the information presented at these sites.

www.mhhe.com

Dedication

I have thrust him bloodied down the hole,
The mirror image of my soul.
Sweating, pulsing, with battered heart,
His dead eyes staring miles apart.

He had taken control for only a time,
Causing a dimness to strained rhyme.
He had caused aberration to word and deed,
No longer to serve me but to lead.

I slew him with a mighty thrust,
Severing his heart as I knew I must.
His shape drifts away, forever lost,
An odd companion I have lost.

Alone I stand, at the door of Forever,
Knowing only that I can never
Chase away the mighty fear
Or wipe away my one last tear.

ABOUT OUR AUTHOR

Anthony L. Liuzzo, J.D., Ph.D. Dr. Anthony L. Liuzzo serves as Professor of Business and Economics and Director of the MBA and ABBA Programs at Wilkes University in Wilkes-Barre, Pennsylvania.

Dr. Liuzzo is a licensed attorney and economist. He earned his Ph.D. in business administration, Master of Philosophy in economics, and MBA in management from New York University; his law degree from St. John's University; and his bachelor's degree in marketing from Fordham University.

Specializing in public policy issues, employment law, and retail sales forecasting, he has been cited on numerous occasions in hundreds of publications, including *CNN, Forbes,* the *New York Times, USA Today,* the *New York Daily News,* the *Philadelphia Daily News,* the *Chicago Tribune,* the *Washington Times,* the *Cincinnati Enquirer,* the *Pittsburgh Post-Gazette,* the *Detroit News,* and the *San Francisco Examiner,* for his views on legal and business issues.

Prior to joining Wilkes, Dr. Liuzzo served as Editor of a scholarly journal and as Associate Professor of Economics and Finance at Manhattan College in New York City. He has been instrumental in creating several successful small businesses.

Dr. Liuzzo is a member of many professional organizations, and currently serves as a member of the Board of Directors for the Family Service Association of Wyoming Valley. He is the author of numerous books and articles that have appeared in scholarly and professional journals.

Brief CONTENTS

Contents

part 4   Commercial Paper   353

part 5   Property   393

Part 6   Business and Technology   465

part 7 Legal Environment
of Business   521

Preface

WELCOME TO *ESSENTIALS OF BUSINESS LAW*

The new, eighth edition of the *Essentials of Business Law* program is a practical, concise, and broad-based introduction to the vibrant field of business law. While continuing to offer all of the features that have made the seven prior editions successful, this new edition now includes a four-color design, new chapters on the U.S. Constitution and bankruptcy law, two new appendices, updated content, and enhanced support materials. Both the traditional areas of law, such as contracts and property, and the emerging areas of law, such as e-commerce and environmental, are covered in short, informative chapters written to capture the essence of each topic. The objective of the text throughout its coverage is ease—ease of use, ease of teaching, ease of assessment, and ease of understanding. It has been developed for those seeking a more fundamental overview of the concepts and principles that are vital to the understanding of business law. Content changes for this edition include:

PRESENTATION AND DESIGN

The design has been updated, and every page of *Essentials of Business Law* has been printed in color, making for a textbook that is modern and visually stimulating, as well as fun and easy to read. Each chapter opens with a photograph that illustrates the chapter topic, and a quote about the topic from a famous individual.

Chapter-by-chapter changes include:

CHAPTER 1

Our System of Law has been revised to expand coverage of the sources of law. Also, the sections on constitutional powers, constitutional amendments, and judicial review have been removed from this chapter because they will be covered in the new chapter on Constitutional Law (Chapter 5).

- New to this chapter: Section on treaties
- New to this chapter: Section on executive orders

CHAPTER 2

Ethics and the Law has been revised to provide more details on codes of ethics.

- New to this chapter: Discussion of stakeholders
- New to this chapter: Example of code of ethics
- New to this chapter: A sample company values statement was added as a figure

CHAPTER 3

Criminal Law has been revised to expand coverage of crimes in the business world.

- New to this chapter: Discussion of the RICO Act of 1970
- New to this chapter: Section on securities fraud

- New to this chapter: Description of Ponzi scheme
- New to this chapter: Example of Ponzi scheme

CHAPTER 4

Tort Law has been revised to provide expanded coverage of the types of negligence.

- New to this chapter: Discussion of intent regarding the tort of conversion
- New to this chapter: Section on negligence *per se*
- New to this chapter: Section on assumption of risk
- New to this chapter: Example of assumption of risk

CHAPTER 5

Constitutional Law is new to the manuscript. The chapter focuses on the following topics:

- Constitutional powers, the process used to amend the Constitution, judicial review, and the doctrine of preemption
- The commerce clause and the full faith and credit clause
- The First Amendment
- The Second Amendment
- The Fourth Amendment
- The Fifth Amendment
- The Eighth Amendment
- The Fourteenth Amendment
- The Sixteenth Amendment

CHAPTER 6

Administrative Law (previously Chapter 5) has been revised to discuss Congress's authority over administrative agencies.

- New to this chapter: Discussion of subpoena
- New to this chapter: Discussion of Congress's power to override unjust rules and regulations introduced by administrative agencies
- New to this chapter: Discussion of Congress's power to dissolve agencies

CHAPTER 7

Introduction to Contracts (previously Chapter 6) has been revised to include a discussion of the sources of contract law.

- New to this chapter: Section on the sources of contract law
- New to this chapter: Discussion of tangible personal property

CHAPTER 8

Offer and Acceptance (previously Chapter 7) has been revised to include additional ways in which an offer may be terminated.

- New to this chapter: Section on termination of an offer by death or incapacity
- New to this chapter: Description of option contract

- New to this chapter: Section on termination of an offer by destruction or illegality
- New to this chapter: Example of termination of an offer by destruction

CHAPTER 9

Mutual Agreement (previously Chapter 8) has been revised to clarify and expand the coverage of Fraud.

- New to this chapter: Expanded discussion of the requirements for fraud cases
- New to this chapter: Discussion of seller disclosure and how it may be used to avoid a case of fraud

CHAPTER 10

Consideration (previously Chapter 9) has been revised to expand discussion of agreements that lack consideration.

- New to this chapter: Section on illusory promise

CHAPTER 11

Competent Parties (previously Chapter 10) has been revised to provide more details on both minors' avoidance of contracts and liability for minors' torts and crimes.

- New to this chapter: Discussion of minors' purchase/sale of real estate under contract
- New to this chapter: Discussion of parental liability for torts committed by children

CHAPTER 12

Legal Purpose of Contracts (previously Chapter 11) has been revised to expand coverage of agreements that are made in violation of public policy.

- New to this chapter: Section on exculpatory clauses
- New to this chapter: Example of an exculpatory clause

CHAPTER 13

Form of Contracts (previously Chapter 12) has been revised to provide more details on the Parol Evidence Rule and on agreements to sell real property.

- New to this chapter: Discussion of exceptions to the Parol Evidence Rule
- New to this chapter: Discussion of an exception to the written requirement for contracts to sell real property

CHAPTER 14

Operation of Contracts, previously Chapter 13, has not been revised.

CHAPTER 15

Discharge of Contracts (previously Chapter 14) has been revised to expand coverage of termination by agreement and remedies for breach of contract.

- New to this chapter: Discussion of contract substitution
- New to this chapter: Discussion of compensatory damages

- New to this chapter: Discussion of consequential damages
- New to this chapter: Discussion of nominal damages

CHAPTER 16

Transfer of Title (previously Chapter 15) has been revised to expand discussion of rights of ownership and the specific time in which transfer of title occurs.

- New to this chapter: Discussion of a person's rights to encumber property
- New to this chapter: Discussion of a party's right to stipulate precisely when a title transfer occurs

CHAPTER 17

Sales (previously Chapter 16) has been revised to describe an additional type of sale and to provide more details on the delivery of purchased goods.

- New to this chapter: Section on consignment sales
- New to this chapter: Discussion of the risks of shipping goods
- New to this chapter: Discussion of insurable interest

CHAPTER 18

Warranties (previously Chapter 17) has been revised to provide more details on warranty disclaimers and the Magnuson-Moss Warranty Act.

- New to this chapter: Discussion of unconscionable contracts
- New to this chapter: Example of an unconscionable contract
- New to this chapter: Section on consumer remedies under the Magnuson-Moss Warranty Act

CHAPTER 19

Agency (formerly Chapter 18) has been revised to expand coverage of the creation of agency and the duties of principals to agents.

- New to this chapter: Discussion of an organization's ability to act as an agent
- New to this chapter: Discussion of principal competence
- New to this chapter: Discussion of durable power of attorney
- New to this chapter: Discussion of third-party rights/remedies in a case wherein an agent commits a tort and/or crime
- New to this chapter: Description of a gratuitous agent
- New to this chapter: Discussion of agency termination by fulfillment of the agency's purpose and by disloyalty

CHAPTER 20

Business Organizations (formerly Chapter 19) has been revised to discuss an additional type of partnership and to expand coverage of limited liability companies.

- New to this chapter: Section on limited liability partnership
- New to this chapter: Discussion of shareholder liability in the event that a corporation is set up to defraud the public

- New to this chapter: Discussion of the formation of limited liability companies
- New to this chapter: Discussion of the taxation of limited liability companies.

CHAPTER 21

Bankruptcy Law is new to the manuscript. The chapter focuses on the following topics:

- Insolvency and default
- The law of bankruptcy
- The provisions and applications of Chapter 7 of the federal bankruptcy law
- The means test and the requirement for debtor education and credit counseling under the Bankruptcy Abuse Prevention and Consumer Protection Act of 2005
- The provisions and applications of Chapter 13 of the federal bankruptcy law
- The major applications of Chapters 9, 11, 12, and 15 of the federal bankruptcy law

CHAPTER 22

Introduction to Commercial Paper (formerly Chapter 20) has been revised to expand and update coverage of regulations that effect commercial paper and the banking industry, and to describe an additional type of commercial paper.

- New to the text: Section on the Check Clearing for the 21st Century Act
- New to the text: Discussion of recovery of lost, stolen, or destroyed cashier's/certified checks pursuant to the UCC
- New to the text: Section on money orders
- New to the text: Discussion of current banking procedures
- New to the text: A more detailed discussion of postdated checks and bank liability for premature payment

CHAPTER 23

Transfer and Discharge of Commercial Paper (formerly Chapter 21) has been revised to include both an additional personal defense and an additional real defense against payment of commercial paper.

- New to this chapter: Section on breach of warranty
- New to this chapter: Section on discharge in bankruptcy

CHAPTER 24

Real and Personal Property (formerly Chapter 22) has been revised to expand coverage of rights in land other than ownership and to provide a more detailed discussion of eminent domain.

- New to this chapter: Section on profits
- New to this chapter: An illustration of a deed
- New to this chapter: Section on condemnation
- New to this chapter: Example of condemnation

CHAPTER 25

Bailments (formerly Chapter 23) has been revised to expand coverage of the characteristics of bailments and to provide a more detailed discussion of common carrier bailments.

- New to this chapter: Section on termination of bailments
- New to this chapter: Expanded discussion of a bailee's duty to care for a bailor's property
- New to this chapter: Discussion of common carrier liability for loss or damage to goods

CHAPTER 26

Landlord-Tenant Relations (formerly Chapter 24) has been revised to expand coverage of both landlord/tenant rights and the law relating to leases.

- New to this chapter: Discussion of the Fair Housing Act
- New to this chapter: Discussion of timing requirements for eviction notices
- New to this chapter: Expanded discussion of tenancy at sufferance
- New to this chapter: A more precise discussion of a landlord's requirements and rights under the warranty of habitability
- New to this chapter: Discussion of a landlord's right to retain a tenant's security deposit

CHAPTER 27

Wills, Intestacy, and Trusts (formerly Chapter 25) has been revised to provide a more precise discussion of the three topics and to provide coverage of advanced health care directives

- New to this chapter: Discussion of ademption
- New to this chapter: Discussion of the varying state requirements for holographic wills
- New to this chapter: Discussion of mental competence in relation to testamentary capacity
- New to this chapter: Section on advanced health care directives
- New to this chapter: Section on durable power of attorney for health care

CHAPTER 28

Intellectual Property (formerly Chapter 26) has been revised to discuss the Economic Espionage Act, to expand coverage of trademarks and copyrights, and to provide more relevant examples in order to stimulate classroom discussion.

- New to this chapter: Discussion of the Economic Espionage Act of 1996
- New to this chapter: Example of the Economic Espionage Act of 1996
- New to this chapter: Discussion of famous trademarks
- New to this chapter: Example of a trademark
- New to this chapter: Example of trade dress infringement
- New to this chapter: Discussion of copyright protection requirements
- New to this chapter: Example of a music copyright violation in cyberspace

CHAPTER 29

Computer Privacy and Speech (formerly Chapter 27) has been revised to update coverage of pertinent regulations.

- New to this chapter: Section on the USA Patriot Act
- New to this chapter: Discussion of the Unlawful Internet Gambling Enforcement Act of 2006
- New to this chapter: Example of internet gambling

CHAPTER 30

Conducting Business in Cyberspace (formerly Chapter 28) has been revised to update and provide more details on securities trading in cyberspace.

- New to this chapter: Section on recent trends in securities trading
- New to this chapter: Example of recent trends in the securities trading industry

CHAPTER 31

The Employer-Employee Relationship (formerly Chapter 29) has been revised to provide more coverage of applicable regulations.

- New to this chapter: Discussion of the misclassification of independent contractors as employees and the resulting consequences
- New to this chapter: Discussion of new laws that shield employers from the risk of liability for defamation related to employee references
- New to this chapter: Section on negligent misrepresentation
- New to this chapter: Section on the Fair Labor Standards Act of 1938

CHAPTER 32

Employment Law (formerly Chapter 30) has been revised to provide expanded coverage of additional employee rights granted by law.

- New to this chapter: Expanded discussion of OSHA penalties
- New to this chapter: Section on the Equal Pay Act
- New to this chapter: Discussion of the Lilly Ledbetter Fair Pay Act of 2009
- New to this chapter: Expanded discussion of the Pregnancy Discrimination Act
- New to this chapter: Section on the Family and Medical Leave Act
- New to this chapter: Section on Unemployment Benefits

CHAPTER 33

Product Liability (formerly Chapter 31) has been revised to discuss new, pertinent product regulations.

- New to this chapter: Discussion of the Tobacco Control Act
- New to this chapter: Example of the Tobacco Control Act
- New to this chapter: Expanded and updated discussion of the requirements for automakers as established by the National Highway Traffic Safety Administration (NHTSA)
- New to this chapter: Example of the requirements imposed by the NHTSA

CHAPTER 34

Professionals' Liability (formerly Chapter 32) has been revised to provide more details on liability for professional malpractice

- New to this chapter: Discussion of Good Samaritan Laws and how they may be applied to medical professionals to shield their liability for professional malpractice

CHAPTER 35

International Business Law (formerly Chapter 33) has been revised to include a section on doing business in foreign countries

- New to this chapter: Discussion of franchising in foreign countries
- New to this chapter: Section on Contracts for the International Sale of Goods (CISG)
- New to this chapter: Section on the foreign application of antitrust law
- New to this chapter: Section on the Foreign Sovereign Immunities Act

CHAPTER 36

Business and the Environment (formerly Chapter 34) has been revised to expand coverage of pertinent regulations/issues.

- New to this chapter: Discussion of discharge permits as required by the Clean Water Act
- New to this chapter: Discussion of the regulations pertaining to underground storage tanks
- New to this chapter: Discussion of the Resource Conservation and Recovery Act
- New to this chapter: Example of ocean pollution

SUPPLEMENTARY MATERIALS

Two new Appendices have been added to the book, and both documents also can be found on the Online Learning Center at www.mhhe.com/liuzzo8e.

- The Constitution of the United States has been added as Appendix A
- Article 2 of the Uniform Commercial Code has been added as Appendix B

MOBILE APPLICATIONS

For the first time, we have used content from the textbook to create a new application that you can download for your iPhone, iPad, or other mobile device. The free application is designed to give another layer of assessment, one that can be used anywhere, any time. The mobile application for *Essentials of Business Law* contains:

- An electronic flashcard exercise that features all of the key terms that appear in the eighth edition, as well as several terms that are related to the Constitution of the United States.
- Additional questions based on the content from the book. Students are encouraged to read the chapter, and then use this application to quiz themselves on their understanding of the material.

NOTE TO STUDENTS

The eighth edition of *Essentials of Business Law* covers the latest developments in the legal field. This text will help you discover a wealth of information and learning opportunities that will give you a clear understanding of business law topics. The text will also help you identify, explain, and apply the principles of business law in your daily life and in the larger world in which you live. The world of business is continually changing, especially with the advent and evolution of the global marketplace. The concepts and principles presented in the text will assist you in understanding those changes as they relate to business law.

The chapters in *Essentials of Business Law* are organized in a concise and easy-to-read way. Numerous examples applying the law to real-world situations will assist you in understanding important concepts, while key term definitions are provided throughout the text for your reference. The end-of-chapter assessments will help you apply your knowledge and gauge your understanding of the material as you progress, and the extra resources accompanying the text will provide useful and easy-to-use tools to supplement your appreciation of the material.

NOTE TO INSTRUCTORS

What sets *Essentials of Business Law* apart from other programs available is its concise organizational nature and supplementary materials. Chapters are succinct, making it simple for you to plan presentations and teach the course. Each chapter offers an abundance of assesment tools that will help you evaluate your students' progress. The new edition offers expanded coverage of current or emerging areas in the business law field, including employment, bankruptcy, e-commerce, environmental, and international law. In addition, the number of key terms has been increased to include both legal and nonlegal definitions. As a result, *Essentials of Business Law* offers you and your students the coverage of essential topics that many larger, more expensive book programs miss entirely.

The eighth edition has been expanded and updated to include a variety of teaching tools that make it simple for you to organize your classroom discussions, effectively communicate the important business law concepts in each chapter, and assess your students' grasp of the material. The book is accompanied by an Online Learning Center, complete with an Instructor's Manual, a Test Bank, PowerPoint slides, and Instructor's Notes for each chapter. Students can also access the Online Learning Center and complete quizzes to gauge their progress. Each tool makes planning and teaching the course easier than ever.

Acknowledgments

I would like to thank the reviewers who have contributed their time and ideas to the development of the eighth edition. My sincere appreciation goes to the following individuals:

Bonnie Bolinger
Ivy Tech Community College

Dr. Joyce Brooks
King's College

Jeff Bruns
Bacone College

Murray Brunton
Central Ohio Technical College

Barbara Desautels
Hesser College

Konstantinos Diamantis
Tunxis Community College

Donna Donathan
Huntington Junior College

John Gray
Faulkner University

Diane Hagan
Ohio Business College

Christie Highlander
Southwestern Illinois College

Thomas Hughes
University of South Carolina

Jill Jasperson
Utah Valley University

Steven Kaber
Baldwin-Wallace College

Jill Kingsbury
Metropolitan Community Colleges –
Maple Woods

Gilbert Logan
Bryant & Stratton College

Kirsten Mast
The College of Idaho

Debra McCarthy
Central Lakes College

James McCord
Huntington Junior College

Donna McCurley
Gadsden State Community College

Kristin Mueller
Ivy Tech Community College

William Padley
Madison Area Technical College

Cathy Steiner
DuBois Business College

Fran Tannenbaum
NVCC Woodbridge Campus

Matthew Thisse
Dorsey Business Schools

Lori Whisenant
C.T. Bauer College of Business
University of Houston

Robert Wible
Bradford School

I would also like to extend special thanks to my graduate assistant, David Valenti, whose patient and painstaking efforts contributed enormously to the readability and accuracy of the material contained in this text. Finally, I would like to acknowledge the fine work of the many individuals at McGraw-Hill/Irwin, who unselfishly provided their invaluable counsel and wisdom, enabling this edition to become a reality.

A GUIDED TOUR

The eighth edition of *Essentials of Business Law* is designed to ensure that students will not only learn fundamental applications of business law, but also will be able to put those basics into practice after reading a multitude of real-world examples and performing several skill assessment activities.

"A concise, well written, introduction into Business Law that focuses on essential knowledge regarding the various topics. An excellent textbook for college students embarking into the subject of Business Law."

—*Fran Tannenbaum, Northern Virginia Community College: Woodbridge Campus*

CHAPTER OPENING QUOTE

Each chapter opens with a lighthearted but thoughtful quote. The quotes come from a variety of sources, including famous judges, lawyers, entertainers, and business-people.

OUR SYSTEM OF LAW

"As long as I have any choice, I will stay only in a country where political liberty, toleration, and equality of all citizens before the law are the rule."

Albert Einstein, noted scientist

LEARNING OUTCOMES

After studying this chapter and completing the assessments, you will be able to

1.1 Discuss the application of law in today's world.

1.2 Provide examples of how the application of law affects (a) one's personal or social life, (b) business or business operations, and (c) governments.

1.3 Identify the principal sources of law in the United States.

1.4 Explain the reasons for the preparation of the Uniform Commercial Code.

1.5 Cite and describe the major classifications of law.

1.6 Distinguish moral law from legal obligations.

1.7 Describe the structure of our federal and state court systems.

LEARNING OUTCOMES

Learning Outcomes outline the focus of the chapter and provide a roadmap for the material ahead. Each is tied directly to a main heading in the chapter, as well as a corresponding chapter summary point, to help reiterate important topics throughout.

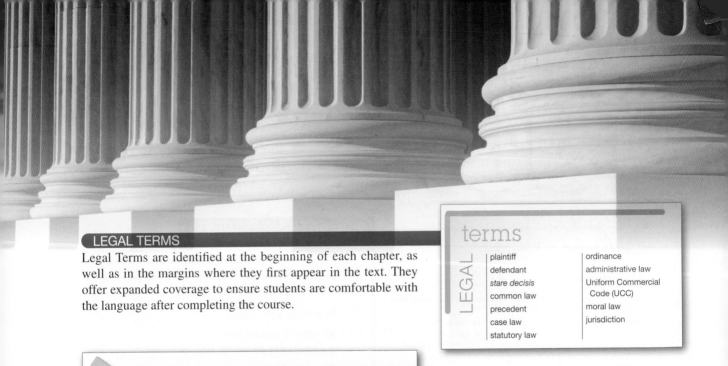

LEGAL TERMS

Legal Terms are identified at the beginning of each chapter, as well as in the margins where they first appear in the text. They offer expanded coverage to ensure students are comfortable with the language after completing the course.

LEGAL terms

plaintiff
defendant
stare decisis
common law
precedent
case law
statutory law

ordinance
administrative law
Uniform Commercial
  Code (UCC)
moral law
jurisdiction

EXAMPLE 2.1

▶ Senior executives of a multimillion-dollar energy company, Enron Corporation, and its outside accounting firm, Arthur Andersen LLP, were found to have engaged in massive unethical and illegal behavior involving questionable accounting practices, fraud, deception, insider trading, and attempts to influence politicians and the media. According to widespread media coverage, executives who knew the firm was headed for bankruptcy were quietly selling their shares of stock while encouraging employees to retain and even buy additional shares. Employees' individual investments in Enron's plummeting stock suffered enormous losses, as did their pension funds similarly invested. It was charged that such financial skulduggery could have happened only with the complicity of Enron's outside accounting firm.

EXAMPLES

Examples throughout the chapter help students understand concepts in a real-world context. Each creates a scenario that ties directly to a key topic, ensuring students will be able to recognize and apply what they have learned in their careers.

"I particularly like these examples because they are real life cases that explain the material that the student just read. My students have said the examples help them to understand the Principles of Law."

—*Kristin Mueller,*
Ivy Tech Community College

CHAPTER SUMMARIES

Chapter Summaries correspond to particular performance objectives and chapter headings, making quick reference and retention of key concepts easy.

"Excellent overview of the material just covered. Short, concise, and to the point."

—*Christie Highlander,*
Southwestern Illinois College

CHAPTER SUMMARY

1. It is important to understand certain essential legal principles because they affect both one's business and personal life. Accountants, for example, need to know that if they do their work carelessly and cause someone to sustain a loss, they could be sued. A person who is planning to rent an apartment or buy a home needs to know his or her legal rights as they relate to property.

2. Examples of how the application of law affects a person's personal and social life can be seen everywhere from the foods eaten, the medicines used, the goods purchased, to the clothing worn. Examples of how the law affects business can be seen in zoning ordinances, regulation of environmental pollution, and licensing laws. Examples of how the law affects the federal government include laws providing for funding for building highways or for low-income housing, or requiring that states, counties, or municipalities maintain them.

3. The sources of law in the United States are the Constitution, executive orders, treaties, common

law, precedent, case law, statutory law, and administrative law.

4. To address conflicts in business law between states, the UCC was prepared in 1952. The UCC is a set of laws that govern various commercial transactions and are designed to bring uniformity to the laws of the states.

5. Law in the United States is typically classified as constitutional law, civil law, criminal law, administrative law, and international law.

6. Moral law is concerned with the unenforceable obligations that people have to one another; legal obligations are those required by enacted statutes and other laws.

7. The structure of the federal and state court systems includes courts of original jurisdiction (federal district courts and state courts) and appeals courts (federal circuit courts of appeals, the U.S. Supreme Court, and state appellate courts).

A GUIDED TOUR

CHAPTER ONE ASSESSMENT

MATCHING LEGAL TERMS

Match each of the numbered definitions with the correct term in the following list. Write the letter of your choice in the answer column.

a. administrative law
b. appellate court
c. civil law
d. common law
e. criminal law
f. defendants

g. executive order
h. moral law
i. original jurisdiction
j. plaintiffs
k. precedents
l. statutory law

m. *stare decisis*
n. trial court
o. Uniform Commercial Code

1. A legally binding directive issued by the president. 1. ___
2. The portion of the law based on the decisions of the old English courts. 2. ___

CHAPTER ASSESSMENTS

Chapter Assessments sharpen students' critical thinking, decision-making, teamwork, technology, and communication skills and aid in student retention. Assessments include:

- Matching Key Terms
- Multiple Choice Quiz
- True/False Quiz
- Discussion Questions
- Thinking Critically about the Law
- Case Questions
- Case Analysis
- Legal Research

THE ONLINE LEARNING CENTER (OLC)

The Online Learning Center follows the text chapter by chapter with digital content to accompany and enhance the book. Assets include self-grading quizzes, review material, and interactive exercises for students to test themselves on core outcomes.

The instructor's side of the OLC contains useful resource materials, including an Asset Map (a tool designed to help instructors organize their courses efficiently), an Instructor's Manual, and PowerPoint slides. The full version of the Uniform Commercial Codes is also available to review or download for students and instructors.

ESSENTIALS OF
BUSINESS LAW

Introduction to Law

chapter **1**

Our System of Law

After studying this chapter and completing the assessments, you will be able to

1.1 Discuss the application of law in today's world.

1.2 Provide examples of how the application of law affects (a) one's personal or social life, (b) business or business operations, and (c) governments.

1.3 Identify the principal sources of law in the United States.

1.4 Explain the reasons for the preparation of the Uniform Commercial Code.

1.5 Cite and describe the major classifications of law.

1.6 Distinguish moral law from legal obligations.

1.7 Describe the structure of our federal and state court systems.

terms

LEGAL

plaintiff	ordinance
defendant	administrative law
stare decisis	Uniform Commercial
common law	Code (UCC)
precedent	moral law
case law	jurisdiction
statutory law	

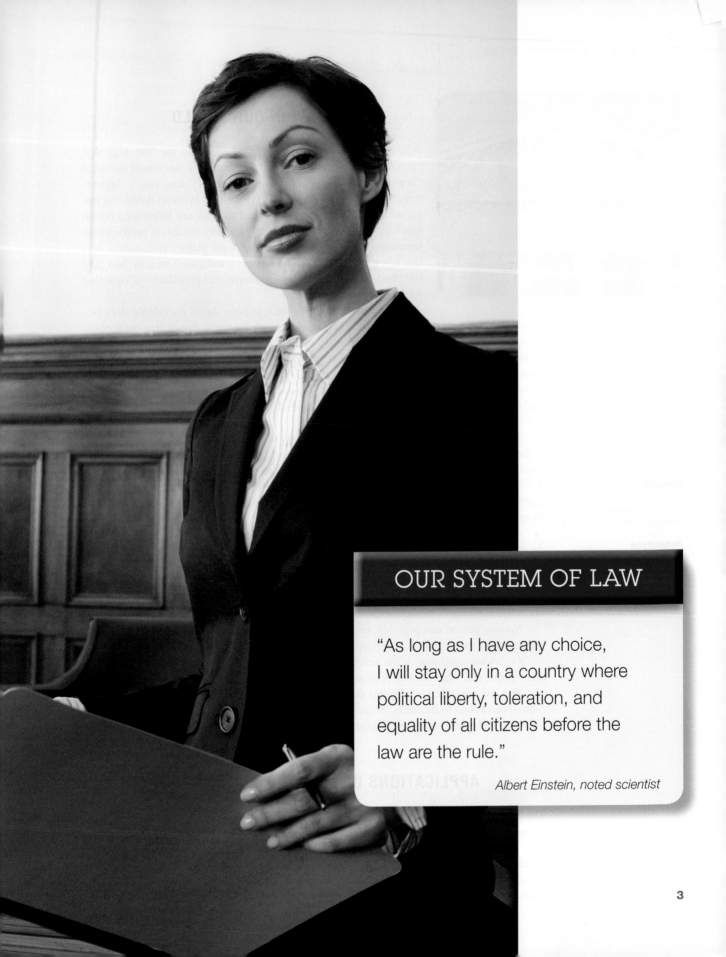

OUR SYSTEM OF LAW

"As long as I have any choice,
I will stay only in a country where
political liberty, toleration, and
equality of all citizens before the
law are the rule."

Albert Einstein, noted scientist

The US Supreme Court Building.

1.1   THE LAW IN OUR WORLD

When students in their 20s were asked to say the first thing that came to mind when they heard the word *law*, responses included "cops and robbers," "courtroom," "narcs," "drug raid," "legislators," "speed limit," and "traffic violation." Without doubt, the impressions that most people have of the law are influenced not so much by actual experience, but by the way the law is portrayed on television and in movies. Sometimes the picture is distorted. Justice always seems to triumph, the "good guys" usually win, and the "bad guys" ultimately are caught and punished—a view that society wishes were true.

Unfortunately, movies and television shows provide the only picture many people get of the law. What people do not see are the many day-in, day-out applications of the law that deal with such ordinary matters as an automobile driver charged with having caused injury to another driver, or one corporation suing another corporation over responsibility for defective merchandise. In real life, the administration of justice can be much less exciting than is often portrayed. There are areas of the law that do not hinge on clear-cut "right" or "wrong" but on an ill-defined middle ground. Still, justice and law are hallmarks of a free society in today's world.

The fact of the matter is that our system of law functions largely outside the spotlight of public attention. Every business day, in every city, town, and village in this country, courts are in session, juries are being selected, and attorneys are busy seeking favorable decisions for their clients, who might be either a **plaintiff**, the person who brings a lawsuit against another, or a **defendant**, the person against whom a lawsuit is brought or who is charged with a violation of the law.

plaintiff
The party who begins a lawsuit by filing a complaint in the appropriate court.

defendant
The party against whom a lawsuit is brought and from whom recovery is sought.

Although the ordinary applications of law are not quite as exciting as a television drama, it is important to understand certain essential legal principles because they affect both your business and your personal life. Accountants, for example, need to know that if they do their work carelessly and cause someone to sustain a loss, they could be sued. Just as important, a person who is planning to rent an apartment or buy a home needs to know his or her legal rights as they relate to property.

No one person can possibly know the entire body of law. Even learned judges and lawyers tend to specialize in certain fields of law. The average person should, however, strive to understand some of the general principles of law, how to avoid common problems and pitfalls, and when to seek professional help.

The law presented in this text deals primarily with the general principles of law and their applications to business. Some chapters focus on personal applications of the law, however, and others treat ethical aspects of personal and business behavior.

1.2   APPLICATIONS OF LAW

The effects of law are felt throughout society. Indeed, some aspects of the law apply to all persons, institutions, and organizations.

PERSONAL APPLICATIONS OF LAW

Imagine, for a moment, how the law affects just one day in your life. The alarm clock that awakens you in the morning is set to a time that is regulated by a law establishing standard time zones. Various federal and state laws regulate the purity and wholesomeness of your breakfast foods. The clothing you wear is labeled in compliance with governmental regulations. Your right to drive a car is regulated by state laws, and speed limits and other traffic laws are often the responsibility of state or local officials. You know that no one else may occupy your home while you are away at school or work because the law protects your property rights. The safety and freedom you enjoy are possible because you live in a nation of order—and that order is a result of laws passed for the benefit of the people and the protection of their rights.

BUSINESS APPLICATIONS OF LAW

If your personal life is influenced by law, think of how much more businesses, and those who work for businesses, are affected by law. Every business must comply with many federal, state, and local laws that are primarily aimed at regulating business activity. A firm that wishes to set up business in a particular community may find that there are laws that prohibit such activities. For example, local zoning ordinances might prohibit the operation of a noisy factory in a residential area. State and federal laws prohibit or regulate the operation of certain businesses that might pollute the environment. Still other laws require that businesses provide safe working conditions for employees or demand that only qualified persons perform certain jobs. State laws, for instance, require that barbers and pharmacists pass examinations to be licensed.

GOVERNMENT APPLICATIONS OF LAW

Legislatures at all levels of government pass many laws that apply only to businesses and individuals, but some laws apply specifically to governments. For example, the federal government may pass a law that provides funding for building highways or for low-income housing. The same law may require that states, counties, or municipalities maintain them.

1.3 SOURCES OF LAW

The ever-changing body of law that affects everyone in our country has arisen from a number of sources. As a result, laws sometimes conflict with one another. The way these conflicts are resolved will be discussed in this chapter.

CONSTITUTIONAL LAW

In our country, the principles and ideals that protect individual liberty and freedom are incorporated in the Constitution of the United States (the federal Constitution). This historic document gives the federal government certain reasonable powers and, at the same time, clearly limits the use of those powers. In addition, each state has a constitution of its own that gives certain powers to the various levels of government within that state. Like the federal Constitution, state constitutions provide safeguards for the rights of individuals within that particular state. You will learn more about the Constitution of the United States and the important foundation it provides to our legal system in Chapter 5 (see Appendix A).

The United States Constitution.

EXECUTIVE ORDERS

An executive order is a legally binding directive issued by the president with the intent to change the manner in which federal agencies and officials operate so as to improve the practices of the federal government. For example, an executive order was issued in 1957 when President Eisenhower ordered federal troops to enforce the Supreme Court's ruling to desegregate the school system.

TREATIES

A treaty is a written agreement between two or more countries that serves to establish terms of an international relationship. Treaties become legally binding when they are approved by two-thirds of the Senate (see Chapter 35).

COMMON LAW

After the Revolutionary War, one of the most difficult tasks faced by our newly independent nation was to establish a system of law. Because the original states were formerly English colonies, it is not surprising that the new states adopted the system of laws that had been used in England for hundreds of years—that is, relying on previous legal decisions when similar disputes arose. This practice of relying on previous decisions is known as *stare decisis*, which means "to stand on decided cases." The English system is known as the common law and still influences legal decisions in the United States today.

stare decisis
The practice of relying on previous decisions in which similar disputes arose.

common law
The body of recorded decisions that courts refer to and rely upon when making later legal decisions.

precedent
A model case that a court can follow when facing a similar situation.

PRECEDENT

A precedent is a court decision on which later courts rely in similar cases. In some instances, a court may be influenced by precedent; in other cases it may not. Whether a court follows a precedent, or decides to overrule it, depends on the court that has ruled on the case and whether the previous case was decided by the highest court in the same state. Decisions made by the U.S. Supreme Court, for example, must be followed by other courts.

Court decisions are recorded in writing so that lawyers and judges can refer to them in preparing or hearing a case. These decisions are published in books called reporters, and many of these decisions are available online. Each case decision is identified by a citation, which includes the names of the parties involved followed by the volume number, the name of the reporter, and the beginning page number of the case. For example, the case of *Milkovich v. News-Herald*, 473 N.E.2d 1191, is reported in volume 473 of the *Northeastern Reporter, Second Series*, beginning on page 1191.

CASE LAW

Sometimes a statute or a common law precedent may be difficult to apply to certain cases or, with the passing of time, may take on different meaning. An existing statute or an

Court decisions are published in books called reporters.

accepted precedent may be based on outmoded standards of justice. In such cases, a court may disregard earlier interpretations of a statute or a principle of common law, or it may interpret them differently. The court's decisions in these cases influence later cases because they too become precedents that may be followed in similar cases. The effects of these decisions have been called case law.

case law
The effects of court decisions that involve the same or similar facts.

STATUTORY LAW

Both federal and state constitutions are general statements of the powers of governments and the rights of individuals. The specific applications of powers and rights are provided for in laws enacted by federal, state, and local governments. Each state constitution provides for a legislature that represents the people. These legislatures have the power to enact laws so long as they do not conflict with either the federal or the state constitution. The laws passed by Congress and by state legislatures are called statutes, and the field of the law that deals with these statutes is known as statutory law. A law that is passed by a local government, such as a city council, is often called an ordinance.

statutory law
The field of law involving statutes, which are laws passed by Congress or by state legislatures.

Not only do statutes provide the specific applications of the powers and rights in the constitutions, they also allow governments to respond to particular circumstances. For example, when the federal and state constitutions were written, cellular telephones and automobiles were not even imagined, much less matters to be regulated. Yet after these were developed, various legislatures passed statutes that restricted the use of cellular telephones while driving.

ordinance
A law that is passed by a local government, such as a city council.

ADMINISTRATIVE LAW

Protection of the rights and freedom of individuals and organizations is well established by the federal and state constitutions, by statutory law, and by common law. Still, today's complex society and system of justice present special needs that require certain laws that include their own administrative machinery. Sometimes when a federal, state, or local legislative body enacts a law, it also sets up an organization to establish rules and enforce them. Administrative law is the body of rules, regulations, and decisions created by administrative agencies.

administrative law
The body of rules, regulations, and decisions created by administrative agencies.

The practice of establishing specialized administrative agencies has several advantages. For example, it relieves the police and the courts from having to establish and enforce regulations that are often highly technical. Administrative agencies include federal agencies such as the National Labor Relations Board, state agencies such as public service commissions, and local agencies such as boards of health. These agencies have in common the authority to establish rules that have the force of law, to maintain "courts" that are often called appeal boards, and to conduct "trials" that are often called hearings. Because administrative law has become such an important part of our legal system, an entire chapter will be devoted to it.

1.4 UNIFORM COMMERCIAL CODE

When the United States was primarily a farming nation and there was relatively little commerce between states, it did not matter that the state constitutions and statutes differed from state to state. As trade between the states increased, however, so did the problems caused by the conflict in business laws among the different states. For example, a businessperson knowing the laws of his or her state had little difficulty so long as customers were all from the same state. But when business was conducted with customers in many states, he or she had to know the law in all of them.

Uniform Commercial Code (UCC)
A set of laws that govern various commercial transactions and that are designed to bring uniformity to the laws of the states.

To solve this problem, the Uniform Commercial Code (UCC) was prepared in 1952 by the National Conference of Commissioners on Uniform State Laws. The UCC is a set of laws that govern various commercial transactions and are designed to bring uniformity to the laws of the states. Over a period of 15 years, 49 states adopted the UCC as part of their state law. Not every state has adopted the entire UCC, and often state courts have differing interpretations of their UCC sections. For example, Louisiana, having been a French territory and therefore greatly influenced by French civil law, has adopted only parts of the Code. Because the UCC is so widely accepted, this book is based on it. For an in-depth look at Article 2 of the UCC, the section designed to regulate the law relating to sales of goods, see Appendix B.

1.5 CLASSIFICATION OF LAWS

The various laws, regardless of origin, can be grouped into several broad classifications, each of which represents a legal specialty. Frequently a lawyer will specialize in one of these areas.

- *Constitutional law* is the study of the federal Constitution, its interpretation by the federal courts, and its relationship to existing laws.
- *Civil law* is the study of the rights and obligations of individuals and includes the law of property, the law of contracts, and the law of torts.
- *Criminal law* is concerned with acts against society (criminal acts) and the regulation of criminal activity.

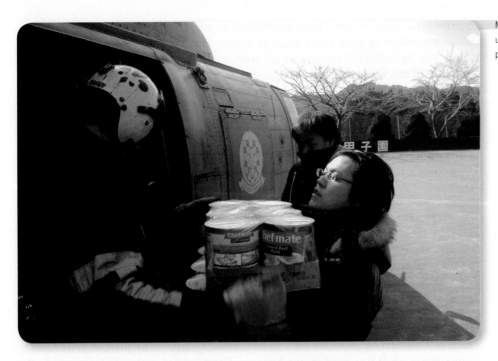

▶ *Administrative law* is concerned with the conduct of governmental administrative agencies and their regulations. Examples are tax laws and laws dealing with transportation and trade.

▶ *International law* is concerned with the conduct of nations in their relations with other nations.

1.6 MORAL LAW

Since earliest times, people have recognized that they are to a certain extent responsible for one another and have obligations to one another beyond those required by the law. For example, a person who sees someone drowning has a moral obligation to try to save him or her, and a person who hears someone screaming for help in the night has a moral duty to at least call the police. Such obligations are based on moral law—that is, the "law" concerned with the unenforceable obligations that people have to one another. Many legal obligations are based on moral obligations, but not all moral obligations are legally enforceable; a person's conscience is often the only means of enforcement.

moral law
The "law" concerned with the unenforceable obligations that people have to one another.

1.7 A SYSTEM OF COURTS

Some of our laws came from sources that were not originally concerned with human freedom. However, most legal scholars agree that today's laws provide adequate protection of the rights of the individual. But the mere existence of laws is not enough.

There must be a means of administering the law to protect the rights of individuals and businesses and to curtail the activities of wrongdoers. In this country, courts and governmental agencies have been established to administer the law. The federal and state constitutions and the entire body of written law would be of little value to individuals and businesses if there were no provision for enforcing the law. Police alone cannot fulfill this function. The federal and state constitutions provide for the establishment of a system of courts that ensure citizens' rights and enforce federal and state statutes.

COURT JURISDICTION

jurisdiction
The authority of a court, as granted by a constitution or legislative act, to hear and decide cases.

The authority or power of a court to hear cases, as granted by a constitution or legislative act, is known as the court's jurisdiction. A court may be limited in its powers to certain kinds of cases or to certain geographical areas. A court has original jurisdiction if it is authorized to hear and decide a case when it is first presented. If a court has the power to review the decisions of another court, it has appellate jurisdiction (the authority to hear appeals).

Courts that are given the power to hear only certain kinds of cases have special jurisdiction. Examples are family courts, traffic courts, and tax courts.

FEDERAL COURTS

The U.S. Constitution provides for a federal court system: "The judicial power of the United States, shall be vested in one Supreme Court, and in such inferior courts as the Congress may from time to time ordain and establish."

The court system that has developed has various levels. The Supreme Court of the United States is the highest court in the federal system. It serves as the court of original jurisdiction for certain kinds of cases, such as those in which a state is one of the parties. The Supreme Court rules on the constitutionality of laws by hearing selected cases that test those laws. The Supreme Court also hears appeals from the highest state courts. However, the Court actually hears only a small percentage of appeals because it has no legal obligation to review decisions of lower courts, except in very limited cases.

The federal district courts have original jurisdiction in cases involving federal statutes and in cases when the parties are citizens of different states and the amount involved is greater than $75,000. Every state has at least one federal district court.

Most appeals from the district courts go to one of the 13 circuit courts of appeals. The decisions of the circuit courts are usually final, although further appeal to the U.S. Supreme Court is possible. Appeals of the decisions of federal administrative agencies, such as the Federal Trade Commission (FTC), are also made to the U.S. Circuit Courts of Appeals.

The federal court system also includes specialized courts that hear only certain kinds of cases. Three of these specialized courts are the U.S. Tax Court, the U.S. Bankruptcy Court, and the U.S. Claims Court. Figure 1.1 gives an overview of the federal court system.

STATE COURTS

State court systems vary, but there are certain basic similarities in all state court systems. All states have general trial courts, which are courts of original jurisdiction, authorized to hear cases not otherwise restricted to specialized courts. General trial courts handle nearly all important disputes involving contracts, criminal law, and corporations. Trial courts in a state may be large municipal courts, with such specialized areas of jurisdiction as traffic violations, juvenile conduct, and domestic relations, or they may be small

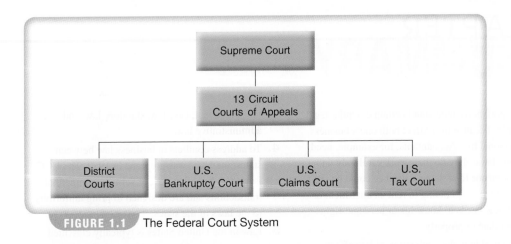

The Federal Court System

justice-of-the-peace courts called magistrate courts, established to hear certain minor violations of law.

If one of the parties in a case feels that he or she did not have a fair trial in the court of original jurisdiction, he or she can, with the aid of an attorney, seek an appeal in a state appellate court, which hears appeals from the trial courts. The names of appellate courts vary in different states. Beyond the courts of appeals are higher-level courts, often called supreme courts, which make final determinations on matters of law. In some less populous states that have no intermediate court of appeals, the state supreme court also serves as a court of appeals. Figure 1.2 gives an overview of the state court system.

Many communities have special courts to handle cases involving small amounts of money. Where these courts exist, there is usually a limit, ranging from $1,000 to $15,000, on the amount of the claim. Because there is a limit on the amount of money that can be involved, these courts are often called small claims courts. The proceedings usually are quite informal, and the parties involved typically are required or encouraged to appear without lawyers to represent them.

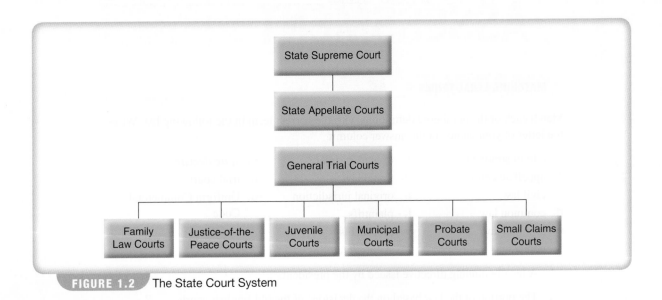

The State Court System

CHAPTER
SUMMARY

1. It is important to understand certain essential legal principles because they affect both one's business and personal life. Accountants, for example, need to know that if they do their work carelessly and cause someone to sustain a loss, they could be sued. A person who is planning to rent an apartment or buy a home needs to know his or her legal rights as they relate to property.

2. Examples of how the application of law affects a person's personal and social life can be seen everywhere from the foods eaten, the medicines used, the goods purchased, to the clothing worn. Examples of how the law affects business can be seen in zoning ordinances, regulation of environmental pollution, and licensing laws. Examples of how the law affects the federal government include laws providing for funding for building highways or for low-income housing, or requiring that states, counties, or municipalities maintain them.

3. The sources of law in the United States are the Constitution, executive orders, treaties, common law, precedent, case law, statutory law, and administrative law.

4. To address conflicts in business law between states, the UCC was prepared in 1952. The UCC is a set of laws that govern various commercial transactions and are designed to bring uniformity to the laws of the states.

5. Law in the United States is typically classified as constitutional law, civil law, criminal law, administrative law, and international law.

6. Moral law is concerned with the unenforceable obligations that people have to one another; legal obligations are those required by enacted statutes and other laws.

7. The structure of the federal and state court systems includes courts of original jurisdiction (federal district courts and state courts) and appeals courts (federal circuit courts of appeals, the U.S. Supreme Court, and state appellate courts).

CHAPTER ONE
ASSESSMENT

MATCHING LEGAL TERMS

Match each of the numbered definitions with the correct term in the following list. Write the letter of your choice in the answer column.

a. administrative law
b. appellate court
c. civil law
d. common law
e. criminal law
f. defendants

g. executive order
h. moral law
i. original jurisdiction
j. plaintiffs
k. precedents
l. statutory law

m. *stare decisis*
n. trial court
o. Uniform Commercial Code

1. A legally binding directive issued by the president.   1. _____

2. The portion of the law based on the decisions of the old English courts.   2. _____

3. A judicial body that has original jurisdiction in cases involving state law.

3. _____

4. Court decisions that later courts tend to follow.

4. _____

5. Those who bring suit against others.

5. _____

6. A judicial body empowered by law to review the findings of a lower judicial body.

6. _____

7. The practice of a court to follow previous decisions.

7. _____

8. The category of law concerned with acts against society.

8. _____

9. The authorization of a judicial body to hear certain types of cases when they are first brought to court.

9. _____

10. The legal specialty concerned with the rights and obligations of individuals.

10. _____

11. A group of laws dealing with business transactions in a consistent manner that have been adopted by most of the states.

11. _____

12. The legal specialty concerned with the relationship between businesses or individuals and government agencies.

12. _____

13. The branch of the law concerned with the laws passed by Congress and by state legislatures.

13. _____

14. The law concerned with the unenforceable obligations that people have to one another.

14. _____

15. Those against whom a suit is brought or who are charged with a violation of the law.

15. _____

MULTIPLE-CHOICE QUIZ

Select the answer that best completes each of the following statements. Write the letter of your choice in the answer column.

16. In our country, the principles and ideals guarding our individual liberty and freedom are presented in

16. _____

   a. judicial decisions.　　　**c.** the common law.

   b. the federal Constitution.

17. Treaties become legally binding when approved by

17. _____

   a. two-thirds of the Senate.　　**c.** two-thirds of Congress.

   b. one-third of the Senate.

18. If a precedent must be followed by another court, the case was originally decided by

18. _____

   a. small claims court.　　　**c.** the Supreme Court.

   b. trial court.

19. Statutes are laws passed by   19. _____

    a. state and federal legislatures. **c.** old English courts.

    b. the Supreme Court.

20. Laws enacted by local governments such as a city council are
often called   20. _____

    a. statutes.   **c.** declarations.

    b. ordinances.

21. The kind of law that results when a court disregards an existing statute,
an accepted precedent, or a principle of common law, or interprets
them differently, with the result that a new precedent is established,
is known as   21. _____

    a. precedent law.   **c.** case law.

    b. law of court review.

22. The purpose of the Uniform Commercial Code is to provide   22. _____

    a. uniform laws for all states to regulate business transactions in
the states.

    b. regulations to be followed in the sale of uniforms.

    c. laws to regulate international business transactions.

23. Unenforceable obligations that people have to one another are
considered to be an aspect of   23. _____

    a. moral law.   **c.** the law of unenforceable promises.

    b. the law merchant.

24. The authority of a court, as granted by a constitution or
legislative act, is known as the court's   24. _____

    a. mandate.   **c.** territory.

    b. jurisdiction.

25. If a court has the power to review the decisions of another court,
it has   25. _____

    a. appellate jurisdiction.   **c.** overrule authority.

    b. original jurisdiction.

26. Juvenile courts, the U.S. Tax Court, and domestic relations courts
are known as   26. _____

    a. specialized courts.   **c.** courts of original jurisdiction.

    b. justice courts.

27. The court that has original jurisdiction in cases involving federal statutes, and in cases when the parties are citizens of different states, is known as   27. _____

a. federal district court.   **c.** the U.S. Supreme Court.

b. circuit court of appeals.

28. Normally appeals from federal district courts are initially heard by   28. _____

a. the U.S. Supreme Court.   **c.** state supreme courts.

b. circuit courts of appeals.

29. Special courts set up to handle small or minor cases, often with a limit on the amount of the claim, are known as   29. _____

a. circuit courts.   **c.** small claims courts.

b. district courts.

30. State courts that have original jurisdiction for cases not otherwise directed to a specialized court are   30. _____

a. trial courts.   **c.** district courts.

b. circuit courts of appeals.

DISCUSSION QUESTIONS

Answer the following questions and discuss them in class.

31. Describe what contemporary society would be like without the system of laws that currently exists.

_____

_____

32. Explain how law affects (a) your personal or social life and (b) business or business operations.

_____

_____

33. Identify the principal origins of law in the United States.

_____

_____

34. Cite and describe the major classifications of law.

_____

_____

35. Distinguish moral law from legal obligations.

_____

_____

36. Can common law and statutory law operate side by side? What are the advantages of each?

_____

_____

THINKING CRITICALLY ABOUT THE LAW

Answer the following questions, which require you to think critically about the legal principles that you learned in this chapter.

37. Personal Applications of Law Many applications of law primarily affect individuals, such as buying or selling personal property. Critique the amount and kinds of protection provided to individuals and whether you think that the law provides too much protection, limiting individual freedom, or too little protection against harm. What are some examples?

_____

_____

38. Business Applications of Law Consider the numerous laws that affect businesses and evaluate the regulatory climate in which they operate. Does it seem that there are too many regulations or too few? Explain your answer.

_____

_____

39. Government Regulation of Governments Various levels of government enact laws that affect other levels of government. Explain the reason for such seemingly inefficient interrelationships and offer an opinion of whether there might be other ways to achieve the same objectives.

_____

_____

40. _Stare Decisis_ The legal concept of _stare decisis,_ which means "to stand on decided cases," is an important factor in our system of law. Is it possible that previous cases, or precedents, do not always embody the exact same issues, concepts, and present-day circumstances as the current case to which the earlier one is applied and by which the current one is judged? What would you suggest as an alternative to the use of precedents?

_____

_____

41. A Question of Ethics Normally there are no prosecutions for "padding" an expense account, yet it is considered unethical. Should such activity be prosecuted more forcefully?

_____

_____

CASE QUESTIONS

Study each of the following cases. Answer the questions that follow by writing _Yes_ or _No_ in the answer column.

42. Precedent Ferguson was arrested for possession of marijuana in a state where it was illegal. He argued at his trial that the highest court in a neighboring state had ruled a similar law invalid, which would be a binding precedent.

   a. Is Ferguson correct in his belief?   **a.** _____

   b. Can a state's highest court rule that the law of another state is
        not binding in its own state?   **b.** _____

   c. Does a precedent in one state affect the law in another?   **c.** _____

43. Jurisdiction A television station aired a broadcast containing insulting remarks about a local official. The official had the broadcaster charged under a state statute that prohibited making defamatory remarks on public airwaves. The broadcaster argued that the statute was in conflict with the U.S. Constitution's guaranty of free speech. The public official countered that the statute was legal and enforceable.

   a. Can states enact laws that limit free speech?   **a.** _____

   b. Can defamatory remarks be made illegal?   **b.** _____

   c. Can a state statute be in conflict with the U.S. Constitution?   **c.** _____

44. Civil Law Phipps became involved in a case of mistaken identity. A local merchant falsely accused him, in front of people who knew him, of shoplifting. Phipps was charged but not convicted. Angry and embarrassed, yet not wanting to spend money for an attorney, he acted as his own attorney and sued the merchant for false arrest in small claims court.

   a. Can Phipps act as his own attorney?   **a.** _____

   b. Does small claims court have jurisdiction in this case?   **b.** _____

   c. Is there a dollar limit on the kind of case that can be brought to
        small claims court?   **c.** _____

CASE ANALYSIS

Study each of the following cases carefully. Briefly state the principle of law and your decision.

45. **Interpretation of Statute** Muscarello illegally sold marijuana, which he transported in a small truck. Police discovered a handgun in the locked glove compartment of the truck. A provision in the firearms chapter of the federal law demands a five-year required prison term for persons who use or carry a firearm during or related to trafficking in drugs. Muscarello claimed that since the gun was in the locked glove compartment of the truck it did not fall within the description of the word "carry" as used in the statute and that he was not subject to the required five-year prison term. *Did Muscarello violate the firearms chapter of the criminal code?* [*Muscarello v. United States,* 118 S. Ct. 1911 (1998)]

Principle of Law:

_____

_____

Decision:

_____

_____

46. **Contract Essentials** Without first obtaining the required marriage license, Evelyn and Joseph Carabetta were married in a religious ceremony. Thereafter, they lived together as husband and wife. They raised four children, all of whose birth certificates listed Joseph Carabetta as their father. At no time did either party ever deny that they were married. In an action to dissolve the marriage, Evelyn Carabetta claimed that the lack of a marriage license made the marriage void. *Does the lack of a marriage license make the marriage void?* [*Carabetta v. Carabetta,* 438 A.2d 109 (Connecticut)]

Principle of Law:

_____

_____

Decision:

_____

_____

LEGAL RESEARCH

Complete the following activities. Share your findings with the class.

47. Working in Teams In teams of three or four, interview the owners or managers of small businesses to determine the levels of laws—federal, state, or local—to which the firm is subject. Further, ask the interviewee to provide examples.

_____

_____

48. Using Technology Using the Internet and search engines, investigate the operation of small claims courts in your community or one nearby. Determine the kinds of cases typically heard and the limit in dollars involved in cases that these courts are authorized to hear.

_____

_____

chapter **2**
Ethics and the Law

After studying this chapter and completing the assessment, you will be able to

2.1 Cite some examples of how unethical behavior in our world has negatively affected business practices.

2.2 Distinguish among ethics, morals, and values.

2.3 Cite several influences on group and individual values.

2.4 Discuss the relationship between law and ethics.

2.5 Provide examples of responses to ethical issues by business firms, educational institutions, governments, and trade and professional associations.

2.6 Discuss some ways businesses can ensure ethical practices.

LEGAL terms

Sarbanes-Oxley	subculture
ethics	code of ethics
morals	stakeholders
values	whistleblower
culture	

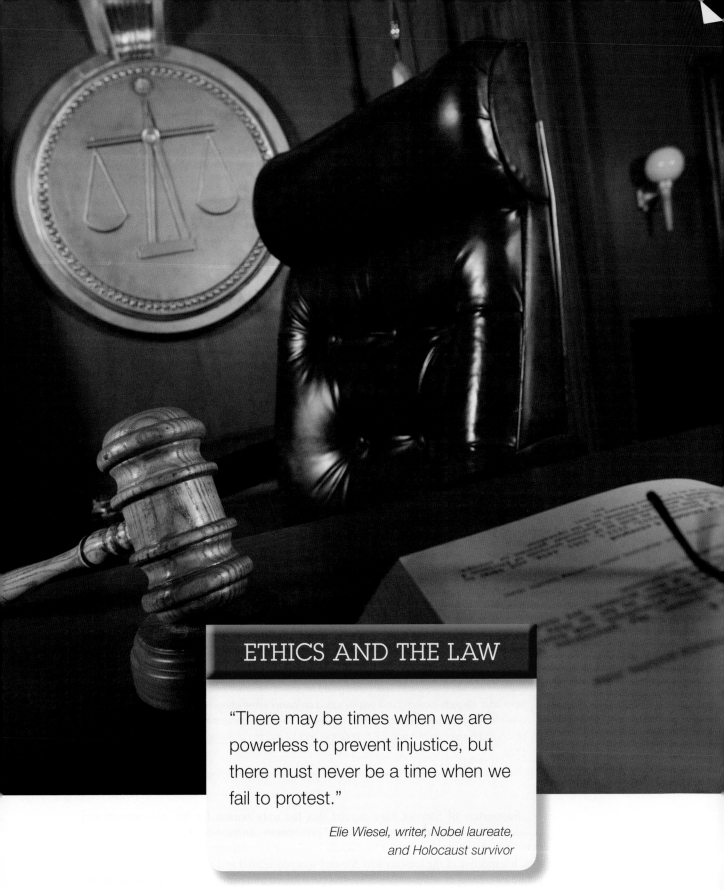

ETHICS AND THE LAW

"There may be times when we are powerless to prevent injustice, but there must never be a time when we fail to protest."

Elie Wiesel, writer, Nobel laureate, and Holocaust survivor

2.1 UNETHICAL BEHAVIOR IN OUR WORLD

It is difficult to read a daily newspaper or watch TV without seeing some reference to ethics—or the lack of them. Such accounts may refer to the latest government purchasing scandal, the wrongful use of insider information for personal gain, or a violation of consumers' interests and rights.

EXAMPLE 2.1

▶ Senior executives of a multimillion-dollar energy company, Enron Corporation, and its outside accounting firm, Arthur Andersen LLP, were found to have engaged in massive unethical and illegal behavior involving questionable accounting practices, fraud, deception, insider trading, and attempts to influence politicians and the media. According to widespread media coverage, executives who knew the firm was headed for bankruptcy were quietly selling their shares of stock while encouraging employees to retain and even buy additional shares. Employees' individual investments in Enron's plummeting stock suffered enormous losses, as did their pension funds similarly invested. It was charged that such financial skulduggery could have happened only with the complicity of Enron's outside accounting firm.

Sarbanes-Oxley
A federal statute that placed an onus on upper management to monitor closely the financial dealings and disclosures of their firms and that established a board to oversee accounting practices in the United States.

The fact that the Enron and Arthur Andersen case dominated the media and resulted in numerous congressional investigations showed the widespread concern with ethical behavior in business. As a result of the attention brought to the public's eye in this and other cases, in 2002 a federal statute, known as Sarbanes-Oxley, was enacted, placing a greater onus on upper management to monitor closely the financial dealings and disclosures of their firms. The law also established a board to oversee accounting practices in the United States. This board reports to the Securities and Exchange Commission, a federal agency. To view a copy of the law, visit http://frwebgate.access.gpo.gov/cgi-bin/getdoc.cgi?dbname=107_cong_bills&docid=f:h3763enr.txt.pdf.

EXAMPLE 2.2

▶ Entrepreneur Martha Stewart was investigated for selling several thousand shares of ImClone stock after allegedly receiving and illegally acting on insider information. Found guilty of a federal crime for lying to investigators, Stewart received a 10-month sentence, split evenly between prison and home confinement; a $30,000 fine; and 19 months of supervision by the probation office.

Supporters of Stewart have argued that the only reason for her prosecution and conviction was her celebrity status. Federal prosecutors, on the other hand, contend that no individual, no matter how powerful, should be allowed to interfere with a federal investigation. Irrespective of the reasons why Stewart was prosecuted and convicted, it is certain that public awareness of white-collar crime has been raised as a result of the media attention this case has received.

Examples also can be found in other professions and in government. In addition, entirely new applications and demands for ethical behavior continue to surface. Environmental ethics, for example, is a growing field as citizens voice their concerns about the pollution of our natural habitat by businesses. Demands for additional government regulation are frequently voiced.

The development of technology has introduced a burgeoning array of ethical questions. Advances in genetics, cloning technologies, and the use of stem cells in medical science, for example, have raised ethical dilemmas unheard of even a decade earlier. Ethical issues involving Internet and computer technology also have prompted people to consider ethical issues such as privacy and free speech on the Internet (see Chapter 29).

The expansion of global markets also has presented today's business professionals with ethical predicaments as they have to cope with different standards of ethics in other countries and cultures. Is it ethical for an American company to do business with a company in an undemocratic country? If an American firm wants to operate a chain of stores in Saudi Arabia, should it offer the same kinds of consumer protection to Saudi consumers as it does to American consumers? These kinds of ethical issues are essential to business law.

Martha Stewart leavesfederal court.

It is evident, then, that we need to reexamine our ethics and to clarify the distinction between what is ethical versus what is legal.

2.2 ETHICS, MORALS, AND VALUES

Both ethics and morals are concerned with standards of right and wrong. Ethics takes a more philosophical approach, examining what is good or bad. Morals are concerned with behavior as judged by society. Ethical theories and moral standards are derived from values—that is, the beliefs or standards considered worthwhile. Clearly, all are, and have always been, important in the creation of an orderly society.

ethics
The philosophical study of what is right and wrong, good and bad.

morals
Beliefs about behavior as judged by society.

values
Beliefs or standards considered worthwhile, and from which a society derives its moral rules.

2.3 SOURCES OF GROUP AND INDIVIDUAL VALUES

There are group values and individual values, both influenced by religions, traditions, and customs. An individual's values are significantly influenced by those held by the groups to which he or she belongs.

There are other influences on the development of individual and group values. Of utmost importance are the values held by a culture—those of a nation or an ethnic group. The American culture, for example, holds that such characteristics as freedom, individualism, family life, fair play, hard work, and honesty are important.

On the other hand, the values held by a subculture—for example, employees of a corporation, or a department within a company—may differ from those of the larger culture.

culture
The set of shared attitudes, values, goals, and practices that characterize a social, racial, religious, or corporate group.

subculture
An ethnic, economic, regional, religious, or social group with attitudes or behaviors that distinguish it from others within a larger culture.

EXAMPLE 2.3

▶ Pedro Gonzalez, a Mexican American living in Texas, works as an accountant for a major corporation in Dallas. As a member of a number of groups, he is influenced by the values of the American culture, but he also is influenced by the special values of the Latino subculture. Since he is Catholic and lives in the Southwest, he is influenced by the values of his religion and by the customs of the geographic area in which he lives. He also is influenced by the values of the corporation for which he works.

2.4 THE RELATIONSHIP BETWEEN LAW AND ETHICS

Unlike law, ethical issues may be multifaceted.

Legal mandates are imposed on individuals or groups by authorities or governments. Ethical considerations, on the other hand, generally spring from within individuals or organizations. However, ethical ideas have been the foundation of much of the legislation enacted by federal, state, and local governments. Consider the role of ethics in the laws that protect consumers against misleading advertising, deceptive labeling, and price-fixing. These laws are clearly based on ethical considerations. Court decisions, too, are frequently influenced by ethics as judges and juries examine the facts of a case and form beliefs about the parties and issues involved.

A distinction between law and ethics is that legal mandates are usually more precise. The law requires individuals and organizations to behave in specified ways, requiring or prohibiting certain acts. Ethical issues may be multifaceted.

EXAMPLE 2.4

▶ The YumBurger chain was faced with the legal requirement of paying its employees a specified minimum wage. It could have simply fulfilled that requirement. However, the management decided, based on ethical considerations, to increase the pay of their workers beyond the mandated wage, feeling the required minimum was inadequate. While this decision might be commendable from an ethical standpoint, it could involve several other ethical issues as well: The cost of the extra pay might result in higher prices for consumers or reduced earnings for shareholders.

2.5 RESPONSES TO ETHICAL ISSUES

The growing awareness of the importance of ethics is evident in the responses of businesses, educational institutions, governments, and trade and professional associations.

RESPONSES OF BUSINESS FIRMS

There is increasing concern about ethics in the business world. Some of this concern is undoubtedly the result of enlightened self-interest, as when corporate executives say that ethical practices are simply good business practices. For example, in voluntarily paying their workers more than the legally required minimum wage, YumBurger also may attract scarce workers in a tight labor market. Other executives may be interested in ethical practices because of the favorable publicity it gives their firms. Corporations may be more concerned about the possible legal consequences of unethical behavior. Businesses concerned with ethics usually focus on their corporate responsibility and the development of codes of conduct.

Corporate Responsibility   The actions of corporations that are intended to demonstrate their wish to behave responsibly take many forms and are conducted under the banner of corporate responsibility. In some cases, the corporation will "adopt" a nearby school and provide equipment and expert personnel to teach particular skills. In other cases, the firm might construct a park, donate funds to a local symphony orchestra, or provide scholarships to a university. In some instances, these actions are little more than thinly veiled public relations efforts to enhance the image of the corporation. In other instances, however, corporate actions reflect a moral and ethical concern with social problems and a sincere effort to improve society.

Critics of corporate social action, however, question whether it is appropriate to commit corporate resources to socially desirable goals. It might be better, they suggest, to maximize earnings for shareholders, who could then use the higher earnings to advance society if they so desire. It is interesting to note that in many states charitable contributions by corporations are legal, while political contributions are not.

Codes of Ethics   Despite a few glaring lapses, many companies today understand the need to maintain ethical standards in their dealings with customers, suppliers, and employees. To do this, some firms or industries establish a code of ethics, sometimes called a *credo* or a values statement, that sets down the principles of ethical behavior expected of personnel in various situations (see figure 2.1). For example, a firm or industry may place a dollar limit on the value of gifts that may be accepted from suppliers doing business with the firm. A code makes clear that the company expects its personnel to recognize the ethical dimensions of corporate policies and actions.

code of ethics
A set of rules that a company or other group adopts to express principles of ethical behavior that are expected of its personnel.

EXAMPLE 2.5

▶ Johnson & Johnson was confronted with a crisis when people in the Chicago area began dying of cyanide poison after taking the firm's Tylenol capsules. Although no connection between the poison and Tylenol was established, Johnson & Johnson recalled the product at great cost. James Burke, chair, said that the established ethics credo was invaluable during this crisis because everyone in the firm knew what the standard of ethics required of them, and personnel at various levels were able to make the necessary decisions quickly.

Many firms expect employees to strictly follow codes; some even require employees to sign contracts annually requiring them to adhere to ethical standards. In such organizations, senior executives will be held to the highest standards for professional and ethical behavior so as to set a benchmark for the firm's stakeholders. A stakeholder is a person or group who may be affected by a firm's actions or decisions, such as employees, owners, shareholders, and customers. Managers should consider relevant stakeholders when establishing codes or engaging in ethical decision making.

stakeholders
People or groups who may be affected by a firm's actions or decisions.

EXAMPLE 2.6

▶ Hewlett-Packard's (HP's) board of directors agreed to request the resignation of company Chief Executive Officer Mark Hurd after discovering he was responsible for engaging in activities considered inappropriate by the company's standards of business conduct. HP's board remained steadfast in upholding the company's ethical and professional standards regardless of the fact that Hurd not only was chairperson and company CEO but also was partially responsible for a company turnaround.

While the areas covered in codes vary from one firm or industry to another, a general list of topics typically includes the following:

▶ Fundamental honesty and adherence to the law.
▶ Product safety and quality.
▶ Health and safety in the workplace.
▶ Possible conflicts of interest.
▶ Employment practices.
▶ Fairness in selling and marketing practices.
▶ Financial reporting.
▶ Supplier relationships.
▶ Pricing, billing, and contracting.
▶ Trading in securities and using insider information.
▶ Payments to obtain business.

Examples of codes of ethics may be found at http://ethics.iit.edu/codes/business.html.

Statement of Values: Family Service Association of Wyoming Valley, Pennsylvania

FSAWV maintains the following values:

We are **accountable.**   We are responsible and accountable to the individual, the family, and the community. We adhere to the national standards of the Council on Accreditation. We are ethically and fiscally accountable to our benefactors. Our integrity has sustained us for over a century.

We are **client-focused.**   We respect the right of self-determination for our clients and our communities. We build trust through compassion and a focus on client needs and potentials. We believe in recovery philosophy and in the recovery of individuals to strengthen families and our community.

We are **professional.**   We are highly trained and knowledgeable in social work and human service practice. Our behavior is professional at all times. We are empathetic to others, and we work diligently to understand and address need. We welcome our customers regardless of circumstance. We strive for diversity with our employees and our partner professionals. We value our century-old tradition of advancing the social work profession through practice and research.

We are **ethical.**   We are committed to the highest standards of ethical behavior toward our consumers. We do not take shortcuts in fulfilling our responsibilities. We build trust through our actions.

FIGURE 2.1   Example of a Values Statement

RESPONSES OF EDUCATIONAL INSTITUTIONS

Educational institutions have responded to the increased need to examine ethics by adding courses, workshops, and programs, and have expanded the study of ethics in existing courses. Typically, topics include fairness in hiring, employment, and promotions; ethical issues in multinational business; ethical issues arising from technology; economic justice; environmental ethics; and ecology.

RESPONSES OF GOVERNMENTS

Governments endeavor to protect consumers and the environment and to influence the ethical behavior of business firms in various ways. For example, governments enact legislation to ensure fair labor practices and to enforce existing statutes. The Federal Sentencing Guidelines also provide an incentive for corporations to act more ethically. Under this mandate, when an employee violates a law in the course of his or her employment, a firm can reduce its possible liability if it can show that it took action to develop moral guidelines for its employees. It can have its potential penalties reduced by millions of dollars. This federal mandate has motivated companies to develop codes of conduct; to appoint high-level personnel (often called *corporate ethics officers*) to oversee compliance and to establish ethics auditing and monitoring systems; and to enforce discipline throughout the firm. Legislators reasoned that if firms integrate ethics into their structure in this way, employees will be less likely to break the law for the company's benefit, and that companies that have taken positive steps to integrate ethics should not be penalized as harshly as those that have not. The guidelines are a response to the public's desire to hold companies to a higher standard, and to impose on white-collar criminals penalties heavier than those previously imposed.

Even the operation of government itself is monitored and regulated. The U.S. Office of Government Ethics, for example, is concerned with the following topics: conflicting financial interests, misuse of position, financial disclosure, impartiality in performing official duties, and other areas of concern. On an international level, federal and state governments require that U.S. firms perform ethically in global markets. For example, the Foreign Corrupt Practices Act prohibits American firms from bribing foreign officials. In addition, diplomatic activities aim to protect American firms from corrupt practices in other countries (see Chapter 35).

RESPONSES OF TRADE AND PROFESSIONAL ASSOCIATIONS

Trade associations develop guidelines for ethical business practices for their diverse memberships. For example, the Direct Marketing Association (DMA) provides self-regulatory standards of conduct for some of the following activities: telephone marketing, sweepstakes, fund-raising, marketing to children, and the collection and use of marketing data. Similarly, the Code of Ethics for the American Alliance of Paralegals is located at http://www.aapipara.org/Ethicalstandards.htm.

2.6 WAYS TO ENSURE ETHICAL PRACTICES

Despite the efforts of the aforementioned groups—businesses, educational institutions, governments, and trade and professional associations—unethical practices persist. Such behavior frequently results in unfavorable public relations, loss of consumer goodwill, and poor employee morale. The threat of legal prosecution and penalties does not eliminate all unethical practices. Sometimes the driving force for reform may be the individual whistleblower.

WHISTLEBLOWING

Our language has a number of derogatory words to describe people who disclose information about wrongdoing. Such terms as "stool pigeon," "stoolie," "fink," "snitch," "rat," and "tattletale" suggest that our society does not regard such behavior highly. But despite society's disdain for informers, certain individuals have been so outraged by what they consider unethical behavior that they have risked widespread condemnation and loss of their jobs to reveal information about the activity. These people are usually termed "whistleblowers."

whistleblower
An employee who discloses to the government, media, or upper management that the company is involved in wrongful or illegal activities.

Typically, a whistleblower is a person who reveals to a governmental authority, or to news media, confidential information concerning some wrongdoing or conduct that he or she regards as unethical. The information may have come to him or her in the course of employment or in other ways. The whistleblower may be a secretary, for example, who knows that his or her boss is cheating customers or the company, or an engineer who knows that a product is unsafe and that purchasers of the product could be injured or killed. Authorities may respond by prosecuting the company. The media may publicize the wrongdoing, which can be equally damaging to a firm.

The whistleblower, too, may be confronted with an ethical dilemma. Often the choice is between remaining silent or revealing information that could result in adverse effects on the firm that may cause many coworkers to lose their jobs.

It is not surprising that retaliation is frequently the result of speaking out. The whistleblower is often regarded as an outcast to the organization or to peers. The federal government and many states have statutes that protect whistleblowers from retaliation. Still, with the possible exception of certain individuals who may have a personal grudge, the usual motivation behind whistleblowing is the outrage to a person's sense of ethics.

INTEGRATION OF ETHICS INTO BUSINESS AND GOVERNMENT

In the abstract, there is agreement that business should be conducted in ways that will not harm the consumer or the environment. What is the most effective way to achieve this? The corporation may indeed adhere to the highest ethical practices, but a new chief executive officer (CEO) or board of directors may discontinue those practices if they reduce profits or otherwise adversely affect the firm. Further government regulation could ensure compliance with ethical standards, but such an arrangement might require a costly and oppressive bureaucracy. The ideal is for responsible individuals, industry organizations, and watchdog groups to encourage corporations and governments to reach mutually agreed-upon ethical practices.

Air traffic control whistle-blower Anne Whiteman. Whiteman was threatened and harassed after reporting air traffic controllers allowing planes to fly in air space less than 1,000 feet apart at the Dallas–Fort Worth Airport, an illegal and dangerous practice.

CHAPTER SUMMARY

1. Examples of how ethics in our world have negatively affected business practices include investors acting on insider information, businesses polluting our natural habitat, and individuals acting unethically in the development of medical and electronic technology. The expansion of global markets also raises some ethical predicaments for business professionals.

2. Ethics is a philosophical approach, examining theories of what is good or bad. Morals are concerned with behavior as judged by society. Values are beliefs or standards considered worthwhile.

3. Individual and group values are influenced by religion, tradition, and customs.

4. Legal mandates are imposed on individuals or groups by authorities or governments. In contrast, ethical considerations generally spring from within individuals or organizations. However, ethical beliefs are the foundation of many of our laws.

5. Business firms respond to ethical concerns by acts of corporate responsibility and the formulation of codes of ethics, or credos. Educational institutions offer courses and workshops and expand their existing programs. Governments endeavor to protect consumers and the environment and to ensure ethical behavior of business firms and the government itself. Trade and professional associations develop guidelines for business and professional members.

6. Some ways business can ensure ethical practices include integrating corporate codes of ethics and relying on whistleblowers. Corporate codes of ethics vary from one firm or industry to another. Whistleblowing is the exposing of an unethical situation to an authority or the media.

CHAPTER TWO ASSESSMENT

MATCHING LEGAL TERMS

Match each of the numbered definitions with the correct term in the following list. Write the letter of your choice in the answer column.

a. code of ethics
b. culture
c. ethics
d. morals
e. subculture
f. values
g. whistleblower

1. A philosophical approach to examining what is good or bad. 1. _____

2. An examination of what is good or bad concerned with behavior as judged by society. 2. _____

3. The beliefs or standards considered worthwhile by an orderly society. 3. _____

4. The sum total of all the learned beliefs, values, and customs that regulate the behavior of members of a particular society.

4. _____

5. A smaller group within a culture.

5. _____

6. A document that sets down a firm's principles of the ethical behavior expected of its employees.

6. _____

7. A person who reveals confidential information concerning some wrongdoing or unethical behavior.

7. _____

TRUE/FALSE QUIZ

Indicate whether each of the following statements is true or false by writing *T* or *F* in the answer column.

8. Unethical behavior has not been a problem in society until recent times.

8. _____

9. Generally, what is unethical is also illegal.

9. _____

10. The term *values* relates to the price of merchandise on sale.

10. _____

11. Personal values can vary from one individual to another.

11. _____

12. People tend to behave in accordance with accepted principles of what is right and wrong that govern the conduct of their group and that reflect the values of the group.

12. _____

13. Public disclosure of a firm's unethical practices can affect other companies as well.

13. _____

14. A whistleblower is a person who calls attention to illegal or unethical behavior.

14. _____

15. A corporate code of ethics might be called a set of guidelines for the ethical behavior expected of employees.

15. _____

16. "Corporate culture" is used to describe the values and standards of acceptable behavior in a corporation.

16. _____

17. The corporate culture may either foster or discourage moral action on the part of its management and workers.

17. _____

18. "Moral standards" include theories holding that a society has certain common, objective, consistent standards that forbid certain behavior as wrong and hold that other behavior is right.

18. _____

DISCUSSION QUESTIONS

Answer the following questions and discuss them in class.

19. Describe the motivation behind the behavior of the executives and personnel at the Enron and Andersen companies described in the text.

_____

_____

_____

20. Identify some typical issues for people who are ethically concerned with the environment.

_____

_____

_____

21. Discuss and provide examples of values that are highly regarded in our society.

_____

_____

_____

22. Suggest several unfavorable consequences facing a business firm that consistently engages in unethical practices.

_____

_____

_____

23. Discuss the relationship between ethics and the law.

_____

_____

_____

24. Discuss several responses by businesses to ethical issues.

_____

_____

_____

THINKING CRITICALLY ABOUT THE LAW

Answer the following questions, which require you to think critically about the legal principles that you learned in this chapter.

25. Whistleblowing A person who blows the whistle on some unethical practice in a firm is often treated as an outcast by his or her coworkers. Why does this occur? Does this mean that the coworkers are less ethical?

26. Codes of Ethics A number of firms accused of unethical behavior had established codes of ethics, or credos, and formal employee orientation programs. It might seem that these efforts had little influence on the practices of the firms. Critique the practice of establishing codes of ethics and suggest ways that their use could be made more effective.

27. **Corporate Responsibility** Critics of corporate social action question whether it is appropriate to commit corporate resources to socially desirable goals. It might be better, they suggest, to maximize earnings for shareholders, who could then use the higher earnings to advance society if they so desire. Critique the arguments of those who advocate direct corporate action to achieve social goals versus the views of those who oppose such action.

28. **Responses of Governments to Ethical Issues** Analyze and critique some current activities of government relating to ethics in business.

29. **A Question of Ethics** The corporate culture exerts a major influence on the ethical behavior of every employee and executive in the firm. Since it is recognized that management largely determines the corporate culture, recommend steps management might take to establish a culture that will instill reasonable standards of ethical behavior for *everyone* in the firm.

CASE QUESTIONS

Study each of the following cases. Answer the questions that follow by writing *Yes* or *No* in the answer column.

30. **Whistleblowing** Ayer, an engineer with product development responsibilities, was confronted with an ethical dilemma. He knew that a product being manufactured by the firm was unsafe for consumer use as a result of cost cutting. He also believed that if he complained to management or to a government body concerned with product safety, he would probably be fired.

   a. If Ayer did nothing, would he still have made an ethical decision?   **a.** _____

   b. If Ayer did nothing because he was concerned that if he complained and manufacturing was suspended many workers would lose their jobs, would he have made an ethical decision?   **b.** _____

   c. Assume Ayer considered blowing the whistle on the firm by releasing information to the newspapers and television networks. Is it likely that such action would have any effect on the firm or on Ayer?   **c.** _____

31. **Illegal Activity** Perkins intended to sell his two-year-old automobile through an advertisement online. Since the car had more than 80,000 miles on it, Perkins reasoned that a buyer would be more willing to purchase the vehicle if he turned back the odometer to 30,000 miles. The car still looked quite new, and Perkins needed the money the sale would bring.

   a. Would turning back the odometer be an ethical action?   **a.** _____

b. If Perkins did not turn back the odometer and the car could not be sold due to the high mileage, and if his family suffered as a result, would Perkins be justified in turning back the odometer to benefit his family?

b. _____

32. **Ethical Decisions** Lackowitz, a college student, was concerned about a final examination. During previous examinations in the same course, he had seen other students cheat and obtain good grades. If he failed the course, he would need to repeat it and pay additional tuition. Also, if he had to repeat the course, his graduation would be delayed one semester, as would his entry into the full-time job market. The financial considerations were of great concern to him.

   a. Would Lackowitz be justified in cheating on the examination?

   a. _____

   b. Could a decision by Lackowitz to inform the instructor about the cheating that he had seen on previous examinations represent an ethical decision?

   b. _____

CASE ANALYSIS

Study each of the following cases carefully. Briefly state the principle of law and your decision.

33. **Deception** Siwek took his new Buick to his dealer for minor repairs. While the car was in the dealer's repair shop, the dealer informed Siwek that the car was equipped with a Chevrolet engine. The standard engine for a car of the model and year in question was a 2.4 litre 4-cylinder manufactured by the Buick division of General Motors. Before the introduction of the year's models, the manufacturer determined that there would not be enough engines built to equip all the Buick models manufactured. For this reason, it was decided to install Chevrolet engines in some Buick cars without disclosing the practice to the buyers. Siwek complained to the Illinois attorney general, who filed a class-action suit against General Motors charging that GM deceived consumers by not informing them of the engine switch.

   Ethical and/or Legal Principle:

   _____

   _____

   Decision:

   _____

   _____

34. **Ethical Responsibility** Quinly and her husband, customers at Greenway Supermarkets, purchased several pounds of filet mignon and checked out their purchases at the newly installed self-scanners. The price listed on the packages of meat

totaled $38; however, when Quinly swiped the packages through the self-scanner, it indicated a price of only $6. Quinly believed that she should inform the management at the supermarket that the computer in the self-scanner had been incorrectly programmed with respect to the price of this product. However, Quinly's husband argued that since the store would be legally obligated to charge the lower price, it was not necessary to call attention to the error. Is Quinly correct in her belief that the ethical course of action is to inform the store?

Ethical and/or Legal Principle:

_____

_____

Decision:

_____

_____

35. **Ethical Violation** Stotts was employed as a technician in the engineering department of Raytron Corporation. All the engineers on staff were required to sign agreements that they would not accept employment with another company in the industry within three years of leaving Raytron. Technicians, who had limited access to company secrets, were not required to sign such agreements. After working at Raytron for about two years, Stotts realized that he was deeply involved in development and had access to the same data as the engineers did. Stotts actively sought a position with Raytron's primary competitor and was hired by Watani Engineering. Because he did not have an engineering degree, he assumed that he had been hired because of his knowledge of Raytron's trade secrets. Did Stotts violate legal or ethical dictates?

Ethical and/or Legal Principle:

_____

_____

Decision:

_____

_____

LEGAL RESEARCH

Complete the following activities. Share your findings with the class.

36. **Working in Teams** One of the important functions of corporate executives is to develop and implement ethical policies for their companies. In groups of four or five, imagine that you are the executives of a major corporation charged with developing

a corporate code of ethics. What are some of the issues you would want to address? Create a list and share them with the class.

_____

_____

37. **Using Technology** Using the Internet and search engines, find news about businesses that are currently facing actual or potential charges of ethical indiscretions. Record your findings and share them with the class.

_____

_____

chapter **3**
Criminal Law

LEARNING OUTCOMES

After studying this chapter and completing the assessment, you will be able to

3.1 Define crime and distinguish between crimes and torts.

3.2 Identify the three major classifications of crimes.

3.3 Discuss several common crimes of particular concern to business and employees.

LEGAL terms

crime	burning to defraud
tort	larceny
treason	robbery
felony	burglary
misdemeanor	bribery
white-collar crime	false pretenses
RICO	forgery
securities fraud	perjury
Ponzi scheme	embezzlement
arson	extortion

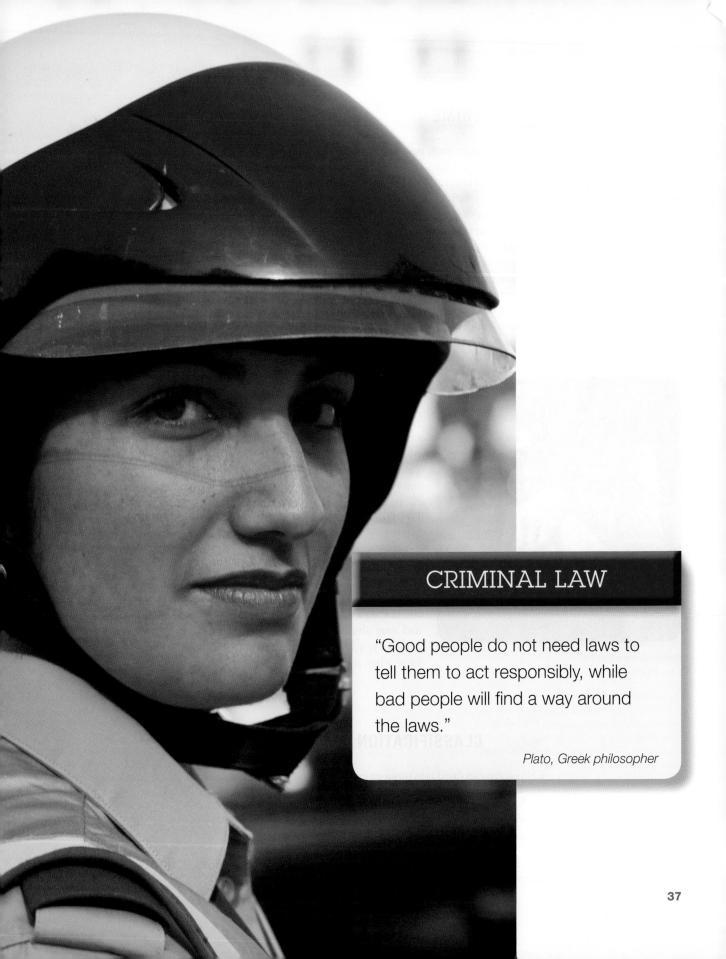

CRIMINAL LAW

"Good people do not need laws to tell them to act responsibly, while bad people will find a way around the laws."

Plato, Greek philosopher

3.1 CRIME

crime
An offense against the public at large punishable by the official governing body of a nation or state.

tort
A private wrong that injures another person's physical well-being, property, or reputation.

The law assures each person certain rights and assigns each person certain duties. As you recall from Chapter 1, the law enforcement authorities of federal, state, and local governments enforce specific laws called *statutes* that are designed to protect the public at large. A violation of a statute is a crime. A private wrong that causes injury to another person's physical well-being, property, or reputation is called a tort.

It is important to note that a certain action can be both a crime and a tort. For example, a person who operates an automobile recklessly or negligently and causes injury to another, or damages his or her property, has committed both the crime of reckless driving and the tort of negligence. The reckless driver can be prosecuted by the appropriate law enforcement authorities for the crime and also can be sued for the tort in a civil court by the person whose property was damaged or who was injured. Chapter 4 is devoted to torts and how they may relate to both your personal and business life.

Certain actions can be both a crime and a tort.

While statutory law determines what is and what is not a crime, many statutes reflect legal principles derived from common law. What makes a particular act, or failure to act, a crime? Why is a certain act, or failure to act, a crime in one state and not in another? Why is a certain act, or failure to act, a crime one day and not the next? These questions can all be answered by one statement: An act, or failure to act, is a crime because the governing statutes say it is. Of course, a high degree of uniformity has emerged among states, so it is uncommon for a particular act to be legal in one state and illegal in another. Also, legislatures attempt to reflect the public interest and will enact legislation that makes a certain act a crime if there is sufficient demand.

In other instances, also reflecting changing public sentiments, legislatures and courts may decide that a particular act previously considered a crime should no longer be viewed as a violation of the law. For example, laws concerning abortion, homosexuality, and drug abuse have been modified considerably in recent years. Similarly, a legislature may repeal statutes, thus making an act legal when it previously had been a crime.

3.2 CLASSIFICATION OF CRIMES

Crimes are classified into three groups according to the seriousness of the offense:

▶ Treason.

▶ Felony.

▶ Misdemeanor.

Federal law and the laws of the states determine the classification and largely specify the punishment.

TREASON

Treason is a major crime defined by the Constitution of the United States as follows: "Treason against the United States shall consist only in levying War against them, or in adhering to their Enemies, giving them Aid and Comfort."

treason
The levying of war against the United States, or the giving of aid and comfort to the nation's enemies.

FELONY

A felony is a serious crime against society, such as murder, arson, larceny, bribery, and embezzlement. It may be punished by execution, by a prison sentence of more than a year, or by a fine.

felony
A crime punishable by death or imprisonment in a federal or state prison for a term exceeding one year.

EXAMPLE 3.1

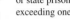

▶ Flogg was an employee of a firm that manufactured expensive electronic equipment. Due to a delay, a truckload of equipment was held at the shipping dock over a three-day weekend. Flogg stole the truck and its contents, intending to drive to another state, sell the equipment, and fly to another country. Unluckily for him, he was caught 75 miles away and ultimately charged with grand larceny, a felony.

MISDEMEANOR

A misdemeanor is a less serious offense than a felony. It is usually punished by a fine and/or imprisonment for no more than one year. Examples of misdemeanors include certain traffic offenses, thefts of small amounts of money, use of illegal measuring devices, and other relatively minor infractions of statutes.

misdemeanor
A less serious crime that is generally punishable by a fine and/or a prison sentence of not more than one year.

EXAMPLE 3.2

▶ Centerport had a local ordinance that prohibited door-to-door sales without a permit. Dowe, without obtaining the permit, began calling on home owners in the town, trying to sell home repairs. When a resident objected, the local police issued Dowe a citation—similar to a traffic ticket—that required him to appear in court, pay a fine, and avoid similar actions until the permit was issued.

3.3 CRIMES IN THE BUSINESS WORLD

Many people associate crime with criminals and gangsters as they are portrayed on television and in the movies. Crimes, however, are not always committed in the sensational style of blazing guns and wild car chases. Often the site of a business crime is the well-appointed office of a corporate executive, his or her private club, or a nearby bar where employees meet after work.

WHITE-COLLAR CRIME

white-collar crime
A term used to describe various crimes that typically do not involve force or violence committed by and against businesses.

White-collar crime is the term used to describe various crimes that typically do not involve force or violence committed by and against businesses. Originally white-collar crime related only to nonviolent crimes against businesses, usually committed by their own employees. The most common white-collar crime was the theft of an employer's funds by employees with access to such funds (embezzlement). In recent years, however, this unofficial category of illegal activity has been applied to nonviolent crimes committed *by* business firms as well as *against* business firms. In this newer, broader application, white-collar crime covers a wide range of crimes, including stock swindles, frauds against insurance companies, credit card fraud, income tax evasion, cyberspace fraud and theft of computer programs, agreements with competitors to fix prices, and others. Depending on its seriousness, a white-collar crime can be either a felony or a misdemeanor and can violate federal or state law.

RICO
One of the most successful laws used to combat white-collar crime, RICO prohibits an organization's employees from engaging in a pattern of racketeering activity.

The Racketeer Influenced and Corrupt Organizations Act of 1970, also known as RICO, is one of the most successful laws used to combat white-collar crime. Originally created to restrict the entry of organized crime into legitimate businesses, RICO prohibits an organization's employees from engaging in a pattern of racketeering activity. Some examples of the wide variety of crimes considered to be racketeering activities are securities fraud, mail fraud, wire fraud, bribery, acts of violence, and embezzlement from pension funds. Under the RICO act, it is easier to both prosecute corrupt organizations and seize assets obtained through corruption. In addition, under RICO, a person who suffers damages to his or her business or property may sue for treble damages, an amount equal to three times actual damages.

SECURITIES FRAUD

securities fraud
A fraud that occurs when a person or company provides false information to potential investors to influence their decisions to buy or sell securities.

Securities fraud occurs when a person or company, such as a stockbroker or investment firm, provides false information to potential investors to influence their decisions to buy or sell securities. In addition, securities fraud encompasses theft of an investor's assets, stock trading based on nonpublic information (see "insider trading" as discussed in Chapter 30), and the wrongful manipulation of financial statements.

EXAMPLE 3.3

▶ Updike, the chief executive officer of Coast-to-Coast Airlines, knew that FlyToday Airlines intended to purchase all outstanding shares of Coast-to-Coast Airlines at a higher price than its current market value. Using insider information, Updike bought as much stock in Coast-to-Coast Airlines as he could afford and resold it to FlyToday Airlines at a huge profit. If discovered, Updike could be charged with the crime of insider trading.

Ponzi scheme
A type of securities fraud in which large gains are promised to investors, but in reality, newer investments are used to provide a return on older investments.

A Ponzi scheme is a type of securities fraud in which large gains are promised to investors; but in reality, newer investments are used to provide a return on older investments. These schemes inevitably collapse over time as older investments eventually become too large to cover with new investments. For more information on Ponzi schemes, visit http://www.sec.gov/answers/ponzi.htm.

EXAMPLE 3.4

► In 2008 Bernard Madoff, former chairman of NASDAQ and owner of an investment firm with more than 4,000 clients, was charged with securities fraud for orchestrating one of the most massive Ponzi schemes to date. Madoff's Ponzi scheme operated for years by promising steady gains to investors during all economic climates; however, the scheme failed when Madoff was unable to meet increased demands for withdrawals resulting from investor uncertainty in the stock market. In the end, total losses to Madoff's investors, including charity organizations, pension funds, celebrities, and average investors, totaled more than $20 billion. The court found Madoff guilty of securities fraud and, because of the egregious nature of his corrupt acts, sentenced him to serve 150 years in a federal prison.

ARSON

The crime of arson is the willful or malicious act of causing the burning of property belonging to another person. Some states have broadened the definition of arson to include the burning of a house by its owner and the destruction of property by other means, such as by explosion. Aside from the few persons who start fires for irrational reasons, most instances of arson are profit related. When the motivation is profit, the arsonist is usually trying to collect money from an insurance company for a building that he or she owns. Most states have statutes that provide for the punishment of persons who burn their own property with the aim of collecting insurance money. Such statutes establish a special category of crime called burning to defraud. To combat these practices, the insurance industry has developed very sophisticated investigation techniques and has an impressive record of assisting in successful prosecutions.

Arson is the willful or malicious act of causing the burning of property belonging to another person.

arson
The willful or malicious act of causing the burning of another's property.

burning to defraud
A special category of crime providing for the punishment of persons who burn their own property with the aim of collecting insurance money.

EXAMPLE 3.5

► Filkins, the owner of a clothing manufacturing firm, was losing money because of unexpected fashion changes. A large inventory of clothing had accumulated before it became apparent that little of it would ever be sold. Desperate, Filkins hired an arsonist to set the building on fire one night when Filkins had an unshakable alibi. The building, inventory, and equipment were insured. Insurance investigators and the fire marshal found evidence of arson and caught the criminal, who identified Filkins as the person who had hired him. The insurance company refused to pay for the loss, and Filkins and the arsonist were both charged with the crime of arson.

larceny
The act of taking and carrying away the personal property of another without the right to do so.

robbery
The taking of property in the possession of another person against that person's will and under threat of bodily harm.

burglary
The illegal entering of another person's premises for the purpose of committing a crime.

LARCENY

Larceny is a broad term that includes most forms of theft—that is, robbery, hijacking, embezzlement, and shoplifting. Larceny is often classified as petty (small) or grand (large), depending upon the value of the stolen property. It is important to distinguish among the various types of larceny. Robbery is defined as the taking of property in the possession of another person against that person's will and under threat of bodily harm—as in the case of a holdup. *Hijacking* is stealing from a vehicle in transit or the vehicle itself; and *shoplifting* is stealing merchandise from a retail store. Burglary is the illegal entering of another person's premises for the purpose of committing a crime.

EXAMPLE 3.6

▶ Jelkin Electronics was in the business of selling and repairing various kinds of electronic equipment such as televisions, stereos, DVD players, and so on. One morning, as he opened for business, the manager discovered that a rear window had been broken, obviously to gain entry during the night, and a number of stereo components had been stolen. The owner immediately called his insurance agent and learned, to his dismay, that his policy covered robbery, but not burglary. The firm suffered the complete loss of the stolen property.

Bribery consists of giving or taking money or property of value with the intent of influencing someone in the performance of his or her duty.

bribery
The act of offering, giving, receiving, or soliciting something of value to influence official action or the discharge of a public duty.

BRIBERY

The crime of bribery consists of giving or taking money or property of value with the intent of influencing someone (usually a public official) in the performance of his or her duty. Some states have enacted laws that also make it a crime to bribe someone other than a public official, such as a purchasing agent employed by a business firm. Both the giver of the bribe and the receiver can be charged with bribery.

EXAMPLE 3.7

▶ Rodriguez was employed as a secretary at Balasen Corporation. She had access to enormous amounts of confidential information, including sales projections, short- and long-range plans, and product development plans. Turner, an executive with a competing firm, initially came to know Rodriguez socially and after a short time recognized the value of the personal contact. An agreement resulted whereby Rodriguez turned over to Turner electronic files containing many confidential documents in exchange for a cash sum. If discovered, both parties could be charged with bribery.

FALSE PRETENSES

The term false pretenses describes a broad category of crimes that involve activities intended to deceive others by making false claims, or to obtain goods by using false pretenses. A number of federal and state statutes govern activities that might be considered false pretenses.

false pretenses
A broad category of crimes that involve activities intended to deceive others or to obtain goods by making false claims.

EXAMPLE 3.8

▶ Rollings operated a small catering and take-out food service. He could see that his business was headed for failure unless he installed additional equipment to increase productivity. For this he needed a bank loan, but he was afraid that he did not own sufficient assets to qualify for the loan. As a result, when Rollings applied for the loan, he claimed that he owned certain equipment that he was actually renting from a restaurant supply company.

A person who makes false statements to a bank for the purpose of obtaining a loan could be prosecuted under the appropriate statute. In Example 3.8, there were no actual "goods," but the bank had extended credit and the credit could be considered a "good."

Another example of the crime of using false pretenses would be a person who continues to purchase goods with a canceled credit card after having been notified of its cancellation.

FORGERY

The crime of forgery consists of wrongfully making or altering the writings of another with the intent to defraud. Forgery could include falsifying a signature on a check or the endorsement (the signature on the reverse side of the check). The act of signing another person's name to a credit card charge slip without permission is also considered forgery. The common practice of a secretary signing a boss's name to letters, however, could hardly be considered forgery, since the secretary signs the letters with the authorization of his or her boss and with the boss's express or implied consent.

forgery
The false making or alteration of a writing with the intent to defraud.

EXAMPLE 3.9

▶ Corcoran was employed as a gas station attendant. One day he noticed that a regular customer, Cosolino, kept a number of oil company credit cards in a wallet in the glove compartment of his car. When Cosolino left his car for repair, Corcoran stole one of the cards and began using it to charge gasoline, tires, and other items at a service station in another town, signing Cosolino's name each time. When he was caught, Corcoran was charged with forgery and other crimes.

PERJURY

The crime of perjury consists of intentionally giving false oral or written statements under oath in a judicial proceeding after having sworn to tell the truth. In some instances, giving false information on a government form is also considered perjury.

perjury
The crime of intentionally giving false oral or written statements under oath in a judicial proceeding after having sworn to tell the truth.

EXAMPLE 3.10

▶ Danvers, a former government official, was called to testify before a congressional committee regarding his activities after leaving government service that might have been in violation of the law. Under oath, he intentionally lied about the extent of these activities. Investigation revealed the untruths in his testimony, and he was charged with and convicted of perjury.

EMBEZZLEMENT

embezzlement
The wrongful taking of money or other property that has been entrusted to a person as a part of his or her job.

The crime of embezzlement may be defined as the wrongful taking of money or other property that has been entrusted to a person as a part of his or her employment. Some jobs, such as accountant, cashier, and bank teller, generally provide more opportunity for embezzlement than other jobs where the employee has little contact with money. The use of computers in business has led to some ingenious schemes for embezzling.

EXAMPLE 3.11

▶ Folsom was employed as a computer programmer at the headquarters of a bank. He secretly programmed the computer so that interest earned on depositors' accounts would be split: Only part of the payment would go to the depositor's account, while a small amount would be placed in an account that Folsom had set up to receive the payments. When he was caught, Folsom was charged with embezzlement.

EXTORTION

extortion
The act of taking or demanding money or other property from someone by using force, threats of force, or economic harm.

The crime of extortion is the act of taking or demanding money or other property from someone by using force, threats of force, or economic harm. The difference between extortion and bribery is that in bribery both parties are willing participants, whereas in extortion one person is willing and the other is unwilling.

Returning to the case of Rodriguez and Turner, discussed in Example 3.7 to illustrate bribery, if Rodriguez had been unwilling to disclose the confidential information and if Turner had threatened to break her legs or burn down her house, the crime would be extortion.

Certain individuals have seized the opportunity for illegal gain by using stolen or counterfeit credit cards.

OTHER BUSINESS-RELATED CRIMES

The number of crimes that involve businesses continues to grow as changes in business practices and technology offer new opportunities for wrongdoers to benefit from illegal or questionable activities.

Credit Card Fraud   Credit cards provide cardholders with many conveniences, but certain individuals have seized the opportunity for illegal gain by using stolen or counterfeit credit cards. Frequently, persons with knowledge of computers access the credit card numbers of consumers who have made purchases on the Internet and use these credit card numbers without authorization. In addition, the practice of obtaining credit cards under false pretenses continues to plague banks, credit card issuers, and consumers.

Identity Theft   Identity theft occurs when an unscrupulous individual steals the name and personal information of someone else by stealing private mail, by obtaining personal data on the Internet, or by soliciting personal information from an unwitting victim over the telephone. The person stealing another's identity does so in order to obtain credit cards and other types of loans, with no intention of ever repaying these. It is, therefore, as important to protect one's identity as it is to protect one's credit cards.

CHAPTER SUMMARY

1. A crime is a violation of a specific statute. A tort is a private wrong that causes injury to another person's physical well-being, property, or reputation.

2. The three classifications of crimes, based on their perceived seriousness, are (a) treason, (b) felonies, and (c) misdemeanors.

3. Many crimes are particularly important to businesses and employees, including the following: white-collar crime, securities fraud, arson, burning to defraud, larceny, robbery, hijacking, shoplifting, burglary, bribery, false pretenses, forgery, perjury, embezzlement, extortion, credit card fraud, and identity theft.

CHAPTER THREE ASSESSMENT

MATCHING LEGAL TERMS

Match each of the numbered definitions with the correct term in the following list. Write the letter of your choice in the answer column.

a. arson

b. bribery

c. burglary

d. extortion

e. felony

f. forgery

g. misdemeanor

h. perjury

i. Ponzi scheme

j. white-collar crime

1. A classification of serious crimes such as murder or arson.   **1.** _____

2. A classification of less serious crimes such as certain traffic offenses.   **2.** _____

3. An act of willful or malicious burning of another's property.

       3. _____

4. The giving or taking of money or property with the intent of influencing, or being influenced, in the performance of an official duty.

       4. _____

5. Wrongfully making or altering the writing of another with the intent to defraud.

       5. _____

6. The taking of someone's property against that person's will under threat of bodily harm.

       6. _____

7. An unofficial category of crime that generally does not involve force or violence.

       7. _____

8. Breaking into and entering another person's property with the intent of committing a felony or stealing property of value.

       8. _____

9. A type of securities fraud in which large gains are promised to investors, but in reality, newer investments are used to provide a return on older investments.

       9. _____

10. Making false oral or written statements under oath.

       10. _____

TRUE/FALSE QUIZ

Indicate whether each of the following statements is true or false by writing *T* or *F* in the answer column.

11. The purpose of criminal law is to compensate injured parties for their losses.

       11. _____

12. If a person's reckless driving results in an automobile accident, he or she can be charged with both a tort and a crime.

       12. _____

13. Treason is a major crime against the federal government consisting of levying war or giving aid and comfort to an enemy.

       13. _____

14. White-collar crime, as distinguished from other types of crime, generally does not involve force or violence.

       14. _____

15. Burning to defraud is a special category of crime committed by persons who burn their own property with the intention of collecting insurance money.

       15. _____

16. Larceny is a broad term that includes most forms of theft.

       16. _____

17. Shoplifting is the term that describes the theft of money by employees, such as accountants or cashiers, who steal money from retail stores.

       17. _____

18. The theft of goods from a vehicle in transit is known as hijacking.

       18. _____

19. In all states, the crime of bribery is limited to giving or taking money or property to influence a public official.

       19. _____

20. The legal term that covers such activities as obtaining goods and other benefits by the use of misleading statements and deception is false pretenses.

       20. _____

21. The crime of perjury is limited to the false swearing under oath before a judge in a federal court.   **21.** _____

22. When employees with access to a firm's money, such as accountants, cashiers, and bank tellers, wrongfully divert funds to themselves or to others, they are usually charged with burglary.   **22.** _____

23. It is always illegal for an executive of a firm to buy or sell the stock of the firm.   **23.** _____

24. A person who profits from the sale of stock as a result of using nonpublic information can be charged with violations of federal law.   **24.** _____

25. The difference between extortion and bribery is that, in extortion, both parties are willing participants in the crime.   **25.** _____

DISCUSSION QUESTIONS

Answer the following questions and discuss them in class.

26. What is the difference between a tort and a crime?

_____

_____

27. What are the three major classifications of crimes?

_____

_____

28. What are some crimes that are particularly applicable to business?

_____

_____

29. What are some acts that were previously considered crimes but are no longer viewed as violations of the law?

_____

_____

30. What are some typical misdemeanors common to most jurisdictions?

_____

_____

31. What are some common examples of white-collar crime?

_____

_____

Answer the following questions, which require you to think critically about the legal principles that you learned in this chapter.

32. **White-Collar Crime** Why do some highly paid business executives engage in illegal practices such as insider trading? What would you recommend to reduce the incidence of such practices?

_____

_____

33. **Burning to Defraud** What would be the effect on the insurance business and the economy if there were no "burning to defraud" statutes?

_____

_____

34. **Embezzlement** Has the use of computers in business increased or reduced the incidence of embezzlement?

_____

_____

35. **Extortion** What is the difference between extortion and bribery?

_____

_____

36. **False Pretenses** What is the intent of someone who is said to engage in activities called "false pretenses"?

_____

_____

37. **A Question of Ethics** Do you think that a U.S. citizen who disagrees with U.S. foreign policy against one of its enemies should be charged with treason for donating money to that enemy's war efforts against the United States? Why or why not?

_____

_____

CASE QUESTIONS

Study each of the cases below. Answer the questions that follow by writing _Yes_ or _No_ in the answer column.

38. **Arson** Williamson owned and operated a restaurant named Plum Pudding. His restaurant had a difficult time competing with Green Apple Snak Shoppe, located across the street. It seemed that whenever Plum Pudding offered a new special price

on a particular meal, its competitor met the price and offered some other inducement as well. As a last desperate effort to remain in business, Williamson hired a "torch" to set fire to the Green Apple. Just as the hired criminal had finished his work, he was apprehended by an off-duty police officer. The hired "torch" admitted his guilt and implicated Williamson.

a. Would Williamson be charged with arson? a. _____

b. Would the hired "torch" be charged with arson? b. _____

c. Is it likely that Green Apple's insurance would pay for the damage? c. _____

d. Is this an example of the crime of extortion? d. _____

39. **False Pretenses** Zaks, the owner of a hairstyling salon, Locks Unlimited, applied for a bank loan to buy new hairdryers and other equipment she felt were needed to attract new customers. To enhance her chances of getting the loan, she told the bank that she owned considerable equipment and furniture, although most of the equipment and furnishings in the shop were actually rented.

a. If Zaks's deception were discovered, is it likely that she could be charged with false pretenses? a. _____

b. If the bank accepted the false statements at face value, did the bank perform responsibly? b. _____

c. Could Zaks be charged with extortion? c. _____

d. Could the banker be charged with bribery? d. _____

40. **Bribery** Gelfis owned and operated Welltech, a janitorial service company that provided services to a number of city and state agencies. Eager to expand his firm and increase his profits, he approached Biondi, the director of purchasing for a state agency, and offered to sell Biondi stock in Welltech at a greatly reduced price. It was clear to both Gelfis and Biondi that Biondi would be expected to award the janitorial services contract to Welltech.

a. If the arrangement were completed, could Gelfis be charged with bribery? a. _____

b. Could Gelfis be charged with burglary? b. _____

c. Could Gelfis be charged with extortion? c. _____

CASE ANALYSIS

Study each of the following cases carefully. Briefly state the principle of law and your decision.

41. **Larceny, Credit Card Fraud, False Pretenses** Buckley, a worker in a restaurant, stole a credit card from the coat of its owner with the intention of using it to charge goods. He purchased some merchandise at a retail store and paid for these goods by presenting the stolen credit card to the salesperson and signing the name of the person whose name appeared on the card. Was Buckley guilty of a crime? [*Buckley v. Indiana*, 322 N.E.2d 113 (Indiana)]

Principle of Law:

_____

_____

Decision:

_____

_____

42. **Price-Fixing** Tameny had worked for Atlantic Richfield Company (ARCO) for 15 years and had risen to the position of retail sales representative. While he never had a formal contract of employment, his duties included managing relations between ARCO and various independent dealers in his territory. ARCO and some of its agents had been manipulating the retail gasoline prices of ARCO dealers. Those violations of federal and state antitrust laws had resulted in an agreement between ARCO and the courts under which ARCO and its agents agreed to discontinue those activities. Despite this agreement, ARCO continued to pressure Tameny to threaten and persuade dealers to cut their gasoline prices to a point at or below the level specified by ARCO. Tameny refused and was subsequently fired for alleged incompetence and unsatisfactory performance. On appeal, the Supreme Court of California was asked to decide (1) whether an employer's authority over employees included the right to demand that an employee commit a criminal act; (2) whether an employer may force compliance by discharging an employee who refuses to do so; and (3) whether an employee may bring a tort action for wrongful discharge. Will Tameny be successful in his action claiming wrongful discharge? [_Tameny v. Atlantic Richfield Co.,_ 610 P.2d 1330 (California)]

Principle of Law:

_____

_____

Decision:

_____

_____

43. **Insider Trading** Franken, president of Monarch Pharmaceuticals Incorporated, was one of only three persons who knew that one of the firm's experimental drugs had just been approved by the federal government. The drug had been found to cure several serious diseases. As soon as news of the approval became public, Franken reasoned, the price of the firm's stock would increase substantially. He arranged with a friend to buy thousands of shares of the company's stock, hoping to sell at a profit after the price increased as a result of the good news. Can Franken be prosecuted for his actions?

Principle of Law:

_____

_____

Decision:

_____

_____

44. **Forgery** Searle, office manager of Entro Products, had access to the firm's checks to be used in paying for office supplies. However, Searle was not authorized to sign them. Each time he wanted to pay invoices, Searle had to have the firm's president sign them. After some months, he was able to copy the president's signature. He had invoices printed for a nonexistent company, and periodically he made out checks to the fake company and signed the president's signature. Ultimately his wrongdoings were discovered. Is it likely Searle will be prosecuted for his crime?

Principle of Law:

_____

_____

Decision:

_____

_____

LEGAL RESEARCH

Complete the following activities. Share your findings with the class.

45. **Working in Teams** Small and medium-sized businesses are often concerned with crimes that could affect the firm. In teams of three or four, interview one or several business owners or managers and ask them to briefly describe the kinds of crimes they are concerned about and the steps they take to minimize the risk of crime.

_____

_____

46. **Using Technology** Using the Internet and search engines, investigate common internal business crimes committed by employees.

_____

_____

chapter 4
Tort Law

After studying this chapter and completing the assessments, you will be able to

4.1 Explain the nature of torts and identify some common torts.

4.2 Describe defamation.

4.3 Explain the differences between libel and slander.

4.4 Explain the two common defenses to charges of defamation.

4.5 Define nuisance and the types of nuisance charges.

4.6 Describe conversion and explain its main purpose.

4.7 Define negligence and distinguish between the different types of negligence.

4.8 Explain the legal concept of liability and provide examples.

terms

LEGAL

defamation	vicarious negligence
libel	negligence *per se*
slander	contributory negligence
trade libel	comparative negligence
nuisance	assumption of risk
conversion	liable
negligence	vicarious liability
reasonable person	strict liability

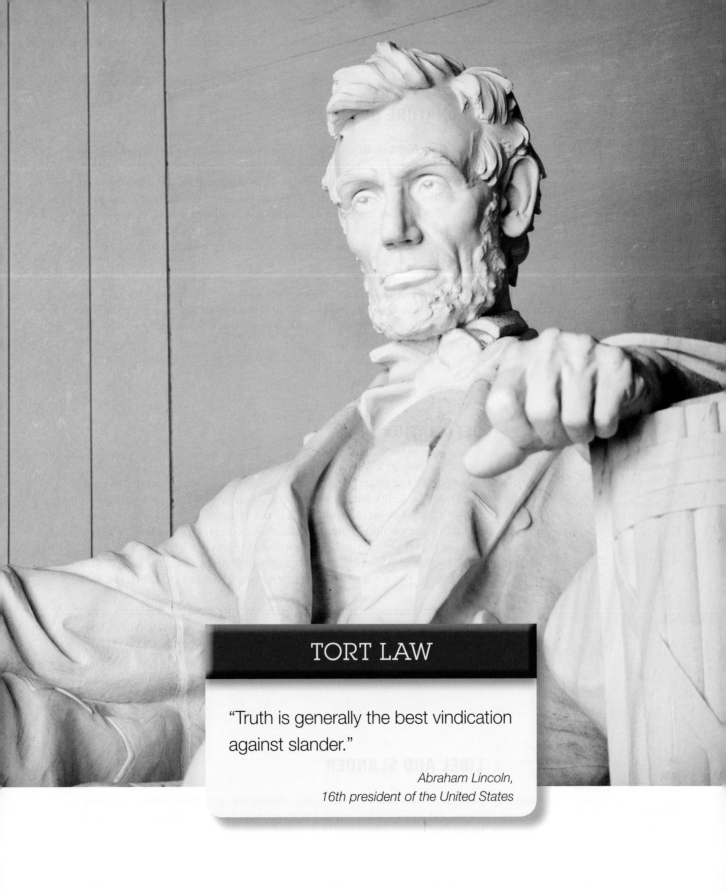

TORT LAW

"Truth is generally the best vindication against slander."

Abraham Lincoln,
16th president of the United States

4.1 THE NATURE OF TORTS

Chapter 3 defined a crime as a violation of the rights of society as a whole, whether an individual is the victim of the crime or there is no identifiable wronged party. A tort, in contrast to a crime, is a violation of the rights of an identifiable individual or business that has been wronged either intentionally or by negligence. For example, when the crime of larceny has been committed and the victim can be identified, then both a crime has been committed and the victim of the larceny has suffered the tort of conversion (the wrongful taking of property). The law of torts does not deal with duties imposed by contract but is concerned only with the violation of private rights.

Whether acting as an individual or as an employee, a person has a responsibility to consider the rights of others. The common torts discussed in this chapter all have some direct or indirect bearing on an individual's personal life and on how he or she performs his or her job. These common torts include defamation, nuisance, conversion, and negligence.

4.2 DEFAMATION

defamation
The harming of a person's reputation and good name by the communication of a false statement.

Defamation is the harming of a person's reputation and good name by the communication of a false statement. For an act to be considered defamatory, it is necessary to show that the statement was made in such a way that others hear or read it. To call someone a thief to the person's face may be an insult, but it is not defamation. A defamatory statement usually holds a person up to hatred, ridicule, or contempt; or causes a person's esteem, respect, or social position to be diminished. Defamation also involves some suggestion of disgrace, and it tends to generate negative feelings about the person who suffers the defamation. For a statement to be defamatory, it must be addressed to a third party.

Occasionally more than one party may be guilty of spreading a defamatory statement. For example, suppose a newspaper reporter includes a previously published defamatory statement in an article. The reporter, along with the party who originally created the false statement, may be found guilty of defamation.

The charge of defamation has been separated into two torts: libel and slander.

4.3 LIBEL AND SLANDER

libel
The spreading of damaging statements in written form, including pictures, cartoons, and effigies.

slander
The spreading of damaging words or ideas about a person, directly or indirectly, in all other forms not considered libel.

Generally, libel is the spreading of damaging statements in written form—including pictures, cartoons, and effigies (likenesses). Defamation on radio, television, and websites is also considered libel.

Slander is the spreading of damaging words or ideas about a person, directly or indirectly, in all other forms not considered libel. Of course the most common form of slander involves spoken words, but slander also can be committed by means of gestures and actions.

CHARACTERISTICS OF LIBEL

Although many libel cases involve defamatory statements published in books, newspapers, magazines, and websites, the possibility of libel also exists in business and personal letters, memos, and catalogs. The libel need not be direct. Subtle suggestion or implication is enough to bring about legal charges. For example, there have been cases in which the use of quotation marks has been interpreted as giving a libelous meaning to otherwise harmless words.

Many libel cases involve defamatory statements published in books, newspapers, magazines, and websites.

EXAMPLE 4.1

▶ Roscoe, a business manager, wrote a memo to his supervisor explaining the absence of one of his female employees. The memo included the words "and I tried to contact the fellow who used to be a 'friend' of hers."

By placing the quotation marks around the word *friend*, Roscoe suggested that the fellow he referred to was really not a friend, but a lover. The important point in this case is that it is not so much the exact wording of the statement that matters, but rather how others—including a jury—might reasonably interpret the statement.

The previous illustration, based on an actual case, may not seem very damaging, given today's more liberal standards of social behavior; but the same principle can apply to other situations. Suppose that a supervisor had written a memo stating, "I don't know what became of the laptop computer, but you might want to check with Fred Chaffee; he has been known to 'borrow' things before."

Another example of how a statement might be interpreted as damaging a person's reputation can be seen in the following case, in which no statement was made, but the implication was damaging nevertheless.

EXAMPLE 4.2

▶ The First National County Bank noticed shortages of money and asked its employees to submit to polygraph (lie detector) tests. One employee, Baxter, was unable to pass the test, and the bonding company refused to renew her bond (a form of insurance that protects a firm from losses due to employee dishonesty). The local newspaper learned of the problems at the bank and interviewed the president, who mentioned that some employees were no longer working because the insurance company would not issue bonds for them. When the newspaper printed the story, Baxter sued the bank, charging libel.

Even though the newspaper account did not mention Baxter by name, she charged that people who knew her and knew that she was no longer working at the bank would assume that she had been involved in the shortages of money.

Most cases of libel are not quite as unusual as those previously described. Many problems simply involve thoughtless written remarks or unfounded gossip. Other problems arise when employers make negative statements when providing references for employees.

EXAMPLE 4.3

▶ Evans and her secretary did not get along well. When the secretary resigned to take a job with another firm, Evans was happy to see her leave. The secretary's new employer sent a routine inquiry form to Evans to verify the secretary's claims of prior employment. The form provided spaces in which to answer the routine questions and also a section for other comments. Evans, who still disliked her former secretary and intended to damage her reputation, added "untrustworthy and dishonest." The new employer discharged the secretary and pointed to Evans's comment as the reason. The secretary brought suit, charging libel.

In recent years, the threat of libel suits by former employees who are unhappy with the references given by former employers has gotten so serious that many firms refuse to respond to any inquiry about former workers—even those who have good records.

CHARACTERISTICS OF SLANDER

Slander is the term that describes almost all defamation that cannot be classified as libel. Slander includes spoken words, gestures, actions, and even omissions. Most cases of slander involve thoughtless statements that reflect on another person's good name and reputation. Since oral statements, unless recorded, cannot be reproduced as evidence, some people tend to speak carelessly about others without realizing that anyone hearing a slanderous statement can be called upon later to testify to having heard it.

EXAMPLE 4.4

▶ Feely, a sales manager, was speaking with a group of employees and customers at a convention when the name of a former salesperson, Tummer, came up. Feely said that Tummer was incompetent and had cheated on his expense account, even though this had never been proven. One of those in the group reported the statement to Tummer and agreed to swear to the fact that Feely had made the statement. Tummer brought suit, charging slander.

The tort of slander does not require a directly defamatory statement. Gestures and actions can sometimes be equally damaging. Consider Example 4.5, in which no defamatory words were spoken.

EXAMPLE 4.5

▶ Mason entered a variety store, examined various articles of merchandise, and then left the store. Conant, the store manager, suspecting that Mason had stolen something, followed her into the street, where—in full view of several bystanders—he ordered her to stop. He then searched her and examined her handbag. Finding nothing, he released her and returned to the store. Mason believed that Conant, by his actions and gestures, had falsely accused her of being a thief. She brought suit for damages to her reputation, charging slander.

Although the store manager did not actually call the customer a thief, by his actions he implied as much. Cautious businesspersons, given a similar situation, would quietly ask the shopper to return to the store and consent to a search in the privacy of the manager's office. Obviously the damages that result from a slanderous statement are influenced by the number of people who hear it. Many people are careful to avoid making such statements publicly before large groups. However, making a defamatory statement to even a single person might still provide the basis for legal action.

EXAMPLE 4.6

▶ Hamm, the sales manager of Linn Products, dictated an angry memo to Pennington, one of her salespersons. In the memo she called Pennington a "thief," among other things. Shortly thereafter, Pennington left the employ of Linn and brought suit, charging slander. Hamm argued that she had dictated a confidential memo, without sending copies to third parties, and that she had not damaged Pennington's reputation because the defamatory words had not been heard or seen by anyone else. Pennington claimed that Hamm had dictated the memo to a secretary, and in so doing had slandered him. The court decided that Hamm had indeed slandered Pennington.

TRADE LIBEL

In conducting business, a firm and its owners have the right to remain free from false and malicious statements by others that may cause a loss or damage to the reputation of the firm, the owners, the products produced, or the merchandise carried or manufactured by the firm. The tort of trade libel is similar to traditional defamation but deals with an individual's title to property, or to the quality or conduct of a business.

trade libel
Defamation that deals with an individual's title to property, or to the quality or conduct of a business.

EXAMPLE 4.7

▶ Philo sent an e-mail message to several suppliers claiming that his competitor, Willit, was about to file for bankruptcy and go out of business. The statements were without foundation since Willit's business was prosperous and there was no likelihood of a bankruptcy. Because such an untrue statement could damage his business, Willit could sue Philo, charging trade libel.

HUMOR AND SLANDER

It might seem that a quick apology and a "sorry, just kidding" might be enough to avoid some charges of slander. Not so! Consider the following case, where the subject of a seemingly harmless remark did not think it was funny.

EXAMPLE 4.8

▶ A radio station was sued as a result of its broadcast of a listener call-in program that invited listeners to nominate a person or a business for the title of "dodo of the day." A listener, who identified herself only as "Bonnie," called to nominate her insurance agent, Lawrence Faro, as the "dodo of the day." She claimed that after she consulted him about a damaged windshield, he advised her to throw a brick through her windshield to make the claim large enough that the insurance company would pay it. Faro denied knowing a customer named Bonnie and sued the radio station for defamation.

4.4   DEFENSES TO DEFAMATION

There are two common defenses to charges of defamation: (1) truth and (2) privilege. If a defamatory statement can be proved to be true, the person who claims that he or she was defamed cannot recover damages. However, a person engaged in business should still be careful, since it is often expensive to go to court in order to prove the truth of a statement. The expense can be avoided by being cautious in the first place.

Similarly, if the person accused of defamation had a special privilege in making the defamatory statement, such as an attorney in a court proceeding who accuses a witness of lying, the defamed person cannot recover damages.

nuisance
An unlawful interference with the enjoyment of life or property.

4.5   NUISANCE

The law gives everyone the right to enjoy his or her land without unreasonable interference from others.

An unlawful interference with the enjoyment of life or property constitutes a nuisance. The law gives everyone the right to enjoy his or her land without unreasonable interference from others. A person who acts in a way that denies this right to a specific person or persons has created a *private nuisance*. A *public nuisance,* by comparison, affects the community or the general public. Creating a nuisance does not mean taking another's property—only detracting from the enjoyment of it. A person can be charged with creating a private nuisance by causing loud noises, creating foul odors, shining bright lights, or diverting a stream.

EXAMPLE 4.9

▶ Springs Manufacturing Company had operated a small factory in the town of Burlingame for many years and was regarded as a responsible firm that created no problem for the community. It even employed 30 townspeople. In an effort to expand the company's business, management decided to begin making a line of goods that required a fairly noisy stamping process. The families in the immediate area complained loudly about the noise. Management took the position that the noise was the price the community had to pay for the economic benefits of having the plant located there.

Example 4.9 illustrates the tort of nuisance. It also illustrates the tough choices people must sometimes make between seeking relief from a nuisance and having to do without some offsetting benefit. The law recognizes that when people live together in a society such as ours, not all people can have their own way. The benefits to one person must be balanced against the inconvenience to another.

4.6 CONVERSION

The law gives each person the right to own and use personal property without interference from others. When this right is denied or abridged by another, the wrongdoer is said to have committed the tort of conversion. This tort can involve a wrongful taking, a wrongful detention, or an illegal assumption of ownership. Conversion may involve removal, damage, destruction, or unauthorized use of another person's property. A shoplifter commits the crime of larceny as well as the tort of conversion. Note, however, that unlike larceny, conversion can occur without intent. For example, if a student accidentally takes a friend's laptop computer under the mistaken assumption that it is his or her own, the student has committed the tort of conversion—regardless of the student's lack of intent. A lawsuit charging a person with conversion provides the victim with the means of collecting money damages from someone who steals personal property. It is one thing to have a dishonest employee arrested, found guilty of the crime of larceny, and punished; but a criminal action does not return the stolen goods or money. A tort action for conversion is one way to help replace the money or property.

conversion
The wrongful exercise of dominion and control over another's personal property.

EXAMPLE 4.10

▶ Clemente stole Quinn's car. While it was in Clemente's possession, the car was destroyed. Quinn had no insurance on his car because he had intended to sell it. The only way he could recover the cost of the car would be to sue Clemente, charging him with conversion.

4.7 NEGLIGENCE

The tort of negligence is the failure to exercise reasonable care necessary to protect others from risk of harm. The number of lawsuits charging negligence has grown tremendously in recent years, in part because news accounts of large jury awards have encouraged others to

negligence
The failure to exercise necessary care to protect others from unreasonable risk of harm.

sue. Also, there seems to have developed a mind-set that when a person experiences misfortune, someone else ought to pay.

Lawsuits have charged professionals such as doctors, dentists, nurses, pharmacists, lawyers, and accountants with malpractice (a term that is used in cases involving the negligence of professionals—see Chapter 34). Home owners have been sued for negligence for injuries that have occurred on their property. Corporations have been sued for negligent design or manufacture of products that cause injury (see Chapter 33). Schools have been sued for failing to educate students properly, and municipalities have been sued for negligent road design that has contributed to accidents. And, of course, automobile drivers are sued in great numbers for negligent operation of an automobile.

To avoid legal action either as an individual or as an employee, each person must exercise reasonable care and good judgment to avoid causing injury to others. Even so, good judgment and care will not prevent all accidents. It is also important to carry adequate insurance coverage for protection against the financial losses that can result from being adjudged liable for the tort of negligence.

EXAMPLE 4.11

▶ Jensen, employed as a truck driver, was driving a new light truck at 40 miles per hour on a mild day when a tire blew out. As a result, his truck collided with another vehicle and caused both extensive damage to the other vehicle and injury to the driver.

While it is difficult to predict how a jury would decide this case, most reasonable persons would say that Jensen was not negligent. But suppose that Jensen was driving at 70 miles per hour, the tires were worn, the day and pavement were hot, and the truck was heavily loaded. In that case, most people would say that Jensen was negligent. It is not just a particular act that constitutes negligence but the circumstances that surround it.

UNAVOIDABLE ACCIDENT

In theory, all accidents are avoidable. Jensen, the truck driver, could have avoided the accident by simply not driving the truck at all—or by not getting out of bed that morning. But the concept of unavoidable accident is intended to focus attention on whether an accident could have been avoided if the person alleged to be responsible had acted reasonably.

THE "REASONABLE PERSON"

reasonable person
A completely fictitious individual who is assumed to have the judgment and skill one would expect from a person with the strengths and limitations of the person whose behavior is being judged.

The law provides certain ways by which juries can determine if a person has acted negligently. One of these ways is the doctrine of the "reasonable person of ordinary prudence," a completely fictitious individual who is assumed to have the judgment and skill one would expect from a person with the strengths and limitations of the person whose behavior is being judged. While there is no standard reasonable person, a jury is asked to determine how the mythical person would have behaved under the same or similar circumstances. Obviously, one reason the law has kept this imaginary individual alive is to prevent jurors from judging a defendant in terms of how they themselves would have behaved.

KINDS OF NEGLIGENCE

The legal concept of negligence is not quite so simple as deciding if the driver of an automobile was driving negligently. Many cases are far more complex, particularly when the law must decide if one or more third parties also can be held responsible for the negligence.

Vicarious Negligence   The term *vicarious* as used in the law means essentially the same as when it is used generally—that is, to describe an act performed by one person as a substitute for another. Vicarious negligence, therefore, means charging a negligent act of one person to another.

vicarious negligence
Charging a negligent act of one person to another.

EXAMPLE 4.12

► Christensen rented a house from Hoover. After a few months, a dispute developed about the amount of rent owed. Hoover obtained a court order to recover possession of the house. Because Christensen was out of town at the time, Hoover hired a local moving and storage company to remove and store the renter's possessions. After Christensen paid the rent owed, Hoover told the storage company to release Christensen's possessions. Unfortunately, some items were damaged and still others were missing. Christensen sued, and after the trial in favor of Hoover, the Colorado State Supreme Court held on appeal that Hoover was vicariously responsible for the loss that occurred while the goods were in the hands of the moving company. [*Christensen v. Hoover*, 643 P.2d 525 (Colo. 1982)]

In many cases that involve the negligence of an employee, the employer is held responsible provided the employee was performing the tasks he or she was hired to do. (The practical reason is that the employer usually has the money or insurance to settle the suit. There is little to gain from a judgment against an employee who does not have the financial resources to pay the damages.)

Negligence Per Se   Negligence *per se*, which translates to "negligence in or of itself," occurs when a defendant in a case of negligence has violated a law that was enacted in order to prevent the type of injury that occurred. For example, if a defendant, while driving his or her vehicle while intoxicated, strikes another vehicle, he or she may be found liable of negligence *per se*.

negligence *per se*
Negligence *per se* occurs when a defendant in a case of negligence has violated a law that was enacted in order to prevent the type of injury that occurred.

Contributory Negligence   The previous paragraphs described the concept of negligence. Contributory negligence is not an accusation but rather a legal defense by the party who is charged with negligence. In effect, the defendant admits to being negligent but argues that the plaintiff was negligent as well and that the plaintiff's negligence contributed to his or her own injuries. Another term for this principle is *contributory fault*. Under the doctine of contributory negligence, the injured party would not be able to sue successfully if he or she were partly responsible, even in a minor way. Note the case in Example 4.13, involving Alvis and Ribar, in which the trial court rejected Alvis's suit because of his contributory negligence.

contributory negligence
A legal defense that involves the failure of an injured party to be careful enough to ensure personal safety.

Comparative Negligence   Many legislatures and courts have now replaced the doctrine of contributory negligence with the doctrine of comparative negligence. Under this latter doctrine, the injured party bringing the lawsuit is not prevented from recovering damages

comparative negligence
A form of negligence that requires the court to assign damages according to the degree of fault of each party.

even if he or she was partly at fault. The jury determines how much the plaintiff was at fault and reduces the verdict by that amount. For example, if the plaintiff was found to be 10 percent negligent, he or she would get an award 10 percent less than the full damages as determined by the jury.

EXAMPLE 4.13

▶ Alvis was injured while riding in a car driven by Ribar. The car had crashed into a metal barrel anchoring an intersection stop sign at the site of some highway construction. Alvis sued Ribar, the county, and a contractor. The suit was dismissed in the trial court because of contributory negligence; apparently there was some evidence of carelessness on Alvis's part as well (he may not have been wearing his seatbelt). But when the appeal reached the Supreme Court of Illinois, it saw injustice in denying any damage to Alvis simply because he had contributed to his injuries. The supreme court sent the case back to the trial court to let a jury decide the extent to which Alvis had contributed to the accident and to proportion damages accordingly. [*Alvis v. Ribar,* 85 Ill. 2d 1, 421 N.E.2d 886 (Ill. 1981)]

assumption of risk
A defense in a case of negligence in which the defendant demonstrates that the plaintiff voluntarily assumed the risk associated with the dangerous condition caused by the defendant.

Negligence as a Result of Assumption of Risk   Sometimes an injured party in a case of negligence assumes the risk as a result of his or her actions. Assumption of risk is a defense raised by the defendant in a case of negligence in which the defendant demonstrates that the plaintiff voluntarily assumed the risk associated with the dangerous condition caused by the defendant. Often parties voluntarily agree to assume the risk associated with dangerous conditions because the advantageous outcomes involved with such exceed the hazards; thus, the defendant will not be liable for negligence. Consider Example 4.14.

EXAMPLE 4.14

▶ Singh, the owner of a sailboat, contacted O'Shea to inquire about renting a boat slip. O'Shea informed Singh that the only boat slip available was one that was accessible only by walking a nonmaintained, rocky, and steep trail, but that if Singh were willing to sign a rental agreement in which she assumed the risk for any injuries that might result from using the unkept trail, O'Shea would lower the rent substantially. Because Singh enjoyed hiking and could greatly benefit from the monetary savings involved with renting this particular boat slip, Singh signed the rental agreement. Because Singh assumed the risk, the court would not find O'Shea liable for negligence should Singh injure herself while using the access trail.

4.8 LIABILITY

liable
Being judged legally responsible.

When a person has been judged to be responsible for a loss, he or she is said to be liable (not to be confused with *libel,* covered earlier). In most lawsuits, the court must decide if the defendant is liable for the damages as charged. In some instances, the law shields certain persons. In other instances, liability is automatically assumed.

EXAMPLE 4.15

▶ Wimpers was in the business of renting power tools. Woo rented a power saw from him that lacked a standard safety guard. While using the saw, Woo cut off two fingers. Wimpers might be charged with negligence (carelessness) for having rented the tool without the guard. Because of the negligence, he would be held liable (responsible) for the injuries and the payment of damages.

It would be easy to state that all liability results from negligence and all negligence creates liability, but this is not the case. There are instances in which a person is liable even though no negligence has been proved.

VICARIOUS LIABILITY

In some cases, the law holds persons liable for the acts of others, such as when an employer is held responsible for the acts of employees, or when a general contractor is held responsible for acts of a subcontractor. The term for this shifting of responsibility is vicarious liability, and it is related to vicarious negligence, discussed earlier.

vicarious liability
The concept of laying responsibility or blame upon one person for the actions of another.

STRICT LIABILITY

Certain events cause death or injury to others even when no negligence exists. Under a doctrine known as strict liability, people may be liable for injuries to others whether or not they have done something wrong. Examples include damage caused by inherently dangerous activities, events, or animals and might involve domestic pets, fire, water, explosives, or dangerous chemicals.

strict liability
The doctrine under which persons may be liable for injuries to others whether or not they have been negligent or committed an intentional tort. This is liability without the necessity of proving fault.

EXAMPLE 4.16

▶ The Crocker Construction Company was building a highway and found it necessary to use explosives to blast away some rock formations. Employees of the firm were well trained and careful in their work. Despite their care, however, some rock fragments damaged a nearby house. The owner of the house sued the construction company for the damages. Crocker raised the defense that the home owner could not show negligence on the part of the company. Judgment was entered for the home owner because, under the doctrine of strict liability, it was not necessary to show negligence, only that the damage occurred.

The broad range of injuries suffered by employees on the job is another example of strict liability. Workers' compensation laws limit the amount of money employees may recover from their employers for most work-related injuries and illnesses; however, the employer and the firm's insurance company cannot avoid payment by claiming that the employee contributed to his or her own injury or illness, or that he or she assumed the risks of the job.

In recent years, the doctrine of strict liability also has been applied to cases involving injury or death caused by manufactured products, such as machinery—even if the injured person misused the product. Some courts believe that the manufacturer found liable for a

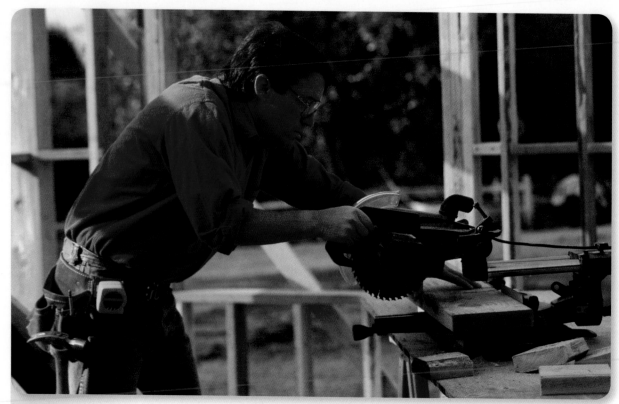

A manufacturer of saws may be liable under the doctrine of strict liability.

product that causes harm is in a better position than the injured person to absorb the costs associated with this injury. Typically the manufacturer's insurance company will pay the damages, and the manufacturer will pass the cost of insurance to all users of the product (see Chapter 33).

A purchaser who is injured by a product has a cause of action by demonstrating merely that (1) the product was defective, (2) the defect was the cause of the injury, and (3) the defect caused the product to be unreasonably dangerous. Strict liability has been recognized and applied in at least two-thirds of the states in this country.

EXAMPLE 4.17

▶ Greenman purchased a power saw for use in his home workshop. He was using the saw when a sliver of wood flew out of the machine and caused him to suffer serious eye injuries. Greenman sued the manufacturer of the machine. The court ruled that the manufacturer was liable under the doctrine of strict liability.

Proponents of strict liability claim that eliminating the need to prove negligence on the part of the manufacturer will encourage manufacturers and sellers to be more concerned with producing safer products. Others argue that the application of strict liability will inhibit the development of new products because of the fear of product liability lawsuits and the high cost of product liability insurance.

CHAPTER SUMMARY

1. A tort is a violation of the rights of an identifiable individual or business that has been wronged either intentionally or by negligence. Common torts include the following: defamation, nuisance, conversion, and negligence.

2. Defamation is the harming of a person's reputation and good name by the communication of a false statement.

3. Libel is the spreading of damaging statements in written form, which include pictures, cartoons, effigies, and any type of media communication. Slander is spreading damaging words or ideas about a person, directly or indirectly, in all other forms not considered libel.

4. Two common defenses to charges of defamation are (1) truth and (2) privilege.

5. Nuisance is an unlawful interference with the enjoyment of life or property. There are two types of nuisance charges in the U.S. system: private and public. A private nuisance occurs when a person acts in a way that denies the right of enjoyment to a specific person or persons. A public nuisance occurs when an entire community or the general public is denied enjoyment as a result of an act.

6. Conversion is a wrongful act against a person's right to own and use personal property. This act can include removal, damage, destruction, or unauthorized use of another person's property. A tort action for conversion is one way to help replace the money or property the victim lost.

7. Negligence is the failure to exercise reasonable care to protect others from risk of harm. Types of negligence include vicarious negligence, negligence *per se,* contributory negligence, comparative negligence, and negligence as a result of assumption of risk.

8. The legal concept of liability involves judging a party legally responsible for a loss or wrong. Examples include being found liable for any of the torts mentioned in this chapter, including defamation, nuisance, conversion, or negligence.

CHAPTER FOUR ASSESSMENT

MATCHING LEGAL TERMS

Match each of the numbered definitions with the correct term in the following list. Write the letter of your choice in the answer column.

a. conversion
b. contributory negligence
c. defamation
d. liability

e. libel
f. negligence
g. nuisance
h. slander

i. tort
j. vicarious liability

1. A broad category of violations of the rights of individuals. 1. _____

2. False written or spoken statements that harm a person's reputation. 2. _____

3. Actions that unreasonably deny someone the enjoyment of his or her land.

3. _____

4. False written statements that harm a person's reputation or good name.

4. _____

5. Actions that physically remove or destroy the personal property of others.

5. _____

6. False spoken statements or actions that damage a person's reputation or good name.

6. _____

7. Carelessness that results in injury to another person or his or her property.

7. _____

8. The state or condition of being responsible for wrong or injury.

8. _____

9. The shifting of responsibility from one person to another.

9. _____

10. A concept that states that one person partially caused his or her own injuries.

10. _____

TRUE/FALSE QUIZ

Indicate whether each of the following statements is true or false by writing *T* or *F* in the answer column.

11. A tort is a violation of the rights of a particular person.

11. _____

12. Tort law is concerned with compensation for losses suffered by injured parties.

12. _____

13. Defamation includes both libel and slander.

13. _____

14. The tort of libel is concerned with injury to a person's reputation caused by false statements that are used in testimony in court.

14. _____

15. A person who defames another individual by exhibiting an insulting drawing in a public place could be charged with libel.

15. _____

16. The tort of slander is concerned with injury to a person's reputation caused by false statements that are spoken.

16. _____

17. Two defenses to charges of defamation are truth and privilege.

17. _____

18. The tort of nuisance does not entail taking another's property, only detracting from his or her enjoyment of it.

18. _____

19. Liability is the state of being responsible for a wrong or injury.

19. _____

20. The tort of conversion is concerned with acts that deny a person the possession of his or her property.

20. _____

21. The tort of negligence is a form of carelessness.

21. _____

22. Vicarious liability means that one person can be held responsible for the negligent acts of another.

22. _____

23. Negligence *per se* occurs when a defendant in a case of negligence has violated a law that was enacted in order to prevent the type of injury that occurred.

23. _____

24. The "reasonable person" doctrine is concerned with the appeal to a jury to assume how a person would behave under the best conditions.

24. _____

25. Under the doctrine of comparative negligence, juries attempt to determine how much in percentage terms the plaintiff was at fault and then reduce the verdict by that amount.

25. _____

DISCUSSION QUESTIONS

Answer the following questions and discuss them in class.

26. Identify several common torts and explain how each might be committed in a business environment.

_____

_____

27. Explain the legal concept of liability and provide examples.

_____

_____

28. Compare contributory negligence with comparative negligence and provide examples of each.

_____

_____

29. Explain vicarious liability and provide an example.

_____

_____

30. Explain strict liability and provide an example.

_____

_____

Answer the following questions, which require you to think critically about the legal principles that you learned in this chapter.

31. Defamation Why is it that public figures find it difficult to successfully sue a publication for libel, whereas private persons have a better chance? Should public figures be required to accept libelous accusations as the price of fame?

_____

_____

32. Trade Libel The law protects businesses against defamatory statements or writings just as it does for individuals. Should there be a different standard for businesses that would permit a firm to attack a competitor?

_____

_____

33. Private Nuisance The law gives a person the right to enjoy his or her land without unreasonable interference from others. If a person plays loud music on his or her property and a neighbor charges him or her with creating a public nuisance, where does the music player's constitutional right to free expression end, and where does the neighbor's right to be free of a private nuisance begin? How would a court decide?

_____

_____

34. Conversion If a person suffers a loss of his or her property as a result of the criminal wrongdoing of another, would it matter whether the thief (wrongdoer) is charged by the victim with the crime of larceny or the tort of conversion?

_____

_____

35. A Question of Ethics Do you believe it is unethical to exaggerate the extent of injuries suffered in an automobile accident resulting from another driver's negligent driving in an effort to increase the amount of a financial settlement that will be paid by an insurance company?

_____

_____

CASE QUESTIONS

Study each of the following cases. Answer the questions that follow by writing _Yes_ or _No_ in the answer column.

36. Libel and Slander Goldman, an ex-convict, was employed in the accounting department of Rogers Products Incorporated. None of his coworkers was aware of his previous conviction and imprisonment, although the president of the firm and

Ruiz, the human resources manager, knew of it. During an office party, Goldman and Ruiz became involved in an argument and Ruiz shouted, "You're an ex-con and a jailbird. We'd be better off without you here."

a. Would Goldman have a basis for a suit for libel? a. _____

b. Would Goldman have a basis for slander? b. _____

c. Did Ruiz violate the professional ethics of his position? c. _____

37. **Negligence** The Sock 'n' Rock Music Store was located in a small shopping mall. In an effort to attract additional customers, the manager of the store installed an outdoor loudspeaker and played rock music at high volume. Nearby stores in the shopping mall objected, claiming that the loud music drove their customers away.

a. Does Sock 'n' Rock have the right to use the rented property as it pleases? a. _____

b. Do the other stores in the mall have a basis for suit, charging private or public nuisance? b. _____

c. Do the other stores in the mall have a basis for suit, charging conversion? c. _____

d. Would a court order preventing the loud music seem to be a good remedy? d. _____

38. **Negligence** Leffingwell engaged the Bartwell Tree Removal Service to cut down and remove a diseased tree from her property. When the work began, it was a calm day. As the work progressed, however, a high wind arose and blew a portion of the tree onto a neighbor's car, causing considerable damage. The neighbor brought suit against Bartwell, charging negligence.

a. Does it seem likely that the accident could have been prevented? a. _____

b. Could the owner of the car be charged with negligence for parking his car in a place where it could be damaged by the falling tree? b. _____

c. Would the neighbor have a sound basis upon which to sue for damages? c. _____

d. Do the circumstances seem to support a defense Bartwell might make claiming that this was an unavoidable accident? d. _____

39. **Conversion** Pratt, a stock-car racing driver, had entered a race to be held several months later. Two days before the race, he left his racing car at a shop to have some last-minute adjustments made. When Pratt went to pick up the car before the race, the shop owner refused to release it until Pratt paid for work that had been done two years earlier on another car. Pratt could not raise the money in time and was unable to participate in the race. As a result he had to forfeit the $75 fee he had paid to enter.

a. Does it seem that the repair shop acted responsibly? a. _____

b. Could Pratt bring suit, charging conversion? b. _____

c. Could Pratt bring suit against the repair shop to recover his $75 entry fee? c. _____

d. Could Pratt have the shop owner arrested for larceny? d. _____

CASE ANALYSIS

Study each of the following cases carefully. Briefly state the principle of law and your decision.

40. **Defamation** At a special meeting, the board of directors of Family Federal Savings & Loan Association asked Newton, its president, manager, and director, to resign. He did so. Shortly thereafter, a reporter for the *Oregon Statesman* talked about Newton's resignation with one of the directors. The very next day, the paper published an article that stated, "The board of directors of the six-branch Family Federal Savings & Loan Association has forced Thomas Newton out of his position as the association's president, charging that he is 'administratively incapable.'" Newton thereupon sued the association and its individual directors for defamation. When a jury awarded him damages, the directors appealed on the ground that the quoted language was not capable of a defamatory meaning. Will the directors succeed in overturning the judgment? [*Newton v. Family FS&L Association,* 616 P.2d 1213 (Oregon)]

41. **Conversion** Rensch left two diamond rings for cleaning at Riddle's Mall in Rapid City, South Dakota. Riddle's had advertised free ring cleaning to the public. When Rensch returned for the rings, he found that a clerk had mistakenly given them to another customer. They were never recovered, and Rensch ultimately sued Riddle. What tort was involved in this case, and is it likely that the court will find for Rensch? [*Rensch v. Riddle's Diamonds of Rapid City,* 393 N.W.2d 269 S.D. (South Dakota)]

Principle of Law:

_____

_____

Decision:

_____

_____

42. **Trade Libel** Robin Williams, famous entertainer and comedian, gave a performance at a San Francisco nightclub, The Great American Music Hall. As part of his comedy routine, he disparaged a particular brand of wine, Rege, by suggesting that it would be a great success if it were directed toward a particular minority group. The discussion of the wine also included certain obscene and vulgar expressions. It seemed that the Rege wine was the target of Williams's jokes. Video and audiotapes were made of the performance and were distributed by the recording company, Polygram Records. Rege brought suit, claiming trade libel. What would be the probable outcome of this suit? Did the fact that the alleged libel took place during a comedy routine alter the case? [*Polygram Records v. Superior Court,* 170 Cal. App. 3d 543 (California)]

Principle of Law:

_____

_____

Decision:

_____

_____

43. **Defamation** Fortrell, an aide in a child care center, was particularly concerned about the behavior of a certain child who frequently fought with and teased
other children at the center. LaRena, the mother of one of the children who had been
a victim of the troublesome child, was at the center one day, and Fortrell explained
that the behavior of the problem child was caused by his mother, Yung, who was
herself unbalanced and unfit to have custody of the child. What Fortrell did not know
was that LaRena was a friend of Yung and reported the conversation to her. Yung
sued Fortrell, charging defamation. Will Yung succeed in a defamation suit?

Principle of Law:

_____

_____

Decision:

_____

_____

LEGAL RESEARCH

Complete the following activities. Share your findings with the class.

44. **Working in Teams** In teams of three or four, interview several property/
casualty insurance agents or claims adjusters (as distinguished from life or health
insurance personnel) to learn more about claims filed against small businesses for
negligence or other torts. Ask what steps or measures might have been taken to
avoid the commission of the tort.

_____

_____

45. **Using Technology** Using the Internet and search engines, investigate a case
involving negligence.

_____

_____

chapter **5**
Constitutional Law

After studying this chapter and completing the assessments, you will be able to

5.1 Explain the difference between express and implied powers; describe the process used to amend the U.S. Constitution; and explain judicial review and the doctrine of preemption.

5.2 Discuss the main provisions of the commerce clause, the full faith and credit clause, and the supremacy clause.

5.3 Describe three provisions of the First Amendment.

5.4 Discuss the current state of constitutional law with respect to the Second Amendment.

5.5 Describe the requirement of probable cause under the Fourth Amendment.

5.6 Identify and explain four protections provided by the Fifth Amendment.

5.7 Provide examples of cases that are addressed by the Eighth Amendment.

5.8 Explain the due process and equal protection clauses of the Fourteenth Amendment.

5.9 Discuss how the Internal Revenue Service administers the collection of income taxes pursuant to the Sixteenth Amendment.

LEGAL terms

express powers	supremacy clause
implied powers	probable cause
Bill of Rights	procedural due process
judicial review	substantive due process
doctrine of preemption	rational basis
commerce clause	intermediate scrutiny
full faith and credit clause	strict scrutiny

CONSTITUTIONAL LAW

"It may be true that the law cannot make a man love me, but it can keep him from lynching me, and I think that's pretty important."

Martin Luther King Jr.,
American civil rights leader

5.1   THE UNITED STATES CONSTITUTION

Every federal statute enacted by Congress, every state statute enacted by state legislatures, every ordinance and code enacted by local municipalities, every administrative law and decision, and every court decision in every case in every jurisdiction—each of these must be consistent with the United States Constitution. This document, although relatively brief (see Appendix A), forms the basis for all American law. This chapter describes several provisions of the Constitution and explains the various ways in which these provisions impact individuals and businesses in the United States.

CONSTITUTIONAL POWERS

Both the federal government and the 50 states' governments have the power to regulate the people who reside within their jurisdictions; and, in addition to the federal Constitution, each state has its own state constitution. This system of government is known as *federalism*. In addition, within the federal government, there are three distinct branches, forming a *separation of powers*. These concepts are discussed in more depth in Chapter 6.

The federal Constitution and state constitutions confer two types of powers on the governments of which they are a part:

express powers
Those that are specifically stated in the federal Constitution.

▶ Express powers are those that are specifically stated. For example, the federal Constitution grants the federal government the explicit powers to raise an army and to impose taxes.

implied powers
Those that have arisen as a result of interpretation of the express powers by the courts.

▶ Implied powers are those that have arisen as a result of interpretation of the express powers by the courts. For example, the federal Constitution gives Congress the implied power to create an agency to explore outer space—something not even imagined by the individuals who wrote the Constitution.

CONSTITUTIONAL AMENDMENTS

Although the drafters of the Constitution were persons of vision, they could not, of course, foresee the changing needs of our country and its people in the many years that were to follow. The Constitution has been amended, or changed, 27 times, and it will probably continue to be amended. Amending the Constitution is an onerous process. Each amendment must be proposed by a two-thirds vote of Congress and ratified, or approved, by the legislatures of three-fourths of our 50 states. It is also possible for an amendment to be initiated by the states. The first 10 amendments are referred to as the Bill of Rights.

Bill of Rights
The first 10 amendments of the U.S. Constitution.

JUDICIAL REVIEW

Both federal and state courts have the power to determine whether laws enacted by legislatures or decisions made by lower courts violate the provisions of the Constitution. If a court decides that a law is contrary to the Constitution, the law can be declared unconstitutional and therefore invalid. The process of deciding if a law is contrary to the Constitution is known as judicial review.

judicial review
The process of deciding if a law is contrary to the Constitution.

THE DOCTRINE OF PREEMPTION

There are several instances in which the Constitution expressly or implicitly provides that Congress has the power to pass legislation. Frequently states and municipalities pass legislation in one or more of these areas, as well. If a state or local law is inconsistent with the federal law, the state or local law may be declared unconstitutional, and the federal law must be followed. This is known as the doctrine of preemption—that is, the federal law preempts, or supersedes, the state law. However, this doctrine applies only in instances where the law in question pertains to a power that the Constitution has expressly or implicitly granted to Congress.

doctrine of preemption
A principle that states that when certain state or local laws are inconsistent with the federal law, the federal law must be followed.

EXAMPLE 5.1

▶ Hazleton, a city in Pennsylvania, saw its population swell from 23,000 to 30,000 during a very short time, largely because of an increase in Latino residents coming from New York and New Jersey. Many were in the country legally, but some were not. The mayor and other city officials, blaming the influx for increases in crime and other problems, passed a series of local ordinances that gave the city the right to fine employers and suspend their business licenses for hiring such immigrants, and requiring anyone over the age of 18, depending on his or her immigration status, to obtain a permit before being allowed to rent an apartment. Numerous laws modeled after the Hazleton ordinances were subsequently passed by states and municipalities throughout the United States. Several groups sued, claiming that the ordinances were invalid. A federal appeals court ruled that because the power to enact immigration laws has been granted to Congress in the Constitution, Hazleton's ordinances were unconstitutional under the doctrine of preemption. (*Lozano v. City of Hazleton*, 496 F. Supp. 2d 477)

5.2 THE COMMERCE CLAUSE, THE FULL FAITH AND CREDIT CLAUSE, AND THE SUPREMACY CLAUSE

The Constitution is divided into major divisions, called *articles;* subdivisions, called *sections;* and in some cases sub-subdivisions, called *clauses.* This chapter addresses three of these particular clauses that have a specific impact on businesses. These clauses are referred to as the commerce clause, the full faith and credit clause, and the supremacy clause.

commerce clause
A provision of the Constitution that grants Congress the power to regulate trade with foreign nations, and among the several states, and with the Indian tribes.

ARTICLE 1, SECTION 8, CLAUSE 3: THE COMMERCE CLAUSE

The commerce clause reads as follows: "The Congress shall have Power . . . to regulate Commerce with foreign Nations, and among the several States, and with the Indian Tribes."

This clause grants Congress the power to regulate commerce among states in order to prevent the restriction of trade activity. Courts have held that the term *commerce*, as used in the Constitution, is defined as the movement or exchange of persons, goods, or information between states.

The commerce clause creates one of the most fundamental powers in the Constitution. Some judges and legal scholars take a broad and expansive view of this clause, and make the claim that Congress has the power to regulate many business activities that would otherwise be left to state legislatures. Others, however, are *strict constructionists*. These individuals maintain that many of the matters that Congress now legislates would be more appropriately left to the states. The commerce clause generates a great deal of intensive legal and political debate; it forms the basis for the division of power between the federal and the state governments, and even between and among the three branches of the federal government (see Chapter 1).

full faith and credit clause
A provision of the Constitution that mandates that each state respect and enforce both the judgments awarded by courts in other states, and the statutes and case law of other states.

supremacy clause
A provision of the Constitution that requires state judges to follow federal law in the event of a conflict with state law.

EXAMPLE 5.2

▶ A number of small, out-of-state wineries challenged Michigan and New York state laws that allowed only in-state wineries to sell directly to consumers. The out-of-state wineries claimed that under the laws, they were unable to compete effectively with the in-state wineries; they incurred additional expenses associated with selling their product solely through retailers. Because the state laws restricted commerce between states, the U.S. Supreme Court held that the laws violated the commerce clause of the Constitution. (*Granholm v. Heald* 544 U.S. 460)

ARTICLE IV, SECTION 1: THE FULL FAITH AND CREDIT CLAUSE

The full faith and credit clause reads as follows: "Full Faith and Credit shall be given in each State to the public Acts, Records, and judicial Proceedings of every other State."

This clause mandates that each state respect and enforce both the judgments awarded by courts in other states, and the statutes and case law of other states (see Chapter 1). The Supreme Court has made a distinction in the level of the respect that must be given. A great deal of respect must be given to the judgments awarded by courts in other states; however, a lower level of respect must be given to another state's statutes and case law.

EXAMPLE 5.3

▶ A handful of states provide that couples who are of the same sex may marry within those states. The question of whether states that do not allow same-sex marriages will be required to recognize same-sex marriages performed in other states, pursuant to the full faith and credit clause, remains undecided.

ARTICLE IV, SECTION 2: THE SUPREMACY CLAUSE

The supremacy clause reads as follows: "This Constitution . . . the Laws of the United States . . . and all treaties made . . . shall be the supreme law of the land; and the judges in every state shall be bound thereby . . ."

This clause, closely tied to the doctrine of preemption, requires state judges to follow federal law in the event of a conflict with state law. According to the supremacy clause, a Supreme Court ruling that involves a constitutional issue is binding on state courts. For instance, in Example 5.2, Michigan and New York state courts must comply with the Supreme Court ruling pertaining to the invalidity of the laws affecting out-of-state wineries. Note that the supremacy clause also requires states to recognize the provisions of U.S. treaties over any conflicting state regulations.

5.3 THE FIRST AMENDMENT

The First Amendment reads as follows: "Congress shall make no law respecting an establishment of religion, or prohibiting the free exercise thereof; or abridging the freedom of speech, or of the press; or the right of the people peaceably to assemble, and to petition the

Government for a redress of grievances." There are several parts to this amendment, three of which are discussed in the following paragraphs.

THE ESTABLISHMENT AND FREE EXERCISE CLAUSES RELATING TO RELIGION

The First Amendment right to freedom of religion is divided into two interconnected pieces, referred to as the *establishment clause* and the *free exercise* clause. The establishment clause makes it unconstitutional for government to recognize a single national religion, or even to create policies or practices that favor one religion over another. The free exercise clause requires that government not interfere with an individual's practicing the religion of his or her choice.

The First Amendment protects freedom of religion.

While the nature of court decisions relating to both of these clauses has changed significantly over time, in general, the current view is that a law is constitutionally permissible provided that it does not unduly burden the practice of religion unless there is a compelling interest. For example, if a specific religion were to encourage the practice of polygamy—that is, simultaneously being married to two or more people—a state might successfully argue that it has a compelling interest in disallowing this practice by passing a law against the crime of bigamy.

FREEDOM OF SPEECH

The First Amendment's freedom of speech clause gives Americans a fundamental right. While individuals certainly have the right to freedom of political or religious speech, this right should be guarded most zealously when the speech is unpopular, upsetting, ignorant, or even anger-provoking. Thus speech that is sexist, racist, ageist, or otherwise offensive is also protected. Similarly, the act of burning the American flag is considered protected speech, and laws prohibiting such acts are unconstitutional.

All speech, however, is not protected under the First Amendment. The following are examples of speech that may constitutionally be limited or silenced: speech that incites imminent danger; child pornography; speech that is legally obscene; speech that threatens physical harm; speech that is defamatory, including both slander and libel (see Chapter 4); interference with works protected by trademark, patent, or copyright law (see Chapter 28); and commercial speech such as deceptive advertising (see Chapter 30).

FREEDOM OF THE PRESS

It would certainly be unconstitutional for a state or municipality to pass a law limiting what a journalist could write or say about a political candidate or issue. However, not all laws pertaining to the news media are unconstitutional. For example, it is constitutionally acceptable for government to tax newspapers. In

The First Amendment gives Americans freedom of speech; but not all speech is protected under this amendment.

> ▶ Speech that incites imminent danger
>
> ▶ Child pornography
>
> ▶ Speech that is legally obscene
>
> ▶ Speech that threatens physical harm
>
> ▶ Speech that is defamatory
>
> ▶ Interference with works protected by trademark, patent, or copyright law
>
> ▶ Commercial speech

FIGURE 5.1   Examples of Speech That May Constitutionally Be Limited or Silenced

addition, the question of whether or not a journalist or a newspaper may be sued for defamation is the subject of Example 5.4.

EXAMPLE 5.4

▶ Sullivan, a police commissioner in Montgomery, Alabama, filed a libel suit against *The New York Times* for publishing allegedly inaccurate information about the Montgomery police department. In overturning a lower court's decision on First Amendment grounds, the Supreme Court held that debate on public issues would be inhibited if public officials could sue for inaccuracies that were made by mistake. The ruling made it more difficult for public officials to bring libel charges against the press because these officials now need to prove that a harmful untruth was printed either maliciously or with a reckless disregard for the truth. (*New York Times v. Sullivan*, 376 U.S. 254)

5.4 THE SECOND AMENDMENT

The Second Amendment reads as follows: "A well regulated Militia, being necessary to the security of a free State, the right of the people to keep and bear Arms, shall not be infringed."

There are several issues associated with this amendment. The first is what is meant by the term "to bear arms." Generally this term has been interpreted to mean "to carry firearms." In addition, much debate has centered on the question of whether the term applies only to military use of arms versus arms held by private citizens. Although some compelling arguments suggest that the term "to bear arms" applies only to the military use of arms, most courts now agree that this right also applies to private citizens.

The right to bear arms is not unlimited, however. Some 21st-century weapons were never imagined by the framers of the Constitution. Once again, interpreting the Constitution is a matter of drawing a line between what is and what is not permissible, balancing rights versus responsibilities.

EXAMPLE 5.5

▶ McDonald, a 76-year-old resident of Chicago, claimed the city's 1982 ban on handguns left him prey to street gangs. In a landmark decision, the Supreme Court held that the right of an individual to "keep and bear arms" protected by the Second Amendment applies to states and ruled that the ban was unconstitutional. However, the opinion also reaffirmed that certain laws are permissible under the Second Amendment, such as those that prohibit the possession of firearms by felons or persons who are mentally ill; those forbidding the carrying of firearms in sensitive places, such as government buildings and schools; or those imposing conditions and qualifications on the commercial sale of arms. (*McDonald v. Chicago*, 130 S. Ct. 3020)

5.5 THE FOURTH AMENDMENT

The Fourth Amendment reads as follows: "The right of the people to be secure in their persons, houses, papers, and effects, against unreasonable searches and seizures, shall not be violated, and no Warrants shall issue, but upon probable cause, supported by Oath or affirmation, and particularly describing the place to be searched, and the persons or things to be seized."

The Fourth Amendment requires that police officers and other government officials (but not private citizens) must have probable cause to be able to conduct a personal or property search. Probable cause may be defined as a reasonable belief that a prudent police officer must have that a suspect has committed, is committing, or is about to commit a crime, thereby giving the officer the authority to conduct a search. All other unreasonable searches and seizures are unconstitutional and invalid. The Supreme Court has ruled that a search occurs only when a person expects privacy in the thing searched, and society believes that expectation is reasonable.

Examples of unreasonable searches and seizures include a detention of longer than 48 hours after a criminal arrest; a nonconsensual extraction of blood; and the gathering of fingerprint evidence in certain circumstances. However, stops of motorists at sobriety checkpoints to investigate possible instances of driving under the influence are not considered unreasonable and are permissible under the Fourth Amendment.

probable cause
A reasonable belief that a prudent police officer must have that a suspect has committed, is committing, or is about to commit a crime, thereby giving the officer the authority to conduct a search.

EXAMPLE 5.6

▶ Concerned that police officers were using their text pagers mostly for personal messages, a police chief decided to read some of them. He discovered that most of the messages sent by one officer were personal in nature. Some of these messages were sent to an ex-wife, others to a female friend. During a one-month period, the chief found that the officer had sent or received 456 messages, but only 57 were work-related. After learning that his messages had been read, the officer sued both the chief and the city, claiming that this action violated the Fourth Amendment. The Supreme Court ruled that public employees have only a limited privacy expectation when using a text pager supplied by the police department, and because the search by the police chief was motivated by a legitimate work-related purpose and because it was not excessive in scope, the search was reasonable. (*City of Ontario v. Quon*, 130 S. Ct. 2619)

5.6 THE FIFTH AMENDMENT

The Fifth Amendment reads, in part, as follows: "No person shall . . . be subject for the same offence to be twice put in jeopardy of life or limb; nor shall be compelled in any criminal case to be a witness against himself, nor be deprived of life, liberty, or property, without due process of law; nor shall private property be taken for public use, without just compensation."

This passage contains four distinct protections from governmental actions:

1. Double jeopardy: the Fifth Amendment does not allow a court to try a criminal defendant more than once for the same offense, whether the first trial has ended in an acquittal or a conviction.

EXAMPLE 5.7

▶ O.J. Simpson, a celebrity and former professional football player, was found not guilty and acquitted in criminal court for the murders of Nicole Brown Simpson and Ronald Goldman. He was subsequently sued for damages in civil court and found liable. Since the first case was criminal, but the second civil, there was no double jeopardy, and the judgment in the civil case did not violate the Fifth Amendment.

2. Self-incrimination: the Fifth Amendment gives individuals the right to refuse to divulge information that could later be used against them in a criminal proceeding. This right to refuse applies to any federal or state legal proceeding, whether criminal, civil, judicial, or administrative.

3. Due process: the Fifth Amendment requires that all persons be granted both procedural and substantive due process. Procedural due process mandates that all persons affected by a legal proceeding receive notice of its subject matter, time, and place and that these proceedings be conducted by a judge who is fair and impartial. Substantive due process mandates that government not unreasonably interfere with an individual's life, liberty, or property rights.

4. Eminent domain: the Fifth Amendment permits the government to take private property, both real and personal, for a public purpose so long as the owner receives just compensation (see Chapter 24).

procedural due process
A Constitutional mandate that all persons affected by a legal proceeding receive notice of its subject matter, time, and place and that these proceedings be conducted by a judge who is fair and impartial.

substantive due process
A Constitutional mandate that government not unreasonably interfere with an individual's life, liberty, or property rights.

5.7 THE EIGHTH AMENDMENT

The Eighth Amendment reads as follows: "Excessive bail shall not be required, nor excessive fines imposed, nor cruel and unusual punishments inflicted."

The Eighth Amendment restricts both the severity and the types of punishments that may be imposed by federal and state governments. The Supreme Court has ruled that punishments

> ▶ A person convicted of armed robbery is sentenced to death.
>
> ▶ A person convicted of shoplifting is sentenced to life in prison.
>
> ▶ A minor is sentenced to life in prison for stealing a car.
>
> ▶ A person convicted of assault and battery is sentenced to death.
>
> ▶ A person convicted of any crime is sentenced to being burned at the stake.

FIGURE 5.2 Examples of Punishments Prohibited under the Eighth Amendment

must be proportionate to the crime committed. The following are examples of punishments prohibited under the Eighth Amendment:

- ▶ A person convicted of armed robbery is sentenced to death.
- ▶ A person convicted of shoplifting is sentenced to life in prison.
- ▶ A minor is sentenced to life in prison for stealing a car.
- ▶ A person convicted of assault and battery is sentenced to death.

In addition, the Supreme Court has found that certain barbarous types of punishment, such as burning at the stake, are prohibited regardless of the type of crime committed.

In addition, the Eighth Amendment mandates that people accused or convicted of crimes are not to be subject to excessive bail. The Supreme Court has found that bail is reasonable when it is not substantially greater than the amount required to guarantee the suspected criminal's appearance in court. However, the Supreme Court has ruled that in extreme cases a court may deny bail altogether.

Finally, the Eighth Amendment prevents the government from imposing an unjustly harsh fine on a person convicted of a crime. If a fine is found to be grossly disproportionate to the crime committed, the fine may be overturned.

EXAMPLE 5.8

▶ Lyle Austin was indicted on four counts of violating South Dakota's drug laws. Austin ultimately pleaded guilty to one count of possessing cocaine with intent to distribute and was sentenced by the state court to seven years' imprisonment. The federal prosecutor then filed an additional lawsuit in federal court, requesting that the court require Austin to forfeit both his mobile home and auto body shop. Austin argued that the forfeiture of these properties would violate the Eighth Amendment. The federal court ruled that forcing Austin to transfer his property to the government under these circumstances did not constitute an excessive fine and thus was not in violation of the Eighth Amendment. (*Austin v. United States*, 509 U.S. 602)

5.8 THE FOURTEENTH AMENDMENT

The Fourteenth Amendment reads, in part, as follows: "No State shall . . . deprive any person of life, liberty, or property, without due process of law; nor deny to any person within its jurisdiction the equal protection of the laws."

While the first 10 amendments, the Bill of Rights, apply to actions of the federal government, the Fourteenth Amendment applies directly to the 50 states. Just as it is impermissible for the federal government to deny an individual either substantive or procedural due process under the Fifth Amendment, it is also unconstitutional for a state to deny an individual due process.

EXAMPLE 5.9

▶ Miranda confessed to a crime during police questioning without knowing he had a right to have an attorney present. Based on his confession, Miranda was convicted. The Supreme Court overturned the conviction, ruling that the due process clause of the Fourteenth Amendment requires that criminal suspects be warned of their rights before they are questioned by police. These rights are the right to remain silent, the right to have an attorney present during questioning, and, if the suspect cannot afford an attorney, the right to have one appointed by the state. The police must also warn suspects that any statements they make may be used against them in a court of law. These are now known as the Miranda warnings. (*Miranda v. Arizona*, 384 U.S. 436)

The Fourteenth Amendment also provides that when states pass laws they must treat all individuals equally. Laws that do not treat all people equally are unconstitutional unless the state can demonstrate the following:

rational basis
A test that measures whether the legislature had a reasonable, and not an arbitrary, basis for enacting a particular statute.

▶ If the law places restrictions on economic or property interests, or if the law discriminates on a basis other than race, sex, national origin, and related categories, the state must show that the law passes the rational basis test. The rational basis test is a standard that measures whether the legislature had a reasonable, and not an arbitrary, basis for enacting a particular statute.

intermediate scrutiny
A test that measures whether a particular statute is substantially related to an important government objective.

▶ If the law discriminates on the basis of sex, or if the law restricts commercial speech, the state must demonstrate that the law passes the intermediate scrutiny test. The intermediate scrutiny test is a standard that measures whether a particular statute is substantially related to an important government objective.

strict scrutiny
A test that measures whether the legislature had a compelling interest for enacting a particular statute.

▶ If the law discriminates on the basis of race or national origin, or if the law infringes on a fundamental constitutional right, the state must show that the law passes the strict scrutiny test. The strict scrutiny test is a standard that measures whether the legislature had a compelling interest for enacting a particular statute.

5.9 THE SIXTEENTH AMENDMENT

The Sixteenth Amendment reads as follows: "The Congress shall have power to lay and collect taxes on incomes, from whatever source derived, without apportionment among the several States, and without regard to any census or enumeration."

Prior to the passage of the Sixteenth Amendment, there were a series of conflicting court decisions regarding the federal government's right to levy an income tax. The Sixteenth Amendment granted the federal government the power to impose and collect a tax on individuals' incomes. The government exercised this power immediately and, by doing so, created a substantial source of revenue.

The Internal Revenue Service (IRS) is a federal agency (see Chapter 6) established by Congress and tasked with administering and collecting federal income tax under the Sixteenth Amendment. The IRS creates and enforces tax laws and improves taxpayers' understanding of these laws. To learn more about the IRS, visit **www.irs.gov**.

CHAPTER SUMMARY

1. Express powers are those that are specifically stated in the federal Constitution; implied powers are those that have arisen as a result of interpretation of the express powers by the courts. Each constitutional amendment must be proposed by a two-thirds vote of Congress and ratified, or approved, by the legislatures of three-fourths of the 50 states. The process of deciding if a law is contrary to the Constitution is known as judicial review. The doctrine of preemption is a principle that states that when state or local laws are inconsistent with a federal law, the federal law must be followed.

2. The commerce clause grants Congress the power to regulate trade with foreign nations, and among the several states, and with the Indian tribes. The full faith and credit clause mandates that each state respect and enforce other states' court judgments, statutes, and case law. The supremacy clause requires state judges to follow federal law in the event of a conflict with state law.

3. The First Amendment's establishment clause makes it unconstitutional for government to recognize a single national religion or to favor one religion over another; its free exercise clause requires that government not interfere with individual religious practice. The First Amendment's freedom of speech clause gives individuals the right to freedom of political or religious speech. The First Amendment's freedom of the press clause allows journalists to write or say whatever they wish about political candidates and issues.

4. Under the Second Amendment, the term "to bear arms" has been interpreted to mean "to carry firearms." Most courts now agree that the right to bear arms applies to private citizens. The right to bear arms is not unlimited, however.

5. The Fourth Amendment requires that police officers and other government officials (but not private citizens) must have probable cause to conduct a personal or property search.

6. Four protections provided by the Fifth Amendment include double jeopardy, self-incrimination, due process, and eminent domain.

7. The Eighth Amendment restricts both the severity and the types of punishments that may be imposed by federal and state governments.

8. Just as it is impermissible for the federal government to deny an individual either substantive or procedural due process under the Fifth Amendment, it is also unconstitutional for a state to deny an individual due process under the Fourteenth Amendment. This amendment also provides that state laws must treat all individuals equally unless the state can demonstrate that a law passes the rational basis test, the intermediate scrutiny test, or the strict scrutiny test.

9. The Internal Revenue Service is a federal agency established by Congress and tasked with administering and collecting federal income tax under the Sixteenth Amendment. The IRS creates and enforces tax laws and improves taxpayers' understanding of the laws.

CHAPTER FIVE
ASSESSMENT

MATCHING LEGAL TERMS

Match each of the numbered definitions with the correct term in the following list. Write the letter of your choice in the answer column.

a. commerce clause   **f.** First Amendment   **k.** probable cause
b. doctrine of preemption **g.** Fourth Amendment   **l.** procedural due process
c. Eighth Amendment   **h.** full faith and credit clause **m.** rational basis test
d. express powers   **i.** implied powers   **n.** strict scrutiny test
e. Fifth Amendment   **j.** judicial review   **o.** substantive due process

1. Rights specifically granted to Congress by the federal Constitution.   1. _____

2. A provision of the Constitution that mandates that each state respect and enforce both the judgments awarded by courts in other states, and the statutes and case law of other states.   2. _____

3. A provision of the Constitution that requires that police officers and other government officials must have probable cause to conduct a personal or property search.   3. _____

4. Rights granted to Congress that have arisen as a result of interpretation of the express powers by the courts.   4. _____

5. A reasonable belief that a prudent police officer must have that a suspect has committed, is committing, or is about to commit a crime, thereby giving the officer the authority to conduct a search.   5. _____

6. A provision of the Constitution that restricts both the severity and the types of punishments that may be imposed by federal and state governments.   6. _____

7. The process of deciding if a law is contrary to the Constitution.   7. _____

8. A constitutional mandate that all persons affected by a legal proceeding receive notice of its subject matter, time, and place and that these proceedings be conducted by a judge who is fair and impartial.   8. _____

9. A test that measures whether the legislature had a compelling interest for enacting a particular statute.   9. _____

10. A principle that states that when certain state or local laws are inconsistent with the federal law, the federal law must be followed.   10. _____

11. A constitutional mandate that government not unreasonably interfere with an individual's life, liberty, or property rights.   11. _____

12. A provision of the Constitution that provides for freedom of religion, freedom of speech, and freedom of the press.   12. _____

13. A provision of the Constitution that grants Congress the power to
regulate trade with foreign nations, and among the several states,
and with the Indian tribes.

13. _____

14. A test that measures whether the legislature had a reasonable,
and not arbitrary, basis for enacting a particular statute.

14. _____

15. A provision of the Constitution that relates to double jeopardy,
self-incrimination, due process, and eminent domain.

15. _____

TRUE/FALSE QUIZ

Indicate whether each of the following statements is true or false by writing *T* or *F* in the
answer column.

16. The federal Constitution has been amended more than 100 times.

16. _____

17. Both federal and state courts have the power to determine whether
laws enacted by legislatures or decisions made by lower courts
violate the provisions of the Constitution.

17. _____

18. The doctrine of preemption applies only in instances where the law
in question pertains to a power that the Constitution has expressly
or implicitly granted to Congress.

18. _____

19. The First Amendment's right to freedom of religion is divided into
two interconnected pieces, referred to as the enterprise clause and
the free exercise clause.

19. _____

20. The Supreme Court has ruled that the term "to bear arms" applies
only to the military use of arms.

20. _____

21. The Supreme Court has ruled that a Fourth Amendment search occurs
only when a person expects privacy in the thing searched, and society
believes that expectation is reasonable.

21. _____

22. The Fifth Amendment does not allow a court to try a criminal
defendant more than once for the same offense unless the first trial
has ended in an acquittal.

22. _____

23. The Eighth Amendment mandates that people accused or convicted
of crimes are not to be subject to excessive bail.

23. _____

24. While it is impermissible for the federal government to deny an
individual due process under the Fifth Amendment, it is not
unconstitutional for a state to deny an individual due process.

24. _____

25. The Sixteenth Amendment granted the federal government power to
impose and collect a tax on individuals' incomes.

25. _____

DISCUSSION QUESTIONS

Answer the following questions and discuss them in class.

26. Describe the process used to amend the Constitution.

_____

_____

27. Provide some examples of speech that may constitutionally be limited or silenced.

_____

_____

28. Provide some examples of laws that are permissible under the Second Amendment.

_____

_____

29. Provide some examples of unreasonable searches and seizures.

_____

_____

30. Describe the circumstances under which a law must pass the rational basis test and the strict scrutiny test.

_____

_____

31. Provide some examples of cases covered under the Eighth Amendment.

_____

_____

THINKING CRITICALLY ABOUT THE LAW

Answer the following questions, which require you to think critically about the legal principles that you learned in this chapter.

32. Full Faith and Credit Clause Why is it important that each state respect and enforce both the judgments awarded by courts in other states, and the statutes and case law of other states?

_____

_____

33. First Amendment Should speech that is sexist, racist, ageist, or otherwise offensive be protected under the First Amendment?

_____

_____

34. Second Amendment Should the right to bear arms be limited to the military use of arms, or should this right also apply to private citizens?

_____

_____

35. Eighth Amendment Should the death penalty be considered cruel and unusual punishment, thus violating the Eighth Amendment?

_____

_____

36. A Question of Ethics Is it ethical for a state legislature to pass a law for the sole purpose of testing its constitutionality?

_____

_____

CASE QUESTIONS

Study each of the following cases. Answer the questions that follow by writing _Yes_ or _No_ in the answer column.

37. First Amendment The town of Homesdale passes an ordinance that requires all retail establishments to remain closed on Christmas Day. Several groups sue, arguing that the ordinance is unconstitutional.

a. Does the ordinance violate the First Amendment of the Constitution?   a. _____

b. Does the ordinance violate the full faith and credit clause of the Constitution?   b. _____

c. Would your answer to either of the previous two questions be different if you learned that over 95 percent of Homesdale's population approves of this ordinance?   c. _____

38. Second Amendment The town of Ericton is considering passing an ordinance that would severely restrict the possession and carrying of firearms.

a. May the ordinance prohibit the possession of firearms by felons?   a. _____

b. May the ordinance prohibit the possession of firearms by persons who are mentally ill?   b. _____

c. May the ordinance prohibit the carrying of firearms in sensitive places, such as government buildings and schools?   c. _____

39. Eighth Amendment In an effort to stem the rising usage of illegal drugs, the town of Zhemville passes an ordinance that mandates that all people found guilty of possessing illegal drugs be flogged.

    a. Does the ordinance violate the Eighth Amendment of the Constitution? **a.** _____

    b. Does the ordinance violate the commerce clause of the Constitution? **b.** _____

    c. Would the ordinance violate the Eighth Amendment of the Constitution if the punishment applied only to people selling, rather than simply possessing, illegal drugs? **c.** _____

CASE ANALYSIS

Study each of the following cases carefully. Briefly state the principle of law and your decision.

40. Fourth Amendment Katz was convicted in federal court under an indictment charging him with transmitting wagering information by telephone from Los Angeles to Miami and Boston, in violation of a federal statute prohibiting gambling. At the trial, the federal prosecutor was permitted, over the objections of Katz's attorney, to introduce evidence of Katz's telephone conversations. These telephone conversations had been overheard by FBI agents who had attached an electronic listening and recording device to the outside of the public telephone booth from which Katz had placed his calls. Did the FBI violate the Second Amendment by listening to Katz's telephone conversations? [*Katz v. United States,* 389 US 347 (California)]

Principle of Law:

_____

_____

Decision:

_____

_____

41. Eighth Amendment While in the custody of the New Castle Youth Development Center (YDC), 17-year-old Betts suffered a tragic spinal cord injury while attempting to make a tackle during a football game. Following the injury, Betts sued YDC and several of its staff members, claiming that his injury resulted from a violation of his Eighth Amendment rights. Was Betts subjected to cruel and unusual punishment while playing football? [*Betts v. New Castle Youth Development Center,* 2009 U.S. District Court (Pennsylvania)]

Principle of Law:

_____

_____

Decision:

_____

_____

42. Sixteenth Amendment The IRS filed a lawsuit against Stern to collect unpaid income taxes, penalties, and interest that had amassed over 10 years. In response, Stern petitioned the court to disallow the IRS from collecting his tax debt, arguing that discrepancies existed between the Constitution and certain Supreme Court cases. Was Stern required to pay federal income taxes pursuant to the Sixteenth Amendment? [*In Re: Peter Kay Stern, Petitioner,* 114 F.3d 1177 (North Carolina)]

Principle of Law:

_____

_____

Decision:

_____

_____

LEGAL RESEARCH

Complete the following activities. Share your findings with the class.

43. Working in Teams In teams of three or four, visit the offices of local college and city newspapers. Ask the reporters and writers to explain the processes they use to verify the truth and accuracy of their reports and articles.

_____

_____

44. Using Technology Using the Internet and search engines, investigate blogs that contain political speech. Make a listing of statements and explain why the speech is protected under the First Amendment.

_____

_____

chapter **6**
Administrative Law

LEARNING OUTCOMES

After studying this chapter and completing the assessment, you will be able to

6.1 Describe the purpose of administrative agencies.

6.2 Discuss the organization of governments and define the specific duties of the three branches of government.

6.3 List and provide examples of the functions of administrative agencies.

6.4 Explain why and how an administrative agency is formed.

6.5 Explain the similarities and differences between administrative agencies and governments.

6.6 Discuss criticism of administrative agencies.

LEGAL terms

administrative agency	judicial branch
legislative branch	subpoena
executive branch	administrative hearing

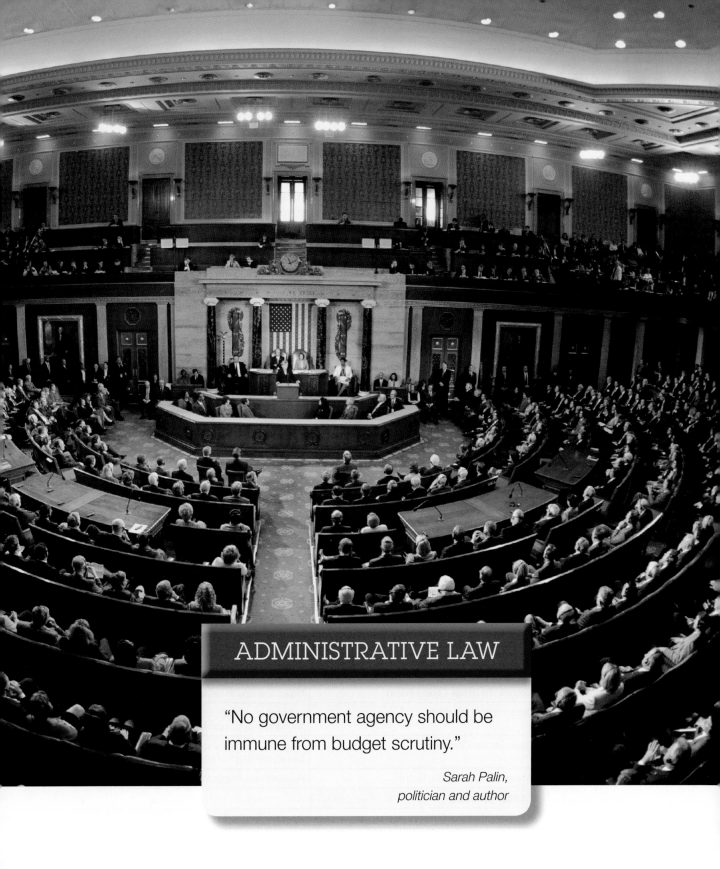

ADMINISTRATIVE LAW

"No government agency should be immune from budget scrutiny."

*Sarah Palin,
politician and author*

6.1 ADMINISTRATIVE AGENCIES

Administrative agencies were introduced in Chapter 1, where the point was made that they affect nearly every individual, business firm, and organization in the country. An administrative agency is a governmental body responsible for the control and supervision of a particular activity or area of public interest. Our society is extraordinarily complex, and no legislature can pass laws specific enough to ensure that all objectives are achieved under all circumstances.

Legislatures lack the time and expertise to make the necessary rules to govern the operations of complex areas of our social and economic life, such as energy, taxation, transportation, environmental pollution, employee safety, and communication. Neither do legislatures have the time or expertise to supervise the many details of these complex areas on a daily basis. As a result, legislatures delegate these responsibilities to administrative agencies, or regulators. These agencies exist at all levels of government: federal, state, and local. Some of the more important agencies are shown in Table 6.1.

TABLE 6.1	Examples of Administrative Agencies
AGENCY	**PURPOSE AND AREA OF REGULATION**
Federal Agencies	
Consumer Product Safety Commission (CPSC)	Establishes safety standards for products.
Equal Employment Opportunity Commission (EEOC)	Protects employees from illegal discrimination.
Environmental Protection Agency (EPA)	Regulates activities that affect the environment.
Federal Communications Commission (FCC)	Regulates radio and television communications.
Federal Trade Commission (FTC)	Regulates antitrust, deceptive advertising, and fair trade practices.
Internal Revenue Service (IRS)	Establishes rules on tax matters and supervises collection of taxes.
Nuclear Regulatory Commission (NRC)	Establishes standards and oversees uses of nuclear energy.
Occupational Safety and Health Administration (OSHA)	Regulates safety and health in the nation's workplaces.
Securities and Exchange Commission (SEC)	Regulates operations of financial markets.
State Agencies	
Alcoholic Beverage Control Board	Issues licenses to sell liquor.
Department of Insurance	Licenses agents and companies; monitors financial soundness of companies.
Public Service Commission	Regulates the provision of electrical power, gas, and water.
Workers' Compensation Board	Regulates payments made to injured workers.
Local Agencies	
Board of Education	Operates local schools.
Board of Health	Inspects food establishments.
Consumer Protection Agency	Regulates businesses; protects consumers' interests.
Department of Weights and Measures	Checks accuracy of scales and other measuring devices.

When a legislature passes a particular law, it often stresses general objectives and guidelines. At the same time, it may create an administrative agency to establish specific rules to be followed by those affected by the law. When the agency is established, the legislature usually specifies the purpose and the powers of the agency, and the actions the agency may take in carrying out the intentions of the law. Administrative agencies have various names, including boards, commissions, and departments. In many respects, administrative agencies are like governments within a government because they combine all three governmental functions: legislative, executive, and judicial.

The legislative branch of the federal government.

 ORGANIZATION OF GOVERNMENTS

To appreciate the similarity of administrative agencies and governments, it will be valuable to review the traditional constitutional governments that operate at the federal, state, and local levels.

Each level of government has three branches: legislative, executive, and judicial. Each branch has specific duties and powers. The organization of administrative agencies often resembles the organization of governments.

LEGISLATIVE BRANCH OF GOVERNMENT

The legislative branch at all levels of government consists of elected representatives who have the responsibility for passing laws that represent the will of the people.

At the federal level, there are two houses of Congress: the House of Representatives and the Senate. At the state level, the legislative branch is often called the general assembly; like the federal Congress, it consists of two houses (except in Nebraska). At the local level, the legislative branch is often called a city council or given a similar name.

legislative branch
The branch of a government body that consists of elected representatives who have the responsibility for passing laws that represent the will of the people.

EXECUTIVE BRANCH OF GOVERNMENT

The executive branch at all levels of government ensures that all enacted legislation is enforced. At the federal level, the executive branch is headed by the president; at the state level, the executive is the governor; and at the local level, the executive is the mayor, county executive, or someone with a similar title.

executive branch
The branch of a government body that consists of an elected executive, including his or her appointed staff.

JUDICIAL BRANCH OF GOVERNMENT

The judicial branch of government determines if there have been violations of the law. It also interprets the law if there are questions about what the law means in particular situations.

At the federal level, there are district courts, appeals courts, and the U.S. Supreme Court. Each state also has several levels of courts: trial courts, appeals courts, and a supreme court. At the local level, there are municipal courts, justice-of-the-peace courts, and magistrate courts.

judicial branch
The branch of a government body that determines if there have been violations of the law and interprets the law if there are questions about what the law means in particular situations.

 FUNCTIONS OF ADMINISTRATIVE AGENCIES

Administrative agencies have been created for a variety of purposes and to fulfill diverse functions. These functions include regulating conduct, satisfying government requirements, disbursing benefits, and providing goods and services.

REGULATING CONDUCT

Often an agency regulates such economic matters as price, entry into a particular geographical area, or entry into a particular kind of business.

EXAMPLE 6.1

▶ Yamoto, a recent college graduate who had majored in insurance and worked part-time for an insurance agency, decided to start his own insurance agency. He learned that before he could enter this kind of business, he would have to pass an examination to test his knowledge of insurance and related law and be licensed by the state insurance department. State insurance regulations require insurance agents to be licensed to make certain that persons in this position are competent to perform their duties and to serve the people who rely on them.

FULFILLING GOVERNMENT REQUIREMENTS

Administrative agencies exist at all levels of government—(see Chapter 5) for example, to collect taxes and to raise revenues through various licensing laws. At the federal level, one of these agencies is the Internal Revenue Service (IRS), which collects taxes needed to operate the federal government.

DISBURSING BENEFITS

A number of governmental agencies distribute subsidies and benefits of various kinds to farmers, persons in need of public assistance, students, individuals who are unemployed, and people who are elderly.

PROVIDING GOODS AND SERVICES

Although the United States is largely a capitalist country, in which the private sector provides most of the goods and services needed by the people, many believe that certain essential services cannot be efficiently provided by the private sector. Some governments at all levels provide goods and services, such as electricity, water, highway maintenance, hospital care, and public housing.

6.4 WHY AND HOW AN ADMINISTRATIVE AGENCY IS FORMED

For illustration, suppose that the consumers in a mythical, medium-sized city called Legis have problems with local businesses. Merchants are cheating customers, scales in stores are inaccurate, businesses that promise to provide certain services do not provide them, advertising is often false and misleading, and auto repair shops overcharge and perform poor-quality work. In short, the consumers in the imaginary city of Legis are having trouble coping with the abuses of the businesses in their community.

As might be expected, many consumers have complained to their elected representatives on the city council. When the need for a change became apparent, the city council decided to pass a consumer protection law. The law required that all businesses in the city of Legis be licensed and also stated that it would be unlawful for businesses to engage in "false advertising, deception, or the employment of unqualified workers to perform auto repair work."

Now let us examine a few aspects of the Legis consumer protection law. The law as passed does not define just what will be considered deceptive. For example, would a furniture store's newspaper advertisement be deceptive if it announced a Presidents' Day sale but failed to mention that the sale would be in effect at its downtown store only and not at its branch stores? Would the advertisement be deceptive if it failed to mention that quantities of certain items were significantly limited? The city council cannot legislate answers to these questions and many more like them. If it tried, it would be tied up for months or years because the legislators have neither the time nor the expertise to cope with these kinds of problems.

The city council knew that the goals of the consumer protection law would not be met by merely licensing businesses unless someone developed answers to such specific questions. Consequently, the law also established a consumer protection agency. The new agency would be headed by a director with the authority to (1) hire experts in various fields to clarify and enforce the law, and to assist in the formulation of agency rules and regulations; (2) license businesses operating in the city of Legis; and (3) establish rules and regulations that businesses will need to follow to maintain their licenses. In addition to establishing the consumer protection agency (CPA), the law required that all businesses would have to be licensed to operate within the city of Legis.

Many cities pass laws requiring that all businesses be licensed.

After the law had been passed, the mayor, with the approval of the city council, hired Savus, a qualified consumer affairs person, to be the head of the CPA. Of course the CPA—like any government entity—needs money to operate. The city council therefore appropriated a certain amount of money that the CPA could use to hire the necessary people, rent office space, pay telephone bills, and so on. The director, Savus, hired experts to develop rules and regulations governing advertising, auto repair shops, and other kinds of businesses.

However, what good would it do for the people of Legis to establish an agency staffed with experts and to make rules and regulations covering the operations of particular businesses if there were no way to enforce the rules? Unfortunately, people do not always obey rules and laws simply because they have been enacted. There must be some authority to ensure that people will obey the rules. In response, statutes have been enacted to grant administrative agencies the power to investigate potential violations of rules or statutes. Accordingly, Savus also hired a group of inspectors to check the accuracy of scales, others to check the truthfulness of newspaper advertising, and so on.

Carrying the example a bit further, suppose that an inspector from the CPA finds that a scale in a supermarket is inaccurate and customers are being overcharged. The inspector notifies the store manager of the condition, but the manager, knowing that the inspector does not have the power of a police officer, points to the door and says, "Get out." What happens next? The inspector would probably report back to the CPA director, informing her that the scale in the store is inaccurate and in violation of rules established by the CPA. The director would likely issue the merchant a subpoena, or an order requiring the recipient to appear at a hearing to provide testimony. To comply with the subpoena, the merchant must attend the hearing at the specified time and place to answer the inspector's complaint. An administrative hearing conducted by an administrative agency is in some respects like an informal court trial, but without a jury. If the merchant refuses to appear, his or her license can be revoked. The CPA director would then notify the regular court prosecutor that the business is operating without the required license—a violation of the law that established the agency. The court could then order the business closed.

subpoena
An order requiring the recipient to appear at a legal proceeding to provide testimony.

administrative hearing
A trial-like judicial proceeding, without a jury, in which an administrative agency rules on matters of the law that the agency is charged with enforcing.

SIMILARITIES AND DIFFERENCES BETWEEN ADMINISTRATIVE AGENCIES AND GOVERNMENTS

Earlier in this chapter we reviewed the three branches of federal, state, and local government—that is, executive, legislative, and judicial. We pointed out that administrative agencies often carry out all three functions. Let us go back to the city of Legis and look at the CPA to see the comparisons between administrative agencies and governments.

SIMILARITIES

There are several significant similarities between administrative agencies and governments.

Executive Function   The executive function of the CPA is performed by the CPA director, Savus, together with her staff of experts, inspectors, and others. The executive function of the CPA includes the daily operations of the agency and the establishment of general policies and objectives.

Legislative Function   The rules and regulations established by the CPA resemble the laws passed by a legislature and have the force of law. This is the legislative function of the administrative agency.

Judicial Function   The activity of the CPA in holding hearings and requiring compliance with its decisions has an effect similar to the decisions made in a regular court of law. This activity is the judicial function of the administrative agency.

DIFFERENCES

While administrative agencies are very much like the three levels of government—federal, state, and local—they also differ in some important respects.

Executive Function   At all three levels of government, the voter has the opportunity to vote the executive into and out of office. Voters elect the president, the governor, and the mayor. Usually, however, voters do not elect the administrator of a regulatory agency. For the most part, the voter has little control over the activities of an administrative agency.

There are two general patterns in the executive organization of an administrative agency. In some agencies, the executive is appointed by and serves at the discretion of the elected executive of the government—the president, the governor, or the mayor—subject to approval by the legislature. At the federal level, examples include the people who head the Department of Transportation, the Department of the Interior, and the Department of Commerce. These executives can be removed from office either with or without cause. In other cases, Congress has created agencies outside the executive branch that are headed by groups or individuals, such as boards or commissions appointed by Congress. Such boards or commissions carry out the executive function of the agency. Once appointed to their multiyear terms, members may not be removed by the president without cause. Examples include appointees of the Federal Trade Commission (FTC) and the Securities and Exchange Commission (SEC).

Legislative Function   At one time there was debate about whether a legislature could delegate to an administrative agency some of the lawmaking authority that some people believed should remain with the legislature. This issue was resolved, and the notion of administrative agencies functioning in a lawmaking role is now widely accepted.

Rules and regulations are established by the agency, not by elected representatives. However, the law requires federal agencies to submit all new rules and regulations to Congress for review. After review, if Congress finds a new rule or regulation to be unjust, Congress can override it. Again, the voter does not have direct control over the legislative function of the administrative agency.

Administrators are usually appointed by the executive with the advice and consent of the legislature. This practice gives the public, through its legislatures, at least some indirect control over the operations of administrative agencies. After administrators have been approved, however, it is generally very difficult to remove them. If the people do not like the way the agency is being run, their only recourse is to bring pressure on the executive or legislative branch to change the agency or to remove the administrator. It is important to note that Congress has the power to dissolve or alter federal agencies; for example, Congress can enact legislation to reduce an administrative agency's funds or its powers.

Judicial Function   The hearings conducted by an administrative agency do not provide for a jury, and the procedures are not as formal as a regular court hearing. Moreover, unlike the judge in a court trial, the "judge" at an administrative agency hearing is not entirely impartial because he or she is determining whether a person or firm has complied with the agency's own rules rather than with statutes enacted by the legislature. There was early debate over whether a legislature could delegate to an administrative agency the authority to function as judge in certain matters. This question was largely settled in the case of *Crowell v. Benson*, 285 U.S. 22 (1932), in which the Supreme Court decided that an administrative agency does have such authority.

The determinations reached at a hearing conducted by an administrative agency can be appealed through the regular court system. As a practical matter, the courts seldom reverse the decisions of the agency unless it can be shown that the agency has clearly abused its authority.

To determine whether an administrative agency has abused its authority, the courts are guided by the statutes that established the agency and by the constitutions of the United States and the individual states.

6.6   CRITICISM OF ADMINISTRATIVE AGENCIES

A number of critics allege that certain administrative agencies have been "captured" by the enterprises they were created to regulate. Because of the economic benefits or burdens that administrative agencies can bestow on a firm or an industry, those regulated have a powerful incentive to secure favorable rulings. In many cases, the need for specialized expertise in a given area can usually come only from the industry being regulated. The insurance industry, for example, is highly complex, and many of the people who have the expertise needed to perform as effective regulators are, or have been, employed by the industry. Some have suggested that the heads of administrative agencies be elected by popular vote, as are some insurance commissioners. However, having these individuals elected would not mean that they would not be influenced as time passed, or that they would not use their positions to further their own economic or political ambitions.

CHAPTER
SUMMARY

1. Legislatures have neither the time nor the expertise to make the necessary rules to govern the operations of complex areas of our social and economic life. Legislatures also lack the time and expertise to supervise the many details of these complex areas on a day-to-day basis. Consequently, legislatures delegate these responsibilities to administrative agencies. There are numerous federal, state, and local administrative agencies. Table 6.1 provides examples of these agencies. A typical administrative agency is a consumer protection agency, which licenses firms, formulates agency regulations, and clarifies and enforces the laws.

2. Each level of government has three branches: legislative, executive, and judicial. Each branch has specific duties and powers. The organization of administrative agencies often resembles the organization of governments. The legislative branch consists of elected representatives who have the responsibility for passing laws that represent the will of the people. The executive branch ensures that all enacted legislation is enforced. The judicial branch determines if there have been violations of the law and interprets the law if there are any questions about what the law means in particular situations.

3. The functions of administrative agencies are regulating conduct in areas such as economic matters and entry into a particular location or industry; fulfilling government requirements such as collecting taxes and raising revenues through various licensing laws; disbursing benefits to agencies or persons; and providing goods and services such as water, highway maintenance, and public housing.

4. The law may establish an administrative agency to protect members of the public who have trouble coping with the abuses of businesses in their communities. Administrative agencies may be headed by a director with the authority to (1) hire experts in various fields to clarify and enforce the law, and to assist in the formulation of agency rules and regulations; (2) license businesses in the city in which they operate; and (3) establish rules and regulations that businesses will need to follow to maintain their licenses.

5. Each level of government has three branches: legislative, executive, and judicial. Each branch has specific duties and powers. The organization of administrative agencies often resembles the organization of governments. However, at all three levels of government, the voter has the opportunity to vote the executive into and out of

office. In contrast, voters do not elect the administrator of a regulatory agency. For the most part, voters have little control over the activities of an administrative agency.

6. Critics allege that administrative agencies are too closely aligned with the enterprises they were created to regulate. In many cases, the need for specialized expertise in a given area can come only from the industry being regulated. Some have suggested that the heads of administrative agencies be elected by popular vote.

CHAPTER SIX
ASSESSMENT

MATCHING LEGAL TERMS

Match each of the numbered definitions with the correct term in the following list. Write the letter of your choice in the answer column.

a. administrative agency   **c.** administrative hearing   **e.** legislative branch
b. executive branch   **d.** judicial branch

1. A branch of government headed by the president, a governor, or a mayor.   **1.** _____

2. A branch of government with responsibility for enacting legislation.   **2.** _____

3. An organization that has executive, legislative, and judicial functions.   **3.** _____

4. A branch of government with responsibility for deciding cases brought before it.   **4.** _____

5. An activity conducted by an administrative agency to receive complaints and to make decisions as to the guilt or innocence of parties charged.   **5.** _____

TRUE/FALSE QUIZ

Indicate whether each of the following statements is true or false by writing *T* or *F* in the answer column.

6. Each level of government usually has three branches: executive, legislative, and judicial.   **6.** _____

7. Executives at all levels of government are elected by the voters.   **7.** _____

8. The heads of administrative agencies at all levels of government are appointed only by the executive branch.   **8.** _____

9. The executive branch of government sees that all enacted legislation is enforced.   **9.** _____

10. The judicial branch of government determines if there have been violations of the law.　**10.** _____

11. There is little similarity between government and the operation of administrative agencies.　**11.** _____

12. The hearings conducted by administrative agencies customarily include trial by jury.　**12.** _____

13. Administrative agencies enforce only laws enacted by legislatures.　**13.** _____

14. The sole purpose of administrative agencies is to regulate business firms.　**14.** _____

15. There is no recourse from the decisions made at an administrative agency hearing.　**15.** _____

16. Once an administrator has been appointed, it is generally difficult to remove him or her from office.　**16.** _____

17. Administrative agencies are found at local, state, and federal levels of government.　**17.** _____

18. In most cases, the individual voter has direct control over administrative agencies.　**18.** _____

19. The courts often reverse the decisions of administrative agencies.　**19.** _____

20. A subpoena is an order requiring the recipient to appear at a legal proceeding to provide testimony.　**20.** _____

DISCUSSION QUESTIONS

Answer the following questions and discuss them in class.

21. Explain the similarities and differences between administrative agencies and governments.

22. Using examples, describe the operation of a typical administrative agency.

23. Name at least three administrative agencies at each level of government: federal, state, and local.

24. Discuss criticism of administrative agencies.

_____

_____

25. Explain why legislatures establish regulatory agencies.

_____

_____

THINKING CRITICALLY ABOUT THE LAW

Answer the following questions, which require you to think critically about the legal principles that you learned in this chapter.

26. Operation of Administrative Agencies Compare and contrast the operation of a government body with the operation of an administrative agency.

_____

_____

27. Judicial Function of an Administrative Agency Compare the procedure followed by an individual appearing as a defendant in a court of law to the procedure followed by an individual charged with a violation of a regulation appearing at a hearing of an administrative agency.

_____

_____

28. Criticism of Administrative Agencies Discuss some current criticism of administrative agencies and evaluate the validity of this view.

_____

_____

29. Impact of Administrative Agencies Individuals as well as businesses are affected by actions of administrative agencies in different ways. Select a particular agency and discuss how the agency affects individuals and businesses.

_____

_____

30. A Question of Ethics Analyze and discuss recourses available to citizens who believe that an executive of an administrative agency is behaving unethically.

_____

_____

Study each of the following cases. Answer the questions that follow by writing *Yes* or *No* in the answer column.

31. Government Regulations For three years, Patterson operated a small restaurant and enjoyed a growing business. His customers were pleased with the food and service. One day an inspector from the city's board of health visited the restaurant to inspect the sanitary conditions in the kitchen. The inspector informed Patterson that he would have to install a tile floor to replace the wooden one in the kitchen because the wooden floor permitted the growth of disease-carrying insects and was, therefore, a health hazard.

   a. Does the board of health have the authority to force Patterson to
make the alteration?   **a.** _____

   b. Can Patterson appeal the order to a regular court with jurisdiction
in the city?   **b.** _____

   c. Can the board of health close the restaurant if Patterson refuses to
comply with the order?   **c.** _____

   d. Does it appear that the board of health is acting in the interest of
the people of the community?   **d.** _____

32. Government Permits Billings lived in a community that required a building permit before any major alterations could be made to residential property. Billings refused to obtain the permit and proceeded to build a garage on her property.

   a. Can the city agency responsible for enforcing the law issue an
order to stop the construction?   **a.** _____

   b. Does it seem likely that the legislation requiring a building
permit was intended to prevent construction?   **b.** _____

   c. Does it seem likely that an appeal to a regular court would be
successful?   **c.** _____

   d. If Billings constructed the garage on her property without obtaining
the permit but met all the requirements of the appropriate building
codes in her city, could the administrative agency require that it be
torn down?   **d.** _____

33. Regulatory Agencies Technology Unlimited operated a small factory, employing 100 workers. The company manufactured special measuring devices that were sold throughout the world to the aircraft industry.

   a. Would federal regulatory agencies have control over any of the
operations of Technology Unlimited?   **a.** _____

   b. Would state regulatory agencies have control over any of the
operations of Technology Unlimited?   **b.** _____

   c. Would local regulatory agencies have control over any of the
operations of Technology Unlimited?   **c.** _____

CASE ANALYSIS

Study each of the following cases carefully. Briefly state the principle of law and your decision.

34. **State Agencies** The law in a particular state provided that the commissioner of insurance had the authority to approve or not approve the rates charged consumers for automobile insurance. The managers of a particular insurance company believed that the services they provided their policyholders were superior to those offered by other companies, and that they should be allowed to charge higher rates than those approved by the commissioner for all companies licensed to sell insurance in the state. At a hearing held in response to the company's request for permission to charge the higher rates, the commissioner considered the request. Does it appear likely that the decisions of the state insurance commissioner will be binding on the company?

    Principle of Law:

    _____

    _____

    Decision:

    _____

    _____

35. **Administrative Hearings** An inspector from the department of weights and measures in a particular city made a routine examination of the gasoline pumps at a service station to check their accuracy. The inspector found that one pump delivered only 4.5 gallons when the meter showed 5 gallons. The inspector sealed the pump and had a subpoena issued, ordering the station owner to report to a hearing to be held the following day. The hearing would be conducted by the commissioner of the department of weights and measures. The operator of the service station claimed that the commissioner lacked authority to compel him to appear at the hearing. Does the commissioner have authority to regulate the operation of the service station?

    Principle of Law:

    _____

    _____

    Decision:

    _____

    _____

36. **Local Agencies** English was an employee of the city of Long Beach, California. His fitness to perform his duties was brought into question by an administrative agency of the city that customarily held hearings where such decisions were made. English was not notified of the hearing. Despite the fact that English was not present, the agency decided that he was unfit to continue his employment. English appealed the decision on the grounds that he was not present at the hearing and that the commission had acted improperly. Does it appear that the administrative agency acted

properly in making a decision affecting a person's employment without his being present? [*English v. City of Long Beach*, 217 P.2d 22 (California)]

Principle of Law:

_____

_____

Decision:

_____

_____

37. **Codes** The New York City charter authorizes the board of health to adopt a health code and to take other appropriate steps to ensure the health of the citizens of the city. The charter states that the code "shall have the force and effect of law." The board took action to provide for the fluoridation of the public water supply. Paduano objected to the plan and brought suit to prevent the water treatment, claiming that the action was discriminatory because it benefited only children and the dental health of children could be achieved in other ways. Is it likely that Paduano would succeed in his action? [*Paduano v. City of New York*, 257 N.Y.S.2d 531 (New York)]

Principle of Law:

_____

_____

Decision:

_____

_____

LEGAL RESEARCH

Complete the following activities. Share your findings with the class.

38. **Working in Teams** Working in teams of three or four, interview officials or supervisors of some department or agency of municipal government—such as the department of weights and measures or board of health. The following are topics that might be included in the interview: the purposes of the agency, how the agency's performance is evaluated, and by whom. Report your findings to the class.

_____

_____

39. **Using Technology** Using the Internet and search engines, locate the website of one of the administrative agencies that affect the lives of individuals and businesses in your community. Identify the kinds of services provided to the community.

_____

_____

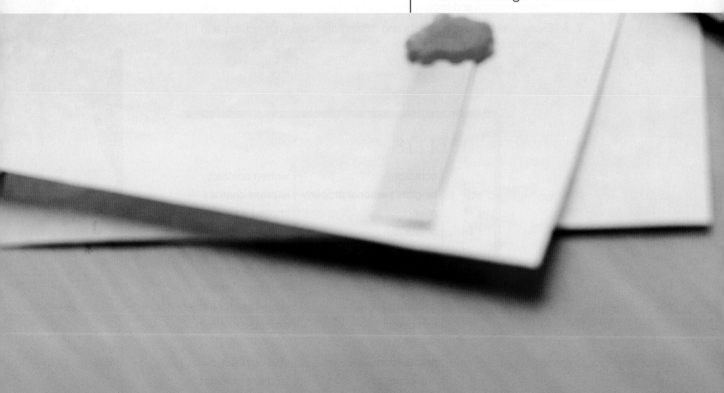

PART 2

CONTRACT

Contracts

chapter **7**
Introduction to Contracts

terms

LEGAL

contract	written contract
tangible personal property	express contract
offer	implied contract
offeror	formal contract
offeree	simple contract
acceptance	entire contract
mutual agreement	divisible contract
consideration	executory contract
competent	executed contract
legality of purpose	valid contract
proper form	void contract
oral contract	voidable contract

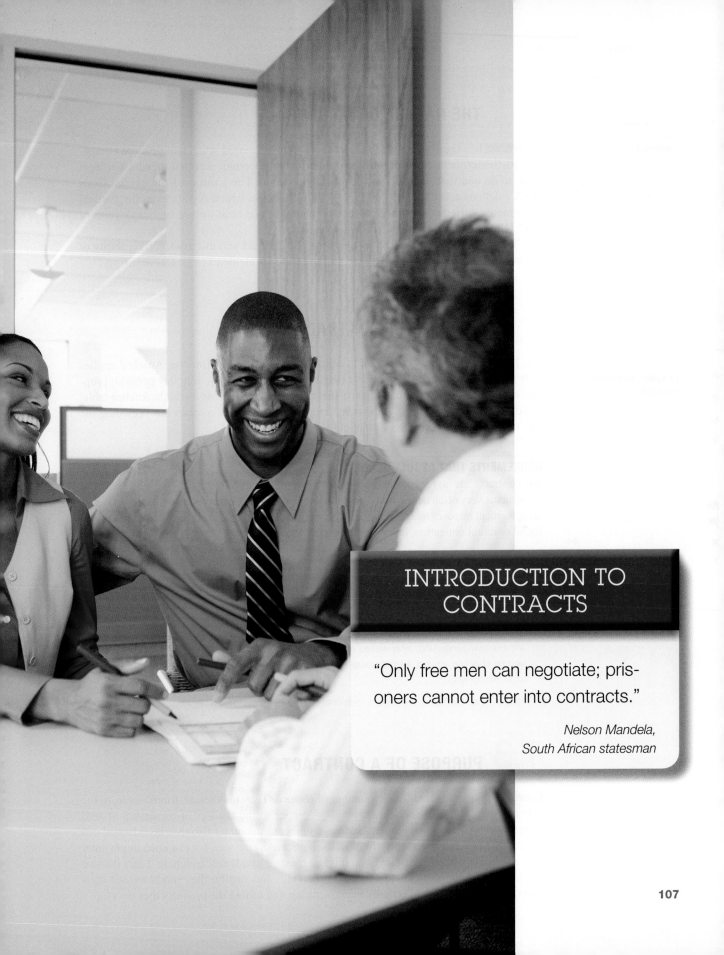

INTRODUCTION TO CONTRACTS

"Only free men can negotiate; prisoners cannot enter into contracts."

Nelson Mandela,
South African statesman

7.1 THE NATURE OF A CONTRACT

contract
A legally enforceable agreement that is created when two or more competent parties agree to perform, or to avoid performing, certain acts that they have a legal right to do and that meet certain legal requirements.

A contract is a legally enforceable agreement that is created when two or more competent parties agree to perform, or to avoid performing, certain acts that they have a legal right to do and that meet certain legal requirements. The Uniform Commercial Code (UCC) defines a contract as "the total legal obligation which results from the parties' agreement as affected by the Uniform Commercial Code or any other applicable rules of law" [UCC 1-201(11)].

This chapter introduces the six elements of a contract and discusses enforceability of contracts. Later chapters will examine each of these six elements in greater detail.

7.2 SOURCES OF CONTRACT LAW

tangible personal property
Personal property that can be moved.

The part of the UCC that is relevant to contract law is Article 2. However, Article 2 applies only to transactions in goods or other tangible personal property. Tangible personal property can be defined as personal property that can be moved, such as a vehicle, kitchen table, or computer. Common law, on the other hand, is the source of contract law regarding the sale of fixed assets, services, or intangibles.

AGREEMENTS THAT RESULT IN CONTRACTS

All contracts are agreements, but not all agreements are contracts. The reason is that agreements very often deal with personal or social matters that cannot be enforced by law. If an agreement imposes a legal obligation, an enforceable contract results; if it imposes only a social or moral obligation, however, it is not a contract and is not legally enforceable.

EXAMPLE 7.1

▶ Allen, an executive secretary, agreed to meet Yung, a college friend from the firm's accounting department, at noon to share a ride to a company-training seminar. Allen failed to keep the appointment, and Yung, who waited an hour for her, missed the seminar. She had no legal course of action against Allen because the agreement was based on a social, rather than a legal, relationship.

7.3 PURPOSE OF A CONTRACT

Contracts may be created for any number of reasons. They may relate, for example, to the sale of merchandise or services, to employment, or to the transfer of ownership of land (real property) or personal property such as a sailboat. A contract also may be extended and revised as needed to reflect the wishes of the parties. An engineer, for example, might enter into a contract with an assistant, who might agree to provide research help. Later the two might broaden the contract to form a partnership; and finally, they might extend their contractual relationship to actually manufacturing and selling the products they develop.

7.4 ELEMENTS OF AN ENFORCEABLE CONTRACT

To be legally enforceable, a contract must contain six elements: (1) offer and acceptance, (2) mutual agreement, (3) consideration, (4) competent parties, (5) legality of purpose, and (6) proper form. If one of these elements is missing, the courts will usually refuse to enforce the contract. Each of these elements will be discussed in this chapter.

OFFER AND ACCEPTANCE

An offer is a proposal made by one party, the offeror, to another party, the offeree, that indicates a willingness to enter into a contract. An acceptance is an indication made by the offeree that he or she agrees to be bound by the terms of the offer.

MUTUAL AGREEMENT

The parties to a contract must have a clear understanding of what they are undertaking. The contract must show mutual agreement, sometimes referred to as a *meeting of the minds*.

CONSIDERATION

In most cases, each party to a contract must promise either to give up something of value that he or she has a legal right to keep, or to do something that he or she is not otherwise legally required to do. This exchange of promises is called consideration. If only one party promises something, such as paying a certain amount of money, and the other party promises nothing, then the agreement lacks consideration. Exceptions to the general rule will be discussed in Chapter 10.

COMPETENT PARTIES

The parties to a contract must be competent—that is, be capable of understanding what they are doing. They must be of legal age and normal mentality. The functioning of a party's mind must not be impaired by injury, mental disease, or the influence of drugs or alcohol.

LEGALITY OF PURPOSE

The intent of the contract must not violate the law. It must have legality of purpose. The courts will not enforce a contract to do something that violates the law (see Example 7.12).

PROPER FORM

Certain contracts, such as those involving the sale of personal property for $500 or more, or those that cannot be fulfilled within a year, must be in writing to be enforceable. Other kinds of contracts must not only be in writing but must also follow a prescribed form, such as containing the signatures of the parties. These requirements for contracts are known as proper form.

These essential elements of a contract will be discussed in more detail in later chapters. At this point it is necessary only to remember that an agreement, to be legally enforceable, must contain these six elements.

offer
A proposal made by one party (the offeror) to another person (the offeree) that indicates a willingness to enter into a contract.

offeror
The person making a proposal.

offeree
The person to whom a proposal is made.

acceptance
An indication made by the offeree that he or she agrees to be bound by the terms of the offer.

mutual agreement
The state of mind that exists between an offeror and an offeree when a valid offer has been accepted, and the parties know what the terms are and have agreed to be bound by them. Mutual agreement is also known as "a meeting of the minds."

consideration
The promise to give up something of value that a party to a contract has a legal right to keep, or to do something that the party is not otherwise legally required to do.

competent
Being mentally capable of understanding the terms of a contract.

legality of purpose
The requirement that the intent of a contract be legal for the contract to be enforceable.

proper form
The requirement that the form of a contract be correct for the terms of the contract to be enforceable.

EXAMPLE 7.2

▶ Rossetti offered to sell his grand piano to Bray for $2,000. Bray agreed to buy it at that price, and the two parties put their agreement in writing. Both Rossetti and Bray were legally competent to enter into a contract. They came to a mutual agreement about the terms of the transaction. Rossetti promised to give up his grand piano in return for Bray's promise to pay $2,000 for it. This was the consideration given by Rossetti and by Bray. Since the agreement involved more than $500, the written contract fulfilled the requirement of proper form. And of course the sale of a grand piano was perfectly legal. Because the agreement satisfied the six elements, a legally enforceable contract resulted.

7.5 KINDS OF CONTRACTS

Contracts may be classified in several ways, depending on the manner in which they are created, expressed, or performed. Thus a contract may be either oral or written; it may be express or implied; it may be formal or simple; and it may be entire or divisible.

ORAL CONTRACTS

oral contract
An agreement that is not in writing or signed by the parties.

Most contracts in business and in private life are simple, unwritten agreements that result from conversation between the parties involved. Even a telephone conversation can result in an enforceable oral contract. An oral contract is one that is not in writing or signed by the parties. That is, it is a real contract created entirely by the conversation of the parties. A person who discusses the terms of a purchase with a salesperson, pays cash for it, and takes the item with him or her is making an oral contract. A person makes many such contracts in a day, and yet each of these simple transactions contains all the elements of a contract.

WRITTEN CONTRACTS

written contract
An agreement that is reduced to writing on a permanent surface.

A written contract is one that is reduced to writing on a permanent surface. Although an oral contract may be just as binding as a written contract, it is advisable to put a contract in writing if the transaction is important or complicated, if the contract involves a large amount of money, or if the contract will extend over a long period of time. Thus, a contract calling for the construction of a building, the installation of expensive machinery, or the payment of a large sum of money for household furnishings should be in writing to protect the parties involved and to prevent a later disagreement over the terms.

The law does not specify any particular form or language to be used. It is sufficient that the parties clearly express themselves in understandable language.

A written contract can be simply a handwritten note, a printed statement, a letter printed from a word processing document, or any other memorandum containing the terms of the agreement, as long as it is signed by the party or parties who wish to be bound by the

A written contract can be simply a handwritten note.

agreement. Some important agreements are not even called contracts, although in fact they are; they may be called simply a "memorandum of agreement" or other such term.

EXAMPLE 7.3

▶ Ward, an editor with a publishing company, had frequent dealings with Michalski, an author with whom the company had a binding contract. During personal meetings and telephone conversations while working together on a book manuscript, a number of agreements concerning matters that were not covered in the existing contract were made. Wishing to strengthen the existing contract and make it more specific, Ward sent Michalski a letter that began, "The purpose of this letter is to reduce to writing the substance of our several discussions in which we agreed . . ." At this point the letter confirmed all the points that needed clarification. The letter concluded with, "if the above reflects our agreements, please sign and date one copy of this letter in the place indicated and return one copy to me at your earliest convenience. The extra copy of the letter is for your files." At the bottom of the page, there was the following: "Accepted and agreed to: _____, Date: _____"

The purpose of this simple business letter was to reduce the possibilities of later disagreement. In the event of a dispute involving an oral contract, the parties must depend on circumstances, or on the testimony of witnesses, to determine the rights of the parties. The problem, of course, is that memories fade, and even witnesses cannot be relied on to recall exactly what was said. With a written contract, these particular problems are eliminated.

EXPRESS CONTRACTS
A contract that specifically states the agreement of the parties, either orally or in writing, is called an express contract. The term is used to distinguish such contracts from others in which the meaning or the intention of the parties is inferred from their actions.

express contract
A contract that explicitly states the agreement of the parties, either orally or in writing.

IMPLIED CONTRACTS
Certain business and personal transactions are neither oral nor written but are nevertheless legally binding. The terms of these agreements are understood from the actions or conduct of the parties, from the customs of the trade, or from the conditions or circumstances, rather than from oral or written words. A transaction of this kind is considered an implied contract. Thus, an implied contract results when a customer asks a merchant to deliver an article to his or her home with no mention of payment. The buyer implies that he or she will pay the market price of the article when it is delivered or when the bill is presented.

implied contract
A contract that does not explicitly state the agreement of the parties but in which the terms of the agreement can be inferred from the conduct of the parties, the customs of the trade, or the conditions or circumstances.

EXAMPLE 7.4

▶ Levy entered a retail office supply store, ordered a copy machine, and left instructions that it was to be delivered to his office. The price of the machine, when payment was to be made, and the exact time of delivery were not discussed.

Example 7.4 provides an illustration of an implied contract. Three implied agreements are involved: (1) that the market price of the copy machine will be paid; (2) that payment will be made on delivery or when it is customary to make payment (depending on the usual relationship of the merchant and the customer or the customs of the business); and (3) that delivery will be made within a reasonable time.

An implied contract results when a person accepts goods or services that cannot reasonably be considered a gift. A person who stands idly by while another confers an unrequested benefit implies a promise to pay a reasonable amount for the benefit. Such a promise of payment, however, is not implied if goods were delivered or the services rendered during the absence of, and without the knowledge of, the recipient.

EXAMPLE 7.5

▶ Cushing drove his car into Jerseyland Auto and asked for a regular tune-up. While he waited for the work to be done, he noticed a second service attendant begin to install a new battery, which he had not ordered. Obviously a mistake had been made, but when it came time to pay his bill, he was charged only for the tune-up and not the battery. When the mistake was discovered the next day, Jerseyland Auto sent Cushing a bill. Cushing will have to pay for the battery. A person who accepts or uses goods not intended for himself or herself has an implied obligation to pay the reasonable value for these goods.

FORMAL CONTRACTS

formal contract
A specialty contract that is written and under seal.

A formal contract, or specialty contract, is a written contract under seal. The seal on a formal contract may consist of simply the word *Seal* or *L.S.* (which means *locus sigilli,* the place of the seal), a scroll, a wafer, or an impression on the paper. Four ways in which a seal may appear are shown in Figure 7.1. Today only a few contracts, such as bonds, mortgages, and deeds conveying title to real estate, are required to have a seal. Many states have stopped using the seal entirely.

SIMPLE CONTRACTS

simple contract
An informal contract made without seal—even though the subject matter of the contract may be extremely complex and may involve huge amounts of money.

A contract that is not formal, whether it is written, oral, or implied, is called a simple contract. That is, a simple contract is an informal contract made without seal—even though the subject matter of the contract may be extremely complex and may involve huge amounts of money.

EXAMPLE 7.6

▶ The laws of a certain state require that every real estate mortgage be in writing and under seal. A mortgage bond was made in this state on the prescribed form by a home owner who printed the letters *L.S.* opposite the signature and thereby fulfilled the legal requirement that the mortgage bond be under seal. A seal may consist of any design adopted for that purpose.

FIGURE 7.1   Four Ways of Indicating a Seal

ENTIRE CONTRACTS

An entire contract, or indivisible contract, has two or more parts. Each part is dependent upon the others for satisfactory performance. Such a contract must be completely performed. The law of sales specifically states that "unless otherwise agreed, all goods called for by a contract for sale must be tendered [offered] in a single delivery and payment is due only on such tender" (UCC 2-307).

entire contract
An agreement that is made up of two or more parts, in which each part is dependent upon the others.

EXAMPLE 7.7

▶ Kibbi Real Estate had planned to move into new offices and ordered 20 new desks and accompanying chairs from Belmont Office Supply. On the delivery date, Belmont delivered only the desks and explained that the manufacturer of the chairs had been experiencing labor difficulties. Belmont, however, demanded immediate payment for the desks. The order for the desks and chairs is an entire contract because these items are usually ordered in sets and the desks are of little use without the chairs. Kibbi Real Estate is not required to pay for the desks until the chairs are delivered.

DIVISIBLE CONTRACTS

A divisible contract is one that is made up of two or more parts, each part being independent of the others. In the case of a contract for the sale of goods, a party to such a contract must be paid upon request for any part of the contract performed as agreed, even though the entire contract is not performed. The law of sales provides that "where the circumstances give either party to a contract for sale the right to make or demand delivery in lots, the price, if it can be apportioned, may be demanded for each lot" (UCC 2-307).

divisible contract
An agreement that is made up of two or more parts, each part being independent of the others.

EXAMPLE 7.8

▶ Schiff, a dealer in playground equipment, placed an order with Play and Grow Company for five playground swings and three freestanding slides. Play and Grow delivered the swings but, because of a shortage of materials, could not deliver the slides until three months later. Schiff must accept and pay for the swings even though the slides were not sent with the swings because the swings can be used without the slides (unlike the previous case, in which the chairs were needed to use the desks).

7.6 STATUS OF CONTRACTS

Contracts frequently have a long life. At any particular time, a contract may be awaiting the first act of the parties to execute its terms, in the process of completion, or completed.

EXECUTORY CONTRACTS

An executory contract is one in which some future act or obligation remains to be performed under its terms. A contract is completely executory if no part of it has been

executory contract
An agreement in which some future act or obligation remains to be performed under its terms.

performed. It is partly executory if some parts have been performed and some have yet to be performed. If an article is ordered and delivered but not yet paid for, for example, the contact is executory since it is completed on the part of the seller but not completed on the part of the buyer.

EXAMPLE 7.9

▶ Tran signed an agreement with the Epsilon Technology Company for the installation of an office computer network. The computers were installed, but because of a shortage of the new models of laser printers covered by the contract, the printers were not installed. The part of the contract dealing with the computers and connecting cables was completed, but the part concerned with the printers was still not completed. The contract is therefore executory.

Where computers, but not accompanying printers, were installed, the contract is considered executory.

executed contract
A record of an agreement that has been completed in all respects by all the parties.

EXECUTED CONTRACTS
A contract in which all of the terms of the agreement have been fully performed by both parties is an executed contract. An executed contract is not really a contract at all. It is more a record of an agreement that has been completed in all respects by all the parties.

EXAMPLE 7.10

▶ Lee, an employed secretary, signed a contract with an employment agency that agreed to find her a new position as an executive secretary. He agreed to pay the agency 50 percent of his first month's salary. The agency found him a position with a brokerage firm, and a month later Lee sent the agency a check for 50 percent of his first month's salary, as he had agreed to do. The contract is now executed, with no part uncompleted.

7.7   ENFORCEABILITY OF CONTRACTS

It is important to determine whether a contract is valid, void, or voidable because not all contracts can be enforced.

valid contract
An agreement resulting in an obligation that is legally enforceable.

VALID CONTRACTS
The vast majority of contracts entered into in any business day are valid. A valid contract is an agreement resulting in an obligation that is legally enforceable. It meets all the requirements of a contract because all six essential elements are present.

EXAMPLE 7.11

▶ Gorbea, the owner of a computer supply company, agreed in writing with the Diaz Sign Company to pay $800 to have a specific sign erected on her property within 30 days. The Diaz Sign Company constructed and installed the sign within the specified time and Gorbea sent the company $800. All the essential elements of a legal contract are present in this case.

Offer and Acceptance   Gorbea offered Diaz Sign Company $800 to erect a specific sign within 30 days. Diaz Sign Company indicated its acceptance of the offer by signing the contract.

Mutual Agreement   There was no confusion regarding the amount, the specifications, or the time limits for completion of the transaction. There was, in effect, a meeting of the minds.

Consideration   Gorbea promised to pay $800, and the Diaz Sign Company promised to build and install the sign.

Competent Parties   Gorbea and the Diaz Sign Company are competent to enter into a legal contract.

Legality of Purpose   The sale and installation of the sign are legal acts. There are no indications of violations of local codes or ordinances.

An agreement that lacks one or more of the essential elements of a contract is a void contract.

Proper Form   The contract concerned the sale of a sign for an amount over $500, and it was in written form.

Now consider the six elements again. If Gorbea offered Diaz Sign Company $800, and Diaz said it would charge $900, there would be no acceptance of the offer. If Gorbea thought she was getting a revolving electric sign and Diaz Sign Company thought she wanted a simple electrically lighted sign, there would not be mutual agreement. If Gorbea did not agree to pay for the sign, consideration would be lacking. If Gorbea were a minor, she would not have the authority to make a binding contract; that is, she would not have been a competent party. If local zoning regulations prohibited the type of sign Gorbea wanted, the contract would not have been for a legal purpose. The UCC requires that contracts for the sale of goods for $500 or more be in writing. If this agreement were not in writing, it would not be enforceable because it would lack proper form.

VOID CONTRACTS

An agreement that lacks one or more of the essential elements of a contract is a void contract from the very beginning. That is, it is not a true contract at all and is therefore unenforceable.

void contract
A contract that is not enforceable from the beginning because it lacks one of the requirements of a valid contract.

EXAMPLE 7.12

▶ Hritzik operated a clothing manufacturing firm and entered into an agreement with an unlawful enterprise that offered to bring illegal aliens into the country to work for Hritzik. When the first truckload of immigrants arrived, a number were seriously ill, rendering them unfit to work. Hritzik wanted healthy workers and refused to pay the agreed-upon price. The enterprise wanted its money. Neither Hritzik nor the importer would have access to any legal remedy since their agreement violated federal immigration laws and was void from the very beginning: It lacked one of the essential elements of a contract—legality of purpose.

VOIDABLE CONTRACTS

voidable contract
An agreement that can be rejected by one of the parties for a legally acceptable reason.

An agreement that may be rejected by one of the parties for a legally acceptable reason is a voidable contract. Such a contract is valid and enforceable unless and until it is rejected by the party who has the right to withdraw. Thus, in a contract between a minor and an adult, the adult must perform his or her part of the agreement, unless and until the minor decides to withdraw from the contract.

EXAMPLE 7.13

▶ Braun, a minor, agreed with Main Street Used Cars to purchase a certain automobile. The dealership must perform as agreed, but Braun, who is not legally a competent party, can withdraw from this voidable contract.

Suppose that Braun was an adult who agreed to buy a certain automobile only if it were repainted blue. Assume also that because of an error the automobile was repainted green. Braun can withdraw from the contract because the seller failed to perform according to the terms of the contract. The contract is voidable at Braun's option. If the color green is not acceptable to Braun, she can withdraw from the contract, or she can insist that the car be repainted blue, or she can accept the car as is but with some settlement, such as a lower price than that to which she originally agreed.

CHAPTER SUMMARY

1. A contract is a legally enforceable agreement.

2. The sources of contract law appear in Article 2 of the UCC and common law.

3. All contracts are agreements, but not all agreements are contracts. In some cases, agreements are of a social nature and are not enforceable by law.

4. Contracts may be created for any number of reasons. They may relate, for example, to the sale of merchandise or services, to employment, or to the transfer of ownership of land (real property) or personal property.

5. The six elements of an enforceable contract are (1) offer and acceptance, (2) mutual agreement, (3) consideration, (4) competent parties, (5) legality of purpose, and (6) proper form.

6. An oral contract is one that is legally enforceable and is created entirely by the conversation of the parties. A written contract is one that is reduced to writing in a permanent form.

Express contracts specifically state the agreement of the parties, either orally or in writing. Implied contracts are agreements, the terms of which are inferred from the conduct of the parties, the customs of the trade, or the circumstances.

A formal contract, or specialty contract, is a written contract under seal. A simple contract is an informal contract made without seal—even though the subject matter of the contract is extremely complex.

An entire contract has two or more parts, each dependent upon the others for satisfactory performance. A divisible contract is one that consists of two or more parts, each part being independent of the others.

7. Contracts frequently have a long life. At any particular time, a contract may be awaiting the first act of the parties to execute its terms, in

the process of completion, or completed. An executory contract is one in which some future act or obligation remains to be performed under its terms. An executed contract is one in which the terms of the agreement have been fully performed by both parties.

8. Valid contracts are agreements resulting in obligations that are legally enforceable. Void contracts are agreements that lack one or more of the essential elements of a contract. Voidable contracts are agreements that may be rejected by one of the parties for a legally acceptable reason.

CHAPTER SEVEN
ASSESSMENT

MATCHING LEGAL TERMS

Match each of the numbered definitions with the correct term in the following list. Write the letter of your choice in the answer column.

a. competent party
b. consideration
c. divisible contract
d. entire, or indivisible, contract
e. executed contract
f. executory contract
g. express contract
h. formal contract
i. implied contract
j. legality of purpose
k. mutual agreement
l. oral contract
m. proper form
n. voidable contract
o. void contract

1. A "meeting of the minds" regarding the rights and obligations of the parties to a contract.   1. _____

2. A person who is of legal age and normal mentality.   2. _____

3. The promises exchanged by parties to a contract.   3. _____

4. A contract that is created entirely through conversation of the parties involved.   4. _____

5. A contract that is understood from the acts or conduct of the parties.   5. _____

6. A written contract that bears a seal.   6. _____

7. A contract with several unrelated parts, each of which can stand alone.   7. _____

8. The requirement that a contract cannot violate the law.   8. _____

9. A contract with several related parts, each dependent on the other parts for satisfactory performance.   9. _____

10. A contract whose meaning is not determined by the conduct of the parties.   10. _____

11. A contract that has not yet been completed by both parties.   11. _____

12. A contract that allows the incompetent party to withdraw.   12. _____

13. A contract that has been fully completed by both parties.   13. _____

14. A contract that lacks an essential element and hence was never
legally a contract.   14. _____

15. A requirement for contracts for the sale of goods for $500 or more.   15. _____

TRUE/FALSE QUIZ

Indicate whether each of the following statements is true or false by writing *T* or *F*
in the answer column.

16. All agreements between two competent parties are contracts.   16. _____

17. Written contracts must be handwritten to be legally enforceable.   17. _____

18. Implied contracts are those dealing only with personal transactions.   18. _____

19. Entire contracts are those composed of several related parts.   19. _____

20. To be legally enforceable, contracts must be in writing.   20. _____

21. Contracts do not need to be stated in legal language.   21. _____

22. Implied contracts are neither oral nor written.   22. _____

23. The terms of express contracts are specifically stated.   23. _____

24. A contract is considered executed as soon as all parties have
performed all parts of it.   24. _____

25. In a contract between a minor and an adult, the adult must
perform his or her part of the agreement unless or until the minor
decides to withdraw.   25. _____

DISCUSSION QUESTIONS

Answer the following questions and discuss them in class.

26. Provide examples of typical offers and acceptances.

_____

_____

27. Parties to a contract must have a clear understanding of what they are undertaking—
a meeting of the minds. Provide an example of two parties who have reached such a
clear understanding.

_____

_____

28. Provide an example of a contracting party offering consideration by doing something that he or she is not legally required to do.

_____

_____

29. The law requires that the parties be competent to enter into a contract. Give an example of a party who lacks competence.

_____

_____

30. The law requires that the purpose of a contract must be legal. Provide an example of a contract that would not be enforceable because it lacks legality of purpose.

_____

_____

31. Provide an example of an agreement that would need to be in writing to be enforceable.

_____

_____

THINKING CRITICALLY ABOUT THE LAW

Answer the following questions, which require you to think critically about the legal principles that you learned in this chapter.

32. Competent Parties The law allows a minor to withdraw from a contract simply because he or she is a minor, whereas the other party is bound if the minor wishes to carry out the contract. Do you think the law is fair in such instances?

_____

_____

33. Implied Contracts Certain business and personal transactions are neither oral nor written but are nevertheless legally binding. The terms of these agreements are understood from the actions or conduct of the parties, from the customs of the trade, or from the conditions or circumstances rather than from oral or written words. Do you think implied contracts should be enforceable?

_____

_____

34. **Legality of Purpose** Some contracts freely entered into by the parties involve activities that have been made illegal by state or federal statutes. Since they are illegal, these contracts are unenforceable. Examples are wagering agreements or lending money at high rates of interest (usury). Do you believe that legislatures should interfere with the free will of contracting parties?

_____

_____

35. **Proper Form** For many years the law has required that certain kinds of contracts, such as those involving $500 or more, be in writing to be enforceable. Should the amount of $500 be increased to reflect the effects of inflation?

_____

_____

36. **A Question of Ethics** Do you think it is unethical for an underage person who looks much older to enter into a contract with another person who in good faith expects the underage party to fulfill the terms of the contract?

_____

_____

CASE QUESTIONS

Study each of the following cases. Indicate whether the contract is executed, executory, or neither, and whether it is valid, voidable, or void, by placing an X in the space provided.

37. **Status of Contract** Knoll and Kalichuk signed an agreement for the sale of Knoll's sailboat. The agreement was complete in all respects, including the provision of time and place of delivery, sale price, and accessories included. On the date agreed for the exchange of payment and delivery of the boat, Knoll informed Kalichuk that he had changed his mind and decided not to sell.

    a. Executed _____   Executory _____   Neither _____

    b. Valid _____   Voidable _____   Void _____

38. **Status of Contract** Arslantian, a suburban homeowner who was involved in a major landscaping project, offered to pay Manley, a county employee, 50 percent of the market price for certain shrubbery belonging to the county parks commission if Manley would deliver it to a meeting place in a shopping mall.

    a. Executed _____   Executory _____   Neither _____

    b. Valid _____   Voidable _____   Void _____

Study each of the following cases. Answer the questions that follow by writing *Yes* or *No* in the answer column, or by writing other answers.

39. **Elements of Contract** Fiscus, age 23, entered into an oral contract with Badger, a 30-year-old bricklayer, for the construction of a backyard barbecue for a fee of $300. The work was completed in two weeks, as agreed.

    a. Is there an offer and an acceptance?   a. _____

    b. Is this a valid contract?   b. _____

    c. Are the parties competent?   c. _____

    d. Name the parties.   d. _____

    e. Is the purpose of the contract legal?   e. _____

    f. What is the purpose?   f. _____

    g. Is there consideration present?   g. _____

    h. What is the consideration?   h. _____

    i. Is there mutual agreement?   i. _____

    j. Explain the purpose of the contract.   j. _____

CASE ANALYSIS

Study each of the following cases carefully. Briefly state the principle of law and your decision.

40. **Elements of Contract** Esposito hired Excel Construction Company to repair a porch roof for $625 while she was out of town on vacation. All terms of the agreement were specified in a written contract, but the agreement failed to specify whether it was the front or rear porch that needed repair. When Esposito returned, she discovered that Excel had repaired the rear porch roof. She refused to pay, claiming that she wanted the front porch roof repaired. Were all essential elements of a contract present, and will Esposito be required to pay for the work that was done?

    Principle of Law:

    _____

    _____

    Decision:

    _____

    _____

41. **Consideration** William Storey Sr. promised his nephew, William Storey II, that he would pay him $5,000 if his nephew avoided drinking, using tobacco, swearing, and playing cards and billiards for money until he became 21 years old. The nephew agreed to the offer and kept his part of the bargain. At the age of 21, he wrote to his uncle and

asked for the $5,000. The uncle acknowledged the promise, praised his nephew for keeping his part of the bargain, but did not pay the money at that time. A short time later, the uncle died. The executor of his estate refused to pay the nephew, claiming that the contract was invalid due to the lack of consideration. Was the nephew's promise to avoid drinking, using tobacco, swearing, and playing cards and billiards for money until he became 21 legal consideration? [*Hamer v. Sidway*, 27 N.E. 256 (New York)]

Principle of Law:

_____

_____

Decision:

_____

_____

42. **Proper Form** Hodge, a 54-year-old employee of a bank, discussed his job and future with Tilley, president of Evans Financial Corporation and his employer. They agreed orally on a number of matters, including job title and location. After eight months on the new job, Tilley became dissatisfied with Hodge's work and discharged him. Hodge immediately sued, claiming that the oral agreement provided for employment until he retired at age 65. Does the length of time needed to fulfill the contract have a bearing on the enforceability of the contract? [*Hodge v. Evans Financial Corp.*, 778 F.2d 794 (District of Columbia)]

Principle of Law:

_____

_____

Decision:

_____

_____

43. **Divisible or Entire Contract** Grogan, a marketing consultant, was hired by Kreger Bottling Company to conduct market research into the taste preferences of consumers in a major city. Before he concluded the project, he was asked to take on the additional task of analyzing the appeal of various shapes of bottles that Kreger was considering for a new line of soft drinks. When the taste test was finished, but before the second project was completed, Grogan submitted his bill for the taste test. Kreger refused to pay until the bottle test was completed. Does Grogan have a basis for demanding payment for the portion of the work done?

Principle of Law:

_____

_____

Decision:

_____

_____

LEGAL RESEARCH

Complete the following activities. Share your findings with the class.

44. **Working in Teams** In teams of three or four, interview several small businesses to learn some of the steps businesspersons routinely follow to avoid problems involving contracts.

_____

_____

45. **Using Technology** Using the Internet and search engines, locate the website of one of several legal databases to expand your depth of knowledge of the legal terms related to the kinds of contracts described in the chapter.

_____

_____

chapter 8
Offer and Acceptance

After studying this chapter and completing the assessment, you will be able to

8.1 Identify the first step in reaching agreement and forming a valid contract.

8.2 Explain and provide examples of the three requirements for a valid offer.

8.3 Distinguish between bids, advertisements, and public offers, and describe how each relates to offer and acceptance.

8.4 Explain and provide examples of the two requirements for a valid acceptance.

8.5 Identify the five ways in which an offer may be terminated.

terms

LEGAL

request for proposal
invitation to trade
public offer
mailbox rule
counteroffer

termination by lapse
 of time
revocation
rejection
option contract

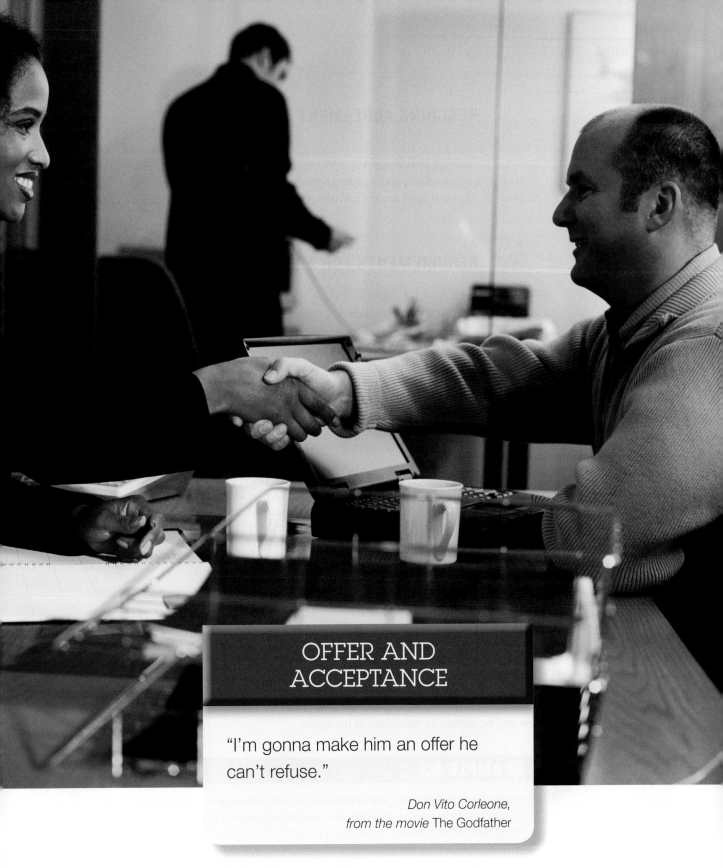

OFFER AND ACCEPTANCE

"I'm gonna make him an offer he can't refuse."

*Don Vito Corleone,
from the movie* The Godfather

8.1 REACHING AGREEMENT

Chapter 7 discussed the six elements of an enforceable contract. The first of these essential elements is offer and acceptance. For a contract to be valid, there must be a proposal that is both offered by the offeror and accepted by the offeree. This chapter addresses the characteristics of offers and acceptances, and describes the ways in which offers are terminated.

8.2 REQUIREMENTS FOR A VALID OFFER

For an offer to be valid, it must be (1) definite and certain, (2) communicated to the offeree, and (3) made with a serious intention that the offeror will be bound by it.

AN OFFER MUST BE DEFINITE AND CERTAIN

To be definite and certain, an offer should specify all the terms and conditions of the contract. Later disagreement can be avoided if the offer is made as specific as possible. Under the Uniform Commercial Code (UCC), however, the omission of one or more essential terms does not necessarily make the offer invalid as long as the contract contains sufficient information to suggest that the parties intended to enter into a contract (UCC 2-204).

According to the UCC, uncertainty with respect to specific terms does not necessarily invalidate a contract. For example, when an offer of sale does not specify a price, it is assumed that the parties intended "a reasonable price at the time set for delivery" (UCC 2-305). Moreover, uncertainty regarding place of delivery, time for shipment, and time for payment does not always invalidate a contract (UCC 2-308, 309, 310). Of course a court resolution of a dispute that arises from uncertainty about contract terms is a difficult way to do business. As a general rule, if an offer is to be definite and certain, it should cover the same points as a good newspaper story: who, what, when, where, and how much.

AN OFFER MUST BE COMMUNICATED

An offeror can make the offer known to the offeree in various ways. The usual means of communication are generally used, including oral communication (in person or by telephone, television, or radio) and written communication (letters, fax, e-mail, or other written forms). Making an offer and having it accepted are such common events in today's business world that people in business frequently use a printed or electronic purchase order upon which the terms of the offer are shown. Purchase orders are usually considered to be offers to buy. In these cases, the buyer of the goods is the offeror and the seller is the offeree. Communication also may be implied by the actions of the parties.

EXAMPLE 8.1

▶ Ellenby, an executive secretary, entered the Metro Stationery store, where he frequently purchased office supplies for his employer. He selected a box of ballpoint pens and several boxes of envelopes and showed them to the owner, who was busy with another customer at the time. The owner nodded and smiled, and the secretary departed from the store. By his action, the executive secretary made an implied offer. The owner of the store, by her conduct, implied that she had accepted the offer and that she would add the charges for his purchases to the employer's account.

AN OFFER MUST INTEND AN ENFORCEABLE OBLIGATION

Offers made in anger or jest, or those made under severe emotional strain, are obviously not made with the intent of entering into a valid, enforceable agreement. The lack of serious intent must, however, be apparent to a reasonable person.

EXAMPLE 8.2

▶ Clayton, a retired executive, was outraged at the amount of a repair bill for his one-year-old car, which was worth about $22,000. He screamed that repair bills were costing him more than the car was worth. He said, "I'll sell this bucket of bolts to anyone for $500." One of the mechanics who heard this quickly offered Clayton five $100 bills. It is doubtful that the mechanic could enforce the sale since a lack of serious intent would be apparent to a reasonable person.

8.3 BIDS, ADVERTISING, AND PUBLIC OFFERS

The requirement of offer and acceptance is usually fairly straightforward in contracts involving just two or perhaps a few parties. However, the issue gets complicated when there is little or no direct contact between the parties, as in the case of bidding, advertising, and public offers.

BIDS AND ESTIMATES

A call for a bid or estimate for materials to be furnished or work to be done is not considered an offer, but rather a request for an offer or an invitation to negotiate that can be accepted or rejected by the person calling for the bid. Such an announcement or solicitation is often called a request for proposal. Many cities and states that wish to enter into a contract with private firms or individuals for the performance of work or the purchase of goods or services require that the lowest bid be accepted. The main purposes of such a regulation are to ensure that the purchaser gets the most economical price and to prevent dishonesty in the form of bribery and kickbacks.

request for proposal
A request for an offer or an invitation to negotiate that can be accepted or rejected by the person calling for a bid.

EXAMPLE 8.3

▶ The board of education of a particular city decided to incorporate a new technology course in its vocational program. Because the course was highly specialized, it was believed that experts would be needed to prepare the new curriculum. Requests for proposals were sent to experts in technology education, and an announcement was published in publications that normally reach specialists in that field.

Note that in Example 8.3, if the board of education's call for bids was considered an offer, and the bids were considered acceptances, then a valid contract would result when the first bid was submitted. Instead the call for bids or proposals was regarded as a solicitation of offers, and thus the proposals submitted were deemed offers.

Sometimes goods are advertised in a newspaper at an incorrect price.

ADVERTISING

An advertisement, such as one that appears every day on television or radio, in a newspaper or a magazine, or on a website, is generally regarded as an invitation to trade, or an invitation to make an offer, rather than a valid offer because it does not contain sufficient words of commitment to sell. Sometimes goods are advertised in a newspaper at an incorrect price. If the error is the fault of the merchant, he or she will be required to honor the lower price. Even if the error is not his or her fault, the merchant may decide to sell the goods as advertised even though this may not be profitable. The reason is usually that the merchant believes it is a good business decision to sell at the advertised price in order to retain public goodwill. Goodwill is worth more than whatever the merchant would gain by enforcing his or her legal rights. If the error is the fault of the newspaper, the merchant may be able to recoup his or her losses from the publication.

If, however, an advertisement contains a positive promise and a positive statement of what the advertiser expects in return, the courts will usually hold that the advertisement is an offer. This is especially true if the word *offer* is used in the advertisement.

invitation to trade
An announcement published for the purpose of creating interest and attracting a response by many people. It is not considered a valid offer because it does not contain sufficient words of commitment to sell.

EXAMPLE 8.4

▶ Surplus Store ran an advertisement in a Minneapolis newspaper that read, "SATURDAY 9 A.M. 2 BRAND NEW PASTEL MINK 3-SKIN SCARFS SELLING FOR $89.50. OUT THEY GO SATURDAY. EACH $1.00. 1 BLACK LAPIN STOLE, BEAUTIFUL, WORTH $139.50 . . . $1.00 FIRST COME, FIRST SERVED." Lefkowitz was the first to present himself on Saturday and demanded the lapin stole for $1.00. Surplus Store refused to sell it to him because of a "house rule" that the offer was intended for women only. Lefkowitz sued and was awarded $138.50. The court held that the words "First come, first served" created a language of promise that is ordinarily lacking in advertisements. [*Lefkowitz v. Great Minneapolis Surplus Store*, 86 N.W.2d 689 (Minnesota)]

PUBLIC OFFERS

When an advertisement offers a reward for information that might lead to the arrest of a criminal or for the return of a lost article, it is regarded as a general offer to the public at large. Acceptance of a public offer by anyone, as indicated by the performance of the act, results in an enforceable contract.

public offer
A general offer to the public at large.

EXAMPLE 8.5

▶ Jamison lost an expensive pedigreed dog while at a park. He placed an advertisement in the *Daily Journal*, offering a $200 reward for the dog's return. This offer is valid, even though it is directed to thousands of readers, only one of whom could accept it.

The number of persons reached by an advertisement has no bearing on the validity of the offer. The purpose of such an advertisement is to reach a person of unknown identity with whom a valid contract can be made.

8.4 REQUIREMENTS FOR A VALID ACCEPTANCE

In order for an acceptance of an offer to be valid, (1) it must be communicated to the offeror and (2) it must be unconditional.

AN ACCEPTANCE MUST BE COMMUNICATED

It is important to determine how an acceptance may be communicated and when such acceptance becomes effective.

Method of Communication   Any of the usual forms of communication, such as telephone, letter, fax, e-mail, text message, and others, may be used in accepting an offer, unless the offer specifies a certain form of communication, such as "Reply by registered mail," "Reply by return mail," or "Reply by e-mail." The UCC states, "An offer to make a contract shall be construed as inviting acceptance in any manner and by any medium reasonable in the circumstances" (UCC 2-206).

When Acceptance Becomes Effective   The general rule is that an acceptance becomes effective when the parties so intend. The offer may explicitly state whether an acceptance is effective when it is sent by the offeree or when it is received by the offeror. If the offer is silent as to the time the acceptance is effective, the mailbox rule states that an acceptance sent via the postal system or by courier is effective when sent. An acceptance communicated by telephone, fax, or telex is effective when received. Courts have been divided on whether an acceptance sent via e-mail or text message is effective when sent or when received.

mailbox rule
A rule that states that an acceptance sent via the postal system or by courier is effective when sent.

EXAMPLE 8.6

▶ Smigel, a Minnesota supplier of oil drilling supplies, sent several of his customers who were located in various parts of the country a letter offering to sell surplus inventory of certain drilling bits for a relatively low price. The offer stated, "Reply by certified mail." On May 14 Perkins sent a certified letter accepting the offer. The letter was received by Smigel on May 17. On May 16 Lukin sent an e-mail message accepting the offer. The e-mail was received the same day, May 16. Smigel must sell his stock to Perkins even though Lukin's acceptance was received first because Perkins used Smigel's specified medium of communication for his acceptance.

Silence as Acceptance   In general, a person cannot be compelled to speak or to write in order to avoid a binding agreement and is under no obligation to reply to an offer. However, silence may indicate assent to an offer when both parties agree beforehand that this is to be the means of acceptance.

EXAMPLE 8.7

▶ In a letter to Westerly Dry Cleaners, Central Solvent, a regular supplier, offered to sell a newly formulated cleaning solvent and stated that it would consider the offer accepted if Westerly did not respond within 10 days. Westerly did not respond, and the solvent was shipped. Central billed Westerly for the solvent and shipping charges. Westerly refused to pay and demanded that the solvent be removed from its premises. Central claimed that Westerly's silence indicated acceptance of the offer. A court would hold that Westerly's silence is not considered an acceptance because Central cannot require the firm to speak.

However, suppose that Westerly and Central had previously agreed that Westerly's failure to turn down Central's written offer for the sale of goods would result in a valid, enforceable contract. In this instance, both parties would have agreed that silence was to be the manner of acceptance. The UCC provides that a "contract for the sale of goods may be made in any manner sufficient to show agreement, including conduct by both parties which recognizes the existence of such a contract" (UCC 2-204).

counteroffer
A response to an offer in which the terms and conditions of the original offer are changed.

AN ACCEPTANCE MUST BE UNCONDITIONAL

A counteroffer—that is, a conditional, or qualified, acceptance of an offer—is generally interpreted as a rejection and is not binding on the parties.

EXAMPLE 8.8

▶ Churchill, the owner of an apple orchard, signed a contract in February to sell the land to Czek but reserved the right to recover the apples when they ripened in the fall. Czek signed the contract but crossed out the words that pertained to the recovery of the apples. In this case there was no contract since Czek did not accept Churchill's offer and his act of crossing out the words constituted a counteroffer.

In a contract, an owner of an apple orchard might reserve the right to recover the apples when they ripen.

The general rule of contract provides that the acceptance of an offer must be the same as the offer, and that if there are any material (important) differences between the offer and the acceptance, the acceptance is regarded as a rejection of the offer. The UCC provides an exception to this rule and states that, between merchants, "a definite and reasonable expression of acceptance or a written confirmation which is sent within a reasonable time operates as an acceptance even though it states terms additional to or different from those offered or agreed upon, unless acceptance is expressly made conditional on assent to the additional or different terms" (UCC 2-207).

The UCC also provides that "additional (or different) terms are to be construed as proposals for addition to the contract, and between merchants, become part of the contract . . . unless the offer expressly limits acceptance to the terms of the offer, they materially alter it; or notification of objection to them . . . is given within a reasonable time after (they) are received" (UCC 2-207).

EXAMPLE 8.9

▶ Wayfar Printers ordered a drum of printing ink from Barlette & Co. On its order, Wayfar stated that delivery must be made by June 1. When Barlette accepted the order, it included the statement "impossible to ship before June 15." The acknowledgment also stated that "if these terms are not acceptable, buyer must notify the seller at once." Wayfar did not complain about the later delivery date. Barlette's acceptance was valid even though it stated terms different from those offered. The UCC states that the different terms become a part of the contract between merchants unless the alterations are material. At times, disagreements can result as to whether or not such different terms are important.

8.5 TERMINATION OF AN OFFER

Offers are terminated by (1) lapse of time, (2) revocation, (3) rejection, (4) death or incapacity, and (5) destruction or illegality.

TERMINATION BY LAPSE OF TIME

When the offeree fails to accept an offer within the time specified, the opportunity to form a contract ends because of a 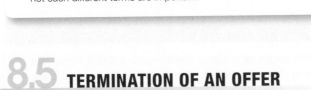termination by lapse of time. When no definite time for acceptance is stated in an offer, it terminates after a reasonable time has passed. What is considered a reasonable time can vary according to the circumstances.

termination by lapse of time
When an opportunity to form a contract ends because the offeree fails to accept an offer within the time specified.

EXAMPLE 8.10

▶ In the early spring, Wilkerson, a wholesaler of sporting goods, offered several dozen of a popular brand of tennis racquets at a specified price to Sportique Stores. Three months later, the store accepted the offer and demanded delivery. Obviously an offer to sell seasonal goods, such as tennis racquets, has a short life and must be accepted long before the passage of three months.

TERMINATION BY REVOCATION

An offer that has been neither accepted nor rejected by the offeree can be revoked, or withdrawn, by the offeror. The offeror may communicate the revocation to the offeree in either spoken or written words. The UCC provides, however, that any written offer by a merchant to buy or sell goods that states that the offer will be held open for a specified time period cannot be revoked during this time period or, if no time period is specified, until a reasonable time has elapsed. An offer that includes specific time limits expires automatically when the time is up unless the offeror chooses to extend the offer (UCC 2-309).

revocation
The calling back of an offer by the offeror before the offer has been accepted or rejected.

EXAMPLE 8.11

▶ Armstrong owned a painting with an appraised value of nearly $100,000. Hoping to sell the work, he placed it in the hands of Westport Galleries for an agreed-upon period of three months for sale at $80,000. After three months, no sale had been arranged. Armstrong took possession of the painting and turned it over to another gallery.

TERMINATION BY REJECTION

rejection
The express or implied refusal by an offeree to accept an offer.

A direct, unqualified rejection, or a refusal to accept, terminates an offer. The offer, once rejected by the offeree, cannot be revived or made into a counteroffer once the communication of the rejection has been received by the offeror. If the offeror acknowledges the rejection but restates the offer, the offeree still has the opportunity to accept, or reject, or make a counteroffer.

EXAMPLE 8.12

▶ Kenna (the offeror) offered to sell his antique car to Fishkin (the offeree) for $40,000. Fishkin sent an e-mail message to Kenna saying, "You know how much I'd like to buy the car, but I simply cannot afford it at this time." Kenna acknowledged Fishkin's rejection of the offer by saying, "I received your note rejecting my offer, but if you want to think about it for another month or two, I'll keep the offer open." By his acknowledgment of Fishkin's rejection and restatement of the offer, Kenna has allowed Fishkin an opportunity to accept the restated offer at a later date.

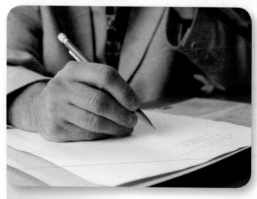

A direct, unqualified rejection terminates an offer.

Just as a qualified acknowledgment of the rejection of an offer serves to keep an offer alive, a qualified rejection may have a similar effect. Suppose, in Example 8.12, Fishkin had said, "Although I'd like to buy your car, I'm pretty sure I won't accept your offer; but I'd like to think about it for a week." The qualified rejection was, in fact, not really a rejection at all.

TERMINATION BY DEATH OR INCAPACITY

Mutual agreement cannot occur if either the offeror or the offeree dies or becomes incompetent. Therefore, an offer is immediately terminated as a result of the death or legal incapacity of either the offeror or the offeree. However, if either the offeror or the offeree is bound by an option contract, the surviving party may still be obligated to the contract. An option contract is one that has a provision to keep an offer open for a certain period of time. In the event of death, the estate of the deceased would be responsible to carry out the provisions of a contract that includes an option.

option contract
A contract that has a provision to keep an offer open for a certain period of time.

TERMINATION BY DESTRUCTION OR ILLEGALITY

If the subject matter of a contract is destroyed or declared illegal after the offer has been made but before it has been accepted, the contract is terminated.

EXAMPLE 8.13

▶ Gipson offered to sell Ramirez her boat for $8,000. While the boat was docked, a storm damaged the boat, causing it to sink. Because the boat was destroyed, the offer was terminated.

CHAPTER SUMMARY

1. The first step in reaching agreement and forming a valid contract is that there must be a proposal that is both offered by the offeror and accepted by the offeree.

2. For an offer to be valid, it must be (a) definite and certain, (b) communicated to the offeree, and (c) made with a serious intention that the offeror will be bound by it. One example would be a salesperson offering a potential buyer an item in a store, putting the terms of sale in clear writing, and signing the document before handing it to the potential buyer for his or her consideration.

3. A call for bids or estimates is not considered an offer, but rather a request for an offer or an invitation to negotiate that can be accepted or rejected by the person calling for the bid. To determine whether an advertisement is an invitation to trade or a valid offer, one should

carefully examine whether the wording in the advertisement contains sufficient words to demonstrate a commitment to sell. If it contains a positive promise and positive statement of what the advertiser expects in return, the courts will usually hold that the advertisement is an offer. When an advertisement offers a reward for information, it is regarded as a general offer to the public at large, and acceptance of a public offer by anyone results in an enforceable contract.

4. A valid acceptance of an offer must be (a) communicated to the offeror and (b) unconditional. An example would be when a buyer informs a seller that she will accept his offer to sell a copy of the daily newspaper for $1.

5. An offer can be terminated by (a) lapse of time, (b) revocation, (c) rejection, (d) death or incapacity, or (e) destruction or illegality.

CHAPTER EIGHT ASSESSMENT

MATCHING LEGAL TERMS

Match each of the numbered definitions with the correct term in the following list. Write the letter of your choice in the answer column.

a. acceptance

b. counteroffer

c. invitation to trade

d. lapse of time

e. mailbox rule

f. offeree

g. offeror

h. public offer

i. request for a proposal

j. revocation

1. A new and different response to an offer.

1. _____

2. A principle that states that an acceptance sent via the postal system or by courier is effective when sent.

2. _____

3. Agreement to a proposal or an offer.

3. _____

4. A call for a bid or estimate for materials to be furnished or work to be done.

4. _____

5. The prevailing legal view of a newspaper advertisement.

5. _____

6. The offeror's rescinding of an offer that has never been accepted by the offeree.

6. _____

7. The party to whom an offer is made.

7. _____

8. The reason for termination of an offer that has not been accepted by the offeree within the time limits specified.

8. _____

9. An offer to large groups of people, only one of whom can accept.

9. _____

10. The person who makes an offer.

10. _____

TRUE/FALSE QUIZ

Indicate whether each of the following statements is true or false by writing *T* or *F* in the answer column.

11. In order for an offer to be valid, it must be definite and certain.

11. _____

12. The person who makes a proposal to enter into a contract is the offeror.

12. _____

13. In order for an acceptance to be valid, it must be communicated to the offeror.

13. _____

14. Requests for proposals and announcements asking for bids or estimates are usually considered legally binding offers.

14. _____

15. According to the UCC, uncertainty with respect to specific terms does not necessarily invalidate a contract.

15. _____

16. A newspaper advertisement of goods for sale is usually considered an invitation to trade.

16. _____

17. If an advertisement contains a positive promise and a positive statement of what the advertiser expects in return, the courts will usually hold that the advertisement is an offer.

17. _____

18. A direct, unqualified rejection terminates an offer.

18. _____

19. An offer that includes specific time limits expires automatically when the time is up unless the offeror chooses to extend the offer.

19. _____

20. The mailbox rule states that an acceptance sent via the postal system or by courier is effective when received by the offeror.

20. _____

DISCUSSION QUESTIONS

Answer the following questions and discuss them in class.

21. What are some circumstances that can lead to uncertainty in offers and acceptances, and how can they be avoided?

_____

_____

22. What are some advantages of written offers and acceptances over spoken ones?

_____

_____

23. Under what circumstances might a specific time be crucial to a transaction that would justify limiting the time for an offer or acceptance?

_____

_____

24. When a definite time for acceptance has not been set, when does the acceptance time terminate?

_____

_____

25. Explain the three requirements of a valid offer.

_____

_____

26. Explain the two requirements of a valid acceptance.

_____

_____

THINKING CRITICALLY ABOUT THE LAW

Answer the following questions, which require you to think critically about the legal principles that you learned in this chapter.

27. Offer Why are newspaper advertisements not considered valid offers?

_____

_____

28. Acceptance Describe the circumstances under which silence on the part of an offeree will be a valid acceptance. Does this seem reasonable and fair?

_____

_____

29. Counteroffer Why does the law interpret a counteroffer that is a conditional or qualified acceptance as a rejection of the offer and not binding on the parties?

_____

_____

30. Termination of an Offer If an offer is rejected, should the offeree have the right to negotiate before the offer is considered terminated?

_____

_____

31. A Question of Ethics Is it appropriate for a city or state official to accept a bid for the performance of work or the purchase of goods or services that is higher than others, even if there are no laws requiring that officials accept the lowest bid?

_____

_____

CASE QUESTIONS

Study each of the following cases. Answer the questions that follow by writing _Yes_ or _No_ in the answer column.

32. Definite and Certain Offer Neto learned that Quan, his neighbor, intended to sell his powerboat. Neto texted Quan stating that he wanted to buy the boat and he would pay a "fair price." A few days later, Quan sold the boat to someone else for a higher price than Neto would have been willing to pay.

a. Does Neto have a legal course of action against Quan?   a. _____

b. Is there anything illegal about this case?   b. _____

c. Can Quan safely ignore Neto's offer because it lacked certainty and definiteness?   c. _____

d. If Neto had specified a price he was willing to pay, would Quan have been obligated to accept it?   d. _____

33. Silence as Acceptance Kallinteris opened a travel agency in her small town. She then received an e-mail message from a local office supply company with which she had no prior dealings wishing her luck with her new business and advising her that she would soon be receiving $250 worth of office supply items, such as file folders, pens, printer cartridges, and so on, unless she informed the company that she did not want these items. Kallinteris did not respond to the e-mail message and received the supplies a few days later.

a. Does Kallinteris's silence constitute an acceptance of the terms of the agreement?

a. _____

b. Does a valid contract between Kallinteris and the office supply company exist?

b. _____

c. If Kallinteris uses the supplies, will she be required to pay for them?

c. _____

34. Termination of an Offer Redmond offered to sell Goosen her used car for $6,000. Goosen could not make up his mind and, finally, after five months, told Redmond that he would accept her offer.

a. Goosen can accept Redmond's offer even though five months have passed.

a. _____

b. Goosen cannot accept Redmond's offer due to the doctrine of revocation.

b. _____

c. Redmond could have required that the offer be accepted within three days.

c. _____

d. Goosen's statement after five months that he wanted to purchase the car for $6,000 is an offer by him that may be accepted by Redmond if she so chooses.

d. _____

CASE ANALYSIS

Study each of the following cases carefully. Briefly state the principle of law and your decision.

35. Bids and Estimates Fletcher-Harlee Corp., a general contractor, solicited bids from subcontractors on various aspects of a building project for which it intended to compete. In response, Pote Concrete Contractors Inc. submitted a written price quotation for providing the concrete for the project. Pote, however, indicated that its price quotation was for informational purposes only. Did Pote's bid constitute a valid offer? [*Fletcher-Harlee Corp. v. Pote Concrete Contractors, Inc.*, 2007 U.S. App. LEXIS 7808 (New Jersey)]

Principle of Law:

_____

_____

Decision:

_____

_____

36. **Counteroffer** Browne offered to sell Houlihan his recently purchased 50-inch plasma screen television set for $6,400. Houlihan sent Browne an e-mail message accepting the offer but asked if she could pay Browne in four equal monthly installments of $1,600. Browne did not acknowledge Houlihan's e-mail and instead sold the television set to Drew for $6,200. Houlihan then purchased a new set for $7,400 and sued Browne for $1,000, the difference in price. Did Houlihan and Browne have a valid contract, and will Houlihan be able to recover $1,000 from Browne?

Principle of Law:

_____

_____

Decision:

_____

_____

37. **Silence as Acceptance** Bell Microproducts, Inc. mailed to McGurn an offer of employment that stated that if McGurn was terminated without cause during the first 12 months of employment, he would receive a severance package worth $120,000. McGurn crossed out the number *12*, replaced it with the number *24*, and signed the contract. Bell did not acknowledge the change that had been made to the contract and hired the applicant. McGurn was terminated without cause 13 months later. Did Bell's silence as to McGurn's counteroffer amount to an acceptance? [*McGurn v. Bell Microproducts, Inc.*, 284 F.3d 86 (Massachusetts).]

Principle of Law:

_____

_____

Decision:

_____

_____

38. **Valid Offer** Sanderson Mart ran an advertisement in the *Daily Tribune* that stated, "Special offer to our customers—3/8-inch Electric Hand Drills, Saturday only—$14.99, only 100 in stock, while they last! Be here when we open for the bargain of the year!" Cruz arrived at the store at 8:00 a.m. when the store opened. The salesperson refused to sell him an electric drill, claiming that he had only two in stock and those were already set aside for another customer—and besides, the advertisement was not really a

binding offer. Will Sanderson be required to sell the electric drill for the advertised price?

Principle of Law:

_____

_____

Decision:

_____

_____

LEGAL RESEARCH

Complete the following activities. Share your findings with the class.

39. **Working in Teams** In teams of three or four, interview a local retailer and ask him or her how, when planning and writing advertising copy, he or she avoids wording that might cause a reader to regard the ad as a definite offer, instead of simply an advertisement.

_____

_____

40. **Using Technology** Using the Internet and search engines, locate web pages that offer goods and services for sale and that specify time periods during which such offers must be accepted.

_____

_____

chapter 9
Mutual Agreement

After studying this chapter and completing the assessment, you will be able to

9.1 List seven ways in which a lack of a meeting of the minds may cause defective agreements.

9.2 Identify the elements of fraud.

9.3 Explain misrepresentation and how it differs from fraud.

9.4 Explain the concept of mistake in the eyes of the law.

9.5 Define undue influence and explain its impact upon the validity of a contract.

9.6 Describe duress and the forms that it may take.

9.7 Define contracts of adhesion and describe the conditions under which these contracts are voidable.

9.8 Define unconscionable contracts.

LEGAL terms

fraud	undue influence
puffing	duress
misrepresentation	contract of adhesion
mistake	unconscionable contract

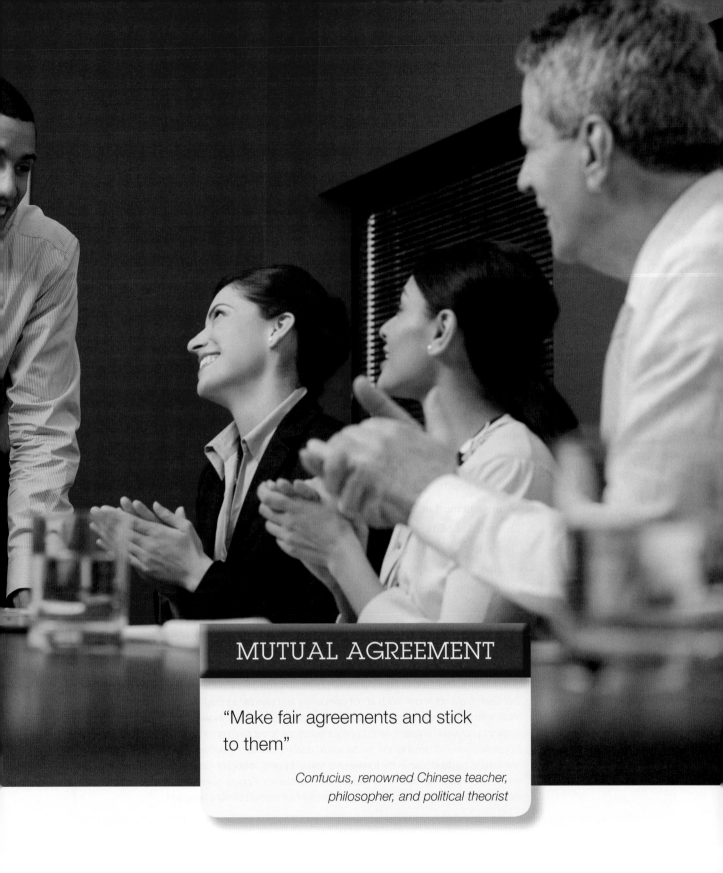

MUTUAL AGREEMENT

"Make fair agreements and stick to them"

Confucius, renowned Chinese teacher, philosopher, and political theorist

9.1 DEFECTIVE AGREEMENTS

In Chapter 7, the six elements of an enforceable contract were discussed. Potential problems with achieving a meeting of the minds, the second of these essential elements, are discussed in this chapter.

Genuineness, or reality, of agreement is said to be present in a contract when there is a true meeting of the minds of the parties. If there is any misunderstanding or if any force or deception is used by either party to obtain the necessary agreement of the other party, the contract is voidable and may be disaffirmed at the option of the injured party. A voidable contract results if agreement of either party is obtained by fraud, misrepresentation, mistake, undue influence, or duress, or if the contract is one of adhesion or is unconscionable. Each of these terms will be explained in this chapter.

9.2 FRAUD

fraud
The intentional misstatement or nondisclosure of a material (essential) fact made by one party in an attempt to influence the actions of another party.

Fraud is the intentional misstatement or nondisclosure of a material fact made by one party in an attempt to influence the actions of another party. It does not matter how the fraud is committed. It may be by spoken or written words or by acts or conduct. Regardless of how the fraud is committed, the party who relies on the misstatement or nondisclosure must suffer a loss as a result of the act.

In order to prove a fraud case, a plaintiff must demonstrate five elements:

1. A misstatement or nondisclosure of a material fact.
2. Knowledge of its falsity or reckless disregard of its truth.
3. Intent to cause the other party to enter into the agreement.
4. Reliance by the injured party.
5. Harm to the injured party (financial, physical, or both).

EXAMPLE 9.1

▶ Eppers went to Micro New Age Computer Store to buy a personal computer so he could process his large collection of digital photos. Donaldson, the owner of the store, quickly sensed that Eppers did not know much about computers and also recognized that Eppers was unfamiliar with how much memory would be necessary to run most available photo-processing software packages. In response to Eppers's questions about the memory of a particular model, Donaldson assured him that the model would accommodate any software on the market and any likely to be developed in the foreseeable future. Eppers, relying on Donaldson's assurances, bought the model that was recommended. To his dismay, Eppers quickly discovered that the memory was inadequate for many popular photo-processing software programs.

Now reexamine the case:

1. Was there a misstatement or nondisclosure of a material fact? Yes, the misstatement was of a material fact. Memory capacity is a vital part of computer equipment.

2. Was the misstatement made intentionally or recklessly? Yes, Donaldson either knew, or should have known, that the memory was inadequate for many programs.

3. Was the misstatement made with intent to deceive Eppers? Yes, Donaldson knew that the memory was important to Eppers.

4. Did Eppers rely on Donaldson's statements and act on them? Yes, Eppers bought the computer that Donaldson recommended.

5. Did Eppers suffer a loss as a result of his reliance on the false statements? Yes, Eppers would need to increase memory at an added cost in order to use the computer as he had intended.

The law allows for a certain amount of "sales talk," or puffing, that is not considered fraudulent.

It is important to recognize the difference between a fraudulent statement and a salesperson's puffing, which is considered a mere expression of opinion. Most salespersons use persuasive statements in an effort to induce a prospective purchaser to buy. In Example 9.1, assume Donaldson also used statements such as "This machine is the best buy in town" and "This computer is as good as the well-known brands." In the eyes of the law, these statements are merely "dealer's talk" and are not considered misstatements of material facts. Puffing refers to generalities and, at times, is directed toward the five senses (the suit looks great, the CD player sounds terrific, the facial tissues feel soft).

Intentional concealment or intentional nondisclosure of material facts (deliberately hiding important information) is just as fraudulent as making false statements. Suppose that, in Example 9.1, Donaldson did not comment on the adequacy of the computer memory but knew from Eppers's comments that he intended to use it with a particular brand of software, and Donaldson knew, or should have known, that the computer sold to Eppers was not adequate. Because Eppers relied on Donaldson's information, it appears that Donaldson was guilty of intentional concealment or intentional nondisclosure. In order to avoid a case of fraud, a seller must disclose pertinent facts that a buyer might not inquire about or notice during a reasonable inspection.

puffing
A general expression of opinion, typically in a sales context, that is used to persuade a prospective purchaser to buy. It does not constitute a misrepresentation of material text.

9.3 MISREPRESENTATION

Misrepresentation is the unintentional misstatement or nondisclosure of a material fact that results in inducing another to enter into an agreement to his or her loss. (Remember that when the misstatement is made knowingly or recklessly, it is, as previously discussed, fraud.)

misrepresentation
A misstatement of a material fact that results in inducing another to enter into an agreement to his or her injury.

It is important to note the distinction between fraud and misrepresentation because the remedy is different. An injured party who can successfully prove fraud may have the contract canceled and bring suit for damages. If the party can prove only misrepresentation, the contract can be canceled, but the injured party cannot sue for additional damages.

EXAMPLE 9.2

▶ Arnold hired BluWater Pool Company to build a swimming pool in his backyard. It was only after construction had begun that Arnold learned from a neighbor that local zoning ordinances prohibited backyard swimming pools in the community. The salesperson for BluWater admitted that he had been thinking about another community where no prohibitions existed. Arnold may void the contract, but he may not seek additional damages because BluWater's misrepresentation was unintentional and innocent.

9.4 MISTAKE

mistake
A belief that is not in accord with the facts.

In the eyes of the law, a mistake is a belief that is not in accord with the facts. Mistakes relating to contracts may be concerned with the nature of the subject matter or the quality of the subject matter. Obviously not every erroneous idea or notion is a mistake, and the law makes it clear that the mistaken belief must concern an existing fact and not a belief about what might happen in the future. Court decisions involving mistakes are often complex, and the courts attempt to determine whether the mistake was "unilateral" (that is, made by only one party) or whether the mistake was "mutual" (that is, made by both parties). For a contract to be dissolved because of a mistake, the law usually requires that both parties be a part of the misunderstanding—that is, the mistake must be mutual.

EXAMPLE 9.3

▶ Chin, a collector of rare paintings, offered to sell a particular Picasso painting (catalog number 1401) to Kovacs for $14,000. When it came time to exchange the painting for the money, it was obvious that Kovacs was expecting a different Picasso (catalog number 1410) and not the catalog number 1401 that Chin had expected to sell. Chin also was surprised because he thought Kovacs wanted to buy catalog number 1401. The contract can be canceled by either party because this was a mutual mistake.

A physician may have the power to control the actions of his or her patients because of a special or confidential relationship.

undue influence
The improper use of excessive pressure by the dominant member of a confidential relationship to convince the weaker party to enter a contract that greatly benefits the dominant party.

9.5 UNDUE INFLUENCE

Sometimes a person has the power to control the actions of another because of a special or confidential relationship to that person. Such relationships are sometimes found between employer and employee, physician or nurse and patient, teacher and student, attorney and client, and so on. When someone uses this power improperly to his or her personal advantage, undue influence is said to exist. A contract resulting from the use of undue influence is voidable at the option of the party wrongfully influenced.

EXAMPLE 9.4

▶ Hsu, a professor of electrical engineering, was working with a foreign student, Placido, on a new ceramic compound in the field of superconductivity. Hsu encouraged his student to continue his research and said that he would undertake to secure the patent on the new compound in both names. Placido was suspicious about the arrangement suggested by Hsu but recognized Hsu's influence over him. Once the patent was issued, Placido realized that it was his work and inventiveness that had resulted in the new compound—and not that of his professor. In this case, the court would likely find that the relationship between professor and student resulted in undue influence.

9.6 DURESS

Duress is the act of applying unlawful or improper pressure or influence to a person in order to gain his or her agreement to a contract. Such pressure can take the form of a threat of bodily harm to an individual or to his or her family, or the threat of serious loss or damage to his or her property. When threats are used to force someone to enter into a contract, the agreement may be dissolved by the injured party.

duress
The act of applying unlawful or improper pressure or influence to a person to gain his or her agreement to a contract.

EXAMPLE 9.5

▶ Brent, the owner of a small trucking company, called on Goodwin, president of Goodwin Manufacturing Company, to sell his company's trucking services. As they concluded their conversation, Brent indicated that it would be a good idea to agree to hire Brent's company to handle Goodwin's trucking needs because other companies that did not utilize Brent's company's services often experienced unexpected fires. Brent's message was clearly a threat, and Goodwin agreed to sign the contract for trucking services. The contract is voidable and could be rescinded by Goodwin because of the duress applied by Brent.

contract of adhesion
A contract drawn by one party that must be accepted as is on a take-it-or-leave-it basis.

9.7 CONTRACTS OF ADHESION

A contract that involves parties who have unequal bargaining power is known as a contract of adhesion. These take-it-or-leave-it contracts are quite common and are normally enforceable. But when enforcement of an otherwise legal contract will result in a significant hardship to one of the parties, courts have considered such agreements to be so unfair as to be unenforceable.

The inequality of bargaining power can exist in contracts that are prepared by one party and simply presented to the other without the opportunity for meaningful negotiation, such as insurance policies or the disclaimers printed on ticket stubs and dry cleaning receipts. Also, some contracts have become so routine that one of the parties may not even

An admission ticket may be a contract of adhesion.

realize that he or she has entered into a contract—an example would be checkroom and luggage receipts or tickets to a parking garage or a theater.

EXAMPLE 9.6

▶ Lorenz brought several expensive shirts to a laundry service for cleaning. A note on the receipt he was given indicated that the establishment was not responsible for goods left over 30 days. Lorenz attempted to pick up his shirts 35 days later and was told that, under the terms of the contract, he was not entitled to their return. The "30 day" clause would be a contract of adhesion, and Lorenz would be entitled to get back his apparel.

9.8 UNCONSCIONABLE CONTRACTS

unconscionable contract
A contract that is so one-sided that it is oppressive and gives unfair advantage to one of the parties.

A contract that is regarded as shockingly unjust or unfair is said to be an unconscionable contract. While courts have long been reluctant to uphold these, more recently the UCC has made such contracts even less likely to be enforced. The Code states, "If the court as a matter of law finds the contract or any clause of the contract to have been unconscionable at the time it was made, the court may refuse to enforce the contract, or it may enforce the remainder of the contract without the unconscionable clause, or it may so limit the application of any unconscionable clause as to avoid any unconscionable result" (UCC 2-302).

When the UCC was written, it was intended that the unconscionable clause would apply only to sales of goods. In recent years, however, virtually the only successful use of unconscionability under the Code has been made by consumers in various kinds of contracts involving such acts as making home improvements, opening a checking account, leasing a gasoline filling station, and leasing an apartment. For example, the UCC has been cited to cancel contracts where one party has written agreements in such a way as to take an obvious unfair advantage of another party who lacked familiarity with the English language.

EXAMPLE 9.7

▶ The sales representative for Frostifresh Corporation sold a freezer to Reynoso, who spoke little English. The salesperson neither translated nor explained the contract, but told Reynoso that the freezer would cost nothing because he would receive a bonus of $25 for each sale made to his friends. The total price of the freezer, made with periodic payments, would have been more than $1,100. The cash price would have been $900, and the wholesale price to the company was $348. The court ruled that the contract was unconscionable and awarded the company a reasonable profit, service and finance charges, and its own cost of $348. [*Frostifresh Corp. v. Reynoso*, 274 N.Y.S.2d 757 (Dist. Ct. 1966), *rev'd on other grounds*, 281 N.Y.S.2d 964 (Sup. Ct. App. Term 1967)]

CHAPTER SUMMARY

1. Seven ways in which a lack of a meeting of the minds may interfere with the legal enforcement of agreements include cases involving (a) fraud, (b) misrepresentation, (c) mistake, (d) undue influence, (e) duress, (f) contracts of adhesion, and (g) unconscionable contracts.

2. Fraud (a) is a misstatement or nondisclosure of a material fact; (b) is made with knowledge of its falsity or with reckless disregard of its truth; (c) is made with the intention of causing the other party to enter into the agreement; (d) is relied on by the injured party; and (e) results in loss to the injured party.

3. Misrepresentation (a) is the unintentional misstatement or nondisclosure of a material fact; (b) results in inducing another to enter into an agreement; and (c) results in loss to the injured party.

4. A mistake is a belief that is not in accord with the facts. Mistakes relating to contracts may be concerned with the nature of the subject matter or the quality of the subject matter.

5. Undue influence is the improper use of power to control the actions of another because of a special or confidential relationship to that person. A contract resulting from the use of undue influence is voidable at the option of the party wrongfully influenced.

6. Duress is the act of applying unlawful or improper pressure or influence to a person in order to gain his or her agreement to a contract. Such pressure can take the form of a threat of bodily harm to an individual or to his or her family, or the threat of serious loss or damage to his or her property.

7. Contracts of adhesion are contracts that involve parties who have unequal bargaining power. When enforcement of an otherwise legal contract will result in a significant hardship to one of the parties, courts have considered such agreements to be so unfair as to be unenforceable.

8. Unconscionable contracts are contracts that are regarded as shockingly unjust or unfair.

CHAPTER NINE ASSESSMENT

MATCHING LEGAL TERMS

Match each of the numbered definitions with the correct term in the following list. Write the letter of your choice in the answer column.

a. contract of adhesion
b. duress
c. fraud
d. intentional concealment
e. misrepresentation
f. mistake
g. mutual agreement
h. puffing
i. unconscionable contract
j. undue influence

1. A contract regarded as shockingly unfair and unjust. 1. _____

2. Domination of a person's will by force or by threat of force or injury. 2. _____

3. A contract characterized by unequal bargaining power of the parties. 3. _____

4. A "meeting of the minds."   4. _____

5. Intentional misstatement of a material fact.   5. _____

6. Purposely not disclosing material facts to a contracting party.   6. _____

7. The power to control the actions of another that results from a special or confidential relationship.   7. _____

8. Unintentional misstatement of a material fact.   8. _____

9. A belief not in accord with the facts that may be concerned with the nature of the subject matter or the quality of the subject matter.   9. _____

10. A mere expression of opinion.   10. _____

TRUE/FALSE QUIZ

Indicate whether each of the following statements is true or false by writing *T* or *F* in the answer column.

11. Fraud may be committed either by spoken or written words or by acts or conduct.   11. _____

12. Intentional concealment of material facts is just as fraudulent as making false statements.   12. _____

13. A contract resulting from the use of undue influence is voidable at the option of the party wrongfully influenced.   13. _____

14. When threats are used to force someone to enter into a contract, the agreement may be dissolved by either party.   14. _____

15. The distinction between fraud and misrepresentation is important because the remedies available to an injured party are different.   15. _____

16. When the UCC was written, it was intended that the unconscionable clause would apply only to contracts for services.   16. _____

17. For a contract to be dissolved because of a mistake, the law usually requires that the mistake be mutual.   17. _____

18. A contract of adhesion is characterized by unequal bargaining power of the parties.   18. _____

19. If a person knowingly makes a false statement of a material fact in a contract with the intent that the other party rely on it, the person making such false statement can be charged with puffing.   19. _____

20. A contract considered shockingly unjust or unfair is an unconscionable contract.   20. _____

DISCUSSION QUESTIONS

Answer the following questions and discuss them in class.

21. List five elements an injured party must prove in order to claim fraud.

_____

_____

22. Explain the distinction between fraud and misrepresentation.

_____

_____

23. Explain the UCC provision relating to when a contract is unconscionable.

_____

_____

24. What are some examples of duress?

_____

_____

25. Persuasive statements based on a salesperson's opinion are referred to as puffing. Provide examples of typical sales situations in which puffing is used.

_____

_____

26. What are some examples of undue influence?

_____

_____

THINKING CRITICALLY ABOUT THE LAW

Answer the following questions, which require you to think critically about the legal principles that you learned in this chapter.

27. Material Fact How should a court decide whether a particular term in a contract is material?

_____

_____

28. **Mistake** Why does the law provide that a mistake must be mutual, and not unilateral, in order for a contract to be voidable?

_____

_____

29. **Undue Influence versus Duress** When does an abuse of power to control the actions of another because of a special or confidential relationship go beyond undue influence and become duress?

_____

_____

30. **Unconscionable Contracts** What criteria should a court use in determining whether a contract is shockingly unjust or unfair and thus unconscionable?

_____

_____

31. **A Question of Ethics** Is the failure to disclose material facts or information to a prospective buyer fair and ethical?

_____

_____

CASE QUESTIONS

Study each of the following cases. Answer the questions that follow by writing *Yes* or *No* in the answer column.

32. **Undue Influence** Guss, a professor at a small college, offered to sell his five-year-old car to Kantrowitz, a student in one of his classes. The price Guss asked was well above market value. Kantrowitz accepted Guss's offer without even test-driving the car.

    a. Is the contract between Guss and Kantrowitz voidable by either Guss or Kantrowitz?   a. _____

    b. Is the contract between Guss and Kantrowitz voidable only by Guss?   b. _____

    c. Is this a contract of adhesion?   c. _____

    d. Is this an example of misrepresentation?   d. _____

33. **Intentional Concealment** Gortino, while trying to sell his house to Stein, was asked if he had ever seen or suspected termites in the house. Gortino replied that he had not and that the house was sound. Several months after Stein had purchased the

house, she learned from neighbors that Gortino had paid for soil treatment to eliminate termites.

a. Can the contract for sale be canceled because of fraud?   **a.** _____

b. Was there a misstatement of a material fact?   **b.** _____

c. Did Stein suffer a loss as a result of Gortino's actions?   **c.** _____

d. Can Stein sue for damages?   **d.** _____

34. **Voidable Contract** Gallagher Restaurant Supply was in the business of leasing equipment to small restaurants. Quezada, the operator of a small diner, leased a coffeemaker from Gallagher. It was only after the contract had been signed that Quezada learned that similar lease agreements with other restaurants were far less costly. Also, the agreement between the parties provided for an accelerated payment of the entire balance if Quezada failed to perform any condition of the lease, "no matter how trivial the condition may be." In addition, Gallagher would be entitled to take back the coffeemaker and collect a 20 percent penalty.

a. Is this an example of a contract signed under duress?   **a.** _____

b. Is it likely that a court would enforce this contract?   **b.** _____

c. Is this an example of a void contract?   **c.** _____

d. Is this an example of a voidable contract?   **d.** _____

CASE ANALYSIS

Study each of the following cases carefully. Briefly state the principle of law and your decision.

35. **Mutual Mistake** Brooking agreed to sell a tract of land to Dover Pool & Racquet Club, Inc., on which Dover planned to build a swim and tennis club. Neither party to the contract knew that just before the contract was signed, the local zoning board of the town in which the land was located published a notice of public hearings on a proposal to amend the zoning in a way that would have prevented Dover from using the land as it had planned to do. Will this contract be enforced? [*Dover Pool & Racquet Club, Inc. v. Brooking*, 322 N.E.2d 168 (Massachusetts)]

Principle of Law:

_____

_____

Decision:

_____

_____

36. **Contract of Adhesion** Weaver, a high school dropout, leased a gas station from American Oil Company and signed a standard agreement prepared by the oil company's lawyers. The lease (contract) contained a clause in fine print that provided that the oil company would not be liable for any injury occurring on the premises regardless of fault. No one representing the oil company called Weaver's attention to the clause or explained it to him. In addition, the lease provided that Weaver would have to pay American Oil for any loss or damages, even if they resulted from the oil company's negligence. An employee of the oil company spilled gasoline on Weaver and his assistant, causing them to be burned and injured. The oil company brought an action seeking to be relieved of liability for the injury and to have Weaver held liable for any damages to the assistant. Will the contract provision for Weaver being held liable be enforced? [*Weaver v. American Oil Co.*, 276 N.E.2d 144 (Indiana)]

    Principle of Law:

    _____

    _____

    Decision:

    _____

    _____

37. **Misrepresentation** Malina, the owner of an old, multistory factory building, offered to lease the building to Larson, a manufacturer. Larson wanted to know whether the construction of the floors was strong enough to support the heavy machinery he planned to install. Malina assured him that the floors would support any machinery brought into the building. After the lease was signed, Larson's engineer studied the construction and reported that the floors would hold only half of the machinery that Larson planned to install. Is Larson bound by the lease?

    Principle of Law:

    _____

    _____

    Decision:

    _____

    _____

38. **Fraud** Power-Sports wished to obtain Harley-Davidson's permission to purchase a motorcycle dealership. Power-Sports provided written and oral statements about its business model, and based upon these statements, Harley-Davidson approved the purchase. Later Harley-Davidson learned that Power-Sports was operating in a manner inconsistent with its statements about its business model. Harley-Davidson sued for damages. Will Harley-Davidson be successful in its lawsuit

against Power-Sports? [*Harley-Davidson Motor Company v. Power-Sports, Inc.*, 319 F.3d 973 (Wisconsin)]

Principle of Law:

_____

_____

Decision:

_____

_____

LEGAL RESEARCH

Complete the following activities. Share your findings with the class.

39. Working in Teams In teams of three or four, visit local dry cleaning establishments, movie theaters, or parking garages. Ask them to allow you to view their receipts, and identify terms that might be viewed as contracts of adhesion.

_____

_____

40. Using Technology Using the Internet and search engines, investigate "unconscionable contracts"; then, with additional research, find examples of existing legislation in several jurisdictions that concern such contracts. Share your findings with the class.

_____

_____

chapter **10**
Consideration

LEARNING OUTCOMES

After studying this chapter and completing the assessment, you will be able to

10.1 Explain consideration and define forbearance.

10.2 Identify and explain the three essential characteristics of valid consideration.

10.3 Describe the kinds of valid consideration, including (a) a promise for a promise, (b) a promise of forbearance, and (c) a pledge or subscription.

10.4 Discuss the situations in which the UCC dispenses with the requirement of consideration in contracts to sell goods.

10.5 Define the term *general release*.

10.6 Identify five kinds of agreements that lack consideration.

LEGAL terms

forbearance	preexisting duty
promisor	gratuitous promise
promisee	illusory promise
pledge	moral consideration
general release	past consideration
barren promise	

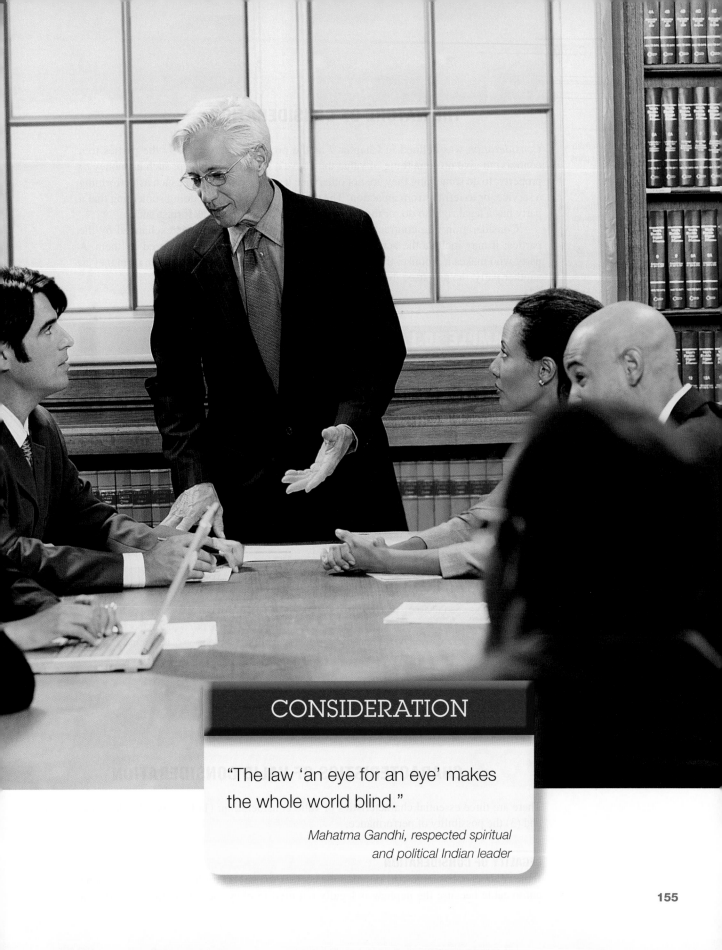

CONSIDERATION

"The law 'an eye for an eye' makes the whole world blind."

Mahatma Gandhi, respected spiritual and political Indian leader

forbearance
The promise to refrain from doing something that a party has a legal right to do.

promisor
In the making of a contract, the party who makes a promise.

promisee
In the making of a contract, the party to whom a promise is made.

10.1   THE NATURE OF CONSIDERATION

Consideration was defined in Chapter 7 as the promises exchanged by the parties to a contract: to give up something of value they have a legal right to keep, such as money or property; to do something they are not otherwise legally required to do, such as performing a service; or to refrain from an action. The promise to refrain from doing something that a party has a legal right to do, or the promise of inaction, is known as forbearance.

Consideration in a contract may be more than just the promises exchanged by the parties; it may include the actual benefit gained and the detriment suffered by them. A party who makes a promise, the promisor, may make a promise to pay a sum of money to another party, the promisee, for the performance of a certain act.

EXAMPLE 10.1

▶ Stein promised to pay his 19-year-old nephew $3,000 on his 22nd birthday if he refrained from smoking cigarettes until he graduated from Northern State College.

This contract is legal and illustrates the promise of forbearance as consideration. Although it seems unlikely that Stein would break his promise or that his nephew would bring suit to collect, it is possible. For example, if Stein were to die before his nephew's 22nd birthday, the executors of his estate might not wish to pay and the nephew might want to sue to collect.

EXAMPLE 10.2

▶ Lund, who owned a tavern, promised to pay $600 to Carposi to install a new satellite dish on Lund's property. In this example, Lund (the promisor) made a promise to pay a sum of money to Carposi (the promisee) for the performance of a certain act. The consideration of the promisor is the money ($600), and the consideration of the promisee is the performance of the act (installing the satellite dish).

10.2   CHARACTERISTICS OF VALID CONSIDERATION

There are three essential characteristics of valid consideration: (1) legality, (2) adequacy, and (3) the possibility of performance.

LEGALITY OF CONSIDERATION

If the contract in Example 10.1 required the nephew to obey all traffic laws, it would not be enforceable because the nephew is legally required to obey these laws anyway. Also, a valid contract does not exist if the consideration is a promise to perform an illegal act or to avoid performing an act that is legally required to be performed.

ADEQUACY OF CONSIDERATION

Traditionally, the courts generally made no attempt to judge whether or not the exchange of promises in a contract was fair—that is, whether there was adequacy of consideration. The law assumed that, as long as no undue pressure was brought to bear, the parties were free to reject a proposed unfair contract. In recent times, however, society has recognized some of the problems associated with contractual relationships in which the unrestricted bargaining power of one party gives him or her an unfair advantage when dealing with another party who lacks the economic power or the education to enter into contracts on an equal footing.

In an attempt to level the playing field, many consumer protection statutes have been passed. The notions of unconscionable contracts (contracts that are shockingly unfair and unjust) and contracts of adhesion (contracts in which the parties have unequal bargaining power) are now widely applied. These concepts were discussed in Chapter 9.

POSSIBILITY OF PERFORMANCE

A legally enforceable contract cannot be based on a promise that is impossible to fulfill. However, a party who promises to do something that is merely difficult to perform, or poses unforeseen expenses, is still bound by the terms of the contract.

EXAMPLE 10.3

▶ Hicky operated a small processing plant that added certain finishing processes to other companies' partially manufactured products. Hicky bid successfully on a job to spray-paint assembled products. Subsequently, Hicky learned that local safety regulations required that spray-painting be done in ventilated paint booths, which Hicky's plant did not have. His choices narrowed down to (1) installing the required booths at great expense; (2) paying considerably higher insurance premiums and fines for violating the regulations; or (3) outsourcing the spray-painting job at additional expense to another company that could meet the ventilation requirements. For all three alternatives, Hicky would lose money on the spray-painting contract. Since the contract is valid and enforceable, if Hicky chose to break the agreement, he would be subject to suit for breach of contract.

10.3 KINDS OF VALID CONSIDERATION

Consideration required in an enforceable contract can take various forms: exchange of promises, forbearance, and pledges or subscriptions.

A PROMISE FOR A PROMISE

As indicated earlier in this chapter, the most common form of valid consideration is the promise of money by one party for the promise of an act by another. Example 10.1, discussed earlier, illustrates this point. It should be noted that the mere promise to act is usually deemed valid consideration. Whether or not the promise is actually carried out is another matter, having to do with the execution of the contract terms and, specifically, with the issue of performance by the parties. The law provides certain remedies to a wronged party where there is partial performance or nonperformance of a promised act (discussed in Chapter 15). A promise of an act by one party in exchange for the promise of an act by another is also considered valid consideration. In other words, the exchange of money is not a requirement.

EXAMPLE 10.4

▶ Carleo promised to repair Mills's car if Mills painted one of Carleo's rooms. The exchange of promises would be considered valid consideration even though no money actually changed hands.

A PROMISE OF FORBEARANCE

Valid consideration is not necessarily either the performance of an act or the payment of money. One party to a contract may, for a variety of reasons, wish to exchange his or her promise to pay money for a promise of inaction from the other party. Many contracts in which part of the consideration is forbearance involve agreements not to compete (to be discussed in greater detail in Chapter 28). Notice that in Example 10.5, part of the consideration is a promise not to act.

EXAMPLE 10.5

▶ Kim agreed to purchase a fruit and vegetable business from Rosen for a certain price if Rosen promised to refrain from opening another fruit and vegetable business in the same town for three years. In this case, Kim's consideration was his promise to pay the agreed selling price for (1) Rosen's business and (2) her promise of inaction, or forbearance. Rosen's consideration was her promise to (1) transfer the business to Kim and (2) avoid opening a similar business in the same town for three years.

A PLEDGE OR SUBSCRIPTION

pledge
A promise to donate money to a church, temple, mosque, hospital, college, cultural institution, or other charitable organization.

Churches, temples, mosques, hospitals, colleges, cultural institutions, charitable organizations, and other groups frequently raise money by asking for a pledge, or subscription (a promise to donate money). Are these pledges enforceable? What is the consideration? What benefit is gained by the person making the pledge? Because these pledges are usually for some worthy cause, the courts have generally held that they are enforceable.

Some courts have held that the consideration given by the charitable institution is the promise to use the money for the purpose for which it was donated. Other courts have held that the consideration is the promises of all the other parties who have donated to the same cause. Still other courts hold that, if the charitable institution has made commitments to spend the money as a result of relying on the promises, the subscrip-

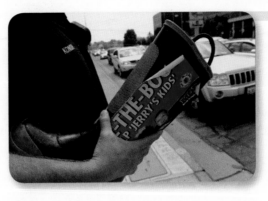

Charitable organizations frequently raise money by asking for pledges.

tions are enforceable. Despite their right to sue for donations promised but never paid, very few charitable organizations sue donors because suing could affect their ability to raise future contributions.

10.4 CONSIDERATION AND THE UNIFORM COMMERCIAL CODE

In some cases that involve contracts to sell goods, the Uniform Commercial Code (UCC) dispenses with the requirement of consideration in certain contracts that involve any of the following:

- ▶ A merchant's written firm offer that provides that the contract is irrevocable.
- ▶ A written discharge of a claim for an alleged breach of contract.
- ▶ Modifications of existing contracts (UCC 2-209).

EXAMPLE 10.6

▶ Sullivan and Baker agreed that Sullivan would sell 5,000 imported shirts to Baker at a certain price to be delivered by May 15. Sullivan learned that he would be unable to meet the delivery date because of transportation delays. He contacted Baker, who agreed to an extension of the time of delivery. Later Baker had a change of heart and demanded that the goods be delivered by the original date. Under the UCC, Baker is bound by the agreed modification even though Sullivan gave no additional consideration for the extension of the delivery date.

10.5 GENERAL RELEASE

Statutes in many states have permitted a person who has a claim against another to give up, or release, his or her claim without an exchange of consideration by making a written statement to that effect. The UCC provides that "any claim or right arising out of an alleged breach can be discharged in whole or in part without consideration by a

General Release

July 1, 20--

The Conway Resort Hotel hereby releases Mary Jacobson from all obligations on her account as of this date.

Conway Resort Hotel

Frank Conway

FIGURE 10.1 General Release

general release
A written agreement in which an aggrieved party can discharge in whole or in part a claim resulting from an alleged breach of contract.

barren promise
A promise to pay an existing debt or to obey the law, or a similar promise of something already owed.

preexisting duty
An obligation that a party is already bound to by law or by some other agreement. The party may not use this as consideration in a new contract.

gratuitous promise
A promise that does not require some benefit in return.

illusory promise
One that consists of an indefinite, open-ended statement purporting to be an agreement.

written waiver or renunciation signed and delivered by the aggrieved party" (UCC 1-107). Such a written agreement is called a general release. Figure 10.1 is an illustration of a general release.

A general release may be regarded as valid consideration if the parties so intend. In such cases, the general release would be viewed as forbearance.

In some states, a general release is supported by consideration only where the original claim that is being released is not regarded by the courts as frivolous; that is, the plaintiff would have had almost no chance of success had the case gone to court. If the original claim is deemed frivolous, there is no forbearance because, in effect, the releasing party is not giving up anything.

10.6 AGREEMENTS THAT LACK CONSIDERATION

Certain agreements are not enforceable because they lack consideration.

BARREN PROMISES
A promise to do something that one is already required to do either by law or by contract represents no additional sacrifice and is not valid consideration. A promise to pay an existing debt or to obey the law, or a similar promise, is called a barren promise; and the obligation to perform acts already required is known as a preexisting duty.

EXAMPLE 10.7

▶ The First State Bank was robbed of more than $300,000 by three armed men. The local bankers' association advertised a reward of $10,000 for the arrest and conviction of each bank robber. In time, all three robbers were convicted. Claims to the reward were made by a number of people, including employees of the bank and the police officers who arrested the robbers. The court ruled that neither the bank employees nor the police were able to collect the reward because they already had a preexisting duty to aid in the capture of the criminals. Another police officer from another county, who had no duty to assist in this case, was allowed to collect the reward.

GRATUITOUS PROMISES

A person who makes a promise without requiring some benefit in return has made a gratuitous promise. Agreements based on such one-sided promises are generally not enforceable. A promise to give a gift is a gratuitous promise—that is, one that is made without receiving anything in return. Because there is no consideration, the promise is not binding. Once a promised gift is presented or delivered, however, the transfer of ownership is complete and consideration is not required (see Chapter 24).

moral consideration
Something that a person is not legally bound to do but that he or she may feel bound to do because of love, friendship, honor, sympathy, conscience, or other reason.

EXAMPLE 10.8

▶ Lopez and Ryan were good friends and golfing enthusiasts. Lopez promised Ryan that when he returned from a golf competition, he would give Ryan the clubs he used in the match. During the competition, he learned the resale value of the clubs was greater than he had originally thought, and he changed his mind. Lopez is under no obligation to fulfill the promise since there was no consideration—that is, it was a gratuitous promise.

ILLUSORY PROMISES

An illusory promise consists of an indefinite, open-ended statement purporting to be an agreement. An illusory promise is neither consideration nor an enforceable agreement. A person who makes an illusory promise never commits to a specific or absolute act. For example, a contractor who is purchasing lumber and tells a lumberyard associate, "If your lumber is high quality, I will buy all of the lumber I need from you," is making an illusory promise.

AGREEMENTS SUPPORTED BY MORAL CONSIDERATION

A person is not legally bound to do what he or she may feel obligated to do because of love, friendship, honor, sympathy, conscience, or some other moral consideration. Some courts, however, will justify the enforcement of some contracts, even though there is no consideration, by stating that there was "moral consideration." A further explanation is that the enforcement of certain contracts is socially beneficial.

A gratuitous promise to give golf clubs to another is generally not enforceable.

EXAMPLE 10.9

▶ Gerber, the owner of Nail Style, a fingernail styling salon, had many financial obligations to suppliers, as well as to the landlord of the building where the salon was located. When the firm failed and Gerber declared bankruptcy, she was legally, but perhaps not morally, relieved of her obligations to pay her creditors. Gerber made a gratuitous promise, based on her own values, to pay the now-forgiven debts from her future earnings. Most courts would agree that the promise is enforceable, even though there was no consideration.

AGREEMENTS SUPPORTED BY PAST CONSIDERATION

Past consideration is a promise to repay someone for a benefit after it has been received. Such a promise is generally not valid consideration and is considered a gratuitous promise, except in cases such as those described in the discussion of moral consideration.

past consideration
A promise to repay someone for a benefit after it has been received.

EXAMPLE 10.10

▶ George Welt promised his brother Frank that he would give him a round-trip ticket to Paris if Frank graduated from a particular college. Frank graduated as agreed, and George gave him the plane ticket. When Frank realized how expensive the ticket was, he promised to pay George one-half of the round-trip fare. Frank later changed his mind and decided not to keep his promise. Frank will not be legally held to his promise since it was based on past consideration.

CHAPTER SUMMARY

1. Consideration is the promises exchanged by the parties to a contract: to give up something of value they have a legal right to keep; to do something they are not otherwise legally required to do; or to refrain from an action. The promise to refrain from doing something that a party has a legal right to do, or the promise of inaction, is known as forbearance.

2. The three essential characteristics of valid consideration are legality, adequacy, and the possibility of performance.

3. Consideration can be based on a promise being exchanged for another promise. It also can be based on forbearance, a party's promise not to do something he or she has a legal right to do. A third kind of valid consideration is a pledge or subscription (a promise to make a donation).

4. The UCC dispenses with the requirement of consideration in contracts to sell goods in the following situations: (a) a merchant's written firm offer that provides that the contract is irrevocable, (b) a written discharge of a claim for an alleged breach of contract, and (c) modifications of existing contracts.

5. A person who has a claim against another may give up, or release, his or her claim without an exchange of consideration by making a written statement to that effect.

6. Five kinds of agreements that lack consideration are (a) barren promises, (b) gratuitous promises, (c) illusory promises, (d) agreements supported by moral consideration, and (e) agreements supported by past consideration.

CHAPTER TEN ASSESSMENT

MATCHING LEGAL TERMS

Match each of the numbered definitions with the correct term in the following list. Write the letter of your choice in the answer column.

a. barren promise
b. consideration
c. forbearance
d. gratuitous promise
e. general release
f. moral consideration
g. past consideration
h. pledge or subscription
i. preexisting duty
j. promise

1. The benefit received and the loss suffered by parties to a contract.

    1. _____

2. A demand of the conscience based on love, friendship, honor, or sympathy.

    2. _____

3. A promise to do what one is already required to do.

    3. _____

4. An offer to confer a benefit on someone without requiring a sacrifice in return.

    4. _____

5. A promise to contribute to a charitable organization.

    5. _____

6. An obligation to perform actions that are already required.

    6. _____

7. An offer to pay for a benefit that has already been received.

    7. _____

8. The act of refraining from exercising a legal right.

    8. _____

9. A written agreement to give up a claim or settle a debt for less than the amount demanded.

    9. _____

10. The party to an agreement who receives a promise.

    10. _____

TRUE/FALSE QUIZ

Indicate whether each of the following statements is true or false by writing *T* or *F* in the answer column.

11. Consideration is one of the elements of a contract.

    11. _____

12. The courts generally do not rule on the adequacy of consideration.

    12. _____

13. A promise of inaction, or forbearance, can be valid consideration.

    13. _____

14. Pledges and subscriptions are never legally enforceable because they lack the element of consideration.

    14. _____

15. A contract in which consideration is based on a promise that is impossible to fulfill cannot be enforced.

    15. _____

16. Preexisting duty refers to existing debts that must be paid.

    16. _____

17. An offer to pay for a benefit after it has been received is enforceable.

    17. _____

18. An agreement based on an illusory promise is enforceable if the purpose of the agreement is legal.

    18. _____

19. A general release allows for the discharge of a debt because it is viewed as forbearance, a form of consideration.

    19. _____

20. No contract is enforceable without consideration.

    20. _____

21. Courts sometimes enforce a contract that lacks consideration because it is socially beneficial.

21. _____

22. The Uniform Commercial Code states that additional consideration is always required in the modification of an existing contract.

22. _____

23. A contract performed because "it is the right thing to do" is an example of forbearance consideration.

23. _____

24. Past consideration is a promise to repay someone for a benefit after it has been received.

24. _____

25. A promise to do something that one is already required to do either by law or by contract is valid consideration.

25. _____

DISCUSSION QUESTIONS

Answer the following questions and discuss them in class.

26. Explain how forbearance can satisfy the requirements of consideration.

27. Explain the three characteristics of valid consideration and provide an example of an agreement having these characteristics.

28. Describe the position generally held by the courts on the matter of adequacy of consideration.

29. Identify four kinds of agreements that lack consideration.

30. Why are courts reluctant to rule on the adequacy of consideration?

31. In some contractual relationships, the bargaining power of one party gives him or her an unfair advantage when dealing with another who might lack the economic power or the education to enter into contracts on an equal footing. What has the law done in an attempt to level the playing field in such cases?

_____

_____

THINKING CRITICALLY ABOUT THE LAW

Answer the following questions, which require you to think critically about the legal principles that you learned in this chapter.

32. **Forms of Consideration** Critique the various exchanges of promises that are legally regarded as acceptable consideration. Your analysis should concentrate on whether each type of consideration facilitates or hinders the execution of a contract.

_____

_____

33. **Invalid Consideration** Since valid consideration is an exchange of promises, it is obvious that a promise to commit an illegal act is not valid consideration. Describe a promise to commit an illegal act that is not legally acceptable.

_____

_____

34. **Consideration—A Promise for a Promise** The most common form of valid consideration is the promise of money by one party for the promise of an act by another. Why is a mere promise deemed adequate in the eyes of the law when consideration based on completed actions might result in fewer disputes?

_____

_____

35. **Consideration—Forbearance** Valid consideration is not necessarily either the performance of an act or the payment of money. One party to a contract, for a variety of reasons, may wish to exchange his or her promise to pay money for a promise of inaction from the other party. Since promises of inaction are often difficult to verify, should promises of forbearance be legally acceptable?

_____

_____

36. **A Question of Ethics** Agreements between parties of unequal bargaining power are known as contracts of adhesion. For example, an apartment house owner presented a tenant with a lease renewal that contained additional and burdensome provisions. The tenant, finding it difficult to move, was forced to accept the lease despite the hardship. Beyond the legal aspects of a contract of adhesion, what are the ethical dimensions to consider in this example?

_____

_____

CASE QUESTIONS

Study each of the following cases. Answer the questions that follow by writing *Yes* or *No* in the answer column.

37. **Adequacy of Consideration** Duggan inherited some nondescript furniture, including an old desk that he sold to Andersen for $50. A short time later he learned that the desk was an antique worth about $500. Duggan brought suit to recover $450, the difference between the sale price and what the desk was really worth.

    a. Will Duggan succeed in this suit?   a. _____

    b. Is the contract between Duggan and Andersen unconscionable?   b. _____

    c. Is the contract void because of the inadequacy of consideration?   c. _____

38. **Forbearance** Helfrich, in a barroom brawl, broke Grady's arm. Grady brought suit against Helfrich for damages. Before the case came to trial, Helfrich offered to give Grady a $500 note, payable in 30 days, as full settlement for all claims Grady had against Helfrich. Grady accepted this offer. When the note came due, Helfrich refused to pay, claiming that there was no exchange of benefits and no consideration.

    a. Is Helfrich correct in his claim that consideration was lacking?   a. _____

    b. Could Grady's action in dropping the suit be regarded as consideration?   b. _____

    c. Is forbearance a form of consideration?   c. _____

39. **Acceptable Consideration** Alfieri, a hunting enthusiast, frequently shot birds in his own and his neighbor's backyard in violation of a city ordinance that prohibited guns being discharged within the city limits. The neighbor offered to pay Alfieri $100 if he would refrain from shooting birds for one year. At the end of the year, the neighbor refused to pay, claiming that there was no consideration.

    a. Will Alfieri succeed in collecting the $100?   a. _____

    b. Is there consideration present in this agreement?   b. _____

    c. Is a barren promise acceptable consideration?   c. _____

CASE ANALYSIS

Study each of the following cases carefully. Briefly state the principle of law and your decision.

40. **Unconscionable Contract** Jackson, a widow who was desperate for money, sold land to her brother, Seymour, for $275. Later Seymour found valuable timber on the land and sold some of it for $2,353. When Jackson realized that the property was worth much more than she had originally thought, she offered to return the sales price with interest. Seymour refused. Jackson sued, claiming fraud—that her brother, upon whom she relied for the management of her affairs, had misrepresented the value of the land. The initial court decision favored Seymour, and the decision was appealed. Is it likely that the court will invalidate the sale of the property? [*Jackson v. Seymour*, 71 S.E.2d 181 (Virginia)]

Principle of Law:

_____

_____

Decision:

_____

_____

41. **Specificity of Consideration** Forrer was an employee of Sears for many years. He eventually left because of health problems and began operating a farm. Sears persuaded Forrer to return to work on a part-time basis, and about one month later promised permanent employment if Forrer gave up the farm and returned to work full-time. Forrer did so, but four months later he was discharged without cause. Forrer sued for damages, lost the case in the trial court, and appealed. Will Forrer be successful in his complaint against Sears? What consideration was promised by Forrer and Sears? [*Forrer v. Sears, Roebuck & Co.*, 153 N.W.2d 587 (Wisconsin)]

Principle of Law:

_____

_____

Decision:

_____

_____

42. **Consideration** The Spring Well Drilling Company entered into a contract with Towne Construction Company to drill a well to supply water to a particular piece of property where Towne was building a house. Spring Well offered no guarantee that water would, in fact, be produced. The drilling proceeded, but no water flowed. Towne refused to pay on the grounds that there was a failure of

consideration. Spring Well sued to collect the agreed fee. Will Spring Well succeed in the suit?

Principle of Law:

_____

_____

Decision:

_____

_____

43. **Validity of Consideration** Maitland, a fund-raiser for Arbor College, solicited contributions for the college's building program. Hamill Manufacturing pledged a contribution to the program. When the company did not pay, Maitland sued. Hamill claimed there was no consideration. Will Maitland be successful in the suit?

Principle of Law:

_____

_____

Decision:

_____

_____

LEGAL RESEARCH

Complete the following activities. Share your findings with the class.

44. **Working in Teams** In teams of three or four, interview officials of religious organizations, hospitals, colleges, cultural and charitable institutions, or any group that raises money by asking for pledges or subscriptions (a promise to donate money). What is the rate of success collecting on these pledges? Have the officials ever attempted to enforce collection by legal means?

_____

_____

45. **Using Technology** Using the Internet and search engines, investigate federal, state, and local laws relating to unconscionable contracts.

_____

_____

chapter **11**
Competent Parties

LEARNING OUTCOMES

After studying this chapter and completing the assessment, you will be able to

11.1 Explain what is meant by contractual capacity and define competent parties.

11.2 Discuss minors' contracts and how the age of majority impacts the legality of contracts.

11.3 Describe the operation of the law as it relates to liability for a minor's torts and crimes.

11.4 Assess the legal status of contracts made by persons who are incompetent.

LEGAL terms

competent party	disaffirmance
contractual capacity	necessaries
minor	ratified
age of majority	emancipation
coming of age rule	abandonment
birthday rule	incompetent

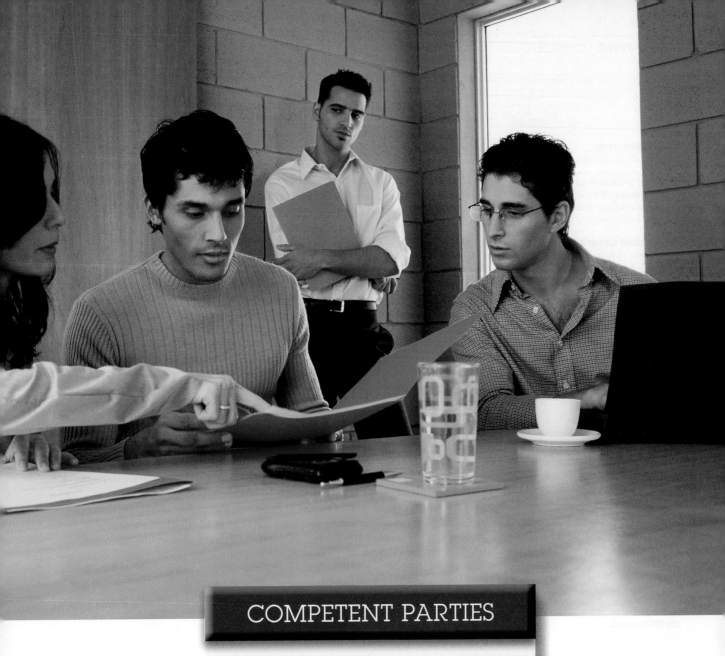

COMPETENT PARTIES

"You got to realize that when I was 20 years old, I had a house, a Mercedes, a Corvette, and a million dollars in the bank before I could buy alcohol legally."

Dr. Dre, record producer and rapper

11.1   THE CAPACITY TO CONTRACT

competent party
A person of legal age and at least normal mentality who is considered by law to be capable of understanding the meaning of a contract and is permitted to enter into a valid contract.

contractual capacity
The ability to make a valid contract.

minor
A person who has not yet reached the age of majority.

Parties to a contract must be competent in both age and mentality. A competent party is a person of legal age and at least normal mentality who is considered by law to be capable of understanding the meaning of a contract. A competent party is said to have contractual capacity—that is, the ability to make a valid contract.

A person who has not yet reached the age of majority is considered a minor, or an infant, in the eyes of the law. Minors and persons who are mentally ill or mentally challenged are usually considered incompetent and lacking in contractual capacity. As a result, they cannot make legally binding contracts, although they are not denied the opportunity to benefit from their legal rights. The responsibility of determining whether a person is competent to contract rests on everyone who enters into a contract with such a person.

11.2   MINORS' CONTRACTS

age of majority
The age at which a person is legally recognized as an adult and is bound by the terms of his or her contract.

coming of age rule
In common law, the view that a person's legal birthday is 12:01 a.m. of the day before his or her actual birthday.

birthday rule
The modern view that a person attains a given age on the anniversary date of his or her birth.

disaffirmance
In contract law, to indicate by a statement or act an intent not to live up to the terms of a contract.

necessaries
Goods and services that are essential to a minor's health and welfare.

The law has always tried to protect young people from adults who might try to take advantage of them. Until individuals reach what is known as legal age, or the age of majority, they are not legally required to carry out most of their contracts (such contracts are voidable, as discussed in Chapter 7). The legal age of majority varies from state to state. In many states it is 18, while in others it is 19 or 21.

Exactly when does a person reach the age of majority? According to the interesting coming of age rule in common law, a person's legal birthday is 12:01 a.m. of the day before his or her actual birthday (see *Mason*, 66 N.C. at 637). Thus, a person who celebrates his or her 18th birthday on April 26, for example, in a state where the age of majority is 18, would become an adult—and legally competent—at 12:01 a.m. on April 25. However, under the modern birthday rule, a person attains a given age on the anniversary date of his or her birth.

AVOIDANCE OF MINORS' CONTRACTS

In contracts between a minor and a competent person, only the minor has the privilege of disaffirmance, or avoidance of the contract; the competent party is bound. However, in contracts for necessaries, such as food, shelter, clothing, employment, and medical care, in many states the minor is bound as well. Also, in general, a minor may not disaffirm a contract for the sale or purchase of real estate.

EXAMPLE 11.1

▶ Blevins, a 45-year-old automobile dealer, agreed to sell Alvarez, a minor, a used car for $1,800. Before the car was delivered, Blevins received a higher offer from another person and attempted to cancel the contract with Alvarez on the grounds that the buyer was a minor. The law permits Alvarez to cancel, or disaffirm, the contract but not Blevins, who is considered a competent party.

RATIFICATION OF MINORS' CONTRACTS

In most cases, whether the contract has not yet been performed (an executory contract) or has been fully performed (an executed contract), the minor may disaffirm the contract if he or she wishes. However, once the minor reaches the legal age of majority, the contract must be either ratified (that is, agreed to) or disaffirmed within a reasonable time. A contract involving a minor can be ratified by an act that shows that the minor party intends to live up to the terms of the contract. Furthermore, if a reasonable period passes after a minor reaches legal age and he or she has said nothing about disaffirming the contract, it is considered ratified in the eyes of the law. In this sense, silence or inaction is the basis for a voidable contract becoming a valid, enforceable contract through ratification.

ratified
An approval of a contract made by a minor after reaching majority.

When a contract is ratified, the entire contract must be ratified, not merely a part of it. Suppose, for example, that the contract involved personal property and had already been performed before the minor reached legal age. In this situation, many states would hold that the minor could either return all (but not part) of the property or money received or demand the return of all (but not part) of the money or property, at any time either before reaching the age of majority or within a reasonable time thereafter.

DISAFFIRMANCE OF MINORS' CONTRACTS

An individual may disaffirm a contract—that is, state his or her intention either orally or in writing not to honor a contract that had been made before reaching legal age. Disaffirmance may be done before reaching the legal age or within a reasonable time after reaching adulthood. The exact time will vary depending on the nature of the contract and current legislation. Disaffirmance, like ratification, may be implied by the acts of the person who has reached legal age and wishes to disaffirm. Disaffirmance might be implied, for example, by failing to make an installment payment. Figure 11.1 shows a sample letter of disaffirmance.

A minor who purchases a used car may disaffirm the contract.

EXAMPLE 11.2

▶ Gibbon, age 17, sold her pickup truck to Deng for $2,800. Shortly after completing the transaction, Gibbon realized that in her eagerness to sell her truck, she had priced it considerably below market value. She then demanded the return of her truck and offered to refund the $2,800 purchase price to Deng. A court would permit Gibbon to disaffirm the contract and get back her truck if she returned the $2,800 to Deng.

If, however, the situation were reversed—that is, Deng, the adult, had sold the truck to Gibbon, the minor, and wanted to cancel the sale—he could not do so if Gibbon were unwilling to cancel the contract.

In some states the minor may avoid the contract even if he or she falsely represented himself or herself as being of age. The minor may then, however, be subject to

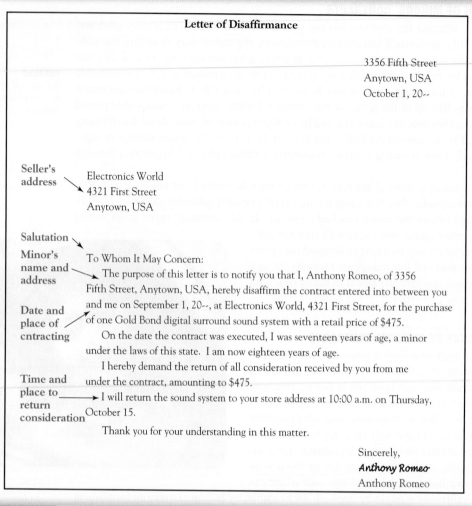

Letter of Disaffirmance

3356 Fifth Street
Anytown, USA
October 1, 20--

Seller's address →

Electronics World
4321 First Street
Anytown, USA

Salutation →

Minor's name and address →

To Whom It May Concern:

The purpose of this letter is to notify you that I, Anthony Romeo, of 3356 Fifth Street, Anytown, USA, hereby disaffirm the contract entered into between you and me on September 1, 20--, at Electronics World, 4321 First Street, for the purchase of one Gold Bond digital surround sound system with a retail price of $475.

Date and place of cntracting →

On the date the contract was executed, I was seventeen years of age, a minor under the laws of this state. I am now eighteen years of age.

I hereby demand the return of all consideration received by you from me under the contract, amounting to $475.

Time and place to return consideration →

I will return the sound system to your store address at 10:00 a.m. on Thursday, October 15.

Thank you for your understanding in this matter.

Sincerely,

Anthony Romeo

Anthony Romeo

FIGURE 11.1 Sample Letter of Disaffirmance

criminal prosecution on the charge of fraud as well as civil liability (damages) for the tort of deceit.

MINORS' ENFORCEABLE CONTRACTS

The law that protects minors from their contractual commitments is not intended to deny them the opportunity to enter into contracts for necessaries that are not provided by their parents, or a guardian. Of course, the nature of the contract must bear some relationship to the minor's individual needs and to his or her social and financial status. As a result of a minor's **emancipation**, he or she assumes many of the rights and obligations of a person of legal age. Emancipation could result from marriage or from voluntary separation of a minor from his or her parents or guardians in order to assume adult responsibilities, such as financial independence. Emancipated minors are generally liable for necessaries purchased for themselves or supplied to a spouse, just as if they were adults.

The law regards actions on the part of the minor that result in emancipation as **abandonment**—that is, a surrender of the special protection given to minors by the law.

emancipation
In contract law, the condition that exists when minors are no longer under the control of their parents and are responsible for their contracts.

abandonment
In contract law, the condition that exists when a minor has left home and given up all rights to parental support.

EXAMPLE 11.3

▶ Eakins was 17 years old and married. A doctor sued him to recover the cost of medical care and surgery provided to him. Eakins did not have medical insurance. The court would hold that Eakins was responsible for the necessaries the doctor provided to him.

If a merchant brings suit to collect payment for merchandise furnished to a minor, the merchant must show that the articles of merchandise are necessaries and that the minor did not already have an adequate supply.

EXAMPLE 11.4

▶ Pineapple Plantation Clothing Store brought suit to recover the cost of clothing sold to Bautista, who was a minor and had refused to pay for the clothing. Bautista already had an ample wardrobe. The store could not recover the cost of the goods because Bautista already had an adequate supply; therefore, the purchases from Pineapple were not necessaries, even though Pineapple had no way of knowing this fact.

A minor is liable only for the reasonable value of necessaries purchased by him or her. If the contract price is more than the sum that the minor should have been charged, he or she can be held responsible only for the lower amount. If the minor has already paid the amount called for in the contract, he or she can recover the amount that was overcharged.

EXAMPLE 11.5

▶ For several years, a druggist charged Matos, a minor, $250 for medication that she needed each month for a chronic disease. The price was three times the price normally charged other purchasers. In this case, a court would enable Matos to recover the amount that she was overcharged.

With the passing years and the growing independence of young people, the courts have recognized that in many instances minors need relatively little protection from the consequences of their youthful decisions. In some cases, the courts have held that contracts made by minors who are nearly adults or that deal with a business are enforceable contracts.

11.3 LIABILITY FOR MINORS' TORTS AND CRIMES

The law does not protect anyone, even a minor, who has committed a tort or a crime. Minors are protected against their own inexperience but not against their own wrongdoing. If a minor injures another person or damages another person's property, he or she may be

Minors are not protected against their own wrongdoing.

liable for such injuries or damages and may be prosecuted by the state in a criminal action. A minor may be held liable for money damages in a tort action when he or she destroys property, appropriates it for himself or herself or for another, causes another person to suffer a money loss through his or her negligence, or persuades another person to break a contract. A minor also can be held liable if he or she makes damaging statements in writing (the tort of libel) or orally (the tort of slander).

EXAMPLE 11.6

▶ McDonnell, who was 17, looked much older because of his large size and full beard. When the merchant asked McDonnell's age, he claimed that he was 18, the age of majority in his state. He bought an MP3 player for $140. After using the player for six months, McDonnell brought it back to the dealer and demanded the return of his money.

In most states, the dealer would have to return the money to McDonnell even though he did not know that he was dealing with a minor. The minor, despite the false representation of his age, may avoid the contract. The dealer, however, may sue him for the tort of fraud and attempt to recover any damages that the dealer suffered. In many states, when a minor disaffirms a contract and returns the goods, he or she can be held liable for damages to the goods.

In most states, parents are not held liable for torts committed by their children; however, if a child causes damage due to a lack of parental supervision, the parent may be held liable for any damages caused by the unsupervised child.

11.4 CONTRACTS OF THE MENTALLY INCOMPETENT

Persons of unsound mind are considered incompetent to make binding contracts because they are assumed to lack the mental capacity to safeguard their own affairs. Consequently, most of their contracts are considered voidable and cannot be enforced against them if they do not carry them out.

A person who is mentally ill may sometimes have lucid periods during which he or she can exercise sound judgment. If the person entered into a contract during a lucid interval and the other party can prove it, such person will be held to the contract. The cause of the incompetence does not matter. The cause might be bipolar disorder, Alzheimer's disease, brain injury, drugs, or alcohol.

A person with mental incompetence is liable for the reasonable value of necessaries that he or she buys, unless he or she can return them. For all other contracts, the person who is mentally incompetent can recover his or her money or property, but the other party's consideration must be returned if possible.

incompetent
Being unable to make binding contracts due to having an unsound mind and being unable to safeguard one's own interests and affairs.

EXAMPLE 11.7

▶ Friedman, an aged recluse, lived alone and had in years past engaged Cullman, a local handyman, to perform various maintenance jobs around his house such as lawn cutting, painting, and minor repairs. Shortly before his death, Friedman had engaged Cullman to make some plumbing repairs. After his death, the administrator of Friedman's estate attempted to avoid paying Cullman's bill, claiming that Friedman was mentally incompetent when he ordered the plumbing repairs. A court would probably require the estate to pay the reasonable value of the repairs.

A contract with a person who has been declared insane by the courts is void even if the other party who contracted with the incompetent individual did not know that he or she had been declared insane by the courts. When a court classifies a person as insane, it appoints a legal guardian to handle his or her affairs. Any contracts the insane person makes thereafter, including contracts that have been made during lucid periods, are considered void, not simply voidable. Nevertheless, if a person who has been declared insane by the court purchases necessaries, most courts will hold the legal guardian liable for their reasonable value.

CONTRACTS OF PERSONS AFFECTED BY DRUGS OR ALCOHOL

If a person makes a contract while so intoxicated by alcohol or affected by drug use that he or she is unable to understand the nature and effect of the contract, it is voidable at his or her option. The law considers the impaired person to have been mentally incompetent at the time the contract was made, and thus he or she is not bound by it. However, if the party, when no longer impaired, and within a reasonable time, chooses to carry out the contract, it has been ratified. If the contract is for necessaries, he or she must pay their reasonable value.

EXAMPLE 11.8

▶ Fogel, while intoxicated, bought a parka from Plymouth Army-Navy Store on credit. When billed, he refused to pay for the garment, claiming that he was so intoxicated at the time he bought it that he did not know what he was doing. If Fogel could not return the parka, he would be required to pay for it because it would be considered a necessary.

If a contract does not involve necessaries, the person who wishes to disaffirm it on the grounds that he or she was intoxicated or affected by drugs when the contract was made must either return the other party's consideration or prove that he or she lost possession of it while still impaired. Obviously, if the person disposed of the other party's consideration after returning to normal, the law would not permit disaffirmance of the contract because the contract had been ratified by the intoxicated person after regaining the power to contract.

CHAPTER SUMMARY

1. Contractual capacity is the ability to make a valid contract. A competent party is a person of legal age and at least normal mentality who is considered by law to be capable of understanding the meaning of a contract.

2. Until individuals reach what is known as legal age, or the age of majority, they are not legally required to carry out most of their contracts. The age of majority is the age at which a person can make binding contracts. Until a person reaches the age of majority, he or she is not legally required to carry out most of his or her contracts because such contracts are voidable. Once the minor reaches the legal age of majority, the contract must be either ratified or disaffimed within a reasonable time.

3. The law does not protect minors who have committed a tort or crime. A minor is held responsible for injury to other persons, damaged property, and damaging statements. In many states, even if a minor disaffirms a contract and returns the goods, he or she can be held liable for any damages to the goods.

4. If a person enters into a contract while so impaired that he or she is unable to understand the nature and effect of the contract, then the contract is voidable at his or her option.

CHAPTER ELEVEN ASSESSMENT

MATCHING LEGAL TERMS

Match each of the numbered definitions with the correct term in the following list. Write the letter of your choice in the answer column.

a. abandonment
b. age of majority
c. contractual capacity
d. competent party
e. disaffirmance
f. emancipation
g. incompetence
h. minor
i. necessaries
j. ratification

1. Items considered essential for a person's well-being, such as food, shelter, clothing, medical care, and employment.   1. _____

2. Affirming, or agreeing to, the terms of a contract entered into previously.   2. _____

3. A person who has not yet reached the age of majority.   3. _____

4. The state of a minor who has married and/or left home that renders the minor responsible for his or her contracts.   4. _____

5. The act of canceling a voidable contract.   5. _____

6. Legal incapacity to make a binding contract.   6. _____

7. Statutory legal age.   7. _____

8. A person of legal age and normal mentality who is capable of
   understanding the meaning of a contract.   8. _____

9. The ability of a party to make a contract.   9. _____

10. A minor's surrender of the special protection given to him or her by
    the law.   10. _____

TRUE/FALSE QUIZ

Indicate whether each of the following statements is true or false by writing *T* or *F* in the answer column.

11. A person's legal birthday is the same as the day on which his or her
    birthday is celebrated.   11. _____

12. An emancipated minor's contracts for necessaries are valid.   12. _____

13. A contract with a minor can be ratified by either party.   13. _____

14. Upon reaching legal age, a minor must ratify earlier completed
    contracts in writing.   14. _____

15. A minor is responsible for his or her torts and crimes.   15. _____

16. Contracts made while a person is intoxicated are voidable by either party. 16. _____

17. A person who is of legal age and at least normal mentality is considered
    a competent party.   17. _____

18. A contract made by a person while intoxicated must be ratified in
    writing within 30 days.   18. _____

19. A minor is considered emancipated, and hence responsible for his or
    her contracts, upon marriage.   19. _____

20. The responsibility of determining whether or not a person is competent
    rests with anyone who enters into a contract with the person.   20. _____

21. The law regards actions of minors that result in emancipation as
    abandonment.   21. _____

22. A minor's disaffirmance must be in writing to be effective.   22. _____

23. Ratification of a minor's contracts must be in writing to be effective.   23. _____

24. In some states a minor may avoid a contract, even if he or she falsely
    represented himself or herself.   24. _____

25. A contract ratification must apply to the entire contract.   25. _____

Answer the following questions and discuss them in class.

26. Discuss what is meant by "age of majority" and how it affects the legal status of minors entering into contracts.

_____

_____

27. How is a contract with a minor affected by the minor's ratification of the contract?

_____

_____

28. A minor is held legally responsible if he or she injures another person or another person's property. Would it make a difference if the injury were accidental?

_____

_____

29. A minor purchased a desk, computer, and printer—all on sale. If the minor later attempted to purchase only the computer, the salesperson could legally refuse to limit the sale to the one item on the grounds of the buyer's minority. In this example, what is the legal principle regarding partial ratification of the minor's contract?

_____

_____

30. A 17-year-old dancer signed a contract for a season with a ballet company. After rehearsals and two performances, the dancer received a better offer from another company. Could she terminate the contract? Why or why not?

_____

_____

31. Contracts made by persons who are mentally incompetent are generally voidable. Are there any exceptions? If yes, explain.

_____

_____

THINKING CRITICALLY ABOUT THE LAW

Answer the following questions, which require you to think critically about the legal principles that you learned in this chapter.

32. Age of Majority The minimum age required under the law for obtaining a driver's license is usually lower than the age for drinking or voting. What is the rationale for this?

_____

_____

33. Minors' Contracts Is it fair that minors' contracts are voidable, whereas those of adults are legally binding?

_____

_____

34. Contracts of Emancipated Minors The contracts of emancipated minors are usually considered legally binding. Give an example to illustrate why this is necessary.

_____

_____

35. Contracts of Persons Who Are Mentally Incompetent If a contract is made by a responsible adult who later becomes mentally incompetent, is the contract enforceable by either party?

_____

_____

36. A Question of Ethics Is it fair and ethical for a minor to take advantage of the protection accorded by the law to breach a contract made with a person who believed the minor to have reached the age of majority?

_____

_____

CASE QUESTIONS

Study each of the following cases. Answer the questions that follow by writing _Yes_ or _No_ in the answer column.

37. Minors' Contracts Nguyen, who was 17 years old, purchased a used boat, agreeing to pay for it in monthly installments over a two-year period. During the next six months, she made 6 of the 24 payments she had agreed to make. The day before she celebrated her 18th birthday, she made the 7th payment. One month later, instead of making the regularly scheduled payment, she attempted to disaffirm the contract, claiming that she was a minor when she made the contract. (Nguyen lived in a state where the age of majority is 18.)

    a. Did Nguyen's first six payments indicate her ratification?   **a.** _____

    b. Is this a contract for necessaries?   **b.** _____

    c. Did the seventh payment serve to ratify the contract?   **c.** _____

    d. Is it likely that Nguyen will be successful in her attempt to disaffirm the contract?   **d.** _____

38. Voidable Contract Caroli, who was 17 years old, signed an agreement to buy a used computer from Egan for $150. While Caroli was on his way to pick up the equipment, Egan got an offer for $250 from someone else. When Caroli arrived with the money to complete the transaction, Egan told him he was unwilling to go through with the agreement because Caroli was a minor.

a. Can Egan cancel the contract?   a. _____

b. Is this a voidable contract?   b. _____

c. Can Caroli cancel the contract?   c. _____

d. If Egan sells the computer to Caroli, can Caroli later return the computer?   d. _____

39. **Contracts of Persons Who Are Mentally Incompetent** Jena, who had been declared insane by the courts, purchased a high-powered sports car for $46,000. Since he made the purchase during a lucid interval, his condition was not evident to the seller. Jena drove the car for several months; subsequently, he returned it to the seller and claimed that his mental condition permitted him to avoid the contract.

a. Was Jena's contract valid at the time of purchase?   a. _____

b. Did Jena's continued use of the car constitute ratification?   b. _____

c. Can the seller claim that the contract was valid because the car was a necessary?   c. _____

d. Will Jena be successful in avoiding the contract?   d. _____

CASE ANALYSIS

Study each of the following cases carefully. Briefly state the principle of law and your decision.

40. **Contracts of Persons Who Are Mentally Incompetent** Staples, following extensive injuries in an automobile accident, was declared mentally incompetent. He imagined himself to be in command of a large army engaged in protecting the country against an invasion. He ordered several large tents, sleeping bags, and other military supplies from a firm that specialized in selling such goods. When he failed to pay for the goods, the firm attempted to seize Staples's bank deposits and his disability pension. Will the military supply firm be successful in its attempt to secure payment?

Principle of Law:

_____

_____

Decision:

_____

_____

41. **Contracts of Emancipated Minors** Doran, a young man of 17, married a 17-year-old woman. After the wedding they moved to another city, where they both found work and began to buy furniture and appliances. When they realized that they

had been unwise in some of their purchases, they attempted to rescind the contracts, claiming they were minors. Will the Dorans be successful in avoiding the contracts?

Principle of Law:

_____

_____

Decision:

_____

_____

42. **Contracts of Persons Who Are Mentally Incompetent** Ortelere, a retired teacher, had built up a substantial amount of funds in her retirement plan before she retired because of "involutional psychosis" (a form of mental illness). She had previously specified that a lowered monthly retirement benefit would be paid to her so that her husband would get some benefit from the retirement plan if she died before he did. After her mental problems began, she changed her payout plan and borrowed from the pension fund. As a consequence of the changes she made, her husband lost his rights to benefits. Two months after she made the changes, she died. The husband sued to reverse the changes his wife had made, claiming that she was not of sound mind when she made them. Will the changes in the plan be voided? [_Ortelere v. Teachers' Retirement Board_, 250 N.E.2d 460 (Wisconsin)]

Principle of Law:

_____

_____

Decision:

_____

_____

LEGAL RESEARCH

Complete the following activities. Share your findings with the class.

43. **Working in Teams** In teams of three or four, interview several retailers of home appliances or furnishings to determine how they ascertain the age of customers who wish to enter into an installment contract for purchases.

_____

_____

44. **Using Technology** Using the Internet and search engines, compare the age of majority provisions in several states. Also, determine the differences in the legal ages required for various activities, such as marriage, driving, voting, and military service.

_____

_____

Legal Purpose of Contracts

LEARNING OUTCOMES

After studying this chapter and completing the assessment, you will be able to

12.1 Discuss legality of purpose in relation to public interest, and classify illegal agreements into three major categories.

12.2 Identify four kinds of agreements that violate statutes.

12.3 Identify five kinds of agreements that violate public policy.

12.4 Explain the provisions of two major laws governing illegal restraint of trade: the Sherman Antitrust Act and the Robinson-Patman Act.

12.5 Discuss four instances where restraints of trade are legally enforceable.

LEGAL terms

blue laws
Sunday agreement
gambling agreement
interest
usury
unlicensed transaction
champerty
exculpatory clause

restraint of trade
monopoly power
Sherman Antitrust Act
Robinson-Patman Act
government-granted
  franchise
franchisor
franchisee

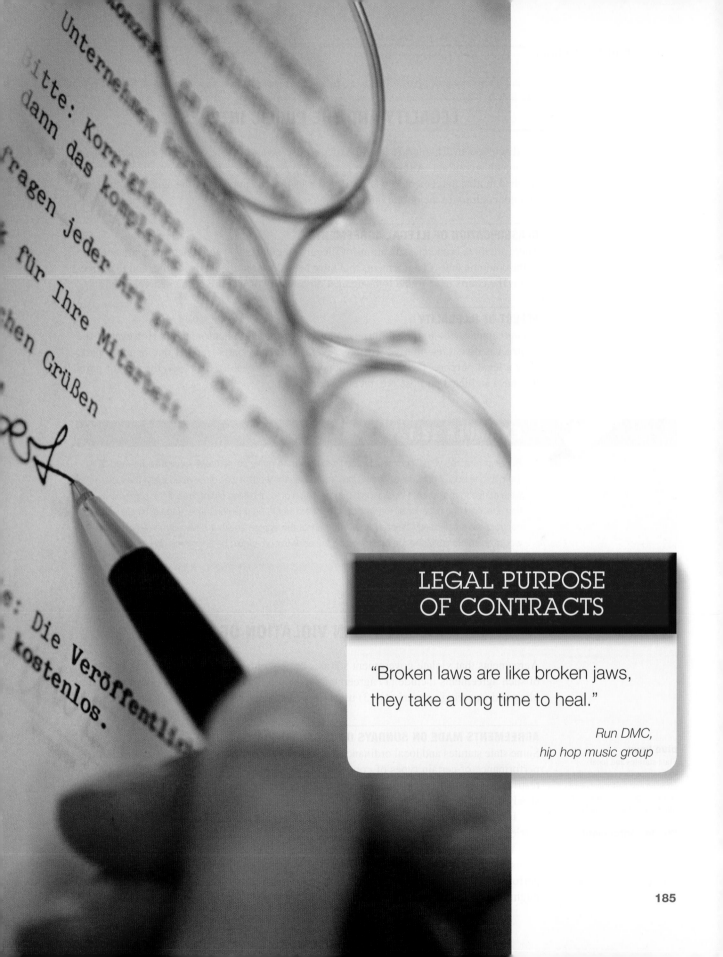

LEGAL PURPOSE
OF CONTRACTS

"Broken laws are like broken jaws,
they take a long time to heal."

Run DMC,
hip hop music group

12.1 LEGALITY AND THE PUBLIC INTEREST

As discussed in Chapter 7, legality of purpose is one of the essential elements of an enforceable contract. Although the parties to a contract are legally competent and have reached mutual agreement, the law still requires that the purpose of the agreement be legal and not contrary to the public interest.

CLASSIFICATION OF ILLEGAL AGREEMENTS

There are three broad classifications of illegal agreements: (1) agreements that are contrary to the common law, (2) agreements that have been declared illegal by statute, and (3) agreements the courts have found to be against the security or welfare of the general public.

EFFECT OF ILLEGALITY

An agreement with an illegal purpose is usually void and unenforceable. However, if the contract is divisible—that is, if it has several unrelated parts—and if one or more parts have a legal purpose, then those components are enforceable. However, the part or parts that have an illegal purpose are not enforceable.

EXAMPLE 12.1

▶ Revak contracted with Sunnyside Home Remodelers to make some major repairs and to add a room to one side of her house. After Sunnyside began the work, it was discovered that if the room were added to the house, Revak would be in violation of local zoning ordinances. If the agreement had specified one price for all the work, the contract would be unenforceable. If the estimate and contract were sufficiently detailed, then the part of the agreement that covered the remodeling would be enforceable and the part involving the added room would be unenforceable.

12.2 AGREEMENTS IN VIOLATION OF STATUTES

Agreements that violate government statutes are not enforceable by the courts. Examples of such agreements include (1) agreements made on Sundays or legal holidays, (2) gambling and wagering agreements, (3) usurious agreements, and (4) unlicensed transactions.

AGREEMENTS MADE ON SUNDAYS OR LEGAL HOLIDAYS

blue laws
State statutes and local ordinances that regulate the creation and performance of certain types of contracts on Sundays and legal holidays.

Sunday agreement
A contract made on a Sunday; in a small number of jurisdictions, such contracts are invalid unless they are ratified on a weekday.

Some state statutes and local ordinances, referred to as blue laws, regulate the creation and performance of certain types of contracts on Sundays and legal holidays. Many of these restrictions originate in religious customs and practices. In recent years, there has been a steady decline in the number of activities that are prohibited on Sundays and holidays.

In a small number of jurisdictions, a contract that is made on a Sunday but is to be carried out on a weekday is invalid. In some states, a Sunday agreement must be ratified on a weekday. The contract is considered ratified if it is performed on a weekday or if the terms are restated on a weekday. Contracts made on a legal holiday can generally be performed on the next business day following the holiday. Examples of contracts that might be made on a Sunday or on a legal holiday and ratified on a weekday are contracts involving the payment of a note, the delivery of merchandise, and the repair of equipment.

GAMBLING AND WAGERING AGREEMENTS

All states have legislation that regulates gambling—that is, risking money or something of value on the uncertain outcome of a future event. A gambling agreement is one in which performance by one party depends on the occurrence of an uncertain event. Some states permit betting on certain kinds of horse or dog races; other states permit state-run lotteries. Where gambling agreements are permitted, the state closely regulates the nature of the betting and usually derives considerable revenue from it. Even in a state that permits betting on horse races, the bets must be placed with state-approved outlets, such as racetracks or off-track betting facilities operated or regulated by the state. Other bets in these states are illegal unless approved by state law and are, therefore, as unenforceable as they would be in a state that permits no gambling at all. (Examples of illegal gambling would include typical office basketball and football pools.) In some states, gambling on Native American reservations is legal.

All states have legislation that regulates gambling.

gambling agreement
An agreement in which performance by one party depends on the occurrence of an uncertain event.

EXAMPLE 12.2

▶ In a state that permits betting on horse races at racetracks and at off-track betting facilities, Cohen bet his friend, Hermann, that a certain horse would win a particular race. The horse lost, but Cohen refused to pay. This bet is unenforceable because it was made privately without compliance with the betting regulations established by the state.

USURIOUS AGREEMENTS

Interest is the charge for the use of borrowed money, generally expressed as an annual percentage of the amount of the loan (principal). Nearly every state has laws that regulate interest charges. If a loan is made at an interest rate higher than that allowed by state law, the lender is guilty of usury, which is defined as charging interest higher than the law permits. Such usurious agreements are illegal and void. In some states, usury laws do not apply to transactions between corporations. In many states, the usury statutes apply to retail installment credit sales and credit card transactions. Most states have varying usury rates, depending on the kind of loan.

interest
The charge for using borrowed money, generally expressed as an annual percentage of the amount of the loan (principal).

usury
Charging interest higher than the law permits.

EXAMPLE 12.3

▶ Nunez purchased a refrigerator from a local appliance dealer. Since he did not have a credit record, he agreed to pay the dealer $100 down and $100 per month for one year from the date of purchase. There were no other benefits to Nunez, such as delivery or an investigation of his credit. The price for a cash transaction would have been only $800. When Nunez computed how much it was costing him to finance the purchase through the dealer, he refused to make any more payments, claiming that the rate of interest was illegal. A court would likely rule that the interest charge was usurious.

UNLICENSED TRANSACTIONS

To protect the public, most states require persons engaged in certain businesses, professions, and occupations to be licensed. The requirements for a license usually include paying an annual fee and passing an examination—written, oral, or both—to ensure competence. Persons in licensed professions and occupations include doctors, dentists, lawyers, nurses, certified public accountants, pharmacists, plumbers, barbers, and teachers. An agreement with a person who does not have the required license is an unlicensed transaction and is generally illegal if the purpose of the statute is regulatory and enforcement of the licensing requirements is clearly in the public interest.

unlicensed transaction
An agreement with a person who does not have a required license.

EXAMPLE 12.4

▶ Joblin, a foreign-trained doctor with years of experience in his own country, was working in a hospital until he could take the required examinations and be licensed to practice in the United States. He also maintained a small practice in his home and provided for some of the medical needs of people in his neighborhood. One patient ran up a large bill and finally refused to pay. Since Joblin was not licensed when he performed these medical services, he has no legal way to collect his fee.

Unlike Example 12.4, however, if the purpose of the licensing requirement is solely to raise revenue for the jurisdiction and not to ensure competence, the absence of a license does not make the agreement void.

12.3 AGREEMENTS AGAINST PUBLIC POLICY

Some agreements are unenforceable because they are contrary to the interests of the public. Examples include agreements that (1) obstruct or pervert justice, (2) restrain marriage, (3) interfere with public service, (4) defraud creditors and other persons, or (5) contain exculpatory clauses.

AGREEMENTS THAT OBSTRUCT OR PERVERT JUSTICE

Among the kinds of agreements that obstruct or pervert justice are the following: (1) an agreement to conceal a crime or not to prosecute a criminal—such as a thief if he or she returns the stolen property; (2) an agreement to encourage a lawsuit in which one or more of the parties have no legitimate interest, called champerty; (3) an agreement to give false testimony or to suppress evidence; (4) an agreement to bribe a juror or a court official; and (5) an agreement to refrain from testifying as a witness in a legal action.

champerty
An agreement to encourage a lawsuit in which one or more of the parties have no legitimate interest.

EXAMPLE 12.5

▶ Blasky, an investor and speculator, agreed to pay a percentage of his profits on stock trading to Gillian, who had access to confidential information. When the scheme was uncovered and Blasky was charged with violating federal securities regulations, he offered $10,000 to Gillian if Gillian would deny knowing about or being involved in Blasky's illegal activities. The contract was clearly unenforceable because it was an agreement to give false testimony.

In Example 12.5, even if the money was paid, neither side could sue the other. A court will not touch an illegal contract even if one party is out the money or service. Courts require that parties to a lawsuit have *clean hands,* meaning that they are not using illegal acts as the basis for their lawsuits.

AGREEMENTS THAT RESTRAIN MARRIAGE

Agreements in restraint of marriage are void. For example, a person's promise to pay money to his or her child on the condition that the child never marries would not be enforceable. If the child agreed to this arrangement and avoided marrying, he or she could not enforce the agreement.

EXAMPLE 12.6

▶ Heath, a lonely widower, wished his only daughter not to marry and offered her $75,000 if she remained single. The agreement would not be enforceable, and neither the father nor his daughter would be obligated to honor the agreement.

AGREEMENTS THAT INTERFERE WITH PUBLIC SERVICE

Agreements that attempt to bribe or interfere with public officials, obtain political preference in appointments to office, pay an officer for signing a pardon, require one of the parties to the agreement to break a law, or influence a lawmaking body for personal gain are examples of agreements that are illegal because they interfere with public service.

Some very clever schemes have been used to influence public officials. These may include giving "no-show" jobs to relatives of political officials, making contributions to political campaigns, and offering "vacations" as bribes. Public officials and those who attempt to influence them are exposed and prosecuted every year. Often these activities do not involve specific contracts but are nevertheless illegal.

An agreement to wrongfully use one's influence is illegal and unenforceable.

EXAMPLE 12.7

▶ Furth, a government official, used his influence with the parking violations bureau to ensure that a particular firm received a contract for parking meters without competitive bidding. The manufacturer of the meters agreed to employ the official as a consultant when he left office. The agreement was clearly illegal and unenforceable.

AGREEMENTS TO DEFRAUD CREDITORS AND OTHER PERSONS

Because agreements to defraud lack the element of legality of purpose, they are void and unenforceable. An example of an agreement to defraud another person might be an agreement to sell or give away property with the intention of defrauding creditors in anticipation of bankruptcy. Consider Example 12.8.

EXAMPLE 12.8

▶ Lachman, who had been operating a retail store at a loss for several years, agreed to sell his brother-in-law inventory worth $100,000 for the modest sum of $1,000, with the understanding that after bankruptcy proceedings were concluded and his creditors were satisfied, the property would be returned to him. An agreement such as this is void and unenforceable.

EXCULPATORY CLAUSES

exculpatory clause
A statement in a contract that releases one party from liability resulting from his or her own negligence throughout the performance of a contract.

An exculpatory clause is a statement in a contract that releases one party from liability resulting from his or her own negligence throughout the performance of the contract. Exculpatory clauses are contrary to public policy; one party is protected from the consequences of his or her own negligence or willful actions, while the other party is not allowed to recover his or her losses. Exculpatory clauses are illegal when used by companies in a business directly related to the public interest, such as banks, public utilities, and transportation providers. It is logical that such businesses should be held accountable for their actions because they impact the safety and well-being of the public they serve.

EXAMPLE 12.9

▶ Wang entered into a contract with Valenti Construction Company to erect an outdoor deck for the sum of $8,000. Attorneys for Valenti Construction placed a clause in the contract that stated that the company would not be liable for any injuries that resulted due to the negligence of the company's workers. Such an exculpatory clause is illegal because it violates public policy.

12.4 ILLEGAL RESTRAINTS OF TRADE

Competition in public sales and in bidding for contracts is essential in our market-oriented economy because the competition of a free market encourages lower prices, improved products, and better service. Unless specifically permitted by law, agreements to suppress or eliminate competition are illegal and unenforceable. These kinds of agreements are said to be in restraint of trade.

Monopoly power is the term used to describe a situation in which one or more people or firms control the market in a particular area or for a certain product. A monopoly is illegal because it results in a restraint of trade.

SHERMAN ANTITRUST ACT

In 1890 Congress passed the *Federal Antitrust Act,* also known as the Sherman Antitrust Act. This law and several amendments to it are still vigorously enforced against large and small businesses. It forbids certain agreements that tend to unreasonably inhibit competition, fix prices, allocate territories, or limit production. Persons or businesses found guilty of such practices are liable to punishment by heavy fines and imprisonment, and the contracts will be judged to be void. While the act does not prohibit firms from growing large as a result of producing good products and utilizing effective management, if a firm's size allows it to dominate a market, the federal government can require it to be split into smaller businesses. Similar antitrust statutes have been passed by most states to prohibit local anticompetitive practices.

restraint of trade
A limitation on the full exercise of doing business with others.

monopoly power
A situation in which one or more people or firms control the market in a particular area or for a particular product.

Sherman Antitrust Act
A federal statute that forbids certain agreements that tend to unreasonably inhibit competition, fix prices, allocate territories, or limit production.

EXAMPLE 12.10

▶ The two pharmacies in the village of Wagonwheels agreed between themselves that they would each serve a particular section of the town and would charge the same low prices for certain prescription medicines. The purpose of the agreement was to create a monopoly and discourage competition from any new store that might wish to open in the town. This agreement would be found to be in restraint of trade and a violation of state law.

ROBINSON-PATMAN ACT

The Robinson-Patman Act of 1936, which amended earlier antitrust legislation, makes it unlawful to discriminate, directly or indirectly, in matters involving product pricing, advertising, and promotion. It specifically prohibits sellers from discriminating among different purchasers of goods of like grade and quality under certain conditions. The purpose of the act is to ensure that no one customer has an advantage over others. A seller of goods can, however, legally charge a certain customer a lower price if the seller can prove that the lower price is a result of savings due to large-quantity sales to that customer. The act does not force a large buyer to give up the advantages resulting from greater efficiency, but rather puts a limit on the use of the economic power that often results from large size.

Robinson-Patman Act
A federal statute that makes it unlawful to discriminate, directly or indirectly, in matters involving product pricing, advertising, and promotion.

EXAMPLE 12.11

▶ Meadowbrook Fuel is a large national company that markets fuel oil in the city of Westerville. The company sells fuel oil in the area surrounding Westerville for a lower price than it does in the city, where it already controls a substantial share of the market and has little competition. The competition in the surrounding area is largely from small companies. Meadowbrook would be in violation of the Robinson-Patman Act for such discriminatory pricing practices.

12.5 LEGAL RESTRAINTS OF TRADE

Although federal and state legislation and many court decisions encourage competition, there are times when agreements in restraint of trade are in the public interest and are legally enforceable.

Trade secrets, trademarks, patents, copyrights, and agreements not to compete are legally enforceable and are discussed in Chapter 28.

GOVERNMENT-GRANTED MONOPOLIES

government-granted franchise

A legal monopoly in which a state or federal government grants a person or firm a license to conduct a specific business, usually an essential service.

A government-granted franchise is another form of legal monopoly in which a state or the federal government grants a firm or person a license to conduct a specific—usually essential—business such as a bus line, railroad, electric power company, cellular telephone company, TV cable service, and so on. Such franchises are granted because it is in the public interest to limit the number of companies operating in an area if those companies provide a necessary service. These legal monopolies (sometimes called *natural monopolies*) are subject to a greater degree of regulation than other businesses and are responsible to administrative agencies, boards, or public service commissions.

PRIVATE FRANCHISES

franchisor

The parent firm in a franchise agreement.

franchisee

The independent company in a franchise agreement.

A government-granted franchise should not be confused with a private franchise, which is a special kind of business organization involving a contractual relationship between a franchisor (the parent firm) and a franchisee (the independent company). In a private franchise, the contractual relationship provides that the franchisor will supply certain services, such as management consulting, to the franchisee and will allow the franchisee to use the franchisor's name, join with others in national advertising, and secure other benefits. The private franchise is a form of business organization that is usually used in businesses such as fast-food chains, motels, automobile dealerships, and gasoline service stations.

An example of a private franchise.

ZONING REGULATIONS

A community may designate certain areas as zones for such uses as light industrial, industrial, commercial, and residential. While zoning regulations are intended to provide security for the citizens of a community, they also may act as legal restraints of trade because they restrict where and how businesses may operate.

ENVIRONMENTAL AND SAFETY REGULATIONS

Federal and state legislatures have enacted statutes to protect the health and welfare of the general population from the effects of pollution of the atmosphere and bodies of water. Safety regulations protect the health and welfare of the general population of a community, customers, and employees. Like zoning regulations, safety and environmental regulations (discussed in Chapters 32 and 36) also serve as legal restraints of trade because they place limits and restrictions on how a firm may operate.

CHAPTER
SUMMARY

1. Although the parties to a contract are legally competent and have reached mutual agreement, the law still requires that the purpose of the agreement be legal and not contary to the public interest. The three major categories of illegal agreements are (a) agreements that are contrary to the common law, (b) agreements that have been declared illegal by statute, and (c) agreements that have been found by the courts to be against the security or welfare of the general public.

2. Four kinds of agreements that violate statutes are (a) agreements made on Sundays or legal holidays, (b) gambling and wagering agreements, (c) usurious agreements, and (d) unlicensed transactions.

3. Five kinds of agreements that violate public policy are those that (a) obstruct or pervert justice, (b) restrain marriage, (c) interfere with public service, (d) defraud creditors and other persons, and (e) contain exculpatory clauses.

4. The Sherman Antitrust Act forbids agreements that tend to unreasonably lessen competition, fix prices, allocate territories, or limit production. The Robinson-Patman Act makes it unlawful to discriminate, directly or indirectly, in matters involving product pricing, advertising, and promotion.

5. Restraints of trade are legally enforceable in the following instances: (a) government-granted franchises, legal monopolies in which a state or the federal government grants a person or firm a license to conduct a specific—usually essential—business; (b) private franchises, special kinds of business organizations involving contractual relationships between franchisors and franchisees; (c) zoning regulations, legal restraints of trade that restrict where and how businesses may operate; and (d) environmental and safety regulations, statutes to protect the health and welfare of the general population.

CHAPTER TWELVE
ASSESSMENT

MATCHING LEGAL TERMS

Match each of the numbered definitions with the correct term in the following list. Write the letter of your choice in the answer column.

a. champerty
b. exculpatory clause
c. franchisor
d. gambling agreement
e. government-granted franchise
f. interest
g. monopoly power
h. restraint of trade
i. unlicensed transaction
j. usury

1. An agreement based on the uncertain outcome of some future event.   1. ____

2. The practice of charging a higher interest rate than that permitted by law.   2. ____

3. An agreement with a person who is required to have, but lacks,
   the approval of the state to practice his or her business, profession,
   or occupation.   3. _____

4. An agreement by a person to encourage or support a lawsuit in which
   he or she has no legitimate interest.   4. _____

5. The ability to control the market in a particular area or for a
   certain product.   5. _____

6. A legal monopoly granted to a firm or person to conduct a specific
   business such as a railroad or electric company.   6. _____

7. Actions or agreements intended to suppress or eliminate competition.   7. _____

8. A statement in a contract that releases one party from liability
   resulting from his or her own negligence throughout the performance
   of a contract.   8. _____

9. The charge for the use of borrowed money.   9. _____

10. A government or parent firm that grants a monopoly to another.   10. _____

TRUE/FALSE QUIZ

Indicate whether each of the following statements is true or false by writing *T* or *F* in the
answer column.

11. A contract is always legal and enforceable as long as the parties are
    competent and they have a mutual understanding.   11. _____

12. An agreement to perform an illegal act is void and unenforceable.   12. _____

13. All states prohibit all forms of gambling.   13. _____

14. Agreements that require the performance of acts against public
    policy are void.   14. _____

15. Agreements that restrain marriage are valid if both parties agree to
    all provisions.   15. _____

16. Agreements in restraint of trade can be prosecuted only under
    federal law.   16. _____

17. The government will always prosecute companies that wield
    monopoly power because competition is always deemed in the
    public's best interest.   17. _____

18. The Robinson-Patman Act prohibits price discrimination.   18. _____

19. The Sherman Antitrust Act prohibits agreements that tend to lessen competition.

19. ____

20. Zoning regulations also may act as legal restraints of trade because they restrict where and how businesses may operate.

20. ____

21. Environmental and safety regulations seldom act as legal restraints of trade even though they limit and restrict how a firm may operate.

21. ____

DISCUSSION QUESTIONS

Answer the following questions and discuss them in class.

22. Explain the enforceability of divisible contracts in which some parts have a legal purpose while other parts have an illegal purpose.

23. Provide an example of an agreement that has been made illegal by statute.

24. Is an illegal agreement enforceable? Why or why not?

25. Why are contracts made with individuals who are required to be licensed, but are not, usually unenforceable?

26. Legislation intended to protect the natural environment can have unexpected consequences and may serve as a disincentive to business. Explain.

27. How does society benefit from the actions of governments granting monopolies for such services as cellular telephone service, railroads, and so on?

THINKING CRITICALLY ABOUT THE LAW

Answer the following questions, which require you to think critically about the legal principles that you learned in this chapter.

28. **Illegal Agreements** Certain kinds of agreements, such as gambling agreements, are illegal or highly regulated. What do you believe is the primary motivation for such prohibitions?

_____

_____

29. **Licensing** Most states require people engaged in certain professions or businesses to be licensed. How do licensing requirements protect the public?

_____

_____

30. **Environmental Protection** Enforcement of laws that are intended to protect the environment sometimes has unforeseen economic effects, such as plant closings and unemployment. How should society attempt to balance environmental and economic issues?

_____

_____

31. **Competition** Various federal and state laws are intended to encourage competition. Analyze and report on the benefits of competition to society.

_____

_____

32. **Restraint of Trade** Zoning regulations have the effect of restraining trade because they limit the activities of certain kinds of businesses. Explain how society benefits from such limitations.

_____

_____

33. **A Question of Ethics** The Robinson-Patman Act prohibits price discrimination. What were the ethical reasons that motivated the passage of this federal statute?

_____

_____

Study each of the following cases. Answer the questions that follow by writing *Yes* or *No* in the answer column.

34. **Gambling Agreements** Pickens was one of a group of four army veterans who met once a month to play poker. On one occasion, Pickens lost more than $1,000 and refused to pay, claiming that gambling debts are uncollectible. The winner claimed that since the state had legalized off-track betting and had begun a lottery, gambling debts were now legal and collectible.

    a. Does the existence of state-approved gambling affect the legality of other forms of gambling?

    a. _____

    b. Can the winner of the gambling activity legally collect his winnings?

    b. _____

35. **Unlicensed Transactions** Rogan, who had worked for eight years as an electrician's helper, tried several times to pass the state-required electrician's test, but he failed each time. Still, he felt that he knew enough about his trade that he could perform the work of an electrician and accepted several jobs that required a fully licensed electrician. Duggan hired Rogan to install the wiring in a room addition. Just as Rogan was beginning work, Duggan learned that Rogan did not have a valid electrician's license and canceled the contract. Rogan claimed that he should be paid anyway because he turned down other employment elsewhere to accept Duggan's work.

    a. Is the contract between Duggan and Rogan enforceable?

    a. _____

    b. Does it seem that Rogan should be paid for the work he and Duggan agreed he would do?

    b. _____

    c. Is Duggan partly to blame because he failed to ask to see Rogan's license?

    c. _____

Study each of the following cases carefully. Briefly state the principle of law and your decision.

36. **Usurious Agreements** Alfino borrowed money from Yakutsk and agreed in writing to pay a rate of interest higher than that allowed by local law. Later, when Alfino was called upon to pay, he refused, claiming that the agreement was void because of the usurious rate. Yakutsk, the lender, sued to collect. Yakutsk agreed to accept the legal rate of interest and felt he was entitled to collect the debt. Alfino believed that the entire debt was void because of the illegality of the original agreement. In view of Yakutsk's willingness to accept

the legal rate of interest, can Alfino be compelled to pay? [*Yakutsk v. Alfino*, 349 N.Y.S.2d 718 (New York)]

Principle of Law:

_____

_____

Decision:

_____

_____

37. **Price Discrimination** Morton Salt Company, a large producer of table salt, had an established price scale for its product based on the quantity of salt ordered in a 12-month period. Thus, a firm that ordered a substantial quantity of salt paid less per package than a store that ordered a smaller quantity. Acting in response to complaints from small firms, the Federal Trade Commission investigated and determined that the lowest price offered by Morton Salt Company, although available to all customers, was practical only for five national customers who purchased in sufficiently large quantities to benefit from the lowest prices established. Would the alleged price discrimination be covered under the Robinson-Patman Act? [*FTC v. Morton Salt Co.*, 334 U.S. 37]

Principle of Law:

_____

_____

Decision:

_____

_____

38. **Illegal Agreement** Jasons decided to declare bankruptcy because his financial situation was desperate and his only property was a nearly new car worth about $14,000. In an attempt to conceal the value of his property, he sold the car to his friend Dane for $2,000. He planned to buy the car back from Dane when the bankruptcy proceedings were concluded. Is the sale of the car a valid contract? Why or why not?

Principle of Law:

_____

_____

Decision:

_____

_____

LEGAL RESEARCH

Complete the following activities. Share your findings with the class.

39. **Working in Teams** In teams of three or four, interview several owners or managers of small businesses. Ask these individuals whether there are legal obstacles that make it more difficult for their businesses to earn a profit.

_____

_____

40. **Using Technology** Use the Internet and search engines to investigate the Sherman Antitrust Act and the Robinson-Patman Act and the various prosecutions under each.

_____

_____

chapter **13**
Form of Contracts

After studying this chapter and completing the assessment, you will be able to

13.1 Describe the requirement of proper form of contracts, and name instances when contracts (a) should not be in writing, (b) should be in writing, and (c) must be in writing.

13.2 Explain how the parol evidence rule affects the addition of supplementary provisions to a written contract.

13.3 Discuss the Statute of Frauds.

13.4 Identify the six types of contracts that the Statute of Frauds requires to be in writing.

13.5 Specify items of information that must be included in a written contract to satisfy the Statute of Frauds.

terms

LEGAL

parol evidence rule
Statute of Frauds
executor
administrator
guaranty

antenuptial or prenuptial
  agreement
auction sale
memorandum

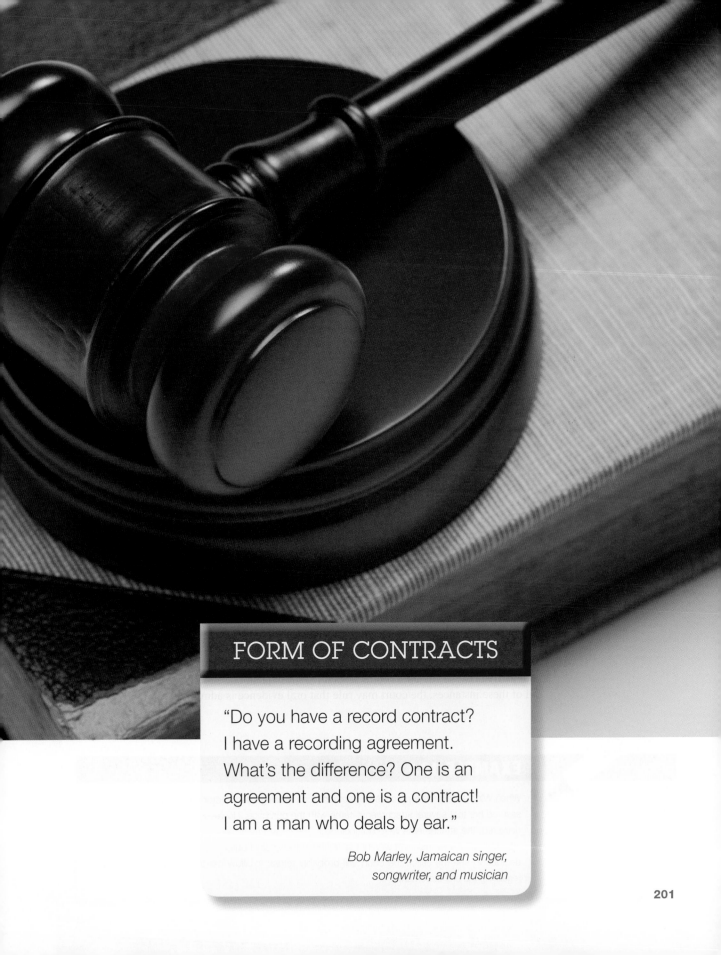

FORM OF CONTRACTS

"Do you have a record contract?
I have a recording agreement.
What's the difference? One is an
agreement and one is a contract!
I am a man who deals by ear."

*Bob Marley, Jamaican singer,
songwriter, and musician*

13.1 THE REQUIREMENT OF PROPER FORM

The essential elements of a valid contract were introduced in Chapter 7. These requirements are (1) offer and acceptance, (2) mutual agreement, (3) consideration, (4) competent parties, (5) legality of purpose, and (6) proper form. Following the introduction of the essential elements, several chapters were devoted to the first five elements. In this chapter, the final element, proper form, is covered.

WHEN CONTRACTS SHOULD BE IN WRITING

The element of proper form requires that certain contracts must be in writing to be enforceable. However, not all contracts should be in writing because many of them are so routine that reducing them to writing would be a waste of time and effort. For example, a written contract is not needed when one is taking a bus ride, purchasing groceries, or ordering a meal in a restaurant. Some contracts *should* be in writing to protect against later disagreement, such as a contract for the purchase of a television. Still others *must* be in writing because the law requires such for the contract to be enforceable.

13.2 THE PAROL EVIDENCE RULE

parol evidence rule
The rule that any spoken or written words in conflict with what the written contract states cannot be introduced as evidence in a court of law.

The word *parol* (not to be confused with the word *parole*) as used in the parol evidence rule simply means "speech" or "words." Parol evidence refers to any supplementary evidence or conditions, written or oral, that a party wants to add to a written contract. The parol evidence rule states that any spoken or written words that are in conflict with what the written contract states cannot be introduced as evidence in a court of law.

There are numerous exceptions to the parol evidence rule. Perhaps the most common exception occurs when oral evidence serves to clear up an ambiguous part of an agreement. Accordingly, oral evidence introduced after a contract is signed is legally accepted if it clarifies some point in the written agreement. The Uniform Commercial Code (UCC) specifically states that the terms of a written contract may not be changed by evidence of any prior agreement but may be explained or supplemented (UCC 2-202).

Some other exceptions to the parol evidence rule apply to (1) incomplete contracts, (2) contracts that contain obvious typographical errors, (3) contracts that are partly written and partly oral, (4) voidable contracts, and (5) subsequent oral modification of contracts. In all of these instances, the court may rule that oral evidence is admissible.

EXAMPLE 13.1

▶ When Wlodyka signed a purchase agreement for a small garden tractor, the salesperson orally assured her that several attachments came with the purchase. However, when the tractor was delivered, the attachments were not included. The seller has no legal obligation to furnish the attachments if their inclusion was not specified in the original purchase agreement. If Wlodyka decides to sue the seller, the court will probably refuse to allow her to introduce testimony regarding the oral statements.

In Example 13.1, if the purchase agreement had included a reference such as "and attachments," oral evidence could have legally been introduced later to identify the specific attachments that were required to be included. In a minority of states, however, even consistent oral statements may not be introduced into evidence if a contract is in writing.

EXAMPLE 13.2

▶ Albano purchased an automobile from McSweyn for $5,000. Not wishing to inform his wife of the real purchase price, Albano asked that the written contract state that the purchase price was only $2,000. McSweyn agreed to this change. When Albano later discovered that the odometer had been modified, he sued for the return of his $5,000. Albano will be allowed to collect only $2,000, the amount specified in the written contract.

13.3 THE STATUTE OF FRAUDS

Like the parol evidence rule, the Statute of Frauds is a confusing name for an important legal principle. The name is taken from the English law of 1677 called "An Act for Prevention of Frauds and Perjuries." The law specifies that certain kinds of agreements must be in writing to be enforceable. While there is some variation in its interpretation, most states agree on the main principle of the statute.

It is important to note that the Statute of Frauds does not prohibit a person from legally entering into oral contracts for certain kinds of agreements; it only specifies that certain contracts must be in writing to be enforceable. The Statute of Frauds applies only to executory contracts—that is, contracts that have yet to be performed. However, once a contract has been completed, it cannot be canceled merely because it was not in writing—even though it should have been.

Statute of Frauds
A law requiring certain contracts to be in writing to be enforceable.

13.4 TYPES OF CONTRACTS THAT MUST BE IN WRITING

The Statute of Frauds specifies six types of contracts that must be in writing to be legally enforceable:

- ▶ Agreements by an executor or administrator to pay the debts of a deceased person.
- ▶ Agreements to answer for the debts of another.
- ▶ Agreements that cannot be completed in less than one year.
- ▶ Agreements made in contemplation of marriage.
- ▶ Agreements to sell any interest in real property.
- ▶ Agreements to sell personal property for $500 or more.

AGREEMENTS BY AN EXECUTOR OR ADMINISTRATOR TO PAY THE DEBTS OF A DECEASED PERSON

executor

A personal representative named in a will to handle matters involving the estate of a deceased person.

administrator

A personal representative named by the court to perform as the executor would in instances in which the deceased person has not left a will.

The law recognizes that there are often many unsettled matters that need to be resolved when a person dies. As will be explained in Chapter 27, an executor is a personal representative named in a will to handle matters involving the estate of the deceased person. An administrator is a personal representative named by the court to perform as the executor would in instances in which the deceased person has not left a will. Either an executor or an administrator has legal authority to arrange for the distribution of the assets of a deceased person, and in such a position may be inclined to promise to pay debts of the deceased personally. The Statute of Frauds requires that such a promise must be in writing to be enforceable.

EXAMPLE 13.3

▶ Dellner was named executor in his father's will. After his father's death, Dellner was attempting to close the estate when a creditor demanded immediate payment of an old debt of $4,000. To avoid embarrassment for other members of the family, Dellner orally advised the creditor that he would pay the debt personally. Such a promise is not enforceable because it is not in writing.

guaranty

A promise to pay the debts or settle the wrongdoings of another if he or she does not make settlement personally.

AGREEMENTS TO ANSWER FOR THE DEBTS OF ANOTHER

A guaranty, or promise, to pay the debts or settle the wrongdoings of another if he or she does not make settlement personally is not enforceable unless it is written.

EXAMPLE 13.4

▶ Mata, the president of Callin Products, Inc., orally promised to pay the corporation's debts from his own resources in an effort to calm several persistent creditors. Under the Statute of Frauds, Mata's promise is not enforceable because it is not in writing.

An oral promise to pay the debts of another is enforceable in some states, however, if the promise is not dependent on the inability or unwillingness of the other party to pay them.

AGREEMENTS THAT CANNOT BE COMPLETED IN LESS THAN ONE YEAR

A contract that obviously cannot be completed within one year must be in writing. If the life of the contract is indefinite and there is a possibility of its being completed within a year, it need not be in writing.

EXAMPLE 13.5

▶ Rizzi, a building contractor constructing a condominium, orally agreed with a food service company to deliver coffee and lunch to the workers on the job until the construction was completed. Six months later, Rizzi canceled the contract. When the food service company complained, Rizzi said that the contract could not possibly have been completed within a year because the schedule called for completion of the condominium in 18 months; and because it was impossible to complete the contract within a year, it must have been in writing to be enforceable.

In Example 13.5, if the building had been scheduled for completion in 9 months but took 14 months because of delays, then the contract would not need to have been in writing to be enforceable.

An exchange of promises made by persons planning to marry is known as a prenuptial agreement.

AGREEMENTS MADE IN CONTEMPLATION OF MARRIAGE

An exchange of promises made by persons planning to marry is known as an antenuptial agreement, sometimes referred to as a prenuptial agreement. Such a contract is enforceable only if it is reduced to writing before the marriage takes place. This law applies to agreements by the parties to accept additional obligations not ordinarily included in the marriage contract.

antenuptial or prenuptial agreement
An exchange of promises made by persons planning to marry.

EXAMPLE 13.6

▶ Kennedy inherited a computer retail store worth several hundred thousand dollars. To ensure that her fiancé was not interested solely in her wealth, she asked him to agree, in writing and before their marriage, that all rights to this property would be hers alone. This agreement, made in contemplation of marriage, is a valid, enforceable contract.

It should be noted that antenuptial agreements often include a provision whereby they expire after a long period of time. Also, antenuptial agreements relating to custody of children in the event of divorce or separation are unenforceable; courts decide custody issues because the welfare of the child is always paramount.

AGREEMENTS TO SELL ANY INTEREST IN REAL PROPERTY

Real property, often called *real estate,* is land and items permanently attached to the land, such as buildings or trees (all other property is considered *personal property*). All contracts to sell real property or any interest in it must be in writing to be enforceable.

There is an exception to the written requirement for contracts to sell real property. This occurs when there has been partial performance of an oral agreement, thus proving the existence of the contract. Let us assume, for example, that the buyer of real property has made significant improvements to the property; paid all, or a portion of, the purchase price; or taken possession of the property. In such a case, a court might rule that partial performance is substantial enough to prove that the contract is enforceable even though it was not in writing.

EXAMPLE 13.7

▶ Abdula agreed to sell a portion of his property to his neighbor, Sasaki. Because they had known each other for many years, they agreed orally on the terms of the contract. When Abdula realized that the property had increased in value over the years, he changed his mind. Sasaki would have no legal recourse, because a contract for the sale of any interest in real property must be in writing.

AGREEMENTS TO SELL PERSONAL PROPERTY FOR $500 OR MORE

auction sale
A sale in which goods are sold to the highest bidder.

The English law of 1677 that served as the basis for the Statute of Frauds provided that a contract of sale for more than 10 pounds sterling had to be in writing. This early law has found its way into today's UCC as a requirement that sales of personal property for $500 or more must be in writing (UCC 2-201). (It should be noted that several states have increased this amount in recent years.) The UCC also has other requirements for written contracts, which are discussed in later chapters.

EXAMPLE 13.8

▶ Suard, the owner of a clothing store, orally agreed to buy a made-to-order display case for $1,200 from Island Fixtures, a manufacturer of display and exhibit equipment. Because of a long-standing relationship between the parties to the contract, neither one demanded that the agreement be in writing. Although either Suard or Island Fixtures could back out of the deal, in most instances they would not because they value their reputations in the community. Legally, however, the contract is unenforceable.

All contracts to sell real property or any interest in it must be in writing to be enforceable.

There are several exceptions to this requirement. Partial or full payment to the seller renders the contract enforceable because it shows the serious intent of the buyer, just as much as a written agreement does.

In Example 13.8, if Suard paid part of the sale price to Island Fixtures at the time of the agreement, both parties would be bound to the contract. Acceptance by the buyer or attempted delivery by the seller of the goods or part of them also indicates the serious intent of the parties and renders the oral contract enforceable.

In auction sales, in which goods are sold to the highest bidder, the sale is completed at the fall of the hammer. The notation in the auctioneer's book, initialed by the buyer, is sufficient to meet the requirements for written contracts. In the case of auction bids made by telephone from another city, the bidder is required to sign an agreement in which he or she agrees to be bound by the telephone bids made. In the case of an online sale, the web page or e-mail is generally regarded as the writing that satisfies the Statute of Frauds (see Chapter 30).

13.5 INFORMATION INCLUDED IN A WRITTEN CONTRACT

Most important contracts are printed and signed by hand by the parties to the agreement. A signature may include any symbol used by a contracting party intending to authenticate a written agreement. This can include, for example, a firm's logo or a purchase order. A valid agreement can be entirely handwritten as long as it is legible. It may even be a series of letters or e-mail messages among several persons. It can be written on almost any surface with any material that makes a discernible mark, such as pen, pencil, or crayon. (Electronically produced and signed contracts will be covered in Chapter 30.)

To satisfy the Statute of Frauds, a written contract or agreement, sometimes called a memorandum, must contain the following information:

memorandum
A written contract or agreement.

1. The names of the parties.
2. The purpose of the agreement.
3. A description of the consideration promised.
4. The date and place where the contract was made.
5. The signatures of the parties.

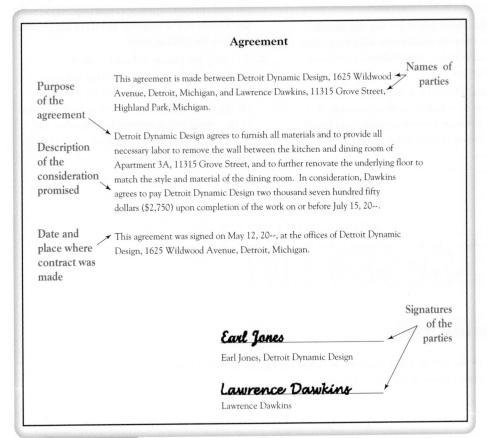

Agreement

Names of parties

Purpose of the agreement → This agreement is made between Detroit Dynamic Design, 1625 Wildwood Avenue, Detroit, Michigan, and Lawrence Dawkins, 11315 Grove Street, Highland Park, Michigan.

Description of the consideration promised → Detroit Dynamic Design agrees to furnish all materials and to provide all necessary labor to remove the wall between the kitchen and dining room of Apartment 3A, 11315 Grove Street, and to further renovate the underlying floor to match the style and material of the dining room. In consideration, Dawkins agrees to pay Detroit Dynamic Design two thousand seven hundred fifty dollars ($2,750) upon completion of the work on or before July 15, 20--.

Date and place where contract was made → This agreement was signed on May 12, 20--, at the offices of Detroit Dynamic Design, 1625 Wildwood Avenue, Detroit, Michigan.

Signatures of the parties

Earl Jones
Earl Jones, Detroit Dynamic Design

Lawrence Dawkins
Lawrence Dawkins

FIGURE 13.1 A Written Contract, or Agreement, Containing Information Sufficient to Satisfy the Statute of Frauds

In addition, written contracts frequently contain the following information:

1. Warranties provided by the seller.
2. An agreement to be bound by the laws of a specific state.
3. An acknowledgment that the buyer has inspected the goods or has waived his or her right to such inspection.
4. The form of acceptable payment (cash, certified check, etc.).

CHAPTER SUMMARY

1. Routine contracts *should not* be in writing because it would be a waste of time and effort. Some contracts *should* be in writing to protect against later disagreement. Still other contracts *must* be in writing because the law requires such for the contract to be enforceable.

2. The parol evidence rule states that any spoken or written words in conflict with what the written contract states cannot be introduced as evidence in a court of law.

3. The Statute of Frauds is a law requiring certain contracts to be in writing to be enforceable. It does not, however, prohibit a person from legally entering into oral contracts for certain kinds of agreements.

4. Contracts that must be in writing to be legally enforceable include agreements (a) by an executor or administrator to pay the debts of a deceased person, (b) to answer for the debts of another, (c) that cannot be completed in less than a year, (d) made in contemplation of marriage, (e) to sell any interest in real property, and (f) to sell personal property for $500 or more.

5. To satisfy the Statute of Frauds, a written contract must include the following five items of information: (a) the names of the parties, (b) the purpose of the agreement, (c) a description of the consideration promised, (d) the date and place where the contract was made, and (e) the signatures of the parties.

CHAPTER THIRTEEN ASSESSMENT

MATCHING LEGAL TERMS

Match each of the numbered definitions with the correct term in the following list. Write the letter of your choice in the answer column.

a. administrator
b. antenuptial or prenuptial agreement
c. auctioneer
d. executor
e. guaranty
f. memorandum
g. parol evidence rule
h. personal property
i. real property
j. Statute of Frauds

1. The law that requires certain types of contracts to be in writing. 1. _____

2. Property other than land and items permanently attached to it. 2. _____

3. The point of law that prevents oral changes to a written contract from being legally enforceable. 3. _____

4. A written contract or agreement. 4. _____

5. The personal representative appointed by a court to distribute the assets of the estate of the deceased. 5. _____

6. Land and items that are permanently attached to it. 6. _____

7. The personal representative named in a will to distribute the assets of the estate of the deceased. 7. _____

8. A promise to pay the debts or settle the wrongdoings of another. 8. _____

9. A person who conducts sales of articles in which individuals bid against one another. 9. _____

10. A contract containing promises made by persons planning to marry. 10. _____

TRUE/FALSE QUIZ

Indicate whether each of the following statements is true or false by writing *T* or *F* in the answer column.

11. Some types of contracts must be in writing to be enforceable. 11. _____

12. The parol evidence rule affects the enforceability of contracts that include oral or written changes in the terms of an existing contract. 12. _____

13. The Statute of Frauds specifies that certain kinds of contracts must be in writing. 13. _____

14. Oral or written evidence cannot legally be introduced to explain unclear portions of a contract. 14. _____

15. A valid contract can be entirely handwritten. 15. _____

16. Promises made in anticipation of marriage are enforceable. 16. _____

17. An agreement to guarantee debts of another generally must be in writing to be enforceable. 17. _____

18. The requirement of writing does not apply in auction sales. 18. _____

19. An agreement that cannot be completed within six months must be in writing. 19. _____

20. An agreement for the sale of personal property for over $500 must be in writing to be enforceable. 20. _____

21. An agreement for the sale of real estate must be in writing to
    be enforceable.   21. _____

22. An agreement by an administrator or executor to pay the debts of
    the deceased must be in writing to be enforceable.   22. _____

23. The Statute of Frauds applies only to contracts that have yet to
    be performed.   23. _____

24. A series of letters or e-mail messages among several persons can
    satisfy the Statute of Frauds.   24. _____

25. A valid contract must be typed, printed, or written in pen.   25. _____

DISCUSSION QUESTIONS

Answer the following questions and discuss them in class.

26. What are the chief provisions of the Statute of Frauds? Can you suggest other
    agreements that also should be in writing?

    _____

    _____

27. What is the minimum dollar amount specified in the Uniform Commercial Code
    as a requirement for written contracts for the sale of personal property? Should this
    amount be greater?

    _____

    _____

28. In auction sales, how is the legal requirement for a written contract satisfied? What
    problems might arise from this arrangement?

    _____

    _____

29. Why do you think a prenuptial agreement dealing with the custody of children
    would not be enforceable?

    _____

    _____

30. Why does the Statute of Frauds apply only to executory contracts—that is, contracts
    that have yet to be performed?

    _____

    _____

THINKING CRITICALLY ABOUT THE LAW

Answer the following questions, which require you to think critically about the legal principles that you learned in this chapter.

31. **Parol Evidence Rule** Even though the parol evidence rule prohibits any oral amendments to a contract, try to envision circumstances when this rule might be unreasonable.

_____

_____

32. **Statute of Frauds** Under the Statute of Frauds, an oral promise to take on the debts of another is enforceable in some states. Can you think of any other activities that might be legally acceptable despite the fact that they are not in writing?

_____

_____

33. **Personal Property** A buyer places a deposit on an item valued at more than $500 but later wishes to cancel the order. Arguing that there is no written contract, could the buyer expect a refund of the deposit?

_____

_____

34. **Statute of Frauds** Why must a contract that obviously cannot be completed within one year be in writing?

_____

_____

35. **A Question of Ethics** A person dies without leaving a will. The administrator of the estate refuses to pay the deceased's debts on the grounds that there is no written evidence of the obligation. Comment on the ethics of this situation.

_____

_____

CASE QUESTIONS

Study each of the following cases. Answer the questions that follow by writing *Yes* or *No* in the answer column.

36. **Statute of Frauds** Coursey orally agreed to sell three acres of land to Oulette for $8,000. After Oulette had paid the $8,000 and the transfer had been officially recorded, Coursey received an offer of $9,000 for the land from another prospective buyer. Hoping to set aside the first transaction so that he could accept the second,

higher, offer, Coursey attempted to cancel the sale to Oulette on the grounds that the Statute of Frauds required a written contract.

a. Does the fact that there is evidence (the recording of the sale) indicate Coursey's agreement to the terms of the sale?

a. _____

b. Will Coursey succeed in canceling the contract of sale?

b. _____

c. Is the contract enforceable?

c. _____

37. **Statute of Frauds** Garcia, an independent computer consultant, was orally engaged by the Eastern Institute of Management, a publisher of management newsletters, to set up an office computer network that included needs assessment, employee training, and a desktop publishing system. The plan envisioned at least 18 months' work. Three months after he began work, Eastern paid Garcia for the work he had done and discharged him in order to hire another consultant, who appeared to have wider experience and greater expertise.

a. Can Eastern Institute legally cancel this agreement?

a. _____

b. If the work could have been done in six months, would the oral contract have been legally enforceable?

b. _____

38. **Parol Evidence Rule** Safran, the owner of an automobile repair shop, placed an order for an engine diagnostic machine from the Mountain Range Equipment Company. The salesperson, Rubinstein, orally assured Safran that a number of test programs for both gasoline and diesel engines would be included as part of the order. When the machine was delivered, the test programs were not included. When the buyer protested, Rubinstein claimed that Safran was mistaken and must have been thinking about another special offer the firm was running.

a. Are the oral promises Rubinstein made that supplement the written contract of sale enforceable?

a. _____

b. Is it likely that Safran will gain legal satisfaction?

b. _____

c. Does the parol evidence rule allow introduction of oral revisions to a contract?

c. _____

CASE ANALYSIS

Study each of the following cases carefully. Briefly state the principle of law and your decision.

39. **Statute of Frauds** Anderson was seriously injured in a traffic accident. Anderson's daughter called a doctor, Lawrence, and told him to "give my father the best care you can give him, and I'll pay whatever you charge." The doctor provided the care, but the father died before the bill was paid. Lawrence attempted to collect for his services from the father's estate. The executor of the estate refused to pay. Lawrence then attempted to collect from the daughter who had guaranteed payment. Is the daughter legally responsible for the debts of her father if the agreement was not in writing? [*Lawrence v. Anderson,* 184 A. 689 (Vermont)]

Principle of Law:

_____

_____

_____

Decision:

_____

_____

_____

40. Parol Evidence Rule Dennison agreed to purchase land from Harden with the understanding that the land contained fruit trees. To prove that there were fruit trees on the property, Harden provided nursery reports stating that Pacific Gold peach trees were growing on the land. When Dennison discovered that the land contained valueless, shrubby trees and only a few of the fruit trees he had been expecting, he sued, charging breach of contract. At the trial, Dennison wanted to introduce the nursery reports as parol evidence to clarify the meaning of the "fruit trees" referred to in the contract. Harden resisted having the nursery report introduced to clarify the contract. Was Dennison successful in his attempt to clarify the contract by adding the terms "fruit trees," or did Dennison get what he agreed to buy? [_Dennison v. Harden,_ 186 P.2d 908 (Washington)]

Principle of Law:

_____

_____

Decision:

_____

_____

41. Contract Essentials Marti, the owner of an expensive sports car, agreed in writing to sell the car to Berini. Because both parties recognized that some necessary engine repairs were needed, their contract did not specify the sales price, intending to determine the cost of repairs first. The cost of repairs was later determined and the final price settled, but the price was never included in the contract. Is this an enforceable contract?

Principle of Law:

_____

_____

Decision:

_____

_____

42. **Statute of Frauds** Wang orally agreed to sell a thoroughbred horse to Presti for $60,000. When Presti sent a check in payment, Wang told him that he intended to hold the check for a month for tax purposes. Wang retained possession of the horse. While the check remained uncashed, a disagreement arose between Wang and Presti. Wang announced that he would not go through with the transaction and that, since the contract was oral, it was unenforceable. Presti claimed that his sending the check was payment and this action made the oral contract valid and enforceable. Wang denied accepting payment. Is Presti's claim, that sending the check made the contract enforceable, valid?

Principle of Law:

_____

_____

_____

Decision:

_____

_____

_____

LEGAL RESEARCH
_____

Complete the following activities. Share your findings with the class.

43. **Working in Teams** There are numerous risks in the preparation of contracts. Some must be written as specified by the Statute of Frauds, while others need not be. In teams of three or four, interview owners or managers of several small businesses and ask about the procedures followed to minimize these risks.

_____

_____

44. **Using Technology** Using the Internet and search engines, investigate the parol evidence rule and the Statute of Frauds in two states. Compare and contrast the rules in the two states.

_____

_____

14

Operation of Contracts

14.1 Identify two instances in which a contract may involve third parties.

14.2 Distinguish between a third-party beneficiary and an incidental beneficiary, and outline the rights of each.

14.3 Interpret the legal concept of assignment of rights.

14.4 Identify three kinds of contracts that may not be assigned.

14.5 Explain the legal concept of delegation of duties.

14.6 Provide examples of contracts that may be assigned by a court of law.

14.7 Discuss novation and how it differs from assignment.

Terms

third-party beneficiary	guarantor	
incidental beneficiary	personal-service contract	
assignment	delegation	
assignor	bankruptcy	
assignee	novation	

chapter **14**
Operation of Contracts

LEARNING OUTCOMES

After studying this chapter and completing the assessment, you will be able to

14.1 Identify two instances in which a contract may involve third parties.

14.2 Distinguish between a third-party beneficiary and an incidental beneficiary, and outline the rights of each.

14.3 Interpret the legal concept of assignment of rights.

14.4 Identify three kinds of contracts that may not be assigned.

14.5 Explain the legal concept of delegation of duties.

14.6 Provide examples of contracts that may be assigned by a court of law.

14.7 Discuss novation and how it differs from assignment.

LEGAL terms

third-party beneficiary	guarantor
incidental beneficiary	personal-service contract
assignment	delegation
assignor	bankruptcy
assignee	novation

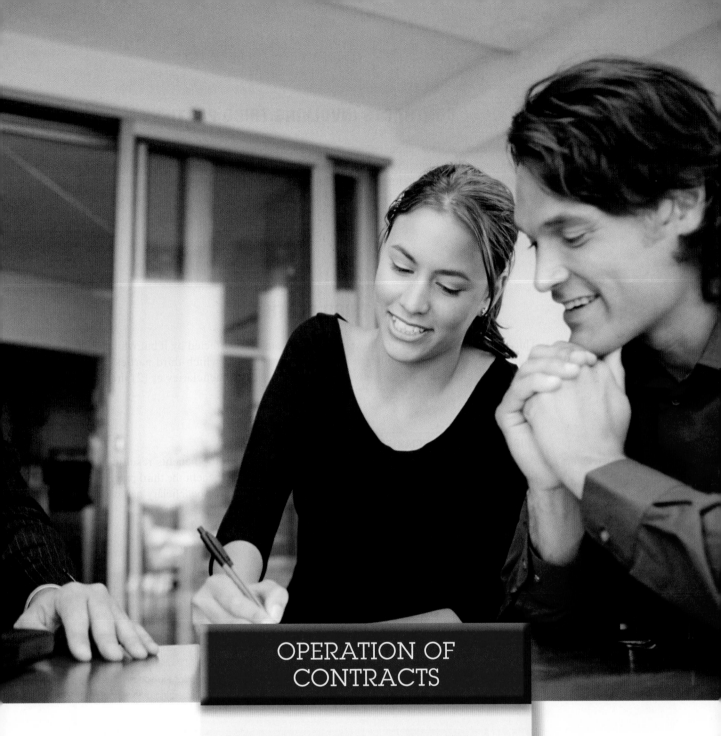

OPERATION OF CONTRACTS

"When two persons are together, two of them must not whisper to each other, without letting the third hear; because it would hurt him."

The prophet Muhammed, founder of the religion of Islam

14.1 CONTRACTS INVOLVING THIRD PARTIES

In the previous chapters about contracts, only contracts between two parties were discussed. The reason is that normally only the two parties to a contract have rights and duties under it. However, there are two important exceptions to this rule: (1) when the purpose of a contract is to benefit a third party and (2) when rights or duties that arise from a contract are legally transferred to a third party.

14.2 RIGHTS OF THIRD PARTIES

Third parties to a contract are those who are in some way affected by it but who are not one of the parties to the contract. There are two ways in which third parties can be affected by a contract: if they are either (1) third-party beneficiaries or (2) incidental beneficiaries.

THIRD-PARTY BENEFICIARIES

third-party beneficiary
A person who is not a party to a contract but is intended by the contracting parties to benefit as a consequence of a contract.

A third-party beneficiary to a contract has a legal right to the benefits resulting from the contract only if it is the intent of the contracting parties to benefit the third party. A life insurance policy is an example of a third-party contract, and the beneficiary named in the insurance policy is legally a third-party beneficiary.

EXAMPLE 14.1

▶ Hamomoto contracted with an artist, Frey, to create a painting of his family's farmhouse for $1,000. The artist was informed that the painting was to be presented to Hamomoto's son as a birthday gift. Just before the painting was finished, Hamomoto died. Frey learned that she could sell the painting through an art gallery for several thousand dollars. She offered to return to Hamomoto's son the portion of the fee that his father had already paid, but the son insisted that Frey fulfill the terms of the contract. The son, who is not one of the contracting parties, is a third-party beneficiary and is entitled to receive the painting.

INCIDENTAL BENEFICIARIES

incidental beneficiary
A person who will benefit as an indirect consequence of a contract, although that was not the intent of the contracting parties.

An incidental beneficiary is one who may benefit as an indirect consequence of a contract, although that was not the intent of the contracting parties. That is, the purpose of the contract is not to confer a benefit to a third party, but a third party does, in fact, benefit from it. Such parties have no rights in the contract, regardless of the size of their gain or benefit.

▶ Sceneview Development Company entered into a contract with Soula Realtors to construct a marina and condominium on the shore of a lake. Philbus owned property adjacent to the planned development. Knowing that the value of his property was about to be greatly enhanced, Philbus began developing his own property and planned to open a number of stores and a restaurant to serve the people who would be attracted to the Sceneview development. However, because of financial difficulties, Sceneview requested, and Soula Realtors agreed, to cancel their contract. Philbus suffered a loss as a consequence of Sceneview's cancellation, but because he is an incidental beneficiary, he has no rights in the contract and no legal course of action.

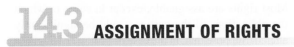

14.3 ASSIGNMENT OF RIGHTS

In most states, the law permits a party to a contract to assign rights—that is, to transfer them to a third party and permit the third party to receive the benefits of the contract. This change of a contract is known as an assignment. The person who transfers his or her rights is known as the assignor; the third party to whom the rights are transferred is known as the assignee. A party to an existing contract may also appoint a third person to perform contractual duties; this appointment is referred to as a delegation(discussed later in this chapter).

A party may transfer his or her rights by assignment, and his or her duties by delegation, subject to several restraints (e.g., prohibition by law and personal-service contracts). It is important to note that the term *duties* means tasks and performance, not responsibilities. A person who agrees in a contract to perform a particular task may generally delegate this task to someone else but is still responsible for getting it done. Consider Example 14.3, in which Higgins transfers his duty to Randall but is still responsible for making certain that the duty is met.

assignment
The transfer of a contract right to a third party who can receive the benefits of the contract.

assignor
The person who transfers his or her rights in an assignment.

assignee
The third party to whom rights are transferred in an assignment.

EXAMPLE 14.3

▶ Higgins, a professor of finance, agreed to conduct a financial planning workshop for Randall, the president of a local club of retirees, for a fee of $1,200. Before conducting the workshop, Higgins assigned his right to the $1,200 to the Holiday Villa Motel, where he had held a number of workshops and to whom he owed $1,500. Holiday Villa was eager to agree to this arrangement because it was concerned about Higgins's ability to pay his bill. When the workshop was finished, Randall simply paid the $1,200 to Holiday Villa instead of to Higgins. Higgins is the assignor and Holiday Villa is the assignee.

FORM OF ASSIGNMENT

In general, an assignment may be either written or oral. However, if the original contract is required to be in writing under the Statute of Frauds, the assignment also must be in writing. Obviously it makes good sense to put important assignments in writing, whether or not required by the Statute of Frauds (see Chapter 13).

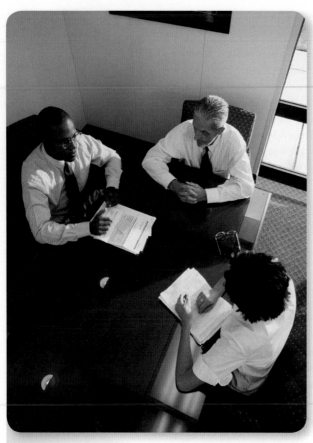

A party to a contract will not be obligated by an assignment made by the other party without his or her knowledge until notified.

NOTICE OF ASSIGNMENT

A party to a contract will not be obligated by an assignment made by the other party without his or her knowledge until notified. In Example 14.3, it is the responsibility of the assignee, Holiday Villa, to notify the other party to the contract, Randall, of the assignment. The burden of investigating claims of assignment then falls on the party notified of the assignment (Randall). After a party (Randall) has received a notice of an assignment, he or she may demand a reasonable time to investigate its validity.

RIGHTS THAT MAY BE TRANSFERRED

Most rights are assignable, except in cases in which the obligations of the parties would be significantly altered. Suppose that, in the case of Professor Higgins's financial planning workshop, Randall contracted with Higgins, but then the retirees vetoed the idea of the workshop altogether—because most of them had modest incomes and little interest in financial planning.

Assume also that, to salvage some value from the workshop to which she was already committed, Randall attempted to assign her right to have the workshop conducted to a local group of bankers. It is likely that this assignment would not be acceptable to Higgins because he would be required to significantly modify his presentation. Usually contracts for personal services are neither assignable nor delegable.

THE ASSIGNOR'S GUARANTY

guarantor
The party who guarantees the promises assigned.

The assignor of a contract right becomes a guarantor—that is, one who guarantees the promises assigned. The Uniform Commercial Code (UCC) states, "No delegation of performance relieves the party delegating of any duty to perform or any liability for breach" (UCC 2-210).

EXAMPLE 14.4

▶ Von Berg, a residential homeowner, entered into a contract with Conant Construction to have a driveway installed. Before construction began, Von Berg learned that a proposed local zoning regulation would no longer allow concrete driveways on her street. Rather than breach her contract with Conant Construction, Von Berg assigned her rights to have the driveway installed to Levi, a friend who owned a similar home nearby. If Conant Construction installed a substandard driveway for Levi, Von Berg, the original assignor of the contract right to have the driveway installed, would be responsible to Levi for Conant's failure to perform properly.

14.4 CONTRACTS THAT MAY NOT BE ASSIGNED

Three types of contracts may not be assigned: (1) contracts that include assignment restrictions, (2) contracts for which assignments are prohibited by law or public policy, and (3) contracts that require personal services.

CONTRACTS THAT INCLUDE ASSIGNMENT RESTRICTIONS

When parties to a contract include in the contract itself a specific provision forbidding assignment, both parties are prevented from assigning their rights or delegating their duties. A contract also may prohibit just one party from assigning or delegating.

CONTRACTS FOR WHICH ASSIGNMENTS ARE PROHIBITED BY LAW OR PUBLIC POLICY

Various state and federal statutes have been enacted to prohibit the assignment of certain contracts. For example, members of the armed services are prohibited from assigning their pay, and many state and local governments prohibit the assignment of salaries of public officials.

CONTRACTS THAT REQUIRE PERSONAL SERVICES

A personal-service contract is one in which services that require a unique skill, talent, ability, and so forth are provided by a specific person. In such a case, the party who hires the specific person to perform certain duties has a substantial interest in having only the hired person perform.

> **personal-service contract**
> A contract in which services that require a unique skill, talent, ability, and so forth are provided by a specific person.

Personal-service contracts may not be assigned. For example, artists, musicians, photographers, and athletes are hired because of their special personal skills, and consequently, their services under a contract may not be delegated to anyone else. In most cases, an employment contract is considered a personal-service contract and may not be assigned.

EXAMPLE 14.5

▶ Janik, vice president of marketing for Maximal Products, hired Papandreau, an inspirational speaker, to address her annual meeting of salespeople. Because of a last-minute scheduling problem, Papandreau canceled her appearance but offered to send her brother to speak in her place. Janik refused the offer, claiming that Papandreau was well known and the salespeople were expecting her unique inspirational message. Should this case reach a courtroom, a court would find in favor of Janik.

14.5 DELEGATION OF DUTIES

Since athletes are hired because of their special personal skills, their services under a contract may not be delegated to anyone else.

Just as a party's rights in a contract can be assigned to another party, a party's duties can be transferred to a third party if the duties do not involve unique skills or abilities.

delegation
The appointment of a third party by a party to an existing contract to perform contractual duties that do not involve unique skills, talents, abilities, and so on.

This transfer is known as a delegation of duties. Even employment contracts may be assigned if there is no relationship of trust or confidence, or any other circumstance that would create a materially greater burden on the party whose services are being assigned.

EXAMPLE 14.6

▶ Rensal Services had a three-year employment contract with Kopelek, an accountant. After Kopelek had been employed for only three months, Rensal Services was sold to Pacific Accountants and Kopelek's contract was assigned to Pacific. Kopelek refused to work for Pacific, claiming that he had a special relationship with Rensal and the working atmosphere was "almost family." The duties assigned to him by Pacific were substantially the same as before the sale of Rensal. Consequently, the assignment of Kopelek's contract would be legally enforceable.

14.6   ASSIGNMENT AND DELEGATION BY LAW

Rights or duties under a contract may be assigned by a court of law when a contracting party dies or becomes bankrupt.

DEATH OF A CONTRACTING PARTY

When a party to a contract dies, all contractual rights are assigned to the administrator or executor of the estate. All rights to the collection of money, to demands for performance, and to the sale or purchase of real or personal property are assigned by law immediately upon the party's death. This assignment does not include personal-service contracts of the deceased that are not delegable because of the unique skills of the deceased.

EXAMPLE 14.7

▶ Zarb, a composer, agreed in writing to sell an original musical score to Olney, a music promoter, for $65,000. One week before the completed score was to be delivered and payment made, Olney was killed in an accident. Meanwhile, Zarb got an offer of $75,000 for the score from a different promoter and as a result stood to gain from not completing the transaction with Olney. The right to purchase the music, however, was assigned by law to Olney's executor, and Zarb must complete the transaction.

In Example 14.7, if Zarb had been killed in the accident, neither Olney nor Zarb's executor would have any rights or duties under the contract, which was for Zarb's personal services.

BANKRUPTCY OF A CONTRACTING PARTY

The laws dealing with bankruptcy provide that the assets and contracts of a bankrupt (legally recognized as unable to pay legitimate debts) person or business be assigned to the trustee in bankruptcy. The trustee is then empowered to sell the assets and exercise contract rights for the benefit of the creditors of the bankrupt person or firm.

bankruptcy
A condition in which a person or business is legally recognized as unable to pay legitimate debts.

14.7   NOVATION

When all parties to a contract agree to a significant change in the contract, the change is called a novation. Such a change actually creates a new contract that is simply based on the earlier one. A novation differs from an assignment in the following ways:

novation
A situation in which all parties to a contract agree to a significant change to a contract.

▶ A novation requires mutual consent of all parties (the original parties to the agreement and any new third parties) just as does a new contract. However, an assignment can be made without the mutual consent of both contracting parties.

▶ A novation transfers all rights and obligations in a contract, but an assignment transfers only the rights of the assignor and leaves the assignor with the duty of fulfilling his or her obligations under the contract.

As a result, a party to a contract who assigns his or her rights or delegates his or her duties to a third party is never free from the contract until it is completely executed. In contrast, if the third party enters the contract as a result of a novation, the party whose rights or duties are assumed is completely relieved of any obligations.

EXAMPLE 14.8

▶ Fortesi and Yellen entered into a contract in which Fortesi agreed to build a garage on Yellen's property. Later they and Zink agreed that Zink will perform Fortesi's obligations, with Yellen expressly releasing Fortesi from the original contract. This is a novation, and Fortesi's obligations are now discharged.

CHAPTER SUMMARY

1. A contract may involve more than two parties (1) when the purpose of a contract is to benefit a third party and (2) when rights or duties that arise from a contract are legally transferred to a third party.

2. A third-party beneficiary to a contract has a legal right to the benefits resulting from the contract only if the contracting parties intend to benefit the third party. An incidental beneficiary is one who may benefit as an indirect consequence of a

contract, although that was not the intent of the contracting parties. An incidental party has no rights in the contract.

3. An assignment occurs when a party to a contract transfers his or her rights under the contract to a third party and permits the third party to receive the benefits of the contract.

4. Three types of contracts that may not be assigned include (a) contracts that include assignment restrictions, (b) contracts for which assignments are prohibited by law or public policy, and (c) contracts that require personal service.

5. A delegation of duties obliges a third party to carry out the tasks and performance under the

terms of the contract, provided they do not involve unique skills or abilities.

6. A court can assign rights and duties under a contract when a contracting party dies or becomes bankrupt.

7. A novation occurs when parties to a contract agree to a significant change in the contract. A novation differs from an assignment because (a) unlike an assignment, it requires the mutual consent of all parties; and (b) a novation transfers all rights and obligations in a contract, but an assignment transfers only the rights of the assignor and still leaves the assignor with the duty of fulfilling his or her obligations under the contract.

CHAPTER FOURTEEN
ASSESSMENT

MATCHING LEGAL TERMS

Match each of the numbered definitions with the correct term in the following list. Write the letter of your choice in the answer column.

a. assignee   e. delegation   i. personal-service contract
b. assignment   f. guarantor   j. third-party beneficiary
c. assignor   g. incidental beneficiary
d. bankrupt   h. novation

1. A significant change in a contract that is made with the mutual consent of all parties.   1. _____

2. The transfer of duties to a third party by a party to a contract.   2. _____

3. A party who would benefit from the performance of a contract, but for whom the contract is not created.   3. _____

4. An outside party for whose benefit a contract is made by other parties.   4. _____

5. A party to a contract who transfers his or her rights to a third party.   5. _____

6. A contract in which services that require a unique skill, talent, ability, or the like are provided by a specific person.

6. _____

7. The state of a person or firm recognized to be unable to pay obligations.

7. _____

8. An outside party to whom contract rights are transferred.

8. _____

9. The transfer of contract rights by one of the parties.

9. _____

10. An assignor who guarantees or stands behind an assignment.

10. _____

TRUE/FALSE QUIZ

Indicate whether each of the following statements is true or false by writing *T* or *F* in the answer column.

11. A third-party beneficiary has a legal right to receive the benefits of a contract if it is the intent of the contract to benefit the third party.

11. _____

12. A third party who benefits incidentally from a contract has a right to the benefits if they exceed $500.

12. _____

13. The law in most states permits the assignment of most contract rights to a third party.

13. _____

14. The court may make assignments for bankrupt persons.

14. _____

15. An assignment must be in writing if the original contract was required by law to be in writing.

15. _____

16. The assignment of certain contracts is prohibited by law.

16. _____

17. It is legally permissible to delegate contract obligations to perform certain tasks.

17. _____

18. Contracts that specifically prohibit assignment in their wording can still be assigned if the assignee is known to be a reputable person.

18. _____

19. Contracts for personal services may not be assigned unless there is agreement to the contrary.

19. _____

20. In most cases, duties required in an employment contract are not
delegable.   20. _____

21. Services of artists, musicians, photographers, and athletes can be
delegated.   21. _____

22. Some assignments are prohibited by public policy.   22. _____

23. Once a person delegates a contractual duty, he or she no longer
has responsibility under the contract.   23. _____

24. A novation is a special kind of assignment where none of the
parties to the contract are required to agree to its terms.   24. _____

25. The assignor of a contract right becomes a guarantor.   25. _____

DISCUSSION QUESTIONS

Answer the following questions and discuss them in class.

26. Distinguish between a third-party beneficiary and an incidental beneficiary.

_____

_____

27. Explain the legal concept of assignment of contracts and provide an example of a
contract that is assignable.

_____

_____

28. Distinguish between the assignment of rights and delegation of duties.

_____

_____

29. Identify the three kinds of contracts that cannot be assigned.

_____

_____

30. Describe the circumstances in which a court might assign rights or duties under a contract.

_____

_____

31. Discuss novation and explain how it differs from assignment.

_____

_____

THINKING CRITICALLY ABOUT THE LAW

Answer the following questions, which require you to think critically about the legal principles that you learned in this chapter.

32. Third-Party Beneficiary Do you think a third-party beneficiary should be required to sign a contract as one of the parties involved?

_____

_____

33. Incidental Beneficiary Should an incidental beneficiary to a contract have any legal recourse if the contract is terminated?

_____

_____

34. Personal-Service Contract Under what circumstances could the duties under a personal-service contract be delegated?

_____

_____

35. Novation What are some advantages of using a novation over a contract assignment?

_____

_____

36. A Question of Ethics Under the law, a bankrupt person is allowed to retain certain property—including his or her residence. Is it ethical for a bankrupt person to use the law to avoid payment on his or her legitimate debts and still retain some, often valuable, property?

_____

_____

CASE QUESTIONS

Study each of the following cases. Answer the questions that follow by writing *Yes* or *No* in the answer column.

37. **Performance Liability** Chang, a florist, contracted with Torres to provide delivery services in the local community. Torres discovered that his vehicles did not have the equipment to handle the work well, so he asked Chang if another delivery service, Rush Truk, would be acceptable to him. After some meetings with Torres and Rush Truk, Chang agreed to the change in delivery services.

    a. Is Torres responsible for the performance of Rush Truk?   **a.** _____

    b. Is this a valid assignment?   **b.** _____

    c. Is this an example of a novation?   **c.** _____

38. **Beneficiary Benefits** Franken, a college student, recognized that she was financially very dependent upon her widowed mother's financial support while she was in college. To protect against the risk of financial loss in the event of her mother's death, Franken persuaded her mother to take out an insurance policy naming her as the beneficiary.

    a. Is Franken an incidental beneficiary?   **a.** _____

    b. Is Franken a third-party beneficiary?   **b.** _____

    c. In the event of the mother's death, would Franken's college be deemed to be a third-party beneficiary?   **c.** _____

39. **Contractual Rights** Westerfield contracted with Bradley Building Company for the construction of a ranch house as a wedding gift for his daughter. Before construction began, Westerfield died and Bradley announced that he would not build the house. Westerfield's daughter brought suit in her own name to compel Bradley to build the house as it had contracted to do.

    a. Does the daughter have any rights in the contract between her father and Bradley Construction Company?   **a.** _____

    b. Can the daughter, a third-party beneficiary, seek to have the court force Bradley Construction Company to construct the house or to pay damages to the daughter?   **b.** _____

40. **Contract Assignment** Rodrigos, the leader of a rock-and-roll group, agreed to provide music for the annual Park College Marketing Club dinner dance. On the night of the dinner dance, however, another, very amateurish group showed up and said that Rodrigos had assigned the contract to them and that they would play the engagement.

    a. Is a person who hires an outside entertainer required to accept the services of a substitute if it is impossible for the original party to perform?   a. _____

    b. Are all contracts assignable?   b. _____

    c. Can contracts for personal services be assigned?   c. _____

CASE ANALYSIS

Study each of the following cases carefully. Briefly state the principle of law and your decision.

41. **Assignable Contracts** A restaurant, Pizza of Gaithersburg, Inc. (PG), agreed with Virginia Coffee Service (VCS) to have vending machines installed in PG's restaurants. The contract was to run for one year and was automatically renewable unless PG gave 30 days' notice. One year later, VCS was sold to Macke Company, including the contract with PG. PG canceled the contract because of the change of ownership. Macke sued PG, claiming that VCS had delegated the duties to Macke and it was performing the duties previously done by VCS. PG claimed that the contract it had with VCS was a personal-service contract and was therefore not assignable. Does Macke Company have a valid argument? [*Macke Co. v. Pizza of Gaithersburg, Inc.*, 270 A.2d 645 (Maryland)]

Principle of Law:

_____

_____

Decision:

_____

_____

42. **Third-Party Beneficiaries** The employees of Powder Power Tools Corp. were represented by a labor union that had negotiated an agreement covering pay rates. A number of employees did not receive the higher rates of pay specified in the union contract. Springer, an employee, brought suit on behalf of those employees who did not receive the higher pay, claiming that they were third-party beneficiaries of the contract. The employer claimed that Springer could not sue because he was

not a party to the contract. Is it likely that Springer will be successful in his suit? [*Springer v. Powder Power Tool Corp.*, 348 P.2d 1112 (Oregon)]

Principle of Law:

_____

_____

Decision:

_____

_____

43. **Lost Benefits** Birmingham Automotive Supply Company entered into a contract with the Excel Construction Company to build a chain-link fence around the property of the auto supply company. Included in the contract was a provision that the fence must be manufactured by Tornado Fence Company. Excel used another brand of fence, and Tornado sued Excel for the loss suffered, claiming that it was a third-party beneficiary to the contract. Will Tornado be successful in its claim of loss suffered?

Principle of Law:

_____

_____

Decision:

_____

_____

44. **Death of a Contracting Party** Weintraub wished to donate a music rehearsal room to Northern College, from which she had graduated. She hired Hazelton, an architect who specialized in acoustics, to design the room. Shortly after the agreement was made, Weintraub died. Hazelton refused to begin work, claiming that his contract was made with Weintraub. Can the college compel Hazelton to complete the work he agreed to do for Weintraub?

Principle of Law:

_____

_____

Decision:

_____

_____

Complete the following activities. Share your findings with the class.

45. Working in Teams   Working in teams of three or four, interview the owners or managers of small businesses to determine whether they typically get involved in contract assignments.

_____

_____

46. Using Technology   Using the Internet and search engines, investigate typical regulations or legislation that governs the assignment of certain contracts. What are some types of contracts typically controlled?

_____

_____

chapter **15**
Discharge of Contracts

LEARNING OUTCOMES

After studying this chapter and completing the assessment, you will be able to

15.1 Identify seven ways in which a contract may be terminated.

15.2 Discuss termination of a contract by agreement.

15.3 Explain the three types of termination by performance.

15.4 Explain termination by impossibility of performance.

15.5 Describe when termination by alteration occurs.

15.6 Identify the circumstances under which a contract would be terminated by operation of law.

15.7 Provide examples of contracts terminated by breach.

15.8 Explain how contracts can be terminated to protect consumers.

15.9 Discuss the remedies for breach of contract, and provide examples of situations that would be appropriate for each remedy.

LEGAL terms

substantial performance
tender of performance
tender of goods
tender of payment
impossibility of performance
frustration of purpose
material alteration
breach of contract

anticipatory breach
mitigate
promissory note
liquidated damages clause
specific performance
restraining order
injunction

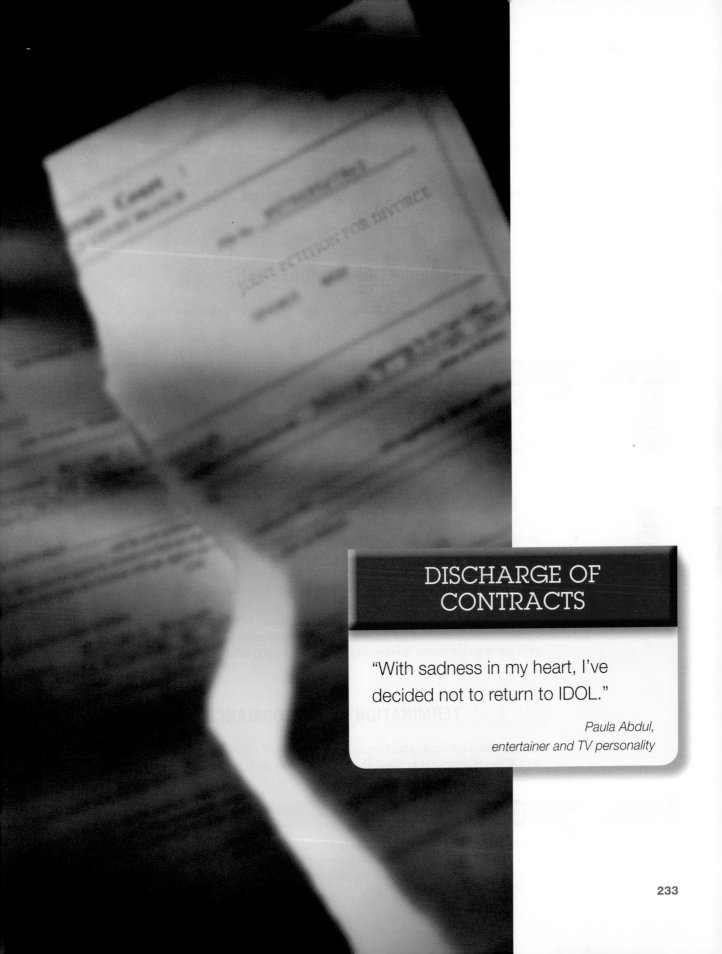

DISCHARGE OF CONTRACTS

"With sadness in my heart, I've decided not to return to IDOL."

Paula Abdul,
entertainer and TV personality

15.1 TERMINATION OF CONTRACTS

Earlier chapters described the formation and operation of contracts. This chapter is concerned with the termination, or end, of contracts.

Contracts may be terminated by (1) agreement, (2) performance, (3) impossibility of performance, (4) alteration, (5) operation of law, (6) breach, and (7) laws and regulations protecting the consumer.

15.2 TERMINATION BY AGREEMENT

A contract may provide for its termination after a certain period of time or upon the occurrence of a certain event.

EXAMPLE 15.1

▶ Office Products agreed to act as a local distributor for the Comet Phone/Fax Company for a period of five years. The agreement required Office Products to sell telephones and fax machines, maintain an inventory of telephone accessories and other supplies, and provide repairs. In this case, the termination was provided for in the contract.

Suppose that after only two years, Office Products found that the distributorship agreement was unprofitable and also that Comet was somewhat disappointed in Office Products' performance. If both firms agreed that cancellation of the contract was the best course of action, the contract could be terminated by mutual agreement even though the original contract did not provide for termination after two years. If, however, only one party was dissatisfied with the contract, both parties would be bound by the terms of the agreement until the specified five years had passed.

Occasionally, instead of agreeing to cancel a contract, both parties may agree to substitute a new contract in place of the original in order to maintain a working relationship. In such a case, the original contract is immediately terminated upon substitution of the new contract.

15.3 TERMINATION BY PERFORMANCE

Complete and satisfactory performance of the terms of a contract will bring about termination. When a contract is fulfilled, there is no need to provide for contract termination.

EXAMPLE 15.2

▶ The Soft Sound Recording Studio agreed to record several radio commercials for Sachley Advertising Agency. When the work was completed on schedule and payment was made, the contract was considered terminated by performance.

SUBSTANTIAL PERFORMANCE

Substantial performance occurs when a party to a contract, in good faith, executes all of the promised terms and conditions of the contract with the exception of minor details that do not materially affect the intent of their agreement. In Example 15.2, if the contract had been largely completed and only small details remained unfinished, then the contract would have been considered substantially performed. Suppose the commercials were completed and the only unfinished work consisted of mailing the duplicated tapes to radio stations. Soft Sound would have substantially performed the contract and would be entitled to payment according to the terms of the contract, less the cost of the mailing.

If an important part of a contract is not performed within the period of time specified, the agreement may be canceled, but the omission of a small detail entitles the injured party to claim only a proportionate reduction in the payment. Some states provide for a remedy only in the event of a material breach, and do not proportion the award.

substantial performance
When a party to a contract, in good faith, executes all of the promised terms and conditions of the contract with the exception of minor details that do not affect the real intent of their agreement.

PERFORMANCE BY PAYMENT OF MONEY

Contracts that require the payment of money are not complete until the amount agreed upon has been paid. If the agreement provides that payment may be made by check, as most payments are, payment by check is considered conditional and subject to collection in cash. A party to a contract who pays by check is not relieved of the obligation for payment under the contract until the cash has been paid by the bank on which the check is drawn.

TENDER AND ITS EFFECT

A tender of performance is an offer to perform and is considered evidence of a party's willingness to fulfill the terms of a contract. If a tender of performance of an act is refused, the person making the offer is relieved of the obligation to perform and may sue the other party for breach of contract.

tender of performance
An offer to perform that is considered evidence of a party's willingness to fulfill the terms of a contract.

EXAMPLE 15.3

▶ Sunset Realty contracted with Clean Sweep to purchase janitorial services, including carpet cleaning, window washing, and general cleaning services. When personnel from Clean Sweep arrived for their evening's work, the manager of Sunset advised them that they would not be needed because a staff meeting was being held in the offices. Clean Sweep made a tender of performance, so although Sunset did not use the services, they were obligated to pay under the contract.

A tender of goods is an offer to provide the goods agreed upon and is considered evidence of a party's willingness to fulfill the terms of a contract. As is true for a tender of performance, if a tender of goods is refused, the person making the offer of goods is relieved of the obligation to provide the goods and may sue the other party for breach of contract.

tender of goods
An offer to provide the goods agreed upon that is considered evidence of a party's willingness to fulfill the terms of a contract.

tender of payment
A money offer of payment of an obligation.

Finally, a tender of payment is an offer of money in payment of an obligation and is considered evidence of a party's willingness to fulfill the terms of a contract. If a tender of payment is refused by the creditor, the debt is not canceled, but penalties and interest cannot be charged beyond the date on which the offer of payment was made.

Valid Tender Certain requirements must be met for tender of money or performance to be valid.

First, tender must be made as specified in the contract. If the contract specifies that payment or performance be made at a certain time or place, or to a particular person, these conditions must be met.

EXAMPLE 15.4

▶ Phin ordered a truckload of Christmas trees from Spruce Tree Company to be delivered to his used car lot on December 5. Because bad weather in Canada and Vermont affected the cutting schedule, the trees were not delivered until December 15. Phin refused delivery, claiming that he had already lost a considerable amount of business he had hoped to get, and he had dismissed the two college students he had hired to sell the trees. Phin had the right to refuse the tender because Spruce Tree failed to meet the conditions of the contract.

The mention of money in a contract implies payment in cash.

Second, when tender of payment is made, it must be for the exact amount. The mention of money in a contract implies payment in cash. Although checks are used in most business transactions, the seller has the right to refuse such a payment and to insist on cash.

Third, if the contract calls for the delivery of specific goods, only the tender of these particular goods will satisfy the contract.

impossibility of performance
When unforeseen circumstances make it impossible to fulfill the terms of a contract; in these cases, the contract is considered void.

15.4 TERMINATION BY IMPOSSIBILITY OF PERFORMANCE

Unforeseen circumstances may make it impossible to fulfill the terms of a contract as originally agreed. In a case of impossibility of performance, the contract is considered void and the parties are discharged.

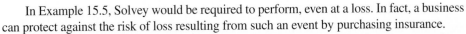

EXAMPLE 15.5

▶ Solvey Brick Company, a manufacturer of standard building bricks used in construction, had a contract to supply several hundred thousand bricks to Ramon Construction. While the contract did not specify the source of the bricks, Solvey assumed that the bricks would be from its own plant. As Solvey was preparing to manufacture the bricks, the plant burned down. Solvey could buy the same type of bricks from another manufacturer and supply them to Ramon at a loss. Most courts would rule that the subject matter was standard bricks, not specific bricks from Solvey's own production facilities, and would not excuse Solvey from its contractual obligations. There was no impossibility of performance.

In Example 15.5, Solvey would be required to perform, even at a loss. In fact, a business can protect against the risk of loss resulting from such an event by purchasing insurance.

The Uniform Commercial Code (UCC) makes a special provision for failure to perform when the goods under contract are destroyed. If the contract covers goods that have been identified (such as a particular article of merchandise), and if the goods are destroyed without fault of either party, the contract is canceled. If the seller's source of supply or means of production creates only a partial inability to perform, the seller may tender only a portion of the goods under contract. Also, if the loss is only partial, the buyer may demand the right to inspect the damaged goods in order to decide whether to reject them or to accept them in their damaged state and claim an allowance for the damages (UCC 2-615).

PERSONAL-SERVICE CONTRACTS

Death or disabling illness of a party to a contract also may render the contract impossible to perform if it can be shown that the contract calls for a special skill or talent possessed by the deceased or ill person. Such personal-service contracts were discussed in Chapter 14.

EXAMPLE 15.6

▶ Iverson, a concert pianist, had a contract to perform at a summer music festival. Before the concert she was stricken with a paralytic stroke and was unable to perform. Because this was a personal-service contract, she was excused from the contract.

On the other hand, a personal-service contract that does not call for a special skill or talent possessed by the deceased or ill person does not excuse performance.

EXAMPLE 15.7

▶ Jackanski, a house painter, had been hired to paint Rollins's colonial-style house. He had already begun work when he fell from a ladder and broke his back. The period of convalescence was estimated at one year. Jackanski is still responsible for painting the house because the skill required is not unique. The court would probably rule that Jackanski could assign the work to another painter—even though the cost might result in a loss to Jackanski.

frustration of purpose
A doctrine that states that where both parties know the purpose of a contract and, through no fault of either party, the reason for the contract no longer exists, the contract is terminated.

FRUSTRATION OF PURPOSE

Closely related to impossibility is the doctrine of frustration of purpose. Where both parties know the purpose of a contract and, through no fault of either party, the reason for the contract no longer exists, the contract is terminated.

EXAMPLE 15.8

▶ Gould contracted with Foxen Limo Services for a chauffer-driven limousine to a nearby city to view game 7 of the World Series. Both parties knew that the purpose of the trip was to attend the baseball game. The series ended four games to two in game 6, and game 7 was never played. Since the purpose of the ride was frustrated and because Gould likely would no longer want to use the limousine company's services, he can terminate the contract.

material alteration
A deliberate change or alteration of an important element in a written contract that affects the rights or obligations of the parties.

15.5 TERMINATION BY ALTERATION

A deliberate change or alteration of an important element in a written contract that affects the rights or obligations of the parties is known as a material alteration and results in termination of the contract.

EXAMPLE 15.9

▶ Perry agreed to buy a vacant lot from Serio for $18,600. When the parties were to close the transaction, it was discovered that the contract to purchase had been changed by Serio to $19,600. Her illegal act of changing the contract not only terminated the contract, but also made Serio subject to criminal prosecution for the crime of forgery.

15.6 TERMINATION BY OPERATION OF LAW

If a law or regulation makes the performance of a contract illegal, the contract is void from the beginning. In fact, there is no contract. If, however, a law is passed *after* the parties enter into a contract that makes performance illegal, the contract is terminated by operation of law.

EXAMPLE 15.10

▶ Burlington, a dealer in shrubbery and trees, agreed with DaVall, a grower in a foreign country, to import several hundred decorative shrubs. To prevent the spread of a plant disease, the U.S. Department of Agriculture enforced a newly created embargo on this variety of shrub and refused to allow the shipment into the country. The parties are released from the agreement because of termination by operation of law.

Laws and regulations that increase the cost of performance, however, do not absolve the parties from their contractual obligations.

Suppose, in Example 15.10, that a new regulation had been passed that required special packaging for imported plants and that this packaging increased the total cost of the plants. In this case, the seller would not be relieved of her obligations, even if the added cost meant that she would lose money on the transaction.

15.7 TERMINATION BY BREACH OF CONTRACT

A breach of contract occurs when a party to a contract refuses to perform as required by the contract or performs in an unsatisfactory manner. There are three common ways in which contracts are breached:

> **breach of contract**
> When a party to a contract refuses to perform as required by the contract or performs in an unsatisfactory manner.

- ▶ Anticipatory breach, sometimes referred to as anticipatory repudiation.
- ▶ Breach resulting from a deliberate or negligent act.
- ▶ Failure to perform an obligation.

ANTICIPATORY BREACH

A party who announces an intention to break a contract is said to create an anticipatory breach. He or she has given notice of intention to break the contract even before being required to perform. Court decisions have allowed the injured party to bring suit for damages at the time of the announcement and have not required the party to wait until the time for performance has passed.

> **anticipatory breach**
> When a party to a contract announces his or her intention to break the contract in the future.

EXAMPLE 15.11

▶ Zikmund, an actress, had agreed to appear in a supporting role in a play scheduled to open on February 1. On December 1, she announced that she would not be available because she had been given a starring role in a motion picture. The producer has a right to initiate a suit on December 1 for anticipatory breach without waiting for the time the contract was to start.

When one party has received notice from the other party of intent to breach, he or she cannot continue with the performance of the work or service covered by the contract; doing so would only increase the amount of damages. When a party breaches a contract, the injured party has the duty to mitigate, or lessen, the amount of damages.

> **mitigate**
> The obligation of the injured party to protect the other party from any unnecessary damages.

EXAMPLE 15.12

▶ Ebersol hired Weston Restorers to restore a 1936 Chevrolet to classic car condition. While Weston was still ordering and manufacturing needed parts, Ebersol announced that he had changed his mind and intended to breach the contract. Weston cannot continue restoring the car and later sue for a greater amount than if he had stopped work at the time when Ebersol breached. He can sue only for damages suffered up to the time he was notified of the anticipatory breach.

The law regarding anticipatory breach does not apply to promises to pay money at some future date.

promissory note
A written promise to pay a specified sum of money.

The law regarding anticipatory breach does not apply to promises to pay money at some future date. A person who renounces an obligation to pay on a promissory note (a written promise to pay a specified sum of money) cannot be sued until after the due date of the first payment on the note, even if such person announces his or her intention to breach before the first payment is due.

BREACH RESULTING FROM A DELIBERATE OR NEGLIGENT ACT

A contract is breached if one party deliberately or negligently stands in the way of performance. For example, if a party who has agreed to sell certain perishable foods negligently allows them to become damaged by freezing, he or she has breached the contract.

EXAMPLE 15.13

▶ Herrera hired Kotley to conduct marketing research at a shopping mall. They agreed that Kotley would interview shoppers selected at random and conduct a survey using a questionnaire. Before the interviews began, Herrera changed his mind and destroyed the questionnaires. The contract was breached by Herrera's deliberate act. Herrera is subject to Kotley's suit for damages—the agreed fee to be paid to Kotley.

FAILURE TO PERFORM AN OBLIGATION

A party who fails to perform contractual obligations, within the time specified or within a reasonable time, has breached the contract. The breach occurs whether the party has completely or partially failed to perform. In the case of complete failure, the contract is terminated. Partial failure to perform may require the nonbreaching party to pay for the work that has already been completed. However, suppose that in Example 15.13, Kotley did have access to the questionnaires but conducted only half the number he had agreed to do. In this situation, it is doubtful that partial work (a survey with only half the responses) would have much, if any, value to Herrera.

15.8 TERMINATION TO PROTECT A CONSUMER

To protect consumers against their own impulsiveness and various questionable sales techniques, a number of federal, state, and local laws and regulations allow consumers to terminate a contract under certain conditions. For example, the federal Consumer Credit Protection Act gives a consumer the right to cancel a credit transaction within three days when the contract requires that the consumer pledge his or her home as a security deposit. Similarly, a Federal Trade Commission (FTC) regulation gives the consumer a "cooling-off" period of three days and the right to cancel contracts for either goods or services made in the consumer's home and to receive a full refund.

15.9 REMEDIES FOR BREACH OF CONTRACT

Each party to a contract has the right to expect complete and satisfactory performance. When such performance is not made, the injured party may sue to recover *compensatory damages,* a sum of money that will compensate for his or her loss. In all such claims for damages, the injured party must determine the damage in terms of money, and the court will determine if the claim is fair and adequate. Compensatory damages are intended to return the injured party to the same position he or she was in before the contract was breached.

EXAMPLE 15.14

▶ Namsang was to be married, and he and his fiancée planned a large reception. After inspecting several restaurants and catering halls, they reached an agreement with Westport Villa for the use of the facilities and for the food and beverage service. A week before the event, Westport canceled the contract, claiming that they had overlooked an earlier commitment. Namsang found alternative facilities but for a fee $1,300 higher. After the event, Namsang sued for damages of $1,300—the difference between the contract price and the higher fee he had to pay as a result of Westport's breach. A court would likely rule in Namsang's favor for $1,300.

Occasionally a court may award *consequential damages* to a plaintiff. Consequential damages are monetary compensation for losses resulting from the special circumstances of a plaintiff that are foreseeable by both parties to a contract. Suppose a contractor breaches a contract by not completing the renovations to a business on time. In this example, the special circumstance is that the business cannot operate while the renovation is taking place. In such a case, a court may award consequential damages to the business to compensate for revenues lost as a result of the business remaining closed.

A court may also award *nominal damages* to a plaintiff in a case where he or she incurred no actual damages as a result of a breach of contract on the part of a defendant.

Nominal damages are small monetary awards, typically $1, that serve to indicate that a plaintiff was wronged by a defendant.

At times, the parties include a statement right in their contract wherein damages are explicitly set in the event one of the parties breaches the agreement. Such a statement is called a liquidated damages clause. Courts will generally enforce liquidated damages clauses provided the damages specified are closely related to the actual damages. Courts will usually not enforce these if the specified damages amount to a penalty or forfeiture.

liquidated damages clause

A statement wherein damages are explicitly set in the event one of the parties breaches an agreement.

SPECIFIC PERFORMANCE

Sometimes a judgment of money damages will not really repay an injured party for a breach of contract. In some cases, the injured party may sue for specific performance—that is, a court order directing a person to perform as he or she agreed to do. To obtain an order of specific performance, the injured party asks the court to order the other party to do what he or she promised to do. For example, if a contract is made for the sale of some unique item, such as an antique, an original painting, or real estate, the buyer can bring an action for specific performance if the seller attempts to breach the contract. A court order for specific performance serves as a remedy in cases in which an award of money damages for a breach of contract cannot adequately compensate the injured party.

specific performance

A court order directing a person to perform—or not perform—as he or she agreed to do in a contract.

Courts almost never order specific performance of a contract for personal services, partly because it is difficult to ensure the performance of someone who is being forced to work after a dispute, in that any loyalty or normal relationship is nearly impossible to achieve. Also, courts do not wish to impose what might be viewed as involuntary servitude.

An order for specific performance may be obtained not only in cases of breach of contract for the sale of unique goods or real estate, but also in cases where the purchaser is not able to obtain the goods called for by the contract elsewhere.

EXAMPLE 15.15

▶ Resol bought and remodeled a restaurant and named it the Packard Roadster. He contracted with Timmons, a collector of classic cars, to purchase a 1932 Packard for $27,000, which he planned to display in the front window of the restaurant. He also registered the restaurant name, had signs made, and ran advertising announcing the grand opening. Sensing an opportunity to sell the vehicle to another buyer for a higher price, Timmons attempted to cancel the contract. Since Resol could not obtain the vehicle elsewhere, he sought an action of specific performance that required Timmons to sell the car as Timmons had agreed to do. Because the product is unique, the court would likely grant the decree of specific performance that Resol requested.

restraining order

A court order prohibiting the performance of a certain act. In some states, a restraining order is temporary.

injunction

A permanent court order prohibiting the performance of a certain act.

RESTRAINING ORDER OR INJUNCTION

Whereas a decree of specific performance is a court order requiring the performance of a certain act, a restraining order, or injunction, is a court order prohibiting the performance of a certain act. In some states, a restraining order is temporary and an injunction is permanent.

EXAMPLE 15.16

▶ Segal sold a heavily wooded parcel of land to Hargett, who claimed that he wanted to use it as a hunting preserve. Hargett agreed to refrain from cutting the trees down for a period of 15 years. One year after the sale, Hargett decided to build a shopping mall on the property, which would require cutting down the trees. Segal began legal action but was concerned that the trees would be destroyed by the time the case was heard. She therefore sought a temporary restraining order to stop all work at the site until the case could be heard.

If, as a result of the legal action taken by Segal, it was found that Hargett had indeed violated his contract, the court could replace the temporary restraining order with a permanent injunction. That would bar Hargett from cutting the trees down for the period specified by the contract. If Hargett failed to obey either the temporary restraining order or the permanent injunction, his actions could result in his being found to be in contempt of court. He could then be fined or even imprisoned.

CHAPTER SUMMARY

1. Contracts may be terminated by (1) agreement, (2) performance, (3) impossibility of performance, (4) alteration, (5) operation of law, (6) breach, and (7) laws and regulations protecting the consumer.

2. A contract can be terminated by agreement if both parties agree that it should end.

3. The three types of termination by performance are (a) substantial performance, in which the contract has been largely completed and only small details remain; (b) performance by payment of money, in which the agreed-upon payment has been paid; and (c) tender of performance, in which there has been an offer to pay the required sum or to perform the required acts.

4. Contracts can be terminated by impossibility of performance when unforeseen circumstances make it impossible to fulfill the terms of a contract as originally agreed.

5. Termination by alteration occurs when an important element in a written contract that affects the rights or obligations of the parties is changed.

6. A contract can be terminated by operation of law if a law passed after the parties entered into a contract makes performance illegal.

7. Contracts terminated by breach occur when a party to a contract refuses to perform as required by the contract or performs in an unsatisfactory manner. Three common ways in which contracts are breached are by (a) anticipatory breach, (b) a deliberate or negligent act, and (c) failure to perform an obligation.

8. Some contracts can be terminated to protect consumers because the law hopes to protect them against their own impulsiveness, questionable sales techniques, and similar problems. For example, the Consumer Credit Protection Act of 1968 gives consumers the right to cancel a credit transaction within three days when the contract requires that the consumer pledge his or her home as a security deposit. Similarly, an FTC regulation gives consumers a "cooling-off" period of three days and the right to cancel contracts made in the consumer's home and to receive a full refund.

9. The remedy of specific performance is a court order that a person perform as he or she agreed to do. The remedy of injunction is a court order that prohibits performance of a certain act.

CHAPTER FIFTEEN
ASSESSMENT

MATCHING LEGAL TERMS

Match each of the numbered definitions with the correct term in the following list. Write the letter of your choice in the answer column.

a. anticipatory breach
b. impossibility of performance
c. material alteration
d. mitigation
e. promissory note
f. specific performance
g. restraining order or injunction
h. substantial performance
i. tender of payment
j. tender of performance

1. A written promise to pay a specified sum of money.   1. _____

2. The completion of a contract except for some small details.   2. _____

3. A change of an important term in a contract that affects the rights or obligations of the parties.   3. _____

4. An offer to perform acts required by a contract.   4. _____

5. An offer of payment made to fulfill the terms of a contract.   5. _____

6. Inability to fulfill the terms of a contract due to unforeseen circumstances.   6. _____

7. Cancellation of a contract due to an announcement of intention to breach prior to the time performance is due.   7. _____

8. A court decree that prohibits the performance of a certain act.   8. _____

9. A court order that directs that a certain act be carried out.   9. _____

10. The duty of an injured party to lessen the amount of damages.   10. _____

TRUE/FALSE QUIZ

Indicate whether each of the following statements is true or false by writing *T* or *F* in the answer column.

11. A contract can be terminated in accordance with provisions in the contract itself.   11. _____

12. A consumer can terminate a contract made in the home with a door-to-door salesperson within three days.   12. _____

13. Complete and satisfactory performance of a contract will bring about its termination.   13. _____

14. A contract must be completely performed in all its details in order to be considered terminated.

14. _____

15. A tender of performance does not relieve a contracting party of his or her obligation to perform.

15. _____

16. A consumer has three days to cancel a contract in which his or her home has been pledged as security.

16. _____

17. Death or disabling illness of a party to a contract terminates the contract if such requires the particular skill or talent of the contracting party.

17. _____

18. A deliberate material alteration of a contract that affects the rights or obligations of the parties is cause for termination of the contract.

18. _____

19. If a law or regulation makes the performance of a contract illegal, the parties are released from their obligations.

19. _____

20. A party to a contract is released from his or her obligations if a law is passed that increases the cost of performing the contract.

20. _____

21. Except for promissory notes, the injured party in a contract may bring suit whenever he or she receives notice that the other party intends to breach the contract.

21. _____

22. A contract is breached if one party deliberately or negligently stands in the way of satisfactory performance.

22. _____

23. When one party to a contract receives notice of the other party's intent to breach, he or she may continue with the performance of work or service covered by the contract, complete such work or service, and then sue for the entire amount of damages.

23. _____

24. An action for specific performance is a request that the court direct a party to perform a particular act agreed upon in a contract.

24. _____

25. A court order directing a person to refrain from performing a particular act is an injunction.

25. _____

DISCUSSION QUESTIONS

Answer the following questions and discuss them in class.

26. Discuss termination of a contract by agreement.

_____

_____

27. Explain how a contract is terminated by performance.

_____

_____

28. Provide an example of a contract terminated by impossibility of performance.

_____

_____

29. Explain how a contract might be terminated by breach.

_____

_____

30. Explain how a contract might be terminated to protect a consumer.

_____

_____

31. Discuss the remedies of specific performance and injunction.

_____

_____

THINKING CRITICALLY ABOUT THE LAW

Answer the following questions, which require you to think critically about the legal principles that you learned in this chapter.

32. Termination by Performance Contract termination by performance seems so final. Do you think that the parties to a contract should be given an opportunity to change their minds if circumstances change after the required performance? Why or why not?

_____

_____

33. Termination by Impossibility of Performance At times, one of the parties to a contract terminated by impossibility of performance suffers some injury or loss as a result. Should the law recognize this possibility and provide some form of redress?

_____

_____

34. **Termination by Breach** The law provides a remedy for a party injured by the breach of a contract. But the usual remedy, a lawsuit that awards money damages, does not always give the injured party the level of redress appropriate to the situation. What other remedies are available, and how effective are they?

_____

_____

35. **Personal-Service Contracts** Death or disabling illness of a party to a personal-service contract requiring a special skill or talent terminates the contract. How would a concert promoter, who had sold tickets and rented a hall, protect against a loss that would likely result from the termination of a contract with a renowned pianist?

_____

_____

36. **A Question of Ethics** To protect consumers against their own impulsiveness and various questionable sales techniques, a number of federal, state, and local laws and regulations allow consumers to terminate a contract under certain conditions. Is it ethical for a consumer to take advantage of this protection, when his or her own good judgment should have suggested avoidance of the contract?

_____

_____

CASE QUESTIONS

Study each of the following cases. Answer the questions that follow by writing *Yes* or *No* in the answer column.

37. **Termination to Protect a Consumer** Bushek signed a contract with Aluminum Window Products Company to replace the windows and wooden window frames of his house with new ones made of aluminum. The salesperson asked Bushek to sign a "routine form" to help ensure that credit would be granted. The following day he read the "routine form" and discovered that he had, in fact, pledged the entire house as security, and if he defaulted on payments, the house could be taken from him.

    a. Is the contract Bushek signed legal?   a. _____

    b. Does Bushek have the right to cancel the contract?   b. _____

    c. If Bushek decides to cancel the contract, is he liable for damages?   c. _____

38. **Substantial Performance** Central City Garage Builders contracted with Morgan for the construction of a two-car garage and an attached greenhouse of similar size. The garage was built on schedule, but, because of a shortage of special

materials, it appeared that the construction of the greenhouse would be delayed for several months. Central City requested payment for the entire contract.

a. Does Central City have a legitimate claim that it had performed substantially?

a. _____

b. Can Central City claim that it was prevented from completing the project because of impossibility of performance?

b. _____

c. Would Central City have a right to request payment for the portion of the contract that was completed?

c. _____

39. **Revoked Contract** Scher, a home owner, purchased a vacuum cleaner from a door-to-door salesperson. When the salesperson demonstrated the machine in her home, it seemed to work quite effectively. After signing the contract, she checked several consumer magazines at the public library and learned that the company was noted for its deceptive practices and that the demonstration machine was specially constructed and not the same type the consumer gets.

a. Does Scher have the opportunity to terminate the contract?

a. _____

b. Was the contract Scher signed a valid one?

b. _____

c. Is the contract voidable?

c. _____

40. **Termination by Breach** Chiu agreed to sell his custom-built sailboat to Graham for $60,000. Before delivery, Chiu received another offer for $68,000 and wrote to Graham that he had decided not to sell his boat after all.

a. Can Graham obtain a decree of specific performance?

a. _____

b. Would a suit for money damages completely satisfy Graham?

b. _____

c. Can Chiu avoid Graham's suit by claiming that he was merely selling to the highest bidder?

c. _____

CASE ANALYSIS

Study each of the following cases carefully. Briefly state the principle of law and your decision.

41. **Impossibility of Performance** Bunge, a grain dealer, contracted with Recker, a farmer, to purchase 10,000 bushels of soybeans at $3.35 per bushel. The contract did not specify where the beans were to have been grown, except that they were to be grown in the United States. As a result of crop failure, Recker was unable to deliver the beans, even with several extensions of the deadline. Finally, Recker admitted that he could not deliver, claiming impossibility of performance. In the meantime, the market price had increased from $3.35, the agreed price, to $5.50 at the time agreed for delivery. Bunge sued for the difference between $3.35 and the market price at the time agreed for delivery. Will Recker be excused from his contractual obligations, or should he be held responsible for delivering as agreed? [*Bunge Corp. v. Recker*, 519 F.2d 449 (8th Cir.)]

Principle of Law:

_____

_____

Decision:

_____

_____

42. **Termination by Agreement** Laclede Gas Company purchased propane gas from Amoco Oil Company and sold it to various residential subdivisions. After the contract had been in operation for some time, Amoco refused to supply any more gas. Laclede was unable to find another supplier willing to enter into a long-term contract such as Laclede had with Amoco. Management of Laclede felt that money damages would not provide a reasonable settlement. What would be a reasonable resolution of Laclede's problem? [*Laclede Gas Co. v. Amoco Oil Co.*, 522 F.2d 33 (8th Cir.)]

Principle of Law:

_____

_____

Decision:

_____

_____

43. **Termination by Performance** Blackburn, a painting contractor, agreed in writing to paint DeSoto's house for a certain price. After the house was painted, DeSoto asked Blackburn to paint his garage. Blackburn had other painting jobs scheduled and refused the additional work. DeSoto felt that his offer of additional work was entitled to higher priority. Is DeSoto correct that the completed contract should entitle him to a higher priority?

Principle of Law:

_____

_____

Decision:

_____

_____

44. **Termination by Breach** Dahl, the owner of a machine shop, agreed to manufacture 22 valves for $460 each for Capobianco. When 6 valves were finished and shipped, Capobianco advised Dahl of his intention to cancel the contract. Dahl went

on to build the remaining valves according to the contract. Will Dahl be successful in his suit for the entire amount?

Principle of Law:

_____

_____

Decision:

_____

_____

LEGAL RESEARCH

Complete the following activities. Share your findings with the class.

45. **Working in Teams** In teams of three or four, interview owners or managers of small businesses to learn some typical contracts in which the firms have been involved and how they were terminated.

_____

_____

46. **Using Technology** Using the Internet and search engines, investigate the Federal Trade Commission's website to learn when contracts may be terminated to protect the consumer.

_____

_____

PART 3

Sales, Agency, and Business Organizations

chapter 16
Transfer of Title

LEARNING OUTCOMES

After studying this chapter and completing the assessment, you will be able to

16.1 Explain how title and certificate of title relate to the concept of ownership.

16.2 Distinguish between the two main types of property, and indicate which one is subject to the law of sales.

16.3 Describe how title passes and discuss how bills of sale, bills of lading, and warehouse receipts are involved in the passing of title.

16.4 Explain when title to goods passes.

16.5 Define the term *conditional sales* and identify the two types of conditions found in contracts for conditional sales.

16.6 Explain the law governing title to lost or stolen goods.

16.7 Define the principle of estoppel and provide examples of how this principle is applied in various situations.

16.8 Discuss sales by persons with possession of, but not title to, goods.

16.9 Describe the passage of title to fungible goods.

LEGAL terms

- title
- bill of sale
- bill of lading
- straight bill of lading
- order bill of lading
- warehouse receipt
- nonnegotiable warehouse receipt
- negotiable warehouse receipt
- conditional sale
- conditions precedent
- conditions subsequent
- estoppel
- remote party
- wrongful possession
- fungible goods

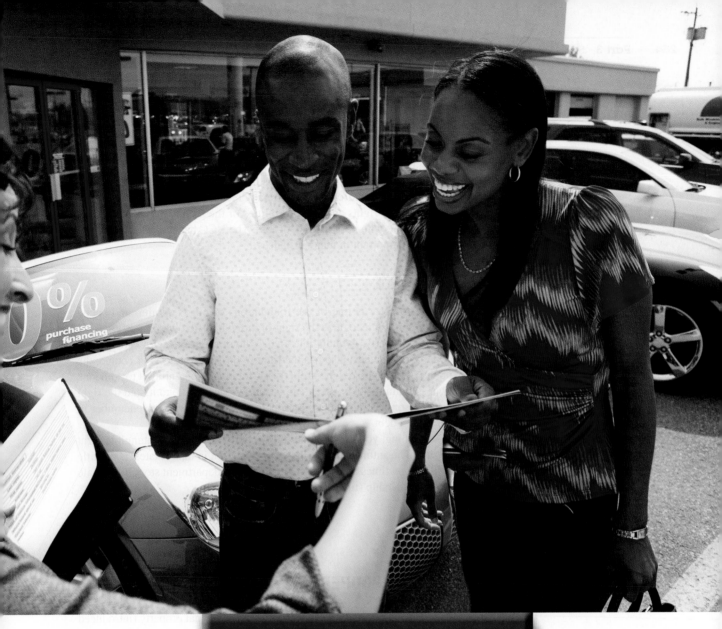

TRANSFER OF TITLE

"Is it not lawful for me to do what
I will with mine own?"

The Bible,
Matthew 20:15

16.1 TITLE

Many business transactions that involve disputes are like a game of musical chairs. The person who is left standing when the music stops is the one who loses. Similarly, legal disputes often involve the determination of who holds title when a loss occurs.

Prior to the adoption of the Uniform Commercial Code (UCC), the concept of title was crucial in determining the rights and responsibilities of the parties to a contract and, perhaps even more important, who bore the risk of loss. The UCC has reduced the significance of title, but it is still important in many instances.

THE RIGHT OF OWNERSHIP

The concept of private property is one of the foundations of our economic and social system. The laws of our country recognize the right of individuals to own property.

title
Ownership and the right to possess something.

Title, as it relates to property, is intangible—you cannot see it or feel it. The person who has title to property (the owner) also has the right to possess it unless, of course, the person has given up the right to possess the property by, for example, renting it to someone else. Thus if you own something—a house, a car, a suit—you have title to it, and the right to sell it. Moreover, a person who has title to a property also has the right to encumber it, or offer it as collateral for a debt.

When you sell something, you sell not only the property but also the intangible right of ownership called *title.* The automobile *certificate of title,* used in many states, is not title but rather proof of title. Sometimes an exchange of letters or a department store bill of sale can be used as proof of ownership (title).

16.2 KINDS OF PROPERTY

The two main classifications of property are real property and personal property (introduced in Chapter 13).

REAL PROPERTY

Real property, sometimes referred to as real estate, is land and all articles permanently attached to it, such as buildings and trees.

PERSONAL PROPERTY

Personal property is all property other than real property, such as automobiles, clothing, computers, and so on. Personal property can be tangible—that is, it can be seen and touched, like the examples just cited; or it can be intangible, such as patents, copyrights, or ownership in a corporation, which cannot be seen or touched. Only personal property—tangible or intangible—is affected by the law of sales and the UCC. Real property is governed by a separate branch of law, to be covered in Chapter 24. Sales of services do not involve either real or personal property; and contracts for such services are considered ordinary contracts.

16.3   HOW TITLE PASSES

There are a variety of ways in which title can pass. Involved in the passage of title are the legal concepts of bill of sale, bill of lading, and warehouse receipt.

BILL OF SALE

A bill of sale is simply a written statement that the seller is passing ownership to the buyer. The bill of sale need not be an elaborate legal document—a handwritten note is just as effective. The important thing to remember is that the description of the goods should be as complete as possible. For example, if you bought a computer from a neighbor, a simple note describing the goods involved in the transaction as "a computer" would probably be adequate. However, if the note included a more complete description, such as "one Apple MacBook Pro, 13 inch: 2.66 GHz, Serial No. 175274," you would be further protected from a claim of ownership by another person.

bill of sale
A written statement that the seller is passing ownership to the buyer.

BILL OF LADING

A bill of lading is a receipt for goods to be shipped, acknowledging that such goods have been received and indicating agreement that the goods will be transported to the destination specified. The bill of lading is prepared by the common carrier, such as a trucking firm, a railroad, or an ocean liner, that has agreed by contract to transport the goods by land or water. In the case of goods shipped by air, an *airbill* is prepared. One copy of the document is signed by the common carrier—when the carrier accepts the goods for shipment.

There are two kinds of bills of lading. The most common is a straight bill of lading, which is simply a receipt but is not negotiable. An order bill of lading, in addition to being a receipt, is negotiable; that is, the order bill of lading is proof of title and can be used to transfer title from one person to another. Such a negotiable order bill of lading can be used to ensure that the carrier will not deliver the goods until the receiver surrenders the original copy of the order bill of lading to the carrier. Because it would be nearly impossible for anyone to possess the original order bill of lading without the shipper's agreeing to it, such a document is proof of ownership. Bills of lading are covered by Article 7 of the UCC.

bill of lading
A receipt for goods to be shipped, acknowledging that such goods have been received and indicating agreement that the goods will be transported to the destination specified.

straight bill of lading
A nonnegotiable receipt for goods to be shipped, acknowledging that such goods have been received and indicating agreement that the goods will be transported to the destination specified.

order bill of lading
A receipt for goods to be shipped that is negotiable and is proof of title that can be used to transfer title from one person to another.

EXAMPLE 16.1

▶ Global Art Importer in New York agreed through a series of e-mail messages to sell 15 expensive paintings to an art gallery in Peoria, Illinois. Global Art received an order bill of lading from the trucking line, turned over the shipment, and notified the Peoria art gallery that the paintings were being shipped. The shipper gave the original order bill of lading to its bank, which in turn sent it to a cooperating bank in Peoria. The Peoria art gallery was instructed by e-mail to pay the agreed-upon sales price for the merchandise to the Peoria bank in order to obtain the original copy of the order bill of lading. When the Peoria art gallery paid the money to the bank, it was given the original order bill of lading, which it then surrendered to the trucking firm upon delivery of the artwork.

A warehouse receipt is used for goods that are being stored.

warehouse receipt
Much like a bill of lading except that the goods are not being shipped but merely stored.

nonnegotiable warehouse receipt
A receipt for the goods to be stored.

negotiable warehouse receipt
Proof of ownership that can be used to transfer title from one person to another.

WAREHOUSE RECEIPT

A warehouse receipt is much like a bill of lading except that the goods involved are not being transported but merely stored. There are two kinds of warehouse receipts. A nonnegotiable warehouse receipt is like a straight bill of lading—it is simply a receipt for the goods to be stored. A negotiable warehouse receipt, like the negotiable order bill of lading, requires that the original copy be presented to the warehouser before the goods will be surrendered to someone claiming them. Also, like an order bill of lading, a negotiable warehouse receipt is proof of ownership.

Suppose that, in Example 16.1, the purchaser of the artwork was located in the same community as the manufacturer. The transaction would be similar to the one in the preceding case. The warehouser would play the same role as the trucking line, but a cooperating bank would probably not be involved in the transaction.

16.4 WHEN TITLE PASSES

Title to goods passes when the parties intend for it to pass. In the event that the intent of the parties is not clear, title passes at the moment when they unconditionally agree to sell specific goods that are in a deliverable state.

INTENT

Since, in the eyes of the law, title passes when the parties intend it to pass, how does a party prove what he or she intended? Suppose that a person bought a boat and arranged to pick it up the following day. Before the buyer had a chance to pick it up, the boat was destroyed by fire. Quite likely, the seller would claim that he intended title to pass at the time of the transaction, thus insisting that the buyer bear the loss. The buyer, on the other hand, would probably say that he intended title to pass when he picked up the boat, arguing that the seller should bear the loss. To minimize the number of such disagreements, certain rules for determining the intent of the parties have been established.

EXAMPLE 16.2

▶ Castelli agreed to purchase Piak's car for $18,000. They both agreed that Castelli would return the following day with license plates and take delivery of the vehicle. In the eyes of the law, title passed at the time of agreement, even though the parties may have taken a few minutes to complete the necessary written documents, such as a bill of sale and the check for payment of the car.

SPECIFIC TIME

Although it may take some time to complete the documents that signify the passing of title, title itself passes in a single instant. While both parties are free to create a contract that stipulates precisely when the transfer of title passes, the law does provide guidelines as to when this occurs.

16.5 CONDITIONAL SALES

A conditional sale is one with contract provisions that specify conditions that must be met by one of the parties. The two types of conditions found in contracts for conditional sales are conditions precedent and conditions subsequent.

conditional sale
A sale with contract provisions that specify conditions that must be met by one of the parties.

CONDITIONS PRECEDENT

When a sales contract provides that specific conditions must be met before title passes, the agreement contains conditions precedent.

Suppose that in Example 16.2, Castelli agreed to purchase Piak's car if Piak had new tires installed. Title would pass when the tires were installed. If anything had happened to the car before the tires were installed, Piak would bear the loss.

conditions precedent
Conditions in a sales contract that must be met before title passes.

CONDITIONS SUBSEQUENT

When a sales contract provides that specific conditions must be met after title has passed, it is said to contain conditions subsequent. A right-of-return provision in a sales contract is an example of a condition subsequent that gives the buyer the right to *revest*, or transfer back, title to the seller if the buyer is not satisfied after making the purchase.

Returning to the case of Castelli and Piak in Example 16.2, suppose that the parties agreed that Castelli would purchase the car but would have the right to return it to Piak if it did not have enough power to pull a travel trailer that Castelli had ordered. Whether the car would be adequate for this purpose would not be known until the trailer was delivered. If the sales contract included this condition and upon delivery of the trailer it was discovered that the car did not have enough power, Piak would be obliged to take the car back and title would be revested in her.

conditions subsequent
Conditions in a sales contract that must be met after title has passed.

16.6 LOST AND STOLEN GOODS

When a person possesses an item, ownership is presumed, but it is possible to have possession of goods without having title, just as it is possible to have title without having possession.

A person who finds an article has good title against anyone except the true owner. Anyone who buys an article from someone who has found it must be prepared to surrender the article to the true owner. However, it is often difficult to prove ownership of a lost article. Local police departments and insurance agents' associations have mounted campaigns to help people identify their property with the use of a tool that engraves identifying information on property. They also have encouraged persons to retain receipts with model and serial numbers of valuable personal property.

EXAMPLE 16.3

▶ Fortuna, while on a business trip, left a laptop computer in an airline waiting room, where it was found by Moreno. Because the computer had a serial number that matched the one on her bill of sale, Fortuna was able to prove ownership and recover her property.

A thief has no title to goods he or she has stolen, and therefore cannot pass title to anyone else. The real owner of stolen goods has not passed title to anyone, and even an innocent purchaser who bought the stolen items in good faith would have to return them to the original owner.

16.7 TRANSFER OF TITLE BY ESTOPPEL

estoppel
A legal bar to using contradictory words or acts in asserting a claim against another.

Under certain circumstances, it is possible for title to goods to be passed by a nonowner who does not have title. In these cases, title is said to pass by estoppel. Estoppel is a legal bar to the use of contradictory words or acts in asserting a claim against another. As the concept of estoppel is used in discussions of title, the titleholder is estopped—legally prevented—from claiming ownership of the property as a result of certain actions taken by the titleholder. UCC 2-202 and UCC 2-403 deal with the rights of persons who acquire questionable title.

For title to pass by estoppel, the purchaser must be able to prove the following:

1. The purchase was made in good faith. That is, the buyer believed the seller to be the real owner or one appointed to act for the real owner.

2. The purchase was made from one in rightful possession.

3. Value was given by the buyer for that which he or she now claims ownership under the principle of estoppel.

EXAMPLES OF ESTOPPEL

The following are examples of how the principle of estoppel is applied.

Transfer of Money or Commercial Paper Made Out to Bearer When the owner of cash or commercial paper, such as a check, makes it payable to bearer, who then gives it to a third person, the original owner cannot demand the return of the money from a third party to whom it was given in exchange for something of value (see Chapter 22).

EXAMPLE 16.4

▶ Schultz gave his brother-in-law, Robb, $150 cash and asked him to buy a DVD player because Robb could use his employee discount. Instead Robb bought himself a suit. Schultz cannot demand the return of the cash from the person who sold the suit.

Transfer of Property to a Seller Dealing in the Same Type of Goods When the owner of goods entrusts property to a person who sells the same type of goods and that person sells the property to an innocent third party, the owner is estopped from recovering the goods from the third party.

EXAMPLE 16.5

▶ Unger left a power lawnmower at a garden shop for repair and service, and the owner of the shop inadvertently sold the mower to another customer. Unger would be estopped from recovering the mower from the purchaser, an innocent third party. Unger can, however, sue the owner of the garden shop for the value of the mower.

Transfer of Property to a Seller Permitted to Appear as the Real Owner   If the owner of property gives possession of it to a second party and allows that person to act as the real owner, the rightful owner cannot recover the property if the second party sells the property to an innocent third party.

Suppose that Unger, in Example 16.5, borrowed a lawnmower from his neighbor to use while his own was being repaired. Without permission, Unger then sold the borrowed mower to a gardener who was working on his lawn. The neighbor would be estopped from recovering the lawnmower from the gardener. However, the neighbor could bring legal action against Unger.

Transfer of Proof of Ownership to an Unauthorized Seller   If the owner of goods entrusts proof of ownership to someone in possession of the goods, the goods cannot be recovered by the true owner from an innocent purchaser.

Returning again to Example 16.5 regarding Unger and the lawnmower, suppose that the neighbor who loaned the mower to Unger also gave him the bill of sale (proof of ownership). If Unger then sold the mower to another neighbor, the rightful owner would be estopped from recovering the mower from the innocent purchaser because Unger, the unauthorized seller, had proof of ownership.

remote party
A person with the right to make legitimate sales as a representative of the owner of the goods, although he or she is not a titleholder.

wrongful possession
When property, such as stolen goods, is transferred without permission of the owner.

16.8 SALES BY PERSONS HAVING POSSESSION

There are instances when individuals have possession of goods, but not title to them, and sell these goods to third persons.

A salesperson in a grocery store is known as a remote party.

SALES BY PERSONS HAVING RIGHTFUL POSSESSION

A salesperson in a retail store, service station, restaurant, and so on is known as a remote party. Such individuals have the right to make legitimate sales as representatives of the owner of the goods, although they themselves are not titleholders. A salesperson has the express or implied permission of the titleholder of the merchandise to sell it. Agents acting on behalf of principals can pass title without holding title themselves (see Chapter 19).

SALES BY PERSONS HAVING WRONGFUL POSSESSION

Unlike the situations described previously, in which possession of goods was transferred with the permission of the owner, situations of wrongful possession occur when property, such as stolen goods, is transferred without permission of the owner. The titleholder, or rightful owner, of stolen goods is never estopped. That is, he or she is never prevented from exercising a claim to the goods, even if the person in possession of them is an innocent purchaser of the property.

EXAMPLE 16.6

▶ Brilley, a shipping clerk employed by Rexeer Auto Parts, stole an automobile engine and sold it to a friend, Petras. After Rexeer Auto discharged Brilley, the owners suspected that Petras had possession of the stolen engine, which they could prove was their property by its serial number. With the aid of the police, they recovered the stolen engine. Even if Petras had sold the engine to Jones, who sold it to Smith, Rexeer Auto could recover the property at any point when it could be found because Rexeer Auto never lost title to it.

16.9 TRANSFER OF TITLE TO FUNGIBLE GOODS

fungible goods
Goods that are generally sold by weight or measure.

Fungible goods are those that are generally sold by weight or measure. Examples include wheat, sugar, flour, gasoline, oil, and so on. A unit of such goods is like any other unit. Consequently, 1,000 gallons of No. 2 fuel oil in a storage tank that holds many thousands of gallons are exactly like all the other gallons of No. 2 oil in the tank. Nevertheless, it is important to determine when title to such fungible goods passes. Generally, the following rules apply:

▶ If goods are ordered and the building, tank, storage yard, or grain elevator from which they are to come is not specified, this general rule of title passing applies: Title passes when the goods become ascertained—that is, when they become clearly identifiable. As a result, when a person simply orders 1,000 gallons of No. 2 fuel oil, title passes when the 1,000 gallons are delivered or at least separated from the larger mass.

▶ If a buyer orders a specific quantity of fungible goods from a specific mass—for example, if the preceding order for fuel oil specified that it be from "Hunterspoint Storage Yard"—title passes at once, even before the portion ordered is separated from the rest. In the eyes of the law, the buyer acquires immediate title to an undivided share of the specific mass because the units of oil are all the same and no selection is necessary to identify the particular units that the buyer is purchasing.

EXAMPLE 16.7

▶ Rural Cannery received an order from Fisk Supermarkets for 1,000 cases of canned peas bearing the Fisk label. The cannery normally packaged such goods for many supermarkets and had an abundant supply of canned peas. After it received this order, the cannery began placing Fisk labels on cans of peas. Title to the canned peas passed to Fisk when the labels were affixed to the cans.

CHAPTER SUMMARY

1. Title, as it relates to property, is intangible. It represents ownership and the right to possess something, unless that right has been given up.

2. Real property is land and all articles permanently attached to it, such as buildings and trees. Personal property is all kinds of property other than real property. Only personal property is governed by the law of sales.

3. There are a variety of ways in which title can pass. A bill of sale is a written statement that the seller is passing ownership to the buyer. A bill of lading is a receipt for goods to be shipped, acknowledging that such goods have been received and indicating agreement that the goods will be transported to the destination specified. A warehouse receipt is like a bill of lading except that the goods involved are not being transported but merely stored.

4. Title to goods passes when the parties intend for it to pass. In the event that the intent of the parties is not clear, title passes at the moment when they unconditionally agree to sell specific goods that are in a deliverable state.

5. A conditional sale is one with contract provisions that specify conditions that must be met by one of the parties. The two types of conditions found in contracts for conditional sales are conditions precedent and conditions subsequent. Conditions precedent are those that must be met before title passes. Conditions subsquent are those that must be met after title passes.

6. A person without good title to goods cannot transfer title, except in cases of transfer of title by estoppel. Someone who finds lost goods has title to them against anyone but the true owner. A thief has no title to goods that he or she has stolen, and consequently cannot pass title, even to innocent purchasers.

7. Estoppel is a legal bar to using contradictory words or acts in asserting a claim against another. Examples of estoppel include transfer of money or commercial paper made out to the bearer, transfer of property to a seller dealing in the same type of goods, transfer of property to a seller permitted to appear as the real owner, and transfer of proof of ownership to an unauthorized seller.

8. Person having rightful possession of goods have the right to make legitimate sales as representatives of the owners of the goods, although they are not titleholders. Persons having wrongful possession of goods have no right to make sales, and the titleholders of these goods are never estopped.

9. Title to fungible goods passes when the goods become clearly identifiable. In cases in which a specific quantity is ordered from a specific mass, title passes at once, even before the portion ordered is separated.

CHAPTER SIXTEEN
ASSESSMENT

MATCHING LEGAL TERMS

Match each of the numbered definitions with the correct term in the following list. Write the letter of your choice in the answer column.

a. bill of sale
b. certificate of title
c. condition subsequent
d. condition precedent
e. estoppel
f. fungible goods
g. order bill of lading
h. personal property
i. real property
j. remote party
k. straight bill of lading
l. warehouse receipt

1. A common carrier's nonnegotiable receipt for goods accepted for shipment.

1. _____

2. A written statement that the seller is passing, or transferring, ownership to a buyer.

2. _____

3. A carrier's receipt for goods accepted for shipment that ensures that the goods will not be delivered unless the original bill of lading is surrendered.

3. _____

4. A provision in a contract that requires the performance of a specific act before title passes.

4. _____

5. A salesperson authorized to sell merchandise for a merchant.

5. _____

6. Land and articles permanently attached to it.

6. _____

7. A provision in a contract that requires the performance of a specific act after title passes.

7. _____

8. A legal bar to the use of contradictory words or acts in asserting a claim against another.

8. _____

9. Goods generally sold by weight or measure, such as grain or gasoline, where each unit is like all others.

9. _____

10. A document that is proof of ownership.

10. _____

11. Possessions other than real property, such as jewelry.

11. _____

12. Evidence of ownership provided by a storage facility.

12. _____

TRUE/FALSE QUIZ

Indicate whether each of the following statements is true or false by writing *T* or *F* in the answer column.

13. A bill of sale must be prepared on a specific legal form.

13. _____

14. Title is proof of ownership as shown by a bill of sale.

14. _____

15. Personal property is land and anything attached to it.

15. _____

16. A straight bill of lading is an instrument used to collect money owed.

16. _____

17. The general rule of law regarding the passing of title is that title passes when the parties intend it to pass.

17. _____

18. A handwritten bill of sale may be an effective legal document.

18. _____

19. Estoppel is a legal principle that can prevent an owner from recovering his or her own property under certain circumstances.

19. _____

20. An airbill is similar to a bill of lading except that it covers a shipment made by air.

20. _____

21. Conditions precedent are required acts that must be performed before title passes.

21. _____

22. A person who finds an article has good title against anyone else except the true owner.

22. _____

23. The owner of cash who entrusts it to another cannot demand the return of the money from a third party to whom the money was given in exchange for something of value.

23. _____

24. Title to goods can never pass to another without the consent of the owner.

24. _____

25. Conditions subsequent are required acts that must be performed after a contract is signed.

25. _____

26. Title to fungible goods passes when they are delivered.

26. _____

27. The owner of personal property cannot recover it from an innocent third party who purchased it from a seller in possession of the property and who was entrusted with proof of ownership by the real owner.

27. _____

DISCUSSION QUESTIONS

Answer the following questions and discuss them in class.

28. Distinguish between real and personal property and indicate which is subject to the law of sales.

_____

_____

29. Explain how title and certificate of title relate to ownership.

_____

_____

30. Explain how title passes and discuss how bills of sale, bills of lading, and warehouse receipts are involved in the passing of title.

_____

_____

31. Explain the law governing title to lost or stolen goods and sales by persons having wrongful possession of goods.

_____

_____

32. Discuss the principle of estoppel and provide examples of how this principle is applied in various situations.

_____

_____

33. Explain the passage of title to fungible goods.

_____

_____

Answer the following questions, which require you to think critically about the legal principles that you learned in this chapter.

34. **Title** An important application of the concept of title relates to who is holding title when a loss occurs. Are there other ways of determining who should bear a loss in a business transaction?

_____

_____

35. **Conditions Precedent** A contract stipulates that certain conditions must be met before title can pass. A seller might wish to hasten the passage of title to minimize the risk of loss and the cost of insurance to indemnify such losses. Consider a typical sales transaction and suggest steps a seller might take to accelerate title transfer.

_____

_____

36. **Estoppel** It seems that passage of title by estoppel might deny the rights of an innocent though inattentive property owner. Should a legitimate titleholder lose title because of his or her inattention?

_____

_____

37. **Remote Parties** How can a buyer in a store know whether he or she is dealing with a titleholder or a remote party? Does it make a difference? Generally, whom does a buyer hold responsible for problems?

_____

_____

38. **A Question of Ethics** Is it ethical for a person who is not a titleholder to act as one who has title to goods, thereby misleading a prospective buyer?

_____

_____

CASE QUESTIONS

Study each of the following cases. Answer the questions that follow by writing _Yes_ or _No_ in the answer column.

39. **Passage of Title** Crowley, a building contractor, ordered 500 bags of cement from Litvak Building Supply. It was agreed that Litvak would deliver to a building site and title would pass when delivery was made. Before the bags of cement could

be loaded on a delivery truck, a train derailment destroyed much of the supply company's inventory.

a. Must Crowley bear the loss and recover damages from the railroad? a. _____

b. Is the requirement of delivery to a building site a condition precedent? b. _____

c. Did title to the bags of cement pass at the time the order was placed? c. _____

40. **Estoppel** Hollander purchased a computer from a pawnshop for use in his real estate office. Several weeks later, Diem, one of Hollander's customers, mentioned that the computer looked familiar and asked if he could examine it. After checking the underside of the machine, he pointed to his Social Security number, which had been engraved on the metal frame by his insurance agent. Diem demanded the return of the computer, claiming that it had been stolen from him and that he could produce the original sales slip.

a. Can Diem legally recover the computer if he could prove that it had been stolen? a. _____

b. Can a rightful owner be estopped from recovering his or her property from an innocent purchaser? b. _____

c. Could the pawnshop have given good title to Hollander? c. _____

41. **Condition Precedent** Fallon agreed in writing to purchase a used truck from Moonlit Motors with the understanding that a snowplow attachment would be added. When Fallon attempted to take delivery of the truck, he found that the plow attachment had not been added. He refused to accept delivery. Moonlit protested that the plow attachment was being shipped from Minnesota and that it would be installed when it arrived. Moonlit demanded that Fallon accept the truck.

a. Can Fallon legally refuse to accept the truck? a. _____

b. Is this an example of a condition precedent? b. _____

c. Is the contract enforceable? c. _____

42. **Certificate of Title** Forell, a resident of Des Moines, purchased a nearly new Buick automobile from a seller in Cleveland for the unusually low price of $4,000. The seller explained that he was in town to take delivery of another automobile that he had just inherited from his late father. The seller produced a certificate of title. After Forell had possession of the Buick for several months, he sold it to Bates for $3,800. After Bates had driven the car for two months, he was stopped by the police for a minor traffic violation. When the police routinely checked the vehicle identification number through their computer, it was discovered that the car had been stolen from Santiago in Cleveland and that the certificate of title was forged. When Santiago learned that his car had been located, he claimed ownership.

a. Will Santiago be able to recover his automobile? a. _____

b. Will the certificate of title Forell obtained from the out-of-town seller entitle him to ownership? b. _____

c. Was Forell a good-faith purchaser? c. _____

CASE ANALYSIS

Study each of the following cases carefully. Briefly state the principle of law and your decision.

43. **Title to Stolen Goods** Patterson was on a group vacation tour when he discovered that his camcorder was not where he had left it on the tour bus. Later on the tour, Patterson noticed another vacationer, Carlsen, with a similar camcorder. When Carlsen was confronted, he claimed that he had found the camcorder at one of the tour bus stops. When Patterson produced a bill of sale with a serial number that matched the one on the disputed camcorder, Carlsen refused to surrender it, claiming that since he had found it, it was his. Will Patterson be able to regain possession of his lost camcorder?

    Principle of Law:

    _____

    _____

    Decision:

    _____

    _____

44. **Remote Party** Kiang, a sales representative working for Prat's Appliances, sold a refrigerator to Pogany. After several weeks, Pogany changed her mind and wanted to repudiate the sales contract. Her argument was that a valid contract did not exist because Kiang did not possess title to the refrigerator and therefore could not convey title to her. Will Pogany be allowed to repudiate the sales contract?

    Principle of Law:

    _____

    _____

    Decision:

    _____

    _____

45. **Passage of Title** Hughes purchased a new Lincoln Continental automobile from Al Greene, Inc., an authorized new car dealership. On the day of the sale, Hughes made a cash down payment and signed a purchase contract and an application for the title certificate. The understanding was that Hughes would take immediate possession of the car and return in a few days for new-car preparation and the installation of a CB radio. On the way home from the dealer, Hughes wrecked the car. The certificate of title had not yet been issued by the state. The buyer, Hughes, claimed that title had not yet passed since the title certificate had not yet been issued. Who must bear the loss? [*Hughes v. Al Greene, Inc.,* 418 N.E.2d 1355 (Ohio)]

Principle of Law:

_____

_____

Decision:

_____

_____

LEGAL RESEARCH

Complete the following activities. Share your findings with the class.

46. Working in Teams In teams of three or four, interview several real estate agents and discuss title and title insurance.

_____

_____

47. Using Technology Using the Internet and search engines, find an instrument of title, such as a bill of sale, bill of lading, or warehouse receipt.

_____

_____

chapter **17**
Sales

After studying this chapter and completing the assessment, you will be able to

17.1 Discuss the concept of title in relation to the law of sales.

17.2 Distinguish between a contract for sale and a contract to sell.

17.3 Identify the classifications of sales contracts, including oral, written, express, and implied.

17.4 Discuss the difference between entire and divisible contracts.

17.5 Describe the special requirements of contracts for labor and materials.

17.6 Discuss trial periods and returns.

17.7 Discuss auction sales, conditional sales, and consignment sales.

17.8 Discuss how the delivery of shipments affects the passage of title, and how FOB shipping point and FOB destination differ.

17.9 Explain both sellers' and buyers' remedies for breach of sales contracts.

LEGAL terms

contract for sale
existing goods
future goods
contract to sell
contract for labor
  and materials
contract for sale with
  the right of return
sale on approval
sale or return

auction without reserve
auction with reserve
conditional sales contract
FOB shipping point
FOB destination
stoppage in transit
specific performance
replevin
cover

SALES

"I'm not impulsive at all—except about buying clothes. That's my biggest weakness."

Alex Rodriguez,
Professional Baseball Player

17.1 THE LAW OF SALES

Because the law of sales affects so many individuals and businesses, Article 2 of the Uniform Commercial Code (UCC) is quite comprehensive. Article 2, however, does not include investment securities (covered by Article 8 of the UCC), real estate, or services. Contracts for services are considered ordinary contracts and are not covered by the UCC.

In the case of transactions that involve both goods and services, courts look to the predominant portion of the contract to determine whether it is a sales contract for goods or a services contract for repairs, which incidentally includes the parts necessary to make the repairs.

The term *title,* introduced in Chapter 16, as used in contracts for sale, refers to ownership. Consequently, having title to something usually means having the right to possess it. However, there are important exceptions. For example, if *A* leases *B* an automobile, *B* has the right to possess the vehicle, but *A* retains ownership. The concept of title is important in the law of sales. Equally important are the remedies for *breach of contract—* that is, breaking a contract.

17.2 CONTRACTS FOR SALE VERSUS CONTRACTS TO SELL

contract for sale
A legally enforceable agreement that has as its purpose the immediate transfer of title to personal property in return for consideration.

A contract for sale is a legally enforceable agreement that has as its purpose the immediate transfer of title to personal property in return for consideration. The contract may be for a present sale of goods or for a sale of future goods—goods that are not yet in existence or manufactured. A sale, according to the UCC, is the passing of title from the seller to the buyer for a price (UCC 2-106). Payment for goods can be in the form of money, or goods, or in the performance of services (UCC 2-304).

EXAMPLE 17.1

> Jesup agreed to sell an amateur radio transmitter to Moncada for $750. Moncada paid the agreed price, and Jesup gave him the equipment.

This is an executed contract for sale, and title (ownership) to the transmitter passed when the money was paid to Jesup. If Moncada, after purchasing the transmitter, left it with Jesup for a day while he arranged delivery and it was damaged, destroyed, or stolen during that time, the loss would be borne by Moncada.

existing goods
Goods that physically exist and are owned by the seller at the time of sale.

Suppose that, in Example 17.1, the parties had agreed that the sale of the radio equipment would be completed when Moncada had passed his FCC amateur's examination. The transaction would be viewed as an agreement in which both parties intended title to pass when Moncada passed the examination. If anything happened to the equipment in the interim, Jesup would suffer the loss.

future goods
Goods that do not exist at the time of the sales transaction but are expected to come into the possession of the seller.

Goods that physically exist and are owned by the seller at the time of sale are considered existing goods. Goods that do not exist at the time of the sales transaction but are expected to come into the possession of the seller are considered future goods.

Examples of such future goods include growing crops and timber, unborn livestock and pets, goods not yet manufactured, and so on. An agreement to sell future goods is considered a <mark>contract to sell</mark>, in contrast to a contract for sale. The distinction between existing and future goods is important because a person cannot sell goods to which he or she does not hold title.

contract to sell
An agreement to sell future goods.

EXAMPLE 17.2

▶ Kierman paid a $500 deposit to Mondrus, a breeder of pedigreed dogs, who agreed to sell Kierman a male puppy from the next litter of his prize terrier for $1,200. Before the terrier gave birth to the expected litter, it was killed in a fire that destroyed the kennel. Kierman demanded the return of his deposit, claiming that title to the puppy did not pass until delivery was made. Mondrus demanded the balance of the agreed price of $1,200, claiming that the unborn puppy belonged to Kierman from the time of their agreement.

The courts have heard many such cases, and in almost every one they have held that title to such future goods remains with the seller. In Example 17.2, Kierman would get back his deposit and Mondrus would bear the loss.

17.3 ORAL, WRITTEN, EXPRESS, AND IMPLIED CONTRACTS

As is true for all contracts, sales contracts may be oral or written, and express or implied. As pointed out in Chapter 13, contracts for $500 or more must be in writing to be enforceable (UCC 2-201). The complete agreement need not be in writing, but there must be some evidence of the intention of the parties. The contract also must be signed by the affected parties.

In a contract to sell unharvested wheat, title remains with the seller.

17.4 ENTIRE AND DIVISIBLE SALES CONTRACTS

Entire and divisible contracts were introduced in Chapter 7, and examples were provided to show the difference between them. The significance of the distinction between entire and divisible sales contracts can be seen in numerous business transactions.

EXAMPLE 17.3

▶ Management Mode, a publisher of newsletters, decided to switch from using an outside typesetter to internal desktop publishing to save the cost of typesetting and to speed up its operation. The firm ordered personal computers from Compu-Writ for each of its editors and writers, appropriate word-processing software, desktop publishing software, in-house training software, and laser printers. Delivery of the equipment and software was scheduled to be made within 30 days of placing the order. However, delivery of the laser printers was delayed for two months.

Because all the components are interdependent and were included in the same order—an entire contract—payment for the contract would not be required until the whole order was filled. Payment for the portion of the order delivered—the computers—would not be due when they were delivered. On the other hand, if the computers and the printers were ordered for separate offices—a divisible contract—payment for the computers would be due when delivery was made, even though delivery of the printers was delayed for two months.

17.5 CONTRACTS FOR LABOR AND MATERIALS

contract for labor and materials
A sales contract for goods of special design, construction, or manufacture.

A sales contract for goods of special design, construction, or manufacture is neither a contract for sale nor a contract to sell. Such a contract is considered a contract for labor and materials. A contract for labor and materials, even though it involves $500 or more, need not always be in writing to be enforceable. This is an exception to the UCC requirement that contracts of $500 or more be in writing. The UCC provides that "if the goods are to be specially manufactured for the buyer and are not suitable for sale to others," the requirement of a written contract does not necessarily apply [UCC 2-201(3)]. The contract will not be binding if the buyer repudiates (cancels) the oral contract and the seller receives the notice before he or she has made either a substantial beginning in manufacturing the goods or commitments for their procurement. If, however, the seller has begun manufacture or made a commitment, the cancellation is not effective [UCC 2-201(3)].

EXAMPLE 17.4

▶ Little Lucy's Bakery orally contracted with Foremost Conveyor Company for the design and construction of a special conveyor system to be installed in the shipping room of the bakery. After the conveyor was designed, built, and ready to be installed, Little Lucy's hired a new manager. The new manager canceled the order, claiming that it was invalid because it was not in writing. Foremost Conveyor can recover damages from the bakery for breach of contract because the cancellation was received after work on the conveyor system had begun.

17.6 TRIAL PERIODS AND RETURNS

While a merchant might prefer to sell for cash with no return privilege, if the seller's competitors are willing to allow prospective customers a trial period or the right of return, the seller also must do so in order to remain competitive. In these kinds of selling arrangements, it is important to determine who owns and has title to the merchandise while it is in the prospective buyer's possession, in the event of loss or damage.

CONTRACT FOR SALE WITH RIGHT OF RETURN

Certain kinds of goods are frequently sold on a trial basis. Because a sales brochure or demonstration may not persuade a businessperson that a certain office machine will be an asset to the business, a short trial period during which the buyer can use the machine is often arranged. A contract for sale with the right of return gives the buyer both title to the goods and the opportunity to return them to the seller at a later time.

contract for sale with the right of return
A contract for the sale of goods that gives the buyer both title to the goods and the opportunity to return them to the seller at a later time.

SALE ON APPROVAL

When a contract provides for the sale of goods subject to the buyer's approval, the transaction is a sale on approval. The goods remain the property of the seller until the buyer has expressed approval of the goods. Title and risk of loss remain with the seller. The buyer may indicate approval orally or in writing, or by retaining the goods for more than a reasonable time.

sale on approval
A contract for the sale of goods subject to the buyer's approval.

EXAMPLE 17.5

▶ The sales representative of Scrub 'n' Clean Equipment was attempting to persuade the manager of River Rock Car Wash to install a new type of car wash brush. The cost of the brushes and uncertainty about their effectiveness made the car wash manager hesitant to make a commitment to buy until he had the opportunity to try the equipment. The sales representative agreed to let the car wash use four brushes for two months on approval.

Both parties in this case agreed to a sale on approval. After using the brushes for a month or two, the car wash manager could agree to purchase them, and at such time title would pass to the car wash. It is not wise for a potential buyer to let the trial period slip by on the assumption that the seller does not mind or that the buyer is getting something for nothing. The buyer must notify the seller of his or her decision to return the goods, if that is the intention, within the time agreed upon for trial of the goods, or within a reasonable time if no time has been agreed upon. If notification is not given during that period, the user's continued, prolonged use of the goods on approval could be interpreted as implied consent to buy, and the user could be held responsible for the goods and be obligated to pay for them.

A bidder's offer is accepted when the auctioneer lets the hammer fall.

SALE OR RETURN

Most goods sold by reputable merchants can be returned for a variety of reasons unless the sale is clearly identified as final or the circumstances of the return are unreasonable. Very often a merchant will agree to a sale or return—that is, an agreement whereby the seller will accept the return of goods at the request of the buyer in order to maintain goodwill rather than because the seller is legally obliged to accept the returned goods. The sale of goods can be made with the understanding that the purchaser takes title to the goods but has the right to return them within a specified or reasonable time. In such cases, the purchaser must assume all the obligations of ownership while the goods are in his or her possession.

sale or return
An agreement whereby the seller will accept the return of goods at the request of the buyer to maintain goodwill, rather than because the seller is legally obliged to accept the returned goods.

Suppose that in Example 17.5, the manager of River Rock Car Wash was sure that the new brushes were what he wanted and needed. Suppose also that the funds were available for the planned purchase of the brushes and that a purchase order for the brushes was issued. If the brushes did not prove satisfactory, the manager could probably still return them. The major distinction between this example and the previous one is that in this instance, title to the brushes is in the hands of the purchaser, who would be held responsible for loss or damage of the equipment. Not only would the parties to the agreement have an interest in who held title, but the insurance carriers for the car wash as well as the supplier, Scrub 'n' Clean, would also have an interest in who held title.

17.7   OTHER KINDS OF SALES

Two additional kinds of sales are auction sales and conditional sales.

AUCTION SALES

Auction sales were introduced in Chapter 13. At an auction sale, the buyer is the party making the offer, or bid. The seller is the owner of the goods, who has engaged an auctioneer to gather bids from interested parties with the intent of selling to the highest bidder. The bidder's offer is accepted when the auctioneer says, "Going once, twice, three times, sold!" and at the same time lets the hammer fall. A bidder may retract a bid at any time before the hammer falls, and such retraction does not revive any previous bid. If a bid is made while the hammer is falling, the auctioneer may use his or her discretion to reopen the bidding or declare the goods sold under the bid made as the hammer was falling [UCC 2-328(2)].

auction without reserve
One at which the goods must be sold to the highest bidder and may not be withdrawn after bidding has begun.

auction with reserve
One that gives the auctioneer the right to withdraw the goods at any time before announcing completion of the sale if reasonable bids are not made.

There have been reported instances of expensive pieces of property being sold at auction for a pittance simply because no one offered a higher bid. This possibility occurs only at an auction without reserve—one at which the goods must be sold to the highest bidder and may not be withdrawn after bidding has begun. An auction with reserve gives the auctioneer the right to withdraw the goods at any time before announcing completion of the sale if reasonable bids are not made. If a *reserve amount* has been established, it is announced by the auctioneer before bidding begins, or is disclosed in posters or catalogs listing the goods to be auctioned. Auction sales are with reserve unless otherwise specified [UCC 2-328(3)].

The legal requirement that sales of personal property for $500 or more be in writing is satisfied by the notations made in the auctioneer's sales book. In the case of telephone bids made from distant branches of the auction house, the bidder must sign an agreement in advance that sets out the conditions under which he or she agrees to pay any accepted bid.

Online auctions are conducted on the Internet; but unlike live auctions during which a buyer can inspect goods to be auctioned, bidders in an online auction rely on the reputation of the seller, photographs that display the goods, and e-mail. Items offered for sale can be offered with a reserve so that the sale price must be equal to or greater than the reserve.

CONDITIONAL SALES

conditional sales contract
A sales contract that includes conditions that must be met either before or after the sale is completed.

Some sales contracts include conditions that must be met either before or after the sale is completed. In most instances, the conditions deal with arrangements for payment. A conditional sales contract is one way of selling merchandise with the condition that title will remain with the seller until the purchase price has been paid. The buyer cannot legally resell goods purchased this way because title has not passed; a person cannot sell goods to which he or she has no title. The seller can *repossess* the goods (take back property through judicial action) if the buyer does not pay in the time agreed.

CONSIGNMENT SALES

A consignment sale occurs when a seller (a consignor) entrusts goods to a merchant (a consignee) who acts under contract as the seller's agent to sell the goods in exchange for a small fee.

17.8 DELIVERY

Many transactions require shipment of the goods purchased. However, shipping goods is not without risk. While goods are in transit, there is a distinct possibility that damage may occur. Any number of unfortunate events may transpire; for example, shifting cargo can cause damage to fragile items; a natural disaster, like a flood or tornado, can destroy or damage goods; a shipper can even lose the goods. Generally a prudent party will make certain that goods are insured against these types of losses; but in order to do so, the party must have an insurable interest in the goods. An insurable interest is the right to insure goods against any potential loss. Sellers have an *insurable interest* in the goods as long they have title to them, whereas buyers are allowed to insure goods even before they obtain title to them [UCC 2-501(1)].

The manner in which the goods are shipped affects the passing of title. Title to goods that are shipped by private carrier or delivered by the seller passes at the time of delivery to the buyer. If the buyer arranges for delivery, title passes when the buyer, or his or her agent, picks up the goods. However, in the case of goods that are shipped by *common carrier*—someone who is in the business of transporting goods (or persons), whether by rail, truck, plane, or any other mode of transportation—title passes to the purchaser according to the conditions that follow.

SALES FOB SHIPPING POINT

The abbreviation *FOB* means "free on board." When goods are sold FOB shipping point, title to the goods passes from the seller to the buyer when the carrier receives the shipment, and it is understood that the buyer will pay the transportation charges. From that point, the goods belong to the buyer, and in the event of loss or damage, the buyer must attempt to recover any loss from the carrier. Further, the buyer is responsible for paying the seller for the merchandise even if he or she never receives it (UCC 2-319).

FOB shipping point
Title to goods passes from the seller to the buyer when the carrier receives the shipment and it is understood that the buyer will pay the transportation charges.

SALES FOB DESTINATION

Title to goods shipped FOB destination passes when the goods are delivered to the buyer. In the event of their loss or damage en route, the seller must attempt to recover any loss from the carrier. In such a case, the cost of transporting the goods is paid to the carrier by the seller but is usually included in the buyer's invoice or is billed to the buyer separately.

This method of shipment offers the buyer an advantage. For example, in case of a lost or damaged shipment, the buyer can quickly call the seller and arrange for a duplicate shipment. The buyer's money is not tied up in goods not received, and the buyer is spared the inconvenience of filing a claim with the carrier.

FOB destination
Title passes from the seller to the buyer when the goods are delivered to the buyer.

17.9 REMEDIES FOR BREACH OF SALES CONTRACTS

The law provides a number of remedies to protect the buyer and the seller in disputes involving sales contracts. It is important to note that remedies are available for only a limited time. The UCC provides a *statute of limitations*—that is, a time limit after which the usual legal remedies are no longer available. The UCC provides that, in the absence of negligence or fraud (for which there may be different statutes of limitations), legal action to remedy a breach of sales contract must be started within four years from the breach (UCC 2-725).

SELLERS' REMEDIES

A seller has a number of remedies at law depending on the circumstances of the case. The most common circumstances are discussed here.

When the Buyer Refuses to Accept Delivery of the Goods   When the buyer refuses to accept delivery of the goods, the seller may do one of the following:

1. Store the goods for the buyer and sue to recover the sales price if the goods are not readily resalable to another customer (UCC 2-704).

2. Resell the goods immediately if they are perishable or if their market value might depreciate rapidly. Also, the seller can sue the buyer for the difference between the price the goods brought in the resale and the price the buyer had agreed to pay for them plus incidental damages (UCC 2-706).

3. Retain the goods and sue the buyer for the difference between the contract price and the market price at the time the buyer refused to honor the contract (UCC 2-706).

EXAMPLE 17.6

▶ Georgio placed an order with Med-Lab Manufacturing Company for specially designed medical laboratory testing equipment. When the equipment was ready for shipment, Georgio notified Med-Lab of her intention to cancel the order. Med-Lab has the right to hold the equipment for Georgio and sue for the agreed-upon purchase price.

If the equipment was not of special design and could be sold to others, Med-Lab could return the equipment to stock for sale to others and sue Georgio for damages resulting from Georgio's breach. In this case, the damages would be limited to the profit Med-Lab would have made on the sale if there had been no breach.

When the Buyer Refuses to Pay the Purchase Price   When the buyer refuses to pay the purchase price, the seller may do one of the following:

1. If the seller still has possession of the goods, he or she can resell them after a reasonable period and sue for any damages incurred.

2. If the merchandise has already been delivered to the buyer, he or she can sue for the purchase price.

EXAMPLE 17.7

▶ Molstad bought a laser printer from Computer Cosmos Company, agreeing to pay cash for it. Computer Cosmos insisted on retaining possession of the printer until the invoice amount was paid in full. When Molstad failed to pay within the agreed-upon time, Computer Cosmos sold the printer to Fishman at a lower price because of a general lowering of prices that took place between the time Molstad agreed to buy and the time it was sold to Fishman. Computer Cosmos sued Molstad for the difference between the price Molstad had agreed to pay and the price paid by Fishman. Computer Cosmos was successful in its efforts to recover this difference.

When the Buyer Is Insolvent   Sometimes, after goods have been shipped to the buyer but before actual delivery has been made by the carrier, the seller learns that the buyer is *insolvent*—that is, the buyer no longer has sufficient assets to pay his or her debts.

When the buyer is insolvent, the UCC provides the seller with the right of stoppage in transit. Stoppage in transit is the right of an unpaid seller to stop goods in transit and order the carrier to hold them for the seller. This right to interrupt the shipment of goods to the buyer exists for both FOB shipping point sales and FOB destination sales (UCC 2-705).

To exercise this right of stoppage in transit, the seller must satisfy the common carrier that the buyer is insolvent. If the seller's information proves unfounded, both the seller and the carrier are subject to suit for damages. For this reason, the carrier should require the seller by contract to accept full responsibility for any loss that it may suffer as a result of a suit by the purchaser.

stoppage in transit
When the buyer is insolvent, the right of an unpaid seller to stop goods in transit and order the carrier to hold them for the seller.

EXAMPLE 17.8

▶ An order of books was en route to Readers' Haven bookstore, timed to arrive in time for a well-promoted author's book-signing party. The seller, Words in Print, notified the carrier not to deliver the books, claiming that it had received information from a reliable source that the buyer, Readers' Haven, was insolvent. Later it was revealed that the information was in error. Both the publisher and the carrier are subject to Readers' Haven's suit for damages.

BUYERS' REMEDIES

The UCC provides a buyer with certain remedies depending on the specific circumstances (UCC 2-711).

When the Wrong Quantity Is Delivered   Should the seller deliver the incorrect quantity of the goods ordered, the buyer has several options. If a smaller quantity of merchandise is delivered than was ordered, the buyer may either reject delivery and sue for damages or accept the quantity delivered and sue for damages, which would be calculated as the lost profits that would have resulted from the sale of the undelivered portion. If a larger quantity of goods is delivered than was ordered, the buyer may reject the entire shipment; accept only what was ordered and reject the rest; or accept the entire shipment and pay for the additional items at the contract price.

To exercise the right of stoppage in transit, the seller must satisfy the common carrier that the buyer is insolvent.

EXAMPLE 17.9

▶ Woodbury Way, an appliance store, ordered 100 microwave ovens from an importer. By mistake, the importer shipped 200. Woodbury Way was delighted to learn that he had an unexpected bargain since the wholesaler's price was going to be increased as a result of changes in the foreign exchange rate. The buyer has the right to keep the entire shipment and pay for all 200 microwaves at the contract price.

When the Goods Are Not as Ordered   In the event that the seller delivers goods that are not as specified in the contract, the buyer may revoke the contract and return the goods that are substantially different from those that were ordered. If the goods have already been paid for, the buyer may demand a refund of the purchase price and, in most states, sue for damages for breach of warranty, a legally binding guarantee (see Chapter 18). Alternatively, the buyer may keep the goods and sue for damages for any loss resulting from the seller's breach of contract. If the goods are of a higher quality than what was ordered, the buyer has the option of either rejecting the order or keeping the order and paying the contract price.

EXAMPLE 17.10

▶ Susuki purchased and paid for a standby electric generator for emergency use at his factory. The seller assured Susuki that the generator would produce enough power to keep his essential operations going during a power failure. When the generator was tested, however, it failed to produce sufficient power. Susuki could demand and obtain a refund. In this instance, Susuki probably could not show that he had sustained additional damages, so a lawsuit would be unlikely.

When the Seller Fails to Deliver the Goods   When title has passed to the buyer for goods the seller has failed to deliver, the buyer has the following remedies:

1. The buyer can sue for damages by bringing a tort action charging conversion. As explained in Chapter 4, conversion is a tort that results when a person has unlawfully assumed ownership of property that belongs to another. The amount of damages sought would be the value of the goods at the time of the seller's failure to deliver.

specific performance
An order that requires the seller to deliver the goods specified in the contract or face being held in contempt of court.

2. If the goods are unique, such as a one-of-a-kind work of art, and the buyer wants the particular goods that are specified in the contract, the buyer can seek a court order of specific performance. Such an order requires the seller to deliver the goods specified in the contract or face being held in contempt of court (UCC 2-716). (See Chapter 15.)

replevin
An action to recover possession of specific goods wrongfully taken or detained by another.

3. Another remedy available to a buyer who wishes to obtain goods that are rightfully his or hers, rather than money damages, is to sue to obtain them by bringing an action of replevin—an action to recover possession of specific goods wrongfully

taken or detained by another (UCC 2-716). In such an action, the court will order the sheriff to seize the goods and deliver them to the buyer.

4. The UCC also permits a buyer to cover—that is, to buy similar goods elsewhere to substitute for those not delivered by the seller. If the buyer chooses to cover, he or she may demand from the seller, as damages, the difference between the cost of cover (what he or she paid for the replacement goods) and the contract price, plus any incidental expenses, less expenses saved as a result of the seller's breach (UCC 2-712).

cover
When the seller fails to deliver the goods, the right of a buyer to buy similar goods elsewhere to substitute for those not delivered by the seller.

EXAMPLE 17.11

▶ Andrews, a retail electronics dealer, purchased and paid for 60 netbooks of an advanced design from a wholesaler. The netbooks were in stock, and delivery was promised. Clearly title had passed. Because of a sharp increase in the manufacturer's prices, the wholesaler refused to deliver the devices as agreed in the contract. Andrews can sue the distributor for the difference between the contract price and the higher market price at the time of the wholesaler's refusal to deliver. If she is seeking money damages, her suit will be an action for conversion. Alternatively, if the devices are in short supply and she is more interested in getting the netbooks than in a money settlement, she can seek an order of specific performance. Or she can institute an action of replevin for delivery of the netbooks. If the netbooks are available elsewhere at a higher price, she could cover by buying them at the higher price and then suing the wholesaler for the difference between the contract price and the price of the cover. The suit also could seek repayment of expenses such as the additional cost of transportation from a distant seller.

If title has not yet passed to the buyer, his or her remedy when the seller refuses to deliver at the time and place stated in the contract is a suit for breach of contract. The amount of damages would be the difference between the contract price and the market price at the time delivery was refused. The UCC also permits recovery of other damages that the buyer can prove, less any expenses saved as a result of the seller's breach (UCC 2-713).

EXAMPLE 17.12

▶ Ho, the owner of a business school, ordered 30 computers from Latimer, a supplier of office equipment, at a price of $875 each. A week before the time agreed for delivery, Latimer got an order for 30 of the same kind of computers from an insurance company that had relocated to the city. The second buyer agreed to pay a price of $1,150 each. Sensing an opportunity to increase his profit, Latimer refused to fill Ho's order. While it would be difficult to determine the amount of damages, Ho could sue for foreseeable damages that might include the lost tuition that would have been paid by students who would have enrolled in the school if the computers had been delivered as promised.

CHAPTER
SUMMARY

1. The term *title*, as it is used in contracts for sale, refers to ownership. Having title to something usually means having the right to possess it.

2. A contract for sale is a legally enforceable agreement that has as its purpose the immediate transfer of title to personal property in return for consideration. A contract to sell is an agreement to sell future goods.

3. Sales contracts may be oral or written, and express or implied.

4. An entire contract is one in which all of the components of the agreement are included in the same order; a divisible contract is one in which components of an agreement are in separate orders.

5. A contract for labor and materials is a sales contract for goods of special design, construction, or manufacture. These contracts need not always be in writing, and they can be canceled before a substantial beginning or commitment to procurement has been made.

6. If a seller's competitors are willing to allow prospective customers a trial period or the right of return, the seller also must do so in order to remain competitive. A contract for sale with the right of return is an agreement that gives the buyer both title to the goods and an opportunity to return them to the seller at a later time. A contract for sale on approval is one in which the goods remain the property of the seller until the buyer has expressed approval of the goods.

7. An auction sale is one in which the buyer is the party making the offer, or bid. A conditional sale is one in which certain conditions must be met before or after the sale is completed. A consignment sale occurs when a seller (a consignor) entrusts goods to a merchant (a consignee) who acts under contract as the seller's agent to sell the goods in exchange for a small fee.

8. In sales FOB shipping point, title to the goods passes from the seller to the buyer when the carrier receives shipment, and it is understood that the buyer will pay the transportation charges. In sales FOB destination, title to goods passes when the goods are delivered to the buyer.

9. Sellers' remedies and buyers' remedies for breach of a sales contract depend on the circumstances. The UCC provides a statute of limitations in which legal action for breach of contract must be started. A seller may seek damages when the buyer refuses to accept delivery of the goods, when the buyer refuses to pay the purchase price, or when the buyer is insolvent. A buyer may seek damages when the wrong quantity is delivered, when the goods are not as ordered, or when the seller fails to deliver the goods.

CHAPTER SEVENTEEN
ASSESSMENT

MATCHING LEGAL TERMS

Match each of the numbered definitions with the correct term in the following list. Write the letter of your choice in the answer column.

a. conditional sales contract

b. contract for labor and materials

c. contract to sell

d. insolvency

e. reserve amount

f. sale on approval

g. sale or return

h. title

i. statute of limitations

j. stoppage in transit

1. Ownership of goods.

1. _____

2. A contract for the sale of goods of special design, construction, or manufacture.

2. _____

3. A contract for sale that gives the buyer the title to goods and the opportunity of returning them to the seller at a later time.

3. _____

4. A sales agreement whereby the seller retains title and the buyer can return the goods.

4. _____

5. An agreement for the sale of future goods.

5. _____

6. An amount used in auction sales that specifies the lowest acceptable bid.

6. _____

7. A sales agreement whereby the seller retains title until the buyer pays for the goods.

7. _____

8. A time limit after which legal remedies are no longer possible.

8. _____

9. A state in which a person is unable to pay his or her debts.

9. _____

10. The right of an unpaid seller to stop goods in transit and order the carrier to hold them for the seller.

10. _____

TRUE/FALSE QUIZ

Indicate whether each of the following statements is true or false by writing *T* or *F* in the answer column.

11. Contracts for sale can be oral or written, express or implied.

11. _____

12. A contract for sale differs from a contract to sell primarily in the point at which title passes.

12. _____

13. In most cases of the sale of future goods, title remains with the seller until the goods are in a deliverable state.

13. _____

14. Goods that physically exist and are owned by the seller at the time of sale are considered existing goods.

14. _____

15. A contract for the sale of various, unrelated articles is considered a divisible contract.

15. _____

16. A contract for labor and materials must always be in writing, regardless of the amount of money involved.

16. _____

17. When goods are sold on approval, the buyer has title during the
trial period.   17. _____

18. The buyer of goods sold on approval can indicate his or her consent
to keep the goods by retaining them for longer than the agreed time
or a reasonable time.   18. _____

19. A buyer whose goods are not delivered within a reasonable time
has the right to "cover"—that is, to purchase substitute goods
from another seller.   19. _____

20. The title to goods sold with right of return passes to the buyer
at the time of sale.   20. _____

21. A contract for special manufacture, construction, or design of
goods is considered a contract for labor and materials.   21. _____

22. The notations in an auctioneer's book of sales of more than $500
satisfies the requirements of the Uniform Commercial Code that
such contracts be in writing to be enforceable.   22. _____

23. A common carrier is a firm in the business of transporting goods
or persons—by rail, truck, plane, or any other mode of
transportation.   23. _____

24. Title to goods shipped FOB shipping point remains with the seller
until delivery is made to the buyer.   24. _____

25. The buyer of goods that have been shipped FOB destination must
bear the loss if the goods are lost or damaged in transit.   25. _____

DISCUSSION QUESTIONS

Answer the following questions and discuss them in class.

26. How can a contract for future goods provide price flexibility for the seller and, at the
same time, provide predictability to the buyer?

_____

_____

27. Why is it important to determine when title passes?

_____

_____

28. A contract for sale with the right of return gives the buyer both title to the goods and the opportunity to return the goods to the seller at a later time. What are the benefits to the seller of this type of sales transaction?

_____

_____

29. When a contract provides for the sale of goods subject to the buyer's approval, the transaction is a sale on approval. What are the benefits to the buyer of this type of sales transaction?

_____

_____

30. Discuss advantages and disadvantages to both sellers and buyers of shipping FOB destination and FOB shipping point.

_____

_____

31. Explain both sellers' and buyers' remedies for breach of contract.

_____

_____

THINKING CRITICALLY ABOUT THE LAW

Answer the following questions, which require you to think critically about the legal principles that you learned in this chapter.

32. Contract for Labor and Materials A contract for labor and materials need not be in writing, even if it is over $500. Does the buyer of the labor and materials enjoy the same level of legal protection as if the contract were in writing?

_____

_____

33. Internet Auction Compare and contrast online auctions with actual live auctions.

_____

_____

34. Sellers' Remedies How might a seller avoid pitfalls in selling to unknown buyers?

_____

_____

35. Buyers' Remedies How might a buyer avoid pitfalls in buying from unknown sellers?

_____

_____

36. A Question of Ethics Is it fair for a buyer to ask a seller to hold merchandise while the buyer shops for a better price?

_____

_____

CASE QUESTIONS

Study each of the following cases. Answer the questions that follow by writing _Yes_ or _No_ in the answer column.

37. Contract for Labor and Materials Rios furnished Stern, a carpenter, with a set of sketches for a cabinet she wanted built. They orally agreed on a price of $1,000, the type of wood to be used, and the delivery date. Before Stern had begun work or obtained the necessary materials, Rios canceled the agreement, saying that she planned to move to another apartment and would not need the cabinet.

    a. Was this a contract for sale?   **a.** _____

    b. Was this a contract for labor and materials?   **b.** _____

    c. Was this a contract to sell?   **c.** _____

    d. Will Stern be successful in a suit for damages?   **d.** _____

38. Divisible or Entire Contracts Miro, the owner of a supermarket, contracted with Market Supply Company for one complete checkout counter, including a cash register. After the counter was installed, but before the cash register was delivered, Market Supply Company demanded payment for the checkout counter. Miro refused to pay, claiming that he had contracted for a complete checkout counter, including the cash register, and he would pay when the cash register was installed.

a. Was this a sales contract?　　　　　　　　　**a.** _____

b. Was this a divisible contract?　　　　　　　　**b.** _____

c. Was this an entire contract?　　　　　　　　 **c.** _____

d. Does Market Supply have grounds for suit to collect for the portion of the order that was delivered?　**d.** _____

39. **Contract for Labor and Materials** Galen, a purchasing agent for Ziff Construction Company, agreed orally with Houk Lumber to purchase 800 double-hung vinyl windows. The agreed price was $40,000. When Ziff Construction lost its financial backing, it had to cancel its plans for the houses it had planned to build. Houk sued to collect the purchase price.

a. Was this a contract for sale?　　　　　　　 **a.** _____

b. Was this a contract for labor and materials?　**b.** _____

c. Did the contract meet the Uniform Commercial Code requirement of writing?　　　　　　　　　　　 **c.** _____

d. Is it likely that Houk would win the lawsuit?　**d.** _____

40. **Sales Contracts** Eamons offered to sell his sailboat, complete with boat trailer, to Fitzgerald for $12,000. Fitzgerald agreed to the offer, gave Eamons a deposit of $500, and said that he would pay the balance when he came back with his car to pick up the boat and trailer. While Fitzgerald was away, the boat caught fire and was destroyed.

a. Was this a contract for sale?　　　　　　　 **a.** _____

b. Did the parties intend title to pass when Fitzgerald picked up the boat?　　　　　　　　　　　　　 **b.** _____

c. Must Eamons bear the loss?　　　　　　　　**c.** _____

d. Was this a contract to sell?　　　　　　　　**d.** _____

CASE ANALYSIS

Study each of the following cases carefully. Briefly state the principle of law and your decision.

41. **Substitute Goods** Gagne made a good living selling snacks, hamburgers, and refreshments at athletic events. He placed a written order with Pacific Container Company for 4,000 Styrofoam containers to be used to package hamburgers. Gagne requested that delivery be made three days before the last big football game of the season, and Pacific promised to meet the date. Two days before the game, the order still had not been delivered. In desperation, Gagne ordered 4,000 similar containers from another firm. When his order from Pacific finally arrived, Gagne refused to

accept delivery or to pay for it. Pacific Container sued to collect the purchase price. Is Pacific likely to collect?

Principle of Law:

_____

_____

Decision:

_____

_____

42. **Auction Sales** Bundeson, a farmer, attended an auction of used farm equipment and successfully bid $1,600 for a tractor. When he returned home, he learned that a real estate developer was eager to buy his farm and build a shopping center on the property. Bundeson agreed to sell his farm, but then realized that he would not need the tractor he had just purchased and that it would be to his advantage to avoid the sale. He notified the auctioneer that he would not go through with the sale because the Uniform Commercial Code required a written contract for personal property sales of $500 or more. Will Bundeson succeed in avoiding the contract?

Principle of Law:

_____

_____

Decision:

_____

_____

43. **Contract for Services** Gates entered into a contract with Mennonite Deaconess Home & Hospital for the installation of a new, "one-ply roofing system." The work was to be done by an installer chosen by Mennonite but approved by Gates. When the work was nearly complete, but before Gates had approved the work, the hospital paid the installer 90 percent of the balance due. After inspection, Gates did not approve, and in addition, the roof leaked and had to be replaced at the hospital's expense. The hospital claimed that Gates was responsible for the quality of the work. Gates claimed that he could not be held accountable because service contracts are not covered by the Uniform Commercial Code. Did the contract involve goods or services, and will Gates be held responsible? [*Mennonite Deaconess Home & Hospital Inc. v. Gates Engineering Co.*, 363 N.W.2d 155 (Nebraska)]

Principle of Law:

_____

_____

Decision:

_____

_____

LEGAL RESEARCH

Complete the following activities. Share your findings with the class.

44. Working in Teams   In teams of three or four, interview owners or managers of small businesses to determine what kinds of contracts they routinely put into writing.

_____

_____

45. Using Technology Using the Internet and search engines, investigate online auctions to determine the operating rules of the various sites.

_____

_____

chapter 18
Warranties

After studying this chapter and completing the assessment, you will be able to

18.1 Identify the various provisions of the law that protect consumers and third parties who suffer physical injuries or financial losses.

18.2 Explain the term *warranty* and distinguish between express and implied warranties.

18.3 Identify the four kinds of express warranties.

18.4 Identify the three kinds of implied warranties.

18.5 Explain the provisions of the Magnuson-Moss Warranty Act.

LEGAL terms

warranty	implied warranty of
express warranty	fitness for a particular
implied warranty	purpose
custom of the	Magnuson-Moss
marketplace	Warranty Act
disclaimer	interstate commerce
implied warranty of	full warranty
merchantability	limited warranty
merchant	lemon laws

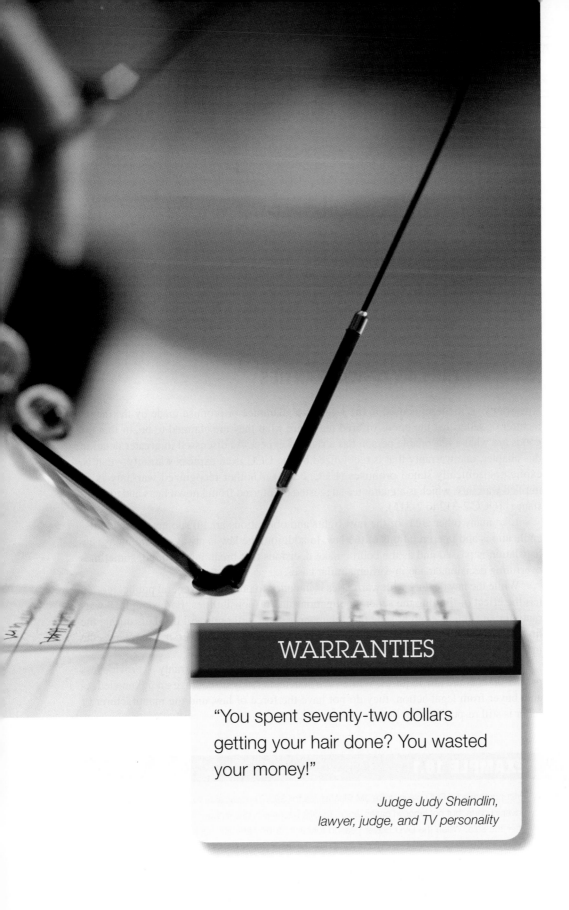

WARRANTIES

"You spent seventy-two dollars getting your hair done? You wasted your money!"

Judge Judy Sheindlin,
lawyer, judge, and TV personality

18.1 PROTECTING CONSUMERS AND THIRD PARTIES

A seller or manufacturer has a significant legal responsibility to buyers and users of goods and services, as well as to third parties. These obligations are covered by the law of sales, contract law, the Uniform Commercial Code (UCC), and tort law. Together, these various provisions of the law provide remedies to buyers and users of goods and services, and to third parties, who suffer physical injuries or financial losses. Two important aspects of the law protecting buyers and users concern warranties and product liability.

Warranties, covered by the law of sales, contract law, and the UCC, provide consumers with remedies when goods that they purchase are not or do not perform as expected. Warranties are addressed in this chapter. Product liability, on the other hand, covered by tort law, provides consumers and users with remedies when they are injured or suffer property damage as a result of defective goods. Product liability is discussed in Chapter 31.

18.2 THE LAW OF WARRANTIES

warranty
A guarantee or promise made by the manufacturer or seller that the goods or services offered really are what they claim to be, or that goods or services are what a reasonable person has a right to expect.

express warranty
An explicit, specifically stated promise.

implied warranty
A guarantee suggested or inferred from known facts and circumstances.

A warranty, as the term is used in the UCC, is a guarantee or promise made by the manufacturer or seller that the goods offered really are what they are claimed to be, or that the goods are what a reasonable person has a right to expect. As discussed in greater detail in this chapter, one warranty that is recognized by the UCC is an express warranty—that is, explicit, specifically stated promises (UCC 2-313). Another recognized warranty is an implied warranty, which is a guarantee suggested or inferred from known facts and circumstances (UCC 2-312 to 2-315).

Like many other areas of the law, rights and obligations are all subject to the courts' applications and interpretations of the law. In addition, the law is always changing as new legislation is passed and as the courts make decisions that break new ground, sometimes overruling decisions made in earlier, similar cases.

While the law dealing with warranties is intended to protect the general public, it often has the effect of limiting the seller's obligations and responsibilities. For example, a warranty for an appliance might state that the manufacturer will replace it if it fails during the first 90 days. While this promise may appear to be a benefit to the buyer, it also relieves the manufacturer of any obligation if the appliance fails after 90 days.

At times, a manufacturer or seller issues statements limiting a warranty to provide less protection than the law requires. While such statements may discourage an unknowledgeable buyer from legal action, they do not have the force of law, and the manufacturer or seller is still responsible for breach of warranty.

EXAMPLE 18.1

▶ Prist purchased a DVD player from JM Electronics for $90. The warranty to which Prist agreed covered parts, but not labor, in cases where repairs became necessary during the first 180 days after the sale. When the DVD player ceased functioning properly after only two months, Prist learned that she would be responsible for $120, the labor portion of the repair bill. Prist recognized that she would be better off just purchasing a new DVD player and that her warranty did not afford her any real protection.

18.3 EXPRESS WARRANTIES

Express warranties can be made in many ways, both orally and in writing, including by promise, description, sample, or model. They also can be made before or after a sale. However, not everything that a salesperson communicates can be construed as a warranty, and sometimes salespeople can disclaim express warranties.

EXPRESS WARRANTY BY PROMISE

An *express warranty* is an explicit, definite promise by the seller that the goods will have certain characteristics. An express warranty that is made by the seller to the buyer and becomes part of the basis of the agreement creates an explicit warranty that the goods will be as promised. If a written warranty is vague and indefinite, the court may apply the custom of the marketplace, or what such a warranty usually means in similar transactions [UCC 2-313(1)(a)].

> **custom of the marketplace**
> What a warranty usually means in similar transactions.

The UCC requirement that the warranty be part of the basis of the agreement has been interpreted to mean that the buyer must have relied on the promise and did not dismiss it as puffing, or sales talk (see Chapter 9).

It is not required that a seller make a specific written or oral statement of warranty for an express warranty to exist. Actions of the seller also may be considered express warranties.

EXAMPLE 18.2

▶ Wiggins, a homeowner, asked Grosso Lumber for 10 sheets of outdoor plywood. The seller delivered the plywood and, by so doing, warranted that the plywood was suitable for outdoor use.

EXPRESS WARRANTY BY DESCRIPTION, SAMPLE, OR MODEL

The UCC states that "any description of goods which is made part of the basis of the bargain creates an express warranty that the goods shall conform to the description" [UCC 2-313(1)(b)]. A manufacturer of electric wire, for example, that accepts orders for No. 8 electric wire would be held to have warranted that the wire shipped will in fact be No. 8.

The UCC also states that any sample or model that "is made part of the basis of the bargain creates an express warranty that the whole of the goods will conform to the sample" or model [UCC 2-313(1)(c)]. A buyer may refuse delivered goods if the goods are not the same as described by the seller or do not conform to the sample or model used by the seller to effect the sale.

EXAMPLE 18.3

▶ Clawson Appliance had on display a General Electric microwave oven Model JE 1590. Prospective buyers were encouraged to examine the appliance, take measurements, and make note of technical specifications. By using a display model as the basis for the sale, Clawson warranted that any of the same model oven it sold would be substantially the same as the one on display.

A sample or model that is made part of the basis of the bargain creates an express warranty that the goods will conform to the sample or model.

THE TIMING OF THE EXPRESS WARRANTY

While most express warranties are made before or during a sales transaction, written or oral statements issued by the seller after the transaction has been completed also can be interpreted as express warranties. Marketers recognize the uneasiness that many buyers experience after having made a buying decision. "Did I make the right decision?" "Should I have purchased the Ford instead of the Acura?" In an effort to reduce this uneasiness, sellers often send out mailings to assure buyers that they did indeed make a wise purchase. These statements, subsequent to the sale, also can be regarded as express warranties.

THE EFFECT OF SELLERS' "PUFFING"

The UCC states that "it is not necessary to the creation of an express warranty that the seller use formal words such as 'warrant' or 'guarantee' or that the seller have a specific intention to make a warranty, but an affirmation merely of the value of the goods or a statement purporting to be merely the seller's opinion or commendation of the goods does not create a warranty" [UCC 2-313(3)]. Consequently, puffing, however sincere and persuasive this sales talk may be, does not constitute a warranty. This is true even if the buyer relies on such statements.

EXAMPLE 18.4

> A salesperson in an appliance store told a customer that the washing machine she was considering "is the best in the world and will be trouble-free for many years to come." Such a statement is considered a mere expression of opinion. Since the statement is mere puffing, it does not form the basis of a warranty and therefore would be unenforceable.

Only when statements of fact about quality of merchandise, construction, price, durability, performance, effectiveness, and safety are made part of the contract and later prove false may the buyer bring action against the seller for breach of express warranty.

DISCLAIMERS OF EXPRESS WARRANTIES

disclaimer
A denial or repudiation in an express warranty that places specific limitations in the warranty.

In an effort to limit the effect of express warranties, some sellers put specific limitations in the warranty. Such a denial or repudiation in an express warranty is known as a disclaimer and serves to limit the effectiveness of a warranty. Suppose, for example, that a manufacturer claims a pump will deliver a certain number of gallons of water per minute. A disclaimer may say, "Warranty does not cover applications where water must be pumped into storage tanks."

Another example of a disclaimer is when oral warranties are given and then followed by a written document containing a disclaimer. This might happen when a salesperson is attempting to be persuasive and promises more orally than the firm is willing to promise in writing. Remember that the *parol evidence rule* would prevent a court from considering such oral statements that were inconsistent in the written document (see Chapter 13).

18.4 IMPLIED WARRANTIES

In addition to the provisions dealing with express warranties, the UCC also makes specific references to implied warranties, which are those warranties not made explicitly but that a buyer might reasonably expect a seller to honor. Implied warranties can relate to either the title or the quality of goods.

TITLE

The UCC provides that "the title conveyed shall be good, and its transfer rightful; and the goods shall be delivered free from any security interest or other lien or encumbrance of which the buyer at the time of contracting has no knowledge" [UCC 2-312(1)(a)(b)]. This simply means the seller promises that

1. He or she is the real owner of the goods offered for sale.
2. The seller has the right to sell the goods.
3. There are no claims or liens of any kind against the goods that might later cause the seller to lose title to someone else who might claim ownership or an interest in the goods.

EXAMPLE 18.5

▶ Futaba bought a used car from Jalik, a college friend, for $4,800. A short time later, a local bank notified Futaba that Jalik owed $700 to the bank, he had used the car as security for the loan, and the indebtedness was recorded at the appropriate county office. As a result, the bank had an interest in the car. Futaba may sue his former friend for his loss on the grounds that the implied warranty of title had been breached.

QUALITY

The law recognizes two types of implied warranties of quality: (1) warranties of merchantability, which are given solely by merchants; and (2) warranties of fitness for a particular purpose, which apply more generally to merchants as well as to others.

Implied Warranty of Merchantability   The law assumes that the goods sold by a merchant/seller are fit to be sold or resold, and therefore carry an implied warranty of merchantability. A merchant is anyone who deals in goods of the kind being sold in the ordinary course of business, or who presents himself or herself as having the skills or knowledge relating to the goods [UCC 2-104(1)]. The UCC provides that when a merchant sells goods, he or she warrants that the goods will:

1. Pass without objection in the trade under the contract description.
2. Be fit for the ordinary purposes for which such goods are sold.
3. Be adequately contained, packaged, and labeled as the agreement may require.
4. Conform to the promises or statements of fact made on the container or label [UCC 2-314(2)].

The implied warranty of merchantability is probably the most important warranty the law provides from the viewpoint of the buyer. It imposes a general duty upon the merchant/seller to furnish goods that are at least of minimum acceptable quality.

implied warranty of merchantability
The law's assumption that goods sold by a merchant/seller are fit to be sold and are adequate for the ordinary purposes for which such goods are sold.

merchant
An individual who deals in goods of the kind being sold in the ordinary course of business, or who presents himself or herself as having the skills or knowledge relating to the goods.

EXAMPLE 18.6

▶ Dos Santos entered a diner and ordered a turkey club sandwich. When she examined it, she noticed a foreign substance, which turned out to be a form of mold. She complained to the manager and, since there was a breach of the implied warranty of merchantability, Dos Santos was provided with a replacement sandwich at no additional charge.

implied warranty of fitness for a particular purpose
The law's assumption that goods are fit for their intended use.

Implied Warranty of Fitness for a Particular Purpose If a seller, at the time of making a contract, knows or has reason to know any particular purpose for which the goods are required and that the buyer is relying on the seller's skill or judgment in selecting or furnishing suitable goods, there is an implied warranty of fitness for a particular purpose (sometimes referred to as *fitness of purpose*). That is, the goods must be fit for the intended purpose (UCC 2-315).

EXAMPLE 18.7

▶ Business Printers, Inc., informed its supplier that it was seeking a new high-speed press that would be suitable for printing high-quality, four-color brochures. Bonhomme, the manufacturer's representative, thinking more of his commission than the needs of his customer, recommended a particular press. When the press was delivered and installed, Business Printers discovered that it printed only in black. Clearly Bonhomme violated the manufacturer's implied warranty of fitness of purpose.

It must be noted, however, that an implied warranty of fitness exists even if the buyer does not expressly inform the seller of his or her intended use of the merchandise. To recover for breach of the implied warranty of fitness of purpose, a buyer must prove that (1) the seller knew or had reason to know the buyer's purpose, (2) the seller knew or had reason to know that the buyer was relying on the seller's skill or judgment, and (3) the buyer did rely on the seller's skill or judgment.

DISCLAIMERS OF IMPLIED WARRANTIES

The two important implied warranties of merchantability and of fitness for a particular purpose may be disclaimed in several ways. The UCC provides specific rules that must be followed by a seller who wants to avoid the responsibility of these implied warranties. A disclaimer of the warranty of merchantability must mention the word *merchantability*. If the disclaimer is in writing, it must be conspicuous; that is, it cannot be buried in the fine print of the contract (UCC 2-316). In fact, most states require a specific type size or mandate that the disclaimer must be in bold print.

Disclaimers of the warranty of fitness for a particular purpose must be in writing and must be conspicuous. Such warranties are excluded by the use of expressions such as "as is" or "with all faults" or other language that would call the buyer's attention to the exclusion of this implied warranty (UCC 2-316).

The court may refuse to enforce unconscionable disclaimers, just as it may refuse to enforce unconscionable contracts as discussed in Chapter 9 (UCC-302). *Unconscionable disclaimers* are ones that are inconspicuous, oppressive, or unfair.

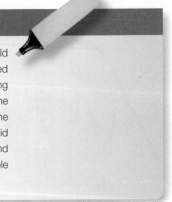

EXAMPLE 18.8

▶ Hao went to an electronics store to shop for a new television. A salesperson at the store told Hao that all new televisions include a 12-month warranty. Hao purchased the set and received the receipt when the television was delivered. Hao hung the television on the wall of her living room and enjoyed it until it stopped working two months later. When Hao made a claim with the store based on the implied warranty of merchantability, the salesperson refused to honor the warranty, pointing out that the receipt contained a disclaimer stating that the warranty was void if the television was installed on a wall. Since Hao had not read the disclaimer on the receipt, and because the disclaimer seems unfair, a court will likely find the disclaimer to be unconscionable and thus unenforceable.

18.5 MAGNUSON-MOSS WARRANTY LEGISLATION

Even with the protection provided by the UCC, consumers were not always protected adequately. The Magnuson-Moss Warranty Act addresses many different kinds of abuses to consumers relating to warranties.

Magnuson-Moss Warranty Act
A federal statute that addresses many different kinds of abuses to consumers relating to warranties.

PROVISIONS OF MAGNUSON-MOSS

The Magnuson-Moss Warranty Act applies only when written warranties are made voluntarily on consumer products that cost more than $25. Under the act, a seller or manufacturer must clearly disclose the details of such warranties to the consumer prior to the purchase of a warranted product. In addition, the act requires that such warranties must be labeled as either "full" or "limited." The act applies only to purchases by consumers of tangible personal property normally used for personal, family, or household purposes, not to commercial or industrial transactions. Because it is a federal statute, the act affects only warranties on products that are sold in interstate commerce—that is, trade between two or more states.

interstate commerce
Trade between two or more states.

The type of warranty to which the act applies is much more narrowly defined than is an express warranty under the UCC. Specifically, warranties covered by the act are (1) any written statement of fact made by a seller to a purchaser relating to the quality or performance of a product and stating that the product is free of defects or that it will meet a specified level of performance over a period of time, or (2) a written promise to "refund, repair, replace, or take other action" if a product fails to meet written specifications.

Obviously express warranties that are not in writing, such as those created by verbal description or by sample, continue to be governed solely by the UCC, even though a consumer transaction is involved.

DISTINCTION BETWEEN FULL AND LIMITED WARRANTY

The Magnuson-Moss Act makes a distinction between a *full warranty* and a *limited warranty*.

Full Warranty A full warranty promises that a defective product will be repaired without charge within a reasonable time after a complaint has been made. If the product cannot be repaired within a reasonable time, the consumer may receive either a replacement product or a refund of the purchase price. The consumer is not required to do anything unreasonable, such as ship a heavy product back to the factory, to obtain warranty service. In addition, a full warranty applies to anyone who owns the product during the warranty period, not just the original buyer. No time limitation can be placed on a full warranty.

full warranty
The promise that a defective product will be repaired without charge and within a reasonable time after a complaint has been made.

Lemon laws are statutes that provide remedies to consumers for products such as automobiles that repeatedly fail to meet certain standards of quality and performance.

limited warranty
A written warranty that does not meet the minimum requirements of a full warranty.

lemon laws
Statutes that provide remedies to consumers for products such as automobiles that repeatedly fail to meet certain standards of quality and performance.

Limited Warranty A written warranty that does not meet the minimum requirements of a full warranty must be designated as a limited warranty. If only a time limitation distinguishes a limited warranty from a full warranty, then the act permits the seller to indicate this fact by such language as "full 12-month warranty."

For additional information regarding the Magnuson-Moss Warranty Act, visit www.ftc.gov/bcp/edu/pubs/business/adv/bus01.shtm#Magnuson-Moss.

REMEDIES

Generally, a consumer who has suffered damages due to a violation of the provisions of the Magnuson-Moss Warranty Act may sue for breach of warranty in state court. If, however, a large number of consumers are injured by the same seller, a *class action lawsuit,* which is a lawsuit collectively filed by many individuals, may be brought against the seller in federal court. In either situation, consumers can recover court costs and attorney's fees if they win the case.

LEMON LAWS

The Magnuson-Moss Warranty Act is sometimes referred to as the *federal lemon law.* In addition to federal law, consumers are also protected by lemon laws enacted by the individual states. Lemon laws are statutes that provide remedies to consumers for products such as automobiles that repeatedly fail to meet certain standards of quality and performance. Lemon laws vary greatly from state to state, and may not necessarily cover used or leased products. "Lemon law" is the common nickname for these laws, but each state has different names for its laws and acts. For additional information about state lemon laws visit www.bbb.org/us/auto-line/state-lemon-laws.

CHAPTER SUMMARY

1. Consumers and third parties are protected by the law of sales, contract law, the UCC, and tort law. Together these various provisions of the law provide remedies to buyers and users of goods and services, and to third parties who suffer physical injuries or financial losses.

2. A warranty is a guarantee made by a manufacturer or a seller that the goods offered for sale are what they are claimed to be, or that the goods are what a reasonable person has a right to expect. An express warranty is explicitly stated, whereas an implied warranty is suggested or inferred from known facts and circumstances.

3. Express warranties can be made both orally and in writing, by promise, description, sample, or model.

4. Implied warranties include that of ownership when title is passed and of merchantability and fitness for a particular purpose in contracts for the sale of goods.

5. The Magnuson-Moss Warranty Act addresses many different kinds of abuses to consumers relating to warranties.

CHAPTER EIGHTEEN
ASSESSMENT

MATCHING LEGAL TERMS

Match each of the numbered definitions with the correct term in the following list. Write the letter of your choice in the answer column.

a. disclaimer
b. express warranty
c. full warranty
d. implied warranty
e. limited warranty
f. product liability
g. custom of the marketplace
h. warranty of fitness for a particular purpose
i. warranty of merchantability
j. warranty of title

1. A warranty provided by law for the protection of the buyer and not specifically included in the agreement. 1. _____

2. An implied warranty that goods are suitable for the specific purpose for which they are sold. 2. _____

3. What a vague or ambiguous warranty usually means in similar transactions. 3. _____

4. A denial or repudiation of an express warranty made at the time of sale. 4. _____

5. An implied warranty that the seller actually owns the goods sold. 5. _____

6. Law that provides consumers and users with remedies when they are injured or suffer property damage as a result of defective goods. 6. _____

7. An implied warranty that goods sold are fit for the ordinary purpose for which they are intended. 7. _____

8. A written or oral promise or statement regarding goods sold. 8. _____

9. Under the Magnuson-Moss Act, a warranty that requires a seller to repair or replace a defective product without charge within a reasonable time. 9. _____

10. Under the Magnuson-Moss Act, the designation that must be used if a warranty does not meet the minimum requirements. 10. _____

TRUE/FALSE QUIZ

Indicate whether each of the following statements is true or false by writing *T* or *F* in the answer column.

11. Warranties are promises or statements made by manufacturers or sellers. 11. _____

12. While the law dealing with warranties is intended to protect the general public, it often has the effect of limiting the seller's obligations and responsibilities. 12. _____

13. Any warranty can be canceled if the seller claims that it is causing him or her to lose money. 13. _____

14. A specific oral promise made by a seller is an implied warranty.

14. _____

15. The Uniform Commercial Code clearly specifies requirements that manufacturers or sellers must follow in making disclaimers.

15. _____

16. Sales talk, or puffing, is considered a warranty.

16. _____

17. The implied warranty of merchantability means that all merchants warrant their goods to be of the highest quality.

17. _____

18. There is an implied warranty of title with the sale of merchandise that means the seller actually owns the goods.

18. _____

19. Custom of the marketplace can be applied by a court when a warranty is vague and indefinite.

19. _____

20. The sale of food involves the implied warranty of merchantability.

20. _____

21. Promises and statements issued after the sale have no effect on the warranty of a product.

21. _____

22. A disclaimer of a warranty of fitness for a particular purpose is effective if it includes expressions such as "as is" or "with all faults."

22. _____

23. The parol evidence rule allows a court to consider oral statements of warranties, even if these are inconsistent with the written express warranties.

23. _____

24. An implied warranty of fitness may exist even if the buyer does not make his or her intended use of the merchandise known to the seller.

24. _____

25. While there are express warranties that relate to quality, there are no implied warranties relating to such.

25. _____

DISCUSSION QUESTIONS

Answer the following questions and discuss them in class.

26. Explain the term *warranty* and distinguish between express and implied warranties.

_____

_____

27. Provide examples of four kinds of express warranties and three kinds of implied warranties.

_____

_____

28. Explain disclaimers of implied warranties and the requirements for them to be legally valid.

_____

_____

29. Explain the provisions of the Magnuson-Moss Warranty Act.

_____

_____

30. Explain the effect of warranties offered after a transaction has been completed.

_____

_____

_____

THINKING CRITICALLY ABOUT THE LAW

Answer the following questions, which require you to think critically about the legal principles that you learned in this chapter.

31. Custom of the Marketplace In the case of a vague or indefinite written warranty, how can a court determine what such a warranty usually means in similar transactions?

_____

_____

32. Disclaimers What is the primary objective of warranty disclaimers?

_____

_____

33. Disclaimers Should the law distinguish between a reasonable basis for a warranty disclaimer and one that attempts to substantially negate the warranty?

_____

_____

34. Oral Warranties How would the law distinguish between oral statements of warranty and puffing?

_____

_____

35. A Question of Ethics Can it be ethically justified for a manufacturer to sell a product with a warranty less than the law requires?

_____

_____

CASE QUESTIONS

Study each of the following cases. Answer the questions that follow by writing _Yes_ or _No_ in the answer column.

36. Warranty Buynoski, the operator of a restaurant, served a dinner to Costas. Costas had nearly finished her soup when she found several metal chips in the bottom of her bowl. When Costas showed the chips to Buynoski, the restaurant owner was very apologetic and offered not to charge for the meal. Costas, still angry at the risk to which she had been exposed, said, "I'll see you in court!"

a. Does Costas have a case involving a warranty?   a. _____

b. Had Buynoski offered an express warranty?   b. _____

c. Could Costas claim an implied warranty of fitness of purpose?   c. _____

37. **Disclaimer** Liang was about to purchase an air-conditioning unit for her apartment at a closeout sale at Center City Appliance. The salesperson assured her that the unit was large enough to cool the apartment she described. The price was right, but she was nervous when the salesperson said, "Remember that you're taking this unit 'as is.'" When she found that the unit would not cool the apartment, she returned to the store, where she claimed that the unit had been sold with an implied warranty of fitness for a particular purpose. The salesperson reminded her that he had said "as is."

a. Can the oral disclaimer void the implied warranty of fitness for
a particular purpose?   a. _____

b. Is there an implied warranty still in effect?   b. _____

c. Is Liang reasonable in her demand?   c. _____

38. **Warranty** Pathek sold a pair of skis to Whelan, making no specific warranties or promises of any kind other than letting Whelan examine and try them. In fact, Pathek did not own the skis; he had only rented them. When the true owner claimed them, Whelan demanded his money back. Pathek defended his actions by stating that he had made no warranty of any kind.

a. Did Pathek give an implied warranty of title?   a. _____

b. Will Whelan be able to recover his money?   b. _____

c. Did Pathek give an express warranty of any kind?   c. _____

CASE ANALYSIS

Study each of the following cases carefully. Briefly state the principle of law and your decision.

39. **Warranty** Walters bought a power lawnmower. Attached to the engine was a tag that read in part, "For 90 days from purchase date Power Engine Company will replace for the original purchaser, free of charge, any part or parts found, upon examination at any factory authorized dealer, to be defective under normal use and service." Two weeks after purchase, the starter mechanism broke, and Walters returned her machine to the factory authorized dealer. Can the dealer be compelled to repair the mower?

Principle of Law:

_____

_____

Decision:

_____

_____

40. Warranty Adano Restaurant Supply, which sells only to commercial customers, sold 200 plastic dishes to Airport Diner. When the owner of the diner attempted to wash the dishes in the dishwasher, they were distorted by the heat. Airport Diner claimed that there was an implied warranty of fitness for a particular purpose, since most restaurants used the same type of dishwasher it did. When the owner bought the dishes from Adano, he assumed that they could be washed with the equipment in his restaurant. Does Airport Diner have a legal remedy?

Principle of Law:

_____

_____

Decision:

_____

_____

41. Disclaimer Ferguson contracted to buy a quantity of knitting yarn. After receipt he cut it and knitted it into sweaters. At this point, he discovered color variations from one piece to another. Ferguson refused to pay the agreed price, claiming that the yarn had been sold with a warranty of merchantability. The seller, Wilson Trading Corporation, sued to collect the contract price and pointed out that the sales contract provided that "no claims . . . shall be allowed if made after weaving, knitting, or processing, or more than ten days after receipt of shipment." Ferguson viewed the time-limit clause as modifying the warranty of merchantability, which was stated explicitly elsewhere in the contract, and that the disclaimer was in conflict with the warranty. Will the disclaimer be viewed as negating the warranty? [*Wilson Trading Corp. v. David Ferguson, Ltd.,* 244 N.E.2d 685 (New York)]

Principle of Law:

_____

_____

Decision:

_____

_____

LEGAL RESEARCH

Complete the following activities. Share your findings with the class.

42. Working in Teams In teams of three or four, visit an appliance retailer. Check the warranties on various products to find out their duration, disclaimers, and any other related information. What safety information is included?

_____

_____

43. Using Technology Using the Internet and search engines, find additional information about the Magnuson-Moss Warranty Act.

_____

_____

chapter **19**
Agency

LEGAL terms

agent	agency by ratification
principal	agency by necessity
contract of agency	agency by operation of law
general agent	
special agent	express authority
power of attorney	implied authority
attorney in fact	apparent authority
durable power of attorney	gratuitous agent
	irrevocable agency

AGENCY

"I don't take every offer that comes along—I get a lot of them. I think sometimes my agent gets mad at me!"

*Serena Williams,
professional tennis player*

19.1 PRINCIPAL–AGENT RELATIONSHIPS

It is often necessary or desirable for a person or firm to be represented by another in business or personal dealings with third parties. This relationship is called a principal–agent relationship. The person who represents another is known as the agent. The person the agent represents or for whom he or she performs duties is called the principal. An agreement between a principal and an agent by which the agent is vested with authority to represent the principal is known as a contract of agency. Many, but not all, employees act as agents of their employers. Often an agent is not specifically referred to as an agent, and similarly, some people or firms referred to as agents or as an agency are not really agents at all. For example, an automobile dealership may be referred to as an agency when the dealer is simply a retailer selling a product made by a manufacturer. As a result, it is important to distinguish between an agency relationship and other forms of relationships.

agent
A person authorized to act on behalf of another and subject to the other's control in dealing with third parties.

principal
A person who authorizes an agent to act on his or her behalf and subject to his or her control.

contract of agency
An agreement between a principal and an agent by which the agent is vested with authority to represent the principal.

WHO MAY APPOINT AN AGENT

Any competent party (a person or a corporation) who has the legal right to perform an act may delegate his or her performance to another by appointing an agent. Certain acts of a personal character, however, such as voting, serving on juries, rendering professional services, and holding public office, may not be delegated to others.

A minor who has appointed an agent may avoid the contract of agency in some states, just as he or she may avoid other kinds of contracts, as discussed in Chapter 11. In some instances, courts have held that minors who operate businesses are bound by the contracts they make. So, too, is a minor who operates a business and whose agent enters into contracts with third parties.

EXAMPLE 19.1

▶ Diego, a minor who owned an automobile repair shop, employed Fogel, an adult, as head mechanic. Fogel contracted with Mid-City Auto Supply for the purchase of needed supplies and equipment. When the order was delivered, Diego refused to accept it. In some states, Diego has a right to avoid the contract, just as if he had entered into the contract himself.

WHO MAY BE APPOINTED AS AN AGENT

Anyone who is legally competent to act for himself or herself may serve as an agent for another. Minors and others who lack the capacity to enter into contracts on their own (discussed in Chapter 11) may still be considered competent to represent other persons as agents if they are capable of properly carrying out the duties of an agency relationship. Additionally, an organization, such as a partnership or corporation, may act as an agent (see Chapter 20).

EXAMPLE 19.2

▶ Jutson, a minor, was employed by Quong as a buyer in the young men's department of a retail clothing store. Jutson's duties included making contracts with third parties in the name of his employer. Jutson's contracts are binding on Quong because of the legal relationship of principal and agent that exists between them. Jutson is expected to exercise good judgment and discretion in making contracts for his employer, just as any other agent would be.

19.2 CLASSES OF AGENTS

Agents are usually classified according to the nature of their relationship with their principals.

GENERAL AGENT
A general agent is a person authorized to assume complete charge of his or her principal's business or who is entrusted with general authority to act for the principal in all business-related matters.

SPECIAL AGENT
A special agent is a person delegated to act only in a particular transaction, under definite instructions, and with specific limits on the scope of his or her authority. Examples of special agents are real estate firms that have been given authority to manage the property of an owner; lawyers who have been given authority to manage the financial affairs of a client; and auctioneers who have been given authority to represent a seller. Typically, the average real estate broker is not acting as an agent if his or her responsibility is limited to locating a buyer or seller of real property.

19.3 CREATION OF AGENCY

An agency may be created by agreement, ratification, necessity, or operation of law.

AGENCY BY AGREEMENT
The most common method of creating an agency is by contract or agreement. A contract of agency usually states the rights and duties of the principal and the agent, the duration of the agency, and any other agreements made between the parties. Generally, an agency contract may be either oral or written, and either express or implied. The requirements of the Statute of Frauds (discussed in Chapter 13) concerning the kinds of contracts that must be in writing also apply to contracts of agency. For example, a contract appointing an agent must be in writing if the appointment is to extend beyond a year.

The legal document that formally creates an agency is called a power of attorney. The precise legal term for the person appointed as agent is attorney in fact. If, for example, Nancy Williams, an agent, signs documents on behalf of Susan McGowan, her principal, the signature is "Susan McGowan, by Nancy Williams, her attorney in fact."

A principal must be competent in order to appoint an agent. In the event a principal becomes incompetent after an agent has been appointed, the power of attorney may be invalidated. A principal should execute a document known as a durable power of attorney if he or she intends for the agent's authority to act on his or her behalf to remain intact in the event the principal becomes incompetent. Alternatively, a durable power of attorney can be used to give an attorney in fact authority to act on behalf of the principal only in the event the principal becomes incompetent. Often, durable power of attorneys are used in health care situations (see Chapter 27).

general agent
A person authorized to assume complete charge of his or her principal's business or who is entrusted with general authority to act for the principal in all business-related matters.

special agent
A person delegated to act only in a particular transaction, under definite instructions, and with specific limits on the scope of his or her authority.

power of attorney
An instrument in writing by which one person, as principal, appoints another person as agent and confers the authority to perform certain specified acts on behalf of the principal.

attorney in fact
The person appointed as agent when the power of attorney is exercised.

durable power of attorney
An instrument that documents a principal's desire for an agent's authority to remain intact in the event the principal is incapacitated; or to become effective only in the event the principal becomes incompetent.

EXAMPLE 19.3

▶ Ogle, the owner of a gift shop, expected to be out of the country for several months on a buying trip to Asia. Although she employed several salespeople, Ogle did not trust any of them to run the business during her absence. She appointed Gross, her brother-in-law, as an agent, by power of attorney, and gave him the authority to hire and discharge employees, renew the lease on her store, set prices, purchase merchandise, and perform other such duties as necessary. The relationship between Ogle and Gross is that of principal and agent, created by power of attorney.

AGENCY BY RATIFICATION

agency by ratification
An agency that results when a principal approves an unauthorized act performed by an agent or approves an act done in the principal's name by an unauthorized person.

An agency by ratification results when a principal (1) approves an unauthorized act performed by an agent or (2) approves an act done in the principal's name by an unauthorized person. The ratification must apply to the entire act; a principal cannot accept the benefits of such a transaction and refuse to accept the obligations that are a part of it. Ratification occurs after the fact, while authorization (in an agency by agreement) occurs before the fact.

EXAMPLE 19.4

▶ Geiser purchased a camera on behalf of a friend, Jacinto, without his knowledge or consent. Geiser asked the dealer to hold the camera until directed to deliver it. When Jacinto learned of the purchase, he could have canceled the purchase. Instead, he notified the dealer to send the camera immediately. By this act, Jacinto ratified the unauthorized purchase. Therefore, Jacinto cannot later refuse to accept and pay for the camera. Jacinto's responsibility dates from the time of the original transaction with Geiser, not from the time of ratification. Jacinto is bound by the contract just as if Geiser had possessed full authority to make it.

AGENCY BY NECESSITY

agency by necessity
An agency that is created when circumstances make such an agency necessary.

An agency by necessity is created when circumstances make such an agency necessary. Although a family relationship does not normally give members of a family the right to act as agents for one another, the law in some states recognizes an agency by necessity when one spouse fails to support the other spouse or their minor children. In these states the spouse acting as agent for the other spouse, may purchase necessities for himself or herself and their children, even against the will of the nonsupporting spouse, and thereby makes the other spouse responsible for payment. Similarly, a minor may purchase necessities if his or her parent fails to provide these.

agency by operation of law
An agency that is created when a court finds the need for an agency to achieve a desired social policy.

AGENCY BY OPERATION OF LAW

An agency by operation of law is created when a court finds the need for an agency to achieve a desired social policy. For example, a child's parent may not be providing the child with certain necessities of life. In this case, a court may appoint an agent, called a *guardian ad litem,* with the authority to purchase whatever necessities the parent has failed to provide. Under such a court-directed agency, the parent would be bound by reasonable contracts made by the agent.

A court may appoint a guardian ad litem, with the authority to purchase whatever necessities the parent has failed to provide.

19.4 AUTHORITY OF AN AGENT

An agent may perform only those acts that have been authorized by the principal or court. If an agent exceeds the authority, he or she can become personally liable unless the unauthorized act was reasonably assumed by a third party to be within the powers delegated to the agent. Just as third parties can be justified in assuming that an agent has certain authority, so, too, an agent can be justified in assuming that he or she has certain authority not specifically stated in the contract of agency. While the courts have an interest in protecting the property and the interests of the principal, they also have an interest in protecting the property and interests of third parties who may have had good reason to rely on the apparent authority of the agent.

The authority of an agent can be express, implied, or apparent.

EXPRESS OR IMPLIED AUTHORITY

The authority of an agent to perform the duties that are specifically stated in the contract of agency is known as express authority—that is, the authority that has actually been given by the principal, either orally or in writing.

Authority also can be implied by the agency relationship. Implied authority is the authority an agent reasonably assumes he or she has that relates to the express authority granted by the principal. If, for example, the agency agreement gives the agent the express authority to purchase goods for the principal, the agent has implied authority to purchase the goods using the principal's credit. It is easy to confuse implied authority with apparent authority, discussed in the following paragraph. Remember that implied authority is the relationship between principal and agent in which the principal implies the authority. This authority is sometimes called incidental authority. For example, if *A* appoints *B* as his agent and asks *B* to purchase a car for him, *B* has the implied authority to fill the tank with gasoline.

express authority
An agent's authority that the principal voluntarily and specifically sets forth as oral or written instructions in an agency agreement.

implied authority
The authority an agent reasonably assumes he or she has that relates to the express authority granted by the principal.

APPARENT AUTHORITY

Apparent authority is the authority that a third party may reasonably assume an agent possesses, despite the fact that the agent does not actually possess such authority. It would be reasonable, for example, for a third party to assume that a retail store manager has the authority to set prices, hire salespeople, and purchase merchandise, because the customs of the business usually give store managers this kind of authority. On the other hand, it would be unreasonable for the owner of a multistory building to assume that a store manager had the authority to sign a 20-year lease.

apparent authority
The authority that a third party may reasonably assume an agent possesses, despite the fact that the agent does not actually possess such authority.

EXAMPLE 19.5

▶ Kertz, the assistant manager of the sporting goods department of a large store, offered customers a 25 percent reduction on the prices of all merchandise in her department during an end-of-season sale, despite the fact that authority to change prices was limited by the store to managers. Since customers (third parties) would be reasonable in assuming that Kertz had authority to reduce prices, the store is bound to these customers under the doctrine of apparent authority.

AGENT'S TORTS AND CRIMES

A principal is liable for the torts and crimes of the agent if they are committed at the direction of the principal or while the agent is performing authorized duties during the ordinary course of the agency. Thus, if an agent makes a fraudulent statement in a contract within the scope of his or her authority, the principal is responsible. In such a case, the third party may either cancel the contract with the principal and recover compensation for losses sustained, or affirm the contract and sue the principal for any monetary damages. Whether an agent commits a tort or crime willfully, recklessly, or negligently, the fact of the principal's liability is the same. Both the principal and the agent may be held liable for an agent's torts or crimes committed while the agent is acting within the scope of his or her authority.

EXAMPLE 19.6

▶ Mamnani, acting as a sales agent in an electronics store owned by Fischer, purchased, and intended to resell, merchandise that Mamnani knew to be stolen. If Fischer knew of the nature of the merchandise, both Mamnani (the agent) and Fischer (the principal) would be subject to criminal prosecution. On the other hand, if only Mamnani knew that the merchandise was stolen, Fischer would not be subject to prosecution since purchasing and selling stolen merchandise was not within the scope of Mamnani's authority.

19.5 DUTIES OF AGENTS, PRINCIPALS, AND THIRD PARTIES

When an agency is created, three parties are affected—the agent, the principal, and the third party. Each of these parties has duties to one another. We now turn our attention to these rights and obligations.

DUTIES OF AGENT TO PRINCIPAL

There are several duties that an agent owes to a principal:

▶ An agent must obey all the principal's reasonable and lawful orders and instructions within the scope of the agency contract.

▶ An agent may not perform any act that would betray the principal's trust.

- An agent may not act for two parties to a contract without the consent of both.

- An agent may not buy his or her own property for the principal, sell the principal's property to himself or herself, or compete with the principal in any way, without the principal's knowledge and consent.

- An agent must possess the qualifications needed to carry out the work of the agency as agreed.

- An agent is liable for losses to the principal resulting from the agent's incompetence.

- An agent must keep accurate accounts of his or her transactions conducted as part of the agency agreement.

- An agent must remit to the principal all profits from contracts made by the agent unless other provisions are made in the agency agreement.

EXAMPLE 19.7

- Basso, a sales representative employed by Gilman Products, was authorized to enter into contracts for the installation of burglar alarms. His responsibilities included negotiating prices for the complete installation and arranging for local workers to install the alarms. General guidelines were established for the usual prices of the equipment sold and the fees to be paid for the installation. On the sale of a system to Ballwin, Basso correctly gauged Ballwin's urgent need for the alarm and his high income. The price quoted was considerably higher than usual for an installation of this kind. Basso was also fortunate in locating a maintenance worker who was willing to do the work for much less than the usual rate. While there was a very substantial profit because of the higher sales price and the lower installation cost, the higher profits all belong to Gilman Products (the principal).

DUTIES OF PRINCIPAL TO AGENT

There are several duties that a principal owes to an agent:

- A principal must pay the agent the compensation agreed to in the contract.

- If a person acts as an agent for more than one party with their knowledge, the agent is entitled to receive compensation from each principal.

- A principal must reimburse the agent for any money advanced by the agent in carrying out the principal's instructions and for debts legally paid to third parties on behalf of the principal.

- A principal must reimburse the agent for any loss or damage suffered by the agent in the legitimate performance of duties.

In all cases where an agent is owed money by the principal and is in possession of the principal's property or goods, the agent may place a lien and refuse to surrender the property or goods to the principal until payment has been made.

Although the majority of agents are paid, it is not necessary for an agent to receive compensation for his or her services in order for an agency relationship to exist. A gratuitous agent is one who acts on behalf of a principal without being paid. One should note, however, that gratuitous agents are held to a lower level of liability than paid agents.

gratuitous agent
One who acts on behalf of a principal without being paid.

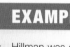

EXAMPLE 19.8

> Hillman was employed as a sales representative for the Common Merchandise Company. As part of his agreement with the company, he received a salary, commission, and traveling expenses. The automobile that Hillman used was supplied by the company. While on a business trip, Hillman finished his work early and took a side trip to visit friends 75 miles off his normal route. A hit-and-run driver damaged the car through no fault of Hillman. It cost $1,500 to have the damages repaired. The company need not reimburse Hillman for the repairs because the cost of these was an expense unrelated to the discharge of his duties and not in the ordinary course of the agency.

A principal is responsible to third parties for all agreements made by the agent on behalf of the principal if the agent acted within the scope of his or her authority.

DUTIES OF PRINCIPAL AND THIRD PARTY TO EACH OTHER

A principal is responsible to a third party for all agreements made by the agent on behalf of the principal if the agent acted within the scope of his or her authority, either express or implied. If, however, the agreement was not authorized by the principal, and if it was apparently (or obviously) outside the scope of the agent's employment, the principal is not liable. The third party is liable to the principal on all lawful contracts made by his or her agent.

EXAMPLE 19.9

> Masoudi, a distributor, whose business was limited to the sale of computers, employed Foxen as a sales representative in a certain territory. Even though Masoudi did not accept trade-ins, Foxen offered Sciamenti an arrangement whereby Foxen would exchange a laptop computer for Sciamenti's used photocopy machine. If Foxen, after taking possession of Sciamenti's photocopy machine, refused to surrender the laptop computer, Sciamenti could not require Masoudi to give it to him. There would be no apparent authority since Sciamenti should have suspected that Foxen's offer was beyond the scope of his actual (express or implied) or apparent authority.

DUTIES OF AGENT AND THIRD PARTY TO EACH OTHER

The relationship between an agent and a third party, and whether an agent can be held personally responsible, are influenced by a number of factors.

Disclosed Principal   When the agent informs the third party that he or she is acting on behalf of another, and makes the third party aware of the identity of the principal, the principal is known as a *disclosed principal.* For example, when an agent signs a contract "Louise Smith, by Susan Jacobs, Agent" or merely signs the principal's name, he or she is acting on behalf of a disclosed principal.

Because the third party knows of the agency and knows the identity of the principal, the agent cannot be held personally responsible as long as the agent acts within the scope of his or her actual authority.

Partially Disclosed Principal   When the agent informs the third party that he or she is acting on behalf of another, but the identity of the principal is unknown to the third party, the principal is known as a *partially disclosed principal.* For example, when the agent signs his or her own name and the title "Agent," he or she is acting on behalf of a partially disclosed principal.

Because the third party does not know the identity of the principal, the agent can be held personally responsible to the third party. If the agent acts with authority (either actual or apparent), and the third party later learns of the identity of the principal, the third party may also hold the principal liable.

Undisclosed Principal   When the agent does not inform the third party that he or she is acting on behalf of another person, the unidentified principal is known as an *undisclosed principal.*

Once again, because the third party does not know the identity of the principal, the agent can be held personally responsible to the third party. Similarly, if the agent acts with authority (either actual or apparent), and the third party later learns of the fact of the agency and the identity of the principal, the third party may also hold the principal liable.

EXAMPLE 19.10

▶ Watanabe, as agent for Bangor Supply, purchased 500 bags of Portland cement from Northwest Cement without disclosing his agent status. After shipment, Watanabe attempted to cancel the order. Northwest Cement can sue Watanabe because he became a party to the contract when he neglected to disclose his principal during his dealings with Northwest. If Northwest Cement learned later that Watanabe was an agent for Bangor, Northwest might choose to sue Bangor instead, or it could sue both Bangor and Watanabe.

19.6 TERMINATION OF AGENCY

Agency is a type of contract and, like other contracts, may be terminated by agreement, by performance, or by operation of law.

An agency contract is terminated by an act of the parties when (1) the principal and the agent have mutually agreed on termination, (2) the principal has dismissed the agent, (3) the agent has given up the position, or (4) the purpose of the agency relationship is fulfilled.

If an agency exists "at will," the principal has the right to revoke the agency agreement and discharge the agent for a reason, such as incompetence, disloyalty, or similar shortcomings, or for no reason at all.

A principal who dismisses an agent must give notice of the termination of the agency to all third parties who are accustomed to doing business with the agent or who have knowledge of the appointment. Failure to do so will render the principal liable on any further contracts made by the agent in the principal's name because the agent would still have apparent authority in the eyes of third parties until they have been notified.

irrevocable agency
An agency contract that cannot be terminated by a principal in which the agent has an interest in the subject matter of the agency in addition to the remuneration that he or she receives for services.

A principal may not revoke an agency contract if the agent has an interest in the subject matter of the agency in addition to the remuneration (e.g., salary, commissions) that he or she receives for services. Such a contract is an **irrevocable agency**, or an *agency coupled with an interest.* An agency agreement that authorizes an agent to sell specific property, deduct commissions, and apply the proceeds toward an outstanding debt that the principal owes the agent is an example of an irrevocable agency. Similarly, partners who have a shared interest in a business are agents for each other and cannot dismiss each other (see Chapter 20).

EXAMPLE 19.11

▶ A manufacturer of office machines offered Irving a three-year exclusive agency to sell a new model of fax machines. Irving accepted the offer and paid the agreed-upon price of $25,000. The manufacturer/principal cannot revoke the agreement until the end of the three-year period. This contract is an example of an agency coupled with an interest.

With the exception of an agency coupled with an interest, the death of either party terminates the agency contract immediately. The agency relationship also may be terminated by insanity, illness, impossibility of performance, disloyalty, or bankruptcy.

19.7 DIFFERENCES BETWEEN PRINCIPAL–AGENT AND EMPLOYER–EMPLOYEE RELATIONSHIPS

The legal principles governing the relationship of principal and agent and of employer and employee are, in many respects, the same. The main difference between principal–agent and employer–employee relationships is an employer's power to control the activities of a non-agent employee. Whereas an agency agreement brings about a relationship between a principal and a third party that results in a contract, an employee who is not also an agent has no such rights or powers. An employee acts under the employer's direction and is subject to the employer's control.

The employer controls not only what shall be done by the employee but also how it shall be done. If, however, an employee is required to perform duties for the employer that necessitate the exercise of judgment and discretion and that result in the establishment of a contractual relationship between the employer and a third party, then the employee has the status of an agent even without a formal contract of agency.

EXAMPLE 19.12

▶ Stein operated an automobile repair shop and frequently sent a senior mechanic, Lopez, to the local auto parts distributor to purchase parts needed for repairs. The cost of the parts was charged to Stein's account, which he paid periodically.

In Example 19.12, Lopez is clearly an employee. Lopez is also Stein's agent, with authority to enter into contracts for the purchase of parts on behalf of the repair shop. If Lopez bought parts for his own use without Stein's permission, the parts distributor could still collect from Stein because an employer is responsible for the acts of employees performed within the scope of the employee's duties, and because the parts distributor would reasonably believe that Lopez had an agent's authority. If Stein had directed Lopez to negotiate an agreement for a quantity discount on parts with the supplier for future purchases, Lopez would be an agent with actual express authority to enter into such an agreement.

Some employees are agents; some are not. Some agents are also employees and some are not. The two relationships are judged independently.

CHAPTER SUMMARY

1. The person who represents another is known as the agent. The person whom the agent represents is called the principal. An agreement between a principal and an agent by which the agent is vested with authority to represent the principal is known as a contract of agency.

2. The major kinds of agents are general agents, persons authorized to assume complete charge of their principal's business; and special agents, persons delegated to act only in particular transactions.

3. An agency can be created by agreement, ratification, necessity, or operation of law.

4. Authority can be express, implied, or apparent. Express authority is the authority of an agent to perform the duties that are specifically stated in the contract of agency. Implied authority is the authority an agent reasonably assumes he or she has that relates to the express authority granted by the principal. Apparent authority is the authority that a third party may reasonably assume an agent possesses, despite the fact that the agent does not actually possess such authority.

5. (a) An agent has a duty to obey all of the principal's reasonable and lawful orders and instructions within the scope of the agency contract. (b) A principal must pay the agent the compensation agreed upon in the contract, must reimburse the agent for any money advanced by the agent in carrying out the principal's instructions and for debts legally paid to third parties, and must reimburse the agent for any loss or damages suffered by the agent in the legitimate performance of duties. (c) A principal is responsible to a third party for all agreements made by the agent on behalf of the principal if the agent acted within the scope of his or her authority, either express or implied. (d) In the case of a disclosed principal, an agent cannot be held personally responsible to a third party as long as the agent acts within the scope of his or her actual authority. In the case of a partially disclosed or undisclosed principal, an agent can be held personally responsible to the third party.

6. Agency can be terminated by agreement, performance, operation of law, or fulfillment of the agency's purpose. Specific reasons may include death, insanity, illness, impossibility of performance, or bankruptcy.

7. The main difference between principal–agent and employer–employee relationships is an employer's power to control the activities of a non-agent employee.

CHAPTER NINETEEN
ASSESSMENT

MATCHING LEGAL TERMS

Match each of the numbered definitions with the correct term in the following list. Write the letter of your choice in the answer column.

a. agent
b. agency by necessity
c. agency by ratification
d. apparent authority
e. attorney in fact

f. express authority
g. contract of agency
h. disclosed principal
i. implied authority
j. irrevocable agency

k. partially disclosed principal
l. power of attorney
m. principal
n. undisclosed principal

1. The party in an agency contract who represents another.

1. _____

2. A principal whose existence and identity are not known to third parties.

2. _____

3. The name given to a legal document that formally creates an agency.

3. _____

4. The party in an agency contract who delegates power to another.

4. _____

5. An agreement between a principal and an agent in which the agent is vested with authority to represent the principal.

5. _____

6. An agency coupled with an interest.

6. _____

7. The authority possessed by an agent that may be reasonably assumed by a third party.

7. _____

8. The authority possessed by an agent that is specifically stated in the agency contract.

8. _____

9. A principal who is known to third parties.

9. _____

10. The precise legal term for an agent.

10. _____

11. The agency that results when a person approves an unauthorized act done in the principal's name by a person who had no authority to act as agent.

11. _____

12. The agency that results when a person fails to support his or her spouse or minor children.

12. _____

13. The authority an agent reasonably assumes he or she has that relates to the express authority granted by the principal.

13. _____

14. A principal whose identity is not known to a third party who knows he or she is dealing with an agent.

14. _____

TRUE/FALSE QUIZ

Indicate whether each of the following statements is true or false by writing *T* or *F* in the answer column.

15. A general agent is a person authorized to assume complete charge of his or her principal's business.

15. _____

16. A competent party may delegate his or her service on a jury to another by appointing an agent.

16. _____

17. An agent is reasonable in assuming that he or she has the authority that is related to the responsibilities covered in the contract of agency.

17. _____

18. An agent is liable to the principal for any losses that result from the agent's neglect or incompetence.

18. _____

19. A principal is liable for an agent's torts and crimes if they were committed in the ordinary course of the agent's performance of authorized duties.

19. _____

20. An agent representing a partially disclosed principal becomes a party to the contract.

20. _____

21. In a contract between an agent and a third party, the agent can be held responsible to the third party if the identity of the principal is not disclosed.

21. _____

22. An employee who performs only mechanical acts under the employer's direction and is subject to the employer's control is still legally an agent.

22. _____

23. Acts of an employee while performing duties of employment are considered the acts of the employer.

23. _____

24. If an agency exists "at will," the principal has the right to revoke the agency agreement and discharge the agent, provided such discharge is for a good reason.

24. _____

DISCUSSION QUESTIONS

Answer the following questions and discuss them in class.

25. Identify the parties to an agency agreement and describe the relationship of the parties.

_____

_____

26. Classify the two major kinds of agents and discuss the four ways in which an agency may be created.

_____

_____

27. Differentiate between disclosed principal, partially disclosed principal, and undisclosed principal.

_____

_____

28. Explain how an agency may be terminated.

_____

_____

29. Differentiate between the principal–agent and employer–employee relationships.

_____

_____

30. Distinguish among express, implied, and apparent authority.

_____

_____

THINKING CRITICALLY ABOUT THE LAW

Answer the following questions, which require you to think critically about the legal principles that you learned in this chapter.

31. **Agency** It is often difficult for a third party to distinguish between an agent and an employee. Are there times when it is important to distinguish between the two? Should there be a clear identification system established?

_____

_____

32. **Agent's Liability** A principal is liable for the torts and crimes committed by an agent if he or she is performing authorized duties. To what extent should the agent also be liable?

_____

_____

33. **Undisclosed Principal** Does it seem likely that a third party would be suspicious if an agent disclosed the existence but not the identity of his or her principal?

_____

_____

34. Employees as Agents Does it place an unnecessary burden on a third party to determine whether he or she is dealing with an employee who has the authority of an agent?

_____

_____

35. A Question of Ethics In some states, an agent's contracts may be voided if he or she is acting for a principal who is a minor. Is this fair to a third party with whom the contract is signed?

_____

_____

CASE QUESTIONS

Study each of the following cases. Answer the questions that follow by writing _Yes_ or _No_ in the answer column.

36. Authority of an Agent Peterman, a resident of Florida, sold a home in California to Oliveras. Peterman hired Fogelman, an attorney-at-law, to represent her at the real estate closing and provided Fogelman with a contract of agency giving Fogelman the authority to sell the home. At the closing, Fogelman also agreed to sell Oliveras an expensive piano owned by Peterman that was still in the home.

a. Does Fogelman have implied authority to sell the piano?　　a. _____

b. Does Fogelman have apparent authority to sell the piano?　　b. _____

c. Is Fogelman a special agent?　　c. _____

d. Is Fogelman an attorney in fact?　　d. _____

37. Apparent Authority A shipper asked a truck driver to deliver a shipment of chemicals and to protect them from freezing while en route. The driver assured the shipper that the chemicals would be carried in heated trucks. When the shipper learned that the shipment had been damaged in transit by freezing, she demanded payment from the trucking company.

a. Did the truck driver have any authority to assure the shipper that the chemicals would be protected from freezing?　　a. _____

b. Would the trucking company be responsible for the damaged chemicals?　　b. _____

c. Did the truck driver have apparent authority?　　c. _____

d. Was the truck driver acting as an agent?　　d. _____

38. Agency by Necessity The Chalmers family lived in poverty. Despite their destitute condition, Mrs. Chalmers bought several articles of jewelry for herself and an expensive painting for their home. When the retailer attempted to collect payment, Mr. Chalmers refused to pay. The merchant claimed that Mrs. Chalmers was acting as an agent for Mr. Chalmers.

a. Is this an example of agency by necessity?   a. _____

b. Is this an example of agency by ratification?   b. _____

c. Will the retailer succeed in collecting from Mr. Chalmers?   c. _____

d. Does the law recognize agency by necessity when a spouse makes essential purchases?   d. _____

CASE ANALYSIS

Study each of the following cases carefully. Briefly state the principle of law and your decision.

39. **Responsibility of Employer** Franklyn, a clerical employee of Woodbury Manufacturing Company, told Buron that he was an agent of the company and made a contract on behalf of Woodbury. Later Woodbury repudiated the contract and claimed that Franklyn had no authority to enter into a contract. Buron then sued Franklyn, who claimed that he thought he had the authority. Will Buron succeed in her suit?

    Principle of Law:

    _____

    _____

    Decision:

    _____

    _____

40. **Undisclosed Principal** Ferrara made a contract with Perret without informing her that he was acting on behalf of National Steel Wire Company. Ferrara had actual express authority, as provided in his contract of agency with National. The contract was breached and Perret sued National. National claimed that Perret could not sue because her contract was with Ferrara, and not with National. Will Perret be successful in her suit against National?

    Principle of Law:

    _____

    _____

    Decision:

    _____

    _____

41. **Agency** Washington purchased an automobile from Courtesy Motor Sales, a Ford automobile dealer. After the car was delivered, she discovered that the car she

thought was new was in fact used and that the odometer had been turned back to conceal the mileage. Washington sued Courtesy and named Ford Motor Company in the suit on the grounds that Courtesy was acting as an agent for the manufacturer. Will Washington succeed in her suit against Ford Motor? [*Washington v. Courtesy Motor Sales, Inc.,* 199 N.E.2d 263 (Illinois)]

Principle of Law:

_____

_____

Decision:

_____

_____

42. **Agency** Blodgett, while walking on a public sidewalk, was injured when a large piece of wood fell from a construction job at the offices of Olympic Savings and Loan Association. The construction work was being done by Drury Construction Company. Blodgett sued both Olympic and Drury, claiming that Drury was an agent for Olympic. Olympic denied both responsibility for the injury and the existence of an agency relationship with Drury. Will Blodgett succeed in her suit against Olympic? [*Blodgett v. Olympic Savings and Loan Association,* 646 P.2d 139 (Washington)]

Principle of Law:

_____

_____

Decision:

_____

_____

LEGAL RESEARCH

Complete the following activities. Share your findings with the class.

43. **Working in Teams** In teams of three or four, interview managers of small real estate agencies. Discuss with these managers the nature of the agent's relationship with the principal, including agent's authority and other matters.

_____

_____

44. **Using Technology** Using the Internet and search engines, investigate "contract of agency" and identify key terms in such a contract.

_____

_____

chapter **20**

Business Organizations

LEGAL terms

sole proprietorship	articles of incorporation
unlimited liability	bylaws
partnership	quorum
winding-up period	subchapter S corporation
joint venture	proxy
joint and several liability	fiduciary responsibility
limited partnership	duty of loyalty
limited liability	duty of care
corporation	limited liability company (LLC)

BUSINESS ORGANIZATIONS

"Remain a corporation and retain control if you like, but behave as a servant leader in a partnership."

Sam Walton,
founder of Walmart

20.1 ORGANIZATIONAL FORMS

Many people in the United States have an entrepreneurial spirit that encourages them to pursue the "American dream" of owning and operating their own business. However, there are numerous responsibilities and decisions that come with accomplishing this objective. Questions such as "Should I begin the business by myself, or share authority with others?" "How can I obtain enough money to keep the business afloat and profitable?" and "Will I have personal responsibility for the debts of the business, and how can I protect myself from creditors and others?" will be addressed in this chapter.

There are several different types of organizational forms that may be selected for a business structure. The organizational forms that are emphasized in this chapter are those that are available to firms that are in business to make a profit for their owners, as distinct from those organizations whose existence is primarily to benefit society.

sole proprietorship
A business owned and operated by one person.

unlimited liability
Legal exposure in which an owner of a business is personally liable for all of the debts and obligations of the business.

Businesses are generally structured as one of the following: (1) sole proprietorship, (2) partnership, (3) corporation, or (4) limited liability company. While different states have variations on these forms, the descriptions and discussion that follow generally apply to all businesses in the United States.

20.2 SOLE PROPRIETORSHIP

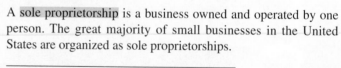

A sole proprietorship is a business owned and operated by one person. The great majority of small businesses in the United States are organized as sole proprietorships.

ADVANTAGES OF A SOLE PROPRIETORSHIP

A person wishing to open a business may elect to organize as a sole proprietorship because these are extremely easy to form. Generally, all the entrepreneur needs to do is obtain a general business license from his or her local municipality, allowing him or her to conduct business in the community. Another advantage to a sole proprietorship is that the owner has complete authority, within the boundaries of the law, for the running of the business and does not need to report to any other person. He or she can be creative and entrepreneurial, and all profits generated will flow directly to the owner. The owner pays income taxes on earned profits at his or her personal rate (although there are some special rules regarding the deductibility of certain expenses). Just as it is quite easy to begin a business as a sole proprietorship, it is also easy to dissolve the business in the event the owner wishes to do so.

A sole proprietorship is a business owned and operated by one person.

DISADVANTAGES OF A SOLE PROPRIETORSHIP

The major disadvantage of a sole proprietorship is the fact that the owner of the establishment has unlimited liability, which means that the owner is personally liable for all of the legal debts and obligations of the business. By having unlimited liability, the owner places his or her assets at risk, whether these assets are personal or business related. Obviously, this is a major consideration and the owner needs to carefully weigh this risk. Accordingly, the owner should consider purchasing liability and other appropriate insurance coverage.

A second disadvantage of a sole proprietorship is the difficulty the owner faces in raising money to finance the operations of the business. Since the owner is managing the business alone, he or she cannot turn to other owners to provide additional funds, should this become necessary to maintain the stability or growth of the company. The owner is often limited to borrowing from creditors who will charge the owner interest and demand repayment of the principal, whether the firm makes a profit or not. Similarly, because the owner is on his or her own, it is often difficult for a sole proprietorship to attract trustworthy employees.

EXAMPLE 20.1

▶ Milotin decided to open his own store, offering ink refills for printer cartridges to local companies. Between his own savings and some borrowing, Milotin believed he had sufficient financing to keep the store as a going concern for two years. Not wishing to share profits or management with any other person, Milotin formed a sole proprietorship; obtained a general business license; purchased liability, fire, and theft insurance; and opened for business.

20.3 PARTNERSHIP

A partnership is a business owned and operated by two or more persons. The shares of the partners might be equal, or they might vary according to an agreement between or among the partners. This would be true for either profits or losses, and it is not even necessary that profits and losses be shared in the same percentages. Similarly, partners, by agreement with one another, share responsibility for managing the affairs of the business.

Dissolution of a partnership is governed by the partnership contract and usually occurs due to (1) the death or disability of one of the partners, (2) the expulsion of one of the partners (at times for cause, and at other times for no cause), (3) illegality of the partnership's business, (4) the retirement of one of the partners, and (5) the bankruptcy of the business. Dissolution is followed by a winding-up period, during which there is an orderly liquidation of the partnership assets.

At times, individuals become partners for only a short period of time, or for only a single project. This activity is defined as a joint venture.

partnership
A business owned and operated by two or more persons.

winding-up period
The time after dissolution of a partnership during which there is an orderly liquidation of the partnership assets.

joint venture
An activity in which individuals become partners for only a short period of time or for only a single project.

ADVANTAGES OF A PARTNERSHIP

Each partner has the right to share in the profits of the business. While the partnership itself does not pay federal income taxes, it does complete an informational tax return, wherein it reports profits or losses to the government and how these profits or losses have been apportioned between or among the partners. Each partner is then required to pay income taxes on those profits (or is entitled to deduct those losses) that have been apportioned to him or her.

Just as each partner has a right to share in the profits of the company, each partner also has a right to share in the value of the firm's assets; that is, all business assets are owned jointly by all partners.

Like a sole proprietorship, a partnership is fairly easy to form, and the owners have complete authority for the running of the business.

DISADVANTAGES OF A PARTNERSHIP

joint and several liability
Legal exposure such that a person with a claim against a general partnership can elect to sue either all of the partners together or any individual partner whom he or she chooses.

As is true for a sole proprietorship, the major disadvantage of a partnership is the fact that each partner has unlimited liability for all legal obligations and debts of the business. Recall from Chapter 19 that each partner is an agent for all other partners, and that when a partner acts with either actual or apparent authority, all other partners become liable for his or her acts. In addition, partners have joint and several liability, which means that a person with a claim against the partnership can elect to sue either all of the partners together or any individual partner whom he or she chooses.

EXAMPLE 20.2

▶ Petrillo and Patel co-owned a bakery in the form of an equal general partnership. The two of them agreed that Petrillo, who worked the morning hours by himself, would be responsible for cleaning the sidewalk in front of the store. After a heavy snowstorm, Petrillo failed to remove the ice, and Weissman, a pedestrian, slipped, sustaining a compound fracture to her leg. Weissman elected to sue only Patel, since he lived in the same town as she. Patel would be found to be liable to Weissman and could recoup his financial losses only by suing his partner, Petrillo.

Example 20.2 illustrates clearly just how risky a business organized as a partnership can be to a partner, especially since he or she is responsible for all authorized or ratified acts by any other partner. Once again, it is extremely important for partnerships to have ample liability and other forms of insurance.

Another disadvantage of the partnership form is the fact that there may be times when partners disagree on how the business should be run. Whether relating to day-to-day operations or major strategic undertakings, sharing authority at times can be difficult when partners are of different minds.

LIMITED PARTNERSHIP

limited partnership
A business in which there are one or more general partners and one or more limited partners.

A limited partnership is a business in which there are one or more general partners (with rights and obligations as described previously) and one or more limited partners. Limited partnerships receive the same tax treatment as all partnerships. Also, as with all partnerships, authority, dissolution, and so forth are governed by the partnership contract.

limited liability
Legal exposure in which an owner of a business is not personally liable for all of the debts and obligations of the business.

Advantage of Being a Limited Partner   The limited partner is attracted to the limited partnership because it provides him or her with limited liability: His or her personal liability for all of the legal debts and obligations of the business is limited to his or her investment in the business.

EXAMPLE 20.3

▶ Jefferson and Aaron were general partners in a business that purchased old homes, remodeled them, and sold them at a profit. Since they needed a large amount of additional financing, they approached Shah, encouraging her to join their partnership. Shah knew very little about the business but saw this as an opportunity for investment. Shah provided a large sum of cash and became a limited partner, thus protecting her personal assets from creditors of the partnership.

Disadvantage of Being a Limited Partner   While the limited partner does not have the disadvantage of unlimited liability, he or she is not able to participate in the overall management of the business, lest he or she be deemed by the courts to be a general partner, and lose his or her limited liability.

In Example 20.3, if Shah were to become actively involved with the remodeling of the homes, a court might well determine that she was a general partner, and her liability could be construed to be unlimited.

LIMITED LIABILITY PARTNERSHIP

A limited liability partnership (LLP) is a type of partnership commonly used by professionals who are in business together. LLPs were created in order to shield a partner's personal assets from a third party's claim of negligence against another partner. Generally, in an LLP, all partners have limited liability for other partners' negligence.

20.4 CORPORATION

A corporation is a business formed as a separate legal entity. Individuals can start a corporation by applying for a charter in one of the 50 states. Corporations are owned by *shareholders,* who purchase shares of stock in the corporation. In order to sell these shares to the general public, it is often necessary that documentation be filed by the corporation with the Securities and Exchange Commission (SEC) (see Chapter 30).

The corporation drafts articles of incorporation that list the general powers of the company. The company usually has bylaws, which provide rules for the meetings of the corporation. A quorum, the minimum number of shares necessary to be present at a meeting, is required for action to be taken.

A corporation is considered a kind of *legal person,* and courts have granted corporations constitutional rights similar to those granted individuals and other organizations, such as freedom of speech, due process of law, and freedom from unreasonable searches and seizures. While, in general, corporations may freely give charitable contributions, political contributions are strictly regulated.

Some states require corporations to have a *corporate seal,* which must be affixed to contracts and other legal documents. Corporations also have a special *tax identification number,* similar to an individual's Social Security number, that identifies them on tax returns, bank records, and other official documents. Generally, corporations are said to *exist in perpetuity:* They continue to live on unless some formal action is taken to discontinue the business.

corporation
A business formed as a separate legal entity.

articles of incorporation
A document that lists the general powers of a corporation.

bylaws
A document that provides rules for the meetings of a corporation.

quorum
The minimum number of shares necessary to be present at a corporate meeting in order for action to be taken.

A corporation is a business formed as a separate legal entity.

ADVANTAGES OF A CORPORATION

The major advantage of a corporation is the fact of limited liability to shareholders. Courts are extremely hesitant to *pierce the corporate veil;* that is, the law assigns responsibility for corporate obligations to shareholders only under very unusual circumstances. For example, the court may hold corporate shareholders liable if the corporation is set up specifically to defraud the public.

Shareholders vote for directors, who are responsible for managing the overall strategy and operations of the firm over the long term.

EXAMPLE 20.4

▶ Costas inherited a large sum of money and wished to invest a portion of the funds in the stock market. Through a broker, she purchased shares of common stock in several corporations whose shares were duly registered with the SEC and traded publicly. Costas's personal assets are shielded from creditors, and her risk is limited to the money she invested in the stock market.

Another advantage to a corporation is the ease with which the company can raise capital. A corporation can obtain additional financing by issuing and selling new shares of stock in the company, without the necessity of altering its organizational form.

DISADVANTAGES OF A CORPORATION

The major disadvantage of a corporation is the fact that the corporation is required to pay separate income taxes at a special corporate rate for any year during which a profit is earned. At the time profits are distributed to shareholders, these may be subject to an additional tax, depending on applicable tax regulations.

A second disadvantage to a corporation is the expense associated with forming and maintaining the company. Corporations are required to keep updated minutes of meetings, provide detailed financial statements to creditors and investors, prepare complex tax returns and SEC filings, and so forth.

SUBCHAPTER S CORPORATION

A subchapter S corporation is a corporation for all purposes as explained previously but with the advantage of being taxed as a partnership. In order to qualify as a subchapter S corporation, the company must comply with tax regulations, such as the restriction that there be a limited number of shareholders, among other requirements.

subchapter S corporation
A corporation that is taxed as a partnership.

CORPORATE DIRECTORS AND OFFICERS

While the shareholders own the corporation, they do not directly manage the activities of the firm. Shareholders vote for *directors,* members of a board who are responsible for managing the overall strategy and operations of the firm over the long term. Frequently, shareholders who cannot attend meetings of the corporation nonetheless vote for directors by signing a proxy, a legal document that transfers the right to vote in a corporate election to another person (remember that, as was explained in Chapter 14, it is not permitted to transfer the right to vote in a political election to another person).

proxy
A legal document that transfers the right to vote in a corporate election to another person.

Directors do not involve themselves in the day-to-day operations of the corporation. Rather, directors appoint *officers,* who exercise control over the normal, routine matters that arise on a daily basis. These officers could include a president, vice presidents, a comptroller, and others.

FIDUCIARY RESPONSIBILITY

Directors and officers have a fiduciary responsibility to the company in which they hold their positions. Fiduciary (from the Latin word for "faith") responsibility means that directors and officers will exercise their authority while working under a duty of loyalty and a duty of care.

fiduciary responsibility
A legal requirement that a person will exercise his or her authority while working under a duty of loyalty and a duty of care.

Duty of Loyalty   The duty of loyalty means that a director has a legal and ethical obligation to administer to the affairs of the corporation with personal integrity, honesty, and candor. Directors are, for example, prohibited from advancing their own personal or outside business interests at the expense of the corporation. Neither can directors use their authority to assist persons outside the corporation when such action would harm the firm.

duty of loyalty
A legal and ethical obligation placed upon a director to administer to the affairs of the corporation with personal integrity, honesty, and candor.

EXAMPLE 20.5

▶ O'Shea, a senior partner in a law firm, also served on the board of directors for a large manufacturing corporation. When the company decided to purchase a new warehouse, O'Shea convinced the board of directors to hire his law firm to handle the transaction for an exorbitant fee. O'Shea has breached his duty of loyalty and violated both his legal and ethical responsibilities.

Duty of Care   The duty of care means that a director has a legal and ethical obligation to act diligently and prudently in conducting the affairs of the corporation. A director is responsible for selecting, monitoring, and evaluating competent management. He or she must promote and advance the policies and strategic initiatives of the firm, while at all times making certain that the implementation of these policies and strategies adheres to principles of law and safety. When a director considers a corporate matter, he or she must make a decision only after fully informed, meaningful deliberation.

duty of care
A legal and ethical obligation placed upon a director to act diligently and prudently in conducting the affairs of the corporation.

EXAMPLE 20.6

▶ Nagy serves on the board of directors for a large software company. Nagy's position on the board requires that she oversee the company's investment portfolio. Nagy enjoys the prestige of serving on this board; however, she frequently fails to review the financial statements provided by the company's accountants or trends taking place in the stock market. As a result, the company's investments perform extremely poorly. By her failure to exercise due care, Nagy is violating both her legal and ethical responsibilities.

20.5 LIMITED LIABILITY COMPANY

limited liability company (LLC)
A relatively new organizational form available in most states that provides all of the owners with limited liability.

A limited liability company (LLC) is a relatively new organizational form currently recognized by all 50 states. Laws governing the formation of LLCs vary from state to state. Thus, it is important to follow the precise requirements of the applicable state law when organizing an LLC. Generally, to organize an LLC, members (owners) draft an operating agreement that governs the business in important matters, such as how the LLC will be managed, the members' rights and responsibilities, and how the LLC is to be dissolved. An LLC is taxed as a partnership for federal tax purposes (state laws vary in terms of state tax treatment). The members of the LLC act as a *management team;* that is, they share in the overall control of the business.

ADVANTAGES OF A LIMITED LIABILITY COMPANY

The LLC provides all members with limited liability, while allowing them to participate in the management of the business. In addition, since the LLC is treated in the same manner as a partnership by the IRS, members can avoid double taxation of earnings. Finally, since it is generally a small company, in most states it is quite easy to form.

	Sole Proprietorship	Partnership	Limited Partnership	Limited Liability Partnership	Corporation	Subchapter S Corporation	Limited Liability Company
Ease of Formation	Yes	Yes	Yes	Yes	No	No	Yes
Tax Advantages	Yes	Yes	Yes	Yes	No	Yes	Yes
Limited Liability	No	No	Yes	Yes	Yes	Yes	Yes
Owners' Ability to Manage	Yes	Yes	Yes/No	Yes	No	No	Yes
Ease of Raising Capital	No	No	No	No	Yes	Yes	No
Separate Legal Entity	No	No	No	No	Yes	Yes	Yes

FIGURE 20.1 Organizational Forms

DISADVANTAGES OF A LIMITED LIABILITY COMPANY

As is true for all small firms, the members of an LLC frequently have difficulty in raising additional funds to expand or maintain the business. Furthermore, as was true for partnerships, there may be times when members of the management team disagree on how the business should be run.

20.6 OTHER ORGANIZATIONAL FORMS

The organizational forms discussed in this chapter are those whose purpose is to earn profits. It must be noted that there are several other organizational forms that exist in the United States whose purpose is to aid society. These organizations are referred to as *not-for-profits* and can include charitable organizations as well as others, such as universities, political parties, labor unions (discussed in Chapter 32), social clubs, and others.

CHAPTER SUMMARY

1. For-profit businesses are generally organized as one of the following forms: (1) sole proprietorship, (2) partnership, (3) corporation, or (4) limited liability company.

2. A sole proprietorship is a business owned and operated by one person. Advantages to organizing as a sole proprietorship include (a) the business is easy to form, (b) the owner has complete authority for the running of the business, (c) all profits generated flow directly to the owner, and (d) the business is easy to dissolve. Disadvantages of organizing as a sole proprietorship include (a) the owner has unlimited liability and (b) the owner faces difficulty in raising money to finance the operations of the business.

3. A partnership is a business owned and operated by two or more persons. Advantages to organizing as a partnership include (a) each partner has the right to share in the profits of the business and (b) each partner has a right to share in the value of the firm's assets. Disadvantages of organizing as a partnership include (a) each partner has unlimited liability for all legal obligations and debts of the business and (b) partners have joint and several liability. The advantage of being a limited partner

is that he or she is provided with limited liability. The disadvantage of being a limited partner is that he or she is not able to participate in the overall management of the business, lest he or she be deemed by the courts to be a general partner. Limited liability partnerships were created in order to shield a partner's personal assets from a third party's claim of negligence against another partner.

4. A corporation is a business formed as a separate legal entity, a kind of legal person. Corporations are owned by shareholders, who purchase shares of stock in the corporation. A corporation drafts articles of incorporation, which list the general powers of the company, and bylaws, which provide rules for the meetings of the corporation. Generally, corporations exist in perpetuity.

5. A limited liability company (LLC), which provides all of the owners with limited liability, is taxed as a partnership for federal tax purposes. The owners of the LLC act as a management team; that is, they share in the overall control of the business.

6. Organizational forms that are not business entities are not-for-profits that include universities, political parties, labor unions, social clubs, and others.

CHAPTER TWENTY
ASSESSMENT

MATCHING LEGAL TERMS

Match each of the numbered definitions with the correct term in the following list. Write the letter of your choice in the answer column.

a. articles of incorporation   **e.** partnership   **i.** sole proprietorship
b. corporation   **f.** joint venture   **j.** subchapter S
c. duty of care   **g.** limited liability company
d. duty of loyalty   **h.** limited partnership

1. A relatively new organizational form available in most states that provides all of the owners with limited liability.   **1.** _____

2. A legal and ethical obligation placed upon a director to administer the affairs of the corporation with personal integrity, honesty, and candor.   **2.** _____

3. A business formed as a separate legal entity.   **3.** _____

4. A business owned and operated by one person.   **4.** _____

5. A business owned and operated by two or more persons.   **5.** _____

6. A legal document that lists the general powers of a corporation.   **6.** _____

7. A type of corporation that is taxed as a partnership.   **7.** _____

8. A legal and ethical obligation placed upon a director to act diligently and prudently in conducting the affairs of the corporation.   **8.** _____

9. A business in which there are one or more general partners and one or more limited partners.   **9.** _____

10. An activity in which individuals become partners for only a short period of time, or for only a single project.   **10.** _____

TRUE/FALSE QUIZ

Indicate whether each of the following statements is true or false by writing *T* or *F* in the answer column.

11. The great majority of small businesses in the United States are organized as limited liability companies.   **11.** _____

12. The major disadvantage of a sole proprietorship is the fact that the owner of the establishment has unlimited liability.   **12.** _____

13. A disadvantage of a sole proprietorship is the difficulty the owner faces in raising money to finance the operations of the business.   **13.** _____

14. In a partnership, the shares of the partners might be equal or they might vary according to an agreement between or among the partners.   **14.** _____

15. In a partnership, it is necessary that profits and losses be shared in the same percentages.   **15.** _____

16. In a partnership, the expulsion of one of the partners must always be for cause.   **16.** _____

17. During the winding-up period, there is an orderly liquidation of the partnership assets.   **17.** _____

18. While a partnership itself does not pay federal income taxes, it does complete an informational tax return.   **18.** _____

19. Each partner is an agent for all other partners.   **19.** _____

20. A limited partner is allowed to participate in the overall management of the business, and at the same time maintain limited liability.   **20.** _____

21. Courts have granted corporations similar constitutional rights to those granted to individuals.   **21.** _____

22. A corporation usually has bylaws, which provide rules for the meetings of the corporation.   **22.** _____

23. Corporations may freely give both charitable contributions and political contributions.   **23.** _____

24. Corporations continue to live on unless some formal action is taken to discontinue the business.   **24.** _____

25. The shareholders who own the corporation directly manage the activities of the firm.   **25.** _____

DISCUSSION QUESTIONS

Answer the following questions and discuss them in class.

26. Identify the four forms in which businesses are generally organized.

_____

_____

27. Name four advantages and two disadvantages of organizing as a sole proprietorship.

_____

_____

28. Identify two advantages and two disadvantages of organizing as a partnership.

_____

_____

29. Explain the differences between a limited partnership and other partnerships.

_____

_____

30. Differentiate among corporate shareholders, directors, and officers.

_____

_____

31. Explain both the duty of loyalty and the duty of care as these pertain to corporate directors and officers.

_____

_____

THINKING CRITICALLY ABOUT THE LAW

Answer the following questions, which require you to think critically about the legal principles that you learned in this chapter.

32. Limited Partnership Is it fair that in a limited partnership, the limited partner enjoys limited liability while the general partner faces unlimited liability?

_____

_____

33. Limited Liability Persons who face unlimited liability (such as sole proprietors and partners) are allowed to purchase insurance to protect themselves from creditors and others. Should the law allow insurance to be used for this purpose?

_____

_____

34. Sole Proprietorship How can a sole proprietor attract employees who are trustworthy?

_____

_____

35. Corporation Corporations have been granted freedom of speech, freedom from unreasonable searches and seizure, and due process of law. Does it make sense that a legal (as opposed to natural) person has these rights?

_____

_____

36. A Question of Ethics Is it ethical for a broker or a financial adviser to earn commissions from investments of corporations of which the broker or financial adviser is also a director?

_____

_____

CASE QUESTIONS

Study each of the following cases. Answer the questions that follow by writing *Yes* or *No* in the answer column.

37. Sole Proprietorship Horvath opened a small convenience store, organizing the business as a sole proprietorship. Since she was concerned that she would not have sufficient financing, she borrowed $20,000 from Blaum, her brother-in-law. When the business began earning profits, Horvath spent these monies on personal items. When her accountant completed her tax return, Horvath was informed that she owed a great deal of money to the government.

a. Is Horvath required to pay taxes herself on the profits from the store? **a.** _____

b. Is Blaum required to pay taxes himself on the profits from the store? **b.** _____

c. Can Blaum legally demand that he be allowed to manage the business's financial matters in the future? **c.** _____

38. Authority of General Partners Felagi and MacWilliams agreed to open a restaurant selling pizza and sandwiches. The business was organized as a partnership, with each partner owning 50 percent and sharing profits and losses equally. The two partners also agreed that each would have actual authority to spend up to $500 for purchases relating to the restaurant without the prior approval of the other partner. Salespersons of a nearby automobile dealership regularly ate lunch in the restaurant and came to know that Felagi was an owner of the establishment. Felagi, without consulting MacWilliams, then signed a contract to purchase a $17,000 vehicle in the partnership's name. MacWilliams later learned of the transaction and refused to honor the contract.

a. Can the automobile dealership sue the partnership to enforce the contract? **a.** _____

b. Can the automobile dealership elect to sue only Felagi to enforce the contract? **b.** _____

c. Can the automobile dealership elect to sue only MacWilliams to enforce the contract? **c.** _____

d. Does Felagi have apparent authority to bind the partnership? **d.** _____

39. Fiduciary Duty Olav, a retired banker, served on the board of directors for a nationally prominent charitable organization. The local chapter of the charity discussed plans to purchase and relocate to a new building across town. Olav approached Mansfield, a close friend, and the two of them quickly closed on a deal for the new building, purchasing it for $1.2 million and placing title in Mansfield's name only. When the matter later came before the board of the charitable organization, Olav encouraged the organization to make an offer of $1.6 million to Mansfield. Olav did not disclose to the board that he would share in the profits of the sale.

a. Is Olav violating his fiduciary duty?

b. Is Olav violating his duty of loyalty?

c. Is Mansfield violating his fiduciary duty?

d. Is this an example of a proxy dispute?

a. _____

b. _____

c. _____

d. _____

CASE ANALYSIS

Study each of the following cases carefully. Briefly state the principle of law and your decision.

40. **Liability of Shareholders** Holley and Holley, an interracial couple, alleged that they were the victims of discrimination in housing as a result of actions by Crank, an employee of Triad, Inc. The Holleys sued Meyer, the sole shareholder, the president, and a broker of Triad, Inc. Meyer argued that he was not personally responsible for the actions of either Triad or its employee, Crank. Will the Holleys be successful in their efforts to hold Meyer personally responsible? [*Holley v. Meyer*, 258 F.3d 1127 (2003)]

Principle of Law:

_____

_____

Decision:

_____

_____

41. **Organization's Constitutional Rights** Dale, an assistant scoutmaster for the Boy Scouts, lost his position when the organization learned that he was gay. Dale contended that he was the victim of discrimination while the Boy Scouts argued that they were exercising their First Amendment right of freedom of expression. Does the organization have First Amendment rights, or will Dale be successful in his suit against the Boy Scouts? [*Dale v. Boy Scouts of America*, 160 N.J. 562, 734 A.2d 1196 (2000)]

Principle of Law:

_____

_____

Decision:

_____

_____

42. Partnership Shares Melvin and his brother Russell Ballantyne formed an oral partnership, which started out as a farming operation but grew into oil and gas exploration. Russell was in charge of the farming operation, while Melvin was in charge of the oil and gas exploration. In practice, and by mutual agreement, the brothers withdrew profits from the partnership that were attributable to each of their respective business pursuits and paid the expenses related to each of their respective activities. In other words, Melvin kept the oil and gas income and paid those expenses, while Russell did the same with the farm income and expenses. However, for tax purposes, Melvin and Russell each reported 50 percent of the partnership's total income, gains, losses, deductions, and credits on their individual federal tax returns. When Melvin died, the partnership automatically dissolved and family relations also took a turn for the worse. A dispute later arose regarding tax liability, and it was the contention of the Internal Revenue Service that there should be a 50–50 split with respect to tax treatment and distribution of the assets from the farming operation. Russell argued that he alone was entitled to the benefits from the farming operation. Is Russell correct in his contention that he alone should be entitled to the benefits from the partnership? [*Estate of Melvin W. Ballantyne, Deceased* (T.C.M. (CCH) 2002-160) (2003)]

Principle of Law:

_____

_____

Decision:

_____

_____

LEGAL RESEARCH

Complete the following activities. Share your findings with the class.

43. Working in Teams In teams of three or four, interview owners of small businesses in your city or town. Ask them to explain why they chose their particular business organizational form.

_____

_____

44. Using Technology Using the Internet and search engines, investigate the tax rules relating to the organizational forms discussed in the chapter.

_____

_____

chapter 21
Bankruptcy

LEARNING OUTCOMES

After studying this chapter and completing the assessments, you will be able to

21.1 Explain the conditions under which individuals and businesses become insolvent and default on their loans.

21.2 Distinguish between a voluntary filing and an involuntary filing in bankruptcy.

21.3 Explain the provisions and applications of Chapter 7 of the federal bankruptcy law.

21.4 Describe the means test and the requirement for debtor education and credit counseling under the Bankruptcy Abuse Prevention and Consumer Protection Act.

21.5 Explain the provisions and applications of Chapter 13 of the federal bankruptcy law.

21.6 Explain the major applications of Chapters 9, 11, 12, and 15 of the federal bankruptcy law.

LEGAL terms

debtor	secured debt
creditor	preferential payment
insolvency	fraudulent transfer
default	Bankruptcy Abuse
bankruptcy	Prevention and
voluntary filing	Consumer Protection
involuntary filing	Act of 2005
liquidation	means test
straight or liquidation	reorganization bankruptcy
bankruptcy	priority debts

BANKRUPTCY

"I don't like the B word."

Donald Trump, real estate developer and
TV personality

21.1 INSOLVENCY AND DEFAULT

Unfortunately, there are times when individuals or businesses face significant financial challenges that cannot be overcome, no matter how responsible these individuals are or how competently these businesses are run. This situation might occur for a variety of reasons: a serious downturn in the economy, significant mismanagement of financial assets, a series of poor investment decisions, a personal tragedy, a failure of health, or the like. An individual or business that owes money is said to be a debtor; an individual or business to which money is owed is said to be a creditor. People familiar with good accounting practices recognize that assets (the value of the property an individual or business owns) should exceed liabilities (the value of what an individual or business owes). On the other hand, insolvency occurs when an individual's or business's liabilities exceed assets.

Unless the insolvent individual or business can quickly correct the problem, insolvency often leads to default, wherein the debtor fails to meet one or more financial obligations to his or her creditors. When this occurs, it becomes important to protect, at least in part, the interests of the creditors who otherwise would not receive most, or even any, of the money they are rightfully owed.

Bankruptcy is the legal state that occurs when a debtor is insolvent, is in default, and is unable to fulfill his or her obligations to pay back his or her creditors. In most instances, when bankruptcy is filed, the debtor's assets are sold and the money is distributed among the debtor's creditors to pay the debt that is owed.

Under federal law, bankruptcy filings must not be made in bad faith—that is, for the sole purpose of defrauding a creditor. In addition, it is illegal for a debtor to knowingly conceal property or to falsify records; both crimes are punishable by fines or imprisonment.

This chapter explains a few of the many provisions of the law that pertains to bankruptcy.

debtor
An individual or business that owes money.

creditor
An individual or business to which money is owed.

insolvency
The state that occurs when an individual's or business's liabilities exceed assets.

default
The state in which a debtor fails to meet one or more financial obligations to his or her creditors.

bankruptcy
The legal state that occurs when a debtor is insolvent, is in default, and is unable to fulfill his or her obligations to pay back his or her creditors.

21.2 THE LAW OF BANKRUPTCY

Bankruptcy filings are governed by Congress under Article 1, Section 8 of the United States Constitution. This section gives Congress the power "to establish . . . uniform laws on the subject of bankruptcies throughout the United States." As a result, Congress passed the *Bankruptcy Code* in 1978 under Title 11 of the United States Code. It is important to recognize that bankruptcies are governed under both federal law and state laws, which vary greatly. Therefore, both debtors and creditors must be acquainted with the provisions of both sets of laws.

Bankruptcy filings can either be voluntary or involuntary. A voluntary filing occurs when the debtor himself or herself files a bankruptcy petition; an involuntary filing occurs when creditors pressure the debtor to file. Bankruptcy cases are administered by the United States Bankruptcy Courts, which are part of the district courts of the United States (see Chapter 1).

Bankruptcy law is divided into *chapters,* which is where they appear in the federal bankruptcy law. While all the chapters relating to bankruptcy law are important, select chapters will be discussed in the following paragraphs.

voluntary filing
A form of bankruptcy that occurs when the debtor himself or herself files a bankruptcy petition.

involuntary filing
A form of bankruptcy that occurs when creditors pressure a debtor to file.

21.3 CHAPTER 7 OF THE FEDERAL BANKRUPTCY LAW

The most common type of bankruptcy filed by individuals and businesses is Chapter 7. After a petition for bankruptcy is filed, a trustee, usually an attorney-at-law who is experienced in handling bankruptcy cases, is appointed. The assets of the debtor then go through

- ▶ Real property used as a residence
- ▶ One motor vehicle
- ▶ Household furnishings
- ▶ Appliances
- ▶ Books
- ▶ Pets
- ▶ Musical instruments
- ▶ Jewelry
- ▶ Trade tools
- ▶ Life insurance contracts
- ▶ Individual retirement accounts
- ▶ Prescription health aids

FIGURE 21.1 Examples of Exempt Property under Federal Law (up to a Specified Dollar Limit)

a process called liquidation, in which the assets are sold to obtain cash. Chapter 7 bankruptcy is sometimes referred to as straight or liquidation bankruptcy. The trustee divides the assets into those that are exempt (that is, those that are protected from the creditors) and those that are nonexempt (that is, those that are not afforded such protection). Examples of exempt property under federal law (up to a specified dollar limit) include the debtor's interest in real property used as a residence; one motor vehicle; household furnishings, appliances, books, pets, and musical instruments; jewelry; trade tools; individual retirement accounts (IRAs); life insurance contracts; and prescription health aids. Unless specifically exempted under federal or state law, all other property is nonexempt.

After the trustee has determined which of the debtor's property is exempt and which is nonexempt, he or she collects the debtor's nonexempt property, sells it, and dispenses the proceeds in a fair manner to protect the interests of the creditors to the fullest extent possible. The trustee is responsible for monitoring the claims of these creditors to be certain that all these claims are proper and legally enforceable.

The trustee also distinguishes between the debts that are secured versus those that are unsecured. A secured debt is a loan for which a specific asset is used as collateral, or pledged. Examples of secured loans are mortgages, which are secured by the real property (the land and the home), and automobile loans, which are frequently secured by the vehicles that have been purchased.

Two types of actions by the debtor are prohibited under bankruptcy law. The first is a preferential payment, in which the debtor gives favorable treatment to one creditor over another. The second is a fraudulent transfer, in which the debtor sells property for an amount far below its market value, thus depriving creditors of the fair value had the property been liquidated by the trustee. A contract that is entered into by the debtor that includes either a preferential payment or a fraudulent transfer is illegal and, therefore, as described in Chapter 12, void.

liquidation
A process in which assets are sold to obtain cash.

straight or liquidation bankruptcy
The name given to a Chapter 7 bankruptcy, in which a trustee collects the debtor's nonexempt property, sells it, and dispenses the proceeds.

secured debt
A loan for which a specific asset is used as collateral.

preferential payment
A transfer of funds in which the debtor gives favorable treatment to one creditor over another.

fraudulent transfer
A transaction in which the debtor sells property for an amount far below its market value.

EXAMPLE 21.1

▶ Wang owned a valuable racehorse worth over $100,000. After a series of poor investment decisions, she became insolvent and realized that she was about to default on her numerous loans. Wang decided to petition the court for Chapter 7 bankruptcy. Prior to the petition, she entered into a contract to sell the racehorse to her cousin for $500. Recognizing that this was a fraudulent transfer, the court held that the contract was void and ordered the racehorse turned over to the trustee. Wang then claimed that the racehorse was really a pet and thus was exempt property. The court rejected this argument as well. The trustee sold the horse for its market value and turned the proceeds over to Wang's creditors.

▶ Student loans

▶ Certain debts for luxuries

▶ Back alimony and child support

▶ Certain cash advances

▶ Most tax debts

▶ Certain debts resulting from driving under the influence

FIGURE 21.2   Examples of Debts That Are Not Discharged

Under Chapter 7, a record of bankruptcy may remain in your credit report for up to 10 years—which might make creditors reluctant to extend funds.

At the conclusion of the process prescribed by Chapter 7, most or all of the debtor's debts are *expunged,* meaning they cease to exist and do not survive the bankruptcy. Examples of debts that are discharged are credit card bills, medical bills, and lawsuit judgments. However bankruptcy law provides that some debts survive the bankruptcy. Examples of debts that are not discharged are student loans, unless repaying them would constitute an extreme hardship to the debtor and his or her dependents; debts of more than $550 to any one creditor for luxuries borrowed within 90 days before filing; back alimony and child support; cash advances of more than $825 taken within 70 days before filing; most tax debts; and debts resulting from an incident in which the debtor kills or injures someone while he or she is driving under the influence of drugs or alcohol.

EXAMPLE 21.2

▶ McAndrew ran up numerous credit card charges and owed a significant amount of money on her student loans. When she lost her job, she petitioned the court for Chapter 7 bankruptcy. McAndrew's credit card debts were expunged, but the debt relating to the student loans survived the bankruptcy, and McAndrew must still pay back these loans.

In Example 21.2, it is important to note that although McAndrew's credit card debts were expunged, a record of her bankruptcy may remain in McAndrew's credit report for up to 10 years—which might make creditors reluctant to extend funds to her during that period. However, some creditors may choose to provide financing to an individual who has recently received a bankruptcy discharge because, in general, a debtor may not file a Chapter 7 bankruptcy if he or she has received a bankruptcy discharge in the last six to eight years.

21.4 THE BANKRUPTCY ABUSE PREVENTION AND CONSUMER PROTECTION ACT OF 2005

Providing the most significant changes to bankruptcy law in nearly 30 years, the Bankruptcy Abuse Prevention and Consumer Protection Act was passed in 2005. This federal law instituted strict rules and eligibility requirements for debtors filing for bankruptcy. Among the many provisions in the law were the application of a new means test and the requirement of debtor education and credit counseling.

Bankruptcy Abuse Prevention and Consumer Protection Act of 2005
A federal law that instituted strict rules and eligibility requirements for debtors filing for bankruptcy.

THE MEANS TEST

The Bankruptcy Abuse Prevention and Consumer Protection Act provides that debtors filing for bankruptcy under Chapter 7 must meet a means test. The means test uses a complex formula that measures an individual's income relative to the median income of the people in the state where he or she resides. The Bankruptcy Abuse Prevention and Consumer Protection Act in effect allows the bankruptcy court to disallow a petition for a Chapter 7 bankruptcy if the individual filing for bankruptcy earns an income that is too high to meet the standards of the means test. In such a case, the debtor might be required to file under a different chapter of the bankruptcy law. For more information about means testing, visit www.justice.gov/ust/eo/bapcpa/meanstesting.htm.

means test
A complex formula that measures an individual's income relative to the median income of the people in the state where he or she resides.

EXAMPLE 21.3

▶ Morris, a highly paid vice president at a large oil company, overextended herself by making too many personal purchases using credit cards, and she found herself unable to pay her numerous credit card bills. Despite discontinuing making purchases on her credit cards, she noticed that her debt nonetheless continued to grow due to the cards' onerous interest and penalty charges. When she finally recognized the importance of personal fiscal responsibility and wished to be debt-free, she filed for bankruptcy under Chapter 7. After Morris underwent a means test, it was determined that her high income made her ineligible to file under this chapter.

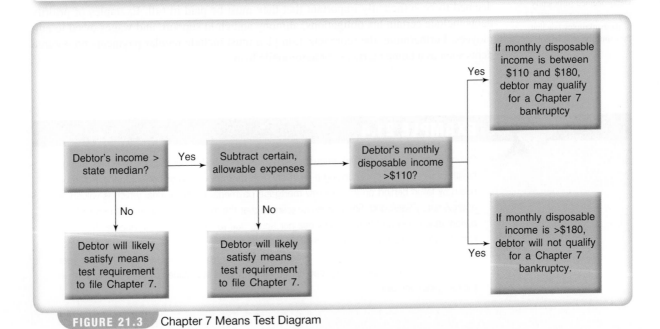

FIGURE 21.3 Chapter 7 Means Test Diagram

DEBTOR EDUCATION AND CREDIT COUNSELING

In addition to the means test, the Bankruptcy Abuse Prevention and Consumer Protection Act requires that a debtor who wishes to file under any chapter of the bankruptcy law must, unless exempt, receive individual or group credit counseling from an approved, not-for-profit, individual or group budget or credit counseling agency. The debtor must obtain a certificate from this agency outlining the assistance in budgeting that the debtor received. The counseling must be performed by telephone or online within 180 days prior to the bankruptcy filing. For a listing of approved agencies, visit www.usdoj.gov/ust.

21.5 CHAPTER 13 OF THE FEDERAL BANKRUPTCY LAW

reorganization bankruptcy

The name given to a Chapter 13 bankruptcy, in which the debtor agrees to pay back all or a portion of his or her debts over a period of from three to five years.

Under the provisions of Chapter 13 of the federal bankruptcy law, the debtor retains his or her property but agrees to pay back all or a portion of his or her debts on an interest-free basis over a period spanning from three to five years. This is quite different from the provisions of Chapter 7, in which the debtor surrenders his or her assets to a trustee. Due to this difference, Chapter 13 bankruptcy is sometimes referred to as a reorganization bankruptcy.

Chapter 13 proceedings are initiated voluntarily, unlike Chapter 7 proceedings, which can be initiated either voluntarily or involuntarily. To be eligible to file for Chapter 13 bankruptcy, a debtor must be able to demonstrate that he or she has an income that is sufficient to pay off his or her debts within the prescribed period, and that the amount of debt that is currently owed does not exceed the specified limits of $1,010,650 for secured debts and $336,900 for unsecured debts. Note that the Bankruptcy Abuse Prevention and Consumer Protection Act also applies to Chapter 13 and requires that the debtor receive the same prefiling counseling as is required under Chapter 7.

priority debts

Debts deemed sufficiently important under Chapter 13 of the bankruptcy law that they must be paid in full.

Under Chapter 13, certain debts are considered to be priority debts. Priority debts are deemed to be sufficiently important that they must be paid in full. Examples of priority debts include certain tax obligations, alimony and child support, and wages owed to employees. Furthermore, the reorganization plan must include regular payments on secured debts such as a home mortgage or automobile loan.

EXAMPLE 21.4

▶ Polumbo incurred a significant amount of expenses on behalf of her mother, who had serious health issues. Although occupying a relatively high-paying position at her company, Polumbo has now fallen behind on the monthly mortgage payments for her home, which is valued at approximately $350,000. She is quite concerned that the mortgage company will bring a legal action against her and that she will lose her home due to foreclosure. She decides to file for Chapter 13 bankruptcy to stop her creditors from repossessing her home. Since her home is not valued over $1,010,650 and since she earns an income, Polumbo is put on a strict four-year repayment plan and is allowed to keep her home as long as she abides by the rules set forth in the reorganization plan.

Under Chapter 13, once the repayment plan is satisfied, all remaining debts that are eligible for discharge are expunged. The debtor must, however, first demonstrate to the bankruptcy court that he or she is current on alimony and child support obligations and that he or she has completed a second budget counseling course with an agency approved by the United States trustee. This second counseling course does not replace, but is in addition to, the prefiling counseling course described earlier in this chapter. For a listing of approved agencies at the trustee's website, visit www.usdoj.gov/ust.

Finally, it is important to point out that some debtors prefer Chapter 13 to Chapter 7 because Chapter 13 allows the debtor to retain nonexempt property.

21.6 CHAPTERS 9, 11, 12, AND 15 OF THE FEDERAL BANKRUPTCY LAW

In addition to Chapter 7, the federal bankruptcy law contains several other chapters that might apply to individuals or businesses that become insolvent and default on their debts. Several of these other chapters are discussed in the following paragraphs.

CHAPTER 9

Chapter 9 bankruptcy involves the adjustment of debts for a municipality. The purpose of this chapter is to provide a municipality with a debt repayment plan, rather than to require the liquidation of municipal assets. A *municipality* in the bankruptcy code is defined as a political subdivision or public agency or instrumentality of a state, including cities, towns, villages, counties, taxing districts, municipal authorities, and school districts.

EXAMPLE 21.5

▶ Officials from the town of Wilkbar find that it is unable to recover from debt incurred from a failed transit system. Among other remedies, the option of a tax raise was rejected, and Wilkbar has no other choice but to file for Chapter 9 bankruptcy. As a result of the bankruptcy, the court finds that the town must create a plan for recovery, which requires Wilkbar to make significant and painful reductions in expenditures on community programs.

CHAPTER 11

While partnerships, sole proprietorships, and individuals all may file for Chapter 11 bankruptcy, this chapter is most commonly used by corporations. In a Chapter 11 bankruptcy, the debtor proposes a reorganization plan in order to pay back creditors over time. Daily business decisions continue to be made and implemented by management, but major decisions must be approved by the bankruptcy court.

EXAMPLE 21.6

▶ Saarsgard Motor Corporation, a publicly traded automobile manufacturer, finds that it is unable to pay its debts but wishes to remain in business. It files for Chapter 11 bankruptcy. The company is forced to restructure its business with the approval of the bankruptcy court and work out a plan to become profitable once again. Saarsgard will continue to be able to conduct its normal business operations and to sell its stocks and bonds to members of the public.

EXAMPLE 21.7

▶ Adelphia Communications Corporation announced that, due to stiff competition in the telecom industry, it was necessary for the company to file for Chapter 11 bankruptcy protection. Soon thereafter, federal prosecutors unveiled a complex scheme by which the company founders illegally siphoned more than $100 million in corporate funds. The decision to file for Chapter 11, rather than Chapter 7 bankruptcy, was made in order to provide the company enough time to secure the sale of a large portion of company assets to other companies in the telecom industry. Under Chapter 7 bankruptcy, Adelphia shareholders and creditors may have fared worse; the immediate liquidation of company assets could have resulted in far greater losses.

Some individuals elect to file bankruptcy under Chapter 11, rather than Chapter 13, because they have high levels of debt—levels that are greater than the debt limits specified by Chapter 13.

CHAPTER 12

During the 1980s, a serious economic downturn in the agricultural sector prompted Congress to amend the bankruptcy code to provide distressed farmers a more favorable alternative to a Chapter 7 bankruptcy proceeding. As a result, Chapter 12 bankruptcy was specifically created to adjust the debts of family farmers or fishers who earn an annual income. Under a Chapter 12 bankruptcy, a plan is created to ensure that these debtors repay their debt over a period spanning from three to five years. The family farmer or fisher can be an individual, corporation, or partnership. To be eligible for a Chapter 12 bankruptcy, a debtor cannot owe more than $1,500,000, with at least 80 percent of these debts being related to farming or fishing. Furthermore, at least 50 percent of the debtor's income must come from his or her farming or fishing activities.

EXAMPLE 21.8

▶ Alessi, who works full-time as a highly paid executive at a local manufacturing company, supplements his income by growing corn on his farm. Alessi now finds that he is facing financial trouble due to ongoing problems in the corn industry, as well as several large purchases he made to satisfy his personal desires. He decides to file for Chapter 12 bankruptcy to help pay his debts but is rejected because only 40 percent of his income is generated from farming activities. Alessi will need to find an alternative way to address his financial predicament.

Chapter 12 bankruptcy was specifically created to adjust the debts of family farmers or fishers who earn an annual income.

CHAPTER 15

Chapter 15 bankruptcy involves ancillary and other cross-border cases. Added to the bankruptcy code by the Bankruptcy Abuse Prevention and Consumer Protection Act, Chapter 15 provides a framework for bankruptcy cases in which foreign countries are involved. The purpose of this chapter is to promote cooperation between U.S. courts and those of foreign countries in bankruptcy cases.

CHAPTER SUMMARY

1. Insolvency occurs when a individual's or business's liabilities exceed assets. Insolvency often leads to default, wherein the debtor fails to meet one or more financial obligations to his or her creditors.

2. Bankruptcy filings are governed by Congress under the U.S. Constitution. A voluntary filing occurs when the debtor himself or herself files a bankruptcy petition; an involuntary filing occurs when creditors pressure the debtor to file.

3. In a Chapter 7 bankruptcy, the assets of the debtor are liquidated to obtain cash. The trustee divides

the assets by whether they are exempt. The trustee collects the debtor's nonexempt property, sells it, and dispenses the proceeds in a fair manner to protect the interests of creditors. At the conclusion of this process, most or all of the debtor's debts are expunged and do not survive the bankruptcy.

4. The Bankruptcy Abuse Prevention and Consumer Protection Act requires that debtors meet a means test that measures an individual's income relative to the median income of the people in the state where he or she resides. In addition, the law requires that a debtor who wishes to file under any

chapter of the bankruptcy law must, unless exempt, receive individual or group credit counseling.

5. Under Chapter 13 of the federal bankruptcy law, the debtor retains his or her property, but agrees to pay back all or a portion of his or her debts interest-free over a period spanning from three to five years.

6. Chapter 9 bankruptcy involves the adjustment of debts for a municipality. In a Chapter 11 bankruptcy, the debtor proposes a reorganization plan to pay back creditors over time. Chapter 12 bankruptcy was specifically created to adjust the debts of family farmers or fishers who earn an annual income. Chapter 15 bankruptcy involves ancillary and other cross-border cases.

CHAPTER TWENTY ONE
ASSESSMENT

MATCHING LEGAL TERMS

Match each of the numbered definitions with the correct term in the following list. Write the letter of your choice in the answer column.

a. assets
b. bankruptcy
c. creditor
d. debtor
e. default

f. insolvency
g. involuntary filing
h. liabilities
i. liquidation
j. means test

k. priority debt
l. reorganization bankruptcy
m. secured debt
n. straight bankruptcy
o. voluntary filing

1. A form of bankruptcy in which the debtor agrees to pay back all or a portion of his or her debts over a period spanning from three to five years.   1. _____

2. A complex formula that measures an individual's income relative to the median income of the people in the state where he or she resides.   2. _____

3. A form of bankruptcy that occurs when creditors pressure a debtor to file.   3. _____

4. The legal state that occurs when a debtor is insolvent, is in default, and is unable to fulfill his or her obligations to pay back his or her creditors.   4. _____

5. An individual or business that owes money.   5. _____

6. An item deemed sufficiently important under Chapter 13 of the bankruptcy law that it must be paid in full.   6. _____

7. The value of the property an individual or business owns.   7. _____

8. An individual or business to which money is owed.

8. _____

9. A form of bankruptcy that occurs when the debtor himself or herself files a bankruptcy petition.

9. _____

10. A debt for which a specific asset is used as collateral.

10. _____

11. The value of what an individual or business owes.

11. _____

12. A form of bankruptcy in which a trustee collects the debtor's nonexempt property, sells it, and dispenses the proceeds.

12. _____

13. The state that occurs when an individual's or business's liabilities exceed assets.

13. _____

14. A process in which assets are sold to obtain cash.

14. _____

15. The state in which a debtor fails to meet one or more financial obligations to his or her creditors.

15. _____

TRUE/FALSE QUIZ

Indicate whether each of the following statements is true or false by writing *T* or *F* in the answer column.

16. Persons familiar with good accounting practices recognize that assets should never exceed liabilities.

16. _____

17. In most instances, when bankruptcy is filed, the debtor's assets are sold and the money is distributed among the debtor's creditors to pay the debt that is owed.

17. _____

18. Bankruptcies are governed under both federal and state law.

18. _____

19. All bankruptcy filings are involuntary.

19. _____

20. Chapter 9 bankruptcy is sometimes referred to as straight or liquidation bankruptcy.

20. _____

21. Chapter 13 bankruptcy is sometimes referred to as reorganization bankruptcy.

21. _____

22. A bankruptcy court may disallow a petition for a Chapter 7 bankruptcy if the individual does not meet the standards of the means test.

22. _____

23. All debtors wishing to file for bankruptcy must receive individual or group credit counseling from an approved, not-for-profit, individual or group budget or credit counseling agency.

23. _____

24. In a Chapter 11 bankruptcy, all daily business decisions must be made and implemented by the bankruptcy court.

24. _____

25. Chapter 12 bankruptcy was specifically created to adjust the debts of family farmers or fishers who earn an annual income.

25. _____

DISCUSSION QUESTIONS

Answer the following questions and discuss them in class.

26. List some examples of exempt property under Chapter 7 of the federal bankruptcy law.

27. Describe the two types of actions by the debtor prohibited under bankruptcy law that were discussed in this chapter.

28. List some examples of debts that are not discharged under a Chapter 7 bankruptcy.

29. Explain the debtor education and credit counseling requirement under the Bankruptcy Abuse Prevention and Consumer Protection Act.

30. List some examples of priority debts under a Chapter 13 bankruptcy.

31. Describe the process used in a Chapter 11 bankruptcy.

Answer the following questions, which require you to think critically about the legal principles that you learned in this chapter.

32. **Exempt Property** Why is some property considered exempt under Chapter 7 of the federal bankruptcy law?

_____

_____

33. **Debtor Education and Credit Counseling** Why does the law require a debtor to receive individual or group credit counseling prior to be allowed to file for bankruptcy?

_____

_____

34. **Chapter 13** Why are certain debts considered to be priority debts under Chapter 13 of the federal bankruptcy law?

_____

_____

35. **Chapter 9** Should municipalities that are mismanaged be allowed to file for bankruptcy?

_____

_____

36. **A Question of Ethics** Is it ethical for an individual to purchase numerous items on credit when he or she knows that bankruptcy is available as an option in the event of a default?

_____

_____

CASE QUESTIONS

Study each of the following cases. Answer the questions that follow by writing _Yes_ or _No_ in the answer column.

37. **Exempt Property** Chen had numerous debts from credit card bills, a home mortgage, and a loan resulting for a second automobile purchased on credit. He filed for bankruptcy under Chapter 7. Chen's assets, in addition to his two

automobiles, included a home, some rare coins, a pet pedigreed dog, and a baby grand piano.

a. Is the second automobile exempt property?   a. _____

b. Are both the dog and the piano exempt property?   b. _____

c. Are the rare coins exempt property?   c. _____

d. Is the home exempt property?   d. _____

38. **Chapter 11** Travel Junction, a corporation, encounters financial difficulties and files for bankruptcy under Chapter 11. The bankruptcy court approves a reorganization plan to pay back creditors over time and begins monitoring the activities of the business.

a. Must Travel Junction receive prior approval from the bankruptcy court to purchase three new desks for the office?   a. _____

b. Must Travel Junction receive prior approval from the bankruptcy court to purchase two new computers for the office?   b. _____

c. Must Travel Junction receive prior approval from the bankruptcy court to purchase a new building with 12 rental apartments?   c. _____

39. **Chapter 13** Brown earned a significant income as a pilot for a major airline. Despite this high income, Brown ran into serious financial difficulties when she invested in a business owned by her brother that failed. Brown filed for bankrutpcy under Chapter 13 to gain some time to get her financial affairs back in order.

a. Will Brown need to receive individual credit counseling prior to be allowed to file for bankruptcy?   a. _____

b. Must Brown demonstrate to the bankruptcy court that the amount of debt that she owes is less than $1,010,650 for secured debts and $336,900 for unsecured debts?   b. _____

c. Must Brown complete a second budget counseling course after the bankruptcy court approves the reorganization plan?   c. _____

CASE ANALYSIS

Study each of the following cases carefully. Briefly state the principle of law and your decision.

40. **Bad Faith** A mere eight days after it was formally incorporated as a business, Schaefer Salt Recovery Inc. (SSR) filed a petition under Chapter 11 of the bankruptcy code. SSR's only assets were mortgages on three properties on which foreclosure actions brought by Segal were pending in court. SSR's vice president and attorney, Khoudary, advised Segal's attorney that the foreclosure actions could not be enforced as a result of the filing. Presumably this was one of the reasons why Khoudary advised Segal's attorney that "Segal was skunked." Segal moved to dismiss the Chapter 11 petition for cause, arguing that the petition had been filed for

the sole purpose of frustrating Segal's efforts to conclude the pending foreclosure actions. Did SSR act in bad faith by filing the petition for bankruptcy, and will Segal be successful in foreclosing on the mortgages? [*In Re: Schaefer Salt Recovery, Inc.*, United States Third Circuit, Docket No. 06-4574 (New Jersey)]

Principle of Law:

_____

_____

Decision:

_____

_____

41. **Discharged Debts** Jensen was involved in a motor vehicle accident with Boyer. Jensen brought suit against Boyer, alleging that her negligence caused the accident. Boyer then brought a countersuit against Jensen, claiming that it was actually Jensen's negligence that caused the accident. Jensen subsequently filed for bankruptcy protection. The bankruptcy court issued a discharge, and Jensen filed a motion to dismiss Boyer's lawsuit due to the bankruptcy discharge. Are lawsuit judgments discharged in a bankruptcy, and will Jensen be successful in having Boyer's claim against him discharged? [*Boyer v. Jensen*, California Court of Appeal, Docket No. B174899 (California)]

Principle of Law:

_____

_____

Decision:

_____

_____

42. **Chapter 11** Following months in which Chrysler experienced deepening losses and received billions in bailout funds from the federal government, the company, now referred to as Old Chrysler, filed a bankruptcy petition under Chapter 11. The filing unsuccessfully sought additional government bailout funds for a restructuring, but the bankruptcy court ultimately settled on a transaction in which most of Old Chrysler's operating assets would be transferred to New Chrysler in exchange for $2 billion in cash and other consideration. In addition, Fiat, another automobile manufacturer, agreed to provide New Chrysler with certain fuel-efficient vehicle platforms, access to its worldwide distribution system, and new management that was experienced in turning around a failing auto company. Financing for the sale would come from the U.S. Troubled Asset Relief Program (TARP) and from Export Development Canada. The United Auto Workers union, the United States Treasury, and Export Development Canada would own the New Chrysler. Fiat, for its contributions, would immediately own 20 percent of the equity with rights to acquire more. Numerous groups appealed, seeking to stop the Chapter 11 bankruptcy from proceeding. Does it seem likely that the appeals court will

support the settlement reached in the bankruptcy court? [*In Re: Chrysler LLC, et al.*, United States Second Circuit, Docket No. 09-2311-bk (New York)]

Principle of Law:

_____

_____

Decision:

_____

_____

LEGAL RESEARCH

Complete the following activities. Share your findings with the class.

43. **Working in Teams** In teams of three or four, listing some events that might occur in the course of an individual's life or a business's transactions that could result in insolvency, default, and bankruptcy.

_____

_____

44. **Using Technology** Using the Internet and search engines, investigate individuals and businesses that have declared bankruptcy, and determine under which chapter(s) these bankruptcies filed. Speculate about the reasons for the bankruptcies and the selection of the particular chapter(s). What types of economic conditions would lead an individual or business to select a particular chapter?

_____

_____

chapter **22**

Introduction to Commercial Paper

LEARNING OUTCOMES

After studying this chapter and completing the assessment, you will be able to

22.1 Explain the characteristics of commercial paper and how it differs from ordinary contracts.

22.2 Distinguish between the two basic kinds of commercial paper: promises to pay (notes) and orders to pay (checks and drafts).

22.3 Identify the parties to commercial paper.

22.4 List and explain the essentials for negotiability of commercial paper.

22.5 List and explain the nonessentials for negotiability of commercial paper.

22.6 Discuss the various kinds of checks and the rules and procedures for stopping payment on a check.

22.7 Discuss electronic funds transfers and provide several examples of these.

LEGAL terms

commercial paper	traveler's check
negotiable instrument	bad check
promissory note	forgery
check	forged check
draft	raised check
negotiability	postdated check
order instrument	stop-payment order
stale check	electronic funds
Check 21	transfer (EFT)
certified check	Electronic Funds Transfer
cashier's check	Act (EFTA) of 1979

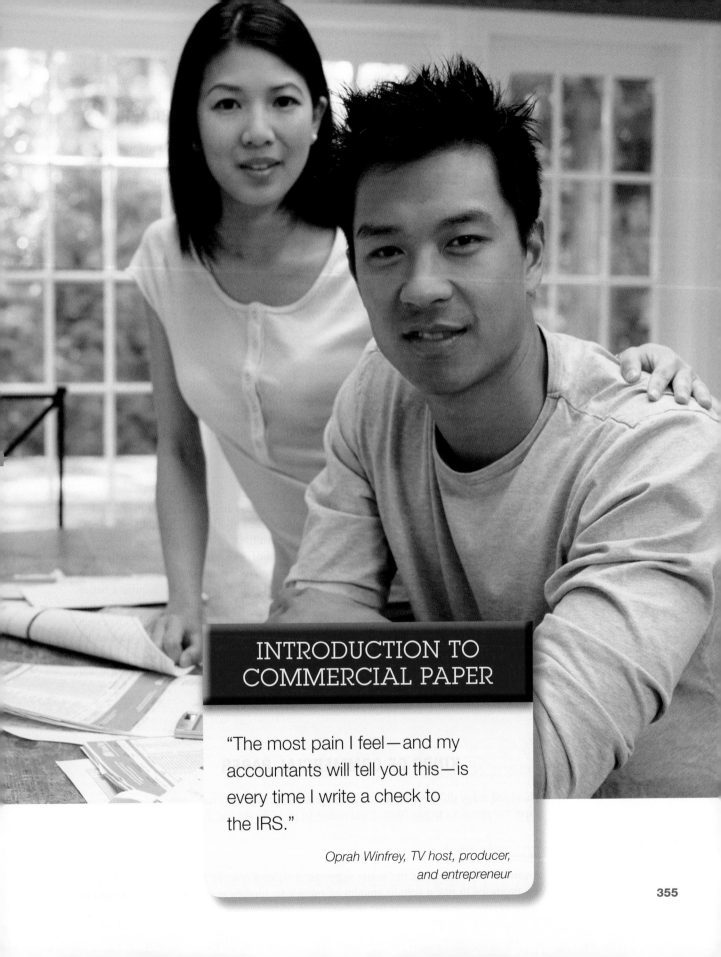

INTRODUCTION TO COMMERCIAL PAPER

"The most pain I feel—and my accountants will tell you this—is every time I write a check to the IRS."

Oprah Winfrey, TV host, producer, and entrepreneur

22.1 CHARACTERISTICS OF COMMERCIAL PAPER

commercial paper
A number of legally binding and commercially acceptable documents that are used to transfer money from one person to another.

Commercial paper is a term widely used in law to describe a number of legally binding and commercially acceptable documents, such as notes, checks, and drafts, that are used to transfer money from one person to another. These documents are negotiable—that is, they are freely transferable—and they circulate throughout our commercial system almost as readily as cash. Commercial paper is sometimes referred to as negotiable instruments. A negotiable instrument is an unconditional written promise to pay, or pay to the order of another party, a certain sum of money on demand or at a definite time. Negotiable instruments are highly trusted and play an important role in everyday individual and business transactions.

negotiable instrument
An unconditional written promise to pay, or pay to the order of another party, a certain sum of money on demand or at a definite time.

Commercial paper (negotiable instruments) forms the basis of contracts, but it differs from ordinary contracts in two important ways: presumption of consideration and assignability.

PRESUMPTION OF CONSIDERATION

The law presumes that commercial paper is issued for value—that is, for consideration. A party to a simple contract who is seeking to enforce the promise contained in the agreement must prove that he or she gave consideration; however, a party to commercial paper who is trying to collect payment does not. Instead the person trying to avoid payment must prove that he or she received no consideration.

NEGOTIABILITY VERSUS ASSIGNABILITY

As described in Chapter 14, ordinary contracts usually may be assigned; but the assignee, or the person to whom rights are transferred, may receive only those rights held by the person making the assignment (the assignor) at the time of the transfer. In addition, the person who has acquired assigned rights to a contract must notify the other party to the contract of the assignment. These conditions do not apply to commercial paper that is being negotiated (transferred). The person to whom commercial paper is transferred may acquire a better right to it than the person who made the transfer. For example, if commercial paper that has been found or stolen is sold (transferred) to an innocent person for value, that person becomes the legal owner with title enforceable even against the rightful owner—unlike the innocent purchaser of found or stolen jewelry, who does not acquire title. In addition, in some cases the person receiving the instrument can receive money on the instrument when the transferring person could not.

22.2 KINDS OF COMMERCIAL PAPER

There are many different kinds of commercial paper. The two basic types of commercial paper are promises to pay (notes) and orders to pay (checks and drafts).

promissory note
A written note or letter in which one person promises to pay a certain amount of money to another at a definite time.

PROMISES TO PAY

A promissory note is, as the name suggests, a written note or letter in which one person promises to pay a certain amount of money to another at a definite time. A simple promissory note would be one saying, "I, John Jones, promise to pay to the order of Frieda Smith $100 in 60 days from the date this note is issued." If Frieda Smith should need the $100 before the 60 days have passed, she could take this written promise to a bank or to another person and, if the bank or other person felt that John Jones would keep his promise, Smith could then transfer, or negotiate, her interest in the promise to the bank, or to the other person, in exchange for $100. Smith would then have the money she needed without having to wait for it, and the bank or the other person would be entitled to receive Jones's $100 at the time promised.

ORDERS TO PAY

There are situations in which a person orders another individual to pay a definite sum of money. This form of commercial paper includes checks (in which a bank is ordered) and drafts (in which a third party is ordered).

Checks   A check is a written order drawn on a bank by a depositor that requests the bank to pay, on demand and unconditionally, a definite sum of money to the bearer of the check or to the order of a specified person. Consider a check for $50 from Frieda Smith to John Jones simply as a letter from Smith to her bank saying, "Dear Ms. Banker: You are in possession of some of my money and I now wish you to pay $50 of it to John Jones." The banker would ask Jones to prove his identity; ask Jones to sign his name on the back of the check—that is, to endorse it—as an indication that he is receiving the $50; and then pay Jones the $50 as directed by Smith. Additional discussion of endorsements is presented in Chapter 23.

check
A written order drawn on a bank by a depositor that requests the bank to pay, on demand and unconditionally, a definite sum of money to the bearer of the check or to the order of a specified person.

Drafts   Whereas a check is a letter to a bank instructing it to pay money to a certain person, a draft, or *bill of exchange,* is an unconditional written order to a person instructing him or her to pay money to another, third person. Drafts are often used in certain kinds of businesses.

draft
An unconditional written order to a person instructing him or her to pay money to another, third person.

EXAMPLE 22.1

▶ Frey traveled for extended periods and, not wanting to delay payments to utility companies during his absences, authorized his attorney to make periodic payments of specified amounts. Frey used drafts to accomplish this objective.

THE MEANING OF "PAY TO THE ORDER OF"

If the check from Frieda Smith to John Jones was worded, "Pay to John Jones . . .," the banker could not do otherwise. But if the check said, "Pay to the order of John Jones . . .," it would mean, "Pay this money to John Jones or do whatever else he wants you to do with it." These few key words, "Pay to the order of," give commercial paper negotiability, or the ability to be transferred freely from one person to another and be accepted as readily as cash. As a result, Jones can tell the banker, "I don't really want the money Smith is telling you to give me. I want you to pay it to Brown instead."

An item of commercial paper containing the key words of negotiability, "pay to the order of," or their equivalent, is an order instrument. Notes, drafts, and checks are all examples of order instruments.

negotiability
The ability to be transferred freely from one person to another and be accepted as readily as cash.

order instrument
An item of commercial paper that contains the key words of negotiability, "pay to the order of," or their equivalent.

22.3 PARTIES TO COMMERCIAL PAPER

The parties involved in a promissory note have particular names. The person who makes the promise is called the *maker*. If the maker has someone else add his or her name to the promise to strengthen it, the other person is known as the *comaker*. The person to whom the promise is made is the *payee*.

Similarly, the parties involved in a draft or a check have particular names. The person who draws or creates the check or draft is called the *drawer*. The person who receives the money is called the *payee*. The person who is ordered to pay the money is called the *drawee* (in the case of a check, the drawee is a bank). Whoever is in possession of commercial paper is called the *holder*. Some holders are called *holders in due course*, to be covered in Chapter 23. The holder can be the payee, the drawee, or the drawer, but obviously only one of these parties can be the holder at one time.

22.4 ESSENTIALS FOR NEGOTIABILITY OF COMMERCIAL PAPER

To be negotiable under the Uniform Commercial Code (UCC), commercial paper must conform to the following requirements [UCC 3-104(1)].

IT MUST BE IN WRITING AND SIGNED BY THE MAKER OR DRAWER

Commercial paper may be handwritten, printed, or written by any other means that will make a mark. The signature may be written either at the bottom or in the body of the instrument, as, "I, Fred Allan, promise to pay . . ." [UCC 1-201(46)].

The device used in writing a note does not affect its negotiability. Anything that will make a mark is satisfactory.

EXAMPLE 22.2

▶ Forgue offered Aiello a $500 note in payment for merchandise she had purchased. The note specified payment within 30 days. Aiello refused to accept the note because of the fact that it was written in red ink, incorrectly assuming that it was not enforceable.

Only the person who writes his or her name on a note as the maker, or on a check or draft as the drawer, is liable for it. The liability is the same even if the person signs a trade name or an assumed name. Thus, in a note bearing the signature "Charles Lamb, Agent for Clark Insurance Company," Lamb is personally liable. The phrase "Agent for Clark Insurance Company" merely describes Lamb. If the note were signed "Clark Insurance Company, by Charles Lamb, Agent," the company would be liable. Lamb would have clearly indicated that he had signed for his employer (see Chapter 19).

IT MUST CONTAIN AN UNCONDITIONAL PROMISE OR ORDER TO PAY A DEFINITE SUM IN MONEY

The promise in a note, or the order in a check or draft, must be unconditional. Statements requiring that certain things be done or that specific events take place before payment make the instrument a simple contract rather than commercial paper. Contrary to popular opinion, an IOU is not a promise to pay; it is merely an acknowledgment of a debt.

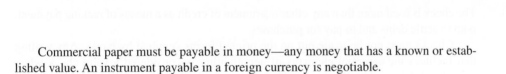

EXAMPLE 22.3

▶ Spiegelgras received a note from an individual who owed him money. The note contained the statement, "Payment to be made from my income tax refund check." This note was not negotiable because payment depended on the Internal Revenue Service agreeing that a refund was due. In case of a lawsuit, this instrument would be considered a simple contract. Suppose that, instead of the provision about the tax refund, the note contained the statement, "This note is in payment of purchases made in January." This latter statement would not affect the negotiability of the note because it does not in any way limit, restrict, or condition payment.

Commercial paper must be payable in money—any money that has a known or established value. An instrument payable in a foreign currency is negotiable.

IT MUST BE PAYABLE ON DEMAND OR AT A DEFINITE TIME

Commercial paper must be payable on demand or at some definite time. A note payable "on or before July 1, 20—, or "one month after sight," or "on presentation" is negotiable because the time of payment is certain.

An instrument payable "within 60 days after death [of a named person]" is not payable at a definite time and is not negotiable. A promise to pay when a person marries or when he or she reaches a certain age is not a promise to pay at a definite time, because the person might never marry or might die before reaching the specified age. In such instances, the instruments are nonnegotiable.

IT MUST BE PAYABLE TO ORDER, TO BEARER, OR TO CASH

Unless an instrument contains words of negotiability such as "payable to bearer" or "payable to the order of" or "payable to cash," it is not negotiable.

A DRAFT OR CHECK MUST NAME OR INDICATE THE DRAWEE WITH REASONABLE CERTAINTY

The person who is expected to pay a draft or check must be named or otherwise indicated in the instrument with reasonable certainty for the instrument to be considered negotiable.

22.5 NONESSENTIALS FOR NEGOTIABILITY OF COMMERCIAL PAPER

Certain items may be omitted from commercial paper without affecting its negotiability. Because consideration is presumed, the words "for value received" are not needed. Also, the consideration or value given by the maker or the drawer need not be specified.

If the date of a note, check, or draft is not indicated, the holder may write in the date when the instrument was issued without affecting its negotiability. If this date is not known, the date when the paper was received is considered the date of issue. Commercial paper may be *antedated* (dated previously) or *postdated* (dated ahead).

The place of business or home of a maker of a note is presumed to be where the instrument was drawn or where it is payable if this information is not given on the paper.

In a note, draft, or check, if the amount payable expressed in figures differs from the sum stated in words, the amount expressed in words is considered the true one. If the sum stated in words is not also expressed in figures, this omission does not affect negotiability.

The numbering of (or the failure to number) commercial paper does not affect its negotiability.

22.6 CHECKS

The check is used more than any other instrument of credit as a means of making payment, both to settle debts and to pay for purchases.

Checks need not be made out on the printed forms supplied by banks. Any writing that includes the essential elements of negotiability is considered a valid check when signed and delivered by the drawer. However, many banks today prefer that the encoded routing number assigned a drawer (depositor) be shown on every check written by him or her. For proper processing through computers and other electronic machinery, these numbers are recommended, although they are not legally necessary. Figure 22.1 shows an example of a check.

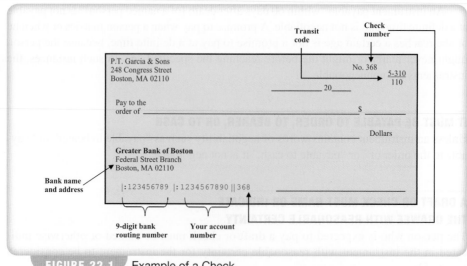

FIGURE 22.1 Example of a Check

RELATIONSHIP BETWEEN BANK AND DEPOSITOR

A check provides a safe means of transferring money and serves as a receipt when paid and canceled by the bank. It may circulate through several persons, banks, and organizations. The bank must honor a check when it is properly drawn against the money the drawer has on deposit or the bank will be liable to the drawer for damages.

PAYMENT OF CHECKS

Checks are always payable on demand. The UCC provides that, with respect to the liability of the drawer, a reasonable length of time for presentation for payment is 30 days after the date appearing on the check or after issue (the date the check is actually written), whichever is later. A bank may pay a check presented more than 30 days after its date, but it is not required to do so. A check presented more than six months after its date is known as a stale check (UCC 4-404). Stale checks will not be honored by banks.

stale check
A check presented more than six months after its date.

EXAMPLE 22.4

▶ Shuster received a check from Cavanagh and immediately presented it to her bank for payment. Cavanagh's bank, for reasons of its own, refused to honor the check, although Cavanagh had sufficient funds on deposit to cover it. Cavanagh can sue her bank for any damages that she may have sustained as a result of the bank's refusal to cash her check.

THE CHECK CLEARING FOR THE 21st CENTURY ACT

The *Check Clearing for the 21st Century Act,* a federal law commonly known as Check 21, became effective in 2004. The law revolutionized the manner in which checks are handled by banks. In the past, banks physically transported checks between the drawee bank and the bank in which they were deposited. Check handling was inefficient, costly, and time-consuming. Check 21 created efficiency in check handling by allowing banks to create digital substitutes of checks to be handled electronically, thereby removing paper checks from the process.

Check 21
The term commonly used to refer to the Check Clearing for the 21st Century Act, a federal law revolutionizing the manner in which checks are handled by banks.

Under Check 21, banks provide checking account customers with copies of the digital check substitutes rather than the original canceled checks. Also, the drawer must be certain funds are immediately available in his or her account to cover a check. Electronic check transfers occur almost instantaneously.

CERTIFIED CHECKS

A merchant who sells goods to a person whose credit standing is not known may request the customer to make payment by certified check, a check that the bank has promised to pay when it is presented for payment. If the drawer's funds on deposit are sufficient to cover the amount of the check, the teller or cashier will write or stamp across the face of the check the word "certified" and the date. The teller will then sign his or her name and title and make an entry in the depositor's account indicating that the depositor's balance has been reduced by the amount of the check. While actual cash is not set aside for the payment of the check, a notation of the transaction is made on the depositor's record. The bank assumes absolute liability for

certified check
A check that the bank has promised to pay when it is presented for payment.

Checks are always payable on demand.

payment. It should be noted that under the UCC, unless otherwise agreed by contract, a bank has no legal obligation to certify a check [UCC 3-411(2)].

Liability for Certified Checks   If a drawer of a check has the bank certify it, he or she remains conditionally liable for payment of the check until the holder can reasonably present it for payment. However, when a check is certified at the request of the payee or holder, while the drawee is still responsible for eventual payment, the drawer and all prior endorsers are released from all liability. The reason is that the payee or holder could have requested payment instead of certification.

EXAMPLE 22.5

▶ Sherwin asked her bank to *stop payment* (a service offered by banks whereby a depositor can have the bank refuse to pay a depositor's check when it is presented for payment by a holder) on a check that she had certified. The bank refused to stop payment, even though the check had not yet been presented for payment.

In Example 22.5 the bank was justified in refusing to honor Sherwin's request. By certifying the check, the bank had assumed absolute liability for its payment. Certification assures the payee or any subsequent holder that the check is genuine and that the bank will honor the check when it is presented for payment.

There is no time limit for the presentation of a certified check for payment. The bank must honor it whenever the holder demands payment.

CASHIER'S CHECKS

cashier's check
A check issued by a cashier or other designated officer of a bank and drawn against bank funds.

A cashier's check, sometimes called an *official check,* a *teller's check,* or a *bank check,* is issued by the cashier or other designated officer of a bank and drawn against bank funds. A depositor may request such a check when, for example, he or she intends to use it to pay for merchandise from an out-of-town dealer who will not accept a personal check.

A cashier's check is made payable either to the depositor who purchases it from the bank or to the person who is to cash it. If the check is made payable to the depositor, he or she endorses it to the person to whom it is being transferred.

The UCC provides for recovery of a lost, stolen, or destroyed certified or cashier's check. If such an event occurs, either the payee or the person who purchased the check may request a full refund from the bank. According to UCC 3-312, if a claim is made for recovery of a cashier's check and that check is not presented for payment within 90 days after the check was made (or 90 days after acceptance of a certified check), the bank will generally issue a refund. If the bank does issue a full refund to either party, it is released from all liability regarding the certified or cashier's check.

TRAVELER'S CHECKS

A traveler's check is a certified check issued in a denomination of $10 or more by certain banks, travel agencies, and financial services companies. The issuer usually charges the purchaser of traveler's checks a fixed rate, perhaps 1 percent, to issue them.

For persons who are traveling, especially in foreign countries, traveler's checks are a safe form in which to carry money because anyone finding or stealing them would have difficulty using them. Only the purchaser who signed the checks when he or she bought them may negotiate them. They are convenient because they are accepted almost all over the world.

To cash a traveler's check, the purchaser countersigns it in the presence of the person who is converting it into cash or accepting it in payment of a purchase. However, with the growing availability of ATMs and the widespread acceptance of credit cards in foreign countries, the use of traveler's checks has declined somewhat in recent years.

MONEY ORDERS

A money order is similar in form to a personal check and may be purchased at a bank or other third-party location. Since the funds are prepaid, much like a cashier's check, a money order is considered a more trusted method of payment than a personal check. A money order, however, is limited in maximum face value. The person who purchases a money order fills in the name of the payee, signs it as the drawer, and retains the receipt.

BAD CHECKS

A bad check is one against a bank in which the drawer has insufficient funds on deposit to cover the check or no funds at all. Most states have statutes making a person who issues a check drawn on a bank in which he or she has no account guilty of the criminal offense of larceny. In some states, it is a criminal offense for a person to intentionally issue a check drawn on a bank in which that person has an account but has insufficient funds on deposit. The law in most states allows the drawer of a check a specified number of days, usually 5 or 10, to deposit funds to cover the check without incurring criminal liability.

FORGED AND RAISED CHECKS

Forgery is the act of fraudulently making or altering a note, check, draft, or some other document, causing the financial loss of another. Both the intent to defraud and the creation of a liability must be proved in order for an act to constitute forgery. A person who commits a forgery is guilty of a crime. A forged check, one signed by a person other than the drawer, and a raised check, one on which the amount has been raised by the payee or bearer, are two of the most common types of forgery.

Liability for Forged Checks A depositor who opens a checking account with a bank must fill out a signature card and leave it on file with the bank. The bank is then assumed to know the depositor's signature and is liable if it pays any checks on which the drawer's signature has been forged. Currently, many banks are transferring signature cards to electronic databases to allow for quick and efficient verification of signatures at all branch locations. The depositor has the

traveler's check
A certified check, useful when traveling in foreign countries, that is issued in denominations of $10 or more by certain banks, travel agencies, and financial services companies.

bad check
A check against a bank in which the drawer has insufficient funds on deposit to cover the check or no funds at all.

forgery
The act of fraudulently making or altering a note, check, draft, or some other document, causing the financial loss of another.

forged check
A check that is signed by a person other than the drawer.

raised check
A check on which the amount has been raised by the payee or bearer.

In some states, it is a criminal offense for a person to intentionally issue a check drawn on an account with insufficient funds.

responsibility of notifying the bank of a forgery within a reasonable time (or a period set by statute) after receiving his or her monthly statement and canceled checks (although many banks have discontinued the practice of returning the actual paper copies of checks). Failure to notify the bank in a timely manner releases the bank from liability.

Because the bank alone has the opportunity to inspect a check at the time of payment, it is liable if it pays a raised check unless the drawer, through carelessness, wrote the check in such a way that it could easily be altered. Although the drawer was careless, if the bank could have readily detected the alteration, it may still be held liable.

Courts have repeatedly held that when a check is drawn in such a careless and incomplete manner that a material alteration can easily be made without the check looking suspect, the drawer has prepared the way for forgery and is liable if it is committed.

EXAMPLE 22.6

▶ On April 15, LaRosa mailed her federal income tax forms with a check payable to the "Internal Revenue Service." She wisely did not make the check payable to "IRS." She recognized that, in the event her check became lost or stolen, "IRS" could easily be altered to "MRS" followed by the finder's or thief's surname.

POSTDATED CHECKS

postdated check
One that is dated later than the date on which the check is written.

A postdated check is one that is dated later than the date on which the check is written. A person may write a postdated check when insufficient funds are in the bank at the time the check is drawn, but the person expects to deposit sufficient funds to cover it by the date on the check. A person also may postdate a check for self-protection when some act is to be completed by the payee before the date of the check. Such a check has the effect of a promissory note at the time it is drawn. It is a mere promise to pay, at a future date, the amount specified. A postdated check may not be cashed by the payee before the date shown on the check.

By accepting a postdated check, the payee agrees not to cash it before the date indicated. However, it is important to note that a bank may honor an otherwise properly payable postdated check before its date unless the drawer has given the bank reasonable notice of the postdating [UCC 4-401]. To avoid a payee cashing a check prior to the date indicated, the drawer must notify his or her bank of the postdating, thus placing the bank on formal notice. If the bank cashes the postdated check after receiving formal notification of the postdated check, the bank can be held liable for any losses incurred by the drawer as a result of the premature payment.

EXAMPLE 22.7

▶ Iamani expected to travel to several foreign countries. Before leaving, he gave his college-bound son a number of postdated checks, one dated for each month of the college semester. The arrangement provided a monthly allowance without the risks associated with making one lump payment.

STOPPING PAYMENT ON CHECKS

A stop-payment order is an instruction a depositor gives to his or her bank not to pay a particular check. The notice can be given at any time before a check is presented for payment. If the bank does not do as requested by the drawer and cashes the check, it is liable to the depositor for the amount paid. A small charge is usually made by the bank for the service of carrying out a stop-payment order [UCC 4-403(1)].

If the drawer of a check dies before the check is paid, the bank may nevertheless honor it. The UCC provides that the death of the drawer of a check does not revoke the authority of the bank to accept, pay, or collect an item or to account for proceeds of its collection until the bank learns of the death and has a reasonable opportunity to act. Even with knowledge of the depositor's death, a bank may pay or certify checks drawn on it before the death and for 10 days thereafter unless ordered to stop payment by a person claiming an interest in the account [UCC 4-405(1)].

stop-payment order
An instruction a depositor gives to his or her bank not to pay a particular check.

22.7 ELECTRONIC FUNDS TRANSFER SYSTEMS

In past years it was said that the use of commercial paper would result in a "cashless" society. There is now speculation that the use of electronic funds transfers may result in a "checkless" society. Electronic funds transfer (EFT) refers to a variety of electronic applications for handling money.

electronic funds transfer (EFT)
A variety of electronic applications for handling money.

APPLICATIONS OF ELECTRONIC FUNDS TRANSFER SYSTEMS

EFT systems offer a variety of convenient and useful applications, including ATMs, point-of-sale systems, and direct deposit and withdrawal, to name a few.

Automated Teller Machines An *automated teller machine (ATM)* performs many functions that tellers in banks do. Typically, a depositor will activate the machine by inserting a plastic card encoded with information to be read by the machine, identify himself or herself by entering a personal identification number (PIN), and choose from a menu of bank transactions. The customer can make inquiries about the status of the account, withdraw cash, make deposits, and transfer funds from one account to another. The usefulness of the customer's identification card is further enhanced when banks are linked by networks that connect different banks into a local, national, or international system. For example, a traveler in California can insert a plastic card into a Los Angeles bank's ATM and withdraw cash and have the withdrawal charged to his or her bank account in New York.

Banks in foreign countries are similarly linked with U.S. banks, and it is possible for a traveler in London, Paris, Rome, or Hong Kong to use an ATM to withdraw local currencies and have the amount charged to his or her account at the prevailing rate of exchange.

An ATM performs many of the functions that a teller in a bank does.

Point-of-Sale Systems A *point-of-sale system* allows a consumer to transfer funds from a bank account to the merchant's bank account to pay for merchandise purchased. The terminal is located at the merchant's place of business.

Direct Deposits and Withdrawals The electronic movement of funds from one bank account to another has many useful applications, such as when an employee authorizes an employer to deposit his or her wages to the employee's bank account electronically instead of paying him or her by cash or check.

Other Applications of EFT Most banks provide customers with the use of an online portal through which they can access information about their accounts, transfer funds from one account to another, and authorize the bank to pay regular bills. Alternatively, bank customers may use pay-by-phone systems to telephone their bank's computer and authorize payment of certain bills and transfer funds to other accounts or to third parties.

The transfer of funds between banks is still another application of EFT. Although this has some usefulness to individual customers, it has far-reaching effects on the worldwide banking system. Because of the speed with which it processes financial settlements, EFT facilitates international trade.

THE ELECTRONIC FUNDS TRANSFER ACT

Electronic Funds Transfer Act (EFTA) of 1979
A federal statute that established the rights, responsibilities, and liabilities of consumers in dealings with financial institutions.

The most comprehensive federal legislation in this area is the Electronic Funds Transfer Act (EFTA) of 1979, which went into full effect in 1980. The act establishes the rights, responsibilities, and liabilities of consumers in dealings with financial institutions. Because the purpose of the act is consumer protection, it does not govern transfers among financial institutions or among businesses.

The EFTA limits consumer liability to $50 if the consumer notifies a card issuer within two days of learning that a card has been lost or stolen. If the customer fails to notify the issuer within two days, the consumer's liability increases to $500.

The EFTA also requires the institution to provide written receipts each time an ATM is used, and monthly statements on which electronic transactions are shown.

CHAPTER SUMMARY

1. *Commercial paper* is a term widely used in law to describe a number of legally binding and commercially acceptable documents, such as notes, checks, and drafts, that are used to transfer money from one person to another. Commercial paper consists of contracts but differs from ordinary contracts in two ways: the presumption of consideration and assignability.

2. Promises to pay consist of a written note or letter in which one person promises to pay a certain amount of money to another at a definite time. Orders to pay typically use an expression such as

"pay to the order of" and give commercial paper negotiability.

3. The parties involved in a promissory note include the maker, the comaker, and the payee. The parties involved in a draft or a check include the drawer, the payee, the drawee, the holder, and the holder in due course.

4. For commercial paper to be negotiable, it must be in writing and signed by the maker or drawer, contain an unconditional promise or order to pay a definite sum of money, be payable on demand or at a definite time, and be payable to order or to

bearer; a draft must name or indicate the drawee with reasonable certainty.

5. Nonessentials for negotiability include the words "for value received" or specific mention of the consideration or its value (because consideration is assumed). Indicating dates, specifying the place of business or home of the maker of the note, and numbering the commercial paper are all nonessential to negotiability.

6. A certified check is a check that the bank has promised to pay when it is presented for payment. A cashier's check is issued by the cashier or other designated officer of a bank and drawn against bank funds. A traveler's check is a certified check issued in a denomination of $10 or more by certain banks, travel agencies, and financial services companies. A depositor at a bank can place a stop-payment order by giving the bank an instruction not to pay a particular check.

7. Electronic funds transfer systems offer convenient and useful electronic money-handling applications, including automated teller machines, point-of-sale systems, and direct deposit and withdrawals, among others.

CHAPTER TWENTY-TWO
ASSESSMENT

MATCHING LEGAL TERMS

Match each of the numbered definitions with the correct term in the following list. Write the letter of your choice in the answer column.

a. bad check
b. draft or bill of exchange
c. cashier's check
d. certified check
e. check
f. drawee
g. drawer
h. holder
i. maker
j. negotiability
k. payee
l. postdated check
m. promissory note
n. raised check
o. stop-payment order

1. A person who is in possession of commercial paper. 1. _____

2. An instrument that is essentially a depositor's order to his or her bank to pay money to a party named on the instrument. 2. _____

3. A characteristic of a credit instrument that allows its transfer from one party to another. 3. _____

4. A type of commercial paper that is essentially a written promise to pay money to a designated party. 4. _____

5. The party to commercial paper who makes a promise to pay. 5. _____

6. The party to commercial paper who is designated as the one to receive payment. 6. _____

7. The party to a draft against whom it is drawn. 7. _____

8. The party who draws a draft against another.   8. _____

9. A check drawn against an account with insufficient funds or against a bank in which the drawer has no funds.   9. _____

10. A check that bears a date later than the date on which the check was written.   10. _____

11. A check for which the bank ensures that the drawer has sufficient funds to make payment.   11. _____

12. A notice to a bank requesting that a certain check not be paid.   12. _____

13. A check drawn against a bank's own funds.   13. _____

14. An unconditional written order from one party to another directing him or her to pay a certain sum to a third party.   14. _____

15. A check on which the amount has been altered to increase it.   15. _____

TRUE/FALSE QUIZ

Indicate whether each of the following statements is true or false by writing *T* or *F* in the answer column.

16. The law presumes that commercial paper was issued for value.   16. _____

17. A subsequent holder of commercial paper can have no greater rights than the original holder.   17. _____

18. The words "pay to the order of" are required for an instrument to have negotiability.   18. _____

19. A stale check is one that is presented six months or more after it was written or issued.   19. _____

20. The main purpose of a certified check is to ensure that funds are on deposit to cover the check.   20. _____

21. A person who adds his or her name to a promissory note to strengthen it is known as a comaker.   21. _____

22. A bank can refuse to honor a depositor's check even if it is properly drawn and there are sufficient funds on deposit.   22. _____

23. A postdated check is one that is written subsequent to the date appearing on the instrument.   23. _____

24. The Uniform Commercial Code provides that a reasonable length of time for demand for payment of a check is one year.

24. _____

25. If a depositor requests in a timely manner that his or her bank stop payment on a check written by the depositor, the bank must bear responsibility if the check is cashed.

25. _____

DISCUSSION QUESTIONS

Answer the following questions and discuss them in class.

26. Explain the two ways in which commercial paper differs from ordinary contracts.

_____

_____

27. Discuss the major differences between the two basic kinds of commercial paper: promises to pay (notes) and orders to pay (checks and drafts).

_____

_____

28. If a checkbook is stolen and checks are written by the thief and cashed, who bears the loss?

_____

_____

29. Discuss the law and liability as applied to bad checks and to forged, raised, and materially altered checks.

_____

_____

30. Discuss circumstances that might require stopping payment on a check.

_____

_____

31. What are the benefits and drawbacks to the consumer of using electronic funds transfers, automated teller machines, and point-of-sale systems?

_____

_____

Answer the following questions, which require you to think critically about the legal principles that you learned in this chapter.

32. **Financial and Banking System** The complexity of the financial and banking system is a bit staggering. What might be done to simplify the system for consumers?

_____

_____

33. **Traveler's Checks** Issuers of traveler's checks encourage buyers to retain unused checks as a form of "emergency fund." Who benefits from this practice and why?

_____

_____

34. **Postdated Checks** Should the practice of writing postdated checks be illegal?

_____

_____

35. **A Question of Ethics** The practice of floating provides an opportunity to "borrow" interest-free by cashing a check for which there are inadequate funds on deposit. If the check writer makes a deposit to cover the check in time to avoid a "bounced check" charge, is this practice ethical?

_____

_____

Study each of the following cases. Answer the questions that follow by writing *Yes* or *No* in the answer column.

36. **Safety of Funds** Bolena sold some valuable jewelry to McGovern, whom she had never met before. She was concerned about whether McGovern's check was good and whether there were sufficient funds on deposit in McGovern's account to cover it.

    a. Would a certified check relieve Bolena's concern?   a. _____

    b. Would a cashier's check relieve Bolena's concern?   b. _____

    c. Would McGovern's promissory note give greater security?   c. _____

37. Parties to a Check Wiggins had a checking account at her local bank. She wrote out a check to Shin, a maintenance worker, in payment for services he had provided.

a. Is Wiggins the drawee?   **a.** _____

b. Is Shin the drawee?   **b.** _____

c. Is her bank the drawee?   **c.** _____

38. Safety of Traveler's Funds Hausen was planning an extensive trip to Europe and wanted to avoid carrying large sums of cash.

a. Would you advise Hausen to carry certified checks?   **a.** _____

b. Would you advise Hausen to carry traveler's checks?   **b.** _____

c. Would you advise Hausen to charge his purchases to his credit card?   **c.** _____

39. Postdated Checks Tandy wanted to issue a check in payment of her rent, due June 1, before leaving on a vacation trip on May 15, but she did not have sufficient funds on deposit in her checking account. Her employer automatically deposits her paycheck to her bank on the last day of each month.

a. Should Tandy issue an antedated check?   **a.** _____

b. Should Tandy issue a postdated check?   **b.** _____

c. Should Tandy borrow money from the bank to pay the rent?   **c.** _____

CASE ANALYSIS

Study each of the following cases carefully. Briefly state the principle of law and your decision.

40. Negotiablity of Note Grove Hotel hired Fortas, an electrical contractor, and paid him with a promissory note for $3,400. The note stated that it was "with interest at prevailing bank rates." Did the stipulation about interest rates affect the negotiability of the note?

Principle of Law:

_____

_____

Decision:

_____

_____

41. **Postdated Check** Graver gave Srau a postdated check for $2,000 as a deposit on a sailboat as acceptance of Srau's offer to sell the boat. Later, after Srau sold the boat to someone else, he claimed that the check was not really part of a binding contract because it was postdated, and thus created a qualified acceptance. Did postdating the check affect its negotiability?

Principle of Law:

_____

_____

Decision:

_____

_____

42. **Refusal to Pay Draft** Higgins was a used car dealer. He purchased a Corvette, giving the seller a draft drawn by him on the First State Bank of Albertville in the amount of $8,115. This draft was later presented by the seller to the bank for payment. Meanwhile, Higgins sold the car to Holsonback, who paid with a draft on the Albertville National Bank in the amount of $8,225. When the Albertville National Bank requested Holsonback to pay the draft, he refused, claiming that there was a problem with the certificate of title. The issue was raised as to whether, under the Uniform Commercial Code, negotiable instruments can be issued conditionally. Did Holsonback have the right to withhold payment on the draft because of the problem with the certificate of title? [*Holsonback v. First State Bank*, 394 So. 2d 381 (Alabama)]

Principle of Law:

_____

_____

Decision:

_____

_____

43. **Negotiable Instruments** After Balkus died intestate, included among Balkus's possessions were bank deposit slips for a savings account owned by him. On each deposit slip was a handwritten notation, "Payable to Ann Balkus Vesley [Balkus's sister] on P.O.D. the full amount and other deposits." Each slip was dated and signed by Balkus. His sister claimed that she was entitled to the money because "P.O.D." meant "payable on death"; the deposits were negotiable instruments; and she was a holder in due course. Are the deposit slips negotiable instruments under the Uniform Commercial Code? [*Estate of Balkus*, 381 N.W.2d 593 (Wisconsin)]

Principle of Law:

_____

_____

Decision:

_____

_____

LEGAL RESEARCH

Complete the following activities. Share your findings with the class.

44. Working in Teams Working in teams of three or four, interview personnel at your local bank to check liability for lost or stolen bank-issued ATM, credit, and debit cards.

_____

_____

45. Using Technology Using the Internet and search engines, investigate legal safe-guards to protect electronic transfer of funds.

_____

_____

chapter **23**

Transfer and Discharge of Commercial Paper

terms

LEGAL

endorsement	without recourse
endorser	holder in due course
endorsee	personal defense
blank endorsement	real defense
bearer instrument	counterclaim
special endorsement	material alteration
restrictive endorsement	presentment
qualified endorsement	dishonored

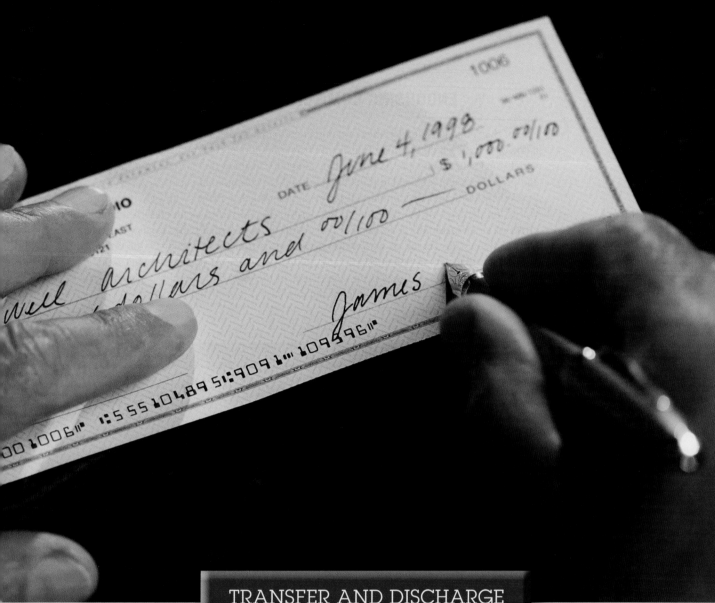

"By the way, lunch is on me. I just
cashed my Nana's birthday checks."

*Jerry Seinfeld, from the
TV series* Seinfeld

23.1   ENDORSING COMMERCIAL PAPER

One of the valuable characteristics of commercial paper in our personal and business lives is the ease with which it can be transferred from one person to another and the ease with which final settlements can be made. This chapter considers the various legal principles and procedures that are used to transfer and discharge commercial paper.

When the holder of commercial paper signs his or her name, with or without other words, on the back of the instrument, this writing is referred to as an endorsement. The effect of an endorsement is to transfer ownership of commercial paper to another. When the transferee (the person to whom the instrument is transferred) receives the endorsed instrument, that person becomes the new holder, or owner, of it. This is what is meant when we say that a paper has been negotiated. In this way, commercial paper takes the place of money for the payment of debts and purchase of goods and services.

endorsement
When the holder of commercial paper signs his or her name, with or without words, on the back of an instrument to transfer ownership to another.

EXAMPLE 23.1

► Hatfield received a check from a customer that read in part, "Pay to the order of Harriet Hatfield . . ." Hatfield signed her name on the back of the check and gave it to Tai. By so doing she transferred (negotiated) the check to Tai, who then became the holder, or owner, of the check.

endorser
The person who signs his or her name to a negotiable instrument.

endorsee
The person to whom a negotiable instrument is transferred.

The endorser of an instrument is the person who signs his or her name on it; the endorsee is the person to whom the instrument is transferred.

Commercial paper is usually endorsed on the back. The endorsement may be written by hand, printed, or even stamped. To be valid, the endorsement must be written for the entire amount stated in the instrument. Attempting to transfer only part of the face value of the negotiable instrument by endorsement invalidates the negotiation.

EXAMPLE 23.2

► Canaan used a check that he had received as a birthday gift to pay for purchases at a retail store. He endorsed the check by printing his name in green ink on the back of it. The merchant refused to accept it, claiming that the endorsement should have been script-written in black or blue ink. The merchant was incorrect. The check was properly endorsed. The intent to transfer ownership was indicated by Canaan's signature. The fact that the signature was printed and in green ink did not affect its validity.

23.2   KINDS OF ENDORSEMENTS

Any of the following endorsements may be used in transferring commercial paper. The choice of endorsement will depend on the purpose of the transfer.

FIGURE 23.1 Example of a Blank Endorsement

BLANK ENDORSEMENT

A blank endorsement is an endorsement where the name of the payee is written by the payee on the back of a negotiable instrument. According to the Uniform Commercial Code (UCC), an instrument endorsed in blank is payable to anyone who is in possession of it; it is called a bearer instrument (UCC 3-111).

Technically, an instrument made payable to bearer is negotiable by delivery only; that is, the bearer is not required to endorse it. As a practical matter, however, banks require the bearer of such an instrument to sign it on the reverse side for purposes of identification.

The UCC also provides that "where an instrument is made payable to a person under a misspelled name or one other than his own, he may endorse in that name or his own or both; but signature in both names may be required by a person paying or giving value for the instrument" (UCC 3-204).

blank endorsement
An endorsement in which the name of the payee is written by the payee on the back of a negotiable instrument.

bearer instrument
An instrument that is payable to anyone who is in possession of it.

EXAMPLE 23.3

▶ Newson received a check with a blank endorsement from a customer. Because of the blank endorsement, the check is a bearer instrument. Newson can negotiate it merely by delivery. But in all probability, anyone accepting the check from Newson would insist that she endorse it as well. The transferee would require this endorsement so that if the check proved to be bad and the bank refused to honor it, Newson would have to pay.

SPECIAL ENDORSEMENT

A special endorsement, or *full endorsement,* is one in which the payee specifies the person to whom, or to whose order, it is to be paid. The instrument can be further negotiated only when it has been endorsed by the specified person.

special endorsement
An endorsement in which the payee specifies the person to whom, or to whose order, it is to be paid.

EXAMPLE 23.4

▶ Porenta requested that a friend, Hartley, cash a dividend check for her. Hartley gave Porenta the money and accepted her check, which Porenta had endorsed in blank. Hartley had just moved to another city and decided to use the check to open a new account at a local bank. To protect himself in case he lost the check before he could open the account, he wrote over Porenta's signature endorsement, "Pay to the order of Thomas Hartley." He had the right to do so and was probably acting prudently.

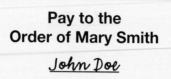

FIGURE 23.2   Example of a Special Endorsement

The UCC specifically provides that the holder of an instrument may convert a blank endorsement into a full endorsement by writing "Pay to the order of [transferee's or holder's name]" over the endorser's signature (UCC 3-204). In Example 23.4, Hartley is the endorsee (transferee) and Porenta is the endorser (transferor).

RESTRICTIVE ENDORSEMENT

restrictive endorsement
An endorsement with a signature to which words have been added restricting further endorsement of the instrument.

A restrictive endorsement is a signature to which words have been added restricting the further endorsement of the instrument. According to the UCC, however, a restrictive endorsement does not prevent further transfer or negotiation of the instrument. The holder has the rights of any purchaser of commercial paper except that he or she must do with the instrument as the endorsement directs (UCC 3-206).

The phrases "For deposit only" and "Pay to [endorser's bank] for deposit only" are examples of restrictive endorsements that are often used when deposits are sent to a bank by messenger or by mail. "Pay Herbert Fredericks only" and "Pay Herbert Fredericks, for collection" are other examples of restrictive endorsements.

EXAMPLE 23.5

▶ While on vacation, Egan received a check in payment of a debt. Because it would be several weeks before she could deposit it personally in her bank, she endorsed it "For deposit only—Patricia Egan," and mailed it to the bank. If the check should be lost in the mail or stolen, it could not be cashed by the holder.

For Deposit Only

John Doe

FIGURE 23.3   Example of a Restrictive Endorsement

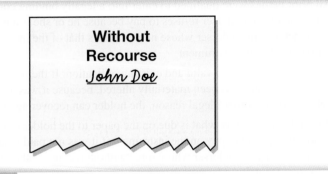

FIGURE 23.4 Example of a Qualified Endorsement

qualified endorsement
An endorsement in which the endorser avoids liability for payment even if the maker or drawer defaults on the instrument.

without recourse
A phrase used to indicate a qualified endorsement.

QUALIFIED ENDORSEMENT

In the case of a qualified endorsement, the endorser avoids liability for payment even if the maker or drawer defaults on the instrument. A qualified endorsement, using a phrase such as "without recourse," can be used together with a blank endorsement or special endorsement. The use of a qualified endorsement does not affect the negotiability of an instrument.

EXAMPLE 23.6

▶ Mustafa, the owner of a furniture store, received a $1,000 promissory note from Huff in payment for merchandise purchased. Worried that Huff might not have sufficient funds to pay the note when it was due, Mustafa offered the note to Casler in payment of a debt at a 25 percent discount on the note on condition that Mustafa be permitted to include the words "without recourse" in her endorsement. If Casler were to accept the offer and Huff failed to pay the note at maturity, Casler could look only to Huff, not to Mustafa, for payment. Mustafa's qualified endorsement would pass title to the note and relieve her of all liability on the note.

23.3 OBLIGATIONS, WARRANTIES, AND DISCHARGE OF ENDORSERS

The endorser of a promissory note or the drawer or endorser of a draft or check is liable for the payment of the instrument if the following conditions are met:

1. It has been properly presented for payment to the maker of the note or to the drawee of the draft or check.
2. Payment has been refused by the maker or drawee.
3. Notice of the refusal has been given to the drawer or endorser.

To ensure the negotiability of commercial paper, the UCC assumes the following warranties in every endorsement (UCC 3-417):

1. The instrument is genuine. If the maker's or drawer's signature is forged, the endorser is liable to a subsequent holder for payment of the paper.

2. All prior parties were qualified to enter into a legally binding contract. If the maker or a prior endorser refuses to pay because he or she is a minor or otherwise incompetent, any endorser whose name follows that of the incompetent party is liable for payment of the instrument.

3. The instrument is for a valid and existing obligation. If the maker refuses to pay because the paper has been materially altered, because it was given for a gambling debt, or for any other illegal reason, the holder can recover against the endorser.

4. The endorser will pay what is due on the paper to the holder or to any subsequent endorser who had to pay on the instrument if it was not paid when presented for payment. Only an endorser who wrote "without recourse" above his or her name is exempt from this warranty.

5. The endorser is the true owner of the paper (has good title to it). If he or she found or stole the paper and transferred it to another by endorsement, the endorser is liable for any loss suffered by the endorsee.

EXAMPLE 23.7

▶ John Lynch received a check in the mail intended for James Lynch, who lived in the same building. Even though John knew that the check was not intended for him, he endorsed it and gave it to a merchant in payment for goods he had purchased. After the merchant deposited the check in the bank, he was informed that payment had been stopped by the drawer. The merchant can hold John Lynch liable for the amount on the basis of Lynch's implied warranty that he had good title to the instrument.

An endorser of an instrument is released from liability by (1) any act that completes the negotiation of the instrument, such as payment; (2) the release of a prior party's obligation or the release of the debtor; (3) the intentional cancellation of the endorser's signature by the holder; (4) a valid tender of payment by a prior party; or (5) an agreement binding on the holder to extend the due date of the instrument.

EXAMPLE 23.8

▶ Kappo executed a note to Wenner in payment of a debt. Wenner then negotiated the note to Wise by endorsing it. When Wise presented the note at maturity for payment, Kappo told him that she would pay the note in full if given two weeks' more time. If Wise were to agree to Kappo's request for an extension of time, Wenner would be discharged from liability.

holder in due course
A holder who has taken a negotiable instrument in good faith and for value, before maturity, and without actual or constructive notice of any defects in the instrument.

23.4 HOLDER IN DUE COURSE

A holder in due course of commercial paper, according to the UCC (UCC 3-302), is one who has taken the paper in good faith and for value, before maturity, and without actual or constructive notice (notice inferred from circumstances) of any defects in the instrument.

He or she is sometimes called a "*bona fide* holder for value without notice" (*bona fide* is a Latin term meaning "in good faith").

For a person to be a holder in due course of a negotiable instrument, the following must be true:

1. The paper must be complete and regular on its face. If it is apparent from the appearance of the instrument that it has been altered, the holder is not considered a holder in due course.

2. The paper must have been acquired on or before the due date. The fact that commercial paper is past due is considered notice that something might be wrong with it. According to the UCC, if the buyer of overdue negotiable paper did not have notice or knowledge that it was overdue, he or she could be a holder in due course. However, a person who accepted a demand instrument (a promissory note payable upon demand) later than a reasonable length of time after it was issued is considered to have been aware that it was overdue (in the case of a check, 30 days is deemed to be a reasonable time).

3. The paper must have been acquired for a valuable consideration. The consideration may have been the reasonable value of the instrument itself, or it may have been any detriment, injury, or loss suffered by the holder in taking the instrument.

4. The paper must have been taken in good faith and for value. A person who has acquired a commercial paper for a sum much smaller than the face value of the instrument appears to have acted in bad faith unless the person can show that he or she acted prudently by checking into the reasons for the low value before accepting it.

Any holder of an instrument, other than the payee, who might know of a fraud or learn of it before negotiating the instrument to a holder in due course cannot later become a similar holder, even if title to the instrument is transferred to him or her from the holder in due course.

EXAMPLE 23.9

▶ Svensson had a $500 note that had been made payable to him by Pappas. He offered the note to Manchester at a 60 percent discount. Simple prudence suggests that Manchester should have tried to find out why Svensson was willing to sell the note at such a low price—or large discount. In short, she should have looked for a defect in the instrument. Without such a search, she would not be considered a holder in due course. If Manchester transferred the instrument before maturity to Cho, who paid value for it, not knowing that Manchester had purchased the note at a 60 percent discount, then Cho would be considered a holder in due course. However, if Manchester later reacquired the note from Cho, Manchester would not be considered a holder in due course because one cannot benefit from one's own wrongdoing.

23.5 DEFENSES AGAINST PAYMENT OF COMMERCIAL PAPER

personal defense
A defense against payment of commercial paper that may be used against any party except a holder in due course.

A defense against payment of commercial paper that may be used against any party except a holder in due course is called personal defense. A defense against payment of commercial paper that claims the instrument was void from the beginning is known

real defense
A defense against payment of commercial paper that claims the instrument was void from the beginning.

as real defense or *absolute defense*. Real defenses may be used by the maker or drawer against any party to a paper, including a holder in due course.

PERSONAL DEFENSES

Personal defenses against payment of commercial paper relate to the acts or circumstances leading to the issue of the paper rather than to the paper itself. These defenses include lack of consideration; fraud, duress, or undue influence; breach of warranty; nondelivery of a completed instrument; nondelivery of an incomplete instrument; payment before maturity; and counterclaim.

Lack of Consideration   Although consideration is presumed to have been given for a promissory note, draft, or check, proof by the maker or drawer that consideration was in fact lacking can be used as a defense against paying the instrument.

EXAMPLE 23.10

▶   Moser gave his brother a 90-day promissory note as a gift. Before the maturity date, he changed his mind, and when the note came due, Moser refused to pay it. If sued on the note by his brother, Moser could avoid paying it by proving lack of consideration as a personal defense.

Fraud, Duress, or Undue Influence   If fraud, duress (threat of harm to person or property), or undue influence was used to induce a person to sign a negotiable instrument, the injured person may use any of these as a personal defense against any person who is not a holder in due course.

The UCC provides that, unless a person who takes an instrument has the rights of a holder in due course, his or her claim for payment is subject to "all defenses of a party which would be available in an action on a simple contract" (UCC 3-306).

BREACH OF WARRANTY

In the event of a breach of warranty, the injured party may assert the breach as a personal defense. If, for example, payment for plumbing repairs is made by check, but the repairs do not meet applicable building codes, the drawer may claim the breach of warranty as a personal defense.

Nondelivery of a Completed Instrument   Sometimes a completed negotiable instrument comes into the possession of an immediate party (the payee indicated on the instrument) before the maker or drawer has delivered it. In such a case, the payee cannot collect on the instrument. If the payee, however, negotiates the instrument to a holder in due course, the new holder in due course can enforce payment by the maker. Thus the personal defense of nondelivery is not valid against a holder in due course.

EXAMPLE 23.11

▶ Tomar, a wholesaler, agreed to accept Brinner's note in payment for goods. When Tomar went to Brinner's office to collect the note, no one was there, but on Brinner's desk Tomar found the completed note made out to him. If Tomar took the note without waiting for delivery by Brinner, he could not enforce payment if Brinner refused to pay it. But if Tomar sold the note to Singh, who becomes a holder in due course, Singh could collect on the instrument from Brinner, who in turn could sue Tomar.

Nondelivery of an Incomplete Instrument   Under the UCC, no distinction is made between lack of delivery of a completed and an incomplete instrument. In either case, it is treated as a personal defense, not effective against a holder in due course (UCC 3-306).

Payment before Maturity   Suppose the maker of an instrument paid it before maturity but failed to get the paper itself back. In this case, he or she would be discharged from further liability to immediate parties (the payees) but would remain liable on the note if it should come into possession of a holder in due course.

Counterclaim   The maker of a note or the drawer of a check or draft may deduct from the amount demanded by an immediate party any amounts owed him or her by the payee. This type of personal defense is called a counterclaim.

> **counterclaim**
> When the maker of a note or other drawer or acceptor of a bill of exchange may deduct from the amount demanded by an immediate party any amounts owed him or her by the payee.

REAL DEFENSES

Real, or absolute, defenses to payment of commercial paper, good against anyone, including holders in due course, include forgery, material alteration, lack of intent to execute commercial paper, incapacity of the parties to contract, bankruptcy, and illegality created by law.

Forgery   Commercial paper on which the signature of the maker or drawer has been forged is void. Even a holder in due course cannot collect on an instrument if he or she obtained title after a forgery. Endorsers of a forged instrument who negotiate the paper are liable. The reason is there are implied warranties of endorsers that an instrument is genuine, that the endorser has good title to it, and that all prior parties had the capacity to contract.

EXAMPLE 23.12

▶ Misuki found a blank check that belonged to Pierce, a neighbor. Misuki filled out the check for $500, made it payable to himself, and signed Pierce's name—a forgery. He then endorsed the check and transferred it to Bader with a special endorsement in payment of a debt. Bader endorsed the check and cashed the check at Pierce's bank. When the forgery is discovered—as it will be when Pierce reviews his monthly statement—the bank must return the money to Pierce's account because it cashed a forged check. It will, however, look to the endorsers, Misuki and Bader, to recover the loss.

material alteration
A deliberate change or alteration of an important element in a written contract that affects the rights or obligations of the parties.

Material Alteration   Any change made to an instrument that affects the rights of the parties is called a material alteration. The maker or drawer is responsible to pay the paper according to its original terms, not the altered terms. Changing the place or date of paper, or adding or changing an interest rate, are examples of material alterations.

The UCC provides that the loss falls upon the party whose conduct in signing a blank instrument made the fraud possible—that is, whose negligence or recklessness invited alterations by subsequent holders (UCC 3-406).

EXAMPLE 23.13

▶ Stirks used a check to pay Moore, a merchant, $100 for a purchase. Moore raised the amount of the check to $1,000, endorsed it, and cashed it at a bank other than the one on which it was drawn. When the check was returned to Stirks's bank for collection, the bank noted the alteration and refused to pay it. The bank that cashed the check can hold Stirks liable only for $100, the amount for which the check was originally drawn.

Lack of Intent to Execute Commercial Paper   A person cannot be held liable, even by a holder in due course, if he or she signs an instrument that is apparently not negotiable and the paper is later fraudulently converted into a negotiable instrument. Fraud in executing an instrument is a real, or absolute, defense, but fraud related to the circumstances surrounding the issuing of a paper and not to the paper itself is a personal defense.

EXAMPLE 23.14

▶ Jackson believed she was signing a receipt for the delivery of an appliance when, in fact, she was signing a note. If she can prove that she had not been negligent and that she was tricked into signing the paper, she may use fraud in the execution of the instrument as a defense. This real, or absolute, defense is good against any holder, including a holder in due course. If instead Jackson had paid for merchandise with a note and later found that the goods were not of the quality contracted for, her defense against payment would be fraud in the making of the contract. This is a personal defense valid against anyone except a holder in due course.

Incapacity of Parties to Contract   An incompetent person, such as a minor, who makes, signs, and delivers a negotiable instrument cannot be held liable for its payment. The real defense of incompetence is valid against anyone, even a holder in due course.

Discharge in Bankruptcy   If a bankruptcy court discharges a debt secured by commercial paper during a bankruptcy proceeding, the maker of the commercial paper is released from all liability associated with it (see Chapter 21). In such a case, the maker of the commercial paper has a real defense against payment.

Illegality Created by Law   Often state statutes expressly declare that commercial paper given for gambling transactions or at usurious rates of interest is void. Paper issued under such circumstances is unenforceable, no matter who holds it.

23.6 PRESENTMENT OF COMMERCIAL PAPER

In order to establish the liability of the endorsers of commercial paper, the holder must engage in what is known as presentment: tendering a note to the maker and demanding its payment, or showing a draft or check to the drawer and requesting its acceptance or payment, on or after the maturity date at the place stated in the instrument.

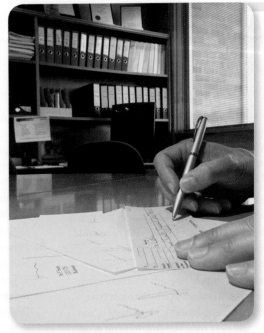

Commercial paper is void when the signature of the maker or drawer has been forged.

presentment
When the holder of a note tenders it to the maker and demands payment, or shows drafts to the drawer and requests its acceptance or payment, on or after the maturity date at the place stated in the instrument.

The UCC states that presentment may be made by mail or at the place of acceptance of payment specified in the instrument. If no place is specified, presentment may be made at the place of business or residence of the party who is to accept or pay. Because the liability of the maker of commercial paper is absolute, presentment and demand are not necessary to bind him or her.

Commercial paper must be presented for payment during business hours on the due date given on the instrument. A demand instrument such as a note or check must be presented for payment within a reasonable time after the date of issue.

EXAMPLE 23.15

▶ Chilton bought merchandise from Ramos and paid with a 60-day note. Ramos negotiated the note to Brill for value. Brill presented the note to Chilton for payment several weeks after the maturity date. When Chilton refused to pay, Brill attempted to collect from Ramos. She could not do so. Ramos, as an endorser, was released from liability when the holder, Brill, failed to present the note for payment when it became due.

dishonored
When a negotiable instrument is not accepted when presented for acceptance, it is not paid when presented for payment at maturity, presentment is excused or waived, or the instrument is past due and unpaid.

23.7 DISHONOR OF COMMERCIAL PAPER

A negotiable instrument is considered dishonored if it is not accepted when presented, if it is not paid when presented for payment at maturity, or if presentment is excused or waived and the instrument is past due and unpaid.

The holder of dishonored commercial paper must give notice of the dishonor immediately—a bank by midnight, and by any other person by midnight of the third business day after dishonor—to the drawer and to all endorsers in order to hold them liable on the instrument. Any drawer or endorser to whom such notice is not given is relieved from liability (UCC 3-508).

CHAPTER SUMMARY

1. The purpose of an endorsement is to transfer ownership of commercial paper from one party to another. When the transferee receives the endorsed instrument, that person becomes the new holder, or owner, of it.

2. There are four kinds of endorsements: (a) a blank endorsement is one in which the name of the payee is written by the payee on the back of a negotiable instrument; (b) a special endorsement is one in which the payee specifies the person to whom, or to whose order, it is to be paid; (c) a restrictive endorsement is a signature in which words have been added restricting further endorsement of the instrument; and (d) a qualified endorsement is one in which the endorser avoids liability for payment even if the maker or drawer defaults on the instrument.

3. The endorser of a promissory note or the drawer or endorser of a draft or check is liable for the payment of the instrument provided it has been properly presented for payment to the maker of the note or to the drawee of the draft or check; payment has been refused by the maker or drawee; and notice of the refusal has been given to the drawer or endorser. The UCC assumes the following five warranties exist in every endorsement: (1) the instrument is genuine; (2) all prior parties were qualified to enter into a legally binding contract; (3) the instrument is for a valid and existing obligation; (4) the endorser will pay what is due on the paper to the holder or to any subsequent endorser who had to pay on the instrument if it was not paid when presented for payment; and (5) the endorser is the true owner of the paper.

4. The four requirements for being a holder in due course are (a) the paper must be complete and regular on its face, (b) the paper must have been acquired on or before the due date, (c) the paper must have been acquired for a valuable consideration, and (d) the paper must have been taken in good faith and for value.

5. Personal defenses against payment of commercial paper can be used against anyone except a holder in due course; real defenses can be used against any party, including a holder in due course. Personal defenses include lack of consideration; fraud, duress, and undue influence; breach of warranty; nondelivery of a completed instrument; nondelivery of an incomplete instrument; payment before maturity; and counterclaim. Real defenses include forgery, material alteration, lack of intent to execute commercial paper, incapacity of the parties to contract, bankruptcy, and illegality created by statute.

6. Presentment of commercial paper occurs when a holder tenders a note to the maker and demands its payment, or shows a draft to the drawer and requests its acceptance or payment, on or after the maturity date at the place stated in the instrument.

7. A commercial paper is deemed dishonored if it is not accepted when presented for acceptance, it is not paid when presented for payment at maturity, or if presentment is excused or waived and the instrument is past due and unpaid.

CHAPTER TWENTY-THREE
ASSESSMENT

MATCHING LEGAL TERMS

Match each of the numbered definitions with the correct term in the following list. Write the letter of your choice in the answer column.

a. bearer instrument	**f.** endorsee	**k.** qualified endorsement
b. blank endorsement	**g.** endorsement	**l.** presentment
c. counterclaim	**h.** endorser	**m.** real, or absolute, defense
d. dishonorment	**i.** material alteration	**n.** restrictive endorsement
e. holder in due course	**j.** personal defense	**o.** special, or full, endorsement

1. An endorsement by which the payee of an instrument transfers it to the order of another person.   1. _____

2. The person who writes his or her name on the back of an instrument.   2. _____

3. The person to whom an instrument is transferred.   3. _____

4. The practice of the holder of commercial paper of writing his or her name on the back of an instrument.   4. _____

5. An endorsement that transfers an instrument but limits the liability of the endorser.   5. _____

6. An endorsement that transfers an instrument to whoever has possession of it.   6. _____

7. An endorsement that limits the transfer of an instrument to a particular person or for a particular purpose.   7. _____

8. A person who has accepted commercial paper in good faith, for value, before maturity, and without notice of any defects in the instrument.   8. _____

9. A claim for not paying commercial paper that relates to the circumstances leading to the issuing of the paper rather than to the paper itself.   9. _____

10. A claim that states that the instrument was void from the beginning.   10. _____

11. The deduction of amounts owed claimed by the maker of a note or the drawer of a draft from the amount demanded by an immediate party.   11. _____

12. Important changes to an instrument that affect the rights of the parties.   12. _____

13. Exhibiting a note to its maker and demanding payment.   13. _____

14. Refusal to pay a commercial paper.   14. _____

15. An instrument that is payable to anyone who is in possession of it.   15. _____

TRUE/FALSE QUIZ

Indicate whether each of the following statements is true or false by writing *T* or *F* in the answer column.

16. The writing a holder puts on the back of a negotiable instrument is known as a negotiation.   16. _____

17. An endorsement of an instrument must be for the entire amount.   17. _____

18. The Uniform Commercial Code attributes an implied warranty to an endorsed instrument that the signature is genuine.   18. _____

19. An endorser of an instrument is released from liability by any act that discharges the instrument, such as payment.   19. _____

20. If it is apparent that an instrument has been altered, the holder is not a holder in due course.   20. _____

21. An instrument endorsed in blank is payable to anyone in possession of it. 21. _____

22. An instrument with a special, or full, endorsement is payable only to the person named in the endorsement.   22. _____

23. A restrictive endorsement prevents further negotiation of an instrument. 23. _____

24. If an instrument endorsed in blank is lost, the finder may not legally negotiate it.   24. _____

25. The words "For deposit only" constitute a blank endorsement.   25. _____

DISCUSSION QUESTIONS

Answer the following questions and discuss them in class.

26. Why would a person who receives a check want to limit its negotiability, and how would this be done?

    _____

    _____

27. Under what circumstances are a minor's checks valid?

    _____

    _____

28. What kind of an endorsement allows an endorser to avoid liability for payment even if the maker or drawer defaults on the instrument?

    _____

    _____

29. Describe the defenses against payment of commercial paper that are concerned with the acts or circumstances leading to the issue of the paper rather than to the paper itself.

_____

_____

30. What is the difference between a contract and a negotiable instrument as it concerns consideration?

_____

_____

31. State statutes usually declare that commercial paper that is given for gambling transactions or at usurious rates of interest is void. Can a person pay off an illegal gambling debt by check?

_____

_____

THINKING CRITICALLY ABOUT THE LAW

Answer the following questions, which require you to think critically about the legal principles that you learned in this chapter.

32. Delivery of Negotiable Instrument If all other requirements of a negotiable instrument have been met except delivery, should payment depend on delivery, and, if so, why?

_____

_____

33. Liability of Endorser The innocent endorser of a forged instrument who negotiates commercial paper is liable. Is this fair?

_____

_____

34. Endorsements Should an endorsement written in pencil be legally acceptable? Why or why not?

_____

_____

35. Material Alteration How do significant changes made in an instrument affect the rights of the parties to it?

_____

_____

36. **A Question of Ethics** Is it ethical for direct mail marketers to include a document that resembles a check made payable to the addressee, when closer examination reveals certain conditions such as "good only toward the purchase of . . ."?

_____

_____

CASE QUESTIONS

Study each of the following cases. Answer the questions that follow by writing _Yes_ or _No_ in the answer column.

37. **Raised Check** Sikonen gave his check for $5 to Rivera, but in so doing he neglected to fill in the customary wavy line following the amount in the words. Rivera endorsed the check to Montana, who easily increased the amount to $500 and then presented the check to Sikonen's bank for payment.

   a. Will Sikonen be required to bear the loss because of his negligence in writing the check?   **a.** _____

   b. Will Rivera have to bear the loss because of his negligence in endorsing a check that could be so easily altered?   **b.** _____

   c. Will the bank be required to bear the $495 loss for cashing an altered check?   **c.** _____

38. **Defenses** Laredo found a checkbook belonging to Waldron, drew a check, signed Waldron's name to it, and gave it to Kelly. The payee, Kelly, endorsed the check to a holder in due course, who presented it to the bank for payment. The bank refused to pay the check.

   a. Will Waldron's account be charged for the check because he lost the checkbook?   **a.** _____

   b. Is forgery a real defense, and may it be used against the claims of a holder in due course?   **b.** _____

   c. Is a holder in due course protected against all types of defenses?   **c.** _____

39. **Stale Check** Church accepted a three-year-old check that Field endorsed to her. When Church presented the check for payment, the bank refused to honor it and informed Church that the account had been closed for a year.

   a. Is a person who accepts a demand instrument, such as a check, subsequent to a reasonable time after issue considered to have been given notice that the instrument is overdue?   **a.** _____

   b. Is the drawer of a check responsible to all holders in due course for a period of seven years?   **b.** _____

   c. Can Church sue the drawer to collect the check?   **c.** _____

CASE ANALYSIS

Study each of the following cases carefully. Briefly state the principle of law and your decision.

40. Bearer Instrument McCutchon wrote a check payable to "cash" while he was in a supermarket. Before he got to the cashier, he realized that he had lost the check. Is this a bearer instrument, payable to any holder?

Principle of Law:

_____

_____

Decision:

_____

_____

41. Personal Defense Poulakis sold a computer using fraudulent means to Welson, who paid for the machine with a promissory note for $1,200. When Welson discovered the fraud, she refused to honor the note when it was presented for payment by a subsequent holder. Welson claimed fraud as a defense. Will Welson succeed in avoiding payment to a holder in due course?

Principle of Law:

_____

_____

Decision:

_____

_____

42. Negotiability Locke gave two promissory notes to Consumer Food, Inc., in payment for merchandise he purchased. The notes said, "Buyer agreed to pay to seller." Consumer Food, Inc., assigned the notes to Aetna Acceptance Corporation. Were these notes negotiable instruments? [*Locke v. Aetna Acceptance Corporation*, 309 So. 2d 43 (Florida)]

Principle of Law:

_____

_____

Decision:

_____

_____

43. **Postdated Check** Gentilotti, father of an illegitimate son, drew a check for $20,000 in 1969 payable to the son's order. The check was dated July 1, 1985, but provided on the face of the check that, should Gentilotti die before that date, "this check shall be payable immediately." Gentilotti issued the check to the son's mother, the legal guardian. Gentilotti died on July 4, 1980. Despite the available funds, the bank, acting on orders of Gentilotti's executor, refused payment when the check was presented. The drawer's executor refused payment on the grounds that the obligation was not due. Was the postdated check valid? [*Smith v. Gentilotti*, 359 N.E.2d 953 (Massachusetts)]

Principle of Law:

_____

_____

Decision:

_____

_____

LEGAL RESEARCH

Complete the following activities. Share your findings with the class.

44. **Working in Teams** Working in teams of three or four, interview personnel at your local bank to describe the circumstances under which the bank might refuse to cash a check drawn on an account held at the bank.

_____

_____

45. **Using Technology** Using the Internet and search engines, find items for sale in which the form of payment accepted is a check. How should such checks be written and endorsed?

_____

_____

Property

24. Real and Personal Property

25. Bailments

26. Landlord–Tenant Relations

27. Wills, Intestacy, and Trusts

chapter **24**

Real and Personal Property

LEARNING OUTCOMES

After studying this chapter and completing the assessment, you will be able to

24.1 Describe the characteristics of property and provide examples of items considered property.

24.2 Distinguish between real and personal property.

24.3 Identify and discuss common ways in which title to personal property can be acquired.

24.4 Discuss the different forms of property ownership.

24.5 Discuss the characteristics of real property.

24.6 Describe ownership interests in real property in terms of freehold and leasehold estates.

24.7 Discuss the transfer of real property, including (a) the various types of deeds, (b) the delivery and recording of deeds, and (c) transfers made through eminent domain and adverse possession.

LEGAL terms

real property

personal property

inter vivos gift

gift *in causa mortis*

accession

severalty

joint tenancy

tenancy by the entirety

tenancy in common

community property

easement

freehold estate

leasehold estate

fee simple

life estate

deed

condemnation

eminent domain

adverse possession

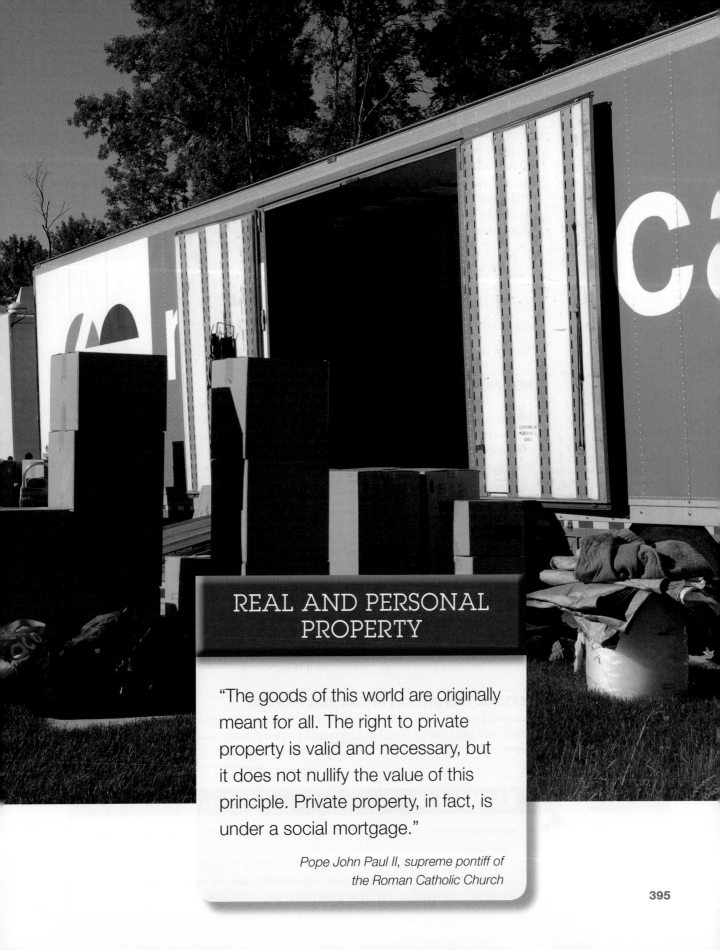

REAL AND PERSONAL PROPERTY

"The goods of this world are originally meant for all. The right to private property is valid and necessary, but it does not nullify the value of this principle. Private property, in fact, is under a social mortgage."

Pope John Paul II, supreme pontiff of the Roman Catholic Church

24.1 CHARACTERISTICS OF PROPERTY

To many people, the term *property* suggests land. Actually, property should be viewed more broadly because it also includes tangible goods such as automobiles, furniture, clothing, and even pets. In addition, there are intangible possessions, such as patents, rights to drill for oil on someone else's land, and copyrights of creative works such as books. These intangible possessions are also property. Consequently, the broad term *property* includes, in addition to land, both tangible and intangible personal property.

24.2 DISTINCTION BETWEEN REAL AND PERSONAL PROPERTY

The law distinguishes between real and personal property and governs each in different ways.

REAL PROPERTY

Under common law, ownership of real property extended from the center of the earth to the highest point in the sky. A person owned not only a portion of the earth's crust but also the ground under it and the airspace above it. As a result, real property comprises land and everything attached to the land. This would include minerals such as oil, iron ore, and others. Real property includes any permanent additions to the land, such as houses, buildings, and trees.

real property
The ground and everything permanently attached to it, including land, buildings, trees, and shrubs; the airspace above and the ground below the land also are included.

personal property
Tangible and intangible property that is not real property.

PERSONAL PROPERTY

Personal property includes all property other than real property, both tangible and intangible. Examples of tangible personal property include furniture, clothing, books, and pets. Examples of intangible personal property include patents, copyrights, goodwill, trademarks, and service marks (discussed in Chapter 28).

REAL PROPERTY CAN BECOME PERSONAL PROPERTY

Because real property consists of land and things permanently attached to it, it follows logically that when things are removed from real property, they become personal property. When a tree is cut down, for example, it becomes personal property. So, too, grain growing in a field becomes personal property when it is harvested.

PERSONAL PROPERTY CAN BECOME REAL PROPERTY

Personal property, such as trees or shrubbery purchased at a nursery, become real property when they are planted. Similarly, personal property items, such as lumber and bricks, become real property when they are used to erect a building on real property.

EXAMPLE 24.1

▶ Blanchard owned one-half acre of vacant property. He hired a contractor to build a house on the property and to plant various trees and shrubs. A year later, Blanchard became dissatisfied with the planting, uprooted the trees and shrubs, and sold them to a neighbor. In this case, the building materials and trees were personal property that became real property. When the trees and shrubs were uprooted, they became personal property once again.

24.3 ACQUIRING TITLE TO PERSONAL PROPERTY

Title to personal property is the actual ownership of property, not just the evidence of ownership, such as a certificate of title (see Chapter 16). Title (ownership) can be transferred from one person to another in a number of ways, including finding lost property, gift, sale, inheritance (see Chapter 27), and other ways that will be discussed later in this chapter.

FINDING LOST PERSONAL PROPERTY

The saying "Finders keepers, losers weepers" has no basis in law. The finder of lost property holds it in trust—that is, in safekeeping, at least for a time, for the real owner. As a result, the finder is a custodian acting for the true owner. The finder of lost property has ownership rights superior to everyone except the true owner.

Responsibility of the Finder A person who finds property has a legal responsibility to make reasonable efforts to return the property to its rightful owner. Statutes in many states provide that if the finder of lost property has made reasonable efforts to locate the owner without success within a period specified by statute, title to the property then transfers to the finder.

Personal property includes all property other than real property, both tangible and intangible.

EXAMPLE 24.2

▶ Chan, while walking through a park, found an envelope containing a bundle of cash and documents that identified the owner. As soon as Chan found and took possession of the envelope, he assumed responsibility for safeguarding the money and returning it to the rightful owner.

Distinction between Lost and Mislaid Property Courts frequently make a distinction between lost and mislaid property. An object has been "mislaid," rather than lost, when it was intentionally left in a certain place and then forgotten by the owner. Objects forgotten in this way are considered to have been transferred willingly and placed in the custody of the person with whom the object was left, and thus are not lost at all. On the other hand, an object that has not been intentionally left in the custody of someone else and then forgotten is considered lost, not mislaid.

EXAMPLE 24.3

▶ McAvoy, a customer in Medina's barbershop, found a briefcase containing certain valuables that had been left there but forgotten by another customer whose identity could not be determined. A dispute arose over who should get the briefcase and its contents. The court awarded possession to Medina, stressing that the owner had intentionally left the briefcase and then forgotten it, and thus had entrusted it to Medina's care.

In a similar but distinct case, an entirely different finding resulted.

EXAMPLE 24.4

▶ Bridges found a parcel of cash on the floor of Hassan's store. Both Bridges and Hassan claimed ownership. The court ruled that the cash was not intentionally left on the floor and that there was no custody on the part of Hassan. Possession was awarded to Bridges.

The distinction between the situations described in Examples 24.3 and 24.4 is that the former case illustrates mislaid property, while the latter case illustrates lost property.

Property Found in Public versus Private Places   Courts also have made a distinction between objects found on a private portion of a person's property and objects found in areas open to the public. The thinking behind the distinction is that an owner of property that is not open to the public is presumed to possess both the place itself and whatever it contains. In an area that is open to the public, however, the finder is more likely to gain ownership of a found object than is the owner of the land.

EXAMPLE 24.5

▶ Patillo, a worker for a swimming pool maintenance company, was cleaning the pool at the Red River Motel when he found a valuable diamond ring. Both Patillo and the owner of the motel, Calkins, claimed ownership. The court decided that since Calkins had the right to say that the pool should be cleaned in any way he thought fit, and to direct what should be done with anything found in the pool, Calkins should be presumed to have the right to exercise control over any object found in or on it. The finder, Patillo, would probably have been granted possession if the ring had been found in the parking lot or on the floor in the motel lobby, since these areas are open to the public.

Statutory Remedies   Many states have enacted statutes that govern who owns lost and mislaid property. Typically, these statutes require the finder of lost or mislaid property to notify a specific government official who maintains records of the property found. If, by the end of a period of time set by statute, the true owner does not claim the property, title to such property is transferred to the finder. If the true owner does not come forward and the finder does not wish to claim ownership, title to the property transfers to the state after the period of time specified in the statute.

ABANDONED PROPERTY

Personal property is considered abandoned when the owner disposes of it with the apparent intention of disclaiming ownership. Title to such property is transferred to the first person who takes control over it.

GIFTS

A *gift* is the voluntary transfer of property by one person to another without consideration or payment of any kind. While gift giving is a common act, it takes on added dimensions

The owner of a horse owns the foal born to the horse.

when viewed from a legal standpoint. Three requirements must be met for property to be transferred as a gift:

1. The *donor* (the person giving the gift) must intend to make a gift.
2. The gift, or a written statement of the donor's intention, must actually be delivered to the *donee* (the person who is to receive the gift).
3. The donee must accept the gift.

Once these three requirements are met, the donor cannot rescind the gift.

Inter Vivos Gifts   An *inter vivos* gift refers to property given while both parties are alive. *Inter vivos* is a Latin term meaning "between the living."

inter vivos gift
A gift between the living that meets all of the legal requirements for a gift.

Gifts *in Causa Mortis*   A gift given by a living person who expects to die from a known cause is known as a gift *in causa mortis,* a Latin term meaning "in contemplation of death." If the donor does not die from the expected cause or dies as a result of some other cause, the gift can be reclaimed by the donor or the donor's estate.

gift *in causa mortis*
A gift, given by a living person who expects to die from a known cause, that meets all of the legal requirements for a gift.

EXAMPLE 24.6

▶ Eisermann suffered from terminal cancer. Recognizing the seriousness of his condition, he signed over several valuable stock certificates to his son, despite the objections of his wife and other children. On the way home from the hospital, he was killed in an automobile accident. The executor of his estate could justifiably claim that the gift *in causa mortis* to the son may be revoked and that the stock certificates should be included in the estate.

ACCESSION

accession
The right of an owner of property to any increase in the property.

Accession is the right of an owner of property such as plants or animals to any increase in the property. The owner of a cow, for example, owns the calves born to the cow.

24.4 OWNERSHIP OF REAL OR PERSONAL PROPERTY

Title (discussed in Chapter 16) is actual ownership, not just evidence of ownership. At this point, different forms of ownership will be introduced. Many of the following descriptions of single- and multiple-person ownership apply to both real and personal property.

SEVERALTY OWNERSHIP

severalty
Ownership of a particular piece of property that is held by one person.

Ownership is held in severalty when all the rights of ownership in a particular piece of property are held by one person. Although one might at first think that the word *severalty* suggests several people, in fact *several* means "separate" in this context.

MULTIPLE OWNERSHIP

For various reasons, it is sometimes desirable for multiple people to own real or personal property jointly. However, certain types of property, such as businesses, boats, cars, and planes, cannot be divided among the owners. Obviously, one of the co-owners of an airplane could not very well claim the wings of the plane and indicate that the engine belonged to the other owner.

joint tenancy
When two or more persons own equal shares of personal property with right of survivorship.

Joint Tenancy   A joint tenancy exists when two or more persons own equal shares of property. The death of one person transfers his or her interest to the surviving joint tenants.

In cases of joint tenancy, the owners are said to have an *undivided interest:* Each owner can claim ownership of the entire estate, subject to the same right of the other joint tenants. Generally, a person's part interest in property may be sold just as a severalty interest may be sold, unless specifically prohibited. To underscore the intention of the parties, agreements generally include the phrase "with right of survivorship." In this sense, "survivorship" means that in the case of one owner's death, ownership of the portion owned by the deceased passes to the survivors.

EXAMPLE 24.7

▶   McGrath and Connell were partners who owned both a retail business and the real property on which the store was built as joint tenants. Each owner had a wife and children. McGrath died and Connell assumed McGrath's ownership of the business and the property. McGrath's wife and children inherited neither of these two assets.

tenancy by the entirety
A form of joint ownership of property by husband and wife in which both have a right to the entire property and the right of survivorship.

Tenancy by the Entirety   A tenancy by the entirety is a form of joint ownership of property by husband and wife in which both have the right to the entire property, and, upon the death of one, the other has title (the right of survivorship).

Tenancy in Common   A tenancy in common is a form of joint ownership of property by two or more persons. The ownership interest of any one of the owners can be sold, transferred, or inherited. The distinction of tenancy in common is that an owner's interest does not pass to the persons who share ownership at the time of his or her death. Rather, the interest of a tenant in common passes to that person's heirs.

tenancy in common
A form of joint ownership of property by two or more persons in which any owner's interest can be sold, transferred, or inherited.

EXAMPLE 24.8

▶ Assume that McGrath and Connell, in the previous example, own the retail business and the real property as tenants in common. McGrath dies, and his share of the jointly held property passes to his heirs.

Community Property   Some states have enacted statutes that provide that property acquired by either one of the spouses during a marriage is the community property of both husband and wife; that is, the property acquired belongs to both parties. Statutes in these states vary in the determination of what happens to property at the time of death or in the case of divorce. Generally, the law provides that property owned by either party before the marriage, or property received as gifts or inheritances by either party during the marriage, remains the property of the individual and does not become community property.

community property
Property acquired during marriage that, in some states, belongs to both husband and wife.

24.5   REAL PROPERTY

Real property is distinguished from personal property in a number of ways. Unlike most forms of personal property, the supply of land is limited. Moreover, land is unique, and one piece of land is not the same as any other. One piece, for example, may contain valuable minerals and another might have little value.

LAND
As previously stated, the law relating to real property treats land as extending down to the center of the earth and also includes things that are permanently attached to it, such as houses, buildings, and trees. Moreover, rights to land include the airspace above the land to an indefinite height, subject to the rights of aircraft in flight that do not pose a hazard to persons or property on the land. Land also includes rights to minerals such as oil, coal, or iron ore, except in states where the state retains an interest in certain minerals.

BUILDINGS AND FIXTURES
A *building* is a structure built on land. Such a structure can be almost any building permanently placed or constructed on or beneath the surface of the land. When items of personal property are added to land or to buildings in such a way that they become a part of these, they are known as *fixtures*. Planted shrubbery and trees and satellite dishes are examples of fixtures.

RIGHTS IN LAND OTHER THAN OWNERSHIP
Rights in land can be separated from the land itself, except in the case of easements. Examples of such rights are discussed in the following paragraphs.

Subterranean Rights   The right to extract minerals, such as oil or coal, from land is known as *subterranean rights*. The right to extract minerals can be sold without altering the ownership of the land itself.

Air Rights   The right to build on or over the land is known as *air rights*. Air rights are of particular significance in crowded urban areas where the right to erect a building over some other use of the land might be sold. An example of such use would be the sale of the right to erect an apartment building over railroad tracks or a highway.

easement
A right or interest in land granted to a party to make beneficial use of the land owned by another.

Easements   An easement is a right or interest in land granted to a party to make beneficial use of the land owned by another. The distinction between easements and other real property rights is that easements "run with the land." That is, they cannot be sold or transferred once they are recorded. An example of an easement is the right granted to a public utility company to enter the land of another to maintain telephone lines or electrical equipment.

Profits   A *profit* is a right to enter another person's land and remove some product of the land or its natural resources. If, for example, an individual has the right to enter a neighboring property to remove timber for his or her logging company, he or she has a profit. A profit includes an implied easement to allow access to the property; but in addition to the easement, a profit is a right to take something of value from the land.

Licenses   The owner of land may grant a party the right to enter the land for a specific purpose. For example, a landowner may grant someone the right to build a temporary stand to sell fruits and vegetables or souvenirs to passing motorists, or the owner of a service station may license someone to sell Mother's Day flowers on a portion of the property. Generally, the landowner receives payment or a share of profits in exchange for the license. Licensing agreements may be written or oral. The temporary interest created in the land does not run with the land.

EXAMPLE 24.9

▶   The Downtowner Motel allowed Rubin to use a small area in the corner of the lobby to display and sell his sculptures. The arrangement required Rubin to pay the motel owner a small commission on any sculptures sold. After several years, the motel manager informed Rubin that the arrangement was over. Rubin disagreed, claiming that the arrangement was a lease. Rubin is incorrect. In this instance, the arrangement is clearly a license, not a lease.

freehold estate
An estate in which a person owns the land for life or forever.

leasehold estate
An estate in which a person has an interest in real property that comes from a lease.

24.6   OWNERSHIP INTERESTS IN REAL PROPERTY

Interests in real property can relate to either ownership or possession. The term *estate* is used to identify the interest or the right a person has in real property. An estate can be either a freehold estate, by which a person owns the land either for life or forever, or a leasehold estate, by which a person has an interest in real property that comes from a lease.

A leasehold estate is not ownership, but only the right to possess real property, subject to the provisions of a lease (see Chapter 26).

FREEHOLD ESTATES

There are a number of ways in which freehold estates can be held that provide absolute (total) ownership lasting either for the lifetime of the holder or forever. Consequently, a holder of a freehold estate in land can transfer the estate (ownership) by sale, by gift, or by leaving it to his or her heirs. A holder of a freehold estate also can create and transfer an interest in the estate that lasts only for a lifetime. Such an estate, called a *life estate,* will be discussed later in the chapter.

Estate in Fee Simple   The owner of a freehold estate who holds it absolutely is said to hold it in fee simple. The owner of a freehold estate who holds real property in fee simple can sell it, give it away, or leave it to his or her heirs. The person to whom it is transferred then owns it in fee simple. The holder of a freehold estate in fee simple is not, however, allowed to use the property in any way that violates local zoning rules, or the rights of others, or restrictive covenants in the deed. For example, a restrictive covenant in a deed may prohibit the alteration, destruction, or removal of a historic structure. Any restrictive covenant must be for a lawful purpose. A restrictive covenant prohibiting a sale because of the race or religion of the prospective buyer, for example, would not be lawful.

fee simple
When an owner of a freehold estate holds it absolutely.

Life Estates   A person who holds a freehold estate (ownership interest) only for his or her lifetime is said to hold a life estate in the property. A life estate is usually created by deed (the document used to transfer ownership in real property) or by inheritance.

If real property is transferred from *A* to *B* for *B*'s lifetime, and *B* dies, the property is then returned to *A,* if he or she is still alive, or to *A*'s heirs. The interest that *A* holds while *B* is still alive is known as a *reversion estate* because the property reverts to *A* upon *B*'s death. But suppose that *A* decides that upon *B*'s death the property should belong to *C. C* is said to have a *remainder estate.*

life estate
A freehold estate in which a person has an ownership interest only for his or her lifetime.

EXAMPLE 24.10

▶ Arnaz, a middle-aged man, owned several houses and was concerned about his older brother's sorry financial situation. The brother had one son, but Arnaz disliked his nephew. Arnaz wished to grant one of his houses to his brother. Instead of granting the brother the house in fee simple, which would mean that the disliked nephew would likely inherit the house upon Arnaz's brother's death, Arnaz granted his brother a life estate in the house. Once the property was granted to the brother, Arnaz had a reversion estate because the property would revert to him. If, however, Arnaz had specified that upon the brother's death, the house was to become the property of Arnaz's daughter, she would then have a remainder estate during Arnaz's brother's lifetime.

LEASEHOLD ESTATES

An estate that does not involve an ownership interest in real property is known as a leasehold estate. A leasehold estate provides the holder with certain rights during the period covered by the lease (see Chapter 26).

24.7 TRANSFER OF REAL PROPERTY

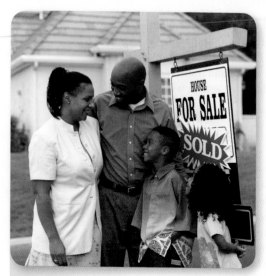

The transfer of real property is, in many ways, more complex than the transfer of personal property. Consequently, a number of specialized terms are used. A deed is the instrument, or document, that conveys an interest in real property between parties. The parties are the *grantor,* the party who conveys real property, and the *grantee,* the party to whom the real property is conveyed. Unlike a contract, no consideration is required to effect a transfer of real property. Real property, like personal property, can be sold or given as a gift during one's life or in the form of an inheritance. A deed, however, is needed in any kind of transfer of ownership.

The transfer of real property is more complex than the transfer of personal property.

deed
The instrument, or document, that conveys an interest in real property between parties.

TYPES OF DEEDS

Deeds can be classified by the kind of ownership interest being transferred.

A *quitclaim deed* transfers whatever interest a grantor has in real property, if any. It states that the grantor claims no interest in the property for which the deed is given. Quitclaim deeds are often used when transferring property to family members or divorcing spouses, or in other transactions between people well known to each other. Quitclaim deeds also are used to resolve questions of full title when a person has a possible but unknown interest in the property. Quitclaim deeds do not warrant good title.

A *warranty deed* is one in which the grantor asserts that he or she has title and that the property is free of the claims of others. There are two kinds of warranty deeds. One is very broad and makes a number of assurances; the other limits the assurances to specific matters.

Deeds are classified by the kind of ownership interest being transferred.

A *bargain and sale deed* simply states that the grantor is transferring the real property to the grantee. No particular warranties are given, but state statutes assume that certain implied warranties are present.

DELIVERY AND RECORDING OF DEEDS

When a deed has been completed and signed by the grantor, it must be delivered to the grantee to bring about a legally enforceable transfer of ownership. While most such deliveries are made in person in the offices of a real estate broker, a bank, a title company, or an attorney, no particular form or place of delivery is required. The deed can be handed in person to the grantee (buyer), mailed to him or her, or given to another person with instructions for delivery.

Recording a deed with the appropriate public official, such as a county recorder of deeds, is not legally required, but it is an important step that notifies everyone of its existence and minimizes the possibility of another person's claim to the property surfacing at a later date.

OTHER TRANSFERS OF REAL PROPERTY

In addition to those just described, there are two other ways in which real property may be transferred: under the doctrines of eminent domain and adverse possession.

Eminent Domain Real property can be taken from an owner by action of government or other public authority for the benefit of the public. Such actions are taken when a governmental body wishes to build a highway or school, for example, and the needed property is privately held. The legal process that occurs when property is taken by the government against the will of the property owner is known as condemnation.

When private property is taken by eminent domain, compensation is made at the fair market value of the property. In recent years, some localities have used the doctrine of eminent domain in a highly controversial manner—to justify the taking of private property for use in economic development, such as when a city takes private homes in order to erect a hotel or shopping center. In the event of a dispute, the owner can pursue remedies available through state and federal courts [see *Kelo v. City of New London*, 545 U.S. 469 (2005)].

condemnation
The legal process that occurs when property is taken by the government against the will of the property owner.

eminent domain
When ownership of real property is taken by the government and the previous owner is compensated at the fair market value of the property.

EXAMPLE 24.11

▶ In 2003 New York State, working with a private developer, unveiled plans to build a new arena complex to house the New Jersey Nets basketball team. Because the 22-acre project did not fit the planned site in Brooklyn, the state exercised its power of eminent domain to acquire necessary properties from their owners. New York State promised redevelopment of a blighted area. However, owners of some of the properties appealed the court's decision. They protested the condemnation of their properties, stating the fact that their properties were not blighted. In 2009 the New York State Supreme Court found that although some of the properties were recently remodeled, including several condominium complexes, there was significant evidence of blight and unsanitary conditions, enough to justify the use of eminent domain to acquire the properties necessary to build the arena.

Adverse Possession Title to land also can be acquired as a result of a person's use of land over a period of time. For title to pass through an adverse possession, it must be proved that there was actual and exclusive continuous possession or use, the possession must have been for a period of years specified by state statute (typically 10 years), possession must have been open and known to the owner, and the land was used with hostility and adversely (that is, without the owner's permission).

adverse possession
When title to land is acquired by a person's exclusive, continuous, open, known, and hostile use of the property over a period of time.

EXAMPLE 24.12

▶ An alley adjacent to a retail store was commonly used by customers to park their cars, without permission but with the alley owner's knowledge. A customer was surprised one day to find that she was blocked from her favorite parking place by a chain. Upon inquiry, the clerk explained that the owner of the alley was required to briefly demonstrate his ownership in order to prevent adverse possession of the alley. The customer would be welcome to park there the following day.

CHAPTER SUMMARY

1. Property includes land; tangible goods such as automobiles, furniture, clothing, and pets; and intangible possessions, such as patents, rights to drill for oil on someone else's land, and copyrights of creative works such as books. Consequently, the broad term *property* includes, in addition to land, both tangible and intangible personal property.

2. Real property is the ground and everything permanently attached to it, including land, buildings, trees, and shrubs. The airspace above and the ground below the land also are included. Personal property is everything, tangible and intangible, that is not real property.

3. A finder of lost property has a responsibility to make a reasonable effort to find the true owner. However, property that is abandoned with the apparent intention of disclaiming it belongs to the first person who takes control of it. An object is considered mislaid, rather than lost, when it has been intentionally left in a certain place and then forgotten by the owner. If an object has not been intentionally left in the custody of someone else, it is considered lost. A gift *inter vivos* is one between the living; a gift *in causa mortis* is given by a living person who expects to die from a known cause.

4. Title is actual ownership, not just evidence of ownership. Different forms of ownership include single- and multiple-person ownership, which apply to both real and personal property. Severalty ownership exists when all the rights of ownership in property are held by one person. Joint tenancy occurs when two or more people own equal shares

in property with the right of survivorship. Tenancy by the entirety is a form of joint ownership by husband and wife in which both have a right to the entire property and the right of survivorship. Tenancy in common is a form of ownership by two or more persons that can be sold, transferred, or inherited. Community property is property acquired during marriage that, in some states, belongs to both husband and wife.

5. The law relating to real property treats land as extending down to the center of the earth and also includes things that are permanently attached to it, such as houses, buildings, and trees. Moreover, rights to land include the airspace above the land to an indefinite height, subject to the rights of aircraft in flight that do not pose a hazard to persons or property on the land. Land also includes rights to minerals such as oil, coal, or iron ore, except in states where the state retains an interest in certain minerals.

6. A freehold estate is one in which a person owns the land for life or forever. A leasehold estate is one in which a person has an interest in real property that comes from a lease. One type of freehold estate is an estate in fee simple, in which the owner of a freehold estate holds it absolutely. A second type of freehold estate is a life estate, in which the owner owns the estate only for his or her lifetime.

7. The transfer of real property may be effected by deed, eminent domain, or adverse possession. A deed is an instrument that conveys an interest in real property between parties. Types of deeds include a quitclaim deed, a warranty deed, and a bargain and sale deed. Real property also can be transferred by eminent domain (when it is taken by the government and the owner is compensated) or adverse possession (when land is acquired as a result of a person's actual, continuous, open, known, and hostile use of land for a certain period of time).

CHAPTER TWENTY-FOUR
ASSESSMENT

MATCHING LEGAL TERMS

Match each of the numbered definitions with the correct term in the following list. Write the letter of your choice in the answer column.

a. accession
b. adverse possession
c. *in causa mortis*
d. eminent domain
e. fee simple

f. freehold estate
g. grantee
h. *inter vivos*
i. joint tenancy
j. leasehold estate

k. life estate
l. quitclaim deed
m. severalty
n. subterranean rights
o. tenancy in common

1. A gift between the living.   1. _____

2. The right of an owner of property to the product of such property—a calf born to a cow, for example.   2. _____

3. Ownership of property held by one person.   3. _____

4. A gift given in anticipation of death.   4. _____

5. A document of transfer of real property.   5. _____

6. Absolute ownership of real property.   6. _____

7. The right of a governmental or public body to acquire privately held real property needed for a public purpose.   7. _____

8. The interest in real property that relates to ownership.   8. _____

9. The person to whom real property is conveyed.   9. _____

10. The interest a person has in real property that lasts until he or she dies.   10. _____

11. The interest in real property that relates to possession.   11. _____

12. A form of co-ownership of property in which one owner's share of the property passes to the other owners upon his or her death.   12. _____

13. The passing of title to land that can result from a nonowner's use of the land.   13. _____

14. Rights that allow a person to extract minerals from land.   14. _____

15. A form of joint ownership of property in which one owner's share of the property can be sold, transferred, or passed to heirs.   15. _____

TRUE/FALSE QUIZ

Indicate whether each of the following statements is true or false by writing *T* or *F* in the answer column.

16. "Property" refers to both personal and real property.

16. _____

17. Fixtures are additions to personal property.

17. _____

18. Personal property can be either tangible or intangible.

18. _____

19. There is no distinction between lost and mislaid personal property.

19. _____

20. A finder of personal property has a responsibility to try to return the property to the rightful owner.

20. _____

21. Title to abandoned property resides with the state.

21. _____

22. Some state statutes provide that property acquired before a marriage is the community property of both husband and wife.

22. _____

23. An easement is the right or interest in land granted for the benefit of one party to make beneficial use of the land of another.

23. _____

24. The person who holds a life estate in real property can sell absolute ownership or pass it on to his or her heirs.

24. _____

25. A grantor of a life estate in real property maintains a reversion estate.

25. _____

DISCUSSION QUESTIONS

Answer the following questions and discuss them in class.

26. Distinguish between real and personal property.

_____

_____

27. Discuss both *inter vivos* gifts and gifts *in causa mortis*.

_____

_____

28. Discuss severalty ownership, tenancy in common, joint tenancy, and community property.

_____

_____

29. Discuss real property as it relates to land, buildings, and fixtures. How does personal property convert to real property?

_____

_____

30. Identify and provide examples of rights in real property.

_____

_____

31. Explain the characteristics of various kinds of deeds, and transfers of real property through eminent domain and adverse possession.

_____

_____

THINKING CRITICALLY ABOUT THE LAW

Answer the following questions, which require you to think critically about the legal principles that you learned in this chapter.

32. Real and Personal Property Why do you think it is necessary to distinguish between real and personal property?

_____

_____

33. Sale of Property The transfer of real property is much more complex than the transfer of personal property. What could be done to simplify real property transactions?

_____

_____

34. Gifts Can a gift given _in causa mortis_ be assumed to be as freely given as a gift given _inter vivos?_ Why or why not?

_____

_____

35. Multiple Ownership of Real Property Various forms of multiple ownership of real property, such as joint tenancy, tenancy by the entirety, tenancy in common, and so on, have evolved from our English legal roots. Are these designations relevant today?

_____

_____

36. **A Question of Ethics** An oceanfront community wanted to limit the use of its beach to residents only. A group contested this exclusion, claiming the ocean was public property. Is it fair for residents to exclude nonresidents from access to the beach?

_____

_____

CASE QUESTIONS

Study each of the following cases. Answer the questions that follow by writing *Yes* or *No* in the answer column.

37. **Property Ownership** Roche and Hecht owned a boat, which they used for weekend fishing trips. Since both were married and had children, they set up their agreement to own the boat in such a way that if either one died, from any cause, the heirs of the deceased party would inherit his interest.

    a. Is this an example of joint tenancy? a. _____

    b. Is this an example of tenancy in common? b. _____

    c. Does Hecht's interest in the boat indicate a severalty interest? c. _____

38. **Found Property** Weber, a customer at a restaurant owned by Hegler, found a wallet on the floor under the table. It contained money but no identification. In an attempt to return it to its rightful owner, she gave it to Hegler with the understanding that if the owner did not return, or could not be located, Weber would claim it. When the owner did not return after a period of a month, Weber claimed the wallet. Hegler refused to give it to Weber, claiming it as his own.

    a. Does Weber have a lawful claim to the wallet? a. _____

    b. Does Hegler have a lawful claim to the wallet? b. _____

    c. Would a court regard the wallet as misplaced? c. _____

39. **Community Property** Prior to their marriage LeRoi and her husband, Pillsbury, each held substantial assets. During their marriage, they jointly purchased a home with the income they earned and LeRoi inherited a substantial amount of money. After four years, they agreed to divorce. The marriage ceremony and divorce action were both in a state with community property laws.

    a. Is the property owned by both husband and wife before marriage considered community property? a. _____

    b. Is LeRoi's inheritance considered community property? b. _____

    c. Is the home considered community property? c. _____

40. **Real and Personal Property** Noguchi and his wife purchased a newly built house that had no lawn or any other landscaping. Over several years, they spent many weekends landscaping with expensive and exotic shrubbery and trees. They

also had a large above-ground pool installed in the yard. Because of a transfer to another city, the Noguchis were forced to sell their home. After the sale but before moving away, the Noguchis began uprooting several shrubs and removing the pool to take these with them. The buyer objected to the removal, claiming that the shrubbery and the pool were real property and were included in the sale of the house. Noguchi claimed that the shrubbery and pool were all personal property.

a. Is the shrubbery real property?   a. _____

b. Is the house real property?   b. _____

c. Is the pool real property?   c. _____

CASE ANALYSIS

Study each of the following cases carefully. Briefly state the principle of law and your decision.

41. **Adverse Possession** Bryer purchased a suburban home. At the time of the sale, the real estate salesperson pointed to a decorative stone fence as the boundary of the property. Because Bryer had several dogs he wanted to keep on his property, he erected a chain-link fence on what he believed to be the property line. His neighbor watched the work being done and did not object. Twenty years later, as a result of a new survey by the town, Bryer was surprised to learn that the fence was 18 inches inside the neighbor's property. Can Bryer claim ownership of all the property on his side of the fence?

Principle of Law:

_____

_____

Decision:

_____

_____

42. **Easement** Rae owned a farm and each summer allowed a neighbor, Fuller, to set up a stand on Rae's property to sell worms to people who drove by on their way to fish in the nearby lake. After 10 years of regularly using the small piece of property, Rae and Fuller had a dispute and Rae forbade Fuller from using his land again. Fuller claimed that he now had the right to continue using the small piece of property as he had in the past, insisting that an easement had been created. Did Fuller's continued use of the property create an easement?

Principle of Law:

_____

_____

Decision:

_____

_____

43. Gifts Harry and Marilyn Owen were divorced after a short marriage and entered into an agreement to divide assets. In addition to the division of personal property as agreed to and as recorded by the court, Marilyn claimed ownership of a Chevrolet automobile and one-half of a $24,000 certificate of deposit, insisting that they were both gifts from her former husband, Harry. Both the car, registered in Harry's name, and the certificate were purchased by Harry before the marriage. He denied having given the car and a one-half interest in the certificate of deposit. Does it appear that the requirements of an *inter vivos* gift have been met, and will Marilyn be awarded the disputed property? [*Owen v. Owen,* 351 N.W.2d 139 (South Dakota)]

Principle of Law:

_____

_____

Decision:

_____

_____

44. Lost and Mislaid Property Paset, a renter of a safety deposit box at Old Orchard Bank and Trust Company, found $6,325 in currency on the seat of a chair in an examination booth in the safety deposit vault. The chair was partially under a table. Paset notified officers of the bank and turned the money over to them. She was told by bank officials that they would try to locate the owner and that she could have the money if the owner was not located within one year. The bank wrote to everyone who had been in the safety deposit vault area on the day of, or on the day preceding, the discovery, stating that property had been found. The money remained unclaimed, and after a year Paset claimed the money under the state statute governing the disposition of lost and found property. The bank refused, claiming that the money was mislaid, not lost, and was therefore property of the bank. Was the money lost or mislaid, and will the court award the money to Paset? [*Paset v. Old Orchard Bank,* 378 N.E.2d 1264 (Illinois)]

Principle of Law:

_____

_____

Decision:

_____

_____

LEGAL RESEARCH

Complete the following activities. Share your findings with the class.

45. Working in Teams Working in teams of three or four, interview personnel at the nearest governmental authority (federal, state, or local) that handles cases of eminent domain, or the taking of private property for public use. Structure the interview so that the process is discussed and ask them about some recent cases.

_____

_____

46. Using Technology Using the Internet and search engines, investigate *Leydon v. Town of Greenwich*, 257 Conn. 318 (2001), relating to the Connecticut court's ruling on a beach access dispute. Discuss the merits of the court's opinion.

_____

_____

chapter **25**
Bailments

After studying this chapter and completing the assessment, you will be able to

25.1 Define and explain the purpose of a bailment.

25.2 Discuss the characteristics of bailments, including the six typical reasons for transferring goods and creating a bailment.

25.3 Distinguish among the four kinds of bailments, and discuss the level of care a bailee is required to give for each one.

LEGAL terms

bailment	bailee's lien
bailor	hotelkeeper
bailee	transient
bailment for the sole benefit of the bailee	common carrier
	consignor
bailment for the sole benefit of the bailor	consignee
	carrier's lien
mutual-benefit bailment	constructive bailment
warehouser	

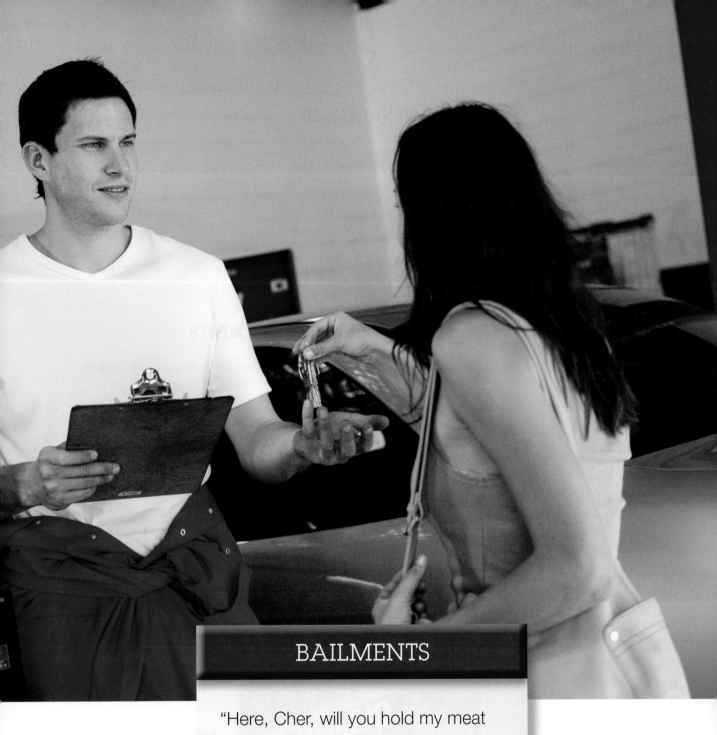

BAILMENTS

"Here, Cher, will you hold my meat purse?"

Lady Gaga,
singer and songwriter

25.1   BAILMENT DEFINED

Earlier chapters have examined numerous kinds of agreements and contracts for many different purposes. A bailment is a special kind of contract that is widely used in business and in personal affairs.

Specifically, a bailment is a transaction in which the owner of tangible personal property transfers the property to another party while still retaining ownership of such. For example, taking clothes to a dry cleaner transfers possession, but not ownership (or title), of the clothes.

bailment
A transaction in which the owner of tangible personal property transfers it (not as a gift) to another party while still retaining ownership.

25.2   CHARACTERISTICS OF BAILMENTS

A bailment allows the owner of personal property to transfer possession of it to another individual for any of the following purposes:

1. *Sale.* For example, a manufacturer ships goods to a retailer to either sell them or return them to the manufacturer (this transaction is known as *consignment*).

2. *Transportation.* For example, a business hires a transporter of goods, a truck line or rail or air carrier, to ship such goods.

3. *Repair or service.* For example, a motorist leaves an automobile at a service station for an oil change.

4. *Rental.* For example, a traveler rents an automobile from a car rental company or skis from a lodge.

5. *Storage.* For example, a company stores goods in a warehouse, a diner places a coat in a checkroom, or a driver leaves a car in a parking lot.

6. *Security for a loan.* For example, a borrower leaves valuable goods with a lender until his or her loan is paid.

bailor
The party in a bailment who retains ownership and transfers possession of the goods.

bailee
The party in a bailment who receives the goods.

In the preceding instances, the person who retains ownership and transfers possession is the bailor and the person who receives the goods is the bailee. The agreement reached between the bailor and the bailee is a bailment.

Taking clothes to a dry cleaner transfers possession, but not ownership, of the clothes.

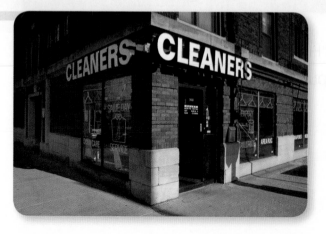

BAILMENT CREATED BY POSSESSION OF GOODS

Actual ownership of goods is not necessary to create a bailment. Anyone in possession of goods can create the bailment relationship and become a bailor—a borrower, a finder, or a thief.

EXAMPLE 25.1

▶ Castro rented a car for use during a business trip. While making a sales call on a downtown firm, Castro parked the car in a parking garage. The parking attendant surrendered the car to someone else by mistake. The parking garage was still responsible for the car and its contents. Although Castro was not the owner, he was a bailor.

BAILEE MUST INTEND TO POSSESS GOODS

The transfer of goods from bailor to bailee must actually take place. Unless there is some other understanding, the bailee must actually accept the goods.

EXAMPLE 25.2

▶ Goldstein had her car serviced regularly at Centre Service Station and knew the owner well. One evening, after the station had closed for the night and all the employees had gone home, Goldstein parked on the station property while she attended a social function. When she returned, the car was gone. The owner of Centre Service denied responsibility because no bailment existed. The service station owner is correct because the station did not accept the car.

BAILEE MUST RETURN IDENTICAL GOODS

Except for a bailment that requires alteration, such as a suit left for cleaning and alterations, or when fungible goods, such as grain or fuel oil, are stored, the identical goods must be returned.

EXAMPLE 25.3

▶ Roth left her smartphone with the Tech Fix store for repair. As a result of an error, her phone was repaired and given to another customer, who left town and could not be located. The owner of the repair shop offered Roth a newer, higher-quality smartphone instead. Roth refused, claiming that the replacement would not be compatible with her hands-free bluetooth car kit. Tech Fix must replace the exact item left for repair or pay damages.

TERMINATION OF BAILMENTS

If a bailment is for a specific term, the bailment ends when the term lapses. Otherwise, a bailment is terminated when its purpose is satisfied, when the parties mutually agree to end it, when either party makes a demand to end it, or if the bailee acts inconsistently with the terms of the bailment.

25.3 KINDS OF BAILMENTS AND CARE DURING CUSTODY

In all types of bailments, the bailee has at least a minimum duty of care to ensure the safety of the bailor's property. The level of care with which a bailee must treat a bailor's goods varies depending on the kind of bailment.

Bailments are often classified into four categories:

1. *Bailments for the sole benefit of the bailee.* An example of this kind of bailment is when one borrows an article, such as a calculator, from a friend.

2. *Bailments for the sole benefit of the bailor.* An example of this kind of bailment is when one agrees to store a friend's car in his or her garage while the friend is out of town.

3. *Bailments for the benefit of both the bailee and the bailor.* An example of this kind of bailment, also called *mutual-benefit bailment,* is when one leaves his or her car with an attendant in a parking garage (see Example 25.1).

4. *Constructive bailments.* An example of this kind of bailment is when goods, such as an umbrella, are thrust upon you by a person who unintentionally leaves property behind in your home.

Parties to a bailment are free to increase or decrease the bailee's duty to care for the bailor's goods by contract.

BAILMENTS FOR THE SOLE BENEFIT OF THE BAILEE

bailment for the sole benefit of the bailee
A bailment relationship in which only the bailee receives any benefit from the relationship.

A bailment for the sole benefit of the bailee usually results in a borrowing/lending transaction. The person who borrows an article (the bailee) gets the only benefit. However, the owner (the bailor) must warn the bailee of any defects or hazards that might exist. Because the bailee is getting something for nothing, the law generally expects the bailee to exercise great or extraordinary care while in possession of the article.

EXAMPLE 25.4

▶ Fordyce lent his car to a friend, Dyani, to use while taking a short trip. Fordyce knew but failed to mention that the brakes were worn and in need of repair. Dyani was injured when the brakes failed and the car crashed into a tree. Fordyce would be held liable for failure to warn Dyani of the unsafe brakes.

However, in Example 25.4, if Dyani had been drinking alcohol and was at fault for the accident, he could be held liable for failing to use great or extraordinary care.

BAILMENTS FOR THE SOLE BENEFIT OF THE BAILOR

bailment for the sole benefit of the bailor
A bailment that exists when the bailor entrusts an article to the bailee for storage or safekeeping without charge, as a favor.

A bailment for the sole benefit of the bailor exists when the owner (the bailor) entrusts an article to another person (the bailee) for storage or safekeeping without being charged. Since the bailee is doing a favor for the bailor, the law requires that he or she exercise only slight care in taking care of the article.

EXAMPLE 25.5

▶ Berens was traveling for several months and asked a friend, Moreno, to care for a valuable painting. Moreno left the painting leaning against the wall in a spare room. While he was out for an evening, the painting was stolen. Moreno would not be liable because he was required to provide only slight care.

MUTUAL-BENEFIT BAILMENTS

By far the most common bailment is the kind in which consideration is present. Recall from Chapter 10 that consideration is the exchange of promises by the parties to an agreement to each give up something of value they have a right to keep, or to do something they are not otherwise required to do.

A mutual-benefit bailment is one in which both the bailee and bailor derive some benefit, and, as a result, each has rights and duties. The bailor has the duty to warn the bailee of any defects in the property that could cause harm. The bailee has the duty to exercise reasonable or ordinary care in the use of the property. Each party has the right to expect the other party to fulfill the duty imposed on him or her.

In Example 25.5, if Moreno had hung the painting in his living room, thereby gaining some benefit, he would have been required to use ordinary care since it would have been a mutual-benefit bailment.

mutual-benefit bailment
A bailment in which both the bailee and the bailor derive some benefit, and, as a result, each has rights and duties.

Bailment for Storage   Both individuals and businesses sometimes need to place articles in storage. The person or firm that provides storage facilities is known as a warehouser. The Uniform Commercial Code (UCC) provides that when goods are turned over to a warehouse for storage, the warehouser will provide a receipt for the goods and will accept the responsibility for loss of, or damage to, the goods caused by a lack of care that a reasonable person would exercise under similar circumstances (UCC 7-204).

warehouser
A person or firm that provides storage facilities.

Parking Lot Bailment   Parking a car in a parking lot or parking garage is a common transaction. It is important to remember, however, that a bailment is created only if the

A bailment is created when the parking lot attendant actually takes control of the vehicle.

parking lot attendant actually takes control of the vehicle. If a customer parks his or her own automobile, locks it, and retains the key, a bailment does not exist—only a license to use the parking space. In most cases, the parking lot has no responsibility for the car. However, even when the customer locks his or her own vehicle and retains the key, if the parking lot provides a substantial number of attendants and makes express or implied assurances that security will be provided, the court may interpret the facts of the case as suggesting that the parking lot had, in fact, gained control of the car and that a bailment existed.

EXAMPLE 25.6

▶ Mandel was often disturbed when he would witness parking lot attendants recklessly driving automobiles with much squealing of tires and racing of engines. For this reason, he preferred to patronize "park-and-lock" garages. On one occasion, he left his vehicle in such a lot, and when he returned he found that the car had been broken into and the radio and cellular telephone had been stolen. The court would find that this was not a bailment because the attendant had no control over the car, and the transaction was merely a license to use the parking space.

Suppose that, in Example 25.6 the parking lot had a number of attendants who were parking and moving the cars of those customers who had left their keys; the attendant admitted that there had been break-ins; and the attendant assured Mandel, "We'll keep an eye on your car." In such a situation, it is likely that a court would find that a bailment did exist, and the parking lot would be liable for the radio and cellular telephone.

Bailment for Work and Services   Whenever one person turns over property to another with the understanding that certain work is to be performed on the property, a bailment for work and services is created. For example, when the owner of an automobile (the bailor) leaves it at a garage (the bailee) to have repairs made, or the owner of fabric (the bailor) turns it over to a tailor (the bailee) to have a garment made, a bailment for work and services is created.

In transactions of this kind, there are actually two legal relationships. The bailor–bailee relationship is concerned with the care of the property. The contractual relationship is concerned with the kind and the quality of work done and the payment for services performed. The bailee in a bailment for work and services is entitled to hold and, if necessary, sell the property if the bailor does not pay for the services or work done. This provision of the law is known as a bailee's lien. (A *lien* is a claim against the property of another as security for a debt.)

bailee's lien
The right of the bailee in a bailment for work and services to hold and, if necessary, sell the property if the bailor does not pay for the services or work done.

EXAMPLE 25.7

▶ Surry instructed the service manager of an automobile service station to perform a tune-up and "check it over carefully and get it ready for the winter." When Surry picked up the car, he got a bill for $385, which included numerous repairs and parts. He refused to pay and the service station refused to release the car, claiming a bailee's lien. The service station has the right to hold the property until Surry (the bailor) pays for the services done. Ultimately, a court would have to decide what services were reasonable to prepare the car for winter.

Hotel Bailments A bailment relationship exists between a guest (as bailor) and a hotel-keeper (as bailee) with regard to the guest's property that is specifically placed in the care of the hotelkeeper. A hotelkeeper, sometimes called an *innkeeper,* is in the business of offering lodgings or temporary shelter to transients. The shelter may be in a hotel, motel, hostel, or bed-and-breakfast. A transient is a guest whose stay is relatively uncertain—a day, a week, a month, or more. Under common law, the hotelkeeper's liability for the property of guests was near absolute, but state statutes today limit a hotel's liability to that of an ordinary bailee or limit liability to the amount listed in a posted notice in the room. Typically, a hotel will have a sign on the room door stating that the hotel's liability extends only to property deposited in the hotel safe. Such statutes also allow the hotel to place a dollar limit on the hotel's liability.

hotelkeeper
A person or firm in the business of offering lodgings or temporary shelter to guests and transients.

transient
A guest whose stay is relatively uncertain.

Common-Carrier Bailments A common carrier is an individual or firm in the business of transporting goods between certain points as allowed by the various state commissions that regulate the carriers. The law requires that a common carrier must accept all shipments that it is authorized to handle. When a shipper, known as the consignor, turns over goods to a common carrier, a mutual-benefit bailment is created that is terminated only when the common carrier delivers the goods to the party designated by the shipper, known as the consignee. The mutual-benefit bailment gives the carrier (the bailee) certain rights and duties:

common carrier
An individual or firm in the business of transporting goods between certain points as allowed by the various state commissions that regulate carriers.

consignor
The person or party shipping goods in a bailment relationship.

consignee
The person or party receiving goods in a bailment relationship.

1. The right to determine and enforce reasonable rules and requirements concerning the operation of its services. For example, a carrier may refuse to accept improperly packed goods or, during certain times of the year, it may refuse to accept goods that could be damaged by freezing temperatures.

2. The right to payment for services provided. The carrier has a legal right to hold a shipment until payment is made. Withholding payment for transportation charges enables the carrier to hold goods on the basis of a carrier's lien.

3. The right to payment from either the consignor or consignee (depending upon the contract of consignment) during the time when the carrier's equipment is rendered unavailable while it is being loaded or unloaded.

carrier's lien
A carrier's legal right to hold a shipment until payment is made.

constructive bailment
A bailment in which goods are thrust upon a bailee who does not have any choice about whether he or she wishes to serve as bailee.

A common carrier is responsible for any loss or damage to goods that occurs while the goods are in its custody. However, a common carrier can avoid liability if goods are lost or damaged as a result of goods improperly packed by the sender, an act of God, or the nature of the goods themselves. A common carrier is permitted by contract to limit the amount of compensation paid in the event of lost or damaged goods.

CONSTRUCTIVE BAILMENTS
There are instances in which goods are thrust upon a bailee who does not have any choice about whether he or she wishes to serve as bailee. An example might be if a guest in your home accidentally leaves behind his or her property, or a package addressed to your neighbor is accidentally delivered to you. Many people would argue that such instances are not bailments at all. Still, the courts have been unwilling to dismiss the idea of bailment altogether. As a result, the idea of involuntary bailment, or constructive bailment, has come about.

The law requires that a common carrier must accept all shipments that it is authorized to handle.

EXAMPLE 25.8

▶ Mr. and Mrs. Burnside were having dinner in the dining room of the hotel in which they were overnight guests. After dinner Mrs. Burnside left her handbag, containing expensive jewelry, at the table. It was then found by the server, who gave it to the cashier. The cashier gave the handbag to the assistant manager, who disappeared with the handbag and its contents. A court would hold that a constructive bailment had been created and that the hotel was responsible for providing reasonable care, which it did not.

CHAPTER SUMMARY

1. A bailment is a special kind of contract that is widely used in business and in personal affairs. Specifically, it is a transaction in which the owner of tangible personal property transfers the property to another party while still retaining ownership of the property.

2. A bailment allows the owner of personal property to transfer possession of it to another individual. The six typical reasons for creating a bailment are sale, transportation, repair or service, rental, storage, and security for a loan.

3. The four types of bailments are as follows:

   (a) A bailment for the sole benefit of the bailee, which occurs when only the bailee benefits from the agreement. Since the bailee is getting something for nothing, he or she is expected to exercise great or extraordinary care in using the property.

   (b) A bailment for the sole benefit of the bailor, which occurs when only the bailor benefits from the agreement. In this case, the bailee receives no benefit and must exercise only slight care.

   (c) A mutual-benefit bailment, in which both the bailee and bailor benefit. In this situation, the bailee is required to exercise reasonable or ordinary care.

   (d) A constructive bailment, which occurs when goods are thrust upon a bailee who does not have a choice about whether he or she wishes to serve as bailee. In constructive bailments, the bailee is usually expected to exercise reasonable care.

CHAPTER TWENTY-FIVE ASSESSMENT

MATCHING LEGAL TERMS

Match each of the numbered definitions with the correct term in the following list. Write the letter of your choice in the answer column.

a. bailee
b. bailment
c. bailor
d. carrier's lien

e. common carrier
f. consignee
g. consignor
h. constructive bailment

i. lien
j. transient

1. A relationship concerned with the transfer and possession of personal property without the passage of title.

1. _____

2. A relationship in which the bailee comes into possession by having goods thrust upon him or her.

2. _____

3. An individual or firm in the business of transporting goods between certain points for anyone.

3. _____

4. A person or firm who ships goods.

4. _____

5. A claim against the property of another as security for a debt.

5. _____

6. A person to whom goods are shipped.

6. _____

7. The person in a bailment relationship who transfers possession of goods to another.

7. _____

8. The person whose stay in a place of lodging is indefinite.

8. _____

9. The claim of a carrier against the owner of property for unpaid transportation charges.

9. _____

10. The person who receives goods as part of a bailment relationship.

10. _____

TRUE/FALSE QUIZ

Indicate whether each of the following statements is true or false by writing *T* or *F* in the answer column.

11. A bailment requires that title pass at the time the bailment is created.

11. _____

12. Bailments can be express or implied.

12. _____

13. Anyone in possession of goods can create a bailment relationship.

13. _____

14. A bailment for the sole benefit of the bailee usually exists in agreements for the rental of equipment.

14. _____

15. In a bailment for the sole benefit of the bailee, the bailee is required to extend only slight care.

15. _____

16. A mutual-benefit bailment does not exist if there is a lack of consideration.

16. _____

17. The Uniform Commercial Code does not cover bailments for storage.

17. _____

18. The bailee in a bailment for work and services is entitled to hold and sell the property if the bailor does not pay for work or services done.   18. _____

19. The relationship between a consignor and a common carrier is a bailment for the sole benefit of the bailor.   19. _____

20. A hotelkeeper has almost total liability for the property of guests.   20. _____

21. When a parking lot operator allows a motorist to lock a car and retain the key, a bailment relationship is created.   21. _____

22. When goods are stored in a warehouse, the warehouser becomes the bailor.   22. _____

23. In a mutual-benefit bailment, the bailee is required to extend extraordinary care.   23. _____

24. When fungible goods are stored, the identical goods must be returned.   24. _____

25. A bailment cannot generally be created without the agreement of both bailor and bailee.   25. _____

DISCUSSION QUESTIONS

Answer the following questions and discuss them in class.

26. Discuss the six typical reasons for transferring goods and creating a bailment.

_____

_____

27. Discuss the importance of acceptance, possession, and return of goods as they apply to bailments.

_____

_____

28. Distinguish between (a) bailment for the sole benefit of the bailee, (b) bailment for the sole benefit of the bailor, (c) mutual-benefit bailment, and (d) constructive bailment, and provide examples of each.

_____

_____

29. Discuss the special requirements of mutual-benefit bailments concerned with (a) storage, (b) parking lots, (c) work and services, (d) hotels, and (e) common carriers.

_____

_____

30. Discuss the level of care a bailee is required to give for each of several kinds of bailments.

_____

_____

31. Discuss constructive bailments and explain how they differ from other kinds of bailments.

_____

_____

THINKING CRITICALLY ABOUT THE LAW

Answer the following questions, which require you to think critically about the legal principles that you learned in this chapter.

32. Mutual Benefit Bailment A car left in a parking garage is damaged and the attendant disclaims responsibility. While in theory the owner of the car (the bailor) would seem to have the law on his or her side, how can he or she prove the claim? In practice, will the owner be able to collect for the damages?

_____

_____

33. Care of Bailments The law of bailments requires that the bailee extend either slight care, reasonable care, or extraordinary care—depending on the circumstances. Why does the law allow such variations?

_____

_____

34. Hotel Bailments A guest's laptop computer is stolen from her hotel room. Should the hotel bear some responsibility for the loss?

_____

_____

35. **Common-Carrier Bailments** Should a common carrier be required to accept *all* goods for shipment that it is authorized to transport? Could there be grounds for refusing some shipments?

_____

_____

36. **A Question of Ethics** A renter of a power tool, ignoring safety warnings, injures himself while using it. The renter later denies that he had seen or read the warnings. The company renting the tool denies any knowledge of the defects in the power tool despite being aware of these defects. Is one party behaving more unethically than the other? Why or why not?

_____

_____

CASE QUESTIONS

Study each of the following cases. Answer the questions that follow by writing *Yes* or *No* in the answer column.

37. **Bailment** Ky operated a service station on a road near the Canadian border. As a favor to customers, he frequently stored, without charge, certain items that travelers preferred not to take into Canada. Rowan had planned to cross the border for a day's visit but did not wish to take with her a bolt of fabric she had in her car. She left the fabric with Ky, saying that she would pick it up later in the day.

    a. Is the service Ky offers a bailment for the sole benefit of the bailee?   **a.** _____

    b. Is Ky the bailor?   **b.** _____

    c. Is Ky required to extend extraordinary care?   **c.** _____

    d. Is Rowan the bailee?   **d.** _____

38. **Bailment** Ziess, a college student, owned some furniture, a portable TV, and a small refrigerator. At the end of the spring semester, she arranged to store her property in a storage room in her dorm building provided by her college for no charge. The college made it clear that all storage was at students' risk.

    a. Is this storage arrangement a bailment for the sole benefit of
    the bailee?   **a.** _____

    b. Is this arrangement a mutual-benefit bailment?   **b.** _____

    c. Can Ziess take any action against the college in the event of loss
    of her property?   **c.** _____

39. **Bailment** Kenworth took his very expensive watch to Gervey Jewelry for repairs and cleaning. During the week in which the watch remained with the jeweler, it was placed in the store's vault each night. One night, burglars were able to bypass the

burglar alarm, break into the store, and use explosives to open the vault. Kenworth's watch was among the goods stolen. Kenworth brought suit, charging that Gervey should have provided greater care in this bailment. Specifically, he charged that Gervey should have had a 24-hour security guard.

a. Is this an example of a mutual-benefit bailment?   a. _____

b. Did Gervey provide at least ordinary care of the bailed property?   b. _____

c. Is it likely that a court would rule in favor of Kenworth?   c. _____

CASE ANALYSIS

Study each of the following cases carefully. Briefly state the principle of law and your decision.

40. Parking Lot Bailment Wall parked his car in the parking lot at O'Hare Airport in Chicago. After he received a parking ticket from a ticket-dispensing machine, an automatic gate was raised and he entered the lot and parked his car in a space of his choosing. On the reverse side of the parking ticket was printed, "This is a lease of parking space only and not a bailment." When he returned the next day, he discovered that his car was missing and was presumed stolen. The car was later found, but it had been extensively damaged by the thieves. Wall brought suit for $1,846, claiming that a bailment existed and that the parking lot operator was responsible. Did a bailment exist, and is the parking lot operator responsible for Wall's loss? [*Clifford L. Wall et al. v. Airport Parking Company of Chicago,* 244 N.E.2d 190 (Illinois)]

Principle of Law:

_____

_____

Decision:

_____

_____

41. Bailment Noble, a resident of Washington, D.C., ordered a stereo tuner from a store in Maine. The unit was shipped and was received by McLean, the receptionist/switchboard operator in Noble's apartment building. She placed the tuner in a small room where packages for tenants were kept. When McLean went off duty at 4 p.m., the package was still in the room. By the next day it was gone; only the empty box in which the unit had been shipped was found outside the building. Noble brought suit, claiming that a bailment existed. The landlord, Bernstein, denied responsibility and pointed out a provision in the lease that the landlord is not responsible for the property of tenants and that, even if an employee of the landlord does store, move, or handle a tenant's property, he or she does so as the tenant's agent. Did a bailment exist, and is Bernstein responsible for the loss? [*Howard Bernstein, et al. v. Richard Noble*, 487 A.2d 231 (District of Columbia)]

Principle of Law:

_____

_____

Decision:

_____

_____

42. **Bailment**   Gilder entered a parking garage enclosed within the Washington Hilton Hotel, where he was directed to a parking space by an attendant. Some of the spaces were designated for park-and-lock, and others were not. He locked the car and kept the keys. When Gilder had entered the garage, he saw a number of employees: a manager, a cashier, and three attendants. After Gilder parked his car, he opened the trunk in plain view of a group of employees, placed his friend's cosmetic bag in it, and locked the trunk. Upon his return, he found the trunk lid damaged from being pried open. Gilder brought suit, charging the garage with failure to provide adequate care. On appeal, the garage denied responsibility, claiming that there was no bailment. Did a bailment exist, and is the garage responsible? [*Parking Management, Inc. v. Mark Gilder*, 343 A.2d 51 (District of Columbia)]

Principle of Law:

_____

_____

Decision:

_____

_____

43. **Bailment**   The Marglin family moved from Indianapolis to New York and rented an apartment smaller than the one they had left. Marglin arranged to have the excess furniture stored at Global Transportation and Storage Company. During the year that the furniture was in storage, Global stored some animal hides near the furniture. When Marglin picked up the furniture, he found that it had a very unpleasant odor. When Marglin complained, Global insisted that it had provided storage as agreed. Marglin brought suit for negligence and claimed that Global had failed to provide the ordinary care required. Will Marglin succeed?

Principle of Law:

_____

_____

Decision:

_____

_____

LEGAL RESEARCH

Complete the following activities. Share your findings with the class.

44. **Working in Teams** In teams of three or four, visit several hotels and motels to determine their policies regarding stolen or missing property. Ask particularly about experiences with guests' complaints.

_____

_____

45. **Using Technology** Using the Internet and search engines, look for legal cases involving bailments and sample bailment contracts. Identify the types of bailments in such cases and contracts.

_____

_____

chapter **26**

Landlord–Tenant Relations

LEARNING OUTCOMES

After studying this chapter and completing the assessment, you will be able to

26.1 Discuss the landlord–tenant relationship.

26.2 Describe the four types of tenant interests in real property.

26.3 Discuss the rights and duties of landlords and tenants.

26.4 Explain several reasons for termination of leases.

26.5 Explain how liability is determined and whether the landlord or tenant is likely to be found liable.

LEGAL terms

landlord	tenancy for years
tenant	tenancy at will
lease	tenancy at sufferance
lessor	warranty of habitability
lessee	mitigate
covenant	quiet enjoyment
conditions	eviction
fair housing act	assignment of lease
periodic tenancy	sublease

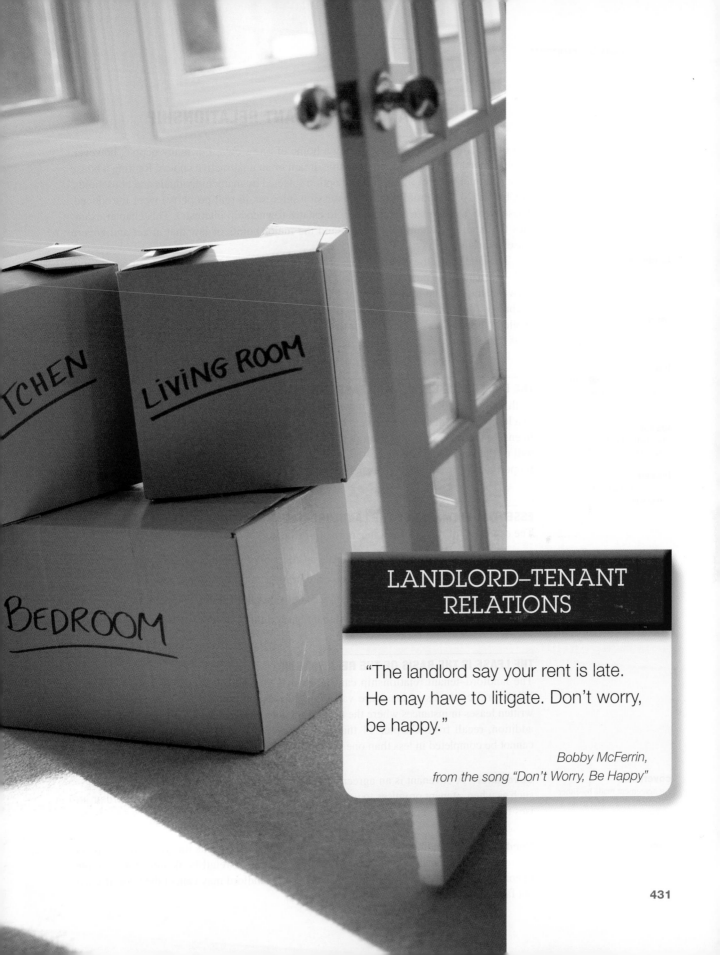

KITCHEN

LIVING ROOM

BEDROOM

26.1   THE LANDLORD–TENANT RELATIONSHIP

Part of the American dream is owning a home of one's own. For many people, however, home ownership is either an unattainable dream or an unattractive choice. Renting a house or an apartment, therefore, is often an option selected by many individuals and households. In Chapter 24, leasehold estates (possession interests in real property) were introduced. These were distinguished from freehold estates (ownership interests). This chapter examines the landlord–tenant relationship and the major points of law that affect and govern leasehold estates.

The landlord is the owner of real property who gives up his or her right of possession, and the tenant is the person who agrees to pay for the use of real property. The relationship between the two involves a tenant's possession, use, and control of real property in exchange for payment of rent. The document in which the terms of the agreement are spelled out is the lease. The landlord is referred to as the lessor, and the tenant is referred to as the lessee.

landlord
The owner of real property who gives up his or her right of possession.

tenant
The person who agrees to pay for the use of real property.

lease
The document in which the terms of a rental agreement are written.

lessor
The landlord in a lease agreement.

lessee
The tenant in a lease agreement.

THE DIFFERENCE BETWEEN A LEASE AND A LICENSE

Both leases and licenses give nonowners certain rights in real property. A lease transfers to a lessee the right of possession; a license does not. A *license* merely gives a person (the licensee) the right to use real property for a specific purpose and can be canceled at the will of the landowner (the licensor). As a result, a lease creates an estate (interest) in real property; a license merely gives permission to use the real property.

ESSENTIAL ELEMENTS OF THE LANDLORD–TENANT RELATIONSHIP

The essentials of the landlord–tenant relationship are

▶ The tenant can occupy a landlord's property only with the consent of the landlord.

▶ The tenant's rights in the property are inferior to those of the landlord.

▶ The property must revert (be returned) to the landlord at the termination of the lease.

▶ The parties must agree that the tenant has a right of immediate possession.

THE LEASE IS THE BASIS OF THE RELATIONSHIP

The landlord–tenant relationship can be created by an express or an implied contract. While oral contracts of lease are valid under common law, most state statutes require written leases in instances where the term of the lease is greater than one to three years. In addition, recall from Chapter 11 that the Statute of Frauds requires that contracts that cannot be completed in less than one year must be in writing to be enforceable.

covenant
An agreement made by either a landlord or a tenant to do certain things.

Covenants   A covenant is an agreement or promise in a lease to do a particular thing— such as when a tenant promises to use the property for certain purposes or a landlord promises to make certain repairs and to ensure the tenant's quiet enjoyment.

conditions
Restrictions that limit the use of the property.

Conditions   A condition, or restriction, included in a lease limits the use of the property. If the lease stipulates that the premises will be used as a retail bookstore, for example, opening a nightclub would not be permissible. The landlord may cancel the lease if a tenant fails to respect the conditions specified.

EXAMPLE 26.1

▶ Whitehorse, the lessee/tenant, leased an apartment from Mirov, the lessor/landlord, for $600 per month. Mirov included in the written lease a statement that pets were not allowed. Whitehorse's promise to pay the rent is a covenant, and the "no pet" clause in the lease is a condition. Mirov can cancel the lease if Whitehorse either fails to pay the rent or allows a dog to live on the premises.

The Law Relating to Leases   The Fair Housing Act prohibits discrimination in housing on the basis of race, color, sex, familial status, national origin, religion, or handicap. Under the Fair Housing Act, it is generally illegal for a landlord to discriminate against these protected classes by refusing to rent property, or by claiming that property is already rented when in fact it is available. It is also illegal for a landlord to alter the terms, privileges, or conditions of a lease so that they are unfavorable to a protected class.

In addition to the Fair Housing Act, under common law, the parties to a lease were relatively free to include whatever terms were acceptable to and agreed upon by the parties. Increasingly, however, leases are subject to many more legal restrictions than they were in the past. Also, since leases are now viewed as contracts, commercial leases are subject to certain provisions of the Uniform Commercial Code (UCC) regarding unconscionability (UCC 2-302).

fair housing act
A federal law that prohibits discrimination in housing on the basis of race, color, sex, familial status, national origin, religion, or handicap.

26.2 TYPES OF TENANT INTERESTS IN REAL PROPERTY

The type of possession interest a tenant has in real property can vary considerably depending on the agreements between the parties and the provisions of the lease. The following types of possession interests are most common.

periodic tenancy
A possession interest in which the lease continues for successive periods for the same length of time.

PERIODIC TENANCY

A periodic tenancy is a possession interest in which the lease continues for successive periods for the same length of time—weekly, monthly, annually, and so forth. A periodic tenancy is somewhat open-ended because it is automatically renewed at the end of the period unless the landlord or tenant gives notice of his or her intent to not renew the lease.

In such a case, either the landlord or tenant must give the other party timely notice in order to comply with applicable state laws. The amount of advanced notice generally equals the term of the lease, but varies greatly from state to state. For example, Connecticut requires a three-day notice prior to the termination of a periodic tenancy, while Delaware requires a 60-day notice.

tenancy for years
The most common type of possession interest in which the lease is for a specific period of time.

TENANCY FOR YEARS

The most common type of possession interest is a tenancy for years. This type of lease is for a specific period of time—weeks, months, years, or the like. A tenancy of this type automatically terminates on the stated expiration date.

Since leases are now viewed as contracts, commercial leases are subject to certain provisions of the UCC.

TENANCY AT WILL

tenancy at will
A possession interest in which no specific time of lease is agreed upon.

A tenancy at will is a possession interest in which no specific time of lease is agreed upon. The lease continues indefinitely until one of the parties notifies the other of a desire to terminate the lease. Most state statutes provide that the landlord must give the tenant a specified minimum number of days' notice of his or her intent to terminate the lease. Sometimes such notice must be in writing.

EXAMPLE 26.2

▶ Commisky was transferred from Chicago to Los Angeles. While she searched for a suitable house, she rented a furnished apartment with the understanding that her stay would be only a few weeks to a few months. She paid rent weekly and could terminate her lease at any time by giving the landlord one week's notice. The lease is an example of a tenancy at will.

TENANCY AT SUFFERANCE

tenancy at sufferance
A tenancy that exists only when a tenant wrongfully extends his or her tenancy beyond the term agreed upon.

A tenancy at sufferance exists only in one limited situation—when a tenant wrongfully extends his or her tenancy beyond the term agreed upon. Tenancy at sufferance is really not a true tenancy at all because the status of the tenant in this situation is uncertain. The landlord can choose either to evict the tenant and treat him or her as a trespasser or to hold the tenant to another term of the lease. Thus, it is important to note that if a tenant extends his or her tenancy by just a few days, the landlord may hold the tenant to a new tenancy—even if the tenancy is unwanted by the tenant.

EXAMPLE 26.3

▶ Segura rented a house from Daly for two years. Uncertain about a pending job relocation, Segura was in no hurry to vacate the premises. At the end of the lease, the two parties had several conversations about Segura staying on, but nothing was agreed upon and no additional rent was paid. Segura's status was that of a tenancy at sufferance. Daly could evict Segura or hold him to another term of the lease, even though Segura had not indicated any desire to renew his lease.

26.3   RIGHTS AND DUTIES OF THE PARTIES

While the rights and duties of the parties are usually stated in the lease (whether the lease is oral or in writing), these rights may be expanded or modified by relevant laws and regulations.

LANDLORD'S WARRANTY OF HABITABILITY

As discussed in Chapter 18, a warranty is a promise or guarantee made by the seller that goods offered for sale are what he or she claims they are—or what a reasonable person has a right to expect. In the case of the landlord–tenant relationship, the law assumes another kind of promise—an implied warranty of habitability. This means that the landlord assures the tenant that the premises are reasonably fit for occupancy and that there are no defects that would impair the health, safety, or well-being of the occupants of the premises. The landlord must also maintain the property in a habitable condition throughout the duration of the lease. Thus, the landlord usually reserves the right to enter and inspect the premises to make any necessary repairs.

warranty of habitability
An implied warranty in which the landlord guarantees that the premises are reasonably fit for occupancy and that there are no defects that would impair the health, safety, or well-being of the occupants.

EXAMPLE 26.4

▶ Dexter had been living in a college dormitory for three years and decided to rent an off-campus apartment for her senior year. Somewhat naïve and eager to be independent, she hurriedly signed a one-year lease and moved in soon afterward. It was not long before she had cause to regret her hasty decision. She discovered that she had the unwelcome company of mice, and there was neither hot water nor heat. In addition, because the door lock was defective and the windows could not be locked, an intruder entered her apartment and stole her laptop computer. When the landlord refused to make necessary repairs, she moved out after one month. The landlord sued, claiming that Dexter had violated the terms of the one-year lease. Dexter claimed that the landlord had breached his warranty of habitability. A court in all likelihood would rule that the landlord had breached the contract by violating the warranty and would agree that Dexter could terminate her lease.

LANDLORD'S RIGHT TO RENT, TO REGAIN POSSESSION, TO EVICT, AND TO RETAIN A TENANT'S SECURITY DEPOSIT

A landlord has the right to collect the agreed-upon rent as provided in the lease. Also, a landlord has the right to regain possession of the property in good condition at the end of the lease. In addition, a landlord has the right, subject to limitations by state statutes and local ordinances, to evict a tenant for nonpayment of rent, illegal use of the premises, or other material violations of the terms of the lease.

Finally, in certain circumstances, a landlord has the right to retain a tenant's security deposit. A security deposit is collected by a landlord to offset his or her losses resulting from tenant-caused property damage or nonpayment of rent. Most states require landlords to provide tenants with a written account of any damages and their subsequent repairs costs within 30 days of the termination of the lease. If a landlord does not provide a tenant with such written account, a tenant will be able to collect his or her security deposit, even if he or she damaged the rental property.

EXAMPLE 26.5

▶ Itoh leased an apartment from Fodor, stating that he would occupy the premises by himself. Within three months, he began using the apartment as a gathering place for drug users. Other tenants complained to Fodor, who shortly thereafter began an eviction action. Fodor would be successful in evicting Itoh.

LANDLORD'S RIGHT TO KEEP FIXTURES AND PERMANENT IMPROVEMENTS

A tenant may wish to make improvements by attaching fixtures to the land or to the premises. Two issues raised by such actions are

1. Does the tenant have the right to make attachments?
2. Does the tenant have the right to remove the fixtures he or she attached at the end of the lease?

Generally, the law gives a tenant the right to make reasonable modifications to the leased property in order to make it suitable for use under the circumstances. For example, it might be quite reasonable for a tenant with a long-term lease to add a patio. On the other hand, it might not be reasonable for a tenant with a one-year lease to add new wiring.

Whether a tenant has the right to remove fixtures at the end of the lease depends largely on whether removing them would damage the landlord's interest.

LANDLORD'S DUTY TO MITIGATE DAMAGES

mitigate
The duty of a landlord to make reasonable efforts to reduce his or her losses resulting from a tenant's abandonment.

In most states, a landlord has a duty to make reasonable efforts to reduce, or mitigate, his or her losses resulting from a tenant's *abandonment* (the voluntary surrender of possession of leased premises). A landlord must make a reasonable effort, for example, to find a new tenant to occupy the abandoned premises. If the landlord fails to make such reasonable effort, the tenant would be relieved of his or her obligation under the lease to pay the rent for the remaining time of the lease.

EXAMPLE 26.6

> Polin rented an apartment for one year for $800 per month. After occupying the apartment for two months, she was transferred to another city and abandoned her rented apartment. The landlord made no attempt to rent the vacated apartment, instead using the time to make repairs and paint it. After nearly a year had passed, the landlord brought suit to collect the rent that would have been paid by Polin had she not abandoned the premises. It is unlikely that a court would award the full amount of lost rent because the landlord had an obligation to mitigate damages (to reduce the loss caused by Polin's abandonment) and to rent the apartment—even at a lower rent. Of course the landlord could sue for the difference between the lower rent and the rent specified in Polin's lease, plus any foreseeable and reasonable expenses associated with finding a new tenant.

TENANT'S RIGHT TO QUIET ENJOYMENT

quiet enjoyment
The right to use the leased premises without unreasonable interferences from the landlord or third parties.

Most written leases provide covenants (promises) of quiet enjoyment of the premises, and in many states, this is an implied right. The right to quiet enjoyment includes the use of the leased premises without unreasonable interference from the landlord or third parties. While the landlord is not always responsible for the actions of third parties over which he or she has no control, some courts have held that the landlord was responsible for the actions of a tenant who denied another tenant his or her right to quiet enjoyment.

EXAMPLE 26.7

▶ Foden, a marriage counselor, leased a ground-floor professional office from Ganley, the owner of an office building. The lease included Ganley's covenant to provide for Foden's quiet enjoyment. The lease also included a condition that the office space would be used only for a professional practice. If Ganley rented an adjoining office to a rock music recording studio, he would have violated his covenant. If Foden changed her line of work and used the property as a nursery school, she would have violated a condition of the lease.

TENANT'S RIGHT TO ACQUIRE AND RETAIN POSSESSION

When agreeing to lease property, the landlord promises that the tenant will have possession of the premises on the agreed-upon date. If the premises are occupied by the previous tenant or under construction, the landlord must take reasonable steps to ensure that the premises are available on the specified date.

The tenant has the right to possession of the leased premises for the duration of the lease. If the landlord interferes with the tenant's right of possession by evicting him or her without a court order of eviction, the tenant has the right to terminate the lease. An eviction is a legal action that denies the tenant the use of the premises. An *actual eviction* occurs when the tenant is denied the physical use of the premises, whether or not such an eviction was approved by a court.

The law gives a tenant the right to make reasonable modifications to the leased property in order to make it suitable for use.

A *constructive eviction* results when the tenant's use or enjoyment of the property has been substantially lessened as a result of certain actions, conditions, or behavior on the part of the landlord or other tenants. A tenant's use or enjoyment would be substantially lessened, for example, by excessive noise, foul odors, or the use of nearby premises for illegal purposes. When the tenant claims constructive, rather than actual, eviction, he or she cannot terminate the lease or stop paying rent unless he or she abandons the premises.

eviction
An action that denies the tenant the use of the premises.

TENANT'S RIGHT TO ASSIGN OR SUBLEASE

Often a tenant will transfer his or her interest in the property to a third person An assignment of lease is a transfer of the tenant's interest in the entire premises for the entire length of the term of the lease. A sublease is a transfer of the tenant's interest for a part of the premises or for a part of the term of the lease. Most leases provide that a tenant may not assign or sublease without the landlord's consent. Also, a provision may be added that a landlord may not unreasonably refuse consent for an assignment or sublease. Of course the landlord is prohibited from refusing consent for reasons that would result in illegal discrimination.

assignment of lease
When a tenant transfers his or her entire interest in the entire premises for the remaining length of the term of the lease.

sublease
A transfer of the tenant's interest in part of the term of the lease and/or part of the premises.

A constructive eviction can
result from excessive noise.

EXAMPLE 26.8

▶ In Example 26.6, Polin had to abandon her apartment as a result of being transferred to another city. Suppose Polin had a friend who agreed to take over the remaining portion of Polin's lease. The arrangement between Polin and her friend would be a sublease. If, however, Polin had learned of the transfer prior to the commencement of the lease, and the friend had agreed to take over the entire premises for the entire period, the arrangement would have amounted to an assignment of lease. Of course the landlord would have the right to approve or disapprove the sublease or assignment, as long as such approval or disapproval was reasonable and not for an illegal reason.

26.4 TERMINATION OF LEASES

A lease may be terminated for several reasons.

LEASE EXPIRATION

The most common reason for termination is the expiration of the lease, whether the tenancy is periodic, for years, or at will. When the lease is terminated for this reason, the landlord is required to return to the tenant any security deposit the tenant had paid unless there are damages to the premises that are above and beyond normal wear and tear.

TENANT'S ABANDONMENT

If the tenant has abandoned the premises, he or she is not relieved of the obligation to pay the agreed-upon rent. If, however, the landlord has violated his or her express or implied duty to provide the tenant with quiet enjoyment, the tenant may abandon the premises under the doctrine of constructive eviction, and this action will terminate the lease.

TERMINATION BY FORFEITURE (BREACH)

Most leases contain a provision that gives the landlord the right to terminate the lease if the tenant fails to pay rent or violates any other material lease provision—for example, making excessive noise, disturbing other tenants, or using residential premises for business purposes. However, the tenant's breach must be *material*—that is, involve an important matter. It is unlikely that a court would allow a termination if the tenant is only a few days late with the rent payment.

26.5 TORT LIABILITY

When a person is injured on leased premises, the question of liability arises. Generally, the person in control of the area in which the injury took place is held to be responsible. The landlord remains in control of common areas, such as hallways, stairways, and laundry rooms.

EXAMPLE 26.9

▶ Bonder, a new tenant in an apartment building owned by Mei, suffered serious injuries when he fell on a broken step while descending a stairway in his apartment building. The landlord was held liable for Bonder's injuries because he was negligent in failing to keep the stairway in good condition.

The tenant is responsible for injuries occurring on his or her own leased premises. For this reason, apartment dwellers' insurance policies are sold to protect the tenant policyholder against liability losses resulting from injuries that occur on the tenant's premises, but not losses that result from injuries that occur in common areas or in the physical structure itself.

EXAMPLE 26.10

▶ While visiting a friend's apartment, McIlhenny tripped on a torn area rug, hit her head on the sharp corner of a table, and was seriously injured. McIlhenny, reluctant to sue her friend, sued the landlord of the building instead, charging him with the tort of negligence. A court would hold that the responsibility for maintaining safe premises was the tenant's, not the landlord's.

CHAPTER
SUMMARY

1. A landlord is an owner of real property who gives up his or her right of possession, and a tenant is a person who agrees to pay for the use of real proerty. The relationship between the two involves a tenant's possession, use, and control of real property in exchange for payment of rent. A lease transfers to a lessee the right of possession. A license does not transfer possession but gives the licensee only the right to use real property and can be canceled at will by the landowner. Covenants are promises by either the landlord or the tenant to do certain things. Conditions are restrictions on the use of the property.

2. The four kinds of tenant interests in real property are the following: (a) periodic tenancy (a possession interest in which the lease continues for the same length of time), (b) tenancy for years (a lease for a specific period of time), (c) tenancy at will (a possession interest in which no specific time of the lease is agreed upon), and (d) tenancy at sufferance (when a tenant wrongfully extends his or her tenancy beyond the term agreed upon).

3. The law imposes on the landlord the warranty of habitability and the duty to mitigate damages if a lease is breached. In return, the landlord has the right to rent, regain possession, evict, and keep fixtures and permanent improvements to the property. Tenants have the right to property that is reasonably fit and safe for occupancy; to the quiet enjoyment of the premises; and to acquire, possess, assign, or sublease the premises subject to the terms of the lease.

4. The most common reason that a lease is terminated is by expiration. Leases also can be terminated by abandonment or by breach of the terms of the lease.

5. Liability is generally determined by who has control of the premises at the time and place of injury. The tenant is responsible for injuries occurring in his or her own leased premises. The landlord is responsible for injuries that occur in common areas.

CHAPTER TWENTY-SIX
ASSESSMENT

MATCHING LEGAL TERMS

Match each of the numbered definitions with the correct term in the following list. Write the letter of your choice in the answer column.

a. abandonment
b. assignment
c. condition
d. covenant
e. eviction
f. lease
g. lessee
h. lessor
i. periodic tenancy
j. quiet enjoyment
k. sublease
l. tenancy at will
m. tenancy at sufferance
n. tenancy for years
o. warranty of habitability

1. The legal term in a landlord–tenant relationship that refers to the landlord.

1. _____

2. The agreement between landlord and tenant.   2. _____

3. The legal term in a landlord–tenant relationship that refers to the tenant.   3. _____

4. A promise made by a landlord or a tenant in a lease.   4. _____

5. A restriction in a lease that allows cancellation if the landlord or tenant fails to honor the limitation.   5. _____

6. A lease in which the lease period continues for successive periods for the same length of time.   6. _____

7. A lease for a specific period of time—weeks, months, years, or the like.   7. _____

8. A lease in which no specific period has been agreed.   8. _____

9. The status when a tenant wrongfully extends tenancy beyond the term of the original lease.   9. _____

10. A landlord's promise that the premises are reasonably fit for occupation and that there are no defects that would impair the health, safety, or well-being of the occupants.   10. _____

11. A tenant's voluntary surrender of possession of leased premises.   11. _____

12. The right of a tenant to use the premises without unreasonable interference from the landlord or third parties.   12. _____

13. An action by the landlord that denies the tenant the use of the premises.   13. _____

14. A transfer of the tenant's interest in the entire premises for the entire term of the lease.   14. _____

15. A transfer of the tenant's interest for part of the premises or for part of the term of the lease.   15. _____

TRUE/FALSE QUIZ

Indicate whether each of the following statements is true or false by writing *T* or *F* in the answer column.

16. A tenant can legally occupy a landlord's property only with the consent of the landlord.   16. _____

17. The tenant's rights in rented property are superior to those of the landlord.   17. _____

18. The landlord–tenant relationship can be created by express or implied contract.   18. _____

19. The unconscionability clause of the Uniform Commercial Code can be applied to the landlord–tenant relationship.   19. _____

20. A tenancy at sufferance describes the relationship that exists when a tenant wrongfully extends his or her stay beyond the terms of the lease.

20. _____

21. A warranty of habitability is the tenant's promise that he or she will inhabit the property according to the terms of the lease.

21. _____

22. If a tenant abandons the premises, the landlord is permitted to continue charging rent while taking no other action.

22. _____

23. The covenant of quiet enjoyment refers to a tenant's promise to remain quiet after 10 p.m.

23. _____

24. A tenant usually has the right to assign or sublease the leased property with the landlord's consent.

24. _____

25. A landlord is liable for all injuries that occur on the leased premises.

25. _____

DISCUSSION QUESTIONS

Answer the following questions and discuss them in class.

26. Discuss the difference between a lease and a license and state the advantages and disadvantages of each.

_____

_____

27. If a tenant chooses to use leased premises for purposes other than the one stipulated in the lease, why would a new agreement be required?

_____

_____

28. If a landlord should fail to make the repairs promised in the lease, what recourse does the tenant have?

_____

_____

29. Should a tenant have the right to remove fixtures he or she has added to the premises? Why or why not?

_____

_____

30. Explain several reasons for termination of leases.

_____

_____

31. Explain how liability for injuries suffered by a tenant's guests in common areas is determined and whether the landlord or tenant is likely to be found liable.

_____

_____

THINKING CRITICALLY ABOUT THE LAW

Answer the following questions, which require you to think critically about the legal principles that you learned in this chapter.

32. Landlord's Rights Under what circumstances should a landlord have the right to withhold his or her permission to assign or sublet premises?

_____

_____

33. Tenant's Rights Most residential leases prohibit the premises being used for business purposes. Would activities such as writing, dressmaking, or accounting be sufficient reason for eviction?

_____

_____

34. Warranty of Habitability What recourse does a tenant have when the landlord fails to provide reasonable habitability?

_____

_____

35. Liability of Landlord Under what circumstances should a landlord be held liable for injuries suffered by a tenant who is a victim of a crime in his or her premises?

_____

_____

36. A Question of Ethics Are tenants justified in withholding rent on the grounds that another tenant's behavior has interfered with their right to quiet enjoyment?

_____

_____

Study each of the following cases. Answer the questions that follow by writing *Yes* or *No* in the answer column.

37. **Tenancy** Maldanado signed a written lease for office space in a commercial building. The lease covered a period of two years and rent was to be paid monthly. At the end of the two years, Maldanado and the landlord began discussions over the terms of a new lease. During the period of negotiations, Maldanado paid the same rent that he had during the original lease, and the landlord accepted the payments.

    a. Was a tenancy at sufferance created?   a. _____

    b. Was the original lease a periodic tenancy?   b. _____

    c. Was a periodic tenancy automatically created during the period
       of negotiations?   c. _____

38. **Landlord Rights** Patsos rented a vacant warehouse for five years with the stated purpose of opening a wholesale meat distribution company. It was necessary to install a number of large refrigerators and other kinds of equipment to process and store meat. At the end of the five years, Patsos decided to build his own warehouse and did not renew the lease. The day he began to remove his equipment, the landlord appeared and stopped the activity, claiming that the refrigerators and other equipment were fixtures because they were permanently installed and thus now belonged to the landlord.

    a. Is it likely that a court would consider the refrigerators and other
       equipment to be fixtures and therefore the property of the landlord? a. _____

    b. Is the determination of whether the landlord's property will suffer
       damage an issue in this case?   b. _____

    c. Is there any way that Patsos could have conducted his business
       without installing the equipment?   c. _____

39. **Conditions of Lease** Perez rented a vacant building, signing a lease indicating that he would open a movie theater. When Perez began operations, the theater specialized in art and classic films. After several months, however, it became apparent that the business was doomed to failure and, in an attempt to salvage his business, Perez changed his policy and began showing adult pornographic films. The change helped the business but attracted a different clientele. The landlord began an eviction action, claiming that Perez had violated the terms of his lease.

    a. Is it likely that the landlord will be successful in evicting Perez? a. _____

    b. Is the landlord asking the court to grant an order for
       constructive eviction?   b. _____

    c. Could the landlord have prevented the disagreement by including
       more specific terms in the lease agreement?   c. _____

> **CASE ANALYSIS**

Study each of the following cases carefully. Briefly state the principle of law and your decision.

40. **Covenants** Knight purchased an apartment building that was occupied by tenants Hallsthammer, Decaprio, and Breit. The day after acquiring the building, Knight informed the tenants that their rent was being increased. A week later, Breit, on behalf of himself and other tenants, informed Knight that the tenants intended to withhold their rent because of the state of disrepair of the building. In their complaint, the tenants cited wall cracks, peeling paint, water leaks, heating and electrical fixture problems, broken or inoperable windows, rodents and cockroaches, and lack of sufficient heat. The tenants accused Knight of a breach of his warranty of habitability, and for this reason they withheld rent payments. Knight defended his actions, stating that the tenants had not given him time to remedy the problems. Does it seem likely that the court would support the actions of the tenants? [*Knight v. Hallsthammer*, 623 P.2d 268 (California)]

    Principle of Law:

    _____

    _____

    Decision:

    _____

    _____

41. **Liability** An intruder entered through a window and raped McCutchen in her apartment. McCutchen sued the landlord, Ten Associates, for failure to provide adequate security and failure to warn her of the risk of intrusion through a window. Ten Associates claimed that they had no way of anticipating an intruder. Evidence was introduced that revealed the landlord knew or should have known of a prior rape and numerous intrusions through apartment windows. Does it appear that Ten Associates was negligent in providing for the security of tenants? [*Ten Associates v. McCutchen*, 398 So. 2d 860 (Florida)]

    Principle of Law:

    _____

    _____

    Decision:

    _____

    _____

42. **Landlord Responsibility** Harmon, the owner of a suburban house, rented it for one year to Wagner and his wife, who had just moved into the city from another state. Two months after moving into the house, the Wagners divorced, and both husband and wife moved to smaller facilities. The house remained vacant for 10 months. At the end of one year, Harmon brought suit to collect the rent for these 10 months. Harmon protested, claiming that the landlord should have tried to rent to someone else. The landlord said that it was Harmon's responsibility to sublease the house. Is it likely that Harmon would be successful in his suit?

Principle of Law:

_____

_____

Decision:

_____

_____

_____

LEGAL RESEARCH

Complete the following activities. Share your findings with the class.

43. **Working in Teams** In teams of three or four, investigate whether your local community has a housing or landlord–tenant court. What are some of the disputes decided by this court?

_____

_____

44. **Using Technology** Using the Internet and search engines, investigate sample leases. What are some of the covenants and conditions typically contained in these leases?

_____

_____

chapter 27
Wills, Intestacy, and Trusts

After studying this chapter and completing the assessment, you will be able to

27.1 Identify the purpose of a will.

27.2 Recognize the language used to describe the various people, and the court, involved with a will.

27.3 Discuss the types of gifts covered by a will.

27.4 Identify the requirements for a valid will.

27.5 Explain how a will is revised or revoked.

27.6 Explain the way the court distributes the estate of someone who dies intestate.

27.7 Discuss advanced health care directives.

27.8 Discuss trusts, including the major types of trusts and the role of a trustee.

LEGAL terms

decedent	ademption
will	devise
testator	holographic will
probate court	nuncupative will
personal representative	testamentary capacity
executor	codicil
administrator	advanced directive
intestate	living will
beneficiary	trust
legacy	trustee
bequest	settlor

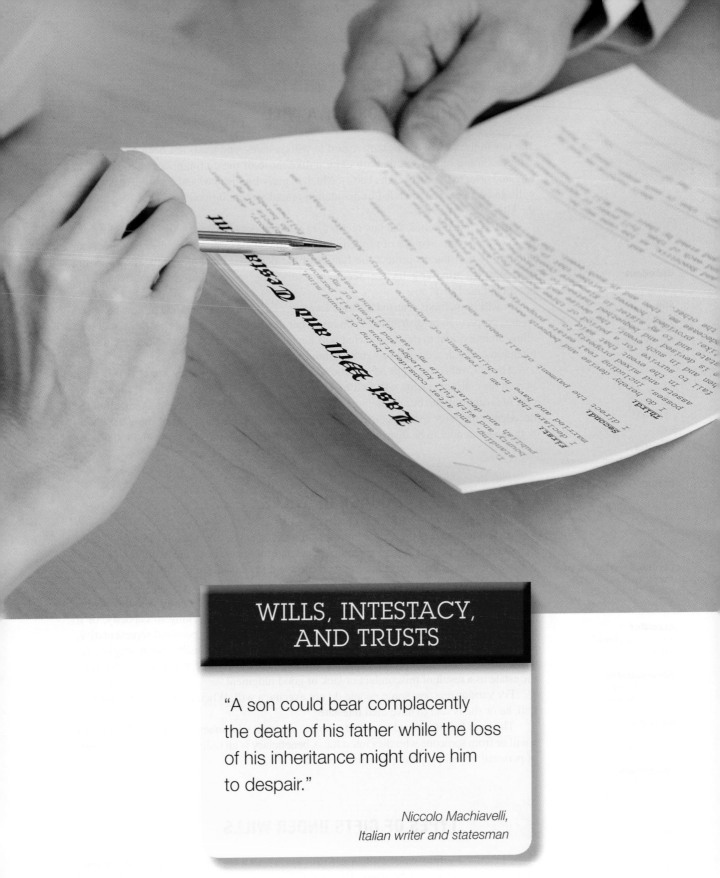

WILLS, INTESTACY, AND TRUSTS

"A son could bear complacently the death of his father while the loss of his inheritance might drive him to despair."

Niccolo Machiavelli,
Italian writer and statesman

27.1 THE PURPOSE OF A WILL

The law in the United States with regard to wills, estates, and trusts has been developed to achieve certain objectives that are quite unlike those of the common law that existed in England prior to the early 20th century. Much of early English law and tradition concerning wills and estates was intended to maintain a feudal system in which all land belonged to the king.

In the United States, the law recognizes the concept of private property and the right of an individual to dispose of property as he or she wishes. Moreover, the law reflects an attempt by the state to protect the family of the deceased person, who is known as the decedent, by providing for the needs of a surviving spouse and children, even if the decedent failed to do so.

A will, sometimes referred to as a *testament,* is a person's declaration of how he or she wishes property to be distributed upon his or her death. The primary purpose of a will is to allow an individual to designate what will happen to his or her property after death. This intention of the decedent is known as *testamentary intent.*

The law, reflecting both recent tradition and current public policy, states that when a person dies, arrangements will first be made to pay his or her final expenses, such as the cost of an appropriate burial, medical expenses, taxes, and legitimate debts. Also, all of the decedent's property will be converted to cash and applied to payment of these expenses, with the remainder to be distributed as the decedent wished or as the law provides.

27.2 THE LANGUAGE OF WILLS

The person who makes the will is known as the testator. The court responsible for accepting a will that meets all statutory requirements and for supervising the operation of a will is known as the probate court. The person responsible for settling the affairs of the decedent is known as the personal representative.

If the personal representative has been named in the will, he or she is known as the executor. If the executor is deceased, declines to serve, or is lacking in capacity, or if the decedent dies without making a will, the court will appoint a personal representative, known as an administrator. The personal representative is responsible for managing the affairs of the estate with prudence. He or she may be held liable for any loss suffered by the estate as a result of misconduct or lack of good judgment.

For various reasons, some people do not execute a will. When a person dies without a will, he or she is said to have died intestate.

The term *heir* is a broad term that refers to a person who inherits property either under a will or from someone who dies intestate. A beneficiary is an individual who receives gifts of personal or real property pursuant to a will.

27.3 TYPES OF GIFTS UNDER WILLS

To be precise, a gift of money under a will is known as a legacy, while a gift of personal property is known as a bequest. Currently, however, the two terms are often used synonymously. A legacy or bequest is *specific,* when it identifies the personal property

decedent
A deceased person.

will
A person's declaration of how he or she wishes property to be distributed upon his or her death.

testator
The person who makes a will.

probate court
The court responsible for accepting a will that meets all statutory requirements and for supervising the operation of a will.

personal representative
The person responsible for settling the affairs of the decedent.

executor
A personal representative named in the will.

administrator
A personal representative appointed by a court.

intestate
The state in which a person dies without a will.

beneficiary
An individual who receives gifts of personal or real property by will.

legacy
A gift of money by will.

bequest
A gift of personal property by will.

given, or *general*, when it does not identify such property. When a bequest is specific, ademption occurs when the personal property is disposed of before the death of the testator. In such a case, the bequest is considered ineffective because a will can distribute only property that the testator owned at the time of his or her death. Finally, a legacy or bequest can be *residuary*, when it provides for the disposition of the balance of the estate. A gift of real property is known as a devise.

ademption
When a specific bequest of personal property is made, but the personal property is disposed of before the death of the testator.

devise
A gift of real property by will.

EXAMPLE 27.1

▶ Pieper drafted a will leaving a large estate, including a power snow blower, to her brother-in-law; $25,000 to her nephew; a summer home to her sister; and the remainder of her estate to her life partner. The power snow blower is a specific bequest, the $25,000 is a general legacy, the summer home is a devise, and the remainder of the estate is a residuary legacy.

27.4   REQUIREMENTS OF A VALID WILL

holographic will
A will that is completely handwritten.

nuncupative will
An oral will.

A will must comply with legal requirements that are intended to ensure that the wishes of the testator are met and that there are no obstacles to the smooth transfer of the property. The law governing wills varies from one state to another, but most states are consistent in specifying certain requirements.

REQUIREMENT OF WRITING

In most cases, a will must be in writing, dated, and signed to be effective. The writing need not be formal, as long as it meets the legal requirements. A holographic will is one that is completely handwritten. Holographic wills have been challenged because they included some words that were not hand-written, such as the letterhead on stationery. As a result, some states require only the material portions and signature to be handwritten in order for a holographic will to be considered valid. Like other wills, a holographic will must be signed and dated.

A nuncupative will, the term used for an oral will, might be valid in only the most unusual circumstances (for example, where the testator was under the imminent danger of death). A tape recording of a decedent's voice, offered as a nuncupative will, would be invalid.

REQUIREMENT OF WITNESSES

A formal, printed will must be signed by the testator and witnessed. In most states, there are no age requirements for witnesses, but they must be legally competent. That is, minors may witness a will as long as they have an adequate understanding of what they are signing and could testify regarding the facts related to the execution of the will if such becomes necessary. The number of witnesses required varies depending upon state law (it usually numbers two or three). It is necessary, however, that the witnesses see the testator sign the document, because they may be called upon later to attest that they actually saw the testator sign. For this reason, it is generally advisable to have witnesses

In most cases, a will must be in writing, dated, and signed to be effective.

who are younger than the testator and who live nearby (not that all younger persons will outlive the testator, but it is more likely that they will). Witnesses generally also must be aware that the document being signed is a will.

Witnesses are expected to be satisfied that the testator is of sound mind at the time of signing. Frequently, testators video themselves and their witnesses during the signing of the will to demonstrate their own competence and the presence of witnesses. However, the video itself is not a valid will. In some states, witnesses cannot also be beneficiaries under the will. There have been instances in some states when wills that have not been witnessed have been accepted as valid.

TESTAMENTARY CAPACITY

testamentary capacity
The requirement that a testator be of sound mind and legal age.

Just as contracts require competent parties, the law relating to wills requires testamentary capacity; that is, a testator must be of sound mind and legal age. There is some variation among the states as to the minimum age. In most states, the age of majority for the purpose of executing a will is 18.

While the testator's age is something that can be determined easily, a person's mental capacity is not so readily provable. It is essential that the testator be of sound mind when the will is made, even though, as often happens, mental capacity may deteriorate with the passing years. From a legal perspective, a testator is considered of sound mind if he or she is adequately rational to understand the act of making a will, realize the nature and disposition of his or her property, and recognize his or her heirs. A person who suffers from mental illness can still be considered of testamentary capacity if he or she makes a will during a lucid period.

If it can be established that the testator lacked testamentary capacity, the will is void.

UNDUE INFLUENCE

The expression *undue influence* (see Chapter 9) describes the pressure that might be applied to a testator to change his or her true wishes for the disposition of property. Undue influence can take many forms, from threats of harm to more subtle suggestions. Very often, it is difficult for a court to decide whether the attention given to an elderly relative, for example, is undue influence or is simply loving concern shown by one of the parties named in the will.

EXAMPLE 27.2

▶ Marley had worked for Phan, a 62-year-old executive, for 15 years as an administrative assistant. When he was 60, Phan had executed a will leaving his entire estate to Marley. Two years later he died. Phan's grown children, who were effectively disinherited by the will, challenged the will, claiming that because of Marley's and Phan's confidential relationship, Marley had exercised undue influence over their father. The court held that the confidential relationship in itself could not be viewed as undue influence. Lacking evidence of undue influence, the will was allowed to stand and the entire estate passed to Marley.

27.5 REVISING AND REVOKING WILLS

During the lifetime of the testator, a number of circumstances may prompt the testator to revise or revoke his or her will. Intended beneficiaries, for example, may die while the testator is alive or may fall out of favor.

REVISIONS

Any alterations to a will, such as erasures, words crossed out, or handwritten insertions, usually invalidate the document. To make legal changes in a will, a separate document, called a codicil, is prepared to revoke, alter, or revise the will. The execution of a codicil has formal requirements and is very much like writing a new will. It must be witnessed and dated. There is no limit on the number of codicils that can be made. In the case of a relatively simple, straightforward will, it is often just as easy to execute an entirely new will. Also, with the use of word processing, it is easy to recall the existing will and make whatever changes are desired. On the other hand, a lengthy, complex will may be more easily revised by writing a codicil.

codicil
A document, separate from the will, in which a person can make legal changes to his or her will.

EXAMPLE 27.3

▶ Kassim, a widower, executed a will in which he left his entire estate to his two children, Robert and Susan, equally. As the years passed, Robert married, fathered three children, and struggled to make ends meet. Susan, on the other hand, remained single and enjoyed great financial success. Kassim felt that Robert needed money more than Susan did. To change the distribution of his estate so that a greater portion went to Robert, Kassim executed a new will.

REVOCATIONS

Many wills include a statement that the testator is revoking all previous wills. Even without such a statement, the most recent will, if valid, automatically revokes all prior wills made by the testator.

Revocations by operation of law can include those that result from marriage or remarriage of the testator, divorce or annulment of a marriage, and the birth or adoption of children after the will was made, all of which can change the disposition of gifts.

27.6 INTESTACY

When a person dies without a will, or had a will that failed to meet the requirements of the law, he or she is said to have died intestate. In such a case, the law of the state in which the deceased person was domiciled (where he or she lived) governs the disposition of his or her property, even though the death may have occurred elsewhere. These laws vary by state. Generally, a surviving spouse and children receive the entire estate. But even this seemingly fair division can create problems, as shown in Example 27.4.

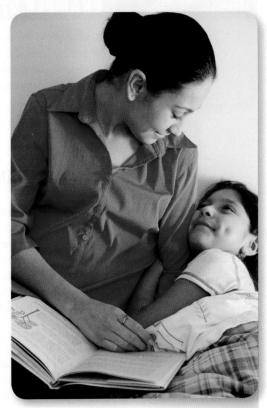

If a person dies without a will, generally the surviving spouse and children will receive the entire estate.

EXAMPLE 27.4

▶ Kaslick, a man of modest means, died intestate, leaving his wife, a full-time homemaker, and two young children. Under state law, Kaslick's estate was divided in half between his wife and their children. Because of their ages, the children's share was held in trust until they reached the age of majority. Since the children's half was not available to her, Kaslick's wife not only had to support herself but her children as well with her one-half of the estate. If Kaslick had prepared a will, he might have left the entire estate, or at least most of it, to his wife, with perhaps a smaller amount to the children.

If a person dies intestate leaving a spouse but no children, the surviving spouse usually receives the entire estate. If there are children but no surviving spouse, the children usually receive the estate. State laws on intestacy also cover other situations, such as when a person dies without either a spouse or children. In these cases, other relatives, including parents, grandchildren, and siblings (brothers and sisters), are then included in the distribution. If no surviving heirs or ancestors of the deceased can be located, the decedent's property passes to the state.

EXAMPLE 27.5

▶ Aiken, a young student with very few assets who believed he did not need a will, was killed in an airplane crash and died intestate. Aiken's estate settled the case with the airline for several hundred thousand dollars. Aiken's father, who had abandoned him as an infant, will likely share in the settlement, despite the fact that Aiken probably would not have wished for this result.

27.7 ADVANCED HEALTH CARE DIRECTIVES

Advancing medical technology can prolong life even when there is little chance of recovery. Many are opposed to their and their loved ones' lives being prolonged by artificial life support. To address these important matters, most states have enacted statutes that allow individuals to execute a device, known as an advanced directive, that documents their expressed wishes regarding their health care in the event that they are incapacitated without hope of recovery. The two most commonly used advanced directives are the living will and the durable power of attorney for health care.

advanced directive
A device that documents an individual's expressed wishes regarding his or her health care in the event that the individual is incapacitated without hope of recovery.

living will
A document in which a person directs his or her physician and/or health proxy to forgo certain extraordinary medical procedures in especially dire circumstances.

LIVING WILLS
A living will is a document in which a person directs his or her physician and/or health proxy to forgo certain extraordinary (heroic) medical procedures if, for example, the person is dying or permanently unconscious. Because statutes regarding advanced directives vary from state to state, a living will must be made following the precise requirements of the applicable state statute in order to be considered valid. The purpose of a valid living will is to permit a terminally ill patient to live or die with dignity and to protect the physician or hospital from liability for sustaining or withdrawing life support.

DURABLE POWER OF ATTORNEY FOR HEALTH CARE

A *durable power of attorney for health care* is a document that appoints an individual as an agent with authority to make health care decisions on behalf of a principal in the event that the principal becomes incompetent. Note that a principal should appoint a capable and trusted individual as his or her attorney in fact; an agent should protect the principal's best interest and not abuse his or her powers. (See Chapter 19.)

27.8   TRUSTS

A trust is a device or mechanism that permits personal or real property to be held by one party, the trustee, for the benefit of another, the *beneficiary*. Some trusts have some of the characteristics of a will in that they allow a person to control the disposition of his or her property after death. One of the benefits of a trust is that it allows the legal title of property to be separated from the benefits of ownership. A trust allows parents, for example, to transfer benefits, such as income derived from property, to children and still withhold actual ownership until the children are older and presumably wiser. In addition, the creation of the trust under these circumstances could result in favorable tax treatment for the parents.

Another use for a trust would be if, for example, Jones put property in trust for Smith's lifetime so that she could benefit from the income the property might produce, and at Smith's death, the property would then pass on to Browne.

> **trust**
> A device or mechanism that permits personal or real property to be held by one party, the trustee, for the benefit of another, the beneficiary.

> **trustee**
> A person who is entrusted with the management and control of another's property or the rights associated with that property.

TYPES OF TRUSTS

There are two main types of trusts. A *testamentary trust* is created by a will. It becomes effective only upon the death of the testator. The names of the parties—beneficiaries and trustee—are specified in the will.

EXAMPLE 27.6

▶ Neurman, a wealthy merchant, was concerned that if he died, his three grown—but irresponsible—children would quickly squander their inheritances. To avoid the problems he foresaw, he established a testamentary trust in his will that provided that upon his death his entire estate, after paying final expenses, would be placed in trust and that the trustee would pay each of his children a yearly allowance.

Note that, in Example 27.6, the final disposition of the property is still undetermined. The question of what happens to the property held in trust when the last of the children dies remains unanswered. To avoid such ambiguity, a trust should provide for final distribution of the property once the objective of the trust has been met.

A *living trust* (also known as an *inter vivos* trust) is established while the person, known as the settlor, who wishes to set up the trust is still alive. The settlor transfers the legal title to the property to the trust to be held for the benefit of either a beneficiary or the settlor himself or herself, possibly providing tax advantages to the settlor.

> **settlor**
> A person who sets up a trust while still alive.

THE ROLE OF THE TRUSTEE

The responsibility of the trustee is that of a fiduciary and, as suggested by the name, is one of great trust. He or she must manage the property according to the wishes of the settlor, who may be deceased. Appointment as a trustee should not be accepted unless one has the temperament, knowledge, and skills necessary to minimize the risks inherent in the position of trustee. Typically, banks, trust companies, attorneys, and other fiduciary organizations offer professional skills in the administration of trusts. Like all other fiduciaries, a trustee has a *duty of loyalty* and a *duty of care* (see Chapter 20 for detailed descriptions of these obligations).

Trustee's Powers   The trustee has certain nondelegable powers granted by law or by the trust instrument itself. Powers usually granted by law include the authority and responsibility to invest trust property; to sell, exchange, or rent property; to contract with others in matters relating to the trust; to borrow funds using trust property as security; and to distribute income to beneficiaries.

Trustee's Duties   The trustee has the duty to maintain appropriate records and to provide a full accounting of the trust property; to pay taxes; and to use good judgment in managing the property, including making good investment decisions. The trustee may purchase securities that are of very low risk and that appear on a document referred to as a *legal list*.

Trustee's Accountability   A trustee whose performance of duty in managing the trust property is called into question can be held liable unless a court rules that the trustee exercised sound judgment.

CHAPTER SUMMARY

1. The purpose of a will is to recognize the concept of private property and give a person the right to dispose of his or her property as he or she wishes. A will is also important for protecting the family of the deceased person.

2. The person who makes the will is known as the testator. The court responsible for accepting a will that meets all statutory requirements and for supervising the operation of a will is known as the probate court. The person responsible for settling the affairs of the decedent is known as the personal representative. If the personal representative has been named in the will, he or she is known as the executor. If the executor is deceased, declines to serve, or is lacking in capacity, or if the decedent dies without making a will, the court will appoint an administrator. A person who dies without a will is said to have died intestate. An heir is a person who inherits property either under a will or from someone who dies intestate. A beneficiary is an individual who receives gifts of personal or real property pursuant to a will. The person who makes the will is known as the testator.

3. A gift of money is known as a legacy and a gift of personal property is known as a bequest, although both terms are often used synonymously. A bequest can be specific, general, or residuary.

4. The requirements for a valid will vary by state but often include that the will be written, dated, signed, and witnessed. The testator also must have testamentary capacity and be free from undue influence. The requirements for testamentary capacity are that the testator be of legal age and of sound mind when the will is created.

5. A codicil is prepared to revoke, alter, or revise a will. The most recent will, if valid, automatically revokes all prior wills made by the testator.

6. When a person dies intestate, the law of the state in which the deceased was domiciled governs the disposition of his or her property. Usually a surviving spouse and children receive the entire estate. If there is no surviving spouse or children, other relatives (including parents, grandchildren, and siblings) are then included in the distribution.

7. Most states have enacted statutes that allow an individual to execute an advanced directive, which documents an individual's wishes regarding his or her health care in the event that the individual is incapacitated without hope of recovery. The two most commonly used advanced directives are the living will and the durable power of attorney for health care.

8. The purpose of a trust is to allow a person to control the disposition of his or her property after death by having it held by one party, the trustee, for the benefit of another, the beneficiary. The two kinds of trusts are a testamentary trust, which is created by a will, and a living trust, which is established while the settlor is still alive. A trustee has a fiduciary duty to manage property according to the wishes of the settlor. Powers usually include the ability to sell, exchange, or rent property; borrow funds; contract with others in matters pertaining to the trust; and distribute income to beneficiaries. Duties include maintaining records of the property, providing a full accounting of trust property, and using good judgment.

CHAPTER TWENTY-SEVEN
ASSESSMENT

MATCHING LEGAL TERMS

Match each of the numbered definitions with the correct term in the following list. Write the letter of your choice in the answer column.

a. beneficiary
b. bequest
c. codicil
d. decedent
e. devise

f. executor
g. holographic will
h. *inter vivos*
i. intestate
j. personal representative

k. residuary
l. settlor
m. testamentary capacity
n. testamentary intent
o. testator

1. The legal term for a deceased person.

1. _____

2. The individual who is either named in a will or appointed by a court to administer an estate.

2. _____

3. A gift of real property left in a will.   3. _____

4. A gift of personal property left in a will.   4. _____

5. The wishes of a person for the distribution of his or her property as
   expressed in a will.   5. _____

6. The person named in a will to administer the estate.   6. _____

7. A person who makes a will.   7. _____

8. A person who receives gifts of personal property in a will.   8. _____

9. The balance of an estate remaining after all other distributions have
   been made.   9. _____

10. A completely handwritten will.   10. _____

11. The requirement that a person be of legal age and sound mind to
    prepare a will.   11. _____

12. A document that revokes, changes, or revises a will.   12. _____

13. The state of a person who dies without a will.   13. _____

14. A trust set up while a person is still living.   14. _____

15. A person who sets up a living trust.   15. _____

TRUE/FALSE QUIZ

Indicate whether each of the following statements is true or false by writing *T* or *F* in the answer column.

16. The probate court is responsible for supervising the operation of a
    will and the settling of an estate.   16. _____

17. When a person dies intestate, the court appoints an executor to
    settle the estate.   17. _____

18. A tape recording is an acceptable form of will.   18. _____

19. Generally, it is good practice to have witnesses to a will who are
    younger than the person making the will.   19. _____

20. A person of any age can make a will.   20. _____

21. Making a codicil has similar requirements to making a new will.   21. _____

22. One of the primary purposes of setting up a trust is to receive favorable tax treatment.

22. _____

23. An *inter vivos* trust is created by a will.

23. _____

24. A trustee who fails to use prudent judgment in managing a trust can be held liable.

24. _____

25. A trustee does not have authority to make investments.

25. _____

DISCUSSION QUESTIONS

Answer the following questions and discuss them in class.

26. Discuss the reasons a person prepares a will.

_____

_____

27. Discuss types of legacies, bequests, and devises covered by a will.

_____

_____

28. Explain each of the requirements of a valid will.

_____

_____

29. Explain why the law requires the testator to have testamentary capacity.

_____

_____

30. Charges of undue influence are frequently made by those who are denied benefits in a will. What steps might a testator take, while still alive, to reduce the likelihood of these charges being made?

_____

_____

31. Explain the way the court distributes the estate of someone who dies intestate.

_____

_____

THINKING CRITICALLY ABOUT THE LAW

Answer the following questions, which require you to think critically about the legal principles that you learned in this chapter.

32. Wills and the Law Should the law dictate that a person must provide for a spouse and children either by a will or by state law of intestacy? Why or why not?

_____

_____

33. Testamentary Intent If a person dies intestate, is there any way his or her heirs could prove what his or her testamentary intent would have been?

_____

_____

34. Holographic Will Why should a holographic will be legally valid while a transcript of a voice or video recorded will is invalid?

_____

_____

35. Trusts What are the alternatives available to a testator who is considering the creation of a testamentary trust?

_____

_____

36. A Question of Ethics A principal who executes a durable power of attorney for health care appoints an attorney in fact to make health care decisions in the best interest of the principal. Suppose the personal beliefs and values of the attorney in fact are in conflict with those of the principal. In the event the principal becomes incompetent, is it ethical for the attorney in fact to make health care decisions for the principal based on his or her own personal beliefs and values, regardless of the principal's?

_____

_____

CASE QUESTIONS

Study each of the following cases and answer the questions that follow by writing *Yes* or *No* in the answer column.

37. **Testamentary Capacity** Gruen suffered from Alzheimer's disease (a form of progressive mental illness that generally occurs during old age) and lived in a nursing home. His sister, whom he had not seen since they were teenagers, instituted proceedings to have him declared mentally incompetent. A physician testified that Gruen was permanently mentally disabled and that his condition would get progressively worse. Gruen's sister was appointed his guardian. Six months later Gruen executed his last will, leaving his entire estate to his sister. When he died, Gruen's other relatives challenged the will, claiming that Gruen had lacked testamentary capacity.

    a. Does it appear that Gruen had testamentary capacity?   a. _____

    b. Does it appear that the will embodied testamentary intent?   b. _____

    c. Does it appear that the sister exerted undue influence?   c. _____

38. **Requirements of a Valid Will** Popov despised lawyers and refused to have one prepare his will. Instead he went online, got information about estate planning, and wrote a will in his own handwriting in which he left his entire estate to his brother and $1 to each of his three children. The will was not witnessed by anyone. After his death, his children challenged its legality and validity.

    a. Are witnesses always necessary for a handwritten will to be valid?   a. _____

    b. Is this an example of a holographic will?   b. _____

    c. Will the validity of the will be rejected by the court because it was not prepared by an attorney?   c. _____

39. **Trusts** Harley set up a trust, naming himself as trustee, and transferred his entire estate to the trust. The trust was intended to provide him with a lifetime income. After his death, the income from the trust was to be paid to his wife. After her death, the income from the trust was to go to three of their four children, after which the trust would be terminated. The trust specifically stated that one child, Nancy, was not named in the trust because other arrangements had been made for her. When the trust began paying to the three children, but not Nancy, she challenged the validity

of the trust, claiming that the trust was a testamentary trust that did not comply with the state statute on wills.

a. Was this a testamentary trust?   a. _____

b. Was this an *inter vivos* trust?   b. _____

c. Will Nancy succeed in overturning the trust?   c. _____

CASE ANALYSIS

Study each of the following cases carefully. Briefly state the principle of law and your decision.

40. **Executor Misconduct**   Corbin was named as executor in his father's will. While going through his late father's papers, he discovered a promissory note made by Fulsom in the amount of $10,000 that reflected a personal loan the decedent had made before he died. Corbin approached Fulsom and indicated that he would accept $5,000 cash in exchange for the note. Obviously Fulsom's payment would not be included in the assets of the estate. One of the heirs discovered the cash payment and brought suit, charging misconduct. Will Corbin be required to cover the loss suffered by the estate?

Principle of Law:

_____

_____

Decision:

_____

_____

41. **Responsibilities of Personal Representatives**   Aversa, the personal representative of her late father's estate, was presented with evidence that there was still $12,000 owing on his automobile. Rather than have the car repossessed, she borrowed $6,000 and refinanced the balance. Objection was made on the grounds that she had exceeded her authority. Is it likely that the court will approve her actions?

Principle of Law:

_____

_____

Decision:

_____

_____

42. **Trustee Responsibilities** The trustees of a labor union pension fund delivered various stocks and bonds to a bank under an agreement that provided that the bank would act as the trustees' agent in investing the fund's assets. The agreement also provided that the bank was "authorized to invest any assets . . . of the investment fund or to dispose of any such asset or property and invest the proceeds of such disposition, as in its absolute and uncontrolled discretion it deem(ed) suitable." The results of the bank's investments were disappointing. The trustees claimed that since trustees may not delegate their power, the bank breached its contract of agency by making unauthorized investment decisions that decreased the value of the fund. Does it appear that the trustees delegated power to the bank to make the investments? [*Local Union 422, U.A. of Joliet, v. The First National Bank of Joliet*, 417 N.E.2d 1077 (Illinois)]

Principle of Law:

___

___

Decision:

___

___

43. **Testamentary Intent** Before Dora Diggs, a widow, died, she left a hand-written document that read, "I want Tom R. Preston and Mattie Price to be the administrators (executors) to settle my estate." Following this she listed various assets. A dispute arose about whether the decedent, Diggs, intended to give Preston and Price general power to dispose of her property. If this were the interpretation, Preston and Price would be the beneficiaries. Other relatives claimed (1) the document was not really a will at all, (2) Diggs merely wanted to name executors, (3) the document lacked testamentary intent, and (4) Diggs died intestate. If this were the case, state intestacy laws would determine the distribution of property. The other relatives would benefit significantly if this position was the decision of the court. Did the disputed document fail to qualify as a will because of the lack of testamentary intent? [*Preston v. Preston*, 617 S.W.2d 841 (Texas)]

Principle of Law:

___

___

Decision:

___

___

LEGAL RESEARCH

Complete the following activities. Then share your findings with the class.

44. Working in Teams In teams of three or four, interview members of the trust department of a local bank to learn how they handle trusts and perform as executors of estates.

_____

_____

45. Using Technology Using the Internet and search engines, investigate cases that embody the terms *testamentary intent, testamentary capacity, holographic will,* and *intestacy.*

_____

_____

chapter **28**
Intellectual Property

LEARNING OUTCOMES

After studying this chapter and completing the assessment, you will be able to

28.1 Discuss intellectual property and explain how it is protected.

28.2 Explain why trade secrets are so important to a firm, and recognize how they may be protected using restrictive covenants and agreements not to compete.

28.3 Discuss when computer software is protected by trade secret law and when it is protected by licensing.

28.4 Distinguish between the types of trademarks.

28.5 Discuss how trademark law can be applied to cyberspace.

28.6 Explain copyrights and how the doctrine of fair use applies to them.

28.7 Describe how copyright law can be applied to software and cyberspace.

28.8 Identify the requirements for obtaining a patent.

28.9 Explain the challenges associated with applying patent requirements to computer hardware and software.

terms

LEGAL

intellectual property

trade secret

electronic espionage act
of 1996

restrictive covenant

agreement not to
compete

trademark

trade dress

cybersquatting

copyright

infringement

fair use

substantial similarity
test

patent

design patent

The Commiss...
and Tradem...

Has received an application for a patent for a new and useful invention. The title and description of the invention are enclosed. The requirements of law have been complied with, and it has been determined that a patent on the invention shall be granted under the law.

Therefore, this

United States Patent

Grants to the person or persons having title to this patent the right to exclude others from making, using or selling the invention throughout the United States of America for the term of seventeen years from the date of this patent, subject to the payment of maintenance fees as provided by law.

Commissioner of Patents and Trademarks

United States Patent [19]

Farrall

[75] Inventor: Donald R. Farrall, Carro...

[21] Appl. No.: 114,297
[22] Filed:
[51] Int. Cl.⁴ ....
[52] U.S. Cl. ....
[58] Field of Search .... 362/2...
       Referen...
[56]   U.S. PATEN...

INTELLECTUAL PROPERTY

"Intellectual property has the shelf life of a banana."

Bill Gates,
founder of Microsoft, Inc.

28.1 INTELLECTUAL PROPERTY DEFINED

intellectual property
Personal property that includes knowledge, ways of doing things, and expressions of ideas.

As described in Chapter 24, individuals and businesses own both real and personal property. Most people think of property as including only tangible items, such as land and buildings (real property); and automobiles, clothing, and cash (personal property). We now examine another form of personal property, which includes knowledge, ways of doing things, and expressions of ideas. This property is commonly referred to as intellectual property or *intellectual capital*. Often the expressions of such intellectual property are stored in computers and on web pages. Intellectual property is protected through the use of trade secrets, trademarks, copyrights, and patents. This chapter addresses how the law protects intellectual property stored on computers and in other locations.

28.2 TRADE SECRETS

trade secret
Specialized knowledge associated with a particular business, including information gained during employment about such matters as manufacturing processes, practices, devices, customer lists, and other confidential information.

A trade secret is specialized knowledge associated with a particular business. It includes information gained during employment about such matters as manufacturing processes, practices, devices, customer lists, and other confidential information that, in the hands of a competitor, would place a firm at a serious disadvantage. The use of a secret process or a scientific formula, for example, might be part of a worker's job, or the work itself might be so critical that disclosing it would result in injury or loss to the employer. When trade secrets are made public, the firm loses the advantage it had while the secrets were undisclosed. Accordingly, most firms take precautions to make certain that their trade secrets remain confidential.

economic espionage act of 1996
A statute that makes the misappropriation or outright theft of trade secrets a federal crime.

In an effort to protect firms from the theft of trade secrets, the Economic Espionage Act of 1996 was passed. This statute makes the misappropriation or outright theft of trade secrets a federal crime. Under the Economic Espionage Act, if the owner of the trade secret took reasonable precautions to protect it from theft, he or she is generally entitled to recover damages resulting from the loss of the advantage provided by the trade secret.

EXAMPLE 28.1

▶ Starwood Hotels Inc. filed suit against Hilton Hotels Corp., claiming that Hilton unlawfully acquired Starwood trade secrets. According to the lawsuit, Hilton executives enticed two senior Starwood executives to steal confidential research and strategic plans, leave the company, and use the data to launch a luxury hotel line for Hilton. If Starwood can substantiate these claims, the company will likely be entitled to recover monetary damages.

PROTECTING TRADE SECRETS

To protect its business and its trade secrets, an employer may, within reasonable bounds, impose restrictions of secrecy on an employee or forbid the employee to work in the same line of business or for a competing firm if he or she leaves the company. This is accomplished by requiring the employee to sign an employment contract, which governs the relationship between the employer and the employee. Often included in this contract is a clause, or paragraph, called a restrictive covenant.

Restrictive Covenants   A restrictive covenant is an agreement in which the employee agrees not to work in similar employment. Nearly all restrictive covenants are enforceable; the most important factor is whether the covenant is reasonable. For example, it would be reasonable for a firm with a highly secret process to require its key people or scientists to agree not to work for a competitor for, say, three years. But if the same company were to require all employees—including shipping clerks, accountants, and maintenance personnel—to sign such an agreement, it would be unreasonable. Similarly, it would be unreasonable to require even key employees to avoid employment with a competitor for 20 years. It also would be unreasonable to restrict such employees from working anywhere in the world, unless perhaps the company could prove that it faced competition internationally. It must be noted that restrictive covenants could be drafted in such a way so as to prevent the employee from working for a competitor even if the employee is terminated, with or without cause.

> **restrictive covenant**
> An agreement in which the employee agrees not to work in similar employment within a certain geographic area or within a specified period of time.

EXAMPLE 28.2

▶ Copley, a scientist with specialized knowledge in the field of superconductivity, was hired by the Conductol Company to work on the development of highly secret ceramics materials. Copley agreed in writing not to work for any other firm within the same state engaged in the same line of research for three years after leaving Conductol. This contract would be enforceable, since Copley's leaving Conductol and joining a competitor would place Conductol at a serious competitive disadvantage because of the possibility of Copley disclosing Conductol's scientific know-how.

Agreements Not to Compete   When an established business is sold, included in the sale are trade secrets that the business owns (for example, the names and addresses of the firm's customers). Accordingly, the contract for sale usually includes an agreement not to compete, similar to the restrictive covenant placed in an employment contract. In this case, the seller agrees not to begin or operate a similar business within a certain geographic area or within a specified period of time. Again, such agreements are generally held valid provided the restrictions are reasonable.

   Such agreements are highly recommended and legally enforceable because the sale of a business includes more than just a firm's physical property, such as land, buildings, inventory, cash, and so on; the sale also includes the firm's *goodwill*—that is, the name and good reputation of the firm.

> **agreement not to compete**
> An agreement in which the seller of a business agrees not to begin or operate a similar business within a certain geographic area or within a specified period of time.

EXAMPLE 28.3

▶ Gavlick agreed to sell her dry cleaning business to Dotzel. The agreement included a provision that Gavlick would not open another dry cleaning business for five years. Two years later, Gavlick opened a dry cleaning business in a community across the state, 300 miles away. Dotzel, still angry at Gavlick for what he considered a bad bargain in terms of the profit potential of the firm, initiated legal action and pointed to the agreement not to compete that prevented Gavlick from opening a similar business within five years. It is doubtful that a court would enforce the agreement because the new firm was located so far away that it would present no real competition.

28.3 APPLICATION OF TRADE SECRET LAW TO COMPUTER SOFTWARE

Some developers of commercial software have attempted to protect against pirated copying by claiming that the program is a trade secret. Since most software is prepared for wide distribution, it is difficult to protect a computer program from being copied by making this argument. However, if a program, such as a complex accounting and budgeting program, is highly specialized and not intended for wide distribution, it would likely be considered a trade secret.

It is important, however, to recognize that a computer program distributed to a limited number of users is usually not sold; rather, the producer of the program generally retains ownership and licenses the use of it.

EXAMPLE 28.4

▶ The Grish Corporation employed 76 workers, each with his or her own desktop computer. Each employee needed access to software such as word processing, database management, spreadsheet, and presentation preparation. The Grish Corporation licensed all of these from Tecknisoft, a computer software firm, and all 76 employees had the software loaded onto their desktops. Included in the license agreement was a promise by Tecknisoft to update all 76 desktops with the latest versions of the software as these became available.

Producers of computer software have an incentive to treat their works as trade secrets, since there is no set time limit on the protection available for trade secrets as there is for trademarks, patents, and copyrights, to be discussed later in this chapter.

Some producers of software sold to the general public that is intended for wide distribution have attempted to use licensing to protect against losses that would result from widespread copying. Frequently, such producers require that individual users who have purchased the software register their ownership. This is often accomplished by requiring the user to access the producer's home page on the web and enter some personal data. Registration then takes place automatically.

28.4 TRADEMARKS

trademark
Any word, name, symbol, or device or combination thereof adopted and used by a manufacturer or merchant to identify his or her goods and distinguish them from goods manufactured or sold by others.

A trademark, according to the *Lanham Trademark Act of 1947,* is "any word, name, symbol, or device or combination thereof adopted and used by a manufacturer or merchant to identify his (or her) goods and distinguish them from goods manufactured or sold by others." Ownership may be designated in advertising or on a label, package, or letterhead by the use of the word *Registered,* the symbol ®, or the symbol ™. Trademark registrations are issued at the federal level by the *U.S. Patent and Trademark Office* of the Department of Commerce for renewable periods of 10 years. The person in whose name a trademark is registered or to whom it has been assigned may prevent others from (1) using the trademark in connection with competing goods, (2) using the trademark in the same or in a similar line of business, or (3) using marks or names so similar to those registered that reasonable people might confuse them. Some famous trademarks have high degrees of consumer recognition and are directly associated with a specific product or service. To prevent the dilution of these trademarks, they are afforded a higher level of protection and may even be shielded from unrelated, noncompeting uses. Some examples of famous trademarks are "Coca-Cola," "Google," and "Nike."

Symbols used to identify services, as distinguished from goods, are called *service marks*. Since the legal requirements for service marks are very similar to those for trademarks, both are often referred to simply as trademarks. The trademark law also protects other such distinguishing identifiers as *trade characters*—fictional characters such as Betty Crocker, the Green Giant, the Pillsbury Doughboy, and the Marlboro man; *trade names*— the name under which a firm does its business, such as Microsoft or General Motors; and *brand names*—the registered names for products such as Windows or Cadillac. In some cases, a firm may use the same trade name and brand name—for example, Quaker Oats Company and Quaker Oats.

EXAMPLE 28.5

▶ The National Football League (NFL) takes a proactive role in preventing the unauthorized commercial use of its trademarked phrases "NFL," "Super Bowl," and "Super Sunday." In lieu of the trademarked phrase "Super Bowl," there have been frequent commercial uses of the phrase "the Big Game." When the NFL attempted to trademark that phrase as well, two colleges that have referred to their game as "the Big Game" for more than 100 years objected. The NFL rescinded its trademark application.

TRADE DESS

Trade dress is a distinctive, nonfunctional feature that distinguishes a merchant's or manufacturer's goods or services from those of another. The trade dress of a product relates

trade dress
A distinctive, nonfunctional feature that distinguishes a merchant's or manufacturer's goods or services from those of another.

Starbucks Coffee Company is a registered trademark of Starbucks Corporation.

to its total image and can include the color of the packaging or the configuration of goods. Examples of trade dress include the packaging for Wonder Bread, the tray configuration for Healthy Choice frozen dinners, and the color scheme of Subway sandwich shops. Seeking protection against trade dress infringements can be vital to the survival of a business.

EXAMPLE 28.6

▶ Anheuser-Busch, in a controversial marketing ploy, produced and distributed Bud Light beer in cans that prominently displayed local colleges' team colors. Some colleges objected to this marketing scheme and informed Anheuser-Busch that the company was infringing on school trade dress. Rather than risk being sued for trade dress infringement, Anheuser-Busch complied with all official requests to cease producing beer cans displaying school colors.

HOW TRADEMARKS ARE LOST

Most firms that have registered trademarks spend considerable amounts of money to research, design, register, and advertise their trademarks. These firms naturally regard them as valuable property and take appropriate measures to protect them. Yet many trademarks have been lost because they were so successful, or so often misused, that they entered the language as ordinary words. That is, to the general public, the trademark came to mean the same as the product, no matter who had manufactured it. Such words that become a common part of the language are called *generic*. Many trademarks that were once the proud possessions of particular companies have been lost in this way. Examples of these former trademarks include *escalator, kerosene, cellophane, aspirin, frisbee,* and *spearmint.*

EXAMPLE 28.7

▶ Escalator was the registered trademark for a moving staircase manufactured by the Otis Elevator Company. The Escalator brand of moving staircase was widely advertised, and the general public began to use the word *escalator* to mean "moving staircase." The manufacturer even advertised in *Architectural Forum* magazine that Otis provided "the utmost in safe, efficient, economical elevator and escalator operation." Because the term *escalator* had become generic, Otis lost its registered trademark.

In Example 28.7, by using the word *escalator* in a generic way, Otis failed to distinguish between the trademark for its own product (escalator) and the generic term for another product (elevator). Otis itself thus helped to prove that *escalator* had become a synonym for "moving staircase." The magazine advertisement was used as evidence in proceedings in the Patent and Trademark Office, which led to the cancellation of the Otis trademark.

PROTECTING A TRADEMARK

Under federal law, the owner of a trademark loses rights to it "when any course of conduct of the registrant, including acts of omission or commission, causes the mark to lose its significance as an indication of origin." It is important that all executives, employees, and the firm's advertising agency try to protect the firm's trademark by following a few basic rules:

▶ *Never use the trademark without the generic name of the product.* A trademark is a proper adjective and should never be used as a common descriptive adjective, verb, or noun. For example, it is incorrect to say "a xerox machine" (common adjective), "Please xerox these papers" (verb), or "The xerox is down the hall" (noun). Correct usage would be "A Xerox photocopy machine," "Please photocopy these papers," and "The Xerox photocopier is down the hall."

▶ *Never use the trademark in the possessive form.* It is incorrect to say, "Ford's excellent performance." The correct form would be "the excellent performance of Ford automobiles."

▶ *Never use the trademark in the plural.* It is incorrect to say, "The doctor prescribed Prozac." The correct form would be, "The doctor prescribed Prozac antidepressant medication."

▶ *Always identify trademarks.* A trademark must always be used in a manner that will distinguish it from the surrounding words. Trademarks should be completely capitalized, given initial capital letters and put in quotation marks, or at least given initial capitals. The generic name should not be capitalized. Correct examples are SECRET deodorant, "Secret" deodorant, and Secret deodorant. Trademarks also may be identified by the symbol ® or ™.

▶ *Continuously monitor the way others use your trademarks.* Most firms use a clipping service that reports periodically on the appearance of a firm's name in publications monitored by the service. Any improper use of the firm's trademarks should be brought to the attention of the editor or writer responsible. Should a challenge to the firm's ownership of a trademark arise, the record of these efforts could be used as evidence that the firm had taken positive action to protect its trademark.

28.5 APPLICATION OF TRADEMARK LAW TO CYBERSPACE

A business needs to be extremely vigilant to ensure that its valuable trademark is protected in cyberspace.

DOMAIN NAMES

A *domain name* is a unique identifier that serves as an address for a web page. It consists of several characters and numerals, followed by a suffix that can be *.com, .org, .gov, .edu,* or the like. It is extremely important to companies that they own the sequence of characters and numerals in order that web users may be properly directed to the company's site, on

A business needs to ensure that its trademark is protected in cyberspace.

which the user may wish to place an order to purchase goods or services, to contact the company, or to find out more about the company's products or business. Accordingly, the law of trademarks applies to the ownership of domain names.

Currently, a private firm is responsible for assigning domain names. An individual or company, however, will not be granted use of a domain name unless he or she first promises not to infringe upon anyone else's trademark.

Registering or using another person's or company's domain name in bad faith for the purpose of earning a profit is referred to as cybersquatting. The *Anti-Cybersquatting Consumer Protection Act of 1999* makes this illegal. One of the many purposes of the law is to prevent someone from buying up domain names and then reselling these back to the companies who own the trademark. To win a lawsuit using this law, a firm would need to demonstrate to the court that

cybersquatting
Registering or using another person's or company's domain name in bad faith for the purpose of earning a profit.

▶ There was bad faith on the part of the cybersquatter.

▶ The company owns the trademark.

▶ The trademark is distinctive.

▶ The domain name being used by the cybersquatter is identical to (or confusingly close to) the trademarked name owned by the complaining party.

28.6 COPYRIGHTS

A copyright is a valid, government-granted protection given to creators of literary, creative, or artistic works such as books, magazines, music, dramatic works, maps, works of art, motion pictures, computer programs, computer games, and videos. In order to receive copyright protection, such works must be (1) original, (2) creative, and (3) expressed in a tangible form. Works produced and copyrighted in one country are protected under the laws of most other countries (see Chapter 35). A copyright cannot prevent the copying of an idea, but only the way it is expressed. Under the current copyright law, a created work is protected for the lifetime of the creator plus 70 years. If the work is produced as a result of the creator's employment, the term is 95 years from the first publication, or 120 years after the creation of the work, whichever is shorter. Material that has been copyrighted is often noted by the symbol ©. If the creator of the work wishes, a formal application for a copyright may be made to the Federal Copyright Office of the Library of Congress. Copying without permission is referred to as infringement.

copyright
A valid, government-granted protection given to creators of literary, creative, or artistic works.

infringement
Copying another's literary, creative, or artistic works without permission.

EXAMPLE 28.8

▶ Harwood was the author of a cookbook. After her book had been published, Harwood discovered another cookbook written by Pauling that was published three years after hers. She noticed that at least one-third of Pauling's book was a direct, word-for-word copy of hers. Harwood or her publisher could bring legal action charging copyright infringement.

FAIR USE

The law sometimes does allow limited copying if such copying falls under the doctrine of fair use. Fair use applies when the copyrighted material is copied without authorization for use in connection with criticism, news reporting, research, education, or parody.

fair use
Limited copying allowed when the copyrighted material is copied without authorization for use in connection with criticism, news reporting, research, education, or parody.

EXAMPLE 28.9

▶ Johansson, the mayor of a city, delivered a speech in which he made several promises. McSwain, a "shock disk jockey" on a local radio station, altered the speech so that it made Johansson appear silly and irresponsible. Since the alterations were clearly made to criticize and parody Johansson's real words, this unauthorized copying would be considered a fair use.

28.7 APPLICATION OF COPYRIGHT LAW TO SOFTWARE AND CYBERSPACE

The *Computer Software Copyright Act of 1980* defines a computer program as a "set of statements or instructions to be used directly or indirectly in a computer in order to bring about a certain act." Pursuant to this law, however, it is not an infringement if the owner of a computer program makes a single copy. Indeed, sellers of computer programs at times encourage the user to make a "working copy" and to safeguard the original CD or disk. The chief concern of software developers is widespread copying and the loss of revenue that would result.

In cases where there is the need to determine whether a person or business has violated the copyright of another, courts use the substantial similarity test. This test is used to determine whether an ordinary reasonable observer comparing two works would have to conclude that the work being questioned was copied from the other. While this test, which applies the judgment of the ordinary reasonable person, seems to resolve most cases involving conventional copyrighted works, the courts rely heavily on the testimony of expert witnesses and professionals in cases involving allegations of computer software copyright infringement.

It should be noted that the substantial similarity test used to determine infringement in computer software cases is nearly identical to that used to judge the claim of a songwriter who alleges that his or her music or lyrics have been wrongfully copied.

substantial similarity test
A test that is used to determine whether an ordinary reasonable observer comparing two works would have to conclude that the work being questioned was copied from the other.

EXAMPLE 28.10

▶ A website named BlueBeat began offering cheap downloads of hundreds of Beatles songs. The owner of BlueBeat claimed that he was the copyright owner of these songs because he altered them with a "psycho acoustic simulation" device. Since the songs sounded almost identical to the original Beatles recordings, the court found in favor of the Beatles' music rights holders and ordered BlueBeat to remove the songs from the website. [*Capitol Records, LLC, et al. v. Bluebeat, Inc., et al.*, Case No. CV 09-8030-JFW (JCx) United States District Court (CA)]

There is no legal distinction between copying from a hard copy and copying electronically. Thus, the individual who downloads a newspaper article from a website or who copies a posting from a blog and then pastes it into a word processing file is liable for infringement. In general, it is also deemed illegal to copy, or even trade, online music without first obtaining permission. The legal issues associated with distributing and sharing online music and other forms of entertainment will be discussed more fully in Chapter 30.

28.8 PATENTS

patent
A valid, government-granted protection awarded to inventors that gives the patent holder the exclusive right to manufacture, use, and sell the invention.

A patent is a valid, government-granted protection awarded to inventors that gives the patent holder the exclusive right to manufacture, use, and sell the invention for 20 years. A patent cannot be renewed. The purpose of patents is to encourage inventors to develop new products and new ideas and to reward them for having done so. Patents, like trademarks, are issued by the U.S. Patent and Trademark Office in Washington, D.C. Patents are issued for devices that are useful, novel, and nonobvious creations. Anyone who manufactures or sells, without permission, a product that has been patented by another can be charged with infringement. A person who profits from unauthorized use of a patented invention is liable to the patent holder for all profits resulting from such unauthorized use and for any other penalties provided by the patent laws.

Historically, patents have been granted for such inventions as machines, processes, or certain chemical compounds, but patents also have been issued for scientifically engineered bacteria as well as genetically engineered life forms. Recently there has been a question as to whether DNA strains should be patentable.

EXAMPLE 28.11

▶ Chakrabarty, a biologist, developed a new strain of bacteria that could alter the nature of crude oil. Recognizing the potential of the discovery for breaking down oil spills, he applied for a patent. Initially the Patent and Trademark Office refused to issue a patent because the development did not meet the usual standards for inventions. After Chakrabarty brought suit, the Patent and Trademark Office widened its qualifications for acceptance, and the patent was issued.

28.9 APPLICATION OF PATENT LAW TO COMPUTER HARDWARE AND SOFTWARE

In order for a patent to be issued, several requirements must be met. The requirements, and their application to computer hardware and software, are described as follows:

▶ *The invention must be a device.* This is a term that has broad application in patent law and may include a design or process. In the case of computer-related inventions, the requirement that an invention be a device is often difficult to meet because many computer features are not devices at all, but rather are based on mathematical formulas or on the manipulation of electronic signals and data.

▶ *The invention must be useful.* Since patent law requires that an invention be useful, in order to be patentable a computer program must be more than just an amusing curiosity.

▶ *The invention must be novel (or new).* Since, to be patentable, a computer program must be original, merely adapting another, similar program would not satisfy the requirement that the invention be novel.

▶ *The invention must be nonobvious.* A computer program, for example, that merely computes the total of a series of numbers would not satisfy the requirement that the device be nonobvious. Since many computer programs are designed to do certain tasks electronically that have previously been done mechanically, it is often difficult to satisfy the novelty and nonobviousness requirements.

EXAMPLE 28.12

▶ Forlee, a secondary school teacher, invented a handheld device for use in grading examination papers. The invention enabled the user to pass the device over a specially designed student answer sheet. The device could identify correct answers, store the information gathered, and then feed the information into a separate personal computer. A specialized program included in the device could enable the computer to generate various statistical analyses of student and class achievement. Forlee applied for a patent for the handheld device, including the computer program. The Patent and Trademark Office would probably grant a patent because, taken together, the device and the computer program meet the requirements that the invention be a device, useful, novel, and nonobvious.

design patent
A patent awarded to individuals or business firms to protect distinctive patterns, figures, and shapes and to prevent unauthorized copying.

DESIGN PATENTS

Combining some of the characteristics of both patents and copyrights, a design patent is awarded to individuals or business firms to protect distinctive patterns, figures, and shapes and to prevent unauthorized copying. Design patents have been issued for soft drink bottles, wine decanters, silverware patterns, and other unique designs. Design patents, however, are granted for periods of less than 20 years.

CHAPTER SUMMARY

1. Intellectual property is a form of personal property. It includes knowledge, ways of doing things, and expressions of ideas. Intellectual property is protected through the use of trade secrets, trademarks, copyrights, and patents.

2. When its trade secrets are made public, a firm loses the advantage it had while the secrets were undisclosed. To protect its trade secrets, an employer or seller of a business may, through a restrictive covenant or an agreement not to compete, impose restrictions of secrecy on an employee or buyer of the business or forbid them from working in the same line of business or for a competing firm.

3. If a computer program is highly specialized and not intended for wide distribution, it would likely be considered a trade secret. A computer program distributed to a limited number of users is usually not sold; rather, the producer of the program generally retains ownership and licenses the use of it.

4. A trademark is any word, name, symbol, or device or combination thereof adopted and used by a manufacturer or merchant to identify his or her goods and distinguish them from goods manufactured or sold by others. Symbols used to identify services, as distinguished from goods, are called service marks. Trade characters are fictional characters; trade names are the names under which a firm does its business; and brand names are the registered names for products. Trade dress is a distinctive, nonfunctional feature that distinguishes a merchant's or manufacturer's goods or services from those of another.

5. A domain name is a unique identifier that serves as an address for a web page. To protect its domain name from a cybersquatter, a firm would need to demonstrate to the court that (a) there was bad faith on the part of the cybersquatter, (b) the firm owns the trademark, (c) the trademark is distinctive, and (d) the domain name being used by the cybersquatter is identical to (or confusingly close to) the trademarked name owned by the complaining party.

6. A copyright is a valid government-granted protection given to creators of literary, creative, or artistic works such as books, magazines, music, dramatic works, maps, works of art, motion pictures, computer programs, computer games, and videos. Fair use applies when the copyrighted material is copied without authorization for use in connection with criticism, news reporting, research, education, or parody.

7. Courts determine whether a person or business has violated the copyright of another's computer software through the use of the substantial similarity test. This test is used to determine whether an ordinary reasonable observer comparing two programs would have to conclude that the software being questioned was copied from the other.

8. To obtain a patent on an invention, it must be a device that is useful, novel, and nonobvious.

9. It is difficult to patent computer-related inventions because many of these are not devices; are mere curiosities; adapt other, similar programs; or are designed to do certain tasks electronically that have previously been done mechanically.

CHAPTER TWENTY-EIGHT
ASSESSMENT

MATCHING LEGAL TERMS

Match each of the numbered definitions with the correct term in the following list. Write the letter of your choice in the answer column.

a. goodwill   **c.** trade secret   **e.** trademark
b. trade name   **d.** brand name

1. Specialized knowledge associated with a particular business.   1. _____

2. The name and good reputation of a firm.   2. _____

3. A word, name, symbol, device, or combination thereof adopted and used by a manufacturer or merchant to identify his or her goods and distinguish them from goods manufactured or sold by others.   3. _____

4. The name under which a firm does its business.   4. _____

5. The registered name for a product.   5. _____

TRUE/FALSE QUIZ

Indicate whether each of the following statements is true or false by writing *T* or *F* in the answer column.

6. A contract in which an employee agrees not to work for a competitor for a reasonable period of time is unenforceable.   6. _____

7. A buyer who purchases a business from a seller receives title to the physical assets but does not gain the goodwill of the business.   7. _____

8. A complex, highly specialized accounting and budgeting software program not intended for widespread distribution would likely be considered a trade secret.   8. _____

9. There is no set time limit on the legal protection available for trade secrets.   9. _____

10. It is illegal for a software producer to require that a user register his or her ownership with the producer.   10. _____

11. Ownership of a trademark is typically noted by using the letter *O* in a circle.

11. _____

12. Trademark registrations are issued by the U.S. Patent and Trademark Office of the Department of Commerce.

12. _____

13. The Green Giant is an example of a trade name.

13. _____

14. Words or terms that become a common part of the language are referred to as *generic*.

14. _____

15. The law relating to trademarks applies equally to the law relating to domain names on the web.

15. _____

16. The Anti-Cybersquatting Consumer Protection Act of 1999 makes cybersquatting illegal even if the cybersquatter acts in good faith.

16. _____

17. Since a copyright covers only an expression in words, works of art cannot be protected under copyright law.

17. _____

18. An infringement is a special form of design patent.

18. _____

19. A person who profits from unauthorized use of a patented invention is liable to the patent holder for all profits resulting from such unauthorized use and for any other penalties provided by the patent laws.

19. _____

20. The courts have ruled that genetically engineered life forms are not patentable.

20. _____

DISCUSSION QUESTIONS

Answer the following questions and discuss them in class.

21. Name five rules that a firm, or its advertising agency, should follow to protect its trademarks.

_____

_____

22. What must a firm prove in court to win a lawsuit filed against a cybersquatter?

_____

_____

23. Give several examples of literary, creative, or artistic works for which a company may be granted a copyright.

_____

_____

24. When does the fair use doctrine apply to copyrighted works?

_____

_____

25. Name the requirements that must be met for an invention to receive a patent.

_____

_____

26. Distinguish between design patents and other forms of patents.

_____

_____

THINKING CRITICALLY ABOUT THE LAW

Answer the following questions, which require you to think critically about the legal principles that you learned in this chapter.

27. **Intellectual Property** Why is it important to society that the law protect intellectual property?

_____

_____

28. **Protecting Trade Secrets** Should an individual who is offered an employment position sign an employment contract that contains a restrictive covenant?

_____

_____

29. **How Trademarks Are Lost** What is the justification for allowing a trademark owned by a company to become generic?

_____

_____

30. **Domain Names** Who should be responsible for assigning domain names: a private company or the federal government?

   _____

   _____

31. **A Question of Ethics** In your opinion, is it acceptable conduct for a firm who publishes adult web sites to take over the domain name of another, well-known company after the time allotted to use that name has expired?

   _____

   _____

CASE QUESTIONS

Study each of the following cases. Answer the questions that follow by writing *Yes* or *No* in the answer column.

32. **Restrictive Covenants** Morales, an oral surgeon in a rural area, wanted to open a second office in a nearby town. She hired Ng, a recently graduated oral surgeon, to operate this new office for three years. The contract of employment specified that Ng would not, during the "three years, or forever thereafter," practice dentistry within the rural area aside from working for Morales. After the three years had passed, Ng left the employ of Morales and opened his own practice of dentistry and oral surgery within the rural area. Morales brought suit, charging Ng with violating the restrictive covenant in their contract of employment.

   a. May Ng argue that the restrictive covenant is void because it lasts for an unreasonably long period of time?   a. _____

   b. May Ng argue that the restrictive covenant is void because it covers an unreasonably large geographic area?   b. _____

   c. May Ng argue that the restrictive covenant is void because it applies to dentists, who are professionals?   c. _____

33. **Trademarks** Hanna developed a refreshing drink using banana extract. She started a business, the Hanna Soft Drink Corporation, and began bottling and selling her soft drinks under the name "Hanna Banana." After a short time, she realized that she would need to protect her intellectual property.

   a. May Hanna register the trade name "Hanna Soft Drink Company"?   a. _____

   b. May Hanna register the brand name "Hanna Banana"?   b. _____

   c. Is it possible that "Hanna Banana" could ever become generic?   c. _____

34. **Copyrights** Legin, a professional writer, discovered that substantial amounts of a copyrighted article he had written 10 years earlier were included in a commercially

published textbook written by Gant. When Legin confronted the publisher of the book, the publishing company denied knowledge of the use of Legin's copyrighted article and also pointed out that the text was intended for educational use.

a. Does Legin have recourse to a legal remedy?

a. _____

b. Does the educational use of the textbook have any bearing on the case?

b. _____

c. Does the fact that the article had been written 10 years earlier affect Legin's copyright protection?

c. _____

CASE ANALYSIS

Study each of the following cases carefully. Briefly state the principle of law and your decision.

35. Application of Trademark Law to Cyberspace Calvin Designer Label developed a website using the terms *Playboy* and *Playmate* to direct users to the site. Calvin also used both terms in the body of its web pages to which users were directed. Playboy Enterprises, Inc. owned the trademarks to both words *Playboy* and *Playmate*. Playboy Enterprises filed a lawsuit seeking to have the court issue an injunction ordering Calvin to cease using the two words. Is the court likely to grant Playboy an injunction? [*Playboy Enterprises, Inc. v. Calvin Designer Label*, 985 F. Supp. 1218 (California)]

Principle of Law:

_____

_____

Decision:

_____

_____

36. Domain Names Webster R. McGee developed a website using the domain name of "Card Service." Cardservice International, Inc., a separate company, maintained that the term used by McGee was confusingly similar to the word owned by Cardservice. Cardservice filed a lawsuit requesting that the court issue an injunction directing McGee to cease using the term "Card Service." Is Cardservice likely to be successful in obtaining the permanent injunction? [*Cardservice International, Inc., v. Webster R. McGee et alia*, 950 F. Supp. 737 (Virginia)]

Principle of Law:

_____

_____

Decision:

_____

_____

37. Copyrights Rural Telephone Service Company was a public utility providing telephone service to several communities in Kansas. Rural published a typical telephone directory consisting of white pages and yellow pages. Feist Publications was a publishing company specializing in publishing telephone directories for large geographical areas. Feist copied much of the white pages of Rural's directory without permission. Rural sued Feist for copyright infringement and won. Feist appealed to the Supreme Court of the United States. Is the Supreme Court likely to rule that Rural's copyright is valid? [*Feist Publications, Inc. v. Rural Telephone Service Company,* 499 U.S. 340 (Kansas)]

Principle of Law:

_____

_____

Decision:

_____

_____

38. Application of Copyright Law to Computers Six freelance writers sold articles for publication in print to a variety of popular newspapers and magazines, including *The New York Times, Newsday,* and *Sports Illustrated.* Nexis allowed computer users to retrieve the online version of these articles, which also were placed electronically onto CD-ROMs. The six freelance writers filed a lawsuit, arguing that, while they had granted permission to have their work appear in print form, they had never granted permission to have their work appear in electronic form. Are the plaintiffs likely to succeed in this lawsuit? [*Tasini v. New York Times Co., et alia,* 972 F. Supp. 804 (New York)]

Principle of Law:

_____

_____

Decision:

_____

_____

LEGAL RESEARCH

Complete the following activities. Share your findings with the class.

39. Working in Teams In teams of three or four, assume that you are the co-owners of a five-star restaurant located in the heart of a large city in the United States. First, draft a clause in a contract that might serve as a restrictive covenant for prospective employees who wish to apply for a server's job. Next, assuming that you will be purchasing a second restaurant from a seller in a different city, draft a covenant not to compete that could be included in the contract for sale.

_____

_____

40. Using Technology Using the Internet and search engines, locate a governmental website that addresses the issue of how to obtain a patent. What information is available on this website? If you had developed or created an invention, would you find the information helpful in protecting your intellectual property?

_____

_____

chapter 29
Computer Privacy and Speech

LEGAL terms

cookie
spyware
phishing
spoofing
hacker
virus
Electronic Communications Privacy Act (ECPA)
USA Patriot Act
Computer Fraud and Abuse Act (CFAA)

worm
Electronic Funds Transfer Act (EFTA) of 1979
public figure
spam
Controlling the Assault of Non-Solicited Pornography and Marketing Act (CAN-SPAM)

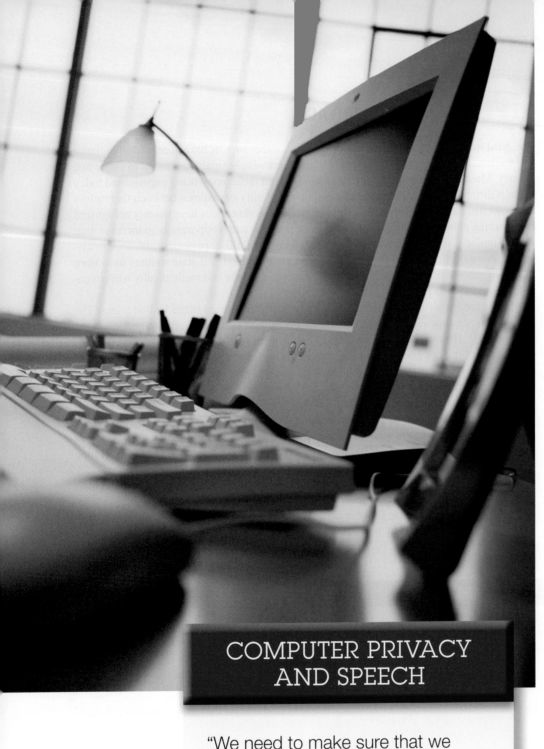

COMPUTER PRIVACY
AND SPEECH

"We need to make sure that we
are better prepared against cyber-
attacks than we turned out to be
against hurricanes."

Hillary Clinton,
United States Secretary of State

29.1 COMPUTER PRIVACY

The great majority of people in the United States either own or have access to a computer and the Internet. As a result, there is a new and increasingly significant threat to individual privacy. Most experts agree that the rapid advances in technology being experienced today make it difficult for people to maintain online anonymity or distance between themselves and powerful interests. Online marketers of products and services have quickly recognized that learning about consumers' online behavior presents a real opportunity to increase their sales. Similarly, there are those in our society who, for thrill or personal gain, seek to discover personal information about individuals. Many federal and state statutes have been passed to address these issues, but laws are developed slowly and methodically while technology expands at a rapid rate.

There are two distinct rights of privacy generally recognized in the United States. The first is a constitutional right to privacy, which is upheld by the U.S. Supreme Court (see Appendix A). However, there is a second kind of privacy that, prior to the prominence of computer use, did not need much protection. This privacy protects information about individuals from widespread distribution. Where people shop, what videos they rent, how much life insurance they have, and what kind of pets they own are all bits of personal information that people may or may not wish to share with others. In the past, when such information was stored in the home, individuals were protected by laws against trespass. No one could enter a home without permission and gather this information. Now that this information is stored on computers and across networks, the law has had a difficult time providing as much protection.

There are also times when people may make statements on the web pertaining to their views on certain issues. These views may be expressed in chat rooms, on websites, on blogs, or in e-mail messages. In most cases, a person's privacy is not protected when he or she makes such statements by using these technologies.

EXAMPLE 29.1

▶ Pietro, who works for Howard Sportswear, received an employee evaluation that was not very laudatory. Pietro, angry that he did not get the raise to which he believed he was entitled, wrote a series of statements in a chat room complaining that his employer treated the employees poorly. The president of Howard Sportswear learned of the postings, and Pietro was fired. There is little that Pietro can do to get his job back.

COOKIES

cookie
A file that is embedded on the hard drive of a computer, often without a person's knowledge, that collects and stores information about the user and his or her online behavior, including websites that have been visited.

A cookie is a file that is embedded on the hard drive of a computer, often without a person's knowledge, that collects and stores information about the user and his or her behavior, including the websites that have been visited. Cookies are an important marketing tool because they allow companies who sell on the web to know which products and services interest a person. While there are currently no federal laws prohibiting the use of cookies when gathering information regarding adults, the *Children's Online Privacy Protection Act* prohibits this practice when minors are involved, unless there is parental consent.

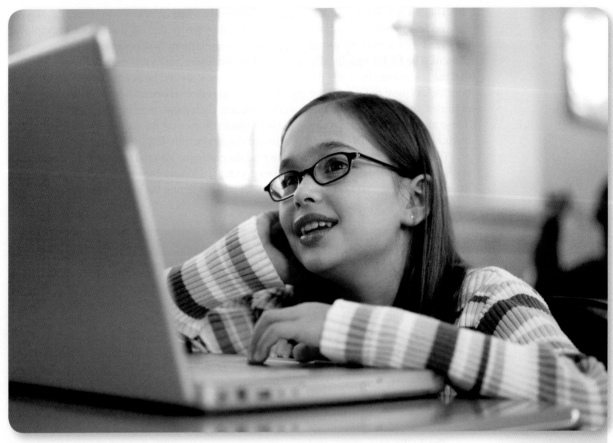

Information gathered from minors through cookies is regulated by the Children's Online Privacy Protection Act.

In addition to cookies, some websites secretly install spyware, which is software that can change a computer's security settings or steal a victim's personal information, such as e-mail addresses, bank account numbers, and credit card numbers. Closely related to spyware are phishing, which is the practice of tricking individuals into disclosing such personal information via e-mail; and spoofing, in which a legitimate website is reproduced to fool users into thinking that they are connected to a trusted site. Again, to address these problems, federal statutes have been proposed but not yet enacted.

Consumers who believe that their right to privacy is being violated by the embedding of software can complain to the Federal Trade Commission, a federal regulatory agency with responsibility to ensure that companies do not use unfair trade practices.

spyware
Software that can change a computer's security settings or steal a victim's personal information, such as e-mail addresses, bank account numbers, and credit card numbers.

phishing
The practice of tricking individuals into disclosing personal information via e-mail.

spoofing
A practice in which a legitimate website is reproduced to fool users into thinking that they are connected to a trusted site.

ELECTRONIC MAIL

Frequently federal and state courts will determine a person's right to privacy by what an individual might reasonably expect under the circumstances. For example, if an individual mails a letter to a friend, he or she could reasonably expect that no one other than the recipient will read the letter. Similarly, persons who provide information via electronic mail (e-mail) from their homes can reasonably expect their statements to be private; hence, the content of e-mail messages is considered protected. The *Electronic Communications Privacy Act (ECPA)* makes it a federal crime to monitor e-mail during real time—when it is being sent or received. It should be pointed out, however, that law enforcement officials may monitor e-mail when they are granted such right by a court.

The law relating to e-mail is applied differently when a person is at work. Employees have no reasonable expectation of privacy while they are on the job, and in fact an employer may read an employee's e-mail at any time, even without first obtaining the employee's consent. The ECPA specifically provides that employers may view e-mail. Despite the fact that the law expressly grants this right to employers, it should be noted that most employers nonetheless have policies to the effect that e-mail sent or received while on the employer's premises, or while using the employer's computer equipment, may be read by the employer. These also may state that an employee is forbidden to encrypt messages or install passwords unknown to the employer or without the employer's permission.

Even if an employer promises not to read the employee's e-mail messages, courts in some states have still ruled that the promise does not create a reasonable expectation of privacy, and the employer may change his or her mind later without letting the employee know.

EXAMPLE 29.2

▶ Jackson, an employee of Chang Manufacturing Co., regularly placed orders for raw materials with Ruiz, an employee of Kleinman Glass Corporation. He spoke frequently on the telephone with her, and they developed a friendly relationship. Jackson then sent Ruiz an e-mail asking her to go out to dinner with him. Jackson's immediate supervisor at Chang read the e-mail, wrote a memorandum disciplining him for violating company policy, and placed a copy of the memorandum in his personnel file. Jackson's discipline would be upheld by a court, and should he apply for another position at a different company, the contents of the e-mail could be disclosed to the prospective employer.

The ECPA also grants an *Internet service provider (ISP)* the right to monitor e-mail messages without the subscriber's consent. Despite possessing this legal right, most ISPs have their subscribers electronically sign a service agreement in which the subscriber acknowledges that the ISP may examine the contents of both sent and received e-mail, and that there is no expectation of privacy.

29.2 COMPUTER CRIME

Many computer crimes, particularly those in which a computer is used as a means of engaging in criminal activity, are simply technologically advanced versions of standard crimes. A bank employee, for example, who programs the bank's computer to make deductions from one or several accounts and to deposit the funds to an account set up and controlled by the employee could be prosecuted for embezzlement even though he or she had not touched actual currency.

Another type of computer crime concerns unauthorized access to computer data. Computers are often linked to other computers by telephone, modems, cable lines, or satellite so that funds or data can be transferred from one to another. While a password is needed to gain access to a computer, often simple, obvious passwords are unwisely chosen, and as a result, unauthorized individuals can easily guess what they are and gain access. Lack of security relating to confidential passwords also results when these keys to entry fall into the wrong hands.

Unauthorized access to computers invites the following violations of rights:

- ▶ Invasion of privacy.
- ▶ Unauthorized use of the computer itself (using another person's property without permission).
- ▶ Manipulation of financial, medical, and other records.
- ▶ Unauthorized access to databases.

EXAMPLE 29.3

▶ City Central College had facilities for student use of computers and access to the Internet. Students had special passwords that enabled them to access an information database through the City Central College Library. Elkin learned Wilbur's password and used it to access the database to gather information for a term paper. The charges incurred by Elkin's unauthorized use of the password appeared on Wilbur's credit card. This use is not very different from Elkin using Wilbur's credit card to purchase merchandise at the local department store.

Examples of unauthorized use of computers include transferring funds from one bank account to another, changing students' grades in college computer files, and crediting accounts for purchases made.

A person who gains unauthorized access to computers, either for mischief or with criminal intent, is called a hacker. For personal gain or simply for the thrill, a hacker may cause the spread of a virus. The term *virus* in this context refers to instructions hidden in software with the potential to cause significant damage to both hardware and software; it has come into use because of the many similarities between these hidden software messages and a biological virus. Like a biological virus, a computer virus can lie dormant in a computer for long periods and spring into action at a predetermined date and time, or when a certain event occurs. Because software provides instructions to a computer, instructions contained in the virus can direct the computer to do any number of things, including erase data, generate data that take up valuable storage space, and conceal the virus itself. Some viruses are little more than a hacker's prank, consisting of instructions that tell the computer to display "Gotcha" or some other message on the screen on a certain date and time. Not all viruses are pranks, however, and some cause major disruptions in computer operations. Frequently, viruses are spread by attaching themselves to the user's e-mail list, located in the computer's address book on the hard drive.

hacker
A person who gains unauthorized access to computers either for mischief or with criminal intent.

virus
Instructions hidden in software with the potential to cause significant damage to both hardware and software.

29.3 COMPUTER CRIME LEGISLATION

Specific computer crime statutes have been enacted by both federal and state legislatures. These statutes include the Electronic Communications Privacy Act, the Computer Abuse and Fraud Act, the Electronic Funds Transfer Act, and other laws that govern cyberspace activities.

A virus has the potential to cause significant damage to both hardware and software.

THE ELECTRONIC COMMUNICATIONS PRIVACY ACT

The Electronic Communications Privacy Act (ECPA) is a statute that addresses hacking and other forms of illegal conduct by making it a federal crime to gain unauthorized access to any communication that is stored on a computer system. This law states that individuals may not gain access without permission to an electronic communication system, or to exceed the authorization they have been granted. It is important to note that in the case of the ECPA, the individual must act intentionally in order to commit a crime. In other words, accidentally intruding on another person's computer files is not a crime under the ECPA.

It is also a crime under the ECPA to disclose to a third party the contents of stored computer information that has been obtained without permission. This is logical; if a person does not have permission to retrieve information, he or she also does not have permission to disclose it to someone else.

Electronic Communications Privacy Act (ECPA)
A federal statute that addresses hacking and other forms of illegal conduct by making it a crime to gain unauthorized access to any communication that is stored on a computer system.

THE USA PATRIOT ACT

The USA Patriot Act (which stands for *United and Strengthening America by Providing Appropriate Tools Required to Intercept and Obstruct Terrorism*) was passed in response to the events that transpired on September 11, 2001. Specific provisions of the USA Patriot Act include (1) lowering the standards required for law enforcement officials and government agents to monitor e-mail and personal electronic information; (2) allowing increased government cybersurveillance; and (3) making it easier to charge persons with serious computer-related crimes.

The USA Patriot Act
A federal statute that lowers the standards required for law enforcement officials and government agents to monitor e-mail and personal electronic information, allows increased government cybersurveillance, and makes it easier to charge persons with serious computer-related crimes.

THE COMPUTER FRAUD AND ABUSE ACT

The Computer Fraud and Abuse Act (CFAA), the first federal computer crime statute in the United States, covers the following areas:

Computer Fraud and Abuse Act (CFAA)
A federal statute that prohibits unlawful access to computers used in national defense, by financial institutions, or by governments.

▶ **National defense.** It is an unlawful use of a computer to gain access to secret information that could affect national security.

▶ **Financial institutions.** It is unlawful to use without authorization a computer to gain access to the financial records of a financial institution—including information held in any file maintained by a consumer reporting agency.

▶ **Government computers.** It is unlawful to access without authorization any department or agency computer used for federal government business.

In addition, the CFAA at times expands upon the ECPA, discussed earlier. While under the ECPA there must be an intent to exceed authorization for a crime to be committed, the CFAA does not require such intent if the intrusion onto another person's computer-stored information causes damage. In other words, even if a person's intent is good, if his or her conduct accidentally causes damage, he or she may be prosecuted for a federal crime under the CFAA.

EXAMPLE 29.4

▶ Witkowski released a worm (a type of virus that replicates itself and uses memory but cannot attach itself to other programs) to demonstrate vulnerabilities in the Maslow Company's computer system. Witkowski created the worm in such a way that its presence could be detected by experts but was not expected to create any problems. Unfortunately for both Witkowski and the Maslow Company, the worm attached itself to the company's mainframe and spread to all the personal computers and terminals in the company, creating millions of dollars in damage due to lost and corrupted files. Witkowski is guilty of violating the CFAA, despite his good intentions.

worm
A type of virus that replicates itself and uses memory but cannot attach itself to other programs.

Electronic Funds Transfer Act (EFTA) of 1979
A federal statute that makes it an offense to use any device that is part of an electronic transfer mechanism to steal money, goods, or services or to alter data, interrupt wire transmissions, or use stolen codes or passwords, when the purpose of such activity is to obtain something of value unlawfully.

THE ELECTRONIC FUNDS TRANSFER ACT

The Electronic Funds Transfer Act (EFTA) of 1979 makes it a federal offense to use any device that is part of an electronic transfer mechanism to steal money, goods, or services or to alter data, interrupt wire transmissions, or use stolen codes or passwords, when the purpose of such activity is to obtain something of value unlawfully.

GENERAL CRIMINAL LAW

Various federal criminal statutes, not originally concerned with computers, are still frequently used to prosecute those who commit computer crimes. The most widely used of these statutes are those that prohibit fraudulent activity using the U.S. mail, known as *mail fraud*. Also used to prosecute computer crime are the statutes that prohibit the use of the telephone and other electronic communication equipment (e.g., a fax machine) for fraudulent activity, known as *wire fraud*.

COMPUTER GAMBLING

Closely related to the issue of computer crime is that of computer gambling. Federal and state laws make most forms of gambling illegal. However, there are numerous exceptions to these regulations in terms of the form of gambling (e.g., state lotteries and horse racing) and the location where the gambling takes place (e.g., Las Vegas and Atlantic City).

The laws governing online gambling vary from state to state, and most states have pending regulations that would severely restrict how and when such gambling may take place. For example, many would argue that even if online gambling were to be legal, it should be restricted to those over 18 years of age. It is important to note that the rules relating to legal purpose and competent parties in contract law apply to agreements made in the form of wagers placed online.

Federal legislation disallows most, but not all, online gambling. For example, multistate lotteries, Native American casinos, and racetracks may continue their operations as before and venture into online forms of gambling as well. It is unclear, however, whether online gambling will be allowed in real time in places like Las Vegas and Atlantic City.

The most recent federal statute to address illegal computer gambling is the *Unlawful Internet Gambling Enforcement Act of 2006* (UIGEA). The UIGEA prohibits online gambling businesses from accepting payments related to Internet gambling in violation of federal or state law, and requires all financial institutions to block payments to unlawful online gambling businesses.

Much more problematic is the issue of how to regulate offshore gambling, where consumer protection laws generally do not apply. Because obtaining jurisdiction over the companies that operate online gambling is difficult, special legislation would need to be enacted to allow federal officials to take action when necessary. It also remains to be seen whether federal regulations will address the way in which the bets are placed—for example, prohibiting the use of credit cards and electronic transfers for the purpose of gambling. The entire issue is not trivial. It is estimated that billions of dollars per year are wagered in online gambling.

EXAMPLE 29.5

▶ Antigua and Barbuda, a small, twin-island nation and haven for the Internet gambling industry, have filed a trade dispute claim against the United States with the World Trade Organization (WTO) (see Chapter 35). Antigua and Barbuda seek to gain access to the American gambling market and to recover a reported $3.4 billion in damages resulting from the United States' blocking Americans' access to offshore gambling websites. Since the United States does not ban all forms of online gambling, the WTO found the United States policy to be discriminatory and ruled in favor of Antigua.

29.4 COMPUTER SPEECH

Many of the laws that protect an individual's right to freedom of speech in traditional contexts, such as in public or in print, also apply to the expression of ideas using computers or network technologies, such as the Internet.

HARMFUL SPEECH

The United States has always had a deep commitment to maintaining an individual's right to *freedom of speech*. Protection afforded to freedom of speech is embodied in the First Amendment to the U.S. Constitution (see Chapter 5). A person's right to make statements that are unpopular, and at times even offensive or annoying, must be zealously guarded.

However, the freedom of speech is not absolute. Laws that prohibit speech, but that would be constitutionally acceptable, include the following:

▶ *Obscene statements.* What constitutes obscenity is the cause of much disagreement. In general, obscenity is that which is judged as such by local community standards.

▶ *Defamatory statements.* Speech that harms a person's reputation is referred to as defamation. This speech would include both slander, which is spoken, and libel, which is written or published (see Chapter 4).

▶ *Certain one-to-one communications.* Several statutes require that telemarketers, for example, cease telephoning when specifically requested.

▶ *Verbal or written threats to person or property.*

▶ *Intentional infliction of emotional distress.* When the objective is to cause another person to sustain severe anxiety, the injured party may sue the offending party.

EXAMPLE 29.6

▶ Goldstein had a long-standing feud with Caione. One evening, Goldstein called Caione and, disguising her voice, pretended to be an official from a local hospital. Goldstein then fabricated a story that Caione's daughter had been in an automobile accident and was severely injured. Caione rushed to the hospital only to learn of the deception. Goldstein is liable to Caione for intentional infliction of emotional distress.

It is important to note that the rules of defamation vary depending on whether one is a public figure. By becoming a public figure, such as a mayor, a baseball star, a rapper, or a rock musician, one implicitly allows others to write about him or her in newspapers and magazines and discuss his or her conduct on television and radio. These same principles hold true in cyberspace. Private figures, but not public figures, would be able to recover damages in the event statements were made about them in chat rooms or blogs. Of course, truth is an absolute defense to a charge of defamation, even in cyberspace.

It is also important to note that the rules of libel vary depending on where the libelous statements are printed. In the case of newspapers, the defamed individual may not recover unless he or she can show that the newspaper acted with actual malice, reckless disregard for the truth, or knowledge by the newspaper that what it printed was false. Recently court cases have held that these same rules apply in cyberspace because numerous news and wire services distribute information online.

public figure
A well-known person who implicitly allows others to write about him or her in newspapers and magazines and discuss his or her conduct on television and radio.

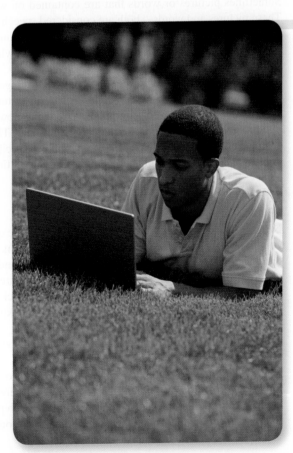

People in cyberspace frequently do not disclose their identities but use fictitious names instead.

LIABILITY OF AN INTERNET SERVICE PROVIDER

When a person is defamed in cyberspace, often he or she is not able to determine the identity of the individual who made the defamatory statements. People in chat rooms, blogs, and in mass e-mails frequently do not disclose their identities but use fictitious names instead.

When individuals learn that someone has posted an untruth about them, especially when such untruth harms them professionally, they often attempt to hold their ISP liable. Courts have consistently held, however, that ISPs are not liable for defamatory statements made while using their service unless they had prior knowledge of such.

EXAMPLE 29.7

▶ Cardone was a well-respected attorney engaging in the practice of divorce law. Cardone represented Mr. Hakim when he was sued by Mrs. Hakim for high alimony payments. Cardone accurately portrayed Mrs. Hakim as guilty of spousal abuse, and no alimony was awarded. Mrs. Hakim, while concealing her identity, posted several notices in a computer forum that stated that Cardone had never actually passed the bar examination. While Cardone strongly suspected that it was Mrs. Hakim who was the author of the untruths, he could not prove it because the ISP refused to disclose Mrs. Hakim's online identity. Cardone then sued the ISP but was unable to recover.

However, suppose we add some additional facts to Example 29.7. One month after Cardone complained to the ISP, Mrs. Hakim struck again, this time depicting Cardone as having a criminal record. Cardone would most likely recover this time against the ISP because it had prior knowledge of the defamation and, as a result, would now have an obligation to protect Cardone from additional defamatory statements.

OBSCENITY

Sometimes pictures or words that are contained on websites are alleged to be obscene. These pictures and words—both are considered speech—are legally obscene if they depict sexual conduct in a manner that is patently offensive under contemporary community standards, appeal to the prurient interest, and, taken as a whole, lack serious literary, scientific, artistic, or political value.

Many experts argue that the problem with this legal definition of obscenity is that it is too vague and ambiguous. As a result, a federal statute passed to regulate websites that contain obscene material or child pornography has now been ruled by the courts to violate due process of law—that is, to be unconstitutional. The dilemma facing many ISPs and search engines is that they are uncertain whether specific web pages, postings, and e-mail content are obscene when matched against this definition.

SPAM

spam
Unsolicited e-mails sent for commercial purposes.

Not all e-mail messages are welcomed, requested, or expected. Unsolicited e-mails sent for commercial purposes are popularly referred to as spam. Spam is undesirable because it can drain an ISP's resources, strain network bandwidth, and clog a user's e-mail folders. Spam should be distinguished from e-mail messages that are sent at the recipient's request; for example, when a person purchases an item from a brick-and-mortar company and provides his or her e-mail address to the seller, it is with the expectation that he or she may receive e-mail solicitations.

Spam is desirable from the originator's point of view because it is inexpensive. It has been estimated that several thousand recipients can be reached with spam for less than $100, while it would cost many thousands of dollars to reach the same number of individuals using a postal service mailing. Suppliers are therefore induced to collect e-mail addresses, often culling these from newsgroups and web pages. It is technologically possible to stop spammers, but such is not commonplace. From a legal standpoint, it is perfectly allowable for a seller to solicit via e-mail.

In 2004 a federal statute, the Controlling the Assault of Non-Solicited Pornography and Marketing Act (CAN-SPAM Act), went into effect. Under this statute, it remains allowable for a seller to solicit via e-mail. However, the law provides that in most situations

▶ E-mail solicitations for products and services must be identified clearly and conspicuously.

▶ Commercial e-mail senders are barred from using misleading or bogus subject lines to conceal their origins.

▶ Commercial solicitations must give the recipient the ability to "opt out" of additional e-mail messages from the sender.

▶ In addition to its legitimate e-mail address, the sender must provide its postal address.

Controlling the Assault of Non-Solicited Pornography and Marketing Act (CAN-SPAM)
A federal statute that limits the circumstances under which commercial e-mail may be utilized.

CHAPTER SUMMARY

1. The rapid advances in technology being experienced today present a new and increasingly significant threat to individual privacy. Cookies can be used to invade a person's privacy because they contain information about an Internet user's behavior, including the sites he or she visits on the web. Spyware can change a computer's security settings or steal a victim's personal information, such as e-mail addresses, bank account numbers, and credit card numbers. Phishing can trick individuals into disclosing personal information via e-mail. E-mail also can be used to violate a person's privacy because it can sometimes be intercepted and read by unintended recipients.

2. Unauthorized access to computers invites the following violations of rights: invasion of privacy; unauthorized use of the computer itself; manipulation of financial, medical, and other records; and unauthorized access to databases.

3. The ECPA is a federal statute that makes it a crime to gain unauthorized access to any communication stored on a computer system. The USA Patriot Act lowers the standards required for law enforcement officials and government agents to monitor e-mail and personal electronic information, allows increased government cybersurveillance, and makes it easier to charge persons with serious computer-related crimes. The CFAA protects the electronic communications systems involved in government, finance, and national defense. The EFTA makes it a federal offense to use a device that is part of an electronic transfer mechanism to steal money, goods, or services or to alter transmissions, steal passwords, and so forth for the purpose of obtaining something of value illegally. Other statutes, many not intended to cover computers, are now applied to computers and networks.

4. While the U.S. Constitution guarantees the First Amendment right to freedom of speech, this right is not absolute. Regulated or prohibited speech includes obscenity, defamation, certain one-to-one communications, threats to person or property, and the intentional infliction of emotional distress. Laws to protect computer users from obscenity and spam are currently developing. Obscene material can be illegal if it is deemed patently offensive by community standards, appeals to prurient interests, and lacks any serious value. Spam is legal but is subject to the provisions of the CAN-SPAM Act.

CHAPTER TWENTY-NINE
ASSESSMENT

MATCHING LEGAL TERMS

Match each of the numbered definitions with the correct term in the following list. Write the letter of your choice in the answer column.

a. defamation   **c.** hacker   **e.** spam

b. worm   **d.** cookie

1. A file that is embedded on the hard drive of a computer, often without a person's knowledge, that collects and stores information about the user.   1. ____

2. A person who gains unauthorized access to a computer either for mischief or with criminal intent.   2. ____

3. A small, self-contained program that invades all computers in a network.   3. ____

4. An unsolicited e-mail sent for commercial purposes.   4. ____

5. Speech that harms a person's reputation.   5. ____

TRUE/FALSE QUIZ

Indicate whether each of the following statements is true or false by writing *T* or *F* in the answer column.

6. Individuals making statements in chat rooms have an absolute right to privacy.   6. ____

7. There are currently no laws prohibiting the use of cookies in the case of adult computer users.   7. ____

8. Employees have no reasonable expectation of privacy while they are at work; hence employers may read their e-mail without first receiving the employee's consent.   8. ____

9. Internet service providers have the legal right to monitor e-mail without the subscriber's consent.   9. ____

10. Employees who transfer money from their employer's account into their own account without authorization can be prosecuted for the crime of embezzlement.   10. ____

11. There are numerous state, but no federal, regulations covering the misuse of computers and data.   11. ____

12. In order to violate the Computer Fraud and Abuse Act, an individual must act with intent. 12. _____

13. Since most forms of gambling are illegal, most forms of online gambling are also illegal. 13. _____

14. Offshore gambling refers to foreign citizens placing bets in casinos located within the United States. 14. _____

15. Slander is a spoken, and libel is a written, form of defamation. 15. _____

16. A newspaper that prints a story about a public figure, with knowledge that the story is untrue, could be held liable for defamation. 16. _____

17. The law mandates that all Internet service providers require subscribers to use their true names when entering cyberspace. 17. _____

18. Pictures and words are legally obscene if they depict sexual conduct in a manner that is patently offensive under contemporary community standards, appeal to the prurient interest, and, taken as a whole, lack serious literary, scientific, artistic, or political value. 18. _____

19. When an individual purchases an item from a brick-and-mortar company and provides his or her e-mail address to the seller, the individual is implicitly consenting to the receipt of e-mail solicitations. 19. _____

20. Spam is illegal in the United States. 20. _____

DISCUSSION QUESTIONS

Answer the following questions and discuss them in class.

21. Explain how the law protecting the privacy of e-mail differs, depending on whether the e-mail is sent from home or from work.

_____

_____

22. Identify at least three typical company policies that restrict e-mail sent or received by employees while on the employer's premises.

_____

_____

23. Name four rights that may be violated when individuals gain access to computers without proper authorization.

_____

_____

24. Give three examples of unauthorized uses of computers that can result in criminal prosecution.

_____

_____

25. Distinguish the Electronic Communications Privacy Act from the Computer Fraud and Abuse Act in terms of intent to commit a crime.

_____

_____

26. Identify five types of laws that restrict speech but would nonetheless be constitutionally permissible.

_____

_____

THINKING CRITICALLY ABOUT THE LAW

Answer the following questions, which require you to think critically about the legal principles that you learned in this chapter.

27. USA Patriot Act Where should the line be drawn between the responsibility of the government to thwart terrorism and the rights of Americans to be free from governmental intrusions into their privacy?

_____

_____

28. Cookies How does the presence of cookies on the hard drive of a user's computer harm an individual's right to privacy?

_____

_____

29. E-mail What justification might there be for an employer to be legally entitled to view an employee's e-mail without the employee's permission?

_____

_____

30. Spam What are some advantages and disadvantages of legally restricting spam in cyberspace?

_____

_____

31. A Question of Ethics Do you believe that it is fair to hold public figures to a different standard of privacy and defamation than private individuals?

_____

_____

CASE QUESTIONS

Study each of the following cases. Answer the questions that follow by writing _Yes_ or _No_ in the answer column.

32. Cookies Comfy Shoes, Inc. maintained a website for the online sale of its products. Comfy carried a complete line of men's, women's, and children's shoes. Included among its many shoe products were children's sneakers. Without obtaining authorization, Comfy placed cookies on the hard drives of all persons visiting its site.

a. Does Comfy have a legal right to place cookies on the computer hard drives of men and women visiting its website?

a. _____

b. Does Comfy have a legal right to place cookies on the computer hard drives of children visiting its website?

b. _____

c. Could users complain to the Federal Trade Commission if they thought their privacy was being violated by Comfy?

c. _____

33. Computer Crime Schroeder, a student at Plymouth College, entered a computer lab on campus, overrode the password system, entered the college's computer without authorization, and changed her grade in a Business Law course from D to a B+.

a. Can Schroeder be charged with the crime of embezzlement?

a. _____

b. Is Schroeder hacking?

b. _____

c. Can Schroeder be charged with unauthorized access to databases?

c. _____

34. Spam WeAreTravel Corp., a retail travel agency doing business in Pennsylvania, regularly sent computer messages to all persons who signed onto the firm's mailing list. In addition, the company sent e-mail to all persons residing in the same town as the agency.

a. Does WeAreTravel Corp. have a legal right to send spam to the persons who signed onto the mailing list?

a. _____

b. Does WeAreTravel Corp. have a legal right to send spam to the persons who are residents of the town in which the company is located?

b. _____

c. Does WeAreTravel Corp. have a legal right to send 200 e-mails per day to these individuals?

c. _____

CASE ANALYSIS

Study each of the following cases carefully. Briefly state the principle of law and your decision.

35. Computer Privacy Timothy R. McVeigh (no relation to the Oklahoma City bomber) was a highly decorated, 17-year veteran of the U.S. Navy. McVeigh was a gay male who, while using an alias, sent an e-mail message to a civilian navy volunteer through AOL. The volunteer searched through AOL's member profile directory and learned some information about the sender; eventually this information and McVeigh's identity found their way to senior officials in the navy. McVeigh was then found to be in violation of the military's policy of "Don't ask, don't tell," an offense that warrants discharge for homosexuality. McVeigh brought suit, attempting to prevent the military from ordering his discharge. Will McVeigh be allowed to offer as an argument that his e-mail to the volunteer cannot be used against him due to his right to privacy? [*McVeigh v. Cohen*, 983 F. Supp. 215 (Washington, D.C.)]

Principle of Law:

_____

_____

Decision:

_____

_____

36. E-mail Michael A. Smith was a regional operations manager for the Pillsbury Company. In this capacity, he regularly used the company's e-mail server. The company regularly assured its employees that all e-mail communications would remain confidential and privileged. While at home, Smith then exchanged e-mail messages with his supervisor. Pillsbury read these e-mail messages, claimed that they were inappropriate and unprofessional, and terminated Smith's employment. Smith brought a lawsuit for wrongful termination, and Pillsbury requested that it be dismissed. Will the court allow Smith's lawsuit to proceed, or will the case be dismissed? [*Smith v. Pillsbury*, C.A. No. 95-5712 (Pennsylvania)]

Principle of Law:

_____

_____

Decision:

_____

_____

37. Computer Crime Legislation Robert Tappan Morris released onto the Internet a worm that spread and multiplied. The worm found its way into computers at several educational and military sites, causing these computers to crash. Morris was charged with violating section 2(d) of the Computer Fraud and Abuse Act of 1986. Morris was able to prove during a jury trial that, while in fact he had released the worm, he did not do so intentionally. Nonetheless, Morris was found guilty of violating the law. He appealed his conviction on the grounds that his access to these educational and military computers was not without authorization since Morris did not intend to access them. Will Morris be successful in his appeal of the guilty verdict? [*United States v. Morris*, 928 F.2d 504 (Washington, D.C.)]

Principle of Law:

_____

_____

Decision:

_____

_____

38. **Liability of an Internet Service Provider** *Rumorville,* a daily online newspaper, was part of a journalism forum on the Internet published by Fitzpatrick. Subscribers to CompuServe, an Internet service provider, had access to *Rumorville.* Skuttlebut was a service that distributed news and gossip about journalism. *Rumorville* published items about Skuttlebut that were alleged to be defamatory and untrue. Skuttlebut sued CompuServe, arguing that this Internet service provider was liable for the defamatory statements carried by the service. Will Skuttlebut be successful in a suit against CompuServe? [*Cubby v. CompuServe*, 776 F. Supp. 135 (New York)]

Principle of Law:

_____

_____

Decision:

_____

_____

LEGAL RESEARCH

Complete the following activities. Share your findings with the class.

39. **Working in Teams** In teams of three or four, draft a federal statute that might be enacted that would address the issue of online gambling. Be certain to include who is covered and what forms of gambling are being regulated.

_____

_____

40. **Using Technology** Using the Internet and search engines, visit a website that provides a free download to detect spyware.

_____

_____

chapter **30**

Conducting Business in Cyberspace

After studying this chapter and completing the assessment, you will be able to

30.1 Identify six key settings in which the law applies to conducting business on the web.

30.2 Discuss the role of the Securities and Exchange Commission in the sale and trading of securities online.

30.3 Explain how the Federal Trade Commission protects consumers from deception in online advertising.

30.4 Identify the copyright issues associated with selling music and other forms of entertainment online.

30.5 Explain how contracts formed online are offered, accepted, and signed.

30.6 Discuss how legal disputes can be settled online using alternative dispute resolution.

30.7 Discuss the current rules pertaining to states' levying sales taxes for purchases made online.

terms

LEGAL

Securities and Exchange Commission (SEC)

Securities Act of 1933

primary market

prospectus

Securities Exchange Act of 1934

secondary market

touting

insider trading

Federal Trade Commission (FTC)

deceptive advertising

Digital Millennium Copyright Act (DMCA) of 1998

Electronic Signatures in Global and National Commerce Act (ESIGN) of 2000

alternative dispute resolution (ADR)

mediation

arbitration

nexus

use tax

Internet Tax Freedom Act

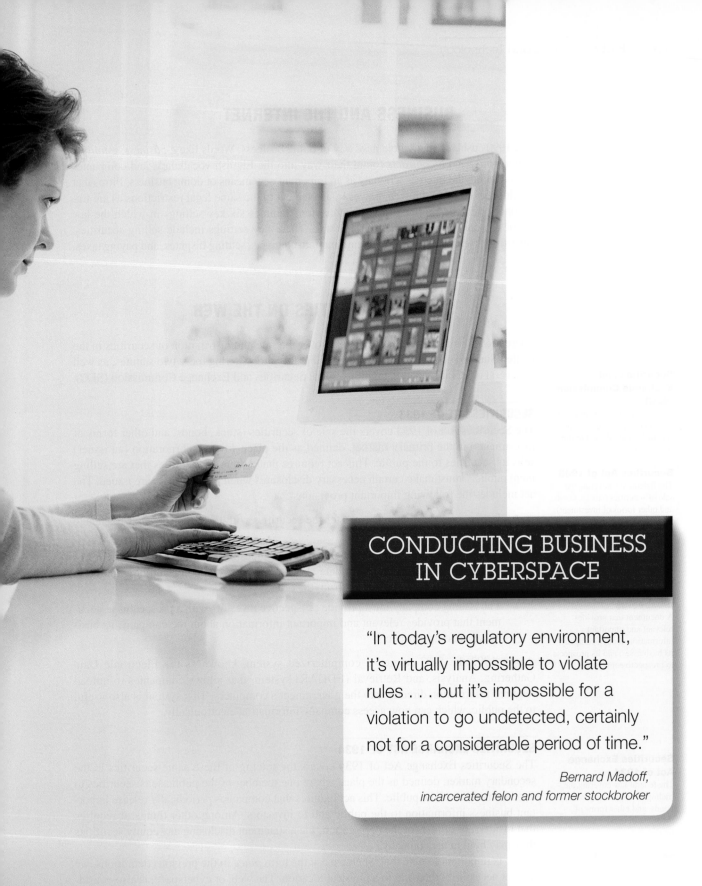

CONDUCTING BUSINESS IN CYBERSPACE

"In today's regulatory environment, it's virtually impossible to violate rules . . . but it's impossible for a violation to go undetected, certainly not for a considerable period of time."

Bernard Madoff,
incarcerated felon and former stockbroker

30.1   BUSINESS AND THE INTERNET

The 1990s ushered in a whole new way of doing business. Words like *e-business, e-tailing, e-marketing,* and *e-contracts* found their way into the English vocabulary, and companies started taking the Internet seriously as an important new means of doing business. Firms that conduct business on the web, however, are subject to the same legal restrictions as are traditional brick-and-mortar firms. This chapter examines six key settings in which the law applies to conducting business on the web. These key settings include selling securities, advertising, selling entertainment, entering into contracts, settling disputes, and paying taxes.

30.2   SELLING SECURITIES ON THE WEB

There are two main federal statutes that cover the sale and distribution of securities in the United States. The federal agency responsible for administering these two statutes, as well as several others laws and regulations, is the Securities and Exchange Commission (SEC).

Securities and Exchange Commission (SEC)
The federal agency responsible for administering the statutes relating to the sale and trading of securities.

Securities Act of 1933
The federal law covering the sale of securities (stocks, bonds, and other forms of investment) in the primary market.

primary market
The place where a corporation (an issuer) sells its securities to the public.

prospectus
A document that provides relevant and important information about a company, its businesses, and its prospects to prospective investors.

SECURITIES ACT OF 1933

The Securities Act of 1933 covers the sale of securities (stock, bonds, and other forms of investments) in the primary market, defined as the place where a corporation (an issuer) sells its securities to the public. This act requires that issuers of securities that are selling them publicly must make certain necessary disclosures when the securities are issued. The act includes the following important provisions:

▶ Issuers of securities must register the securities with the Securities and Exchange Commission.

▶ A registration statement must be filed that includes information about the securities offered, historical and current data about the issuing company, and how the company plans to use the proceeds from the offer.

▶ The issuing company must provide prospective investors with a prospectus, a document that provides relevant and important information about the company, its businesses, and its prospects.

In 1992 the SEC created a computerized system, known as the Electronic Data Gathering, Analysis, and Retrieval (EDGAR) system, that allows companies to upload required information directly into the government's computers. This system is also useful to the public, which can now access company information electronically.

Securities Exchange Act of 1934
The federal law covering the trading of securities (stocks, bonds, and other forms of investment) in the secondary market.

secondary market
The place where one member of the public sells securities to another member of the public.

SECURITIES EXCHANGE ACT OF 1934

The Securities Exchange Act of 1934 covers the trading of these same securities in the secondary market, defined as the place where one member of the public sells securities to another member of the public. This act requires that companies periodically release important business information to the public and to investors. Among other things, it requires that insiders, or officers of the corporation, file a statement disclosing any equity securities they may hold in the company.

It is important to note that when we use the term *place* in the previous definitions, we are not necessarily referring to a physical location. The web, or cyberspace, is also considered a place, and securities are regularly bought and sold electronically.

EXAMPLE 30.1

▶ The Washington Company sold common stock to O'Brien, who held the stock for several years and then resold it at a profit to Gupta. The Washington Company, the issuer in this example, is governed by the 1933 act when it sold the stock to O'Brien and by the 1934 act because O'Brien is legally entitled to resell the stock to Gupta.

The SEC attempts to ensure that prospective investors have access to full and correct information about the companies whose securities they are interested in purchasing. Accordingly, the SEC requires that companies prepare forms and documentation containing financial and other information so prospective investors can, if they so desire, review this information prior to investing money.

Since 1995, the SEC has addressed the issue of selling securities electronically by publishing a series of guidelines relating to such sales. The rules relating to online sales of securities can be summarized as follows:

Securities are regularly bought and sold electronically on the web.

▶ Information that is distributed electronically will satisfy the transmission requirements of the federal securities laws provided that the distribution results in delivery of information substantially equivalent to what the prospective investors would have received in paper form.

▶ There must be timely and adequate notice to prospective investors of the availability of this information.

▶ The electronic delivery must afford access to the information that is comparable to that afforded by paper copies.

▶ There must be evidence to demonstrate that delivery of the information to prospective investors was successful.

The SEC also acts to make certain that investors do not violate the SEC's anti-touting rules. Touting occurs when an investor who owns shares of a company's stock posts notices online—in chat rooms, on web pages, on blogs, and elsewhere—that indicate that the value of the stock will increase. If enough individuals who read these postings believe that the touter is a disinterested expert, the demand for the shares will increase, and the touter has the opportunity to earn large amounts of money by selling the shares at the inflated price.

touting
An activity in which an investor who owns shares of a company's stock posts notices online—in chat rooms, on web pages, on blogs, and elsewhere—that indicate that the value of the stock will increase.

EXAMPLE 30.2

▶ Felmuth, a 15-year-old computer maven, entered chat rooms and placed postings on numerous occasions, pretending to be a financial analyst with an MBA from a respected university. Felmuth falsely implied that she had inside information that the Daya Corporation, a drug manufacturer, was on the verge of a major breakthrough in discovering a cure for a deadly disease. The Daya Corporation's stock rose fivefold in less than a week, and Felmuth made several hundred thousand dollars when she sold the stock for a huge profit. Felmuth is guilty of violating federal securities laws, will be required to repay all profits, and could spend some time in a juvenile detention center.

INSIDER TRADING

insider trading
An illegal activity in which a person who has confidential information about a particular company purchases shares of the company's stock with the intention of selling these shares for a higher price when the information is released to the general public.

Insider trading, a type of securities fraud (see Chapter 3), occurs when a person who has confidential information about a particular company purchases shares of the company's stock with the intention of selling these shares for a higher price when the information is released to the general public. The illegal activity of using insider information for personal gain is considered a "manipulative and deceptive practice," which is illegal under the 1934 act. It is important to note that trading in the stock of the firm by company officials is also called *insider trading,* but as long as it is reported, it is not illegal.

The confidential information may come from various sources. In one case, an individual had prior access to newspaper and magazine articles that, upon publication, affected the price of a company's stock. By making the appropriate investment in the stock of the firm discussed in the news item, the individual experienced a financial windfall. In another case, a top official of a company, having advance knowledge of a development that affected the price of the firm's stock, gave the information to friends and relatives, who then speculated in the company's stock, sharing profits with the wrongdoer. The official used friends and relatives in the scheme because federal law requires upper management to report their trading in the stock of the company with which they are associated.

EXAMPLE 30.3

▶ Chen, president of China Imports, learned that his proposal to expand the firm's operations had been approved by the regulatory authorities and, as a result, China Imports would increase its business considerably. As soon as the news of this development became public, the price of the stock of China Imports would increase. Chen suggested to his brother-in-law that they could share the profit if the brother-in-law bought several thousand shares of the company's stock before the news was made public. By engaging in this illegal activity, Chen has violated federal regulations that prohibit an officer in a corporation from trading in the stock of his corporation without disclosure. Using his brother-in-law to purchase the stock was merely a clumsy attempt to evade the law.

RECENT TRENDS IN SECURITIES TRADING

In recent years, technological improvements that allow real-time market data to be transmitted over cyberspace have altered the way securities trading takes place. Automated trades are frequently transacted by computer programs that analyze market data received in cyberspace. As a result, thousands of trades can now be made within seconds. In light of the impact such advances have had on the securities markets, the SEC is currently attempting to establish new regulations to promote and improve the financial markets.

EXAMPLE 30.4

▶ On May 6, 2010, a large computerized stock trade of $4.1 billion triggered a series of events that resulted in one of the quickest stock market crashes and subsequent recoveries in U.S. history. This market crash, referred to as the "Flash Crash," occurred when a large, computerized stock trade made a sufficient impact on the market to prompt numerous automated trades. These trades flowed into the market at a rate of thousands per second and resulted in an immediate decrease in stock prices. To prevent future occurrences of this phenomenon, the SEC has proposed new regulations aimed at curtailing such rapid-fire trades.

30.3   ADVERTISING ON THE WEB

The federal agency responsible for ensuring that advertising in the United States is truthful is the Federal Trade Commission (FTC). In addition, there are numerous state and local consumer protection agencies, as well as private, not-for-profit companies, that can be of assistance in the event a consumer is misled by a deceptive advertisement.

A deceptive advertisement is defined as one that contains a material (important) misrepresentation, omission, or practice likely to mislead a consumer who acts reasonably under the circumstances.

Ads placed on web pages are required to meet the same standards as ads placed in other media, such as print, billboards, television, and radio. If the FTC determines that a web-based ad is deceptive, it has several options:

► The FTC can issue a cease-and-desist order, in effect compelling the publisher to eliminate the Internet reference.

► The FTC can order an affirmative disclosure, requiring the publisher to revise the web reference to include additional, truthful information.

► The FTC can require corrective advertising, to inform future visitors to the web page that the previous information was deceptive.

► The FTC can seek fines and other civil remedies.

► In extreme cases involving fraud, the FTC can ask the federal Justice Department to file criminal charges, which can lead to imprisonment.

Federal Trade Commission (FTC)
The federal agency responsible for ensuring that advertising in the United States is truthful.

deceptive advertising
An advertisement that contains a material misrepresentation, omission, or practice likely to mislead a consumer who acts reasonably under the circumstances.

EXAMPLE 30.5

► Pluto Stationery sells silver-plated pen and pencil sets for $19.99. On its website, it advertised silver-plated pens for $19.99, and added that there would be a "free" silver-plated pencil provided with the purchase of a pen. Because the pencil is not really free at all, Pluto Stationery is guilty of creating a deceptive ad on its website and can be required to pay a fine.

30.4   SELLING ENTERTAINMENT ON THE WEB

In recent years, it has become quite popular for people to trade and download music and other forms of entertainment (movies, games, etc.) from the web onto compact disks and other digital storage devices. The legal issue associated with this is copyright infringement, discussed in detail in Chapter 28. Because the rightful owners of the music often have not granted permission and do not receive royalties from the pirated music, they have made efforts to stop companies from distributing music online. While the issue is still far from settled, several court decisions have held that copyright infringement takes place even if the company merely provides a forum for music to be "shared" among subscribers.

Another related issue is to what extent Internet service providers (ISPs), discussed in Chapter 29, are liable when a copyright infringement occurs while computer users are online.

It has become quite popular for people to download music from the web onto digital storage devices.

Digital Millennium Copyright Act (DMCA) of 1998
A federal statute that provides that ISPs are not liable for copyright infringements by their subscribers so long as they adhere to certain requirements.

THE DIGITAL MILLENNIUM COPYRIGHT ACT

Among numerous provisions, the federal Digital Millennium Copyright Act (DMCA) of 1998 provides that ISPs are not liable for copyright infringements by their subscribers if they

▶ Adopt and reasonably implement a policy of terminating, in appropriate circumstances, the accounts of subscribers who are repeat infringers.

▶ Accommodate, and do not interfere with, the identification or protection of copyrighted works.

The DMCA further protects ISPs from liability for copyright infringement even for information residing on their users' systems or networks, provided that

▶ The ISP did not have knowledge of the infringing activity.

▶ The ISP did not receive financial benefit directly attributable to the infringing activity.

▶ Upon receiving proper notification of claimed infringement, the ISP expeditiously blocked access to the infringed material.

30.5 ENTERING INTO CONTRACTS ON THE WEB

The ability of parties to enter into agreements in cyberspace raises numerous questions. Offers are readily available on the web, and some questions that may arise include these:

▶ How are offers in cyberspace accepted?

▶ Are agreements entered into on the web contracts of adhesion?

▶ How does a computer user sign a contract made on the web, especially a contract that must be in writing pursuant to the Statute of Frauds?

ACCEPTING OFFERS ON THE WEB

Remember that it is the offeror who determines how offers may be accepted (see Chapter 8). But also remember that silence on the part of the offeree generally does not constitute acceptance of an offer. These same rules are applicable in cyberspace.

Frequently, offers on websites include a button to be clicked by the user with his or her mouse that indicates acceptance. Most courts acknowledge that by clicking the button, the offer has been accepted. It should be pointed out that the button need not explicitly read "I accept." It could, for example, use terms such as "I agree," "Yes," "I consent," or any other expression indicating that the offeree has read the offer and is accepting the terms. Computer users who frequent websites, therefore, should be especially careful to click their mouse only after they have read the entire agreement and accept all of the terms.

Simply visiting a website does not constitute acceptance of an offer that is contained on that website. In other words, silence (not clicking the "I accept" button) does not constitute acceptance on the part of the user.

But what happens when the user has accepted the offer by clicking his or her mouse but has not read all the terms of the agreement?

CONTRACTS OF ADHESION ON THE WEB

In Chapter 9 it was explained that there are many instances when contracts are formed without there being any real negotiating or bargaining by the parties. It also was pointed out that these agreements, termed "contracts of adhesion," are nonetheless valid unless they contain terms that are unreasonable. These same rules apply in cyberspace. If the website visitor has had an ample opportunity to read the terms, and if those terms are not unreasonable, a valid contract exists. Of course, all of the other elements of a contract must be met as well; for example, if the individual accepting the offer is a minor, the contract is voidable, and so forth.

EXAMPLE 30.6

▶ Motomba surfed to a web page for her favorite pop group that indicated that for a $3 monthly fee she could subscribe to a monthly electronic newsletter by clicking the "I subscribe" button. Motomba did not read the lengthy offer but simply clicked the button with her mouse. Later Motomba learned that the terms of the subscriber agreement stated in small print that, in addition to the newsletter, she would receive the latest CD performed by the pop group and would be billed $25. Motomba will be required to pay for the monthly newsletter but will not be required to purchase the CD.

ELECTRONIC SIGNATURES

In Chapter 13 it was explained that the Statute of Frauds requires that certain types of contracts must be in writing and signed by the party to be charged to be enforceable. In addition, even if the Statute of Frauds is not applicable, many parties to contracts prefer them to be in writing so that the terms are clearly spelled out.

Contracts made on the web can easily be reduced to writing by simply printing the portion of the website containing the offer and the important terms of the contract. But how are these written contracts signed?

The Electronic Signatures in Global and National Commerce Act (ESIGN) of 2000, a federal statute, states that electronic contracts containing electronic signatures are just as enforceable as those that are printed on paper. Clicking the computer mouse on the "I agree" button, therefore, constitutes an electronic signature that satisfies the writing requirement of the Statute of Frauds.

Electronic Signatures in Global and National Commerce Act (ESIGN) of 2000
A federal statute that provides that electronic contracts containing electronic signatures are just as enforceable as those that are printed on paper.

Of course, many new technologies are now needed to ensure that the person who is supposedly accepting the contract is actually the person who is clicking the button. Some of these new, emerging technologies include

▶ Allowing the computer user to verify a digital signature using an encrypted code that is registered with a third party.

▶ Providing the computer user with hardware that can read the user's fingerprint or scan the user's retina.

▶ Providing the computer user with hardware that can electronically read the user's handwriting and thus electronically register the user's signature.

Finally, it must be pointed out that ESIGN does not apply to electronic signatures that appear on

▶ Wills, codicils, and related testamentary documents.

▶ Adoption or divorce papers.

▶ Court papers such as orders, pleadings, and motions.

▶ Notices of cancellation or interruption in utility services.

▶ Notices of defaults, repossessions, foreclosures, and evictions.

▶ Notices of cancellation or termination of life or health insurance benefits.

▶ Certain notices relating to recalls of defective products.

▶ Documents relating to the transportation of hazardous materials.

30.6 SETTLING DISPUTES IN CYBERSPACE

alternative dispute resolution (ADR)
A system in which contract disputes and other disagreements are resolved by using means other than a lawsuit.

mediation
A process for dispute resolution in which a neutral third party meets with the disputants in order to have them come to some form of settlement agreement.

arbitration
A process for dispute resolution in which a neutral third party decides a case as if he or she were a judge and jury.

Because it is expensive to proceed against a defendant in a court case, a person who is the victim of a breach of contract will frequently seek to have the dispute resolved using alternative means. Alternative dispute resolution (ADR) is a system in which contract disputes and other disagreements are resolved by using means other than a lawsuit. Means of ADR include mediation, in which a neutral third party meets with the disputants in order to have them come to some form of settlement agreement; and arbitration, in which a neutral third party actually decides a case as if he or she were a judge and jury. (Many "court" shows on television actually depict arbitration proceedings.)

The advantages to ADR include

▶ *Speed.* The matter is resolved quickly.

▶ *Finality.* Unless there is some type of misconduct, ADR results may not be appealed.

▶ *Informality.* ADR does not use the same strict rules of evidence that a court does.

▶ *Privacy.* ADR proceedings are not generally open to the public, as civil trials usually are.

▶ *Financial savings.* Because ADR is faster, with fewer legal motions, witnesses, and so on, they are much less expensive for the disputants than are court trials.

In cyberspace, numerous websites have been established for the purpose of providing forums for both mediation and arbitration of contract disputes. Parties involved in a contract dispute can simply access an Internet search engine to locate an organization that will assist with the ADR process.

30.7 PAYING TAXES ON INTERNET SALES

nexus
The link or tie that a location must have to a sale in order for the location to collect sales tax.

In 1992 the Supreme Court of the United States ruled that a location must have a link or tie to a sale in order for the location to collect sales tax (*Quill v. North Dakota*, 504 U.S. 298). This link or tie is referred to as a nexus. It also must be pointed out that it is the buyer, and not the seller, who pays the sales tax, although it is typically the seller who collects the tax from the buyer and then turns the proceeds over to the state. In other words, a state wishing to collect a sales tax must levy the tax on a buyer who resides within the state and require a seller within the state to collect the tax.

When a consumer shops online, the state in which the consumer resides cannot legally collect the tax, unless the online buyer happens to be purchasing the goods from an online seller who resides within the same state.

EXAMPLE 30.7

▶ Lebeda is a soap crafter who requires lye for her soap making. Because Lebeda resides in a rural area of Pennsylvania, she purchases the lye in quantity online from a manufacturer in California. Lebeda will not be required to pay Pennsylvania sales tax on the lye she purchases.

Many retailers who operate traditional brick-and-mortar enterprises also do business on the web. Because cyberspace is not geographically based in any of the 50 states, some retailers establish separate legal entities for their web-based businesses to avoid collecting sales tax. To compensate for lost sales tax revenue, most states require that consumers who purchase goods out of state must pay a use tax, which is a tax levied on a consumer who uses goods within a state, as opposed to buying them within the state. However, use taxes are extremely difficult to collect on small items sold on the web, and most states do not make efforts to collect use taxes.

The result is that, as of now, states are losing great amounts of tax revenue as a result of web-based sales. Over the next several years, the sales tax laws are certain to be modified to address this issue.

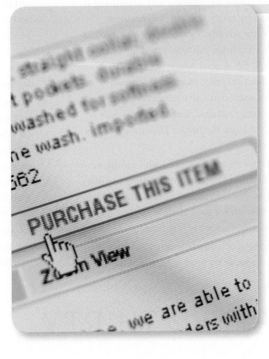

Many retailers who operate traditional brick-and-mortar enterprises also do business on the web.

use tax
A tax to a consumer who uses goods within a state, as opposed to buying them within the state.

TAXING INTERNET ACCESS SERVICES

In 1998 Congress passed the Internet Tax Freedom Act, which established a moratorium on taxing ISPs on the services they provide to computer users. The moratorium, which is a period of time during which no state may levy sales taxes on these ISPs, is currently in effect. Again, many states and localities are seeking changes to the law so that they may begin to tax the monthly fees that people pay for Internet access.

Internet Tax Freedom Act
A federal statute that placed a moratorium on taxing Internet service providers on the services they provide to computer users.

CHAPTER SUMMARY

1. Six key settings in which the law applies to conducting business on the web include selling securities, advertising, selling entertainment, entering into contracts, settling disputes, and paying taxes.

2. For online securities sales, the SEC requires that information distributed electronically to potential investors is to be substantially equivalent to what would have been provided in paper form; access to

information is to be comparable to that afforded by paper copies; there must be adequate notice to prospective investors of the availability of the information; and there must be evidence demonstrating that delivery of information to prospective investors was successful.

3. The FTC protects consumers from deceptive online advertising by ensuring that advertising is truthful and by taking a variety of measures against online advertising that is false or misleading. If the FTC finds that web-based advertising is deceptive, it has several options: It can issue a cease-and-desist order; require an affirmative disclosure; order corrective advertising; seek fines and order civil remedies; and, in severe cases alleging fraud, ask the Justice Department to file criminal charges.

4. The copyright issues associated with selling music and other forms of entertainment online involve the problem that the rightful owners often do not grant permission for its availability online and do not receive royalties when it is pirated.

5. Offers can be made online in much the same way that they are made by other means, and the rules

of acceptance are also similar. For example, by clicking a button that reads "I accept" or something similar, a user can accept and be bound by the terms of an agreement. Silence, or not clicking such a button, cannot be used as grounds for accepting an offer.

6. Advantages of using alternative dispute resolution (ADR) include speed, finality, informality, privacy, and financial savings. Means of ADR include mediation and arbitration. These methods are also available on numerous websites that have been established on the Internet to provide forums for parties to resolve their problems.

7. States are losing a great deal of potential tax revenue because they are not collecting taxes on sales made over the Internet. The reasons include the difficulty of establishing a nexus for the transaction and of collecting use taxes in Internet-based transactions. The Internet Tax Freedom Act established a moratorium on taxing the services that ISPs provide to computer users. However, many states and localities are seeking to change the law so people can be taxed on the monthly fees they pay to have Internet access.

CHAPTER THIRTY
ASSESSMENT

MATCHING LEGAL TERMS

Match each of the numbered definitions with the correct term in the following list. Write the letter of your choice in the answer column.

a. mediation **c.** nexus **e.** arbitration
b. primary market **d.** secondary market

1. The place where a corporation sells its securities to the public. 1. ____

2. The place where one member of the public sells securities to another member of the public. 2. ____

3. A process in which a neutral third party meets with disputants to have them come to some form of settlement agreement. 3. ____

4. A process in which a neutral third party decides a case as if he or she were a judge and jury. 4. ____

5. A location's link or tie to a sale required in order for the location to collect sales tax. 5. ____

Indicate whether each of the following statements is true or false by writing *T* or *F* in the answer column.

6. The Securities and Exchange Commission requires that prospective investors review all of a firm's financial information prior to purchasing any stock in the company.

6. _____

7. Touting occurs when an investor who owns shares of a company's stock posts notices online indicating that the value of the company's stock will increase.

7. _____

8. The Federal Trade Commission is responsible for ensuring that advertising in the United States is truthful.

8. _____

9. A deceptive advertisement is one that contains a material misrepresentation, omission, or practice likely to mislead a consumer who acts reasonably under the circumstances.

9. _____

10. The Federal Trade Commission does not have jurisdiction over advertisements that appear on web pages.

10. _____

11. Companies that provide websites that are forums for music to be shared without permission of the owners may be liable for copyright infringement.

11. _____

12. Most courts will acknowledge that by clicking the "I accept" button, the user has accepted the offer contained on the web page.

12. _____

13. Simply visiting a website can sometimes indicate an acceptance by the user of the terms contained on the site.

13. _____

14. Contracts of adhesion in cyberspace are valid unless they contain terms that are unreasonable.

14. _____

15. An electronic signature will not satisfy the Statute of Frauds.

15. _____

16. The Electronic Signatures in Global and National Commerce Act pertains only to cases in which the offeror and the offeree are from different countries.

16. _____

17. Mediation is a form of alternative dispute resolution in which a neutral party decides a case as if he or she were a judge and jury.

17. _____

18. A disadvantage to alternative dispute resolution is that it is far more time-consuming than litigation.

18. _____

19. A state wishing to collect a sales tax levies the tax on the buyer of goods but usually requires the seller to collect the tax.

19. _____

20. A use tax is a tax to a consumer who uses goods within a state, as opposed to buying them within the state.

20. _____

DISCUSSION QUESTIONS

Answer the following questions and discuss them in class.

21. Compare and contrast the two main statutes that cover the sale and distribution of securities in the United States.

_____

_____

22. State the four rules relating to online sales of securities and explain the importance of these.

_____

_____

23. Evaluate the options that the Federal Trade Commission has in dealing with a firm that has placed a deceptive advertisement online.

_____

_____

24. How can Internet service providers protect themselves against a charge of copyright infringement?

_____

_____

25. Identify types of legal documents for which electronic signatures are not valid and explain why the law excludes these.

_____

_____

26. Name five advantages for individuals who select alternative dispute resolution over litigation and give an example of each.

_____

_____

THINKING CRITICALLY ABOUT THE LAW

Answer the following questions, which require you to think critically about the legal principles that you learned in this chapter.

27. Selling Securities on the Web How can the law better protect individuals who are considering making investments over the web?

_____

_____

28. **Advertising on the Web** Given the enormous amount of advertising placed on the web, what can the Federal Trade Commission do to be certain that all web-based advertising is truthful?

_____

_____

29. **Entering into Contracts on the Web** Why and how are contracts of adhesion especially problematic for offers made on the web?

_____

_____

30. **Electronic Signatures** Describe some ways in which technology might be used to ensure that computer users signing contracts with e-signatures are in fact the persons they are representing themselves to be.

_____

_____

31. **A Question of Ethics** Several representatives of the entertainment media have suggested that a federal statute be enacted that would require all computers sold in the United States to incorporate software that would prevent making digital copies of music and video. Is it fair that consumers would lose the right to use their computers to make additional digital copies, for their own use, of songs and movies that they purchased legally?

_____

_____

CASE QUESTIONS

Study each of the following cases. Answer the questions that follow by writing *Yes* or *No* in the answer column.

32. **Selling Securities on the Web** Mikai developed an exercise device that she sold on a website. Sales were brisk, and she soon discovered that she would need additional funds to purchase materials. She included on the website an invitation to the public to invest in her company by purchasing shares of stock.

   a. Must Mikai register these securities with the Federal Trade Commission? a. _____

   b. If Mikai does not register the securities, can she be charged with violating the Securities Act of 1933? b. _____

   c. Must Mikai provide financial information to investors prior to selling securities online? c. _____

33. **Advertising on the Web** Dragos was interested in obtaining memorabilia relating to her favorite 1980s heavy metal band, Deaf Panther. Through a search engine, Dragos found a company called WebPix, which offered autographed photographs of various celebrities, including Deaf Panther. Dragos ordered the photographs and charged the cost of these to her credit card. The signatures on the pictures turned out to be forgeries.

a. Can Dragos complain to the Federal Trade Commission?   a. _____

b. Can Dragos sue WebPix for breach of contract?   b. _____

c. Can Dragos sue WebPix for a violation of securities law?   c. _____

34. **Settling Disputes in Cyberspace** Kule purchased an antique doll for $700 from Elliott through an auction website known as e-Auction. The description of the doll provided by Elliott stated that it was in "good condition," but when Kule received the doll, she noted that it had a damaged leg. Both Kule and Elliott agreed to be bound by the decision of a representative of e-Auction, who inspected the doll.

a. Is the contract between Kule and Elliott valid despite the fact that it was entered into in cyberspace?   a. _____

b. Is the representative from e-Auction an arbitrator?   b. _____

c. If Kule wishes to resolve the dispute as quickly as possible, would she be better off by filing a lawsuit against Elliott?   c. _____

CASE ANALYSIS

Study each of the following cases carefully. Briefly state the principle of law and your decision.

35. **Selling Securities on the Web** Jonathan G. Lebed was a 15-year-old Internet maven who, over about a six-month period, on 11 separate occasions "engaged in a scheme in which he purchased large blocks of thinly traded stocks and, within hours of making such purchases, sent numerous false and misleading messages over the Internet touting the stocks that he had just purchased." Lebed sold these shares, usually by the next day. From these activities he realized a total profit during the period of $272,826. Is Lebed guilty of violating the securities laws? [*In the Matter of Jonathan G. Lebed, a Minor, through his Guardian*, Administrative Proceeding, File No. 3-10291 (Washington, D.C.)]

Principle of Law:

_____

_____

Decision:

_____

_____

36. **Advertising on the Web** Kenneth Lipsitz sold magazine subscriptions through a friendly and congenial staff located in New York City. Numerous affidavits and complaints alleged either that the magazines never arrived or that they stopped coming long before the subscription was due to expire. Lipsitz was charged with deceptive advertising in New York. Can Lipsitz be found in violation of the New York laws against deceptive advertising even though he sold subscriptions via e-mail and the web? [*People v. Lipsitz*, 663 N.Y.S.2d 468 (New York)]

Principle of Law:

_____

_____

Decision:

_____

_____

37. **Selling Entertainment on the Web** Napster, Inc. provided a free service for visitors to its website that allowed users to share music digitally. Napster did not receive permission from the owners of the music. Several large recording studios that owned much of the music that was being shared filed a lawsuit against Napster, requesting that a federal court order Napster to cease its free online file-sharing service. Will the recording studios be successful in convincing the court to order Napster to cease these operations? [*A&M Records Inc. v. Napster*, 239 F.3d 1004 (California)]

Principle of Law:

_____

_____

Decision:

_____

_____

38. **Entering into Contracts on the Web** Netscape offered all visitors to its website free "SmartLoad" software provided the visitor clicked his or her mouse on a designated box labeled "Download." A reference to a license agreement appeared on the screen in which the "Download" box was located, but the license agreement itself appeared on the next screen. The license agreement contained a clause requiring that any dispute between the parties proceed to arbitration, rather than to court. Six plaintiffs later filed suit against Netscape relating to the software. Netscape demanded that the suit be dismissed and that all the plaintiffs be compelled to have their claims arbitrated instead. Will the plaintiffs be required to have their disputes resolved by an arbitrator, or will the court rule that the license

agreement was not a part of the contract? [*Specht et al. v. Netscape et al.,* 150 F. Supp. 2d 585 (New York)]

Principle of Law:

_____

_____

Decision:

_____

_____

LEGAL RESEARCH

Complete the following activities. Share your findings with the class.

39. Working in Teams In teams of three or four, contact several retail stores in your city or town. Ask them if they maintain websites for consumers. Visit these websites, compare and contrast them, and present to the class your conclusions as to which of these are most effective in encouraging consumers to purchase the retailers' products and services.

_____

_____

40. Using Technology Using the Internet and search engines, find several websites that offer products and services for sale. In addition to clicking an "I accept" button, how are computer users requested to accept offers? List several means.

_____

_____

PART 7

Legal Environment of Business

chapter **31**

The Employer–Employee Relationship

After studying this chapter and completing the assessment, you will be able to

31.1 Describe the duties of an employer and employee to each other.

31.2 Distinguish between employees and independent contractors.

31.3 Explain the doctrine of employment at will.

31.4 List some typical clauses in an employment contract.

31.5 Identify some typical policies contained in an employee handbook.

31.6 Explain how employers expose themselves to legal liability when they provide employee references.

31.7 Discuss the impact of the Fair Labor Standards Act on the employer–employee relationship.

terms

LEGAL

respondeat superior	employee handbook
independent contractor	Fair Labor Standards Act
employment at will	of 1938
employment contract	

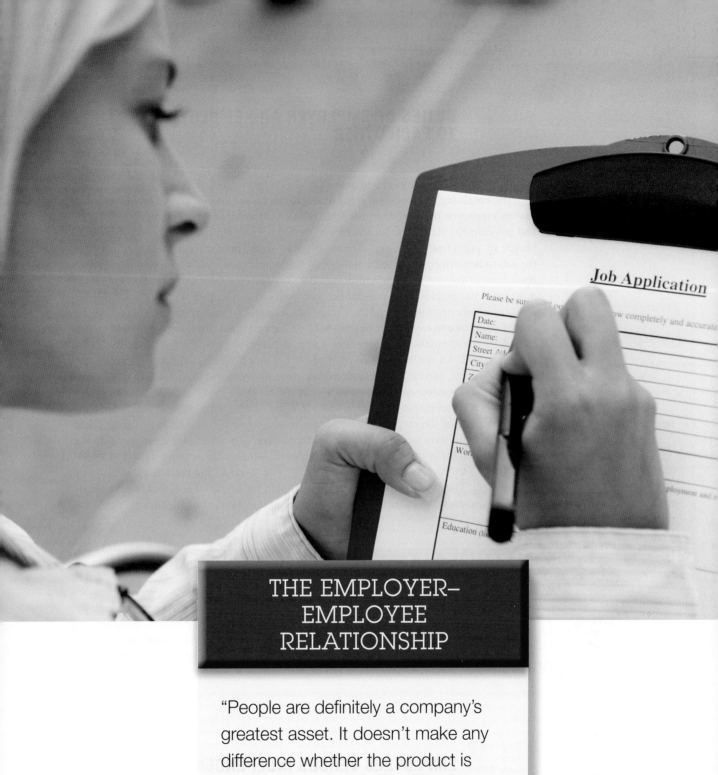

THE EMPLOYER–EMPLOYEE RELATIONSHIP

"People are definitely a company's greatest asset. It doesn't make any difference whether the product is cars or cosmetics. A company is only as good as the people it keeps."

Mary Kay Ash,
founder of Mary Kay Cosmetics Inc.

31.1 DUTIES OF EMPLOYER AND EMPLOYEE TO EACH OTHER

One of the most important legal relationships is that of employer–employee. This chapter examines some of the ways in which the law affects this relationship.

The employer owes several legal duties to his or her employee. An employer must pay an employee the agreed-upon wage, subject to company policy, union contracts, and government mandates, for his or her services. The employer must protect the employee by providing a safe and sanitary place to work, proper tools and machinery for the job to be performed, careful and competent employees with whom to work, and an environment free of discrimination and harassment (see Chapter 32). The employer must warn the employee of any danger that exists in connection with the work. Under *workers' compensation laws* (also covered in Chapter 32), any employee who is injured in the course of employment is permitted to recover compensation for the injury regardless of its cause unless the injury was due to the injured person's gross negligence or intentional act. An employee must obey his or her employer's lawful orders concerning the employment, exercise good faith toward the employer, and do his or her work carefully and conscientiously.

respondeat superior
A legal doctrine that holds that the acts of an employee committed while performing duties are considered the acts of the employer.

The acts of an employee committed while performing employment duties are considered the acts of the employer. This comes from a legal doctrine known as respondeat superior, a Latin term meaning "let the master answer." Therefore, the employer is liable to third parties for injuries caused by an employee, whether the acts are willful or negligent, so long as the acts were committed by the employee within the ordinary course of employment. The employee is also personally liable for wrongful acts that result in injuries to a third party, whether they are intentional or the result of negligence.

EXAMPLE 31.1

▶ Marek was employed in the shipping department of Margo Stores, Inc. Otler, a customer, came to the department to pick up a shipment, and Marek carelessly ran into him with a hand truck and injured Otler's leg. Both Margo Stores and Marek are liable to Otler for the injury. As a practical matter, an injured third party who is interested in receiving a financial settlement will usually sue the employer because the employer generally has more financial resources as well as insurance.

31.2 EMPLOYEES VERSUS INDEPENDENT CONTRACTORS

The distinction between an an employee and an agent was addressed in Chapter 19. Similarly, an employee is also distinct from an independent contractor. It is important to recognize these distinctions because in order to apply the law, a court first needs to determine whether an employer–employee relationship actually existed. In all cases, it is not the worker's title, or the tax treatment he or she receives, that determines whether he or she is an employee. Rather, what the individual does on the job defines the relationship.

INDEPENDENT CONTRACTORS

An independent contractor is a person or firm that performs services for another. Examples of independent contractors include freelance writers and photographers, private-duty nurses, painters, and plumbers. Independent contractors are not under the direct control of the person who engages them. It is important to distinguish between employees and independent contractors because employees usually cannot sue their employers for on-the-job injuries, whereas independent contractors can sue the person with whom they made the contract. An employer is responsible for an employee's torts committed within the scope of employment; the person who engages an independent contractor, on the other hand, is generally not responsible for the independent contractor's torts.

independent contractor
One who contracts to do a job and who retains complete control over the methods employed to obtain completion.

EXAMPLE 31.2

▶ Chu, a retired magazine editor, was engaged by Fifth National Bank to write and edit a monthly employee newsletter. She often spent time in the offices of the bank interviewing various staff members but was paid a flat fee for each issue of the newspaper. Chu is an independent contractor. She would not be considered a member of the bank's staff and did not have the legal status of an employee.

In Example 31.2, if Chu were to libel someone in her newsletter, she, but not the bank, would be responsible for the tort (although the bank would probably be named as a codefendant in a suit). Also, if Chu were injured while in the offices of the bank, unlike an employee, she would not be prevented from suing the bank for its negligence.

A plumber is an example of an independent contractor.

THE INTERNAL REVENUE SERVICE TEST

The Internal Revenue Service (IRS) publishes a kind of test that is used to aid individuals in determining whether a worker fits the status of an employee or an independent contractor. This test includes items such as who provides instruction, training, and tools; who sets hours; who determines where the work is performed and the sequence of work; and how payment is made to the worker. This explicit IRS test aids businesses and individuals in distinguishing employees from independent contractors. Understanding this distinction affects how an individual pays federal income taxes, Social Security taxes, and Medicare taxes. It also determines whether the individual receives a W-2, a tax form provided to employees, or a 1099, a tax form provided to independent contractors.

EXAMPLE 31.3

▶ Pirrone worked for wages of $14 per hour during regularly scheduled hours for Bluesky Travel, answering telephones, responding to e-mail, and greeting clients. At the end of each year, Bluesky sent Pirrone Form 1099 rather than a W-2 form. Pirrone's duties at her job clearly make her an employee, with Bluesky her employer, irrespective of the tax form she was provided.

If the IRS discovers that a company has misclassified employees as independent contractors, it may impose substantial penalties on the company. In a case of a deliberate misclassification, IRS penalties are harsh and may amount to millions of dollars for large companies. Thus, it is crucial to correctly classify workers as either employees or independent contractors.

For additional information relating to the IRS test on employees versus independent contractors, visit www.irs.gov/pub/irs-pdf/p1779.pdf.

31.3 THE DOCTRINE OF EMPLOYMENT AT WILL

employment at will
A doctrine that states that an employer may terminate an employee's employment at any time for a good reason, a bad reason, or no reason at all.

Deeply rooted in U.S. tradition is the doctrine of employment at will, which states that, just as an employee may choose to terminate his or her employment at any time he or she wishes, so too an employer may terminate an employee's employment at any time for a good reason, a bad reason, or no reason at all. Of course, over a long period of time, this doctrine has been eroded by federal, state, and local statutes; by court decisions; and by public policy. Early exceptions to the doctrine disallowed an employee from being terminated for jury duty service, for being called to active duty in the military, and for *whistleblowing* (for example, reporting the employer's criminal acts to the authorities). Later it became illegal to terminate an employee for reasons that amounted to illegal discrimination (see Chapter 32). Today there are numerous reasons for which it would be illegal to terminate an employee.

EXAMPLE 31.4

▶ Smoko worked as a mechanic for Lots and Lots Used Cars. Zlotuca, the manager, ordered him to roll back the odometer on an automobile that was for sale, so that it would command a higher price. Smoko, knowing that such conduct was illegal, refused, and Zlotuca fired him. Smoko sued for lost wages, and Lots and Lots argued that Smoko was employed at will. Smoko will probably be successful in his lawsuit.

31.4 EMPLOYMENT CONTRACTS

There are many instances in which an employer and employee enter into a formal, written employment contract that specifies that the employer agrees to pay, and the employee agrees to work, for a specified period of time at a specified salary. These contracts frequently have clauses related to maintaining confidentiality with respect to trade secrets, restrictive covenants (see Chapter 28), and agreements to arbitrate in the event of a dispute between the parties (see Chapter 30). The U.S. Supreme Court has ruled that arbitration clauses in employment contracts are enforceable provided the employee

employment contract
An agreement that specifies that the employer agrees to pay, and the employee agrees to work, for a specified period of time at a specified salary.

- ▶ Has signed the agreement.
- ▶ Has a reasonable time to file a claim.
- ▶ Has access to the same remedies that a court could provide.
- ▶ Has access to an arbitrator with expertise in employment law.
- ▶ Has the right to be represented by an attorney.
- ▶ Does not have to pay the cost of arbitration.

EXAMPLE 31.5

- ▶ Perez and One Furry Creation, a dog grooming store, entered into an employment contract wherein Perez would be employed for one year as a groomer at a salary of $400 per week. When Perez received her first paycheck, she noticed that the amount of salary was only $300. When Perez complained, she was immediately fired. Perez filed a lawsuit, and One Furry Creation argued that it was company policy that all employee claims go to arbitration. Since Perez never agreed to the policy, she will be allowed to have her case resolved by a court rather than an arbitrator.

31.5 EMPLOYEE HANDBOOKS

Many employers provide employees with employee handbooks, manuals that contain the many policies of the firm. In some states, the provisions contained in the handbook are considered a kind of contract between the employer and the employee, while in other states, legislatures and courts have made it clear that employee handbooks are not to be construed as contracts.

employee handbook
A manual published by an employer that contains the many policies of the firm.

Typically, the employee handbook contains the following information:

- ▶ *History* of the company, including its mission and philosophy.
- ▶ *Hiring procedures,* including a statement that the company complies with federal and state antidiscrimination laws.
- ▶ *Hours of employment,* including how schedules are crafted and time card policies.
- ▶ *Payment of salaries,* including the conditions under which employees may receive advances.
- ▶ *Salary increments and promotions,* including procedures for employee evaluation and appeals that may be available.

▶ *Termination procedures,* including exit interviews and the requirement that employees must return all company property.

▶ *Benefits,* including those legally required—unemployment insurance, Social Security contributions, and workers' compensation; and those not legally required—such as medical insurance, disability insurance, vacation and personal days, sick leave, holidays, education benefits, and profit sharing.

▶ *Leaves of absence,* including maternity leave, jury duty, military leave, and leaves for marriage or religious purposes.

▶ *Safety and security,* including medical and security emergencies, vandalism, tobacco and alcohol policies, drug testing, and computer usage and passwords.

▶ *Miscellaneous policies,* including parking regulations, lost and found, employee dress codes, eating and drinking on company premises, telephone usage, business travel, and employees' right to access their personnel files.

EXAMPLE 31.6

▶ Hegde was employed for five months by a medium-size accounting firm. She was planning a European holiday for next year and was interested in knowing how much vacation time the company offered. She consulted the employee handbook, which provided the information she needed to make her plans.

31.6 EMPLOYEE REFERENCES

Often employers are asked to provide references for employees who are currently working for them or who have worked for them in the past. Employers need to be extremely careful in how they respond to these requests. Providing either negative or incomplete references can subject a previous employer to three kinds of lawsuits brought by either former employees or prospective employers: invasion of privacy, defamation, and negligent misrepresentation.

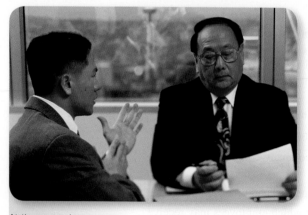

At times, employers are asked to provide references for employees.

INVASION OF PRIVACY

Disclosing personal, irrelevant information about a former employee amounts to invasion of privacy, irrespective of whether such information is true or false. An employer can safely disclose information about a current or former employee in the following areas:

▶ The employee's prior employment and educational history.

▶ The employee's character as such relates to the job (teamwork, leadership abilities, etc.).

▶ The employee's performance capabilities.

▶ The employer's willingness to rehire the employee.

EXAMPLE 31.7

▶ Verret applied for a position at a local bank, using her former manager, Goldstein, as a reference. When the human resources manager at the bank telephoned Goldstein to learn more about Verret's employment history, Goldstein explained that Verret had engaged in an extramarital affair and was about to get divorced. When the bank did not hire Verret, she sued Goldstein for invasion of privacy.

DEFAMATION

In general, a current or former employee may sue his or her employer for defamation if the employer provides information to a third party that is untrue, irrespective of whether it relates to the employee's job performance. Such defamation is considered slander, if spoken, or libel, if written (see Chapter 4).

EXAMPLE 31.8

▶ Lund applied for a position at a local bank, using his former manager, Panganibin, as a reference. When the human resources manager at the bank telephoned Panganibin to learn more about Lund's employment history, Panganibin lied and stated that Lund had stolen money from his employer. When the bank did not hire Lund, he sued Panganibin for slander, a form of defamation.

It is important to note that many states have enacted laws to shield employers from the risk of liability for defamation, provided the previous employer has a good-faith belief that the statements made in the reference are truthful.

NEGLIGENT MISREPRESENTATION

Occasionally employers attempt to reduce their risk of liability in providing references by withholding negative reference information or simply not responding to reference requests. However, if a prospective employer hires an employee based on an incomplete reference, and then suffers damages that may have been avoided had the previous employer provided an accurate reference, the prospective employer may sue the previous employer for negligent misrepresentation.

EXAMPLE 31.9

▶ Central State University fired Baez, one of the clerks in its registrar's office, for stealing money paid by students for their tuition. Baez later applied for a position as a financial aid officer at Kingsman College and, knowing that her former employer had a policy of not providing references, used Central State as a reference. Baez was hired by Kingsman and a short time later stole several thousand dollars and fled the country. Kingsman would probably be successful in a lawsuit against Central State for negligent misrepresentation.

31.7 FAIR LABOR STANDARDS ACT OF 1938

Fair Labor Standards Act of 1938 (FLSA)
The FLSA is a law that sets standards for the minimum age an employee can be, the minimum wages an employee can earn, and the rate at which an employee is paid if he or she works more than a certain number of hours in a given workweek.

The Fair Labor Standards Act of 1938 (FLSA) is a law that sets standards for the minimum age an employee can be, the minimum wages an employee can earn, and the rate at which an employee is paid if he or she works more than a certain number of hours in a given workweek. Currently the federal minimum wage is $7.25, and the overtime pay rate for employees who work more than 40 hours in a workweek is one and a half times their regular wages.

Many industries are covered by FLSA; however, four categories of employees are excluded from coverage: executives, professional employees, outside sales associates, and administrative employees. Of course independent contractors are not covered by the provisions of the FLSA.

CHAPTER SUMMARY

1. An employer must pay an employee the agreed-upon wage for his or her services and provide the employee with a safe and sanitary workplace, proper tools for the job to be performed, careful and competent employees with whom to work, and an environment free of discrimination and harassment. The employer also must warn an employee of any danger that exists in connection with the work. The employee must obey his or her employer's lawful orders concerning employment, exercise good faith toward the employer, and do his or her work carefully and conscientiously.

2. Unlike employees, independent contractors can sue their employer for on-the-job injuries. An employer is also liable for an employee's torts, but not those of an independent contractor, that are committed within the scope of employment. The Internal Revenue Service publishes a test to aid individuals in determining whether a worker fits the status of an employee or an independent contractor.

3. The doctrine of employment at will states that, just as an employee may choose to terminate his or her employment at any time he or she wishes, so too an employer may terminate an employee's employment at any time for a good reason, a bad reason, or no reason at all.

4. Employment contracts frequently have clauses related to maintaining confidentiality with respect to trade secrets, restrictive covenants, and agreements to arbitrate in the event of a dispute between the parties.

5. Typically, an employee handbook contains the history of the company, hiring procedures, hours of employment, payment of salaries, salary increments and promotions, termination procedures, benefits, leaves of absence, safety and security, and miscellaneous policies.

6. Employers who are asked to provide references for employees need to be extremely careful. Providing either negative or incomplete references can subject a previous employer to three kinds of lawsuits brought by either former employees or prospective employers: invasion of privacy, defamation, and negligent misrepresentation.

7. The FLSA is a law that sets standards for the minimum age an employee can be, the minimum wages an employee can earn, and the rate at which an employee is paid if he or she works more than a certain number of hours in a given workweek.

CHAPTER THIRTY-ONE
ASSESSMENT

MATCHING LEGAL TERMS

Match each of the numbered definitions with the correct term in the following list. Write the letter of your choice in the answer column.

a. 1099
b. employment at will
c. employment contract
d. employee handbook
e. independent contractor
f. respondeat superior
g. W-2

1. An agreement that specifies that the employer agrees to pay, and the employee agrees to work, for a specified period of time at a specified salary.   1. _____

2. A tax form provided to employees.   2. _____

3. A person or firm that performs services for another.   3. _____

4. A tax form provided to independent contractors.   4. _____

5. A doctine that states that, just as an employee may choose to terminate his or her employment at any time he or she wishes, so too an employer may terminate an employee's employment at any time.   5. _____

6. A manual published by an employer that contains the policies of the firm.   6. _____

7. A legal doctrine that holds that the acts of an employee committed while performing employment duties are considered the acts of the employer.   7. _____

TRUE/FALSE QUIZ

Indicate whether each of the following statements is true or false by writing *T* or *F* in the answer column.

8. Acts of an employee while performing duties of employment are considered the acts of the employer.   8. _____

9. Workers' compensation laws are designed to ensure that all employees are paid fairly.   9. _____

10. Independent contractors are under the direct control of the person who engages them.   10. _____

11. An independent contractor can sue the person with whom he or she made the contract.   11. _____

12. The doctrine of employment at will has been eroded by federal, state, and local statutes; by court decisions; and by public policy.   12. _____

13. Arbitration clauses in employment contracts are never enforceable.   13. _____

14. In some states, the provisions contained in an employee handbook are considered a kind of contract between the employer and the employee.   14. _____

15. In some states, legislatures and courts have made it clear that employee handbooks are not to be construed as contracts.   **15.** ____

16. A current or former employee may sue his or her employer for defamation if the employer provides information to a third party that is untrue, irrespective of whether it relates to the employee's job performance.   **16.** ____

DISCUSSION QUESTIONS

Answer the following questions and discuss them in class.

17. Describe the duties of an employer and employee to each other.

_____

_____

18. Distinguish between independent contractors and employees.

_____

_____

19. List some exceptions to the doctrine of employment at will.

_____

_____

20. Describe the conditions under which arbitration clauses in employment contracts are enforceable.

_____

_____

21. List some items typically found in an employee handbook.

_____

_____

22. Identify the standards established by the Fair Labor Standards Act of 1938.

_____

_____

THINKING CRITICALLY ABOUT THE LAW

Answer the following questions, which require you to think critically about the legal principles that you learned in this chapter.

23. Duties of Employer Should an employer be held liable for an employee's negligent act even though the employer is not at fault?

_____

_____

24. **Employees versus Independent Contractors** Does it place an unnecessary burden on a third party to determine whether he or she is dealing with an employee or an independent contractor?

   _____

   _____

25. **Employment at Will** Should the law allow an employer to fire an employee without having a good reason?

   _____

   _____

26. **Employee Handbooks** Should promises made in an employee handbook legally bind an employer?

   _____

   _____

27. **A Question of Ethics** When providing a reference for a former employee, is it ethical to withhold truthful negative information for fear of being sued?

   _____

   _____

CASE QUESTIONS

Study each of the following cases. Answer the questions that follow by writing Yes or No in the answer column.

28. **Duty of Employer** Zanucky was employed by a furniture store as a driver of a delivery truck. While making a delivery, he negligently drove through a red light, and the delivery truck struck a vehicle operated by Gittins, who was injured in the accident.

   a. Can Gittins sue Zanucky for her injuries?   **a.** _____

   b. Can Gittins sue the furniture store for her injuries?   **b.** _____

   a. Can the furniture store sue Zanucky for damages to the truck?   **c.** _____

29. **The Doctrine of Employment at Will** Packerd owned a restaurant that employed several employees as servers. When sales began to decline, Packerd decided to fire three servers. He selected Artemuk, who had numerous complaints about her service; Bednerz, who would soon be leaving for jury duty; and Tondruck, who had just been called up for active military service.

   a. May Packerd legally fire Artemuk?   **a.** _____

   b. May Packerd legally fire Bednerz?   **b.** _____

   c. May Packerd legally fire Tondruck?   **c.** _____

30. **Employee Handbooks** Killian was hired as a human resources manager for a company that employed about 75 people. She decided that it would be a good idea to publish an employee handbook explaining the many policies of the firm. She began to consider what provisions the handbook should have.

   a. Should the employee handbook have a section on procedures for employee evaluation and appeals?

   a. _____

   b. Should the employee handbook have a section on the Internal Revenue Service test?

   b. _____

   c. Should the employee handbook have a section on the number of vacation and personal days available to employees?

   c. _____

CASE ANALYSIS

Study each of the following cases carefully. Briefly state the principle of law and your decision.

31. **Employment Arbitration** The GDGS Corporation adopted an arbitration policy and announced it to its employees via e-mail. The policy stated that arbitration was the exclusive means of resolving legal disputes between employees and the company. When Campbell, one of the employees of GDGS, was fired, he filed a lawsuit against the company despite the fact that he was aware of the policy. GDGS insisted that the case go to arbitration. Will Campbell be required to take his claim to arbitration, or can the case be heard by a court? [Campbell v. General Dynamics Government Systems Corp., 321 F. Supp.2d 142 (Massachusetts)]

Principle of Law:

_____

_____

Decision:

_____

_____

32. **Invasion of Privacy** Dasey was employed as a state trooper by the Massachusetts Department of State Police. In his employment application, Dasey stated that he had not used illegal drugs during the previous five years. Later, during an unrelated homicide investigation, a videotape surfaced that depicted Dasey smoking marijuana. Dasey was fired for lying on his application. He filed a lawsuit alleging, among other things, that he had been denied his right to privacy. Has Dasey's privacy been invaded, and will Dasey be successful in his lawsuit? [Dasey v. Anderson et al., 304 F.3d 148 (Fed. 1st Cir. 2002)]

Principle of Law:

_____

_____

Decision:

_____

_____

33. **Employees versus Independent Contractors** Wojewski, a cardiothoracic surgeon, became a member of the medical staff at Rapid City Regional Hospital. Wojewski's staff status entitled him to admit patients, use the hospital's facilities, and perform surgery. Wojewski could also use nurses to assist him in surgery. Wojewski leased separate office space and maintained his own staff, whom he hired and paid. Medical staff membership required Wojewski to provide appropriate patient care, abide by medical staff bylaws, prepare required medical records, abide by ethical principles, attend an orientation program, participate in continuing medical education, and schedule operating room time. Wojewski also agreed to take calls from the emergency room for heart-related emergencies. Wojewski billed his patients directly, and the patients remitted payments directly to him. The hospital did not issue a form W-2 or 1099 to Wojewski and did not pay his Social Security taxes or provide benefits, such as health and malpractice insurance. When Wojewski had a dispute with the hospital, he argued that he was afforded protection as an employee. Does Wojewski hold the legal status of an employee? [Wojewski v. Rapid City Regional Hospital, Inc., 450 F.3d 338 (Fed. 8th Cir., 2006)]

Principle of Law:

_____

_____

Decision:

_____

_____

LEGAL RESEARCH

Complete the following activities. Share your findings with the class.

34. **Working in Teams** In teams of three or four, interview managers of local businesses. Ask them if they have ever provided a negative reference for a former employee.

_____

_____

35. **Using Technology** Using the Internet and search engines, investigate the Internal Revenue Service to determine how the agency distinguishes between employees and independent contractors.

_____

_____

chapter **32**

Employment Law

After studying this chapter and completing the assessment, you will be able to

32.1 Discuss federal and state laws that protect employees, including workers' compensation and the Occupational Safety and Health Act.

32.2 Identify the major federal statutes concerning discrimination in employment, and identify several forms of conduct that can constitute sexual harassment.

32.3 Discuss labor unions and the rights of employees, unions, and employers under federal law.

32.4 Discuss an employee's rights to medical leave and unemployment benefits.

terms

workers' compensation
exclusive remedy
Occupational Safety and Health Act of 1970
Occupational Safety and Health Administration (OSHA)
ergonomics
affirmative action plans
Civil Rights Act of 1964
Title VII
Equal Employment Opportunity Commission (EEOC)
Equal Pay Act of 1963
Age Discrimination in Employment Act of 1967

Pregnancy Discrimination Act of 1978
Americans with Disabilities Act (ADA) of 1990
Civil Rights Act of 1991
sexual harassment
National Labor Relations Board (NLRB)
collective bargaining agreement
wildcat strike
slowdown
lockout
Family Medical Leave Act of 1993
unemployment insurance

EMPLOYMENT LAW

"Society as a whole benefits immeasurably from a climate in which all persons, regardless of race or gender, may have the opportunity to earn respect, responsibility, advancement, and remuneration based on ability."

Sandra Day O'Connor,
former associate justice of
the U.S. Supreme Court

32.1 WORKER SAFETY AND HEALTH

Numerous federal and state laws protect employees from accidents and sicknesses that are job-related. At the state level, there are workers' compensation statutes, which pertain to how a worker may recover damages for work-related injuries and illnesses. At the federal level, several statutes require that employers maintain a safe and healthful work environment. The most important of these federal statutes is the Occupational Safety and Health Act of 1970.

WORKERS' COMPENSATION

workers' compensation
A type of insurance that allows employees to recover damages for work-related injuries and illnesses without having to prove negligence on the part of the employer.

Workers' compensation is a type of insurance that allows employees to recover damages for work-related injuries and illnesses without having to prove negligence on the part of the employer.

EXAMPLE 32.1

▶ Seely, an employee of Gorr Floors, installed carpeting in customers' homes. After an installation, and while on the way back to the Gorr warehouse, Seely stopped at a local tavern for a few beers. He then became engaged in a dispute with another patron and was struck in the face, resulting in the loss of several of Seely's teeth. Seely is not able to file for workers' compensation because his injury is not work-related. He is, however, allowed to try to collect damages for his injuries from the other patron, or perhaps from the owner of the tavern for failing to provide a safe environment.

exclusive remedy
A doctrine that states that an employee who sustains a work-related injury or illness can recover damages only through workers' compensation and may not file a lawsuit against his or her employer.

   Because workers' compensation is mandatory in most industries, and because it provides employees with nearly automatic recovery, it is considered to be the exclusive remedy: an employee who sustains a work-related injury or illness can recover damages only through workers' compensation and may not file a lawsuit against his or her employer.

EXAMPLE 32.2

▶ Kwan was injured when he tripped on a slippery floor while working for Sherwin Mini-Markets. Kwan sued Sherwin, arguing that she should be allowed to recover for her injuries due to Sherwin's negligence in not maintaining a dry floor. Kwan's case will be dismissed because workers' compensation is her exclusive remedy.

   Of course, the fact that an employee is prohibited from suing his or her employer for a work-related injury or illness does not preclude the employee from suing a third party, even if the injury or illness occurred while the employee was on the job.

EXAMPLE 32.3

▶ LeBlanc worked in an office where an outside contracting company was painting the walls. While LeBlanc was walking to the office conference room, a paint can fell from scaffolding and struck him in the head, causing a concussion. LeBlanc may file a workers' compensation claim against his employer and also may file a lawsuit against the contracting company. Should LeBlanc be successful in his lawsuit against the contracting company, his employer (or its insurance company) will be reimbursed for any monies paid to LeBlanc under the workers' compensation claim.

It must be pointed out, however, that employees may still sue their employers if the employer's intentional or grossly negligent conduct caused the injury or illness.

In recent years, the number of workers' compensation claims that have been filed has increased dramatically, causing a large increase in costs associated with the program. Many employees have filed claims for stress-related illnesses, which are compensable if the stress was not the result of the employee's ordinary duties on the job. Many employers have *employee assistance programs* in place, a company benefit that provides opportunities for counseling and stress reduction.

Workers' compensation provides that employees may recover damages for work-related injuries.

Occupational Safety and Health Act of 1970
A federal statute designed to promote safety and health in the workplace.

EXAMPLE 32.4

▶ Lorenz worked as a teller at a bank. An individual entered the bank building, pointed a pistol at her head, and ordered her to turn over the money in her till. Lorenz complied and, fortunately, was not harmed. Subsequently, Lorenz needed to take time off from her position to attend counseling. This stress-related condition is compensable under workers' compensation.

OCCUPATIONAL SAFETY AND HEALTH ACT

The Occupational Safety and Health Act of 1970 was passed to promote safety and health in the workplace. The law created a federal agency, the Occupational Safety and Health Administration (OSHA), to administer its many provisions. OSHA requires that companies maintain records of employee work-related accidents and sicknesses

Occupational Safety and Health Administration (OSHA)
The federal agency that administers the many provisions of the Occupational Safety and Health Act of 1970.

OSHA inspects workplaces to be certain worksites comply with safety and health standards.

and post data regarding these every February. OSHA inspects workplaces (at times using administrative search warrants to gain entry) to be certain that these worksites comply with safety and health standards. In the event violations are found to exist, OSHA can impose penalties ranging from fines to closing the facility; however, in extreme cases, such as those in which deliberate and repeat violations result in a fatality, penalties may reach $500,000 plus prison time. OSHA also requires that all violations be corrected, and often will revisit the facility to ensure that the unsafe conditions have been corrected.

As a response to OSHA standards, companies are paying greater attention to the developing science of ergonomics, which deals with designing workplaces to promote safety and health. Examples would include desk and office chair design, computer screen protections, tilted keyboards, and so forth.

ergonomics
A developing science that deals with designing workplaces to promote safety and health.

32.2 DISCRIMINATION IN EMPLOYMENT

Numerous federal, state, and local statutes prohibit employers from discriminating in employment. Discrimination against employees who are members of a protected class is illegal throughout the employment process, including outreach (for example, how the employer advertises the position), hiring, job classification, salary, promotions, benefits, discipline, layoffs, termination, and so on. At times, under federal and state law, companies must maintain and report detailed records to demonstrate that their employment practices are nondiscriminatory. These reports are referred to as affirmative action plans.

affirmative action plans
Detailed records that demonstrate that an employer's practices are nondiscriminatory.

Civil Rights Act of 1964
A federal statute designed to protect individuals from illegal discrimination.

THE CIVIL RIGHTS ACT OF 1964

The Civil Rights Act of 1964 is a federal statute designed to protect individuals from illegal discrimination. This law is divided into parts, referred to as *titles,* that prohibit discrimination in various situations. Discrimination in employment is covered in Title VII of the law.

Title VII
The portion of the Civil Rights Act of 1964 that deals with discrimination in employment.

The Civil Rights Act of 1964 created the Equal Employment Opportunity Commission (EEOC), a federal agency responsible for administering laws prohibiting discrimination in employment. Since 1972, the EEOC has had standing to sue companies that are alleged to be in violation of the law.

Equal Employment Opportunity Commission (EEOC)
A federal agency responsible for administering laws prohibiting discrimination in employment.

Discrimination in employment is prohibited on the basis of race, creed, color, sex, and place of national origin. Over the years, these classes have been expanded to include others, to be discussed later in this chapter.

EXAMPLE 32.5

▶ Bruno applied for a clerical position at Larkville National Bank and Trust. During her interview with the human resources manager, she was questioned about where her husband worked and whether she planned to have children. When she hesitated in responding, she was informed that she would not be offered the position. Bruno complained to the EEOC, which will likely impose penalties on the bank for discriminating on the basis of sex in the hiring process.

THE EQUAL PAY ACT OF 1963

The Equal Pay Act of 1963 (EPA), enacted prior to Title VII, was the first federal statute to address discrimination against women in the workplace. The act prohibits any employer from engaging in wage discrimination based on sex. Under this law, all employees performing substantially similar jobs must be compensated equally. However, there are some situations in which wage disparity between sexes is permissible, such as when wages are based on seniority or tenure within an organization. In lawsuits under the Equal Pay Act, the statute of limitations resets each time an employer issues a discriminatory paycheck to an employee (the *Lilly Ledbetter Fair Pay Act of 2009*).

Equal Pay Act of 1963 (EPA)
A statute that prohibits any employer from engaging in wage discrimination based on sex.

THE AGE DISCRIMINATION IN EMPLOYMENT ACT

The Age Discrimination in Employment Act of 1967 is a federal statute designed to protect individuals from illegal discrimination in employment on the basis of age. The protected class created pursuant to this statute is persons over the age of 40. It should be noted that several states have laws making it illegal to discriminate on the basis of age against persons who are over the age of 21.

Age Discrimination in Employment Act of 1967
A federal statute designed to protect individuals from illegal discrimination in employment on the basis of age.

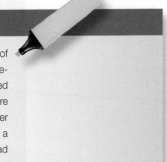

EXAMPLE 32.6

▶ Bookshire was a 67-year-old manager for a telecommunications company. Over a period of 42 years, he rose from being a mailroom clerk to a manager, attaining significant salary increments during his tenure. Senior management officials within the company repeatedly commented to Bookshire that, to retain his position, he would need to improve his technology skills. Bookshire underwent an extensive company training program, performing admirably, and took computer courses at a nearby college as well. Nonetheless, Bookshire was terminated and replaced by a 21-year-old applicant with no experience, at a significantly lower salary than Bookshire had earned. Bookshire filed a complaint with the EEOC, which will likely impose penalties on the company for discriminating in employment on the basis of age.

THE PREGNANCY DISCRIMINATION ACT

The Pregnancy Discrimination Act of 1978 is a federal statute designed to protect individuals from illegal discrimination in employment on the basis of pregnancy. Under the act employers must treat women affected by pregnancy in the same manner as any other employee who suffers from a temporary disability.

Pregnancy Discrimination Act of 1978
A federal statute designed to protect individuals from illegal discrimination in employment on the basis of pregnancy.

EXAMPLE 32.7

▶ Yashiv worked on an assembly line for a manufacturer of plastic containers. The position required that she stand on her feet for long hours. She performed her duties well and continually received outstanding evaluations. Yashiv then informed the company that she had become pregnant and requested a temporary transfer to a clerical position that was vacant and for which she was qualified. The company refused, and when Yashiv entered the latter stages of her pregnancy, she was no longer able to perform her assembly-line duties. The company then terminated her employment. Yashiv filed a complaint with the EEOC, arguing that the company should have honored her reasonable request for a temporary transfer. The EEOC will likely impose penalties on the company for discriminating in employment on the basis of pregnancy.

THE AMERICANS WITH DISABILITIES ACT

Americans with Disabilities Act (ADA) of 1990
A federal statute designed to protect individuals from illegal discrimination in employment on the basis of disability.

The Americans with Disabilities Act (ADA) of 1990 is a federal statute designed to protect individuals from illegal discrimination in employment on the basis of disability. The ADA defines *disability* as a physical or mental impairment that substantially limits one or more of the major activities of life. Persons considered disabled under the ADA would include individuals who are sight impaired, are hearing impaired, or use a wheelchair. Persons who have diseases such as cancer, diabetes, alcoholism, AIDS, epilepsy, manic depression, or schizophrenia are protected under this law. Also protected from discriminatory practices by employers are persons who were prior (not current) drug users or who have learning disabilities or psychologically based eating disorders.

The ADA requires that employers make reasonable accommodation for an otherwise qualified employee with a disability.

The ADA also protects persons who are not currently disabled but who have a record of a covered disability. In addition, the statute protects persons who have a relationship with an individual who has a covered disability (for example, if the employee's spouse is HIV positive). Furthermore, even if an employer incorrectly believes that an employee has a covered disability, the employee is then protected from discriminatory practices.

The ADA requires that employers make reasonable accommodation for an otherwise qualified employee with a disability, unless to do so would cause undue hardship. Courts have been asked on numerous occasions to determine what constitutes a "disability," a "reasonable accommodation," and an "undue hardship."

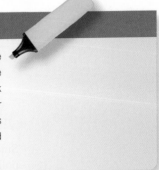

EXAMPLE 32.8

▶ Chambers worked for Jaeger Department Stores as a salesperson. Like all store employees, he was entitled to a one-hour lunch break period. Because Chambers was a diabetic and because he was not allowed to have food at his post, he requested that he be given four 15-minute break periods in lieu of the one-hour break period so that he could maintain a healthy blood sugar level. Because diabetes is a covered disability, and because this reasonable accommodation is not likely to cause undue hardship for the employer, Jaeger Department Stores will be required under the ADA to grant Chambers's request.

THE CIVIL RIGHTS ACT OF 1991

The Civil Rights Act of 1991 is a federal statute that provides two important additional remedies to an employee who can prove that he or she was a victim of discrimination:

Civil Rights Act of 1991
A federal statute that provides additional remedies to an employee who can prove that he or she was a victim of discrimination.

1. An employee may collect *punitive damages* (in effect, to punish the employer).
2. An employee may recover for emotional distress associated with being the victim of discrimination.

SEXUAL HARASSMENT

Sexual harassment is unwelcome sexual attention, whether verbal or physical, that affects an employee's job condition or creates a hostile working environment. Sexual harassment is a form of discrimination on the basis of sex and is illegal under federal and state law. Same-sex harassment is also illegal.

sexual harassment
Unwelcome sexual attention, whether verbal or physical, that affects an employee's job condition or creates a hostile working environment.

There are numerous forms of sexual harassment. Examples may include:

▶ *Unwelcome sexual advances,* such as repeated propositions for dates by a supervisor, coworker, or even a third party (such as a delivery person), whether these occur on or off company premises.
▶ *Coercion,* such as asking for a date while implying either a promise of benefit or threat of reprisal.
▶ *Favoritism,* such as granting a promotion as a result of a relationship (even if the relationship was consensual).
▶ *Indirect harassment,* such as an employee who continually witnesses other employees being sexually harassed.
▶ *Physical conduct,* such as unseemly gestures or touching.
▶ *Visual harassment,* such as graffiti or inappropriate photographs and pictures.
▶ *Verbal harassment,* such as improper teasing, joking, and so forth.

If a case of sexual harassment winds up in court, the employer can attempt to defend against this lawsuit by demonstrating that there was an effective sexual harassment program in force. An effective sexual harassment program is one that:

1. Is in writing and communicated to the employees.
2. Defines sexual harassment and declares a "no tolerance" policy.
3. Establishes a complaint procedure.
4. Trains, educates, and sensitizes employees.

5. Provides for prompt and thorough investigation of complaints.
6. Includes corrective action, including discipline.

32.3 LABOR UNIONS

Since the 1930s, labor unions have played a vital role in both the U.S. economy and its politics. Although the number of employees in the private sector who are members of labor unions has declined in recent years, it is important to understand the rights under the law that pertain to employees, unions, and employers. All of these rights are protected by the National Labor Relations Board (NLRB), a federal agency responsible for administering laws relating to labor unions. A select sample of these rights follows.

National Labor Relations Board (NLRB)
A federal agency responsible for administering laws relating to labor unions.

RIGHTS OF EMPLOYEES

Under federal law, employees have the right to form, join, and assist a labor union (or not to do so) and the right to bargain collectively through representatives of their own choosing. They also have the right not to be discriminated against because of their union activities. In addition, employees have the right to vote for union leadership in democratically held elections. If an employee has a dispute with his or her union, he or she may retain an attorney and file a lawsuit. Employment contracts (discussed in Chapter 31) that limit these rights are unenforceable.

RIGHTS OF THE UNION

The union has the right to represent all employees of a company who are a part of the bargaining unit. The union then has the right to negotiate a contract with the employer, called a collective bargaining agreement, that covers all terms and conditions of employment. During the negotiation process, the union has the right to ensure that the employer *bargains in good faith,* making an honest effort to reach an agreement. In the event an agreement is not reached, the union has the right to call a strike. At times, employees engage in a wildcat strike—a strike without the union's consent, or a slowdown—employees report to work but intentionally decrease their productivity.

collective bargaining agreement
A contract between a union and an employer that covers all terms and conditions of employment.

wildcat strike
A strike without the union's consent.

slowdown
An action wherein employees report to work but intentionally decrease their productivity.

lockout
An action by which an employer does not allow employees to return to work in the event a collective bargaining agreement is not reached.

RIGHTS OF THE EMPLOYER

The employer has the right to be free from *featherbedding* (hiring unproductive workers) and *secondary boycotts* (being targeted by a union when the union's dispute is really with another employer). During the negotiation process, the employer has the right to ensure that the union *bargains in good faith.* In the event an agreement is not reached, the employer has the right to engage in a lockout—that is, not allow employees to return to work.

32.4 ADDITIONAL EMPLOYEE RIGHTS

While numerous additional employee rights are granted to employees as a result of federal and state legislation, two notable rights are the right to medical leave and the right to unemployment benefits.

FAMILY AND MEDICAL LEAVE ACT

The Family and Medical Leave Act of 1993 (FMLA) is a federal statute that provides eligible employees with the right to take up to 12 weeks of unpaid leave for personal medical reasons or to care for a child, spouse, or parent. The FMLA applies to all employers with 50 or more employees. To be eligible, an employee must have worked for his or her current employer for at least 1,250 hours in the previous year.

UNEMPLOYMENT BENEFITS

Unemployment insurance provides financial stability, in the form of unemployment compensation, to eligible employees who lose their jobs. In the United States, unemployment insurance is established by state and federal statutes that create a system whereby employers are required to pay federal and state unemployment insurance taxes. Laws pertaining to unemployment compensation vary from state to state; however, generally, in order for employees to be eligible to receive unemployment compensation, they must have lost a job through no fault of their own, and they must meet the minimum state requirements for wages or time worked during an established period. To learn more about the specifics of unemployment compensation, visit http://www.dol.gov/dol/topic/unemployment-insurance.

Family and Medical Leave Act of 1993 (FMLA)
A federal statute that provides eligible employees with the right to take up to 12 weeks of unpaid leave for personal medical reasons or to care for a child, spouse, or parent.

unemployment insurance
Unemployment insurance provides financial stability, in the form of unemployment compensation, to eligible employees who lose their jobs.

CHAPTER SUMMARY

1. Workers' compensation is a type of insurance that provides that employees may recover damages for work-related injuries and illnesses without having to prove negligence on the part of the employer. It is considered to be the exclusive remedy: An employee who sustains a work-related injury or illness can recover damages only through workers' compensation and may not file a lawsuit against his or her employer. The Occupational Safety and Health Administration administers the many provisions of the Occupational Safety and Health Act. OSHA requires that companies maintain records of employee work-related accidents and sicknesses, inspects workplaces for safety and health standards, and, in the event violations are found to exist, can impose penalties ranging from fines to closing the facility.

2. The major federal statutes designed to protect individuals from discrimination in employment are the Civil Rights Act of 1964, the Age Discrimination in Employment Act of 1967, the Pregnancy Discrimination Act of 1978, the Americans with Disabilities Act of 1990, and the Civil Rights Act of 1991. Forms of conduct that can constitute sexual harassment include unwelcome sexual advances, coercion, favoritism, indirect harassment, physical conduct, visual harassment, and verbal harassment.

3. Under federal law, employees have the right to form, join, and assist a labor union (or not to do so), the right to bargain collectively, the right not to be discriminated against because of their union activities, the right to vote for union leadership in democratically held elections, and the right to retain an attorney and file a lawsuit. The union has the right to represent all employees who are a part of the bargaining unit, the right to negotiate a collective bargaining agreement, the right to ensure that the employer bargains in good faith, and the right to call a strike. The employer has the right to be free from featherbedding and secondary boycotts, the right to ensure that the union bargains in good faith, and the right to engage in a lockout.

4. Two notable employee rights are the right to medical leave and the right to unemployment insurance. The Family and Medical Leave Act of 1993 (FMLA) is a federal statute that provides eligible employees with the right to take up to 12 weeks of unpaid leave for personal illness or to care for a child, spouse, or parent. Unemployment insurance provides financial stability, in the form of unemployment compensation, to eligible employees who lose their jobs.

CHAPTER THIRTY-TWO
ASSESSMENT

MATCHING LEGAL TERMS

Match each of the numbered definitions with the correct term in the following list. Write the letter of your choice in the answer column.

a. Civil Rights Act of 1964
b. EEOC
c. Equal Pay Act of 1963
d. Family Medical Leave Act of 1993
e. OSHA

1. A federal agency that promotes safety and health in the workplace. 1. _____

2. A federal statute that provides eligible employees with the right to take up to 12 weeks of unpaid leave. 2. _____

3. A federal statute designed to protect individuals from illegal discrimination. 3. _____

4. A statute that prohibits any employer from engaging in wage discrimination based on sex. 4. _____

5. A federal agency responsible for administering laws prohibiting discrimination in employment. 5. _____

TRUE/FALSE QUIZ

Indicate whether each of the following statements is true or false by writing *T* or *F* in the answer column.

6. An employee may sue a third party for a work-related injury or illness, even if the injury or illness occurred while the employee was on the job. 6. _____

7. Federal law requires that employers establish employee assistance programs. 7. _____

8. In recent years, the number of workers' compensation claims that have been filed has increased dramatically, causing a large increase in costs associated with the program. 8. _____

9. Stress-related illnesses are compensable under workers' compensation if the stress was not the result of the employee's ordinary duties on the job. 9. _____

10. OSHA can impose a fine for a health or safety violation, but does not have the authority to close a business. 10. _____

11. Discrimination in employment is covered in Title III of the Civil Rights Act of 1964. 11. _____

12. The protected class created pursuant to the Age Discrimination in Employment Act is persons over the age of 50. 12. _____

13. Persons who are living with AIDS are not protected by the provisions of the Americans with Disabilities Act. 13. _____

14. Employees who are victims of illegal discrimination may recover for lost earnings but not for emotional distress. 14. _____

15. Employees who are victims of illegal discrimination may recover punitive damages. 15. _____

16. Improper teasing, joking, and so forth can constitute sexual harassment. 16. _____

17. A company may terminate an employee because the employee has joined a labor union. 17. _____

18. Under federal law, during contract negotiations, employers are required to bargain in good faith, while unions are not. 18. _____

19. An employer has the right to be free from featherbedding. 19. _____

20. In the event a collective bargaining agreement between a union and an employer is not reached, the employer has the right to engage in a lockout. 20. _____

DISCUSSION QUESTIONS

Answer the following questions and discuss them in class.

21. Describe the major provisions of workers' compensation laws.

_____

_____

22. Explain how OSHA ensures that companies maintain safe and healthful work environments.

_____

_____

23. Identify parts of the employment process in which discriminatory practices are illegal.

_____

_____

24. How does the Americans with Disabilities Act define *disability?* Provide some examples.

_____

_____

25. Define *sexual harassment* and identify some forms of conduct that can constitute it.

_____

_____

26. List the rights of employees who are members of labor unions.

_____

_____

THINKING CRITICALLY ABOUT THE LAW

Answer the following questions, which require you to think critically about the legal principles that you learned in this chapter.

27. Workers' Compensation Is it fair that workers do not have the right to sue their employers for negligence?

_____

_____

28. OSHA Should OSHA require that all safety violations be corrected, even if the cost of correcting a violation is extremely high?

_____

_____

29. ADA Should persons with relatively minor disabilities, such as being required to wear corrective lenses, be considered disabled under the ADA?

_____

_____

30. Sexual Harassment Should it be illegal for a supervisor to ask his or her subordinate for a date?

_____

_____

31. Labor Unions How can the NLRB determine whether an employer is bargaining in good faith?

_____

_____

32. A Question of Ethics If a union and a company have agreed to a collective bargaining agreement, is it ethical for employees who disagree with its terms to engage in a slowdown?

_____

_____

CASE QUESTIONS

Study each of the following cases. Answer the questions that follow by writing _Yes_ or _No_ in the answer column.

33. The Americans with Disabilities Act Melski was a truck driver with a large shipping company. Pursuant to company policy, all drivers were required to undergo random drug testing. After being tested, Melski was informed that the results were positive. Melksi admitted to being addicted to cocaine, and her employment was terminated. Melski sued, arguing that she was disabled.

a. Is Melski protected under the Americans with Disabilities Act?   **a.** _____

b. Must the shipping company make reasonable accommodation for Melski?   **b.** _____

c. Is the shipping company required to provide Melski with the services of an employee assistance program?   **c.** _____

34. Labor Unions Widra was a cashier at a large clothing store in her town. Believing her wages were below those offered by the store's competitors, she began to speak with her coemployees about the possibility of becoming affiliated with a national union. The manager of the clothing store heard about these conversations and warned her not to have these discussions. When Widra refused, the manager fired her.

a. Does Widra have the right to discuss the possibility of becoming affiliated with a union despite her manager's objections?   **a.** _____

b. Does the manager have the right to warn Widra not to have these discussions?   **b.** _____

c. Does Widra have the right to hire an attorney to represent her?   **c.** _____

d. Would it matter if the wages at the clothing store were higher than those of competitors?   **d.** _____

35. Workers' Compensation Garafolo was employed as a salesclerk at a liquor store. An armed robber entered the store one day and demanded the cash in the register. When Garafolo hesitated, the robber struck him with a pistol, causing a deep laceration. The robber left without further incident, and Garafolo was treated in the emergency room of a nearby hospital, receiving several stitches. At the insistence of his physician, Garafolo then visited a therapist, who treated him for stress.

a. Can Garafolo collect workers' compensation for the laceration he suffered during the robbery?

a. _____

b. Can Garafolo collect workers' compensation for the stress he experienced as a result of the robbery?

b. _____

c. If Garafolo collects any form of workers' compensation, and the robber is later apprehended, could Garafolo sue the robber for both the laceration and the stress?

c. _____

CASE ANALYSIS

Study each of the following cases carefully. Briefly state the principle of law and your decision.

36. **Workers' Compensation** Ryder, a police officer in Philadelphia, was alone in his patrol car when he received a radio call of a "man with a gun." Ryder was the first officer to arrive and was confronted by a suspect brandishing an AR-15 semiautomatic rifle pointed at him. Ryder was able to subdue him and place him into the back of his police cruiser. Backup units arrived approximately 12 minutes after the initial call. The weapon used by the suspect was later found fully loaded with the safety off. Subsequently, Ryder began to experience severe anxiety and stress from answering routine police calls, feeling that either he would be killed or have to kill somebody. A physician diagnosed Ryder as having posttraumatic stress disorder. Would Ryder be entitled to benefits under workers' compensation laws? [*Ryder v. City of Philadelphia,* 2930 C.D. 1997 (Pennsylvania)]

Principle of Law:

_____

_____

Decision:

_____

_____

37. **Sexual Harassment** Gentry, an employee of Export Packaging Company, reported directly to Broughton. Gentry alleged among other things that, during a period of approximately four months, Broughton subjected her to "40 hugs, 15 shoulder rubs, [and] a kiss on her cheek." She also alleged that she was referred to as a "sex-retary." Gentry sued her employer for sexual harassment, and the jury awarded her both compensatory and punitive damages. The company appealed.

Will the company be successful in setting aside the award for damages? [*Gentry v. Export Packaging Company,* 238 F.3d 842 (Texas)]

Principle of Law:

_____

_____

Decision:

_____

_____

38. **Labor Unions** Roll and Hold Warehouse, the employer, began circulating a new company policy relating to employee attendance. The union representing the company's employees objected to the policy, claiming that it had never been negotiated. The company argued, among other things, that the policy was not material (important) and, therefore, that it did not need to be negotiated. The union charged the company with violating the law by failing to negotiate all terms and conditions of employment and by failing to bargain in good faith. Is the union correct in its position that the attendance policy should have been negotiated and that the company failed to bargain in good faith? [*NLRB et al. v. Roll and Hold Warehouse and Distribution Corporation,* 162 F.3d 513 (California)]

Principle of Law:

_____

_____

Decision:

_____

_____

LEGAL RESEARCH

Complete the following activities. Share your findings with the class.

39. **Working in Teams** In teams of three or four, interview several local businesses. Ask them how they maintain a safe and healthful workplace.

_____

_____

40. **Using Technology** Using the Internet and search engines, navigate to the web pages of your state to determine the criteria under which a worker may receive unemployment benefits.

_____

_____

Product Liability

LEARNING OUTCOMES

After studying this chapter and completing the assessment, you will be able to

33.1 Describe product liability and the tort upon which it is based.

33.2 Discuss several bases of claims often used against manufacturers and sellers in product liability lawsuits.

33.3 Identify the kinds of businesses that can be charged with product liability.

33.4 Explain the legal reasoning behind the concept of strict liability.

33.5 Describe three ways in which the federal and state governments reduce unreasonable risk of injury and death associated with consumer products.

33.6 Summarize the testing procedure required by the Food and Drug Administration in order to gain approval to sell a drug.

33.7 Identify examples of consumer products regulated by the Consumer Product Safety Commission.

33.8 Describe how federal and state statutes regulate tobacco products, and explain some provisions of the Master Settlement Agreement.

33.9 Describe how the National Highway Traffic Safety Administration is responsible for the safety of automobiles sold in the United States.

LEGAL terms

- product liability
- product flaw
- failure to warn
- design defect
- strict liability
- Food and Drug Administration (FDA)
- Consumer Product Safety Commission (CPSC)
- Master Settlement Agreement
- National Highway Traffic Safety Administration (NHTSA)

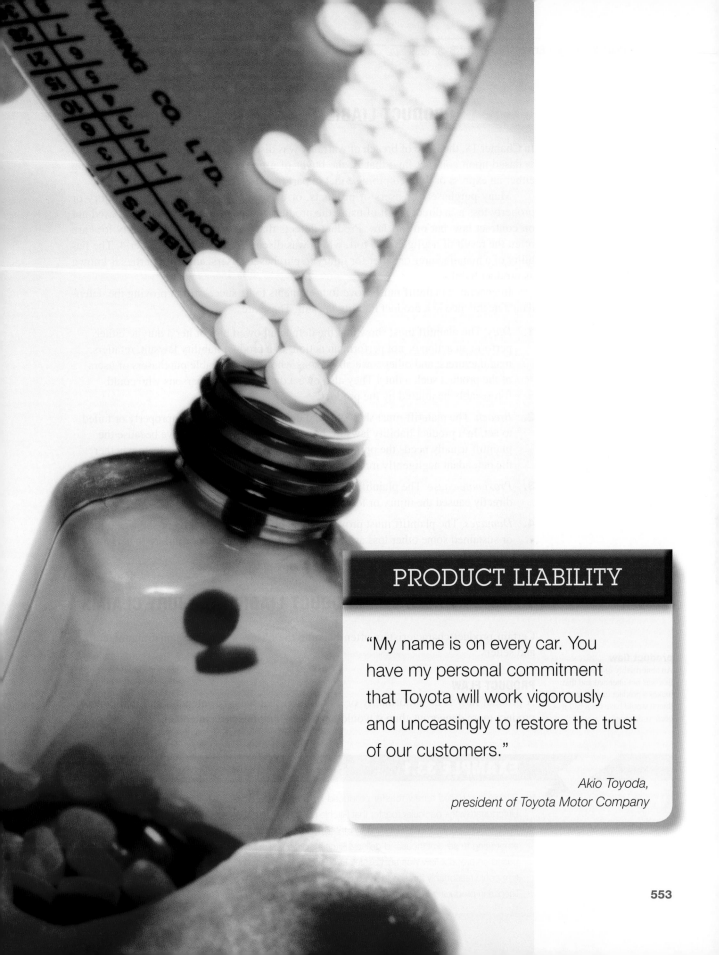

PRODUCT LIABILITY

"My name is on every car. You have my personal commitment that Toyota will work vigorously and unceasingly to restore the trust of our customers."

Akio Toyoda,
president of Toyota Motor Company

33.1 PRODUCT LIABILITY AND TORT LAW

In Chapter 18, the issue of breach of warranty was discussed. A breach of warranty lawsuit is based upon contract law; that is, the buyer of a product sues the seller for breaching either an express or implied promise that in part formed the basis of a contract.

Many purchasers or users of products, or even third parties, who sustain injury or property loss as a direct result of using the product, however, file a civil lawsuit based not on contract law, but on tort law. Product defects that cause injury and property loss are often the result of negligence, a tort, which was discussed in detail in Chapter 4. The liability of a manufacturer or seller for injury to purchasers, users, and third parties is known as product liability.

product liability
The liability of a manufacturer or seller for injury to purchasers, users, and third parties.

In general, a plaintiff must prove four elements to be successful in proving the defendant's negligence in a product liability lawsuit. These are

1. *Duty.* The plaintiff must show that the defendant owed him or her a duty to either perform an action or not perform an action. In a product liability lawsuit, retailers, manufacturers, and others owe all persons who are foreseeable purchasers or users of the product such a duty. They also owe a duty to all third persons who could foreseeably be injured by the product.

2. *Breach.* The plaintiff must show that the defendant either acted improperly or failed to act. In a product liability lawsuit, breach is often difficult to prove because the plaintiff usually needs the opinions of expert witnesses who can evaluate whether the defendant negligently manufactured or sold the product.

3. *Proximate cause.* The plaintiff must show that the defendant's act or failure to act directly caused the injury or loss.

4. *Damages.* The plaintiff must prove, as in all civil lawsuits, that he or she was injured or sustained some other loss as a result of the defendant's act or failure to act.

33.2 BASES FOR PRODUCT LIABILITY INJURY CLAIMS

Certain product characteristics often become the bases of claims against manufacturers and sellers.

product flaw
An abnormality or a condition that was not intended and that makes a product more dangerous than it would have been had it been as intended.

PRODUCT FLAW

A product flaw is an abnormality or a condition that was not intended and that makes a product more dangerous than it would have been had it been as intended.

EXAMPLE 33.1

▶ Ritchie purchased a new toaster produced by a reputable household appliance manufacturer. Unfortunately, the particular toaster that Ritchie purchased had a defect in the wiring system. When Ritchie plugged the toaster into the electrical socket, a fire erupted, causing damage to his home amounting to several thousand dollars. Ritchie's product liability lawsuit against the manufacturer based on product flaw was successful. Even though the manufacturer had never met Ritchie, the firm could reasonably foresee that a purchaser would plug in the toaster. The manufacturer's negligence in producing this particular toaster proximately caused the damage to Ritchie's property.

FAILURE TO WARN

Manufacturers and sellers have a duty to advise purchasers and users of dangers inherent in a product. A failure to warn is a dereliction of this duty.

failure to warn
The dereliction of a duty to advise purchasers and users of dangers inherent in a product.

EXAMPLE 33.2

▶ Poggi purchased a container of hot coffee from a fast-food retailer. When she entered her automobile with the coffee, the contents of the cup spilled onto her lap, causing third-degree burns. Poggi's product liability lawsuit based on failure to warn was successful. The retailer had a duty to warn purchasers and users that the contents were extremely hot and that extraordinary care in handling the container was required.

DESIGN DEFECT

Manufacturers have a duty to design products in a manner that is not negligent. A design defect is a fault in a product that creates a hazardous condition that causes injury.

A design defect is a hazardous condition that exists throughout an entire product line, as opposed to a product flaw, discussed previously, which is an abnormality or condition in a single unit of the product.

design defect
A fault in a product that creates a hazardous condition that causes injury.

EXAMPLE 33.3

▶ An automobile manufacturer produced cars in the United States that had the feel of a "European model." The accelerator pedal was not elongated but had the same shape as the brake pedal. In addition, both the accelerator pedal and the brake pedal were located slightly to the left of where these would be positioned on other cars. Several drivers were involved in accidents, claiming unintended acceleration. In reality, these drivers had been inadvertently applying pressure to the accelerator rather than to the brake. The drivers' suits for product liability based on design defect were successful. Shaping the accelerator pedal in the manner that had been done and positioning the accelerator and brake pedals to the left were considered design defects.

33.3 WHO CAN BE HELD LIABLE FOR PRODUCT-RELATED INJURIES?

In a product liability case, the most obvious target of an injured party is the manufacturer of the defective product. However, others in the distribution channel also may be found liable, including retailers, wholesalers, manufacturers of component parts, assemblers of products, endorsers of products, licensors of trademarks, and licensors of patents.

Retailers are particularly vulnerable when the product manufacturer is insolvent or is a corporation that has been dissolved or is unreachable—such as a manufacturer in a foreign country. Consequently, retailers need to be particularly careful to choose product manufacturers that act responsibly and are also financially secure.

33.4 STRICT LIABILITY

As discussed earlier, under traditional tort law, the injured party must prove that the manufacturer was negligent in producing a product. It is often difficult for injured parties to prove negligence for a number of reasons, and the defenses of manufacturers are often very effective. The financial burden to society and the hardships suffered by injured parties that result are of grave concern to many legal scholars and jurists.

Courts in some states have held that it should not be necessary for an injured person to prove negligence on the part of the manufacturer. They have expressed the notion that the producer is in a better position than the user of a product to prevent injuries because the company has the opportunity and expertise to design safe products. Also, they believe that the manufacturer is in a position to pay for the damages suffered by a user of a product, regardless of whether the firm was in fact negligent, because the manufacturer can buy insurance that pays the injured party. The company can then pass on the cost of insurance to all users of the product. This legal reasoning has given rise to the doctrine of strict liability—that is, liability without the necessity of proving fault.

Today the concept of strict liability is generally accepted, although its application from state to state varies greatly. In some states, strict liability applies only to products that are *inherently dangerous,* such as firearms, fireworks, knives, and so forth. In other states, the doctrine applies only when the manufacturer is in violation of a statute.

strict liability
The doctrine under which persons may be liable for injuries to others whether or not they have been negligent or committed an intentional tort. This establishes liability without the necessity of proving fault.

In a product liability case, the most obvious target of an injured party is the manufacturer of the defective product.

100%
complete &
balanced
nutrition for
growth
& maintenance

With Beef, Bacon & Cheese
Dog Food
NET WT 13.2 OZ (374 g)

Despite the advent of strict liability, there is considerable activity in various state legislatures with a view toward *tort reform* and other efforts to curb abuses of the system. One consequence of strict liability is that companies are sometimes hesitant to introduce new or innovative products because of the fear of liability lawsuits.

33.5 PRODUCT SAFETY

The previous sections of this chapter related to lawsuits that are filed as a result of a product causing injury or loss to a purchaser, user, or third party. The remaining sections of this chapter address some of the federal statutes and administrative rules that are in effect to promote safety for consumers and users of products.

The federal and state governments enact these numerous statutes and rules to reduce unreasonable risk of injury and death associated with consumer products. This is achieved by governments' providing safety information to the public, developing voluntary and mandatory standards, and pursuing recalls of dangerous products. The following provides a small sample of requirements that manufacturers and retailers face as they sell various types of products in the United States. For additional information on these and other types of products, visit http://www.cpsc.gov/cgi-bin/regs.aspx.

33.6 DRUGS

The federal agency responsible for the safety of food and drugs sold in the United States is the Food and Drug Administration (FDA). The FDA requires that all drugs sold be thoroughly tested to ensure that they are both safe and effective. After experimentation in the laboratory and animal studies, pharmaceutical companies subject drugs to four phases of testing:

Food and Drug Administration (FDA)
The federal agency responsible for the safety of food and drugs sold in the United States.

▶ In *Phase I,* a small number of people are tested to determine safety and dosage and to identify side effects that result from taking the drug.

▶ In *Phase II,* the effectiveness of the drug is measured by comparing subjects who receive the drug to those who receive a *placebo* (usually a water pill that will have no impact).

▶ In *Phase III,* the safety and effectiveness of the drug are evaluated in trials involving a great number of people.

▶ In *Phase IV,* continued testing occurs subsequent to FDA approval of the drug.

The process of FDA approval has come under some criticism in recent years, as concerns over the costs and length of time for obtaining approval of prescription drugs have emerged. For a drug to be approved, it is estimated that it costs a pharmaceutical company approximately $700 million and takes about 12 years for the process to unfold. Interestingly, only one of 5,000 chemicals ultimately is approved for sale as a drug, and only one-third of approved drugs become profitable. Furthermore, one-fifth of all drugs that are approved have alleged safety problems.

Because of the costs and time involved in the manufacture of prescription drugs, they have become very expensive to consumers. Many individuals have turned to the Internet, seeking drugs from Canada and other countries. Several unscrupulous firms sell drugs online, offering weaker dosages, mislabeled drugs, and illegal drugs, often from unlicensed pharmacies or firms misrepresenting their facilities as being in Canada. It is expected that federal and state statutes will continue to address this situation.

Furthermore, a pharmaceutical company earns most of its profits from a drug only during the time that the patent for the drug is effective, either 17 or 20 years, depending on the coverage of the patent (see Chapter 28). After the patent expires, other companies may produce alternative versions of the drug, referred to as *generics.* To recoup its costs, therefore, it is necessary that the pharmaceutical company charge high prices that will allow it to continue its research and development (*R&D*) on this and other drugs.

Advertising of drugs is legal, so long as detailed information about the drug being advertised is disclosed. The Federal Trade Commission (FTC) is responsible for ensuring that advertising is truthful (see Chapter 30). Pharmaceutical companies may advertise a drug only for the ailment for which it was approved for use. Doctors, however, may prescribe a drug for other purposes as they deem appropriate (referred to as *off-label* uses).

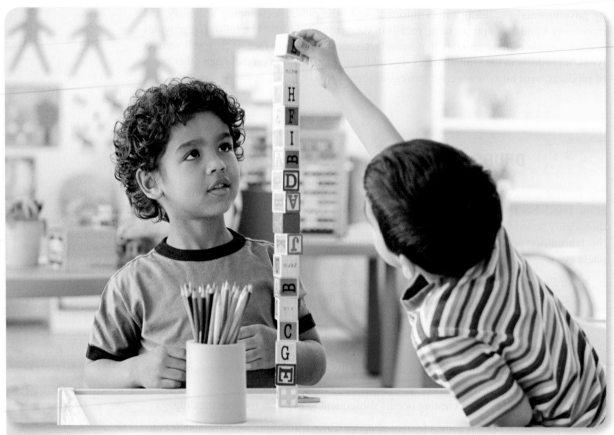

Toys are regulated by the CPSC.

33.7 CONSUMER PRODUCTS

Consumer Product Safety Commission (CPSC)
The federal agency responsible for the safety of consumer products sold in the United States.

The federal agency responsible for the safety of consumer products sold in the United States is the Consumer Product Safety Commission (CPSC). Examples of products that are regulated by the CPSC include clothing, hazardous household cleaners and substances, electronic devices, appliances, furnishings, building materials, toys, and other juvenile products.

Some consumer products with restrictions on them include the following:

▶ Wool products, fur products, and textile fiber products—all of which must be properly labeled and identified.

▶ Flammable products—which must incorporate flame-retardant materials.

▶ Hazardous substances—those that are toxic, corrosive, irritant, or flammable, which must be properly labeled with appropriate warnings.

▶ Children's toys—which may not contain electrical, thermal, or mechanical hazards.

▶ Paint—which generally may not contain lead.

▶ Radiation-emitting products—such as televisions, computer screens, cellular telephones, and microwave ovens, which must contain appropriate safeguards.

The CPSC regularly conducts tests of these products and other consumer products sold in the United States. If the agency determines that a product is dangerous, it can order the manufacturer to recall it. For additional information, visit the agency's website at www.cpsc.gov.

33.8 TOBACCO

Numerous federal and state statutes strictly regulate cigarettes and other tobacco products. Federal law disallows advertising of these products on television and radio, and FTC regulations require disclosure of tar and nicotine levels on cigarette packages. In addition, all cigarette packages must contain a warning from the surgeon general regarding the dangers of smoking.

In 1997 the major cigarette manufacturers in the United States entered into a contract, referred to as the Master Settlement Agreement, in which the companies agreed not to engage in certain advertising strategies. The companies agreed not to advertise using cartoon characters (such as Joe Camel); not to place advertising on billboards or stadium signs; not to pay for product inclusion in films and television shows; not to provide free caps, T-shirts, and so forth; not to distribute free samples of cigarettes; and not to target youth markets by sponsoring concerts, athletic events, and so on. The companies also support the American Legacy Foundation, which provides education regarding the dangers of addiction to tobacco products.

The *Tobacco Control Act* gives the FDA authority to regulate tobacco products in order to discourage children and young adults from smoking. The FDA has introduced new labeling restrictions/requirements for packaging and has banned the production, distribution, and sale of flavored cigarettes.

Master Settlement Agreement A contract in which the major cigarette manufacturers in the United States agreed not to engage in certain advertising strategies.

EXAMPLE 33.4

▶ Djarum, an Indonesian clove cigarette manufacturer, responded to the FDA ban on flavored cigarettes by introducing a new line of clove cigars in the United States. Like cigarettes, these small cigars are filtered and contain paper in the wrapping. Because the FDA's ban on flavored cigarettes applies to any product that matches a cigarette's profile, it is illegal to sell or distribute Djarum clove "cigars" in the United States.

33.9 AUTOMOBILES

The federal agency responsible for the safety of automobiles sold in the United States is the National Highway Traffic Safety Administration (NHTSA).

The NHTSA

▶ Requires that automobiles contain appropriate safety features, such as air bags, seat belts, and so forth.

▶ Routinely proposes both stricter crash test requirements for automakers and, as technology advances, new regulations to provide vehicle occupants with maximum safety benefits.

▶ Investigates potential safety defects in automobiles and has the authority to require automakers to issue recalls to repair dangerous defects and, in extreme cases, cease production of automobiles.

National Highway Traffic Safety Administration (NHTSA) The federal agency responsible for the safety of automobiles sold in the United States.

EXAMPLE 33.5

▶ The NHTSA received hundreds of reports from consumers describing the unintended, sudden acceleration of their Toyota vehicles, which were equipped with computer-controlled accelerators. An initial investigation determined that the automobiles' floor mats had a tendency to push on the gas pedals and were at least partially responsible for the acceleration problems. However, despite a recall by Toyota to replace the floor mats, consumers continued to report new incidents of sudden acceleration—some resulting in fatal crashes. Finally, Toyota executives revealed that the company had traced the problem to a faulty plastic part in the accelerator pedal. Since Toyota did not have enough replacement parts in stock to issue a comprehensive recall, the NHTSA ordered Toyota to cease production of automobiles and imposed a fine of $16.4 million, the maximum allowable.

While the NHTSA administers to the safety of automobiles, the responsibility of controlling automobile emissions rests with the Environmental Protection Agency (see Chapter 36).

The NHTSA is responsible for the safety of automobiles sold in the United States.

CHAPTER SUMMARY

1. Product defects that cause injury and property loss are often the result of negligence, a tort. The liability of a manufacturer or seller for injury to purchasers, users, and third parties is known as product liability. The four elements that generally prove the defendant's negligence in a product liability lawsuit are duty, breach, proximate cause, and damages.

2. A product flaw is an abnormality or a condition that was not intended and that makes a product more dangerous than it would have been had it

been as intended. A failure to warn is a dereliction of a duty to advise purchasers and users of dangers inherent in a product. A design defect is a fault in a product that creates a hazardous condition that causes injury.

3. Manufacturers, retailers, wholesalers, manufacturers of component parts, assemblers of products, endorsers of products, licensors of trademarks, and licensors of patents are the kinds of businesses that can be charged with product liability.

4. The doctrine of strict liability arose because courts believe that the manufacturer is in a better position than the user of a product to prevent injuries and that the manufacturer is in a position to pay for the damages suffered by a user of a product, regardless of whether the firm was in fact negligent, because the manufacturer can buy insurance that pays the injured party.

5. The federal and state governments enact numerous statutes and rules to reduce unreasonable risk of injury and death associated with consumer products. This is achieved by governments' providing safety information to the public, developing voluntary and mandatory standards, and pursuing recalls of dangerous products.

6. The FDA requires that, after experimentation in the laboratory and animal studies, pharmaceutical companies subject drugs to four phases of testing: (a) Phase I, during which a small number of people are tested to determine safety and dosage and to identify side effects that result from taking the drug; (b) Phase II, during which the effectiveness of the drug is measured by comparing subjects who receive the drug to those who receive a placebo; (c) Phase III, during which the safety and effectiveness of the drug are evaluated in trials involving a great number of people; and (d) Phase IV, continued testing that occurs subsequent to FDA approval of the drug.

7. Examples of consumer products regulated by the CPSC include wool products, fur products, and textile fiber products; flammable products; hazardous substances; children's toys; paint; and radiation-emitting products.

8. Numerous federal and state statutes strictly regulate cigarettes and other tobacco products. Federal law disallows advertising of these products on television and radio, and FTC regulations require disclosure of tar and nicotine levels on cigarette packages. In addition, all cigarette packages must contain a warning from the surgeon general regarding the dangers of smoking. In the Master Settlement Agreement, the major cigarette manufacturers in the United States agreed not to advertise using cartoon characters; not to place advertising on billboards or stadium signs; not to pay for product inclusion in films and television shows; not to provide free caps, T-shirts, and so forth; not to distribute free samples of cigarettes; not to target youth markets by sponsoring concerts, athletic events, and so on; and to support a foundation that provides education regarding the dangers of addiction to tobacco products.

9. The NHTSA requires that automobiles contain appropriate safety features, such as air bags, seat belts, and so forth; routinely proposes stricter crash test requirements for automakers and, as technology advances, new safety regulations; and investigates potential safety defects in automobiles and has the authority to require automakers to issue recalls to repair dangerous defects and, in extreme cases, cease production of automobiles.

CHAPTER THIRTY-THREE
ASSESSMENT

MATCHING LEGAL TERMS

Match each of the numbered definitions with the correct term in the following list. Write the letter of your choice in the answer column.

a. product flaw
b. design defect

c. strict liability
d. Master Settlement Agreement

e. product liability
f. failure to warn

1. A fault in a product that creates a hazardous condition that causes injury. **1.** _____

2. Liability without the necessity of proving fault.

2. _____

3. The liability of a manufacturer or seller for injury to purchasers, users, and third parties.

3. _____

4. An abnormality or a condition that was not intended and that makes a product more dangerous than it would have been had it been as intended.

4. _____

5. The dereliction of a duty to advise purchasers and users of dangers inherent in a product.

5. _____

6. A contract in which the major cigarette manufacturers in the United States agreed not to engage in certain advertising strategies.

6. _____

TRUE/FALSE QUIZ

Indicate whether each of the following statements is true or false by writing *T* or *F* in the answer column.

7. Both breach of warranty and product liability lawsuits are based on tort law rather than contract law.

7. _____

8. The four elements of a product liability lawsuit are duty, breach, proximate cause, and damages.

8. _____

9. A design defect is a hazardous condition that exists throughout an entire product line.

9. _____

10. An alteration that a buyer makes in a product is known as a product flaw.

10. _____

11. Manufacturers and retailers have a duty to warn users of dangerous or hazardous characteristics of products.

11. _____

12. Only manufacturers can be held liable in product liability lawsuits.

12. _____

13. The manufacturer is in a better position than the user of a product to prevent injuries because the company has the opportunity to design safe products.

13. _____

14. One consequence of strict liability is that companies are sometimes hesitant to introduce new or innovative products because of the fear of liability lawsuits.

14. _____

15. In Phase II of the drug-testing process, the effectiveness of the drug is measured by comparing subjects who receive the drug to those who receive a placebo.

15. _____

16. It is perfectly safe to purchase prescription drugs over the Internet.

16. _____

17. Advertising of drugs is legal, so long as detailed information about the drug being advertised is disclosed.

17. _____

18. The Consumer Product Safety Commission regularly conducts tests of consumer products sold in the United States.

18. _____

19. Under the terms of the Master Settlement Agreement, cigarette packages must contain a warning from the surgeon general regarding the dangers of smoking.

19. _____

20. The National Highway Traffic Safety Administration has the responsibility of controlling automobile emissions.

20. _____

DISCUSSION QUESTIONS

Answer the following questions and discuss them in class.

21. Describe product liability and the tort upon which it is based.

_____

_____

22. Identify the kinds of business that can be charged with product liability.

_____

_____

23. Explain the legal reasoning behind the concept of strict liability and weigh its consequences for businesspeople and consumers.

_____

_____

24. Summarize the testing procedure required by the Food and Drug Administration in order to gain approval to sell a drug.

_____

_____

25. Identify examples of consumer products regulated by the Consumer Product Safety Commission.

_____

_____

26. Explain some provisions of the Master Settlement Agreement.

_____

_____

THINKING CRITICALLY ABOUT THE LAW

Answer the following questions, which require you to think critically about the legal principles that you learned in this chapter.

27. Failure to Warn Is it obvious to the reasonable consumer that disposable containers containing coffee and other beverages are hot? Should retailers be required to warn customers to exercise care in handling these containers?

_____

_____

28. Who Can Be Held Liable Where should the responsibility lie for product safety: manufacturers, retailers, users, or government regulators?

_____

_____

29. Strict Liability Why would a company that is subject to strict liability be hesitant to introduce new or innovative products?

_____

_____

30. Drugs Should the federal and state governments allow consumers to purchase drugs from Canada and other countries on the Internet?

_____

_____

31. Tobacco Because tobacco is known to cause health problems, should it be illegal to use?

_____

_____

32. A Question of Ethics Is it ethical for a pharmaceutical company to charge high prices for prescription drugs when these drugs are needed by persons who cannot afford them and whose lives depend upon them?

_____

_____

CASE QUESTIONS

Study each of the following cases. Answer the questions that follow by writing _Yes_ or _No_ in the answer column.

33. Failure to Warn Kriz, an elderly man who was quite overweight, purchased a power lawnmower from a nationally known retailer. To start the lawnmower, the user needed to bend down to draw the starter cord. When Kriz bent over, he suffered a heart attack. Kriz sued the retailer, arguing that the lawnmower should have contained a warning advising older, overweight users not to bend over.

a. Is this lawsuit an example of a product liability based upon product flaw?　　　　a. ＿＿＿

b. Is this lawsuit an example of a product liability based upon design defect?　　　　b. ＿＿＿

c. Will Kriz be required to prove that the lawnmower was the proximate cause of his ailment?　　　　c. ＿＿＿

34. **Who Can Be Held Liable** Eddington operated a toy store and carried merchandise from both domestic as well as foreign manufacturers. As the holiday season approached, he found that he could reduce his costs by importing a stuffed toy from a developing country. One of the toys was responsible for an injury to a child, and the parents brought a product liability suit against Eddington. He claimed that he was unaware of the defects of the toy because he did not manufacture it but only sold it.

a. Do the parents of the injured child have the right to sue Eddington instead of the manufacturer?　　　　a. ＿＿＿

b. Can a retailer be held liable for defective products?　　　　b. ＿＿＿

c. Is there anyone else who could be named in the suit?　　　　c. ＿＿＿

35. **Drugs/Failure to Warn** Parker, a person with no medical training, gave a prescription drug to Fishman, a friend, to alleviate back pain Fishman had been experiencing. After taking the drug, Fishman drove his automobile, became disoriented, and struck a telephone pole with his vehicle. Fishman sued, claiming he had never been warned about the drug's side effects.

a. Can Fishman recover the costs associated with the accident from the manufacturer of the drug?　　　　a. ＿＿＿

b. Can Fishman recover the costs associated with the accident from Parker?　　b. ＿＿＿

c. Can Fishman recover the costs associated with the accident from the Food and Drug Administration?　　　　c. ＿＿＿

d. Was Fishman a foreseeable user of the drug?　　　　d. ＿＿＿

CASE ANALYSIS

Study each of the following cases carefully. Briefly state the principle of law and your decision.

36. **Drugs/Failure to Warn** Merck, a major pharmaceutical company, produced a popular painkiller called Vioxx. Despite the drug being approved by the FDA, several studies linked usage of it to cardiovascular risks relating to heart attacks and strokes. Internal e-mails indicated that, for approximately four years, the company was aware that academics and others had concerns over the drug's safety. Finally Merck voluntarily discontinued distribution of Vioxx. Several lawsuits were then

brought by the families of those who had suffered heart attacks after taking the drug. Will the lawsuits against Merck be successful?

Principle of Law:

_____

_____

Decision:

_____

_____

37. **Tobacco** From the early 1950s until his death from smoking-related lung cancer in 1997, Williams smoked cigarettes, primarily the Marlboro brand, eventually developing a habit of three packs a day. At that point, he spent half his waking hours smoking and was highly addicted to tobacco, both physiologically and psychologically. Although, at the urging of his wife and children, he made several attempts to stop smoking, each time he failed, in part because of his addiction. When his family told him that cigarettes were dangerous to his health, he replied that the cigarette companies would not sell them if they were as dangerous as his family claimed. When one of his sons tried to get him to read articles about the dangers of smoking, he responded by finding published assertions that cigarette smoking was not dangerous. However, when Williams learned that he had inoperable lung cancer, he felt betrayed, stating, "Those darn cigarette people finally did it. They were lying all the time." He died about six months after his diagnosis. Williams's widow sued, demanding both compensatory and punitive damages, claiming that the manufacturer of the cigarettes was responsible for her husband's death. Is Williams's widow likely to be successful in her lawsuit? [*Philip Morris USA, Inc. v. Williams*, 540 U.S. 801, 124 S. Ct. 56, 157 L. Ed. 2d 12 (Oregon)]

Principle of Law:

_____

_____

Decision:

_____

_____

38. **Automobiles/Design Defect** Grimshaw, a 13-year-old girl, was a passenger in a Ford Pinto driven by a neighbor. The Pinto stalled and, while motionless, was hit from behind by another car. Moments later, the Pinto's fuel tank exploded, with the result that the driver was killed and Grimshaw was burned over 90 percent of her body. Grimshaw's family sued Ford Motor Company, claiming that Ford was negligent in designing the Pinto so that the fuel tank was in a dangerous position, with "conscious disregard of public safety." The jury awarded the family of the driver $666,000 and Grimshaw $2,841,000 as compensation for her injuries. In addition, the jury awarded Grimshaw another $125,000,000 as punitive damages (that is, to punish Ford). Ford appealed the decision. Will the decision of the jury be upheld?

[*Grimshaw et al. v. Ford Motor Company*, 119 Cal. App. 3d 757, 1981 Cal. App. LEXIS 1859, 174 Cal. Rptr. 348 (California)]

Principle of Law:

_____

_____

Decision:

_____

_____

LEGAL RESEARCH

Complete the following activities. Share your findings with the class.

39. **Working in Teams** In teams of three or four, interview several local businesses to learn what types of complaints they have received regarding defective products. Are these complaints examples of product flaw, failure to warn, or design defect?

_____

_____

40. **Using Technology** Using the Internet and search engines, navigate to the websites of several cigarette manufacturers. What warnings regarding tobacco use do these companies provide?

_____

_____

chapter **34**
Professionals' Liability

LEARNING OUTCOMES

After studying this chapter and completing the assessment, you will be able to

34.1 Explain the characteristics of a professional.

34.2 Distinguish between the malpractice of professionals and other forms of negligence by nonprofessionals.

34.3 Explain how the elements of a malpractice lawsuit are applied to professionals.

34.4 Provide examples of professional malpractice that might be caused by health care providers, accountants, financial planners, architects and engineers, attorneys, insurance agents and brokers, and others.

34.5 Explain how professionals protect themselves against the losses that might result from being found liable for malpractice or negligence.

terms

LEGAL

professional
malpractice
Good Samaritan laws
loss of consortium
churning

statute of limitations
title insurance
whole life insurance
term insurance

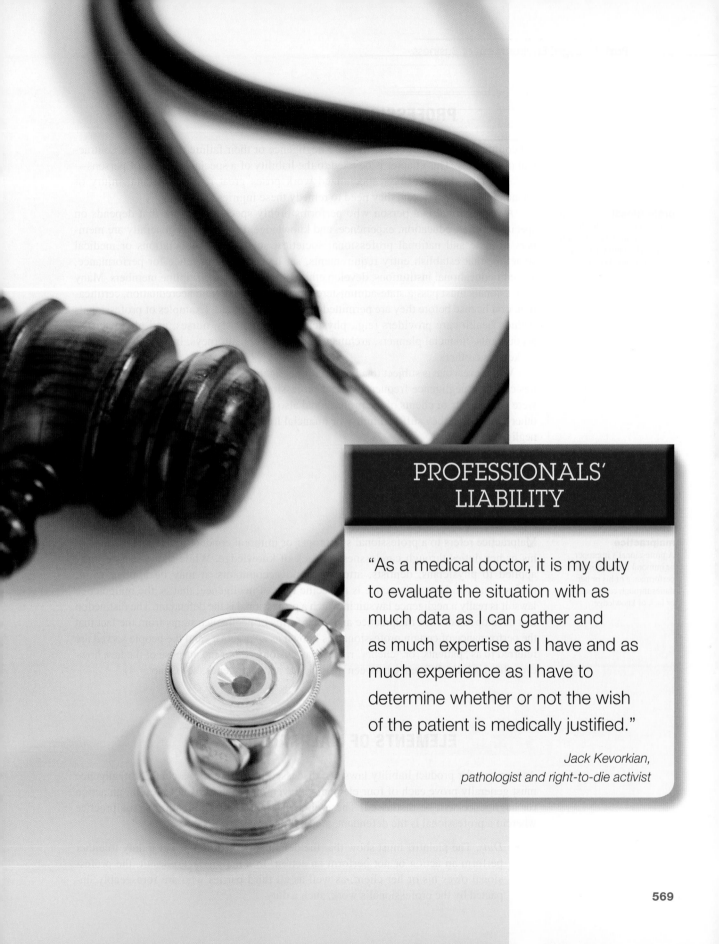

PROFESSIONALS' LIABILITY

"As a medical doctor, it is my duty to evaluate the situation with as much data as I can gather and as much expertise as I have and as much experience as I have to determine whether or not the wish of the patient is medically justified."

Jack Kevorkian,
pathologist and right-to-die activist

34.1 PROFESSIONALS

All competent parties are liable for their negligence or their failure to meet their contractual obligations. This chapter is devoted to the liability of a special category of persons—professionals—because their specialized work poses great risk of personal injury or financial loss to others, and they need to remedy these injuries and losses.

professional
A person who does highly specialized work that depends on special abilities, education, experience, and knowledge.

A professional is a person who performs highly specialized work that depends on special abilities, education, experience, and knowledge. Professionals generally are members of state and national professional societies, such as bar associations or medical societies, that establish entry requirements, set levels of competence for performance, accredit educational institutions, develop ethical standards, and discipline members. Many professionals must pass a state-administered examination and gain accreditation, certification, or a license before they are permitted to work in their field. Examples of professionals include health care providers (e.g., physicians, psychiatrists, nurses, and pharmacists), accountants, financial planners, architects and engineers, attorneys, insurance agents and brokers, and others.

While everyone is subject to a lawsuit for negligence, suits by injured or damaged parties charging negligence frequently target professionals. In some cases, third parties who were not patients or clients of the professional also can sue if they are able to show, among other things, that they suffered injury or financial loss as a direct result of a professional's negligence.

34.2 MALPRACTICE

malpractice
A professional's improper or immoral conduct in the performance of his or her duties through carelessness or lack of knowledge.

Malpractice refers to a professional's improper or immoral conduct in the performance of his or her duties through carelessness or lack of knowledge. While the term is usually applied to physicians, dentists, attorneys, and accountants, it may be applied to all professionals. In law, malpractice is a specific type of negligence; that is, the malpractice lawsuit is really a negligence lawsuit in which a professional is the defendant. The distinction that developed between malpractice and other forms of negligence stems from the fact that the performance of certain professionals is known as a "practice" and the people served are referred to as "patients" or "clients" rather than customers. For the purpose of the law, however, there is little difference between malpractice and negligence (see Chapter 4).

34.3 ELEMENTS OF MALPRACTICE

As was true for product liability lawsuits, discussed in Chapter 33, a claim of negligence must generally prove each of four elements; if even one of these is not present, an action for negligence will be dismissed. These elements, and their application to malpractice wherein a professional is the defendant, are as follows:

▶ *Duty.* The plaintiff must show that the defendant owed him or her a duty to either perform an action or not perform an action. In a malpractice lawsuit, the professional owes his or her client, as well as all third parties who are foreseeably impacted by the professional's work, such a duty.

▶ *Breach.* The plaintiff must show that the defendant either acted improperly or failed to act. In determining whether a defendant has breached his or her duty in a malpractice lawsuit, the defendant's act or failure to act is measured against the standard of care required by a reasonable professional in the same field. As a result, breach is often difficult to prove because the plaintiff will need the opinions of (often reluctant) expert witnesses in the same field who can evaluate whether the defendant acted negligently.

▶ *Proximate cause.* The plaintiff must show that the professional defendant's act or failure to act directly caused the injury or loss.

▶ *Damages.* The plaintiff must prove, as in all civil lawsuits, that he or she was injured or sustained some other loss as a result of the professional defendant's act or failure to act.

34.4 LIABILITY FOR PROFESSIONAL MALPRACTICE

The following discussion explains how specific professionals can commit malpractice or engage in behavior that might result in a charge of negligence.

LIABILITY OF HEALTH CARE PROVIDERS

A medical professional commits malpractice when his or her actions demonstrate that he or she has failed to observe accepted standards of performance and, as a result, the patient suffers injury or death. It is important to note, however, that certain laws exist to shield medical professionals from malpractice claims during extreme circumstances. For example, many statutes provide medical professionals who render emergency care or treatment to injured individuals outside the scope of their regular employment immunity from malpractice lawsuits. Known as Good Samaritan laws, these statutes vary significantly from state to state. However, they usually will not protect a medical professional from a malpractice lawsuit if he or she acts in a reckless manner while providing emergency care or treatment.

Good Samaritan laws
Statutes that provide medical professionals who render emergency care or treatment to injured individuals outside the scope of their regular employment immunity from malpractice lawsuits.

loss of consortium
In a lawsuit by a spouse, a request for damages for loss of companionship.

Physicians   A physician's malpractice might involve his or her failure to render a correct diagnosis of a patient's condition, failure to order appropriate tests, failure to prescribe appropriate medications, or failure to render an accurate prognosis. Medications prescribed must be appropriate in terms of what is needed to effect a remedy and with due concern for possible side effects and allergic reactions. A physician also can be liable for failing to inform a patient of the risks involved in a particular treatment or surgery, or of available alternatives. Physicians also must have the informed consent of their patients prior to rendering treatment (exceptions may apply in emergency situations).

Typically, the malpractice of a physician does not cause injury or loss to third parties, except in cases where the physician's negligence results in a patient's death or permanent disability. In the case of a patient's death, the physician can be held liable to a surviving spouse, children, or parents for wrongful death. If the physician's negligence results in either a patient's death or disability, a spouse may request damages for loss of consortium, or the loss of companionship.

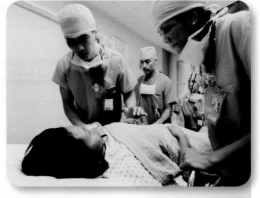

A physician can be liable for failing to inform a patient of the risks involved in a particular surgery.

Psychiatrists   Psychiatrists and other counselors, such as clergy, psychologists, and social workers, who learn from a patient that he or she intends to do harm to another have the legal responsibility to inform the possible victim and the appropriate authorities. Failure to do so is considered malpractice and is also unethical.

Nurses   Even though nurses customarily work under the supervision of physicians, a nurse can be found negligent, for example, for incorrectly administering prescribed medications or failing to properly monitor a patient's condition.

EXAMPLE 34.1

▶ Simmons, a nurse-anesthetist, was charged with negligence in administering a spinal anesthetic that resulted in a patient's paralysis. Expert testimony introduced at the trial showed that it was standard practice in the area to place a pillow under the patient's head when giving a spinal anesthetic to prevent the rise of the anesthetic into the spinal canal. Because Simmons failed to use the pillow, she was held to have been negligent.

Pharmacists   Pharmacists who dispense drugs other than those specifically prescribed by authorized professionals such as physicians also can be charged with malpractice if the incorrectly dispensed drugs cause injury to the legal user. Pharmacists are also liable if they dispense multiple medications that, when taken together, cause injury.

LIABILITY OF ACCOUNTANTS

Accounting professionals are liable to their clients and to third parties when they fail to observe established standards for their profession and if such failure has caused clients or third parties to suffer a loss.

For example, an accountant is liable to a client when, as a result of his or her negligence, the accountant fails to discover or conceals evidence that a client's employee has been embezzling funds. Likewise, an accountant is also liable if he or she fails to file appropriate and timely tax returns with the result that penalties are assessed against the client.

Previously, it was generally held that an accountant had a responsibility only to his or her client. Now, in almost all states accountants' liability has grown to the point that they have been found liable to third parties who have relied on the accountant's work, such as creditors (e.g., banks, suppliers, bondholders) or investors (e.g., shareholders, partners).

EXAMPLE 34.2

▶ The accounting firm of Casey and Ming prepared an analysis and audit of the Referral Publishing Company that was used in securing a loan from First National Bank. The analysis and audit incorrectly depicted Referral as a solvent firm in good financial condition. First National relied on the report and approved the loan. When Referral Publishing failed, the loan could not be repaid. First National sued Casey and Ming, charging negligence. Casey and Ming claimed that the bank had no course of action against them because they had been retained by Referral Publishing and their only duty of care was to their client. Because the use of the analysis and audit in securing a loan from a bank was a reasonably foreseeable event, First National did, indeed, have a cause of action against Casey and Ming.

In Example 34.2, if Casey and Ming's inaccurate audit resulted from their own deliberate actions, and with full knowledge of the inaccuracies, it would not have been the tort of negligence but rather the tort of fraud, and may have subjected the accounting firm and the partners to criminal prosecution as well as civil liability.

LIABILITY OF FINANCIAL PLANNERS

Financial planning is a profession in which practitioners attempt to advise their clients, who can be either individuals or businesses, on the best ways to manage their financial affairs. The work of financial planners involves an initial analysis of the client's personal and financial situation—including age, income, dependents, assets, and debts—as well as the client's desire to accept or avoid risk. The analysis leads to recommendations that typically involve insurance, investments, and pensions. When the client relies on the financial planner's recommendations and suffers a loss, the financial planner can be sued for negligence, but each of the four elements of negligence must be proved.

EXAMPLE 34.3

▶ Hoover, who had just inherited a large sum of money, engaged the services of Orio, who was certified as a financial planner. After a careful analysis of Hoover's financial and personal situation, Orio recommended that Hoover invest in several specific mutual funds. Quite unexpectedly, the stock market declined and Hoover lost several thousand dollars. He sued Orio for malpractice. However, Orio was able to prove that her financial advice had been sound and met the standards for professionals in her field. Hoover's suit was unsuccessful.

Most lawsuits against financial planners involve one or more of the following:

▶ Churning: the financial planner's unreasonably excessive buying or selling of securities to generate commissions.

▶ *Unauthorized trading:* the financial planner's exceeding his or her authority as agreed to by contract between the financial planner and the client.

▶ *Unsuitability:* the financial planner's recommendation of investments that are inconsistent with the client's particular situation, needs, and desires.

▶ *Fraud or misrepresentation:* the financial planner's intentional or negligent misstatement or nondisclosure of a material fact relating to an investment.

▶ *Transfer of account problems:* the financial planner's deliberate obstruction of the client's desire to transfer one or more accounts to another professional.

▶ *Failure or delay in processing:* the financial planner's neglect in complying with the client's wishes to purchase or sell securities in a timely fashion.

churning
A financial planner's unreasonably excessive buying or selling of securities to generate commissions.

LIABILITY OF ARCHITECTS AND ENGINEERS

Architects design and supervise the construction of buildings and other large structures. Engineers usually design devices or installations of a complex nature, such as bridges and power-generating stations. The engineering profession includes a number of specialties, including mechanical, electrical, and civil engineering. Each specialty involves work that, if done negligently, could result in injury to others. Both architects and engineers

Architects are subject to lawsuits for negligence if their work results in injury to parties with whom they have contracted.

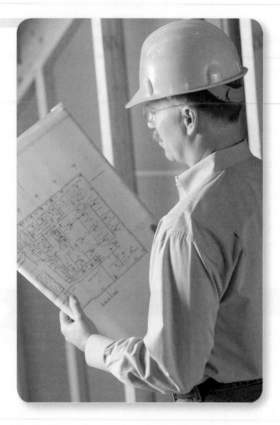

are subject to lawsuits for negligence if their work results in injury to parties with whom they have contracted or to third parties.

Typically, architects and engineers are licensed by states and must demonstrate their competence by passing various examinations and providing evidence of a certain level of education. These professionals do not actually build structures but design them and often supervise the construction. If an architect, for example, negligently designs a building and supervises its construction, and during or after construction it turns out that some of the windows fall out on windy days, the architect is liable both to the firm that hired the architect and to any innocent passerby who may have been killed or injured by the falling windows, and for wrongful death to the spouse, children, or parents of the innocent victim.

EXAMPLE 34.4

▶ Vokes hired the architectural firm of Wilkins and Co. to design and supervise the construction of a four-bedroom colonial house. Two years after the house was completed and Vokes and his family had moved in, Vokes noticed cracks in the foundation. A consulting engineer determined that the house had been built on unstable soil and consequently would continue to settle and ultimately be uninhabitable. Vokes demanded that Wilkins and Co. correct the problem, charging negligence for failing to conduct the soil tests that would be customary for this kind of project. If the problem could not be corrected, Vokes could collect monetary damages.

LIABILITY OF ATTORNEYS

An attorney is liable to a client if he or she fails to exercise due care in handling a client's affairs. If the attorney is in general practice, the standard of performance is that of other attorneys engaged in similar practices in the area. If the attorney is in a specialized practice, such as real estate, family law, or immigration law, it is the performance of other attorneys engaged in similar practice by which he or she will be judged.

An attorney can be found to have committed malpractice if he or she fails to act in a timely fashion in filing claims or bringing suit before the statute of limitations (a legal time limit) expires. Malpractice also can be established if an attorney fails to properly investigate matters related to a client's case, such as seeking clear title to property in real estate matters or interviewing witnesses in criminal matters.

statute of limitations
A legal time limit in which to initiate a lawsuit.

Most instances of attorney malpractice involve only the attorney and his or her client. In recent years, however, in some states, third parties have successfully sued attorneys who have negligently drawn wills with the result that a third party failed to inherit property as was intended. In other cases, attorneys have been held liable to third parties when an attorney planned an estate in such a way that higher taxes were required as a result of the attorney's malpractice.

title insurance
A form of insurance that assures the buyer of real property that there are no other claims to the ownership.

EXAMPLE 34.5

▶ Montoya, an attorney, was engaged by Jallon to handle the legal matters concerning the purchase of a residence. Jallon was in a hurry to move into the house and, knowing this, Montoya neglected to conduct a proper title search or to purchase title insurance, a form of insurance that assures the buyer of real property that there are no other claims to ownership. Two years later, when Jallon attempted to sell the house, the buyer's attorney complained that the title to the property included an *easement* (the right of access to the property) that gave the town the right to extend a road through a portion of the backyard. The buyer was willing to purchase the property despite this impediment but at a greatly reduced price. Jallon sued Montoya, charging malpractice, and sought damages for the amount of the difference between the lower selling price and the price at which the property could have been sold without the impediment to the title.

LIABILITY OF INSURANCE AGENTS AND BROKERS

Insurance agents (representatives of specific companies) and insurance brokers (representatives of insurance buyers who deal with multiple companies) are deemed to possess superior knowledge of insurance and to have the ability to use their expertise to protect buyers against various kinds of losses. As a result, buyers of insurance look to agents and brokers to recommend appropriate coverage. When an agent or broker fails to recommend appropriate insurance and the buyer suffers a financial loss that could have been prevented or lessened, the agent or broker can be charged with negligence.

whole life insurance
A relatively costly form of life insurance protection that includes a savings feature.

term insurance
A form of pure life insurance with no savings feature.

Malpractice on the part of insurance agents and brokers generally relates to either their failure to recommend the purchase of the right kind of insurance to protect against a specific type of loss or their failure to recommend appropriate amounts of coverage. Malpractice of agents and brokers can occur with all forms of insurance, including life, health, automobile, fire, theft, flood, disability, renter's, property, key person, and casualty. An agent or broker must be able to explain each of these to his or her client and make the appropriate recommendation. For example, the agent or broker must distinguish to his or her client whole life insurance, a relatively costly form of life insurance protection that includes a savings feature, from term insurance, a form of pure life insurance with no savings feature.

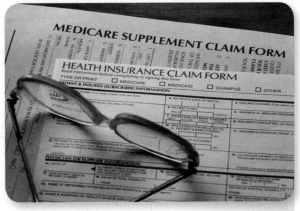

Buyers of insurance look to agents and brokers to recommend appropriate coverage.

EXAMPLE 34.6

▶ Gurchi was concerned about the welfare of his wife and two children and what would happen to them in the event of his untimely death. He discussed his concerns with a life insurance agent, who recommended a whole life policy with a face value of $100,000. For the same cost, Gurchi could have purchased $700,000 of term insurance. Within a year Gurchi was killed in an automobile accident. The proceeds of the policy, $100,000, barely replaced Gurchi's earnings for two years. When the widow realized how little benefit she received as compared to the benefits she would have received had her late husband purchased term insurance, she sued the agent and the insurance company whom the agent represented, charging that the agent had sold her husband an inappropriate form of insurance. During the trial, it was revealed that the agent earned a higher commission for selling the whole life policy than he would have received for selling the term policy. Both the agent and the company were found liable for negligence.

EXAMPLE 34.7

▶ Petras was involved in an accident with an uninsured driver. Petras then learned that his own insurance policy had only minimum coverage that was inadequate to cover his loss. He also learned that for an additional $25 per year, he could have had maximum coverage that would have covered the complete loss. Petras sued the agent for malpractice for failing to inform him about the other insurance options available.

OTHER PROFESSIONALS' LIABILITY

Most other types of professionals are subject to lawsuits for negligence when they fail to perform according to the standards expected of them. Educators and their schools have been sued for failure to educate students to an expected level. Travel agents have been sued for selling substandard hotels and tours.

Directors and officers of corporations have been successfully sued for breach of their duty of loyalty and duty of care (see Chapter 20), resulting from negligence, error, or omission. Shareholders of corporations have sued directors and officers, demanding reimbursement from the company for financial losses resulting from an action or inaction by the director or officer. Lawsuits also have been brought by third parties such as creditors, competitors, and the government.

34.5 REDUCING PROFESSIONALS' RISK OF LIABILITY

Nearly all professionals carry some form of liability insurance to protect against the possibility of being adjudged negligent. However, professionals need to consider additional precautions. Many professional groups conduct workshops and training sessions to help members of the profession reduce the risks that lead to negligent actions and the lawsuits that frequently result. Associations of insurance agents, for example, instruct their members on how best to conduct themselves in dealing with clients in order to minimize the risk of negligence. Many states require continuing education for certain professionals in order for the individuals in the professions to retain their licenses.

CHAPTER SUMMARY

1. A professional is a person who performs highly specialized work that depends on special abilities, education, experience, and knowledge. Professionals generally are members of state and national professional societies, such as bar associations or medical societies, that establish entry requirements, set levels of competence for performance, accredit educational institutions, develop ethical standards, and discipline members. Many professionals must pass a state-administered examination and gain accreditation, certification, or a license before they are permitted to work in their field.

2. Malpractice is a specific type of negligence; that is, the malpractice lawsuit is really a negligence lawsuit in which a professional is the defendant. The distinction that developed between malpractice and other forms of negligence stems from the fact that the performance of certain professionals is known as a "practice" and the people served are referred to as "patients" or "clients" rather than customers.

3. In a malpractice lawsuit, the professional owes his or her client, as well as all third parties who are foreseeably impacted by the professional's work, a duty to either perform an action or not perform an action. In determining whether a defendant has breached his or her duty, the defendant's act or failure to act is measured against the standard of care required by a reasonable professional in the same field. The plaintiff must show that he or she was injured or sustained some other loss as a direct result of the professional defendant's act or failure to act.

4. Examples of professional malpractice include a physician who fails to prescribe the proper treatment, a psychiatrist who fails to alert the authorities and intended victim of a client's plan to cause harm, an accountant who fails to file a tax return in a timely manner, a financial planner who fails to explain investment risks, an architect who fails to design a structure with proper materials, an attorney who fails to inform a client of his or her legal options, and an insurance agent who fails to recommend the correct kind of insurance.

5. Professionals can protect themselves against the possibility of being adjudged negligent by purchasing liability insurance. In addition, many professional groups conduct training to help members of the profession reduce the risks that lead to negligent actions and the lawsuits that frequently result. Many states require continuing education for certain professionals to retain their licenses.

CHAPTER THIRTY-FOUR ASSESSMENT

MATCHING LEGAL TERMS

Match each of the numbered definitions with the correct term in the following list. Write the letter of your choice in the answer column.

a. malpractice **c.** term insurance **e.** whole life insurance
b. professional **d.** title insurance

1. A form of pure life insurance with no savings feature. **1.** ____

2. A professional's improper or immoral conduct in the performance of his or her duties through carelessness or lack of knowledge. **2.** ____

3. A person who performs highly specialized work requiring special
   abilities, education, experience, and knowledge.   3. _____

4. A form of insurance that assures the buyer of real property that there are
   no other claims to the ownership.   4. _____

5. A relatively costly form of life insurance protection that includes a
   savings feature.   5. _____

TRUE/FALSE QUIZ

Indicate whether each of the following statements is true or false by writing *T* or *F* in the
answer column.

6. While the term *malpractice* is usually applied to physicians, dentists,
   attorneys, and accountants, it may be applied to all professionals.   6. _____

7. Good Samaritan laws provide medical professionals who render routine
   care or treatment to individuals immunity from malpractice lawsuits.   7. _____

8. The four elements of a malpractice lawsuit are duty, breach, proximate
   cause, and damages.   8. _____

9. In determining whether a defendant has breached his or her duty in a
   malpractice lawsuit, the defendant's act or failure to act is measured
   against the standard of care required by a reasonable professional in
   the same field.   9. _____

10. A psychiatrist who learns from a patient that the patient intends to do
    harm to another has the legal duty to inform the intended victim or
    the authorities.   10. _____

11. A pharmacist can be sued if he or she dispenses multiple medications
    that, when taken together, cause injury.   11. _____

12. Nurses cannot be found to be negligent because they work under the
    direct supervision of a doctor.   12. _____

13. A financial planner can be sued for deliberately obstructing his or her
    client's desire to transfer one or more accounts to another professional.   13. _____

14. Accounting professionals have a duty only to their client.   14. _____

15. An accountant who deliberately falsifies financial data can be charged
    only with negligence.   15. _____

16. An insurance agent or broker can be charged with negligence only
    if he or she cancels a policy against the wishes of the owner.   16. _____

17. An insurance agent or broker can be charged with negligence for failing
    to recommend appropriate amounts of insurance coverage.   17. _____

18. An architect who designs a building that is later destroyed in a windstorm cannot be charged with negligence because architects have no control over the weather.

18. _____

19. Clergy cannot be charged with negligence.

19. _____

20. Directors and officers of corporations can be charged with breach of their duty resulting from action or inaction.

20. _____

DISCUSSION QUESTIONS

Answer the following questions and discuss them in class.

21. Discuss why the malpractice of professionals is considered more serious by society than negligence by nonprofessionals.

_____

_____

22. Of the four elements of negligence, is one of them more critical than the others?

_____

_____

23. Explain how the malpractice or negligence of a professional might cause injury to third parties.

_____

_____

24. Identify a financial loss suffered by a third party for which an accountant can be found liable.

_____

_____

25. Distinguish between insurance agents and brokers. Do you think that one should bear greater responsibility than the other for advising buyers about their insurance needs?

_____

_____

26. What are some ways that professionals can reduce their risk of negligence lawsuits?

_____

_____

Answer the following questions, which require you to think critically about the legal principles that you learned in this chapter.

27. **Licensing of Professionals** Does the licensing of professionals guard against negligence? Advance arguments for and against.

   _____

   _____

28. **Malpractice Insurance** Does having malpractice insurance lessen the care taken by professionals?

   _____

   _____

29. **Malpractice Insurance** Because most professionals carry liability insurance, what is the role of the insurance industry in promoting the competence of professionals?

   _____

   _____

30. **Churning** Where should the line be drawn between a reasonable number of securities transactions and churning?

   _____

   _____

31. **A Question of Ethics** The purchase of life insurance often involves the client choosing between whole life insurance, which includes a savings feature, and term insurance, which provides only protection. The sales commission also varies depending on the type of policy. Is it ethical for an insurance company to base the agent's commission on the type of policy sold, regardless of the buyer's needs?

   _____

   _____

Study each of the following cases. Answer the questions that follow by writing _Yes_ or _No_ in the answer column.

32. **Liability of Accountants** Weiss, an accountant, prepared the usual accounting records for Malucic, the owner of a clothing store. Malucic entered into negotiations with Walling for the sale of the business, using the records prepared by Weiss to justify a high purchase price. After the transaction was complete, Walling discovered that the business potential had been greatly exaggerated and there was little chance

the clothing store would ever reach the potential suggested by the records. After discussing the matter with his own accountant, Walling concluded that he had been deceived by Weiss's financial reports.

a. Does Walling have a course of action against Malucic?   a. _____

b. Does Walling have a course of action against Weiss?   b. _____

c. Do accountants have a responsibility to persons other than their clients?   c. _____

33. **Liability of Physicians** Philasen underwent minor surgery for the removal of his tonsils. Serious complications developed when he was administered penicillin, to which he was allergic. The doctor denied responsibility because he did not know about the allergy.

a. Does it seem that Philasen has a cause of action against the doctor?   a. _____

b. Does it seem that Philasen has a cause of action against the hospital?   b. _____

c. Was Philasen partly responsible for failing to voluntarily tell the doctor about his allergy?   c. _____

34. **Liability of Architects** Cho, an architect, designed a large ranch-type house for Spadacini. Within two years after construction, the house began to tilt to one side. Cho argued that he was not to blame as the house was designed properly and that the problem was due solely to the negligence of the contractor. Spadacini produced the original contract, which called for Cho to supervise the work of the contractor.

a. Can the architect be held responsible for the substandard work of the contractor?   a. _____

b. Does the architect have a course of action against the contractor?   b. _____

c. Can Spadacini share some of the blame for not supervising the work as well?   c. _____

CASE ANALYSIS

Study each of the following cases carefully. Briefly state the principle of law and your decision.

35. **Liability of Attorneys** Smith was represented by Lewis, an attorney, in a divorce action against her husband, General Smith. General Smith was employed by the California National Guard and, as a state employee, belonged to the State Employees' Retirement System. Lewis advised Smith that her husband's retirement benefits were not community property and thus would not be considered in the divorce litigation or distributed by the trial court. Six months after the divorce was final, Lewis petitioned the court to amend the decree because of his mistake in not including the retirement benefits as community property in the divorce action. It was pointed out that major authoritative reference works, which attorneys routinely consult for a brief and reliable discussion of the law, provided that vested retirement benefits were generally subject to community property

treatment. The court refused Lewis, and Smith brought suit against her attorney for malpractice. Will Lewis be found to be liable for malpractice? [*Smith v. Lewis,* 530 P.2d 589 (California)]

Principle of Law:

_____

_____

Decision:

_____

_____

36. **Liability of Architects** During construction at Alma College, an inadequately reinforced wall of an excavation caved in and killed Clark, a worker employed by Beard, the general contractor. The contract between the architect, Sarvis, and Beard provided that Sarvis had supervisory authority over the construction and thus had the responsibility for the safety of all workers at the site. The administrator of Clark's estate brought suit against Sarvis, charging negligence. Will a suit against the architect succeed? [*Swarthout v. Beard,* 190 N.W.2d 373 (Michigan)]

Principle of Law:

_____

_____

Decision:

_____

_____

37. **Liability of Insurance Agents** Mansfield contacted his insurance agent and asked him to obtain an automobile insurance liability policy to be effective as of February 10. On February 14, Mansfield was involved in an accident while operating his car. The agent provided a policy with an effective date of February 24, which did not cover the loss resulting from the accident. Mansfield charged the agent with a breach of the contract to procure insurance as well as negligence in the performance of his responsibilities. Will Mansfield succeed in his suit? [*Mansfield v. Federal Services Finance Corp.,* 111 A.2d 322 (New Hampshire)]

Principle of Law:

_____

_____

Decision:

_____

_____

38. **Liability of Financial Planners** Chard completed an educational program in financial planning and was awarded the certification offered by a national association of financial planners. He set up a business to offer his financial planning services to the general public. One of his first clients, Roblee, sought Chard's advice on investments and insurance. Chard prepared a written report that included a recommendation to purchase shares in a real estate venture. Because Chard neglected to verify the financial status of the real estate venture, Roblee lost a significant amount of the money he had invested in the venture. With almost no prospect of ever recovering the investment, he sued Chard, charging negligence. Is Roblee likely to succeed in the suit?

Principle of Law:

_____

_____

Decision:

_____

_____

LEGAL RESEARCH

Complete the following activities. Share your finding with the class.

39. **Working in Teams** Working in teams of three or four, interview local insurance agents and brokers to learn about various forms of insurance, such as life, health, automobile, fire, theft, flood, disability, renter's, property, key person, casualty, professional liability, and so forth.

_____

_____

40. **Using Technology** Using the Internet and search engines, investigate a case of professional liability and the basis upon which it was decided.

_____

_____

chapter **35**

International Business Law

After studying this chapter and completing the assessment, you will be able to

35.1 Discuss global business and cite reasons for the increased need for international law.

35.2 Define *international law* and identify its major sources.

35.3 Discuss the doctrine of comity.

35.4 Explain the purposes of several major international trade institutions.

35.5 Discuss the international legal environment and state how trade sanctions and embargoes, export and import controls, and boycotts are utilized by governments to achieve economic and political ends.

35.6 Discuss the Foreign Corrupt Practices Act, the treaty known as Contracts for the International Sale of Goods, and the Foreign Sovereign Immunities Act.

35.7 Discuss the international laws governing intellectual property.

LEGAL terms

international law	trade sanctions
comity	tariff
transnational institutions	quota systems
General Agreement on Tariffs and Trade (GATT)	boycott
World Trade Organization (WTO)	Foreign Corrupt Practices Act (FCPA)
International Monetary Fund (IMF)	Contracts for the International Sale of Goods (CISG)
World Bank	Foreign Sovereign Immunities Act (FSIA)
North American Free Trade Agreement (NAFTA)	World Intellectual Property Organization (WIPO)
European Union (EU)	

INTERNATIONAL BUSINESS LAW

"Mr. Gorbachev, tear down this wall!"

Ronald Reagan,
40th president of the United States

35.1 GLOBAL BUSINESS

The increasing volume of international trade and tourism, the globalization of the market-place, the growing incidence of multinational business organizations, and cultural exchanges have given rise to the need for international law. Although the use of English as the language of business is increasing, cultural differences, disparate legal systems, and fluctuating exchange rates remain major obstacles to conducting business internationally.

35.2 WHAT IS INTERNATIONAL LAW?

international law
The broad study of the legal systems of major countries, treaties, practices, tariffs and nontariff trade barriers, and import and export quotas.

International law is the broad study of the legal systems of major countries, treaties, practices, tariffs and nontariff trade barriers, and import and export quotas. Also included in the study of international law are organizations—national and international—that regulate personal and commercial activity and facilitate international trade.

SOURCES OF INTERNATIONAL LAW
To fully appreciate the complex legal relationships that exist among nations, it is important to recognize that international law often develops to address the many issues that emerge from international trade.

International laws resulting from the trading relationships among nations have a rich history. In ancient times, the Romans ruled the Western world; however, contrary to popular belief, their reign was based primarily on economic, rather than on military, might. Exercising control over trade through the Roman legal system (the international law of the day) allowed the Roman government to rule the world by maintaining order and peace. The philosophy of Roman international law controlling trade and commerce in a peaceful way came to be known as *Pax Romana* (Roman peace), and the phrase itself appeared on their minted coins.

While signing peace treaties is as old as war, efforts to negotiate peaceful solutions to international disputes culminated in the formation of the League of Nations following World War I. Unfortunately, the League was short-lived and failed to prevent another war. Following World War II, the world's nations again organized a forum for peaceful negotiations and established the United Nations—an organization that now is involved in such diverse social and economic functions as the International Labour Organization (ILO), the Food and Agriculture Organization (FAO), and the General Agreement on Tariffs and Trade (GATT).

In modern times, customary practices and treaties are the major sources of international law, and these are recognized in the Statute of the International Court of Justice (Article 38). Over 200 sovereign nations have the capacity to negotiate treaties and create legal obligations.

In the United States, Article II of the Constitution states that treaties are negotiated by the president and must be ratified by two-thirds of the senators present (see Appendix A). However, in practice, other methods are sometimes used.

comity
A discretionary doctrine that holds that the courts of one country should refrain from deciding cases involving the acts of persons from another country.

transnational institutions
Organizations whose purpose is to maintain legal and economic order in trade.

35.3 APPLYING OTHER COUNTRIES' LAWS— THE DOCTRINE OF COMITY

A major legal principle involved in international law is the doctrine of comity, which holds that the courts of one country should refrain from deciding cases involving the acts of persons from another country. The doctrine is discretionary, and courts of individual countries decide whether or not to apply it based on the facts of each case.

35.4 INTERNATIONAL TRADE INSTITUTIONS

Trade among nations remains a vital ingredient in the economic health of the world's population. While countries are sovereign and create and interpret their own sets of laws, the goal is that trade be governed by transnational institutions, whose purpose is to maintain legal and economic order in trade. These transnational institutions are established contractually by several countries that agree to be legally bound by the rules of the organization. A discussion of some of these transnational institutions follows.

THE WORLD TRADE ORGANIZATION

In 1947, an international agreement called the General Agreement on Tariffs and Trade (GATT) was entered into by a multitude of nations. Among its many provisions, GATT provided a set of rules to ensure that there is no discrimination in trade by its signatories and also spelled out a process for resolving international trade disputes. Pursuant to GATT, a country can be granted "normal trade relations" status by its neighbors in order to maintain an efficient and effective means of managing imports (goods from another country coming into the nation) and exports (goods being sold to other countries by companies from within the nation).

By 1995 tariffs had become far less commonplace, and most nations came to recognize that GATT was no longer sufficient. Accordingly, the new World Trade Organization (WTO) was formed. The WTO is responsible for overseeing the implementation of all multinational trade agreements negotiated now or in the future.

In addition to GATT (described previously), the WTO has authority for

▶ GATS: the General Agreement on Trade in Services.

▶ TRIPS: agreements on trade-related aspects of intellectual property rights.

▶ TRIMS: Trade Related Investment Measures.

THE INTERNATIONAL MONETARY FUND

In 1944 several nations formed the International Monetary Fund (IMF). The purpose of this organization is to maintain a stable environment for the economies and the currencies of its members by providing protection against large fluctuations in the value of one currency versus another.

Most international experts agree that the IMF has performed its job admirably to date, but the IMF has come under great pressure due to various economic downturns in several nations. The IMF also is criticized for failing to respond adequately to the economic challenges created in the early 1990s, subsequent to the dissolution of the Soviet Union and the heavy borrowing by developing countries during the mid-1990s.

THE WORLD BANK

In 1944, to provide relief to the countries suffering from the ravages of World War II, the International Bank for Reconstruction and Development was created. Now popularly

General Agreement on Tariffs and Trade (GATT)
An international agreement that provides a set of rules to ensure that there is no discrimination in trade by its signatories and also spells out a process for resolving international trade disputes.

World Trade Organization (WTO)
An organization with responsibility for overseeing the implementation of all multinational trade agreements negotiated now or in the future.

International Monetary Fund (IMF)
An organization whose purpose is to maintain a stable environment for the economies and the currencies of its members by providing protection against large fluctuations in the value of one currency versus another.

A transnational institution's purpose is to maintain legal and economic order in trade.

World Bank

The popular name given to the International Bank for Reconstruction and Development, an organization that works closely with the International Monetary Fund to ensure that developing countries have access to funds to stimulate their economies.

North American Free Trade Agreement (NAFTA)

An economic agreement aimed at promoting and facilitating trade among the United States, Canada, and Mexico.

European Union (EU)

An entity that established a legal and political relationship among its members that promotes economic growth as well as social and cultural affiliations.

referred to simply as the World Bank, this organization works closely with the IMF to ensure that developing countries have access to funds to stimulate their economies.

The World Bank also has come under a great deal of criticism for the following reasons:

▶ It has often provided funds to countries with arguably corrupt regimes that have squandered the funds rather than provide real relief to their economies.

▶ It has provided funds to developing countries, but, despite the large inflow of money, major improvements in these economies have not been realized.

REGIONAL TRADE ORGANIZATIONS AND AGREEMENTS

In addition to the previously described worldwide organizations, numerous regional agreements and entities exist for the purpose of providing legal, political, and economic processes to maintain an orderly relationship among the members.

For example, to promote trade, the United States, Canada, and Mexico have agreed to follow the rules of the North American Free Trade Agreement (NAFTA). Unlike many other regional agreements, the focus of NAFTA is strictly on economic trade rather than on the political interrelationships among the three countries. The agreement provides that

▶ The NAFTA countries will ensure that none of their national or local laws discriminate against the goods of the other countries.

▶ Each country will have greater market access within the borders of the other two.

▶ Some tariffs and import and export restrictions will be eliminated.

The euro (€) is the monetary currency of the European Union.

In 1994, 12 countries in Europe formed what is expected to eventually become "Euroland," an economic and political integration of the members into one entity. As a step in this direction, the European Union (EU) established a legal and political relationship among its members that promotes economic growth, as well as social and cultural affiliations. An example of the kind of interconnection among the members is the inauguration of the *euro* (€), the monetary currency of the EU. Table 35.1 shows the 27 member states of the EU. Table 35.2 lists the countries that use the euro.

TABLE 35.1   Countries in the European Union
▶ The European Union is composed of 27 independent sovereign countries that are known as member states: Austria, Belgium, Bulgaria, Cyprus, the Czech Republic, Denmark, Estonia, Finland, France, Germany, Greece, Hungary, Ireland, Italy, Latvia, Lithuania, Luxembourg, Malta, the Netherlands, Poland, Portugal, Romania, Slovakia, Slovenia, Spain, Sweden, and the United Kingdom.
▶ There are four official candidate countries: Croatia, Iceland, Republic of Macedonia, and Turkey.
▶ The western Balkan countries of Albania, Bosnia and Herzegovina, Kosovo, Montenegro, and Serbia are officially recognized as potential candidates.

TABLE 35.2	Countries Using the Euro
Andorra	Luxembourg
Austria	Malta
Belgium	Monaco
Cyprus	Montenegro
Finland	Netherlands
France	Portugal
Germany	San Marino
Greece	Slovakia
Ireland	Slovenia
Italy	Spain
Kosovo	Vatican City

35.5 THE INTERNATIONAL LEGAL ENVIRONMENT

Companies that conduct business in several countries face the challenge of having to comply with a variety of legal systems that sometimes conflict with one another.

The United States, for example, requires that foreign firms that conduct business here comply with all of the regulations that govern American companies. Likewise, many American companies doing business internationally face the challenge of adapting to local customs and practices.

EXAMPLE 35.1

▶ Kleinsdorf, Inc., a German automobile manufacturing company, is opening a plant in the United States. Kleinsdorf will be required to follow all Environmental Protection Agency regulations pertaining to emissions, all National Labor Relations Board regulations pertaining to employees' right to join unions, and all Occupational Safety and Health Administration regulations pertaining to employee accident and sickness prevention.

In addition, companies that conduct business in other countries are frequently required to follow the laws of the country in which their headquarters are located.

EXAMPLE 35.2

▶ NuCloz Corp., a U.S. firm, entered into a contract with the Xiang Company, a Chinese firm, in which Xiang agreed to manufacture men's designer shirts. NuCloz learned that Xiang did not obtain the necessary permission from the designer of the shirts who owned the trademark. Irrespective of the law in China, NuCloz could be liable for the tort of trademark infringement, and for the crime of counterfeiting in the United States, unless NuCloz desists from selling the shirts bearing the designer's logo.

TRADE SANCTIONS AND EMBARGOES

trade sanctions
Legal restrictions, such as embargoes, placed on trade to achieve desired political results.

Many governments place legal restrictions on trade to achieve desired political results. Countries that enact laws prohibiting trade with specific countries are said to be using trade sanctions, sometimes referred to as *embargoes*. These activities by nations are acceptable under international law, and are indeed incorporated in the charter of the United Nations. The charter also expressly allows trade sanctions and embargoes by regional organizations, such as the Organization of American States, the Organization for African Unity, and the Arab League.

EXPORT AND IMPORT CONTROLS

tariff
A form of tax, or other restrictions, on imports or exports to attain economic results, such as protecting domestic industries or facilitating the production of certain crops.

In addition to trade sanctions and embargoes, at times a country will impose a tariff, a form of tax, or other restrictions, on imports or exports to attain economic results, such as protecting domestic industries or facilitating the production of certain crops.

Export licenses can be used as an adjunct to national security. The United States, for example, requires that exporters obtain a license prior to shipping certain goods to purchasers in other countries. If the product being sold is considered a threat to national security, for example, the export license will be denied and the exporter will not be allowed to fulfill the contract.

In addition, many countries, to maintain a positive balance of trade (i.e., ensuring that the monetary value of exports exceeds that of imports), place restrictions on the numbers and kinds of products that may enter their nation. These restrictions are referred to as quota systems.

quota systems
Restrictions on the numbers and kinds of products that may enter into a nation.

GOVERNMENTAL ACTIONS

Many governments attempt to maintain control over the actions of foreign businesses operating within their countries by controlling the ownership of the foreign companies' assets. These attempts can take three forms:

1. *Expropriation* is the act of a host country taking title to all of the assets of a foreign company. In this case, the host country compensates the owners of the foreign company.

2. *Confiscation,* as is the case with expropriation, also involves the host country taking title to all of the assets of the foreign company. However, in the case of confiscation, no compensation is given to the owners of the foreign company.

3. *Domestication* occurs when the host country mandates that at least partial ownership of the foreign company be sold to local citizens or companies prior to the foreign company's conducting business within the host country's borders.

boycott
Citizens' refusal to purchase goods made by a particular business—for example, a business located in another country.

BOYCOTTS

At times, citizens of a particular country refuse to purchase goods made by businesses located in other countries. This action, whether supported by the government or not, is referred to as a boycott.

EXAMPLE 35.3

▶ Morandim Corporation, a Canadian company, manufactures chemicals and regularly sells these to firms in the Middle East. Several of its customers, who are Arabic, organized a boycott and now refuse to purchase Morandim chemicals unless the company agrees to provide written documentation demonstrating that it does not conduct business with firms in Israel.

35.6 DOING BUSINESS IN FOREIGN COUNTRIES

Organizations that opt to conduct business in foreign countries must follow numerous laws and regulations. These include the Foreign Corrupt Practices Act; the treaty relating to the Contracts for the International Sale of Goods; and the Foreign Sovereign Immunities Act.

THE FOREIGN CORRUPT PRACTICES ACT

In some countries, it is perfectly acceptable and indeed expected that there will be payments made to individuals in order to secure their business. In the United States, however, this type of activity amounts to bribery, which is both illegal and ethically unacceptable. In 1977 the United States passed the Foreign Corrupt Practices Act (FCPA), a federal statute designed to provide executives of American companies with rules and restrictions relating to paying persons in foreign countries to expedite business in these foreign nations. Because customs and practices vary so greatly between countries, the law has helped numerous executives recognize what is and what is not acceptable conduct for U.S. firms, irrespective of acceptable ethical standards in the foreign country.

The FCPA makes it unlawful to bribe foreign government officials to obtain or retain business. Illegal activities include direct bribes paid by U.S. companies, as well as bribes paid through intermediaries. Bribes include money, gifts, or anything of value paid to a foreign governmental official or to a foreign political party.

The FCPA makes it clear that in order to violate the law, the payment must be made "corruptly." The statute defines "corruptly" as "connoting an evil motive or purpose, an intent to wrongly influence the recipient."

While many executives have complained that they are unfairly restrained when doing business in foreign countries, most experts maintain that by reducing bribery, the quality of goods and services produced abroad increases, while international prices are kept at optimal levels. Most would agree that U.S. companies are simply being held to ethical standards generally accepted by the American people.

In 1988 the FCPA was amended so that corporations and their executives were less likely to be prosecuted for making payments to foreign officials. This amendment was intended to offset what was viewed as an unfair advantage enjoyed by firms from other countries that had no such restraints.

CONTRACTS FOR THE INTERNATIONAL SALE OF GOODS

Sometimes parties to an international transaction disagree over the legal provisions of the contract based on the laws of their native countries. These disagreements can delay and stifle international business. To resolve such problems, a treaty known as the United Nations Convention on Contracts for the International Sale of Goods (CISG) was drafted to establish a universal set of legal procedures to be applied to contracts covering international transactions.

Countries that have signed the treaty are bound to the terms of the CISG. Because the United States has ratified this treaty, the CISG supersedes the provisions of the Uniform Commercial Code (UCC) in certain cases. Note that the CISG differs from the UCC in

Foreign Corrupt Practices Act (FCPA)
A federal statute designed to provide executives of American companies with rules and restrictions relating to paying persons in foreign countries to expedite business in these foreign nations.

Contracts for the International Sale of Goods (CISG)
A treaty created to establish a universal set of legal procedures to be applied to contracts covering international transactions.

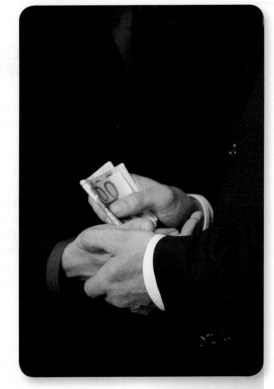

In some countries outside the United States, it is perfectly acceptable and indeed expected that there will be payments made to individuals in order to secure their business.

only a few areas. For example, the CISG does not have a written requirement for contracts involving more than $500, whereas the UCC has a written requirement for such contracts (see Chapter 7 and Appendix A).

FOREIGN SOVEREIGN IMMUNITIES ACT

In the United States, it had been tradition that foreign sovereign nations were granted immunity from all lawsuits brought by private individuals. However, the Foreign Sovereign Immunities Act (FSIA), a federal law passed in 1976, established certain exceptions to foreign sovereign immunity. Under this statute, a U.S. court may allow a lawsuit against a foreign sovereign nation to proceed provided the plaintiff can prove that the foreign nation engaged in one or more of the following:

▶ Commercial activity that occurred in the United States in connection with foreign activity.

▶ Commercial activity outside the United States that caused a direct effect on U.S. commerce.

▶ Commercial antitrust actions (see Chapter 12).

▶ Expropriation, terrorism, or torture.

▶ Other torts committed in the United States.

Foreign Sovereign Immunities Act (FSIA)
A federal law passed in 1976 that established certain exceptions to foreign sovereign immunity.

35.7 INTERNATIONAL LAW AND INTELLECTUAL PROPERTY

Individuals, as well as companies, have rights and duties in foreign countries. These rights and duties are increasingly important in the context of the international laws governing intellectual property.

Intellectual property includes both artistic and industrial property rights. Copyrights, patents, and trademarks are the principal areas involved (see Chapter 28). Related to these rights is industrial "know-how" or technology—particularly in developing countries where technology is transferred between firms in different countries that have joint venture agreements. Nations and businesses have long had an interest in maintaining an orderly process by which intellectual property rights are protected.

The World Intellectual Property Organization (WIPO), a specialized agency of the United Nations, is an international organization that administers numerous treaties concerning protection of intellectual property rights. In 1994 the WIPO announced the formation of a center for the arbitration of disputes involving intellectual property rights.

World Intellectual Property Organization (WIPO)
A specialized agency of the United Nations that administers numerous treaties concerning protection of intellectual property rights.

COPYRIGHTS

Copyrights protect the authors or creators of literary, artistic, or musical works and (in some countries) computer programs. These laws prohibit the reproduction or alteration of an author's work without his or her permission. Copyrighted materials are given at least minimal protection in most countries.

PATENTS

Patents are a statutory privilege granted by a nation to inventors for a fixed period of years to exclude all others from manufacturing, using, or selling a patented product without permission from the inventor. A U.S. firm can take advantage of world markets by licensing foreign firms to either manufacture a patented product or use an innovative manufacturing process in the manufacture of a product. A firm might seek *parallel patents* in each of the countries that maintains a patent system.

TRADEMARKS

Trademarks, trade names, service marks, and certification marks are valuable tools used by businesses to identify their products and services. In most cases, the treatment of these valuable properties in international commerce does not greatly differ from domestic treatment. Trademarks are viewed as property and thus can be transferred or licensed to others. Although not true in the United States, in most countries registration is a prerequisite for ownership and protection of the mark. Often a foreign licensee must meet certain product quality requirements so that the use of the mark does not deceive the consumer or lessen the value of the mark to the owner.

CHAPTER SUMMARY

1. Giving rise to the need for international law are the increasing volume of international trade and tourism, the globalization of the marketplace, the growing incidence of multinational business organizations, and cultural exchanges.

2. *International law* may be defined as the broad study of the legal systems of major countries, treaties, practices, tariffs and nontariff trade barriers, and import and export quotas. Also included in the study of international law are organizations—national and international—that regulate personal and commercial activity and facilitate international trade. The sources of international law in modern times are customary practices and treaties, which are recognized in the Statute of the International Court of Justice. Over 200 sovereign nations have the capacity to negotiate treaties and create legal obligations.

3. The doctrine of comity holds that the courts of one country should refrain from deciding cases involving the acts of persons from other countries. The doctrine is discretionary, and courts of individual countries decide whether or not to apply it based on the facts of each case.

4. The World Trade Organization is responsible for overseeing the implementation of all multinational trade agreements negotiated now or in the future. The International Monetary Fund maintains a stable environment for the economies and the currencies of its members by providing protection against large fluctuations in the value of one currency versus another. The World Bank ensures that developing countries have access to funds to stimulate their economies. The North American Free Trade Agreement governs economic trade among the United States, Canada, and Mexico. The European Union represents a legal and political relationship among its members that promotes economic growth, as well as social and cultural affiliations.

5. Trade sanctions and embargoes, export and import controls, and boycotts are all measures used by governments and citizens of one country to restrict the economic activities of businesses from other countries, by not allowing these foreign firms free access to markets.

6. The Foreign Corrupt Practices Act is a federal statute designed to provide executives of American companies with rules and restrictions relating to paying persons in foreign countries to expedite business in these foreign nations. The treaty known as Contracts for the International Sale of Goods (CISG) was created to establish a universal set of legal procedures to be applied to contracts covering international transactions. The Foreign Sovereign Immunities Act is a federal law that established certain exceptions to foreign sovereign immunity.

7. Copyrights, patents, and trademarks are the principal areas involved in international laws governing intellectual property. Copyrighted materials are given at least minimal protection in most countries. Through the use of patents, a U.S. firm can take advantage of world markets by licensing foreign firms to either manufacture a patented product or use an innovative manufacturing process in the manufacture of a product. The treatment of trademarks in international commerce does not greatly differ from domestic treatment in most cases.

CHAPTER THIRTY-FIVE
ASSESSMENT

MATCHING LEGAL TERMS

Match each of the numbered definitions with the correct term in the following list. Write the letter of your choice in the answer column.

a. comity
b. transnational institutions
c. General Agreement on Tariffs and Trade
d. World Trade Organization
e. International Monetary Fund
f. North American Free Trade Agreement
g. European Union
h. trade sanctions and embargoes
i. import and export controls
j. tariffs
k. quota systems
l. Foreign Corrupt Practices Act

1. Restrictions on the numbers and kinds of products that may enter a nation. 1. _____

2. An organization that provides protection against large fluctuations in the value of one currency versus another. 2. _____

3. A doctrine that holds that the courts of one country should refrain from deciding cases involving the acts of persons from another country. 3. _____

4. Organizations established contractually by several countries that agree to be legally bound by the rules of the organization. 4. _____

5. Government use of legal restrictions on trade to achieve desired political results. 5. _____

6. Agreement that provides a set of rules to ensure that there is no discrimination in trade by its signatories. 6. _____

7. An entity established to achieve economic and political integration of member countries. 7. _____

8. A form of tax, or other restrictions, on exports or imports to attain economic results, such as protecting domestic industries or facilitating the production of certain crops. 8. _____

9. An organization responsible for overseeing the implementation of all multinational trade agreements negotiated now or in the future. 9. _____

10. A broad category that includes various activities, including licensing the sale of some goods to foreign buyers, intended to affect the balance of trade. 10. _____

11. An agreement among the United States, Canada, and Mexico that
    focuses strictly on economic trade.   11. _____

12. A U.S. law that makes it unlawful to bribe foreign government
    officials to obtain or retain business.   12. _____

TRUE/FALSE QUIZ

Indicate whether each of the following statements is true or false by writing *T* or *F* in the
answer column.

13. International law is the broad study of the legal systems of major
    countries, treaties, practices, tariffs and nontariff trade barriers, and
    import and export quotas.   13. _____

14. There is little or no relationship between international law and
    international trade.   14. _____

15. The activities of the United Nations are limited to international law.   15. _____

16. The doctrine of *comity* holds that the courts of one country should
    refrain from deciding cases involving the acts of persons from
    another country.   16. _____

17. The purpose of transnational institutions is to maintain legal and
    economic order in trade.   17. _____

18. The purpose of the International Monetary Fund is to provide a
    clearinghouse for checks drawn on foreign banks.   18. _____

19. The European Union established a legal and political relationship
    among its members that promotes economic growth, as well as social
    and cultural affiliations.   19. _____

20. In some countries, it is common that there will be payments made
    to individuals in order to secure their business.   20. _____

21. The United Nations Convention on Contracts for the International
    Sale of Goods is a treaty created to establish a universal set of legal
    procedures to be applied to contracts covering international transactions. 21. _____

22. Most countries recognize U.S. patents but not copyrights.   22. _____

DISCUSSION QUESTIONS

Answer the following questions and discuss them in class.

23. Cite reasons for the increased need for international law in recent years.

    _____

    _____

24. Discuss some of the ways international trade is regulated by international law.

_____

_____

25. What are some reasons for trade sanctions and embargoes? How do they differ from export and import controls?

_____

_____

26. How do tariffs protect domestic industries, and how do they hinder world trade?

_____

_____

27. Discuss the goals of NAFTA and the means it uses to achieve these goals.

_____

_____

28. Discuss five exceptions to foreign sovereign immunity pursuant to the Foreign Sovereign Immunities Act.

_____

_____

THINKING CRITICALLY ABOUT THE LAW

Answer the following questions, which require you to think critically about the legal principles that you learned in this chapter.

29. **Laws and Culture** Assuming that the law of a country reflects its customs, identify and discuss selected laws in foreign countries and how customs influenced the enactment of these laws.

_____

_____

30. **International Financial Institutions** Discuss the goals and criticisms of the IMF and the World Bank.

_____

_____

31. **Trade Sanctions** Because trade sanctions often affect the people of a country more severely than their government, are sanctions a good way of achieving political goals?

_____

_____

32. **GATT** Pursuant to GATT, countries could receive "normal trade relations" status based on economic criteria. Later this designation was awarded to countries that had achieved specific human rights objectives. Should economic inducements be used to foster moral goals?

_____

_____

33. **A Question of Ethics** Should the FCPA impose U.S. ethical standards on the activities of U.S. businesses in international trade, even though this law may put these businesses at a competitive disadvantage with their foreign counterparts?

_____

_____

CASE QUESTIONS

Study each of the following cases. Answer the questions that follow by writing _Yes_ or _No_ in the answer column.

34. **International Court** Katsoulas, a U.S. car dealer, had a contract with a Korean automobile manufacturer for the delivery of several cars. When the manufacturer failed to deliver the cars as promised, Katsoulas threatened to bring the case to the International Court of Justice for a determination.

    a. Does Katsoulas have a course of action against the car manufacturer? **a.** _____

    b. Can Katsoulas successfully pursue his threat to take his complaint to the International Court of Justice? **b.** _____

    c. If Katsoulis is unsuccessful in his threat to take his case to the International Court of Justice, does he have other avenues of redress? **c.** _____

35. **Foreign Government Control** Straley Corporation, a manufacturer of hand tools, had been exporting its products to several countries in Europe for 10 years and decided to establish a manufacturing operation there. The directors of the company met to select a country in which to begin operations. After much discussion, the board selected the country of Alvinia as the site. Following the selection, additional research revealed that the government of Alvinia had a record of taking over foreign businesses. Even if the government took over the firm, would any of the following types of appropriation be acceptable to the company?

    a. Expropriation. **a.** _____

    b. Confiscation. **b.** _____

    c. Domestication. **c.** _____

36. **Foreign Corrupt Practices Act** Bryerly, a U.S. sales representative for a U.S. firm, Zoom Airplane Company, was attempting to close a deal with a foreign government for the purchase of 14 jet reconnaissance planes. He knew that competitors from two other countries were also bidding for the contract. Eager for

the business, he offered a bribe to the government official who would be instrumental in making the decision.

a. Can Bryerly be prosecuted under the Foreign Corrupt Practices Act? **a.** _____

b. If salespersons from other countries can bribe officials, and those from the United States cannot, are the U.S.-based personnel arguably at a competitive disadvantage? **b.** _____

c. Are there other inducements Bryerly could legally offer the official? **c.** _____

CASE ANALYSIS

Study each of the following cases carefully. Briefly state the principle of law and your decision.

37. Treaties Before boarding an El Al Israel Airlines flight from New York to Tel Aviv, Tseng, a passenger, was physically subjected to an intrusive security search. Although not injured bodily, Tseng sued El Al for damages, asserting, among other charges, assault and false imprisonment. A federal court dismissed the case on the basis of the Warsaw Convention, a treaty that precludes a passenger from maintaining an action for damages resulting from personal injury when the claim does not satisfy certain conditions for liability. The Convention expressly does not "permit recovery for psychic or psychosomatic injury." Will Tseng be successful in her suit? [*El Al Israel Airlines, Ltd. v. Tsui Yuan Tseng,* 122 F.3d 99, reversed]

Principle of Law:

_____

_____

Decision:

_____

_____

38. Trademarks Johnson, a passionate bicyclist, wanted to go into the business of manufacturing high-quality bicycles. He found that both labor and component parts were quite inexpensive in Taiwan. Even adding the shipping charges to the United States, it was economically advantageous to assemble the bicycles in Taiwan. He chose the name "Winner's Choice" and a logo that he registered with the Taiwan government. Business boomed, but his success was his downfall when his bicycles caught the attention of an American corporation that manufactured motorcycles and had previously registered the same trademark in the United States. The American firm brought suit against Johnson contending that he violated the Lanham Act, which regulates trademarks. Johnson maintained that his was a foreign company and therefore not subject to U.S. trademark laws. Is Johnson correct in his defense?

Principle of Law:

_____

_____

Decision:

_____

_____

39. **Boycotts** Yikes, a U.S.-based manufacturer of shoes, had plants in several
    countries in Southeast Asia and enjoyed considerable success in world markets as
    a result of a number of factors, including its excellent products, low prices, efficient
    production, low labor costs, and widespread consumer product acceptance. In the
    midst of its success, a grassroots group took exception to the corporation's poli-
    cies, particularly the firm's labor policies, which the grassroots group referred to as
    "sweatshop" conditions. The grassroots group set up a website on which numerous
    disparaging criticisms and a call for a worldwide boycott of Yikes's products were
    disseminated. In the opinion of Yikes management, the criticisms were without
    merit; yet the unfavorable publicity that would surely result from a defamation
    suit against the grassroots organization did not seem to offer much encouragement
    either. The mass media joined the fray, and Yikes became increasingly defensive.
    The company mounted a public relations campaign to defend its practices. What
    would be a recommended course of action for Yikes?

    Principle of Law:

    _____

    _____

    Decision:

    _____

    _____

LEGAL RESEARCH

Complete the following activities. Share your findings with the class.

40. **Working in Teams** In teams of three or four, interview local small and medium-
    size businesses to learn about the experiences of the interviewees in dealing with
    various aspects of international law.

    _____

    _____

41. **Using Technology** Using the Internet and search engines, investigate the terms
    and international organizations discussed in this chapter.

    _____

    _____

chapter **36**

Business and the Environment

ic Vehicle Fueling Station

BUSINESS AND THE ENVIRONMENT

"Driving hybrid cars is the new way to go. Anyone can do it, no matter how old."

Paris Hilton,
socialite and entrepreneur

36.1 THE DEVELOPMENT OF ENVIRONMENTAL PROTECTION

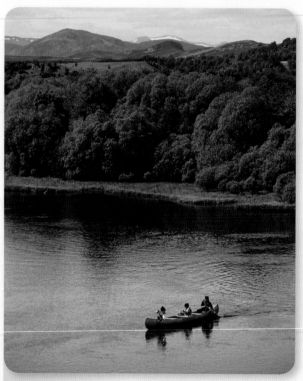

There are laws that protect the abundance of natural resources in the United States.

The United States has been blessed with an abundance of natural resources, including waterways, wetlands, precious minerals, arable land, wildlife, coal, and forests. It was recognized early in the country's history that laws needed to be enacted to protect our physical environment.

Early federal statutes dealing with environmental issues concerned themselves primarily with conservation of forests and wildlife. Because manufacturing had not yet reached a stage that caused significant harm to the environment, few laws regulated business activities with respect to the environment.

In the 1960s this view changed. Citizens of the United States began to insist that strict environmental laws be enacted to maintain purity of air and water. The first Earth Day was celebrated on April 22, 1970, and became a symbol of the political activism of the time. It was realized that the operations of business firms significantly impacted the environment. As businesses manufacture goods for use by consumers, pollution is an unfortunate by-product. What is problematic for policymakers is balancing the importance of allowing businesses to produce at optimal levels while maintaining a watchful eye over the environment.

Today environmental regulation is a distinct area of the law, and firms strive to comply with myriad statutes, regulations, and ordinances that cover the relationship between businesses and the environment.

36.2 GOVERNMENT'S REGULATION OVER ITSELF

National Environmental Policy Act (NEPA) of 1970
A federal statute that requires that any project with significant federal involvement (such as federal financing) must have an approved environmental impact statement prior to the commencement of any work on the project.

environmental impact statement (EIS)
An assessment of the environmental consequences of a planned project that must be approved prior to commencement of any project with significant federal involvement (such as federal financing).

In an effort to ensure that the federal government itself does not contribute to the destruction of the environment, Congress passed the National Environmental Policy Act (NEPA) of 1970. This law requires that any project (such as a dam, a stadium, a canal, or a highway) with significant federal involvement (such as federal financing) must have an approved environmental impact statement (EIS) prior to the commencement of any work on the project. The Council on Environmental Quality issues guidelines for EISs. To be approved, an EIS must provide responses to several questions:

▶ What is the environmental impact of the proposed project?

▶ What negative environmental effects will result from the proposed project?

▶ What are the alternatives to the proposed project (including taking no action)?

▶ What short-term and long-term destruction of environmental resources will result from the proposed project?

▶ What irreversible and irretrievable commitments of resources will be consumed by the proposed project?

EXAMPLE 36.1

▶ Several groups in New York proposed that a new highway be constructed in New York City, to be called Westway. Plans for the highway included destruction of some old wooden piers located in the Hudson River. Destroying the piers could have had an adverse impact on the striped bass whose habitat was in the river. It was alleged that the EIS failed to adequately address the striped bass issue, and Westway was never built.

36.3 GOVERNMENT REGULATION OF BUSINESS

In 1970 Congress created the Environmental Protection Agency (EPA), which has the responsibility of regulating business activities as these relate to the environment. The EPA

▶ Conducts environmental research.

▶ Assists states and municipalities with grants and technical advice.

▶ Administers the federal pollution laws that cover businesses.

Environmental Protection Agency (EPA)
The federal agency that conducts environmental research, assists states and municipalities with grants and technical advice, and administers the federal pollution laws that cover businesses.

36.4 MAJOR FEDERAL LEGISLATION PROTECTING THE ENVIRONMENT

Important federal legislation aimed at protecting the environment includes the Clean Air Act, the Clean Water Act, and the Comprehensive Environmental Response, Compensation, and Liability Act, also known as Superfund.

THE CLEAN AIR ACT

The Clean Air Act of 1970 was created with recognition of the fact that pollution sometimes crosses the boundary lines of local jurisdictions and extends into two or more states. In effect, this law emphasized that when it comes to protecting the environment, state regulation is insufficient and federal law is needed. At the international level, environmental protection is attained by treaties among countries (see Chapter 35).

Pursuant to the Clean Air Act, all states are required to develop air quality standards that are at least as rigorous as the federal standards. Such standards include

Clean Air Act of 1970
A federal statute that requires all states to develop air quality standards that are at least as rigorous as the federal standards. This statute sets primary and secondary standards and regulates both stationary and mobile pollution.

▶ *Primary standards,* which protect human life and health.

▶ *Secondary standards,* which protect property, vegetation, climate, and aesthetic values.

In addition, the Clean Air Act covers two forms of pollution:

▶ *Stationary pollution,* which is caused by factories and other production facilities. This form of pollution is sometimes corrected by the use of scrubbers on smokestacks.

▶ *Mobile pollution,* which is caused by automobiles, trains, airplanes, and so forth. This form of pollution is in part addressed by the EPA monitoring automobile manufacturers to ensure that they meet the standards for minimum gasoline mileage.

In 1990 the Clean Air Act was amended with a law exceeding 1,100 pages. These amendments require that emissions from automobiles contain fewer pollutants, that gasoline sold in the United States be cleaner, and that factories install new technologies to reduce the discharge of pollutants into the air.

THE CLEAN WATER ACT

Clean Water Act of 1972
A federal statute that sets minimum standards for water purity.

The Clean Water Act of 1972 set minimum standards for water purity in a manner similar to the Clean Air Act described previously. Included in such standards is "fishable and swimmable," an intermediate standard of water quality that allows U.S. navigable waterways to be used for propagation of fish, shellfish, and wildlife, and also allows such waterways to be used for recreational purposes.

The ultimate goal of the Clean Water Act is to eliminate the discharge of pollutants into the nation's waters. Under the Clean Water Act, both municipalities and major industries that discharge wastewater must obtain a permit, which states the maximum amount of pollutants that may emitted into a waterway.

EXAMPLE 36.2

▶ An offshore oil drilling rig, owned by BP and operating in the Gulf of Mexico, exploded in 2010. The partially drilled well then began spewing up to an estimated 60,000 barrels of oil per day. After several months, BP was successful in its efforts to permanently cap the well. However, the leak resulted in a massive oil slick that substantially damaged coastal areas and marine life. BP was found to be in violation of the Clean Water Act and may be subject to civil fines.

SUPERFUND

Superfund
A federal statute (also known as the Comprehensive Environmental Response, Compensation, and Liability Act) that regulates the dumping of waste onto land.

In 1980 Congress passed the *Comprehensive Environmental Response, Compensation, and Liability Act (CERCLA)*. More popularly referred to as Superfund, this law regulates the dumping of waste onto land. If business firms illegally dump waste material, they can be held responsible for three times the actual cost of the cleanup.

Superfund designates specific sites, placing them on the *National Priorities List* and mandating that these locations be cleaned up by their owners. The EPA has authority to

Superfund regulates the dumping of waste onto land.

▶ Conduct cleanups when immediate action needs to be taken.

▶ Enforce penalties against potentially responsible parties.

▶ Ensure community involvement.

▶ Involve states.

▶ Ensure long-term protectiveness.

The law also created a *Hazardous Substance Trust Fund* to help defray costs in addressing environmentally scarred land. Despite the national attention paid to this problem, however, applying the provisions of Superfund has not been an easy process, nor has it met with uniform success.

EXAMPLE 36.3

▶ The Yellow Rock Coal Company went bankrupt in 1977. Yellow Rock owned 20,000 acres of environmentally damaged land and had numerous creditors who had not been paid. The land was designated as a Superfund site. A not-for-profit company called Earth Saviors received a federal grant to purchase the land but will need to engage in a massive cleanup before reclaiming the land for use as a park and wildlife preserve.

36.5 LAWSUITS BY PRIVATE CITIZENS

In the event a business firm creates pollution or damages the environment, in addition to being required to pay a fine, it may be held liable to private persons as well. There are several theories of law under which a private individual may bring a lawsuit against a business for creating pollution.

NEGLIGENCE

Negligence is a tort that allows a plaintiff to bring a lawsuit against a defendant under state law for causing personal injury or property damage (see Chapter 4). Businesses that create pollution frequently cause injury to people or damage to their property, and these businesses may be found liable by a court for the tort of negligence.

NUISANCE

Most states have laws prohibiting the creation of a nuisance, a condition that affects a person's health, causes property damage, or interferes with a person's well-being (see Chapter 4).

Businesses that cause pollutants to enter the air or water are in fact creating a nuisance. There are two categories of nuisances:

▶ A public nuisance is created when the nuisance impacts public property, such as a navigable river or a state park. If a business causes pollution that enters a river or park, members of the public could file a lawsuit.

▶ A private nuisance is created when the nuisance impacts private property, such as a residence. If a business causes pollution that enters a person's private property, the affected individual could bring a lawsuit. Generally, state laws mandate that the affected individual must notify the business in writing of the pollution's impact. If the business does not correct the problem, the affected individual may abate the nuisance (reduce the negative impact) on his or her own and charge the business for the work.

public nuisance
A nuisance that impacts public property.

private nuisance
A nuisance that impacts private property.

EXAMPLE 36.4

▶ Festa owned a home adjacent to a small manufacturing company owned by Hedberg that placed numerous bags of unprotected trash near the property line. Festa observed the presence of vermin on her property and wrote Hedberg a letter requesting the removal of the trash—that is, the abatement of the private nuisance. When Hedberg refused to attend to the problem, Festa hired a company to remove the trash and sent Hedberg the bill.

TRESPASS

Trespass is the unauthorized entry onto another person's property. Businesses that cause pollution are, in effect, sending pollutants onto another person's land or water. Most states recognize a cause of action for particle trespass, accepting the theory that businesses are trespassing on another person's property with their pollution particles.

36.6 TYPES OF POLLUTION

The most widely discussed forms of pollution are those that affect air, water, and land, discussed in some detail earlier in this chapter. However, numerous other types of pollution and environmental issues are of great concern to society and are the subject of federal statutes.

NOISE POLLUTION

Excess noise (as measured in decibels) can affect people's health and well-being. Exposure to loud noise for extended periods can affect an individual's ability to hear, can cause mood swings, and is even alleged to injure fetuses. Noise pollution also may result in lower real estate values, as homeowners who live near airports can frequently attest.

PESTICIDE CONTROL

There are currently over 600 chemicals used in the preparation of over 50,000 pesticides. The continued use of a pesticide often causes insects to become immune to the chemical compounds, and as a result the pesticide becomes ineffective. Stronger pesticides must then be created. In addition, many individuals are not comfortable with having their food grown in environments wherein pesticides are used.

SOLID WASTE DISPOSAL

Most products are packaged in containers and wrappers that require disposal. The sheer volume of this waste material makes it extremely difficult to manage its disposal. Accordingly, numerous municipalities require that businesses and homeowners recycle paper, plastic, glass, and metal products. Of course, the time and money necessary to manage a recycling program efficiently and effectively to some extent offsets the value of the program itself. Accordingly, it is well accepted that longer-term solutions must be found. Many companies are going "green," making products and packaging them in environmentally friendly ways. These companies have quickly discerned the positive public relations value of their concern for the environment.

The advancement of technology has contributed to the problem of solid waste disposal. It is estimated that an astounding 100 million cellular telephones are taken out of circulation each year, 25 million of which end up as solid waste. Nearly 90 percent of retired computers sit in landfills or storage. Although there are no federal laws currently addressing e-waste, several states have passed statutes and the EPA has drafted rules relating to recycling cathode ray tubes (traditionally used in televisions and computer monitors).

TOXIC SUBSTANCE DISPOSAL

Of great concern is the quantity of waste materials that can cause great harm to humans who are exposed to them. These toxic substances include medical waste and chemicals. Pursuant to the *Toxic Substance Control Act of 1976,* manufacturers are required to test chemicals thoroughly prior to introducing them into commerce. These tests must be conducted to determine the chemicals' effect on human health and on the environment.

In addition, the *Resource Conservation and Recovery Act of 1976 (RCRA)* governs the storage and disposal of toxic substances. Under the RCRA, the EPA has the authority to regulate facilities that generate, transport, treat, store, or dispose of hazardous waste. The EPA requires such facilities to abide by a "cradle-to-grave" tracking system in which toxic substances are continuously tracked from the point of generation to the point of disposal.

EXAMPLE 36.5

► During the 1950s, a surge in the construction of new gasoline stations resulted in the burial of an enormous number of gasoline storage tanks across the nation. These unprotected steel tanks had an expected life of 30–50 years; however, many of these tanks corroded rapidly and failed much sooner. In the mid-1980s the EPA established regulations that required owners of such tanks to upgrade or replace them with corrosion-resistant tanks that have the capacity to be monitored for future leaks.

NATURAL RESOURCE CONSERVATION

The United States has extraordinary forests and wetlands that have great aesthetic and economic value. Often policymakers struggle with designing laws and regulations that can protect these resources without disturbing the natural ecological order. An example of this is the policy that provides that forest fires that are started by an act of nature (e.g., a lightning strike) are allowed to continue to burn so long as the fire does not threaten human life and personal property. However, there is much debate about the propriety of allowing a fire to burn, sometimes out of control, so as not to disturb the ecosystem.

ACID RAIN

Sulfur emissions, created primarily by manufacturing plants located in the central portion of the United States, cause pollutants to be discharged into the atmosphere and result in so-called acid rain. Because the jet stream flows from west to east, hardest hit by acid rain are the populated areas in the northeast portion of the United States and Canada. Acid rain creates problems for forests and crops, kills fish, and destroys the paint finishes on automobiles.

acid rain
A form of pollution caused by the discharge of sulfur emissions into the atmosphere.

36.7 A CHANGING GLOBAL ENVIRONMENT

Several factors influence the changing global climate, including the release of carbon dioxide into the atmosphere, the destruction of rain forests, and the destruction of the ozone layer.

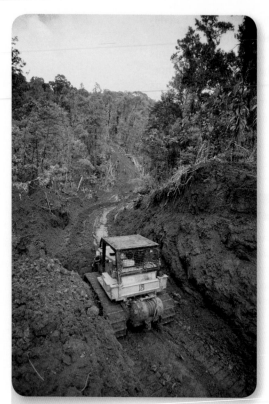

There has been a growing recognition that economic interests are causing the gradual destruction of the rain forests.

greenhouse effect
The rising of global temperatures due to the increased burning of fossil fuels that has loaded the atmosphere with heat-trapping carbon dioxide.

THE GREENHOUSE EFFECT

There has been great concern that global temperatures are increasing over time. Many scientists believe that the increased burning of fossil fuels (coal, gas, and oil) has loaded the atmosphere with heat-trapping carbon dioxide (CO_2), creating global warming, a condition known as the greenhouse effect. The resulting rising temperatures can melt the polar icecaps, causing rising sea levels throughout the world. The result will be damage to coastal areas, as well as a host of ecological changes to the environment.

DESTRUCTION OF RAIN FORESTS

In recent years, there has been a growing recognition that economic interests are causing the gradual destruction of the world's rain forests found in tropical climates. This deforestation alters the distribution and circulation of water, which in turn can lead to drought, flooding, soil erosion, and changes in wind and ocean currents and in rainfall distribution. Another serious result of deforestation is that absorption of carbon dioxide from the atmosphere is substantially reduced.

DESTRUCTION OF THE OZONE LAYER

It is now recognized that the release of chlorofluorocarbons into the air has damaged the ozone layer in the atmosphere. A hole in the ozone layer is most manifest over the South Pole and is causing concern over its potential impact on human health. Chlorofluorocarbons are present primarily in aerosol cans and in freon, a cooling substance historically found in refrigerators and air conditioners.

Because the ozone layer protects the environment from the ultraviolet rays of the sun, damaging this protective shield could well lead to major problems for agricultural products, forests, and wildlife. Holes in the ozone layer can affect human health by causing skin cancer and other disease.

36.8 OTHER ENVIRONMENTAL ISSUES

As our knowledge of our universe increases, so does our recognition of environmental problems. There is growing concern about biodiversity and ocean and space pollution.

BIODIVERSITY

Of concern to environmentalists is the notion that thousands of species are becoming extinct at an alarming rate. It is estimated that since the year 1600, approximately 260 animal species, 370 insect species, and 380 vascular plants have become extinct. Numerous federal statutes have been passed protecting some of these endangered species, but many individuals argue that not enough is being done and that not all species are being protected adequately.

OCEAN POLLUTION

A developing environmental problem is that of ocean dumping, in which waste material is illegally deposited into the waters far off coastal areas. Currently, ocean dumping is allowed under limited circumstances. The EPA is charged with the responsibility of selecting appropriate sites and types of waste that may be discarded into the oceans by U.S. organizations.

SPACE POLLUTION

Environmentalists have recently turned their attention to the increased amount of "space junk" that is orbiting the planet. Satellites no longer in use or in disrepair continue to circle the Earth. It is now estimated that there are 10,000 of these satellites in orbit. In 2008 a U.S. Navy missile scored a direct hit on the fuel tank of a dying spy satellite orbiting 130 miles over the Pacific Ocean, eliminating a toxic threat to people on Earth.

CHAPTER SUMMARY

1. Early federal statutes dealing with environmental issues concerned themselves primarily with conservation of forests and wildlife. In the 1960s, citizens of the United States began to insist that strict environmental laws be enacted to maintain purity of air and water. Today environmental regulation is a distinct area of the law, and firms strive to comply with myriad statutes, regulations, and ordinances that cover the relationship between businesses and the environment.

2. Government regulates itself in the area of environmental protection through the National Environmental Policy Act, which requires that any project with significant federal involvement have an approved environmental impact statement prior to the commencement of any work on the project.

3. The Environmental Protection Agency regulates business activities as these relate to the environment. The EPA conducts environmental research, assists states and municipalities with grants and technical advice, and administers the federal pollution laws that cover businesses.

4. Pursuant to the Clean Air Act, all states are required to develop air quality standards that are at least as rigorous as the federal standards. The Clean Water Act sets minimum standards for water purity in a manner similar to the Clean Air Act. Superfund states that business firms that illegally dump waste material can be held responsible for three times the actual cost of the cleanup. In addition, Superfund designates specific sites, mandating that these locations be cleaned up by their owners.

5. Theories of law under which a private individual may bring a lawsuit against a business for creating pollution include negligence, public nuisance, private nuisance, and trespass.

6. Types of pollution that are of great concern to society include air pollution, water pollution, illegal dumping of waste onto land, noise pollution, pesticide control, solid waste disposal, toxic substance disposal, natural resource conservation, and acid rain.

7. Several factors that influence the changing global climate include the greenhouse effect, destruction of the rain forests, and destruction of the ozone layer.

8. Other environmental issues for which there is growing concern include biodiversity, ocean pollution, and space pollution.

CHAPTER THIRTY-SIX
ASSESSMENT

MATCHING LEGAL TERMS

Match each of the numbered definitions with the correct term in the following list. Write the letter of your choice in the answer column.

a. National Environmental Policy Act

b. environmental impact Statement

c. Environmental Protection Agency

d. Clean Air Act

e. Clean Water Act

f. Superfund

g. public and private nuisance

h. particle trespass

i. acid rain

j. greenhouse effect

1. A law that requires, prior to the commencement of any work, a declaration of the impact any major project will have on the environment.   1. _____

2. Increasing global temperatures that result from increasing amounts of carbon dioxide released into the atmosphere.   2. _____

3. A law that sets minimum standards for water purity.   3. _____

4. A federal agency with responsibility for regulating business activities as they relate to the environment.   4. _____

5. Activities that negatively impact public or private property.   5. _____

6. A cause of action that accepts the theory that a business can illegally enter another person's property with its pollution.   6. _____

7. A condition resulting from the discharge of pollutants into the atmosphere that creates problems for forests and crops, kills fish, and destroys the paint finishes on automobiles.   7. _____

8. A declaration required before beginning construction of a major project that describes the impact of the project on the environment.   8. _____

9. A law that regulates the dumping of waste onto land and designates specific sites, mandating that these locations be cleaned up by their owners.   9. _____

10. A law that sets minimum standards for air purity.   10. _____

TRUE/FALSE QUIZ

Indicate whether each of the following statements is true or false by writing *T* or *F* in the answer column.

11. The United States lacks the abundance of natural resources that many other countries have.   11. _____

12. Environmental regulation is not yet a distinct area of the law.   12. _____

13. The Clean Air Act of 1970 deals only with pollution within the boundaries of each state.

13. _____

14. Included in the Clean Water Act are standards for water quality that allow navigable waterways to be used for the propagation of wildlife and for recreational purposes.

14. _____

15. Applying the provisions of Superfund has been an easy process, and it has had uniform success.

15. _____

16. Businesses that create pollution frequently cause injury to people or damage to their property, and these businesses may be found liable by a court for the tort of negligence.

16. _____

17. A public nuisance is created when a nuisance impacts public property, such as a navigable river or a state park.

17. _____

18. Many states recognize a cause of action for "particle trespass," accepting the theory that businesses are trespassing on another person's property with their pollution particles.

18. _____

19. Excess noise (as measured in decibels) cannot affect human health and well-being.

19. _____

20. Pursuant to the Toxic Substance Control Act of 1976, manufacturers are required to test chemicals thoroughly prior to introducing them into commerce.

20. _____

DISCUSSION QUESTIONS

Answer the following questions and discuss them in class.

21. Explain how the federal government regulates itself in the area of environmental protection.

_____

_____

22. Identify several types of pollution that environmental laws regulate. Which ones do you consider most important?

_____

_____

23. How does Superfund defray costs of cleaning polluted sites?

_____

_____

24. Discuss tort remedies that individuals can use against polluters.

_____

_____

25. The release of carbon dioxide into the atmosphere, the destruction of the rain forests, and the destruction of the ozone layer adversely affect the atmosphere. Can additional domestic relations or international treaties halt the continuing damage more effectively?

_____

_____

26. Despite the warnings on containers of toxic substances, injuries and accidents still occur. Should there be additional regulations, or are there other ways to protect individuals?

_____

_____

THINKING CRITICALLY ABOUT THE LAW

Answer the following questions, which require you to think critically about the legal principles that you learned in this chapter.

27. EPA Discuss the EPA guidelines for preparing an environmental impact statement before a project can be approved. Are they adequate?

_____

_____

28. Environmental Legislation What are some of the specific rules imposed by the Clean Air Act and Clean Water Act? Should these be more stringent?

_____

_____

29. Hazardous Substances Some substances offer both benefits and hazards. How should responsible individuals, corporations, scientists, and regulators weigh the gains and risks of these products?

_____

_____

30. Recycling Separating and recycling plastic, glass, paper, and metal are costly for municipalities. Should these recycling collections be continued, or should the funds be spent on other environmental objectives?

_____

_____

31. A Question of Ethics Most people agree that protection of the environment is an ethical issue. Society is frequently confronted with the conflict between achieving environmental goals and the economic impact on corporations, consumers, and taxpayers. How should this dilemma be addressed?

_____

_____

CASE QUESTIONS

Study each of the following cases. Answer the questions that follow by writing _Yes_ or _No_ in the answer column.

32. Environmental Protection Agency (EPA) An electric power company was charged by the EPA with violating the Clean Air Act by allegedly polluting a small town. To solve the allegations of environmental abuse, the company simply purchased the entire town, maintaining that it needed the land to expand its plant. By buying all of the homes, however, the company believes it now avoids the potential of lawsuits by the EPA and other individuals.

a. Does buying the homes of residents and the entire town mitigate the pollution problem?   **a.** _____

b. Does the agreement of the residents to sell their homes solve the potential pollution problems for those who live downwind?   **b.** _____

c. Is the company acting in an ethical manner?   **c.** _____

33. Private Nuisance LeatherLux Corporation, a manufacturer of upscale handbags, had been in business for 20 years and was considered a model corporate citizen. Expanding, the company developed new tanning processes that resulted in noxious fumes and odors being released into the atmosphere. The once-welcome company was no longer viewed as a good neighbor. A number of nearby residents lodged a written complaint with LeatherLux, detailing the impact of the pollution, as required by state law. LeatherLux ignored their plea. When the fumes and odors continued unabated, the residents decided to take action.

a. Do the residents have a cause of action against LeatherLux?   **a.** _____

b. It is likely that a court will rule in favor of the residents?   **b.** _____

c. May the residents complain to the EPA?   **c.** _____

34. Toxic Substances ChemPlus Corp. manufactured DeCorr, an industrial chemical widely used to treat various metals to retard corrosion. Weston was working in a small shop immersing metal parts in a container of DeCorr when a quantity of the chemical spilled on him. After washing off the chemical, Weston developed a painful rash and blisters. A supervisor contacted ChemPlus and was told that the company had no liability for Weston's injuries because there were adequate warnings on the containers. Calls to the Environmental Protection Agency were equally unavailing because the manufacture of DeCorr was in compliance with the Toxic Substance Control Act of 1976.

a. If Weston can prove that he did not read the warning label, will he be able to recover for his injury?

a. _____

b. Does the Toxic Substance Control Act require that all chemicals be entirely safe?

b. _____

c. Are Weston's injuries the result of the greenhouse effect?

c. _____

CASE ANALYSIS

Study each of the following cases carefully. Briefly state the principle of law and your decision.

35. **Environmental Protection Agency** Midwest Suspension and Brake supplied rebuilt brake shoes for heavy-duty trucks. During an EPA inspection, numerous emissions of asbestos were documented, and detectable amounts of asbestos were found on the shop floor. The EPA then issued a "finding" that the company had violated the Clean Air Act by releasing hazardous air pollutants. The EPA issued an administrative order (AO) requiring that (1) wastes fall into a sturdy cardboard box, instead of falling to the floor; (2) the box be securely closed and wrapped so that it would not leak when discarded; and (3) the box bear a warning label. The AO also required that the floor be vacuumed, not swept, and that the vacuum residue be tightly sealed before disposal. Finally, the AO mandated that asbestos waste be separately disposed of, without compacting, at a landfill. Midwest agreed to comply with the Clean Air Act and the AO.

   Later EPA inspections found that the conditions at the Midwest facility had not been materially corrected. Asbestos-containing materials were being dropped on the shop floor, and the floor was being broom cleaned rather than vacuumed. Because Midwest had failed to correct the problems, the EPA filed suit against it in federal court, seeking injunctive relief as well as civil penalties of up to $25,000 per day for each violation. The federal district court found that Midwest had violated the Clean Air Act and ordered it to pay a $50,000 civil penalty. Midwest appealed, contending, among other things, that it did not fall under the Clean Air Act. Should Midwest be bound by the dictates of the Clean Air Act? [*United States v. Midwest Suspension and Brake,* 49 F.3d 197 (6th Cir. 1994)]

Principle of Law:

_____

_____

Decision:

_____

_____

36. Environment/Wildlife Bronx Reptiles, Inc. imported live animals, including reptiles, into the country approximately twice per week. Edelman, the owner, knew of the International Air Transport Association guidelines for importing wildlife—how specific species should be shipped and the container requirements. Yet over the years, his company has been cited, and civil fines had been paid for numerous violations. Dead animals included iguanas and boa constrictors from Colombia and small mammals from Egypt. When frogs from the Solomon Islands were found dead, Bronx Reptiles Inc. was convicted of a misdemeanor for violating a statute that made it illegal to "knowingly caus(e) a 'wild animal' to be transported to the U.S. under inhumane or unhealthful conditions." Edelman countered that because frogs were reptiles, and not wild animals, they were not covered by the statute. The judge ruled that frogs are, in fact, amphibians and, in any event, fall within the statutory proscription. Given Edelman's belief that the statute did not apply to frogs, is it possible to prove that Edelman "knowingly" caused the inhumane conditions? [*United States of America v. Bronx Reptiles, Inc.*, 949 F. Supp. 2d 481 (E.D. N.Y. 1998)]

Principle of Law:

_____

_____

Decision:

_____

_____

37. National Environmental Policy Act The Forest Service planned extensive timber cutting in a part of the Green Mountain National Forest but did not prepare an environmental impact statement. A coalition of conservation organizations and environmentalists, believing that the action would have potential negative impact on black bears, whose habitat would be disturbed, and endanger the neotropical bird population, filed a lawsuit to compel the Forest Service to prepare the EIS. The district court found that the Forest Service had failed to consider all relevant factors when determining the environmental significance of its proposed action and was directed to prepare a site-specific EIS and enjoined from further timber harvesting and road building until completion of the EIS. Is it likely that the court will rule in favor of the coalition? [*National Audubon v. Hoffman,* 917 F. Supp. 280 (D. Vt. 1995)]

Principle of Law:

_____

_____

Decision:

_____

_____

LEGAL RESEARCH

Complete the following activities. Share your findings with the class.

38. Working in Teams In teams of three or four, check labels on various products such as chemicals, cleansers, insecticides, and herbicides. Look for warnings and EPA information. Discuss your findings.

_____

_____

39. Using Technology Using the Internet and search engines, investigate the Environmental Protection Agency. In what types of activities is this federal agency involved?

_____

_____

APPENDIX A

THE CONSTITUTION OF THE UNITED STATES

We the People of the United States, in Order to form a more perfect Union, establish Justice, insure domestic Tranquility, provide for the common defence, promote the general Welfare, and secure the Blessings of Liberty to ourselves and our Posterity, do ordain and establish this Constitution for the United States of America.

ARTICLE I

SECTION 1

All legislative Powers herein granted shall be vested in a Congress of the United States, which shall consist of a Senate and House of Representatives.

SECTION 2

The House of Representatives shall be composed of Members chosen every second Year by the People of the several States, and the Electors in each State shall have the Qualifications requisite for Electors of the most numerous Branch of the State Legislature.

No Person shall be a Representative who shall not have attained to the Age of twenty five Years, and been seven Years a Citizen of the United States, and who shall not, when elected, be an Inhabitant of that State in which he shall be chosen.

Representatives and direct Taxes shall be apportioned among the several States which may be included within this Union, according to their respective Numbers, which shall be determined by adding to the whole Number of free Persons, including those bound to Service for a Term of Years, and excluding Indians not taxed, three fifths of all other Persons. The actual Enumeration shall be made within three Years after the first Meeting of the Congress of the United States, and within every subsequent Term of ten Years, in such Manner as they shall by Law direct. The Number of Representatives shall not exceed one for every thirty Thousand, but each State shall have at Least one Representative; and until such enumeration shall be made, the State of New Hampshire shall be entitled to chuse three, Massachusetts eight, Rhode-Island and Providence Plantations one, Connecticut five, New-York six, New Jersey four, Pennsylvania eight, Delaware one, Maryland six, Virginia ten, North Carolina five, South Carolina five, and Georgia three.

When vacancies happen in the Representation from any State, the Executive Authority thereof shall issue Writs of Election to fill such Vacancies.

The House of Representatives shall chuse their Speaker and other Officers; and shall have the sole Power of Impeachment.

SECTION 3

The Senate of the United States shall be composed of two Senators from each State, chosen by the Legislature thereof for six Years; and each Senator shall have one Vote.

Immediately after they shall be assembled in Consequence of the first Election, they shall be divided as equally as may be into three Classes. The Seats of the Senators of the first Class shall be vacated at the Expiration of the second Year, of the second Class at the Expiration of the fourth Year, and of the third Class at the Expiration of the sixth Year, so that one third may be chosen every second Year; and if Vacancies happen by Resignation, or otherwise, during the Recess of the Legislature of any State, the Executive thereof may make temporary Appointments until the next Meeting of the Legislature, which shall then fill such Vacancies.

No Person shall be a Senator who shall not have attained to the Age of thirty Years, and been nine Years a Citizen of the United States, and who shall not, when elected, be an Inhabitant of that State for which he shall be chosen.

The Vice President of the United States shall be President of the Senate, but shall have no Vote, unless they be equally divided.

The Senate shall chose their other Officers, and also a President pro tempore, in the Absence of the Vice President, or when he shall exercise the Office of President of the United States.

The Senate shall have the sole Power to try all Impeachments. When sitting for that Purpose, they shall be on Oath or Affirmation. When the President of the United States is tried, the Chief Justice shall preside: And no Person shall be convicted without the Concurrence of two thirds of the Members present.

Judgment in Cases of Impeachment shall not extend further than to removal from Office, and disqualification to hold and enjoy any Office of honor, Trust or Profit under the United States: but the Party convicted shall nevertheless be liable and subject to Indictment, Trial, Judgment and Punishment, according to Law.

SECTION 4

The Times, Places and Manner of holding Elections for Senators and Representatives, shall be prescribed in each State by the Legislature thereof; but the Congress may at any time by Law make or alter such Regulations, except as to the Places of chusing Senators.

The Congress shall assemble at least once in every Year, and such Meeting shall be on the first Monday in December, unless they shall by Law appoint a different Day.

SECTION 5

Each House shall be the Judge of the Elections, Returns and Qualifications of its own Members, and a Majority of each shall constitute a Quorum to do Business; but a smaller Number may adjourn from day to day, and may be authorized to compel the Attendance of absent Members, in such Manner, and under such Penalties as each House may provide.

Each House may determine the Rules of its Proceedings, punish its Members for disorderly Behaviour, and, with the Concurrence of two thirds, expel a Member.

Each House shall keep a Journal of its Proceedings, and from time to time publish the same, excepting such Parts as may in their Judgment require Secrecy; and the Yeas and Nays of the Members of either House on any question shall, at the Desire of one fifth of those Present, be entered on the Journal.

Neither House, during the Session of Congress, shall, without the Consent of the other, adjourn for more than three days, nor to any other Place than that in which the two Houses shall be sitting.

SECTION 6

The Senators and Representatives shall receive a Compensation for their Services, to be ascertained by Law, and paid out of the Treasury of the United States. They shall in all Cases, except Treason, Felony and Breach of the Peace, be privileged from Arrest during their Attendance at the Session of their respective Houses, and in going to and returning from the same; and for any Speech or Debate in either House, they shall not be questioned in any other Place.

No Senator or Representative shall, during the Time for which he was elected, be appointed to any civil Office under the Authority of the United States, which shall have been created, or the Emoluments whereof shall have been encreased during such time; and no Person holding any Office under the United States, shall be a Member of either House during his Continuance in Office.

SECTION 7

All Bills for raising Revenue shall originate in the House of Representatives; but the Senate may propose or concur with Amendments as on other Bills.

Every Bill which shall have passed the House of Representatives and the Senate, shall, before it become a Law, be presented to the President of the United States: If he approve he shall sign it, but if not he shall return it, with his Objections to that House in which it shall have originated, who shall enter the Objections at large on their Journal, and proceed to reconsider it. If after such Reconsideration two thirds of that House shall agree to pass the Bill, it shall be sent, together with the Objections, to the other House, by which it shall likewise be reconsidered, and if approved by two thirds of that House, it shall become a Law. But in all such Cases the Votes of both Houses shall be determined by yeas and Nays, and the Names of the Persons voting for and against the Bill shall be entered on the Journal of each House respectively. If any Bill shall not be returned by the President within ten Days (Sundays excepted) after it shall have been presented to him, the Same shall be a Law, in like Manner as if he had signed it, unless the Congress by their Adjournment prevent its Return, in which Case it shall not be a Law.

Every Order, Resolution, or Vote to which the Concurrence of the Senate and House of Representatives may be necessary (except on a question of Adjournment) shall be presented to the President of the United States; and before the Same shall take Effect, shall be approved by him, or being disapproved by him, shall be repassed by two thirds of the Senate and House of Representatives, according to the Rules and Limitations prescribed in the Case of a Bill.

SECTION 8

The Congress shall have Power to lay and collect Taxes, Duties, Imposts and Excises, to pay the Debts and provide for the common Defence and general Welfare of the United States; but all Duties, Imposts and Excises shall be uniform throughout the United States;

To borrow Money on the credit of the United States;

To regulate Commerce with foreign Nations, and among the several States, and with the Indian Tribes;

To establish an uniform Rule of Naturalization, and uniform Laws on the subject of Bankruptcies throughout the United States;

To coin Money, regulate the Value thereof, and of foreign Coin, and fix the Standard of Weights and Measures;

To provide for the Punishment of counterfeiting the Securities and current Coin of the United States;

To establish Post Offices and post Roads;

To promote the Progress of Science and useful Arts, by securing for limited Times to Authors and Inventors the exclusive Right to their respective Writings and Discoveries;

To constitute Tribunals inferior to the supreme Court;

To define and punish Piracies and Felonies committed on the high Seas, and Offences against the Law of Nations;

To declare War, grant Letters of Marque and Reprisal, and make Rules concerning Captures on Land and Water;

To raise and support Armies, but no Appropriation of Money to that Use shall be for a longer Term than two Years;

To provide and maintain a Navy;

To make Rules for the Government and Regulation of the land and naval Forces;

To provide for calling forth the Militia to execute the Laws of the Union, suppress Insurrections and repel Invasions;

To provide for organizing, arming, and disciplining, the Militia, and for governing such Part of them as may be employed in the Service of the United States, reserving to the States respectively, the Appointment of the Officers, and the Authority of training the Militia according to the discipline prescribed by Congress;

To exercise exclusive Legislation in all Cases whatsoever, over such District (not exceeding ten Miles square) as may, by Cession of particular States, and the Acceptance of Congress, become the Seat of the Government of the United States, and to exercise like Authority over all Places purchased by the Consent of the Legislature of the State in which the Same shall be, for the Erection of Forts, Magazines, Arsenals, dock-Yards, and other needful Buildings;—And

To make all Laws which shall be necessary and proper for carrying into Execution the foregoing Powers, and all other Powers vested by this Constitution in the Government of the United States, or in any Department or Officer thereof.

SECTION 9

The Migration or Importation of such Persons as any of the States now existing shall think proper to admit, shall not be prohibited by the Congress prior to the Year one thousand eight hundred and eight, but a Tax or duty may be imposed on such Importation, not exceeding ten dollars for each Person.

The Privilege of the Writ of Habeas Corpus shall not be suspended, unless when in Cases of Rebellion or Invasion the public Safety may require it.

No Bill of Attainder or ex post facto Law shall be passed.

No Capitation, or other direct, Tax shall be laid, unless in Proportion to the Census or enumeration herein before directed to be taken.

No Tax or Duty shall be laid on Articles exported from any State.

No Preference shall be given by any Regulation of Commerce or Revenue to the Ports of one State over those of another; nor shall Vessels bound to, or from, one State, be obliged to enter, clear, or pay Duties in another.

No Money shall be drawn from the Treasury, but in Consequence of Appropriations made by Law; and a regular Statement and Account of the Receipts and Expenditures of all public Money shall be published from time to time.

No Title of Nobility shall be granted by the United States: And no Person holding any Office of Profit or Trust under them, shall, without the Consent of the Congress, accept of any present, Emolument, Office, or Title, of any kind whatever, from any King, Prince, or foreign State.

SECTION 10

No State shall enter into any Treaty, Alliance, or Confederation; grant Letters of Marque and Reprisal; coin Money; emit Bills of Credit; make any Thing but gold and silver Coin a Tender in Payment of Debts; pass any Bill of Attainder, ex post facto Law, or Law impairing the Obligation of Contracts, or grant any Title of Nobility.

No State shall, without the Consent of the Congress, lay any Imposts or Duties on Imports or Exports, except what may be absolutely necessary for executing it's inspection Laws: and the net Produce of all Duties and Imposts, laid by any State on Imports or Exports, shall be for the Use of the Treasury of the United States; and all such Laws shall be subject to the Revision and Controul of the Congress.

No State shall, without the Consent of Congress, lay any Duty of Tonnage, keep Troops, or Ships of War in time of Peace, enter into any Agreement or Compact with another State, or with a foreign Power, or engage in War, unless actually invaded, or in such imminent Danger as will not admit of delay.

ARTICLE II

SECTION 1

The executive Power shall be vested in a President of the United States of America. He shall hold his Office during the Term of four Years, and, together with the Vice President, chosen for the same Term, be elected, as follows:

Each State shall appoint, in such Manner as the Legislature thereof may direct, a Number of Electors, equal to the whole Number of Senators and Representatives to which the State may be entitled in the Congress: but no Senator or Representative, or Person holding an Office of Trust or Profit under the United States, shall be appointed an Elector.

The Electors shall meet in their respective States, and vote by Ballot for two Persons, of whom one at least shall not be an Inhabitant of the same State with themselves. And they shall make a List of all the Persons voted for, and of the Number of Votes for each; which List they shall sign and certify, and transmit sealed to the Seat of the Government of the United States, directed to the President of the Senate. The President of the Senate shall, in the Presence of the Senate and House of Representatives, open all the Certificates, and the Votes shall then be counted. The Person having the greatest Number of Votes shall be the President, if such Number be a Majority of the whole Number of Electors appointed; and if there be more than one who have such Majority, and have an equal Number of Votes, then the House of Representatives shall immediately chuse by Ballot one of them for President; and if no Person have a Majority, then from the five highest on the List the said House shall in like Manner chuse the President. But in chusing the President, the Votes shall be taken by States, the Representation from each State

having one Vote; A quorum for this purpose shall consist of a Member or Members from two thirds of the States, and a Majority of all the States shall be necessary to a Choice. In every Case, after the Choice of the President, the Person having the greatest Number of Votes of the Electors shall be the Vice President. But if there should remain two or more who have equal Votes, the Senate shall chuse from them by Ballot the Vice President.

The Congress may determine the Time of chusing the Electors, and the Day on which they shall give their Votes; which Day shall be the same throughout the United States.

No Person except a natural born Citizen, or a Citizen of the United States, at the time of the Adoption of this Constitution, shall be eligible to the Office of President; neither shall any Person be eligible to that Office who shall not have attained to the Age of thirty five Years, and been fourteen Years a Resident within the United States.

In Case of the Removal of the President from Office, or of his Death, Resignation, or Inability to discharge the Powers and Duties of the said Office, the Same shall devolve on the Vice President, and the Congress may by Law provide for the Case of Removal, Death, Resignation or Inability, both of the President and Vice President, declaring what Officer shall then act as President, and such Officer shall act accordingly, until the Disability be removed, or a President shall be elected.

The President shall, at stated Times, receive for his Services, a Compensation, which shall neither be increased nor diminished during the Period for which he shall have been elected, and he shall not receive within that Period any other Emolument from the United States, or any of them.

Before he enter on the Execution of his Office, he shall take the following Oath or Affirmation:—"I do solemnly swear (or affirm) that I will faithfully execute the Office of President of the United States, and will to the best of my Ability, preserve, protect and defend the Constitution of the United States."

SECTION 2

The President shall be Commander in Chief of the Army and Navy of the United States, and of the Militia of the several States, when called into the actual Service of the United States; he may require the Opinion, in writing, of the principal Officer in each of the executive Departments, upon any Subject relating to the Duties of their respective Offices, and he shall have Power to grant Reprieves and Pardons for Offences against the United States, except in Cases of Impeachment.

He shall have Power, by and with the Advice and Consent of the Senate, to make Treaties, provided two thirds of the Senators present concur; and he shall nominate, and by and with the Advice and Consent of the Senate, shall appoint Ambassadors, other public Ministers and Consuls, Judges of the supreme Court, and all other Officers of the United States, whose Appointments are not herein otherwise provided for, and which shall be established by Law: but the Congress may by Law vest the Appointment of such inferior Officers, as they think proper, in the President alone, in the Courts of Law, or in the Heads of Departments.

The President shall have Power to fill up all Vacancies that may happen during the Recess of the Senate, by granting Commissions which shall expire at the End of their next Session.

SECTION 3

He shall from time to time give to the Congress Information of the State of the Union, and recommend to their Consideration such Measures as he shall judge necessary and expedient; he may, on extraordinary Occasions, convene both Houses, or either of them, and in Case of Disagreement between them, with Respect to the Time of Adjournment, he may adjourn them to such Time as he shall think proper; he shall receive Ambassadors and other public Ministers; he shall take Care that the Laws be faithfully executed, and shall Commission all the Officers of the United States.

SECTION 4

The President, Vice President and all civil Officers of the United States, shall be removed from Office on Impeachment for, and Conviction of, Treason, Bribery, or other high Crimes and Misdemeanors.

ARTICLE III

SECTION 1

The judicial Power of the United States shall be vested in one supreme Court, and in such inferior Courts as the Congress may from time to time ordain and establish. The Judges, both of the supreme and inferior Courts, shall hold their Offices during good Behaviour, and shall, at stated Times, receive for their Services a Compensation, which shall not be diminished during their Continuance in Office.

SECTION 2

The judicial Power shall extend to all Cases, in Law and Equity, arising under this Constitution, the Laws of the United States, and Treaties made, or which shall be made, under their Authority;—to all Cases affecting Ambassadors, other public Ministers and Consuls;—to all Cases of admiralty and maritime Jurisdiction;—to Controversies to which the United States shall be a Party;—to Controversies between two or more States;—between a State and Citizens of another State;—between Citizens of different States;—between Citizens of the same State claiming Lands under Grants of different States, and between a State, or the Citizens thereof, and foreign States, Citizens or Subjects.

In all Cases affecting Ambassadors, other public Ministers and Consuls, and those in which a State shall be Party, the supreme Court shall have original Jurisdiction. In all the other Cases before mentioned, the supreme Court shall have appellate Jurisdiction, both as to Law and Fact, with such Exceptions, and under such Regulations as the Congress shall make.

The Trial of all Crimes, except in Cases of Impeachment, shall be by Jury; and such Trial shall be held in the State where the said Crimes shall have been committed; but when not committed within any State, the Trial shall be at such Place or Places as the Congress may by Law have directed.

SECTION 3

Treason against the United States, shall consist only in levying War against them, or in adhering to their Enemies, giving them Aid and Comfort. No Person shall be convicted of Treason unless on the Testimony of two Witnesses to the same overt Act, or on Confession in open Court.

The Congress shall have Power to declare the Punishment of Treason, but no Attainder of Treason shall work Corruption of Blood, or Forfeiture except during the Life of the Person attainted.

ARTICLE IV

SECTION 1

Full Faith and Credit shall be given in each State to the public Acts, Records, and judicial Proceedings of every other State. And the Congress may by general Laws prescribe the Manner in which such Acts, Records and Proceedings shall be proved, and the Effect thereof.

SECTION 2

The Citizens of each State shall be entitled to all Privileges and Immunities of Citizens in the several States.

A Person charged in any State with Treason, Felony, or other Crime, who shall flee from Justice, and be found in another State, shall on Demand of the executive Authority of the State from which he fled, be delivered up, to be removed to the State having Jurisdiction of the Crime.

No Person held to Service or Labour in one State, under the Laws thereof, escaping into another, shall, in Consequence of any Law or Regulation therein, be discharged from such Service or Labour, but shall be delivered up on Claim of the Party to whom such Service or Labour may be due.

SECTION 3

New States may be admitted by the Congress into this Union; but no new State shall be formed or erected within the Jurisdiction of any other State; nor any State be formed by the Junction of two or more States, or Parts of States, without the Consent of the Legislatures of the States concerned as well as of the Congress.

The Congress shall have Power to dispose of and make all needful Rules and Regulations respecting the Territory or other Property belonging to the United States; and nothing in this Constitution shall be so construed as to Prejudice any Claims of the United States, or of any particular State.

SECTION 4

The United States shall guarantee to every State in this Union a Republican Form of Government, and shall protect each of them against Invasion; and on Application of the Legislature, or of the Executive (when the Legislature cannot be convened), against domestic Violence.

ARTICLE V

The Congress, whenever two thirds of both Houses shall deem it necessary, shall propose Amendments to this Constitution, or, on the Application of the Legislatures of two thirds of the several States, shall call a Convention for proposing Amendments, which, in either Case, shall be valid to all Intents and Purposes, as Part of this Constitution, when ratified by the Legislatures of three fourths of the several States, or by Conventions in three fourths thereof, as the one or the other Mode of Ratification may be proposed by the Congress; Provided that no Amendment which may be made prior to the Year One thousand eight hundred and eight shall in any Manner affect the first and fourth Clauses in the Ninth Section of the first Article; and that no State, without its Consent, shall be deprived of its equal Suffrage in the Senate.

ARTICLE VI

All Debts contracted and Engagements entered into, before the Adoption of this Constitution, shall be as valid against the United States under this Constitution, as under the Confederation.

This Constitution, and the Laws of the United States which shall be made in Pursuance thereof; and all Treaties made, or which shall be made, under the Authority of the United States, shall be the supreme Law of the Land; and the Judges in every State shall be bound thereby, any Thing in the Constitution or Laws of any State to the Contrary notwithstanding.

The Senators and Representatives before mentioned, and the Members of the several State Legislatures, and all executive and judicial Officers, both of the United States and of the several States, shall be bound by Oath or Affirmation, to support this Constitution; but no religious Test shall ever be required as a Qualification to any Office or public Trust under the United States.

ARTICLE VII

The Ratification of the Conventions of nine States, shall be sufficient for the Establishment of this Constitution between the States so ratifying the Same.

The Word, "the," being interlined between the seventh and eighth Lines of the first Page, the Word "Thirty" being partly written on an Erazure in the fifteenth Line of the first Page, The Words "is tried" being interlined between the thirty second and thirty third Lines of the first Page and the Word "the" being interlined between the forty third and forty fourth Lines of the second Page.

Attest William Jackson
Secretary

Done in Convention by the Unanimous Consent of the States present the Seventeenth Day of September in the Year of our Lord one thousand seven hundred and Eighty seven and of the Independence of the United States of America the Twelfth In witness whereof We have hereunto subscribed our Names.

The Bill of Rights: A Transcription   Note: The following text is a transcription of the first 10 amendments to the Constitution in their original form. These amendments were ratified December 15, 1791, and form what is known as the Bill of Rights.

Amendment I [1791]   Congress shall make no law respecting an establishment of religion, or prohibiting the free exercise thereof; or abridging the freedom of speech, or of the press; or the right of the people peaceably to assemble, and to petition the Government for a redress of grievances.

Amendment II [1791]   A well regulated Militia, being necessary to the security of a free State, the right of the people to keep and bear Arms, shall not be infringed.

Amendment III [1791]   No Soldier shall, in time of peace be quartered in any house, without the consent of the Owner, nor in time of war, but in a manner to be prescribed by law.

Amendment IV [1791]   The right of the people to be secure in their persons, houses, papers, and effects, against unreasonable searches and seizures, shall not be violated, and no Warrants shall issue, but upon probable cause, supported by Oath or affirmation, and particularly describing the place to be searched, and the persons or things to be seized.

Amendment V [1791]   No person shall be held to answer for a capital, or otherwise infamous crime, unless on a presentment or indictment of a Grand Jury, except in cases arising in the land or naval forces, or in the Militia, when in actual service in time of War or public danger; nor shall any person be subject for the same offence to be twice put in jeopardy of life or limb; nor shall be compelled in any criminal case to be a witness against himself, nor be deprived of life, liberty, or property, without due process of law; nor shall private property be taken for public use, without just compensation.

Amendment VI [1791]   In all criminal prosecutions, the accused shall enjoy the right to a speedy and public trial, by an impartial jury of the State and district wherein the crime shall have been committed, which district shall have been previously ascertained by law, and to be informed of the nature and cause of the accusation; to be confronted with the witnesses against him; to have compulsory process for obtaining witnesses in his favor, and to have the Assistance of Counsel for his defence.

Amendment VII [1791]   In Suits at common law, where the value in controversy shall exceed twenty dollars, the right of trial by jury shall be preserved, and no fact tried by a jury, shall be otherwise re-examined in any Court of the United States, than according to the rules of the common law.

Amendment VIII [1791]   Excessive bail shall not be required, nor excessive fines imposed, nor cruel and unusual punishments inflicted.

Amendment IX [1791]   The enumeration in the Constitution, of certain rights, shall not be construed to deny or disparage others retained by the people.

Amendment X [1791]   The powers not delegated to the United States by the Constitution, nor prohibited by it to the States, are reserved to the States respectively, or to the people.
   Note: The capitalization and punctuation in this version are from the enrolled original of the Joint Resolution of Congress proposing the Bill of Rights, which is on permanent display in the Rotunda of the National Archives Building, Washington, DC.

The Constitution: Amendments 11–27   Constitutional Amendments 1–10 make up what is known as The Bill of Rights. Amendments 11–27 are listed next.

Amendment XI [1795]   Note: Article III, section 2, of the Constitution was modified by Amendment XI.
   The Judicial power of the United States shall not be construed to extend to any suit in law or equity, commenced or prosecuted against one of the United States by Citizens of another State, or by Citizens or Subjects of any Foreign State.

Amendment XII [1804]   The Electors shall meet in their respective states and vote by ballot for President and Vice-President, one of whom, at least, shall not be an inhabitant of the same state with themselves; they shall name in their ballots the person voted for as President, and in distinct ballots the person voted for as Vice-President, and they shall make distinct lists of all persons voted for as President, and of all persons voted for as Vice-President, and of the number of votes for each, which lists they shall sign and certify, and transmit sealed to the seat of the government of the United States, directed to the President of the Senate;— the President of the Senate shall, in the presence of the Senate and House of Representatives, open all the certificates and the votes shall then be counted;—The person having the greatest number of votes for President, shall be the President, if such number be a majority of the whole number of Electors appointed; and if no person have such majority, then from the persons having the highest numbers not exceeding three on the list of those voted for as President, the House of Representatives shall choose immediately, by ballot, the President. But in choosing the President, the votes shall be taken by states, the representation from each state having one vote; a quorum for this purpose shall consist of a member or members from two-thirds of the states, and a majority of all the states shall be necessary to a choice. [And if the House of Representatives shall not choose a President whenever the right of choice shall devolve upon them, before the fourth day of March next following, then the Vice-President shall act as President, as in case of the death or other constitutional disability of the President.—]* The person having the greatest number of votes as Vice-President, shall be the Vice-President, if such number be a majority of the whole number of Electors appointed, and if no person have a majority, then from the two highest numbers on the list, the Senate shall choose the Vice-President; a quorum for the purpose shall consist of two-thirds of the whole number of Senators, and a majority of the whole number shall be necessary to a choice. But no person constitutionally ineligible to the office of President shall be eligible to that of Vice-President of the United States.

Amendment XIII [1865]

SECTION 1

Neither slavery nor involuntary servitude, except as a punishment for crime whereof the party shall have been duly convicted, shall exist within the United States, or any place subject to their jurisdiction.

SECTION 2

Congress shall have power to enforce this article by appropriate legislation.

Amendment XIV [1868]

SECTION 1

All persons born or naturalized in the United States, and subject to the jurisdiction thereof, are citizens of the United States and of the State wherein they reside. No State shall make or enforce any law which shall abridge the privileges or immunities of citizens of the United States; nor shall any State deprive any person of life, liberty, or property, without due process of law; nor deny to any person within its jurisdiction the equal protection of the laws.

SECTION 2

Representatives shall be apportioned among the several States according to their respective numbers, counting the whole number of persons in each State, excluding Indians not taxed. But when the right to vote at any election for the choice of electors for President and Vice-President of the United States, Representatives in Congress, the Executive and Judicial officers of a State, or the members of the Legislature thereof, is denied to any of the male inhabitants of such State, being twenty-one years of age,* and citizens of the United States, or in any way abridged, except for participation in rebellion, or other crime, the basis of representation therein shall be reduced in the proportion which the number of such male citizens shall bear to the whole number of male citizens twenty-one years of age in such State.

SECTION 3

No person shall be a Senator or Representative in Congress, or elector of President and Vice-President, or hold any office, civil or military, under the United States, or under any State, who, having previously taken an oath, as a member of Congress, or as an officer of the United States, or as a member of any State legislature, or as an executive or judicial officer of any State, to support the Constitution of the United States, shall have engaged in insurrection or rebellion against the same, or given aid or comfort to the enemies thereof. But Congress may by a vote of two-thirds of each House, remove such disability.

SECTION 4

The validity of the public debt of the United States, authorized by law, including debts incurred for payment of pensions and bounties for services in suppressing insurrection or rebellion, shall not be questioned. But neither the United States nor any State shall assume or pay any debt or obligation incurred in aid of insurrection or rebellion against the United States, or any claim for the loss or emancipation of any slave; but all such debts, obligations and claims shall be held illegal and void.

SECTION 5

The Congress shall have the power to enforce, by appropriate legislation, the provisions of this article.

Amendment XV [1870]

SECTION 1

The right of citizens of the United States to vote shall not be denied or abridged by the United States or by any State on account of race, color, or previous condition of servitude.

SECTION 2

The Congress shall have the power to enforce this article by appropriate legislation.

Amendment XVI [1913]   The Congress shall have power to lay and collect taxes on incomes, from whatever source derived, without apportionment among the several States, and without regard to any census or enumeration.

Amendment XVII [1913]   The Senate of the United States shall be composed of two Senators from each State, elected by the people thereof, for six years; and each Senator shall have one vote. The electors in each State shall have the qualifications requisite for electors of the most numerous branch of the State legislatures.

When vacancies happen in the representation of any State in the Senate, the executive authority of such State shall issue writs of election to fill such vacancies: Provided, That the legislature of any State may empower the executive thereof to make temporary appointments until the people fill the vacancies by election as the legislature may direct.

This amendment shall not be so construed as to affect the election or term of any Senator chosen before it becomes valid as part of the Constitution.

Amendment XVIII [1919]   [Repealed by Amendment XXI]

SECTION 1

After one year from the ratification of this article the manufacture, sale, or transportation of intoxicating liquors within, the importation thereof into, or the exportation thereof from the United States and all territory subject to the jurisdiction thereof for beverage purposes is hereby prohibited.

SECTION 2

The Congress and the several States shall have concurrent power to enforce this article by appropriate legislation.

SECTION 3

This article shall be inoperative unless it shall have been ratified as an amendment to the Constitution by the legislatures of the several States, as provided in the Constitution, within seven years from the date of the submission hereof to the States by the Congress.

Amendment XIX [1920]   The right of citizens of the United States to vote shall not be denied or abridged by the United States or by any State on account of sex.

Congress shall have power to enforce this article by appropriate legislation.

Amendment XX [1933]

SECTION 1

The terms of the President and the Vice President shall end at noon on the 20th day of January, and the terms of Senators and Representatives at noon on the 3d day of January, of the years in which such terms would have ended if this article had not been ratified; and the terms of their successors shall then begin.

SECTION 2

The Congress shall assemble at least once in every year, and such meeting shall begin at noon on the 3d day of January, unless they shall by law appoint a different day.

SECTION 3

If, at the time fixed for the beginning of the term of the President, the President elect shall have died, the Vice President elect shall become President. If a President shall not have been chosen before the time fixed for the beginning of his term, or if the President elect shall have failed to qualify, then the Vice President elect shall act as President until a President shall have qualified; and the Congress may by law provide for the case wherein neither a President elect nor a Vice President shall have qualified, declaring who shall then act as President, or the manner in which one who is to act shall be selected, and such person shall act accordingly until a President or Vice President shall have qualified.

SECTION 4

The Congress may by law provide for the case of the death of any of the persons from whom the House of Representatives may choose a President whenever the right of choice shall have devolved upon them, and for the case of the death of any of the persons from whom the Senate may choose a Vice President whenever the right of choice shall have devolved upon them.

SECTION 5

Sections 1 and 2 shall take effect on the 15th day of October following the ratification of this article.

SECTION 6

This article shall be inoperative unless it shall have been ratified as an amendment to the Constitution by the legislatures of three-fourths of the several States within seven years from the date of its submission.

Amendment XXI [1933]

SECTION 1

The eighteenth article of amendment to the Constitution of the United States is hereby repealed.

SECTION 2

The transportation or importation into any State, Territory, or Possession of the United States for delivery or use therein of intoxicating liquors, in violation of the laws thereof, is hereby prohibited.

SECTION 3

This article shall be inoperative unless it shall have been ratified as an amendment to the Constitution by conventions in the several States, as provided in the Constitution, within seven years from the date of the submission hereof to the States by the Congress.

Amendment XXII [1951]

SECTION 1

No person shall be elected to the office of the President more than twice, and no person who has held the office of President, or acted as President, for more than two years

of a term to which some other person was elected President shall be elected to the office of President more than once. But this Article shall not apply to any person holding the office of President when this Article was proposed by Congress, and shall not prevent any person who may be holding the office of President, or acting as President, during the term within which this Article becomes operative from holding the office of President or acting as President during the remainder of such term.

SECTION 2

This article shall be inoperative unless it shall have been ratified as an amendment to the Constitution by the legislatures of three-fourths of the several States within seven years from the date of its submission to the States by the Congress.

Amendment XXIII [1961]

SECTION 1

The District constituting the seat of Government of the United States shall appoint in such manner as Congress may direct:

A number of electors of President and Vice President equal to the whole number of Senators and Representatives in Congress to which the District would be entitled if it were a State, but in no event more than the least populous State; they shall be in addition to those appointed by the States, but they shall be considered, for the purposes of the election of President and Vice President, to be electors appointed by a State; and they shall meet in the District and perform such duties as provided by the twelfth article of amendment.

SECTION 2

The Congress shall have power to enforce this article by appropriate legislation.

Amendment XXIV [1964]

SECTION 1

The right of citizens of the United States to vote in any primary or other election for President or Vice President, for electors for President or Vice President, or for Senator or Representative in Congress, shall not be denied or abridged by the United States or any State by reason of failure to pay poll tax or other tax.

SECTION 2

The Congress shall have power to enforce this article by appropriate legislation.

Amendment XXV [1967]

SECTION 1

In case of the removal of the President from office or of his death or resignation, the Vice President shall become President.

SECTION 2

Whenever there is a vacancy in the office of the Vice President, the President shall nominate a Vice President who shall take office upon confirmation by a majority vote of both Houses of Congress.

SECTION 3

Whenever the President transmits to the President pro tempore of the Senate and the Speaker of the House of Representatives his written declaration that he is unable to discharge the powers and duties of his office, and until he transmits to them a written declaration to the contrary, such powers and duties shall be discharged by the Vice President as Acting President.

SECTION 4

Whenever the Vice President and a majority of either the principal officers of the executive departments or of such other body as Congress may by law provide, transmit to the President pro tempore of the Senate and the Speaker of the House of Representatives their written declaration that the President is unable to discharge the powers and duties of his office, the Vice President shall immediately assume the powers and duties of the office as Acting President.

Thereafter, when the President transmits to the President pro tempore of the Senate and the Speaker of the House of Representatives his written declaration that no inability exists, he shall resume the powers and duties of his office unless the Vice President and a majority of either the principal officers of the executive department or of such other body as Congress may by law provide, transmit within four days to the President pro tempore of the Senate and the Speaker of the House of Representatives their written declaration that the President is unable to discharge the powers and duties of his office. Thereupon Congress shall decide the issue, assembling within forty-eight hours for that purpose if not in session. If the Congress, within twenty-one days after receipt of the latter written declaration, or, if Congress is not in session, within twenty-one days after Congress is required to assemble, determines by two-thirds vote of both Houses that the President is unable to discharge the powers and duties of his office, the Vice President shall continue to discharge the same as Acting President; otherwise, the President shall resume the powers and duties of his office.

Amendment XXVI [1971]

SECTION 1

The right of citizens of the United States, who are eighteen years of age or older, to vote shall not be denied or abridged by the United States or by any State on account of age.

SECTION 2

The Congress shall have power to enforce this article by appropriate legislation.

Amendment XXVII [1992]   No law, varying the compensation for the services of the Senators and Representatives, shall take effect, until an election of representatives shall have intervened.

UNIFORM COMMERCIAL CODE
Article 2—Sales

PART 1

Short Title, General Construction and Subject Matter

SECTION 2–101. SHORT TITLE

This Article shall be known and may be cited as Uniform Commercial Code—Sales.

SECTION 2–102. SCOPE; CERTAIN SECURITY AND OTHER TRANSACTIONS EXCLUDED FROM THIS ARTICLE

Unless the context otherwise requires, this Article applies to transactions in goods; it does not apply to any transaction which although in the form of an unconditional contract to sell or present sale is intended to operate only as a security transaction nor does this Article impair or repeal any statute regulating sales to consumers, farmers or other specified classes of buyers.

SECTION 2–103. DEFINITIONS AND INDEX OF DEFINITIONS

1. In this Article unless the context otherwise requires
   a. "Buyer" means a person who buys or contracts to buy goods.
   b. "Good faith" in the case of a merchant means honesty in fact and the observance of reasonable commercial standards of fair dealing in the trade.
   c. "Receipt" of goods means taking physical possession of them.
   d. "Seller" means a person who sells or contracts to sell goods.

2. Other definitions applying to this Article or to specified Parts thereof, and the sections in which they appear are:

   "Acceptance." Section 2–606.
   "Banker's credit." Section 2–325.
   "Between merchants." Section 2–104.
   "Cancellation." Section 2–106(4).
   "Commercial unit." Section 2–105.
   "Confirmed credit." Section 2–325.
   "Conforming to contract." Section 2–106.
   "Contract for sale." Section 2–106.
   "Cover." Section 2–712.
   "Entrusting." Section 2–403.
   "Financing agency." Section 2–104.
   "Future goods." Section 2–105.
   "Goods." Section 2–105.
   "Identification." Section 2–501.
   "Installment contract." Section 2–612.
   "Letter of Credit." Section 2–325.
   "Lot." Section 2–105.
   "Merchant." Section 2–104.
   "Overseas." Section 2–323.
   "Person in position of seller." Section 2–707.
   "Present sale." Section 2–106.
   "Sale." Section 2–106.
   "Sale on approval." Section 2–326.
   "Sale or return." Section 2–326.
   "Termination." Section 2–106.

3. The following definitions in other Articles apply to this Article:

   "Check." Section 3–104.
   "Consignee." Section 7–102.
   "Consignor." Section 7–102.
   "Consumer goods." Section 9–109.
   "Dishonor." Section 3–502.
   "Draft." Section 3–104.

4. In addition Article 1 contains general definitions and principles of construction and interpretation applicable throughout this Article.

As amended in 1994.

SECTION 2–104. DEFINITIONS: "MERCHANT"; "BETWEEN MERCHANTS"; "FINANCING AGENCY"

1. "Merchant" means a person who deals in goods of the kind or otherwise by his occupation holds himself

629

out as having knowledge or skill peculiar to the practices or goods involved in the transaction or to whom such knowledge or skill may be attributed by his employment of an agent or broker or other intermediary who by his occupation holds himself out as having such knowledge or skill.

2. "Financing agency" means a bank, finance company or other person who in the ordinary course of business makes advances against goods or documents of title or who by arrangement with either the seller or the buyer intervenes in ordinary course to make or collect payment due or claimed under the contract for sale, as by purchasing or paying the seller's draft or making advances against it or by merely taking it for collection whether or not documents of title accompany the draft. "Financing agency" includes also a bank or other person who similarly intervenes between persons who are in the position of seller and buyer in respect to the goods (Section 2–707).

3. "Between merchants" means in any transaction with respect to which both parties are chargeable with the knowledge or skill of merchants.

SECTION 2–105. DEFINITIONS: "TRANSFERABILITY"; "GOODS"; "FUTURE" GOODS; "LOT"; "COMMERCIAL UNIT"

1. "Goods" means all things (including specially manufactured goods) which are movable at the time of identification to the contract for sale other than the money in which the price is to be paid, investment securities (Article 8) and things in action. "Goods" also includes the unborn young of animals and growing crops and other identified things attached to realty as described in the section on goods to be severed from realty (Section 2–107).

2. Goods must be both existing and identified before any interest in them can pass. Goods which are not both existing and identified are "future" goods. A purported present sale of future goods or of any interest therein operates as a contract to sell.

3. There may be a sale of a part interest in existing identified goods.

4. An undivided share in an identified bulk of fungible goods is sufficiently identified to be sold although the quantity of the bulk is not determined. Any agreed proportion of such a bulk or any quantity thereof agreed upon by number, weight or other measure may to the extent of the seller's interest in the bulk be sold to the buyer who then becomes an owner in common.

5. "Lot" means a parcel or a single article which is the subject matter of a separate sale or delivery, whether or not it is sufficient to perform the contract.

6. "Commercial unit" means such a unit of goods as by commercial usage is a single whole for purposes of sale and division of which materially impairs its character or value on the market or in use. A commercial unit may be a single article (as a machine) or a set of articles (as a suite of furniture or an assortment of sizes) or a quantity (as a bale, gross, or carload) or any other unit treated in use or in the relevant market as a single whole.

SECTION 2–106. DEFINITIONS: "CONTRACT"; "AGREEMENT"; "CONTRACT FOR SALES"; "SALE"; "PRESENT SALE"; "CONFORMING" TO CONTRACT; "TERMINATION"; "CANCELLATION"

1. In this Article unless the context otherwise requires "contract" and "agreement" are limited to those relating to the present or future sale of goods. "Contract for sale" includes both a present sale of goods and a contract to sell goods at a future time. A "sale" consists in the passing of title from the seller to the buyer for a price (Section 2–401). A "present sale" means a sale which is accomplished by the making of the contract.

2. Goods or conduct including any part of a performance are "conforming" or conform to the contract when they are in accordance with the obligations under the contract.

3. "Termination" occurs when either party pursuant to a power created by agreement or law puts an end to the contract otherwise than for its breach. On "termination" all obligations which are still executory on both sides are discharged but any right based on prior breach or performance survives.

4. "Cancellation" occurs when either party puts an end to the contract for breach by the other and its effect is the same as that of "termination" except that the cancelling party also retains any remedy for breach of the whole contract or any unperformed balance.

SECTION 2–107. GOODS TO BE SEVERED FROM REALTY: RECORDING

1. A contract for the sale of minerals or the like (including oil and gas) or a structure or its materials to be removed from realty is a contract for the sale of goods within this Article if they are to be severed by the seller but until severance a purported present sale thereof which is not effective as a transfer of an interest in land is effective only as a contract to sell.

2. A contract for the sale apart from the land of growing crops or other things attached to realty and capable of severance without material harm thereto but not described in subsection (1) or of timber to be cut is a contract for the sale of goods within this Article whether the subject matter is to be severed by the buyer or by the seller even though it forms part of the realty at the time of contracting, and the parties can by identification effect a present sale before severance.

3. The provisions of this section are subject to any third party rights provided by the law relating to realty records, and the contract for sale may be executed and recorded as a document transferring an interest in land and shall then constitute notice to third parties of the buyer's rights under the contract for sale.

As amended in 1972.

PART 2

Form, Formation and Readjustment of Contract

SECTION 2–201. FORMAL REQUIREMENTS; STATUTE OF FRAUDS

1. Except as otherwise provided in this section a contract for the sale of goods for the price of $500 or more is not enforceable by way of action or defense unless there is some writing sufficient to indicate that a contract for sale has been made between the parties and signed by the party against whom enforcement is sought or by his authorized agent or broker. A writing is not insufficient because it omits or incorrectly states a term agreed upon but the contract is not enforceable under this paragraph beyond the quantity of goods shown in such writing.

2. Between merchants if within a reasonable time a writing in confirmation of the contract and sufficient against the sender is received and the party receiving it has reason to know its contents, it satisfies the requirements of subsection (1) against such party unless written notice of objection to its contents is given within 10 days after it is received.

3. A contract which does not satisfy the requirements of subsection (1) but which is valid in other respects is enforceable

   a. if the goods are to be specially manufactured for the buyer and are not suitable for sale to others in the ordinary course of the seller's business and the seller, before notice of repudiation is received and under circumstances which reasonably indicate that the goods are for the buyer, has made either a substantial beginning of their manufacture or commitments for their procurement; or

   b. if the party against whom enforcement is sought admits in his pleading, testimony or otherwise in court that a contract for sale was made, but the contract is not enforceable under this provision beyond the quantity of goods admitted; or

   c. with respect to goods for which payment has been made and accepted or which have been received and accepted (Sec. 2–606).

SECTION 2–202. FINAL WRITTEN EXPRESSION: PAROL OR EXTRINSIC EVIDENCE

Terms with respect to which the confirmatory memoranda of the parties agree or which are otherwise set forth in a writing intended by the parties as a final expression of their agreement with respect to such terms as are included therein may not be contradicted by evidence of any prior agreement or of a contemporaneous oral agreement but may be explained or supplemented

a. by course of dealing or usage of trade (Section 1–205) or by course of performance (Section 2–208); and

b. by evidence of consistent additional terms unless the court finds the writing to have been intended also as a complete and exclusive statement of the terms of the agreement.

SECTION 2–203. SEALS INOPERATIVE

The affixing of a seal to a writing evidencing a contract for sale or an offer to buy or sell goods does not constitute the writing a sealed instrument and the law with respect to sealed instruments does not apply to such a contract or offer.

SECTION 2–204. FORMATION IN GENERAL

1. A contract for sale of goods may be made in any manner sufficient to show agreement, including conduct by both parties which recognizes the existence of such a contract.

2. An agreement sufficient to constitute a contract for sale may be found even though the moment of its making is undetermined.

3. Even though one or more terms are left open a contract for sale does not fail for indefiniteness if the parties have intended to make a contract and there is a reasonably certain basis for giving an appropriate remedy.

SECTION 2–205. FIRM OFFERS

An offer by a merchant to buy or sell goods in a signed writing which by its terms gives assurance that it will be held open is not revocable, for lack of consideration, during the time stated or if no time is stated for a reasonable time, but in no event may such period of irrevocability exceed three months; but any such term of assurance on a form supplied by the offeree must be separately signed by the offeror.

SECTION 2–206. OFFER AND ACCEPTANCE IN FORMATION OF CONTRACT

1. Unless otherwise unambiguously indicated by the language or circumstances

   a. an offer to make a contract shall be construed as inviting acceptance in any manner and by any medium reasonable in the circumstances;

   b. an order or other offer to buy goods for prompt or current shipment shall be construed as inviting acceptance either by a prompt promise to ship or by the prompt or current shipment of conforming or non-conforming goods, but such a shipment of non-conforming goods does not constitute an acceptance if the seller seasonably notifies the buyer that the shipment is offered only as an accommodation to the buyer.

2. Where the beginning of a requested performance is a reasonable mode of acceptance an offeror who is not notified of acceptance within a reasonable time may treat the offer as having lapsed before acceptance.

SECTION 2–207. ADDITIONAL TERMS IN ACCEPTANCE OR CONFIRMATION

1. A definite and seasonable expression of acceptance or a written confirmation which is sent within a reasonable time operates as an acceptance even though it states terms additional to or different from those offered or agreed upon, unless acceptance is expressly made conditional on assent to the additional or different terms.

2. The additional terms are to be construed as proposals for addition to the contract. Between merchants such terms become part of the contract unless:

   a. the offer expressly limits acceptance to the terms of the offer;

   b. they materially alter it; or

   c. notification of objection to them has already been given or is given within a reasonable time after notice of them is received.

3. Conduct by both parties which recognizes the existence of a contract is sufficient to establish a contract for sale although the writings of the parties do not otherwise establish a contract. In such case the terms of the particular contract consist of those terms on which the writings of the parties agree, together with any supplementary terms incorporated under any other provisions of this Act.

SECTION 2–208. COURSE OF PERFORMANCE OR PRACTICAL CONSTRUCTION

1. Where the contract for sale involves repeated occasions for performance by either party with knowledge of the nature of the performance and opportunity for objection to it by the other, any course of performance accepted or acquiesced in without objection shall be relevant to determine the meaning of the agreement.

2. The express terms of the agreement and any such course of performance, as well as any course of dealing and usage of trade, shall be construed whenever reasonable as consistent with each other; but when such construction is unreasonable, express terms shall control course of performance and course of performance shall control both course of dealing and usage of trade (Section 1–205).

3. Subject to the provisions of the next section on modification and waiver, such course of performance shall be relevant to show a waiver or modification of any term inconsistent with such course of performance.

SECTION 2–209. MODIFICATION, RECISSION AND WAIVER

1. An agreement modifying a contract within this Article needs no consideration to be binding.

2. A signed agreement which excludes modification or rescission except by a signed writing cannot be otherwise modified or rescinded, but except as between merchants such a requirement on a form supplied by the merchant must be separately signed by the other party.

3. The requirements of the statute of frauds section of this Article (Section 2–201) must be satisfied if the contract as modified is within its provisions.

4. Although an attempt at modification or rescission does not satisfy the requirements of subsection (2) or (3) it can operate as a waiver.

5. A party who has made a waiver affecting an executory portion of the contract may retract the waiver by reasonable notification received by the other party that strict performance will be required of any term waived, unless the retraction would be unjust in view of a material change of position in reliance on the waiver.

SECTION 2–210. DELEGATION OF PERFORMANCE; ASSIGNMENT OF RIGHTS

1. A party may perform his duty through a delegate unless otherwise agreed or unless the other party has a substantial interest in having his original promisor perform or control the acts required by the contract. No delegation of performance relieves the party delegating of any duty to perform or any liability for breach.

2. Unless otherwise agreed all rights of either seller or buyer can be assigned except where the assignment would materially change the duty of the other party, or increase materially the burden or risk imposed on him by his contract, or impair materially his chance of obtaining return performance. A right to damages for breach of the whole contract or a right arising out of the assignor's due performance of his entire obligation can be assigned despite agreement otherwise.

3. Unless the circumstances indicate the contrary a prohibition of assignment of "the contract" is to be construed as barring only the delegation to the assignee of the assignor's performance.

4. An assignment of "the contract" or of "all my rights under the contract" or an assignment in similar general terms is an assignment of rights and unless the language or the circumstances (as in an assignment for security) indicate the contrary, it is a delegation of performance of the duties of the assignor and its acceptance by the assignee constitutes a promise by him to perform those duties. This promise is enforceable by either the assignor or the other party to the original contract.

5. The other party may treat any assignment which delegates performance as creating reasonable grounds for insecurity and may without prejudice to his rights against the assignor demand assurances from the assignee (Section 2–609).

PART 3

General Obligation and Construction of Contract

SECTION 2–301. GENERAL OBLIGATIONS OF PARTIES

The obligation of the seller is to transfer and deliver and that of the buyer is to accept and pay in accordance with the contract.

SECTION 2–302. UNCONSCIONABLE CONTRACT OR CLAUSE

1. If the court as a matter of law finds the contract or any clause of the contract to have been unconscionable at the time it was made the court may refuse to enforce the contract, or it may enforce the remainder of the contract without the unconscionable clause, or it may so limit the application of any unconscionable clause as to avoid any unconscionable result.

2. When it is claimed or appears to the court that the contract or any clause thereof may be unconscionable the parties shall be afforded a reasonable opportunity to present evidence as to its commercial setting, purpose and effect to aid the court in making the determination.

SECTION 2–303. ALLOCATION OR DIVISION OF RISKS

Where this Article allocates a risk or a burden as between the parties "unless otherwise agreed," the agreement may not only shift the allocation but may also divide the risk or burden.

SECTION 2–304. PRICE PAYABLE IN MONEY, GOODS, REALTY, OR OTHERWISE

1. The price can be made payable in money or otherwise. If it is payable in whole or in part in goods each party is a seller of the goods which he is to transfer.

2. Even though all or part of the price is payable in an interest in realty the transfer of the goods and the seller's obligations with reference to them are subject to this Article, but not the transfer of the interest in realty or the transferor's obligations in connection therewith.

SECTION 2–305. OPEN PRICE TERM

1. The parties if they so intend can conclude a contract for sale even though the price is not settled. In such a case the price is a reasonable price at the time for delivery if

   a. nothing is said as to price; or

   b. the price is left to be agreed by the parties and they fail to agree; or

   c. the price is to be fixed in terms of some agreed market or other standard as set or recorded by a third person or agency and it is not so set or recorded.

2. A price to be fixed by the seller or by the buyer means a price for him to fix in good faith.

3. When a price left to be fixed otherwise than by agreement of the parties fails to be fixed through fault of one party the other may at his option treat the contract as cancelled or himself fix a reasonable price.

4. Where, however, the parties intend not to be bound unless the price be fixed or agreed and it is not fixed or agreed there is no contract. In such a case the buyer must return any goods already received or if unable so to do must pay their reasonable value at the time of delivery and the seller must return any portion of the price paid on account.

SECTION 2–306. OUTPUT, REQUIREMENTS AND EXCLUSIVE DEALINGS

1. A term which measures the quantity by the output of the seller or the requirements of the buyer means such actual output or requirements as may occur in good faith, except that no quantity unreasonably disproportionate to any stated estimate or in the absence of a stated estimate to any normal or otherwise comparable prior output or requirements may be tendered or demanded.

2. A lawful agreement by either the seller or the buyer for exclusive dealing in the kind of goods concerned imposes unless otherwise agreed an obligation by the seller to use best efforts to supply the goods and by the buyer to use best efforts to promote their sale.

SECTION 2–307. DELIVERY IN SINGLE LOT OR SEVERAL LOTS

Unless otherwise agreed all goods called for by a contract for sale must be tendered in a single delivery and payment is due only on such tender but where the circumstances give either party the right to make or demand delivery in lots the price if it can be apportioned may be demanded for each lot.

SECTION 2–308. ABSENCE OF SPECIFIED PLACE FOR DELIVERY

Unless otherwise agreed

a. the place for delivery of goods is the seller's place of business or if he has none his residence; but

b. in a contract for sale of identified goods which to the knowledge of the parties at the time of contracting are in some other place, that place is the place for their delivery; and

c. documents of title may be delivered through customary banking channels.

SECTION 2–309. ABSENCE OF SPECIFIC TIME PROVISIONS; NOTICE OF TERMINATION

a. The time for shipment or delivery or any other action under a contract if not provided in this Article or agreed upon shall be a reasonable time.

b. Where the contract provides for successive performances but is indefinite in duration it is valid for a reasonable time but unless otherwise agreed may be terminated at any time by either party.

c. Termination of a contract by one party except on the happening of an agreed event requires that reasonable notification be received by the other party and an agreement dispensing with notification is invalid if its operation would be unconscionable.

SECTION 2–310. OPEN TIME FOR PAYMENT OR RUNNING OF CREDIT; AUTHORITY TO SHIP UNDER RESERVATION

Unless otherwise agreed

a. payment is due at the time and place at which the buyer is to receive the goods even though the place of shipment is the place of delivery; and

b. if the seller is authorized to send the goods he may ship them under reservation, and may tender the documents of title, but the buyer may inspect the goods after their arrival before payment is due unless such inspection is inconsistent with the terms of the contract (Section 2–513); and

c. if delivery is authorized and made by way of documents of title otherwise than by subsection (b) then payment is due at the time and place at which the buyer is to receive the documents regardless of where the goods are to be received; and

d. where the seller is required or authorized to ship the goods on credit the credit period runs from the time of shipment but post-dating the invoice or delaying its dispatch will correspondingly delay the starting of the credit period.

SECTION 2–311. OPTIONS AND COOPERATION RESPECTING PERFORMANCE

1. An agreement for sale which is otherwise sufficiently definite (subsection (3) of Section

2. 2–204) to be a contract is not made invalid by the fact that it leaves particulars of performance to be specified by one of the parties. Any such specification must be made in good faith and within limits set by commercial reasonableness.

3. Unless otherwise agreed specifications relating to assortment of the goods are at the buyer's option and except as otherwise provided in subsections (1) (c) and (3) of Section 2–319 specifications or arrangements relating to shipment are at the seller's option.

4. Where such specification would materially affect the other party's performance but is not seasonably made or where one party's cooperation is necessary to the agreed performance of the other but is not seasonably forthcoming, the other party in addition to all other remedies

   a. is excused for any resulting delay in his own performance; and

   b. may also either proceed to perform in any reasonable manner or after the time for a material part of his own performance treat the failure to specify or to cooperate as a breach by failure to deliver or accept the goods.

SECTION 2–312. WARRANTY OF TITLE AND AGAINST INFRINGEMENT; BUYER'S OBLIGATION AGAINST INFRINGEMENT

1. Subject to subsection (2) there is in a contract for sale a warranty by the seller that

   a. the title conveyed shall be good, and its transfer rightful; and

   b. the goods shall be delivered free from any security interest or other lien or encumbrance of which the buyer at the time of contracting has no knowledge.

2. A warranty under subsection (1) will be excluded or modified only by specific language or by circumstances which give the buyer reason to know that the person selling does not claim title in himself or that he is purporting to sell only such right or title as he or a third person may have.

3. Unless otherwise agreed a seller who is a merchant regularly dealing in goods of the kind warrants that the goods shall be delivered free of the rightful claim of any third person by way of infringement or the like but a buyer who furnishes specifications to the seller must hold the seller harmless against any such claim which arises out of compliance with the specifications.

SECTION 2–313. EXPRESS WARRANTIES BY AFFIRMATION, PROMISE, DESCRIPTION, SAMPLE

1. Express warranties by the seller are created as follows:

   a. Any affirmation of fact or promise made by the seller to the buyer which relates to the goods and becomes part of the basis of the bargain creates an express warranty that the goods shall conform to the affirmation or promise.

   b. Any description of the goods which is made part of the basis of the bargain creates an express warranty that the goods shall conform to the description.

   c. Any sample or model which is made part of the basis of the bargain creates an express warranty that the whole of the goods shall conform to the sample or model.

2. It is not necessary to the creation of an express warranty that the seller use formal words such as "warrant" or "guarantee" or that he have a specific intention to make a warranty, but an affirmation merely of the value of the goods or a statement purporting to be merely the seller's opinion or commendation of the goods does not create a warranty.

SECTION 2–314. IMPLIED WARRANTY: MERCHANTABILITY; USAGE OF TRADE

1. Unless excluded or modified (Section 2–316), a warranty that the goods shall be merchantable is implied in a contract for their sale if the seller is a merchant with respect to goods of that kind. Under this section the serving for value of food or drink to be consumed either on the premises or elsewhere is a sale.

2. Goods to be merchantable must be at least such as

    a. pass without objection in the trade under the contract description; and

    b. in the case of fungible goods, are of fair average quality within the description; and

    c. are fit for the ordinary purposes for which such goods are used; and

    d. run, within the variations permitted by the agreement, of even kind, quality and quantity within each unit and among all units involved; and

    e. are adequately contained, packaged, and labeled as the agreement may require; and

    f. conform to the promise or affirmations of fact made on the container or label if any.

3. Unless excluded or modified (Section 2–316) other implied warranties may arise from course of dealing or usage of trade.

SECTION 2–315. IMPLIED WARRANTY: FITNESS FOR PARTICULAR PURPOSE

Where the seller at the time of contracting has reason to know any particular purpose for which the goods are required and that the buyer is relying on the seller's skill or judgment to select or furnish suitable goods, there is unless excluded or modified under the next section an implied warranty that the goods shall be fit for such purpose.

SECTION 2–316. EXCLUSION OR MODIFICATION OF WARRANTIES

1. Words or conduct relevant to the creation of an express warranty and words or conduct tending to negate or limit warranty shall be construed wherever reasonable as consistent with each other; but subject to the provisions of this Article on parol or extrinsic evidence (Section 2–202) negation or limitation is inoperative to the extent that such construction is unreasonable.

2. Subject to subsection (3), to exclude or modify the implied warranty of merchantability or any part of it the language must mention merchantability and in case of a writing must be conspicuous, and to exclude or modify any implied warranty of fitness the exclusion must be by a writing and conspicuous. Language to exclude all implied warranties of fitness is sufficient if it states, for example, that "There are no warranties which extend beyond the description on the face hereof."

3. Notwithstanding subsection (2)

    a. unless the circumstances indicate otherwise, all implied warranties are excluded by expressions like "as is," "with all faults" or other language which in common understanding calls the buyer's attention to the exclusion of warranties and makes plain that there is no implied warranty; and

    b. when the buyer before entering into the contract has examined the goods or the sample or model as fully as he desired or has refused to examine the goods there is no implied warranty with regard to defects which an examination ought in the circumstances to have revealed to him; and

    c. an implied warranty can also be excluded or modified by course of dealing or course of performance or usage of trade.

4. Remedies for breach of warranty can be limited in accordance with the provisions of this Article on liquidation or limitation of damages and on contractual modification of remedy (Sections 2–718 and 2–719).

SECTION 2–317. CUMULATION AND CONFLICT OF WARRANTIES EXPRESS OR IMPLIED

Warranties whether express or implied shall be construed as consistent with each other and as cumulative, but if such construction is unreasonable the intention of the parties shall determine which warranty is dominant. In ascertaining that intention the following rules apply:

a. Exact or technical specifications displace an inconsistent sample or model or general language of description.

b. A sample from an existing bulk displaces inconsistent general language of description.

c. Express warranties displace inconsistent implied warranties other than an implied warranty of fitness for a particular purpose.

SECTION 2–318. THIRD PARTY BENEFICIARIES OF WARRANTIES EXPRESS OR IMPLIED

Note: If this Act is introduced in the Congress of the United States this section should be omitted. (States to select one alternative.)

Alternative A   A seller's warranty whether express or implied extends to any natural person who is in the family or household of his buyer or who is a guest in his home if it is reasonable to expect that such person may use, consume or be affected by the goods and who is injured in person by breach of the warranty. A seller may not exclude or limit the operation of this section.

Alternative B   A seller's warranty whether express or implied extends to any natural person who may reasonably be expected to use, consume or be affected by the goods and who is injured in person by breach of the warranty. A seller may not exclude or limit the operation of this section.

Alternative C   A seller's warranty whether express or implied extends to any person who may reasonably be expected to use, consume or be affected by the goods and who is injured by breach of the warranty. A seller may not exclude or limit the operation of this section with respect to injury to the person of an individual to whom the warranty extends.

As amended in 1966.

SECTION 2–319. F.O.B. AND F.A.S. TERMS

1. Unless otherwise agreed the term F.O.B. (which means "free on board") at a named place, even though used only in connection with the stated price, is a delivery term under which

    a. when the term is F.O.B. the place of shipment, the seller must at that place ship the goods in the manner provided in this Article (Section 2–504) and bear the expense and risk of putting them into the possession of the carrier; or

    b. when the term is F.O.B. the place of destination, the seller must at his own expense and risk transport the goods to that place and there tender delivery of them in the manner provided in this Article (Section 2–503);

    c. when under either (a) or (b) the term is also F.O.B. vessel, car or other vehicle, the seller must in addition at his own expense and risk load the goods on board. If the term is F.O.B. vessel the buyer must name the vessel and in an appropriate case the seller must comply with the provisions of this Article on the form of bill of lading (Section 2–323).

2. Unless otherwise agreed the term F.A.S. vessel (which means "free alongside") at a named port, even though used only in connection with the stated price, is a delivery term under which the seller must

    a. at his own expense and risk deliver the goods alongside the vessel in the manner usual in that port or on a dock designated and provided by the buyer; and

    b. obtain and tender a receipt for the goods in exchange for which the carrier is under a duty to issue a bill of lading.

3. Unless otherwise agreed in any case falling within subsection (1)(a) or (c) or subsection

4. the buyer must seasonably give any needed instructions for making delivery, including when the term is F.A.S. or F.O.B. the loading berth of the vessel and in an appropriate case its name and sailing date. The seller may treat the failure of needed instructions as a failure of cooperation under this Article (Section 2–311). He may also at his option move the goods in any reasonable manner preparatory to delivery or shipment.

5. Under the term F.O.B. vessel or F.A.S. unless otherwise agreed the buyer must make payment against tender of the required documents and the seller may not tender nor the buyer demand delivery of the goods in substitution for the documents.

SECTION 2–320. C.I.F. AND C. & F. TERMS

1. The term C.I.F. means that the price includes in a lump sum the cost of the goods and the insurance and freight to the named destination. The term C. & F. or C.F. means that the price so includes cost and freight to the named destination.

2. Unless otherwise agreed and even though used only in connection with the stated price and destination, the term C.I.F. destination or its equivalent requires the seller at his own expense and risk to

   a. put the goods into the possession of a carrier at the port for shipment and obtain a negotiable bill or bills of lading covering the entire transportation to the named destination; and

   b. load the goods and obtain a receipt from the carrier (which may be contained in the bill of lading) showing that the freight has been paid or provided for; and

   c. obtain a policy or certificate of insurance, including any war risk insurance, of a kind and on terms then current at the port of shipment in the usual amount, in the currency of the contract, shown to cover the same goods covered by the bill of lading and providing for payment of loss to the order of the buyer or for the account of whom it may concern; but the seller may add to the price the amount of the premium for any such war risk insurance; and

   d. prepare an invoice of the goods and procure any other documents required to effect shipment or to comply with the contract; and

   e. forward and tender with commercial promptness all the documents in due form and with any indorsement necessary to perfect the buyer's rights.

3. Unless otherwise agreed the term C. & F. or its equivalent has the same effect and imposes upon the seller the same obligations and risks as a C.I.F. term except the obligation as to insurance.

4. Under the term C.I.F. or C. & F. unless otherwise agreed the buyer must make payment against tender of the required documents and the seller may not tender nor the buyer demand delivery of the goods in substitution for the documents.

SECTION 2–321. C.I.F. OR C. & F.: "NET LANDED WEIGHTS"; "PAYMENT ON ARRIVAL"; WARRANTY OF CONDITION ON ARRIVAL

Under a contract containing a term C.I.F. or C. & F.

1. Where the price is based on or is to be adjusted according to "net landed weights," "delivered weights," "out turn" quantity or quality or the like,

unless otherwise agreed the seller must reasonably estimate the price. The payment due on tender of the documents called for by the contract is the amount so estimated, but after final adjustment of the price a settlement must be made with commercial promptness.

2. An agreement described in subsection (1) or any warranty of quality or condition of the goods on arrival places upon the seller the risk of ordinary deterioration, shrinkage and the like in transportation but has no effect on the place or time of identification to the contract for sale or delivery or on the passing of the risk of loss.

3. Unless otherwise agreed where the contract provides for payment on or after arrival of the goods the seller must before payment allow such preliminary inspection as is feasible; but if the goods are lost delivery of the documents and payment are due when the goods should have arrived.

SECTION 2–322. DELIVERY "EX-SHIP"

1. Unless otherwise agreed a term for delivery of goods "ex-ship" (which means from the carrying vessel) or in equivalent language is not restricted to a particular ship and requires delivery from a ship which has reached a place at the named port of destination where goods of the kind are usually discharged.

2. Under such a term unless otherwise agreed

   a. the seller must discharge all liens arising out of the carriage and furnish the buyer with a direction which puts the carrier under a duty to deliver the goods; and

   b. the risk of loss does not pass to the buyer until the goods leave the ship's tackle or are otherwise properly unloaded.

SECTION 2–323. FORM OF BILL OF LADING REQUIRED IN OVERSEAS SHIPMENT; "OVERSEAS"

1. Where the contract contemplates overseas shipment and contains a term C.I.F. or C. & F. or F.O.B. vessel, the seller unless otherwise agreed must obtain a negotiable bill of lading stating that the goods have been loaded in board or, in the case of a term C.I.F. or C. & F., received for shipment.

2. Where in a case within subsection (1) a bill of lading has been issued in a set of parts, unless otherwise

agreed if the documents are not to be sent from abroad the buyer may demand tender of the full set; otherwise only one part of the bill of lading need be tendered. Even if the agreement expressly requires a full set

   a. due tender of a single part is acceptable within the provisions of this Article on cure of improper delivery (subsection (1) of Section 2–508); and

   b. even though the full set is demanded, if the documents are sent from abroad the person tendering an incomplete set may nevertheless require payment upon furnishing an indemnity which the buyer in good faith deems adequate.

3. A shipment by water or by air or a contract contemplating such shipment is "overseas" insofar as by usage of trade or agreement it is subject to the commercial, financing or shipping practices characteristic of international deep water commerce.

SECTION 2–324. "NO ARRIVAL, NO SALE" TERM

Under a term "no arrival, no sale" or terms of like meaning, unless otherwise agreed,

a. the seller must properly ship conforming goods and if they arrive by any means he must tender them on arrival but he assumes no obligation that the goods will arrive unless he has caused the non-arrival; and

b. where without fault of the seller the goods are in part lost or have so deteriorated as no longer to conform to the contract or arrive after the contract time, the buyer may proceed as if there had been casualty to identified goods (Section 2–613).

SECTION 2–325. "LETTER OF CREDIT" TERM; "CONFIRMED CREDIT"

1. Failure of the buyer seasonably to furnish an agreed letter of credit is a breach of the contract for sale.

2. The delivery to seller of a proper letter of credit suspends the buyer's obligation to pay. If the letter of credit is dishonored, the seller may on seasonable notification to the buyer require payment directly from him.

3. Unless otherwise agreed the term "letter of credit" or "banker's credit" in a contract for sale means an irrevocable credit issued by a financing agency of good repute and, where the shipment is overseas, of good international repute. The term "confirmed credit" means that the credit must also carry the direct obligation of such an agency which does business in the seller's financial market.

SECTION 2–326. SALE ON APPROVAL AND SALE OR RETURN; CONSIGNMENT SALES AND RIGHTS OF CREDITORS

1. Unless otherwise agreed, if delivered goods may be returned by the buyer even though they conform to the contract, the transaction is

   a. a "sale on approval" if the goods are delivered primarily for use, and

   b. a "sale or return" if the goods are delivered primarily for resale.

2. Except as provided in subsection (3), goods held on approval are not subject to the claims of the buyer's creditors until acceptance; goods held on sale or return are subject to such claims while in the buyer's possession.

3. Where goods are delivered to a person for sale and such person maintains a place of business at which he deals in goods of the kind involved, under a name other than the name of the person making delivery, then with respect to claims of creditors of the person conducting the business the goods are deemed to be on sale or return. The provisions of this subsection are applicable even though an agreement purports to reserve title to the person making delivery until payment or resale or uses such words as "on consignment" or "on memorandum." However, this subsection is not applicable if the person making delivery

   a. complies with an applicable law providing for a consignor's interest or the like to be evidenced by a sign, or

   b. establishes that the person conducting the business is generally known by his creditors to be substantially engaged in selling the goods of others, or

   c. complies with the filing provisions of the Article on Secured Transactions (Article 9).

4. Any "or return" term of a contract for sale is to be treated as a separate contract for sale within the statute of frauds section of this Article (Section 2–201) and as contradicting the sale aspect of the contract within the provisions of this Article on parol or extrinsic evidence (Section 2–202).

SECTION 2–327. SPECIAL INCIDENTS OF SALE ON APPROVAL AND SALE OR RETURN

1. Under a sale on approval unless otherwise agreed

    a. although the goods are identified to the contract the risk of loss and the title do not pass to the buyer until acceptance; and

    b. use of the goods consistent with the purpose of trial is not acceptance but failure seasonally to notify the seller of election to return the goods is acceptance, and if the goods conform to the contract acceptance of any part is acceptance of the whole; and

    c. after due notification of election to return, the return is at the seller's risk and expense but a merchant buyer must follow any reasonable instructions.

2. Under a sale or return unless otherwise agreed

    a. the option to return extends to the whole or any commercial unit of the goods while in substantially their original condition, but must be exercised seasonably; and

    b. the return is at the buyer's risk and expense.

SECTION 2–328. SALE BY AUCTION

1. In a sale by auction if goods are put up in lots each lot is the subject of a separate sale.

2. A sale by auction is complete when the auctioneer so announces by the fall of the hammer or in other customary manner. Where a bid is made while the hammer is falling in acceptance of a prior bid the auctioneer may in his discretion reopen the bidding or declare the goods sold under the bid on which the hammer was falling.

3. Such a sale is with reserve unless the goods are in explicit terms put up without reserve. In an auction with reserve the auctioneer may withdraw the goods at any time until he announces completion of the sale. In an auction without reserve, after the auctioneer calls for bids on an article or lot, that article or lot cannot be withdrawn unless no bid is made within a reasonable time. In either case a bidder may retract his bid until the auctioneer's announcement of completion of the sale, but a bidder's retraction does not revive any previous bid.

4. If the auctioneer knowingly receives a bid on the seller's behalf or the seller makes or procures such a bid, and notice has not been given that liberty for such bidding is reserved, the buyer may at his option avoid the sale or take the goods at the price of the last good faith bid prior to the completion of the sale. This subsection shall not apply to any bid at a forced sale.

PART 4

Title, Creditors and Good Faith Purchasers

SECTION 2–401. PASSING OF TITLE; RESERVATION FOR SECURITY; LIMITED APPLICATION OF THIS SECTION

Each provision of this Article with regard to the rights, obligations and remedies of the seller, the buyer, purchasers or other third parties applies irrespective of title to the goods except where the provision refers to such title. Insofar as situations are not covered by the other provisions of this Article and matters concerning title become material the following rules apply:

1. Title to goods cannot pass under a contract for sale prior to their identification to the contract (Section 2–501), and unless otherwise explicitly agreed the buyer acquires by their identification a special property as limited by this Act. Any retention or reservation by the seller of the title (property) in goods shipped or delivered to the buyer is limited in effect to a reservation of a security interest. Subject to these provisions and to the provisions of the Article on Secured Transactions (Article 9), title to goods passes from the seller to the buyer in any manner and on any conditions explicitly agreed on by the parties.

2. Unless otherwise explicitly agreed title passes to the buyer at the time and place at which the seller completes his performance with reference to the physical delivery of the goods, despite any reservation of a security interest and even though a document of title is to be delivered at a different time or place; and in particular and despite any reservation of a security interest by the bill of lading

    a. if the contract requires or authorizes the seller to send the goods to the buyer but does not require him to deliver them at destination, title passes to the buyer at the time and place of shipment; but

    b. if the contract requires delivery at destination, title passes on tender there.

3. Unless otherwise explicitly agreed where delivery is to be made without moving the goods,

    a. if the seller is to deliver a document of title, title passes at the time when and the place where he delivers such documents; or

    b. if the goods are at the time of contracting already identified and no documents are to be delivered, title passes at the time and place of contracting.

4. A rejection or other refusal by the buyer to receive or retain the goods, whether or not justified, or a justified revocation of acceptance revests title to the goods in the seller. Such revesting occurs by operation of law and is not a "sale."

SECTION 2–402. RIGHTS OF SELLER'S CREDITORS AGAINST SOLD GOODS

1. Except as provided in subsections (2) and (3), rights of unsecured creditors of the seller with respect to goods which have been identified to a contract for sale are subject to the buyer's rights to recover the goods under this Article (Sections 2–502 and 2–716).

2. A creditor of the seller may treat a sale or an identification of goods to a contract for sale as void if as against him a retention of possession by the seller is fraudulent under any rule of law of the state where the goods are situated, except that retention of possession in good faith and current course of trade by a merchant-seller for a commercially reasonable time after a sale or identification is not fraudulent.

3. Nothing in this Article shall be deemed to impair the rights of creditors of the seller

    a. under the provisions of the Article on Secured Transactions (Article 9); or

    b. where identification to the contract or delivery is made not in current course of trade but in satisfaction of or as security for a pre-existing claim for money, security or the like and is made under circumstances which under any rule of law of the state where the goods are situated would apart from this Article constitute the transaction a fraudulent transfer or voidable preference.

SECTION 2–403. POWER TO TRANSFER; GOOD FAITH PURCHASE OF GOODS; "ENTRUSTING"

1. A purchaser of goods acquires all title which his transferor had or had power to transfer except that a purchaser of a limited interest acquires rights only to the extent of the interest purchased. A person with voidable title has power to transfer a good title to a good faith purchaser for value. When goods have been delivered under a transaction of purchase the purchaser has such power even though

    a. the transferor was deceived as to the identity of the purchaser, or

    b. the delivery was in exchange for a check which is later dishonored, or

    c. it was agreed that the transaction was to be a "cash sale," or

    d. the delivery was procured through fraud punishable as larcenous under the criminal law.

2. Any entrusting of possession of goods to a merchant who deals in goods of that kind gives him power to transfer all rights of the entruster to a buyer in ordinary course of business.

3. "Entrusting" includes any delivery and any acquiescence in retention of possession regardless of any condition expressed between the parties to the delivery or acquiescence and regardless of whether the procurement of the entrusting or the possessor's disposition of the goods have been such as to be larcenous under the criminal law.

    [Publisher's Editorial Note: If a state adopts the repealer of Article 6—Bulk Transfers (Alternative A), subsec. (4) should read as follows:]

4. The rights of other purchasers of goods and of lien creditors are governed by the Articles on Secured Transactions (Article 9) and Documents of Title (Article 7).

    [Publisher's Editorial Note: If a state adopts Revised Article 6—Bulk Sales (Alternative B), subsec. (4) should read as follows:]

5. The rights of other purchasers of goods and of lien creditors are governed by the Articles on Secured Transactions (Article 9), Bulk Sales (Article 6) and Documents of Title (Article 7).

As amended in 1988.

PART 5

Performance

SECTION 2–501. INSURABLE INTEREST IN GOODS; MANNER OF IDENTIFICATION OF GOODS

1. The buyer obtains a special property and an insurable interest in goods by identification of existing

goods as goods to which the contract refers even though the goods so identified are non-conforming and he has an option to return or reject them. Such identification can be made at any time and in any manner explicitly agreed to by the parties. In the absence of explicit agreement identification occurs

a. when the contract is made if it is for the sale of goods already existing and identified;

b. if the contract is for the sale of future goods other than those described in paragraph (c), when goods are shipped, marked or otherwise designated by the seller as goods to which the contract refers;

c. when the crops are planted or otherwise become growing crops or the young are conceived if the contract is for the sale of unborn young to be born within twelve months after contracting or for the sale of crops to be harvested within twelve months or the next normal harvest season after contracting whichever is longer.

2. The seller retains an insurable interest in goods so long as title to or any security interest in the goods remains in him and where the identification is by the seller alone he may until default or insolvency or notification to the buyer that the identification is final substitute other goods for those identified.

3. Nothing in this section impairs any insurable interest recognized under any other statute or rule of law.

SECTION 2–502. BUYER'S RIGHT TO GOODS ON SELLER'S INSOLVENCY

1. Subject to subsection (2) and even though the goods have not been shipped a buyer who has paid a part or all of the price of goods in which he has a special property under the provisions of the immediately preceding section may on making and keeping good a tender of any unpaid portion of their price recover them from the seller if the seller becomes insolvent within ten days after receipt of the first installment on their price.

2. If the identification creating his special property has been made by the buyer he acquires the right to recover the goods only if they conform to the contract for sale.

SECTION 2–503. MANNER OF SELLER'S TENDER OF DELIVERY

1. Tender of delivery requires that the seller put and hold conforming goods at the buyer's disposition and give the buyer any notification reasonably necessary to enable him to take delivery. The manner, time and place for tender are determined by the agreement and this Article, and in particular

a. tender must be at a reasonable hour, and if it is of goods they must be kept available for the period reasonably necessary to enable the buyer to take possession; but

b. unless otherwise agreed the buyer must furnish facilities reasonably suited to the receipt of the goods.

2. Where the case is within the next section respecting shipment tender requires that the seller comply with its provisions.

3. Where the seller is required to deliver at a particular destination tender requires that he comply with subsection (1) and also in any appropriate case tender documents as described in subsections (4) and (5) of this section.

4. Where goods are in the possession of a bailee and are to be delivered without being moved

a. tender requires that the seller either tender a negotiable document of title covering such goods or procure acknowledgment by the bailee of the buyer's right to possession of the goods; but

b. tender to the buyer of a non-negotiable document of title or of a written direction to the bailee to deliver is sufficient tender unless the buyer seasonably objects, and receipt by the bailee of notification of the buyer's rights fixes those rights as against the bailee and all third persons; but risk of loss of the goods and of any failure by the bailee to honor the non-negotiable document of title or to obey the direction remains on the seller until the buyer has had a reasonable time to present the document or direction, and a refusal by the bailee to honor the document or to obey the direction defeats the tender.

5. Where the contract requires the seller to deliver documents

a. he must tender all such documents in correct form, except as provided in this Article with respect to bills of lading in a set (subsection (2) of Section 2–323); and

b. tender through customary banking channels is sufficient and dishonor of a draft accompanying the documents constitutes non-acceptance or rejection.

SECTION 2–504. SHIPMENT BY SELLER

Where the seller is required or authorized to send the goods to the buyer and the contract does not require him to deliver them at a particular destination, then unless otherwise agreed he must

a. put the goods in the possession of such a carrier and make such a contract for their transportation as may be reasonable having regard to the nature of the goods and other circumstances of the case; and

b. obtain and promptly deliver or tender in due form any document necessary to enable the buyer to obtain possession of the goods or otherwise required by the agreement or by usage of trade; and

c. promptly notify the buyer of the shipment. Failure to notify the buyer under paragraph (c) or to make a proper contract under paragraph (a) is a ground for rejection only if material delay or loss ensues.

SECTION 2–505. SELLER'S SHIPMENT UNDER RESERVATION

1. Where the seller has identified goods to the contract by or before shipment:

   a. his procurement of a negotiable bill of lading to his own order or otherwise reserves in him a security interest in the goods. His procurement of the bill to the order of a financing agency or of the buyer indicates in addition only the seller's expectation of transferring that interest to the person named.

   b. a non-negotiable bill of lading to himself or his nominee reserves possession of the goods as security but except in a case of conditional delivery (subsection (2) of Section 2–507) a non-negotiable bill of lading naming the buyer as consignee reserves no security interest even though the seller retains possession of the bill of lading.

2. When shipment by the seller with reservation of a security interest is in violation of the contract for sale it constitutes an improper contract for transportation within the preceding section but impairs neither the rights given to the buyer by shipment and identification of the goods to the contract nor the seller's powers as a holder of a negotiable document.

SECTION 2–506. RIGHTS OF FINANCING AGENCY

1. A financing agency by paying or purchasing for value a draft which relates to a shipment of goods acquires

to the extent of the payment or purchase and in addition to its own rights under the draft and any document of title securing it any rights of the shipper in the goods including the right to stop delivery and the shipper's right to have the draft honored by the buyer.

2. The right to reimbursement of a financing agency which has in good faith honored or purchased the draft under commitment to or authority from the buyer is not impaired by subsequent discovery of defects with reference to any relevant document which was apparently regular on its face.

SECTION 2–507. EFFECT OF SELLER'S TENDER; DELIVERY ON CONDITION

1. Tender of delivery is a condition to the buyer's duty to accept the goods and, unless otherwise agreed, to his duty to pay for them. Tender entitles the seller to acceptance of the goods and to payment according to the contract.

2. Where payment is due and demanded on the delivery to the buyer of goods or documents of title, his right as against the seller to retain or dispose of them is conditional upon his making the payment due.

SECTION 2–508. CURE BY SELLER OF IMPROPER TENDER OR DELIVERY; REPLACEMENT

1. Where any tender or delivery by the seller is rejected because non-conforming and the time for performance has not yet expired, the seller may seasonably notify the buyer of his intention to cure and may then within the contract time make a conforming delivery.

2. Where the buyer rejects a non-conforming tender which the seller had reasonable grounds to believe would be acceptable with or without money allowance the seller may if he seasonably notifies the buyer have a further reasonable time to substitute a conforming tender.

SECTION 2–509. RISK OF LOSS IN THE ABSENCE OF BREACH

1. Where the contract requires or authorizes the seller to ship the goods by carrier

   a. if it does not require him to deliver them at a particular destination, the risk of loss passes to the buyer when the goods are duly delivered to the carrier even though the shipment is under reservation (Section 2–505); but

b. if it does require him to deliver them at a particular destination and the goods are there duly tendered while in the possession of the carrier, the risk of loss passes to the buyer when the goods are there duly so tendered as to enable the buyer to take delivery.

2. Where the goods are held by a bailee to be delivered without being moved, the risk of loss passes to the buyer

   a. on his receipt of a negotiable document of title covering the goods; or

   b. on acknowledgment by the bailee of the buyer's right to possession of the goods; or

   c. after his receipt of a non-negotiable document of title or other written direction to deliver, as provided in subsection (4)(b) of Section 2–503.

3. In any case not within subsection (1) or (2), the risk of loss passes to the buyer on his receipt of the goods if the seller is a merchant; otherwise the risk passes to the buyer on tender of delivery.

4. The provisions of this section are subject to contrary agreement of the parties and to the provisions of this Article on sale on approval (Section 2–327) and on effect of breach on risk of loss (Section 2–510).

SECTION 2–510. EFFECT OF BREACH ON RISK OF LOSS

1. Where a tender or delivery of goods so fails to conform to the contract as to give a right of rejection the risk of their loss remains on the seller until cure or acceptance.

2. Where the buyer rightfully revokes acceptance he may to the extent of any deficiency in his effective insurance coverage treat the risk of loss as having rested on the seller from the beginning.

3. Where the buyer as to conforming goods already identified to the contract for sale repudiates or is otherwise in breach before risk of their loss has passed to him, the seller may to the extent of any deficiency in his effective insurance coverage treat the risk of loss as resting on the buyer for a commercially reasonable time.

SECTION 2–511. TENDER OF PAYMENT BY BUYER; PAYMENT BY CHECK

1. Unless otherwise agreed tender of payment is a condition to the seller's duty to tender and complete any delivery.

2. Tender of payment is sufficient when made by any means or in any manner current in the ordinary course of business unless the seller demands payment in legal tender and gives any extension of time reasonably necessary to procure it.

3. Subject to the provisions of this Act on the effect of an instrument on an obligation (Section 3–310), payment by check is conditional and is defeated as between the parties by dishonor of the check on due presentment.

As amended in 1994.

SECTION 2–512. PAYMENT BY BUYER BEFORE INSPECTION

[1995 Amendments to text indicated by strikeout and underline]

1. Where the contract requires payment before inspection non-conformity of the goods does not excuse the buyer from so making payment unless

   a. the non-conformity appears without inspection; or

   b. despite tender of the required documents the circumstances would justify injunction against honor under of this Act (Section 5–109(b)).

2. Payment pursuant to subsection (1) does not constitute an acceptance of goods or impair the buyer's right to inspect or any of his remedies.

SECTION 2–513. BUYER'S RIGHT TO INSPECTION OF GOODS

1. Unless otherwise agreed and subject to subsection (3), where goods are tendered or delivered or identified to the contract for sale, the buyer has a right before payment or acceptance to inspect them at any reasonable place and time and in any reasonable manner. When the seller is required or authorized to send the goods to the buyer, the inspection may be after their arrival.

2. Expenses of inspection must be borne by the buyer but may be recovered from the seller if the goods do not conform and are rejected.

3. Unless otherwise agreed and subject to the provisions of this Article on C.I.F. contracts (subsection (3) of Section 2–321), the buyer is not entitled to

inspect the goods before payment of the price when the contract provides

    a. for delivery "C.O.D." or on other like terms; or

    b. for payment against documents of title, except where such payment is due only after the goods are to become available for inspection.

4. A place or method of inspection fixed by the parties is presumed to be exclusive but unless otherwise expressly agreed it does not postpone identification or shift the place for delivery or for passing the risk of loss. If compliance becomes impossible, inspection shall be as provided in this section unless the place or method fixed was clearly intended as an indispensable condition failure of which avoids the contract.

SECTION 2–514. WHEN DOCUMENTS DELIVERABLE ON ACCEPTANCE; WHEN ON PAYMENT

Unless otherwise agreed documents against which a draft is drawn are to be delivered to the drawee on acceptance of the draft if it is payable more than three days after presentment; otherwise, only on payment.

PART 6

Breach, Repudiation and Excuse

SECTION 2–601. BUYER'S RIGHTS ON IMPROPER DELIVERY

Subject to the provisions of this Article on breach in installment contracts (Section 2–612) and unless otherwise agreed under the sections on contractual limitations of remedy (Sections 2–718 and 2–719), if the goods or the tender of delivery fail in any respect to conform to the contract, the buyer may

a. reject the whole; or

b. accept the whole; or

c. accept any commercial unit or units and reject the rest.

SECTION 2–602. MANNER AND EFFECT OF RIGHTFUL REJECTION

1. Rejection of goods must be within a reasonable time after their delivery or tender. It is ineffective unless the buyer seasonably notifies the seller.

2. Subject to the provisions of the two following sections on rejected goods (Sections 2–603 and 2–604),

    a. after rejection any exercise of ownership by the buyer with respect to any commercial unit is wrongful as against the seller; and

    b. if the buyer has before rejection taken physical possession of goods in which he does not have a security interest under the provisions of this Article (subsection (3) of Section 2–711), he is under a duty after rejection to hold them with reasonable care at the seller's disposition for a time sufficient to permit the seller to remove them; but

    c. the buyer has no further obligations with regard to goods rightfully rejected.

3. The seller's rights with respect to goods wrongfully rejected are governed by the provisions of this Article on Seller's remedies in general (Section 2–703).

SECTION 2–603. MERCHANT BUYER'S DUTIES AS TO RIGHTFULLY REJECTED GOODS

1. Subject to any security interest in the buyer (subsection (3) of Section 2–711), when the seller has no agent or place of business at the market of rejection a merchant buyer is under a duty after rejection of goods in his possession or control to follow any reasonable instructions received from the seller with respect to the goods and in the absence of such instructions to make reasonable efforts to sell them for the seller's account if they are perishable or threaten to decline in value speedily. Instructions are not reasonable if on demand indemnity for expenses is not forthcoming.

2. When the buyer sells goods under subsection (1), he is entitled to reimbursement from the seller or out of the proceeds for reasonable expenses of caring for and selling them, and if the expenses include no selling commission then to such commission as is usual in the trade or if there is none to a reasonable sum not exceeding ten per cent on the gross proceeds.

3. In complying with this section the buyer is held only to good faith and good faith conduct hereunder is neither acceptance nor conversion nor the basis of an action for damages.

SECTION 2–604. BUYER'S OPTIONS AS TO SALVAGE OF RIGHTFULLY REJECTED GOODS

Subject to the provisions of the immediately preceding section on perishables if the seller gives no instructions within a reasonable time after notification of rejection the buyer may store the rejected goods for the seller's account or reship them to him or resell them for the seller's account with reimbursement as provided in the preceding section. Such action is not acceptance or conversion.

SECTION 2–605. WAIVER OF BUYER'S OBJECTIONS BY FAILURE TO PARTICULARIZE

1. The buyer's failure to state in connection with rejection a particular defect which is ascertainable by reasonable inspection precludes him from relying on the unstated defect to justify rejection or to establish breach

   a. where the seller could have cured it if stated seasonably; or

   b. between merchants when the seller has after rejection made a request in writing for a full and final written statement of all defects on which the buyer proposes to rely.

2. Payment against documents made without reservation of rights precludes recovery of the payment for defects apparent on the face of the documents.

SECTION 2–606. WHAT CONSTITUTES ACCEPTANCE OF GOODS

1. Acceptance of goods occurs when the buyer

   a. after a reasonable opportunity to inspect the goods signifies to the seller that the goods are conforming or that he will take or retain them in spite of their non-conformity; or

   b. fails to make an effective rejection (subsection (1) of Section 2–602), but such acceptance does not occur until the buyer has had a reasonable opportunity to inspect them; or

   c. does any act inconsistent with the seller's ownership; but if such act is wrongful as against the seller it is an acceptance only if ratified by him.

2. Acceptance of a part of any commercial unit is acceptance of that entire unit.

SECTION 2–607. EFFECT OF ACCEPTANCE; NOTICE OF BREACH; BURDEN OF ESTABLISHING BREACH AFTER ACCEPTANCE; NOTICE OF CLAIM OR LITIGATION TO PERSON ANSWERABLE OVER

1. The buyer must pay at the contract rate for any goods accepted.

2. Acceptance of goods by the buyer precludes rejection of the goods accepted and if made with knowledge of a non-conformity cannot be revoked because of it unless the acceptance was on the reasonable assumption that the non-conformity would be seasonably cured but acceptance does not of itself impair any other remedy provided by this Article for non-conformity.

3. Where a tender has been accepted

   a. the buyer must within a reasonable time after he discovers or should have discovered any breach notify the seller of breach or be barred from any remedy; and

   b. if the claim is one for infringement or the like (subsection (3) of Section 2–312) and the buyer is sued as a result of such a breach he must so notify the seller within a reasonable time after he receives notice of the litigation or be barred from any remedy over for liability established by the litigation.

4. The burden is on the buyer to establish any breach with respect to the goods accepted.

5. Where the buyer is sued for breach of a warranty or other obligation for which his seller is answerable over

   a. he may give his seller written notice of the litigation. If the notice states that the seller may come in and defend and that if the seller does not do so he will be bound in any action against him by his buyer by any determination of fact common to the two litigations, then unless the seller after seasonable receipt of the notice does come in and defend he is so bound.

   b. if the claim is one for infringement or the like (subsection (3) of Section 2–312) the original seller may demand in writing that his buyer turn over to him control of the litigation including settlement or else be barred from any remedy over and if he also agrees to bear all expense and to satisfy any adverse judgment, then unless the buyer after seasonable receipt of the demand does turn over control the buyer is so barred.

6. The provisions of subsections (3), (4) and (5) apply to any obligation of a buyer to hold the seller harmless against infringement or the like (subsection (3) of Section 2–312).

SECTION 2–608. REVOCATION OF ACCEPTANCE IN WHOLE OR IN PART

1. The buyer may revoke his acceptance of a lot or commercial unit whose non-conformity substantially impairs its value to him if he has accepted it

    a. on the reasonable assumption that its non-conformity would be cured and it has not been seasonably cured; or

    b. without discovery of such non-conformity if his acceptance was reasonably induced either by the difficulty of discovery before acceptance or by the seller's assurances.

2. Revocation of acceptance must occur within a reasonable time after the buyer discovers or should have discovered the ground for it and before any substantial change in condition of the goods which is not caused by their own defects. It is not effective until the buyer notifies the seller of it.

3. A buyer who so revokes has the same rights and duties with regard to the goods involved as if he had rejected them.

SECTION 2–609. RIGHT TO ADEQUATE ASSURANCE OF PERFORMANCE

1. A contract for sale imposes an obligation on each party that the other's expectation of receiving due performance will not be impaired. When reasonable grounds for insecurity arise with respect to the performance of either party the other may in writing demand adequate assurance of due performance and until he receives such assurance may if commercially reasonable suspend any performance for which he has not already received the agreed return.

2. Between merchants the reasonableness of grounds for insecurity and the adequacy of any assurance offered shall be determined according to commercial standards.

3. Acceptance of any improper delivery or payment does not prejudice the aggrieved party's right to demand adequate assurance of future performance.

4. After receipt of a justified demand failure to provide within a reasonable time not exceeding thirty days such assurance of due performance as is adequate under the circumstances of the particular case is a repudiation of the contract.

SECTION 2–610. ANTICIPATORY REPUDIATION

When either party repudiates the contract with respect to a performance not yet due the loss of which will substantially impair the value of the contract to the other, the aggrieved party may

    a. for a commercially reasonable time await performance by the repudiating party; or

    b. resort to any remedy for breach (Section 2–703 or Section 2–711), even though he has notified the repudiating party that he would await the latter's performance and has urged retraction; and

    c. in either case suspend his own performance or proceed in accordance with the provisions of this Article on the seller's right to identify goods to the contract notwithstanding breach or to salvage unfinished goods (Section 2–704).

SECTION 2–611. RETRACTION OF ANTICIPATORY REPUDIATION

1. Until the repudiating party's next performance is due he can retract his repudiation unless the aggrieved party has since the repudiation cancelled or materially changed his position or otherwise indicated that he considers the repudiation final.

2. Retraction may be by any method which clearly indicates to the aggrieved party that the repudiating party intends to perform, but must include any assurance justifiably demanded under the provisions of this Article (Section 2–609).

3. Retraction reinstates the repudiating party's rights under the contract with due excuse and allowance to the aggrieved party for any delay occasioned by the repudiation.

SECTION 2–612. "INSTALLMENT CONTRACT"; BREACH

1. An "installment contract" is one which requires or authorizes the delivery of goods in separate lots to be separately accepted, even though the contract contains a clause "each delivery is a separate contract" or its equivalent.

2. The buyer may reject any installment which is nonconforming if the non-conformity substantially impairs the value of that installment and cannot be cured or if the non-conformity is a defect in the required documents; but if the non-conformity does

not fall within subsection (3) and the seller gives adequate assurance of its cure the buyer must accept that installment.

3. Whenever non-conformity or default with respect to one or more installments substantially impairs the value of the whole contract there is a breach of the whole. But the aggrieved party reinstates the contract if he accepts a non-conforming installment without seasonably notifying of cancellation or if he brings an action with respect only to past installments or demands performance as to future installments.

SECTION 2–613. CASUALTY TO IDENTIFIED GOODS

Where the contract requires for its performance goods identified when the contract is made, and the goods suffer casualty without fault of either party before the risk of loss passes to the buyer, or in a proper case under a "no arrival, no sale" term (Section 2–324) then

a. if the loss is total the contract is avoided; and

b. if the loss is partial or the goods have so deteriorated as no longer to conform to the contract the buyer may nevertheless demand inspection and at his option either treat the contract as avoided or accept the goods with due allowance from the contract price for the deterioration or the deficiency in quantity but without further right against the seller.

SECTION 2–614. SUBSTITUTED PERFORMANCE

1. Where without fault of either party the agreed berthing, loading, or unloading facilities fail or an agreed type of carrier becomes unavailable or the agreed manner of delivery otherwise becomes commercially impracticable but a commercially reasonable substitute is available, such substitute performance must be tendered and accepted.

2. If the agreed means or manner of payment fails because of domestic or foreign governmental regulation, the seller may withhold or stop delivery unless the buyer provides a means or manner of payment which is commercially a substantial equivalent. If delivery has already been taken, payment by the means or in the manner provided by the regulation discharges the buyer's obligation unless the regulation is discriminatory, oppressive or predatory.

SECTION 2–615. EXCUSE BY FAILURE OF PRESUPPOSED CONDITIONS

Except so far as a seller may have assumed a greater obligation and subject to the preceding section on substituted performance:

a. Delay in delivery or non-delivery in whole or in part by a seller who complies with paragraphs (b) and (c) is not a breach of his duty under a contract for sale if performance as agreed has been made impracticable by the occurrence of a contingency the non-occurrence of which was a basic assumption on which the contract was made or by compliance in good faith with any applicable foreign or domestic governmental regulation or order whether or not it later proves to be invalid.

b. Where the causes mentioned in paragraph (a) affect only a part of the seller's capacity to perform, he must allocate production and deliveries among his customers but may at his option include regular customers not then under contract as well as his own requirements for further manufacture. He may so allocate in any manner which is fair and reasonable.

c. The seller must notify the buyer seasonably that there will be delay or non-delivery and, when allocation is required under paragraph (b), of the estimated quota thus made available for the buyer.

SECTION 2–616. PROCEDURE ON NOTICE CLAIMING EXCUSE

1. Where the buyer receives notification of a material or indefinite delay or an allocation justified under the preceding section he may by written notification to the seller as to any delivery concerned, and where the prospective deficiency substantially impairs the value of the whole contract under the provisions of this Article relating to breach of installment contracts Section 2–612), then also as to the whole,

   a. terminate and thereby discharge any unexecuted portion of the contract; or

   b. modify the contract by agreeing to take his available quota in substitution.

2. If after receipt of such notification from the seller the buyer fails so to modify the contract within a reasonable time not exceeding thirty days the contract lapses with respect to any deliveries affected.

3. The provisions of this section may not be negated by agreement except in so far as the seller has assumed a greater obligation under the preceding section.

PART 7

Remedies

SECTION 2–701. REMEDIES FOR BREACH OF COLLATERAL CONTRACTS NOT IMPAIRED

Remedies for breach of any obligation or promise collateral or ancillary to a contract for sale are not impaired by the provisions of this Article.

SECTION 2–702. SELLER'S REMEDIES ON DISCOVERY OF BUYER'S INSOLVENCY

1. Where the seller discovers the buyer to be insolvent he may refuse delivery except for cash including payment for all goods theretofore delivered under the contract, and stop delivery under this Article (Section 2–705).

2. Where the seller discovers that the buyer has received goods on credit while insolvent he may reclaim the goods upon demand made within ten days after the receipt, but if misrepresentation of solvency has been made to the particular seller in writing within three months before delivery the ten day limitation does not apply. Except as provided in this subsection the seller may not base a right to reclaim goods on the buyer's fraudulent or innocent misrepresentation of solvency or of intent to pay.

3. The seller's right to reclaim under subsection (2) is subject to the rights of a buyer in ordinary course or other good faith purchaser under this Article (Section 2–403). Successful reclamation of goods excludes all other remedies with respect to them.

As amended in 1966.

SECTION 2–703. SELLER'S REMEDIES IN GENERAL

Where the buyer wrongfully rejects or revokes acceptance of goods or fails to make a payment due on or before delivery or repudiates with respect to a part or the whole, then with respect to any goods directly affected and, if the breach is of the whole contract (Section 2–612), then also with respect to the whole undelivered balance, the aggrieved seller may

a. withhold delivery of such goods;

b. stop delivery by any bailee as hereafter provided (Section 2–705);

c. proceed under the next section respecting goods still unidentified to the contract;

d. resell and recover damages as hereafter provided (Section 2–706);

e. recover damages for non-acceptance (Section 2–708) or in a proper case the price (Section 2–709);

f. cancel.

SECTION 2–704. SELLER'S RIGHT TO IDENTIFY GOODS TO THE CONTRACT NOTWITHSTANDING BREACH OR TO SALVAGE UNFINISHED GOODS

1. An aggrieved seller under the preceding section may

a. identify to the contract conforming goods not already identified if at the time he learned of the breach they are in his possession or control;

b. treat as the subject of resale goods which have demonstrably been intended for the particular contract even though those goods are unfinished.

c. Where the goods are unfinished an aggrieved seller may in the exercise of reasonable commercial judgment for the purposes of avoiding loss and of effective realization either complete the manufacture and wholly identify the goods to the contract or cease manufacture and resell for scrap or salvage value or proceed in any other reasonable manner.

SECTION 2–705. SELLER'S STOPPAGE OF DELIVERY IN TRANSIT OR OTHERWISE

1. The seller may stop delivery of goods in the possession of a carrier or other bailee when he discovers the buyer to be insolvent (Section 2–702) and may stop delivery of carload, truckload, planeload or larger shipments of express or freight when the buyer repudiates or fails to make a payment due before delivery or if for any other reason the seller has a right to withhold or reclaim the goods.

2. As against such buyer the seller may stop delivery until

a. receipt of the goods by the buyer; or

b. acknowledgment to the buyer by any bailee of the goods except a carrier that the bailee holds the goods for the buyer; or

c. such acknowledgment to the buyer by a carrier by reshipment or as warehouseman; or

d. negotiation to the buyer of any negotiable document of title covering the goods.

3. a. To stop delivery the seller must so notify as to enable the bailee by reasonable diligence to prevent delivery of the goods.

b. After such notification the bailee must hold and deliver the goods according to the directions of the seller but the seller is liable to the bailee for any ensuing charges or damages.

c. If a negotiable document of title has been issued for goods the bailee is not obliged to obey a notification to stop until surrender of the document.

d. A carrier who has issued a non-negotiable bill of lading is not obliged to obey a notification to stop received from a person other than the consignor.

SECTION 2–706. SELLER'S RESALE INCLUDING CONTRACT FOR RESALE

1. Under the conditions stated in Section 2–703 on seller's remedies, the seller may resell the goods concerned or the undelivered balance thereof. Where the resale is made in good faith and in a commercially reasonable manner the seller may recover the difference between the resale price and the contract price together with any incidental damages allowed under the provisions of this Article (Section 2–710), but less expenses saved in consequence of the buyer's breach.

2. Except as otherwise provided in subsection (3) or unless otherwise agreed resale may be at public or private sale including sale by way of one or more contracts to sell or of identification to an existing contract of the seller. Sale may be as a unit or in parcels and at any time and place and on any terms but every aspect of the sale including the method, manner, time, place and terms must be commercially reasonable. The resale must be reasonably identified as referring to the broken contract, but it is not necessary that the goods be in existence or that any or all of them have been identified to the contract before the breach.

3. Where the resale is at private sale the seller must give the buyer reasonable notification of his intention to resell.

4. Where the resale is at public sale

a. only identified goods can be sold except where there is a recognized market for a public sale of futures in goods of the kind; and

b. it must be made at a usual place or market for public sale if one is reasonably available and except in the case of goods which are perishable or threaten to decline in value speedily the seller must give the buyer reasonable notice of the time and place of the resale; and

c. if the goods are not to be within the view of those attending the sale the notification of sale must state the place where the goods are located and provide for their reasonable inspection by prospective bidders; and

d. the seller may buy.

5. A purchaser who buys in good faith at a resale takes the goods free of any rights of the original buyer even though the seller fails to comply with one or more of the requirements of this section.

6. The seller is not accountable to the buyer for any profit made on any resale. A person in the position of a seller (Section 2–707) or a buyer who has rightfully rejected or justifiably revoked acceptance must account for any excess over the amount of his security interest, as hereinafter defined (subsection (3) of Section 2–711).

SECTION 2–707. "PERSON IN THE POSITION OF A SELLER"

1. A "person in the position of a seller" includes as against a principal an agent who has paid or become responsible for the price of goods on behalf of his principal or anyone who otherwise holds a security interest or other right in goods similar to that of a seller.

2. A person in the position of a seller may as provided in this Article withhold or stop delivery (Section 2–705) and resell (Section 2–706) and recover incidental damages (Section 2–710).

SECTION 2–708. SELLER'S DAMAGES FOR NON-ACCEPTANCE OR REPUDIATION

1. Subject to subsection (2) and to the provisions of this Article with respect to proof of market price (Section 2–723), the measure of damages for non-acceptance or repudiation by the buyer is the

difference between the market price at the time and place for tender and the unpaid contract price together with any incidental damages provided in this Article (Section 2–710), but less expenses saved in consequence of the buyer's breach.

2. If the measure of damages provided in subsection (1) is inadequate to put the seller in as good a position as performance would have done then the measure of damages is the profit (including reasonable overhead) which the seller would have made from full performance by the buyer, together with any incidental damages provided in this Article (Section 2–710), due allowance for costs reasonably incurred and due credit for payments or proceeds of resale.

SECTION 2–709. ACTION FOR THE PRICE

1. When the buyer fails to pay the price as it becomes due the seller may recover, together with any incidental damages under the next section, the price

   a. of goods accepted or of conforming goods lost or damaged within a commercially reasonable time after risk of their loss has passed to the buyer; and

   b. of goods identified to the contract if the seller is unable after reasonable effort to resell them at a reasonable price or the circumstances reasonably indicate that such effort will be unavailing.

2. Where the seller sues for the price he must hold for the buyer any goods which have been identified to the contract and are still in his control except that if resale becomes possible he may resell them at any time prior to the collection of the judgment. The net proceeds of any such resale must be credited to the buyer and payment of the judgment entitles him to any goods not resold.

3. After the buyer has wrongfully rejected or revoked acceptance of the goods or has failed to make a payment due or has repudiated (Section 2–610), a seller who is held not entitled to the price under this section shall nevertheless be awarded damages for non-acceptance under the preceding section.

SECTION 2–710. SELLER'S INCIDENTAL DAMAGES

Incidental damages to an aggrieved seller include any commercially reasonable charges, expenses or commissions incurred in stopping delivery, in the transportation, care and custody of goods after the buyer's breach, in connection with return or resale of the goods or otherwise resulting from the breach.

SECTION 2–711. BUYER'S REMEDIES IN GENERAL; BUYER'S SECURITY INTEREST IN REJECTED GOODS

1. Where the seller fails to make delivery or repudiates or the buyer rightfully rejects or justifiably revokes acceptance then with respect to any goods involved, and with respect to the whole if the breach goes to the whole contract (Section 2–612), the buyer may cancel and whether or not he has done so may in addition to recovering so much of the price as has been paid

   a. "cover" and have damages under the next section as to all the goods affected whether or not they have been identified to the contract; or

   b. recover damages for non-delivery as provided in this Article (Section 2–713).

2. Where the seller fails to deliver or repudiates the buyer may also

   a. if the goods have been identified recover them as provided in this Article (Section 2–502); or

   b. in a proper case obtain specific performance or replevy the goods as provided in this Article (Section 2–716).

3. On rightful rejection or justifiable revocation of acceptance a buyer has a security interest in goods in his possession or control for any payments made on their price and any expenses reasonably incurred in their inspection, receipt, transportation, care and custody and may hold such goods and resell them in like manner as an aggrieved seller (Section 2–706).

SECTION 2–712. "COVER"; BUYER'S PROCUREMENT OF SUBSTITUTE GOODS

1. After a breach within the preceding section the buyer may "cover" by making in good faith and without unreasonable delay any reasonable purchase of or contract to purchase goods in substitution for those due from the seller.

2. The buyer may recover from the seller as damages the difference between the cost of cover and the contract price together with any incidental or consequential damages as hereinafter defined (Section 2–715), but less expenses saved in consequence of the seller's breach.

3. Failure of the buyer to effect cover within this section does not bar him from any other remedy.

SECTION 2–713. BUYER'S DAMAGES FOR NON-DELIVERY OR REPUDIATION

1. Subject to the provisions of this Article with respect to proof of market price (Section 2–723), the measure of damages for non-delivery or repudiation by the seller is the difference between the market price at the time when the buyer learned of the breach and the contract price together with any incidental and consequential damages provided in this Article (Section 2–715), but less expenses saved in consequence of the seller's breach.

2. Market price is to be determined as of the place for tender or, in cases of rejection after arrival or revocation of acceptance, as of the place of arrival.

SECTION 2–714. BUYER'S DAMAGES FOR BREACH IN REGARD TO ACCEPTED GOODS

1. Where the buyer has accepted goods and given notification (subsection (3) of Section 2–607) he may recover as damages for any non-conformity of tender the loss resulting in the ordinary course of events from the seller's breach as determined in any manner which is reasonable.

2. The measure of damages for breach of warranty is the difference at the time and place of acceptance between the value of the goods accepted and the value they would have had if they had been as warranted, unless special circumstances show proximate damages of a different amount.

3. In a proper case any incidental and consequential damages under the next section may also be recovered.

SECTION 2–715. BUYER'S INCIDENTAL AND CONSEQUENTIAL DAMAGES

1. Incidental damages resulting from the seller's breach include expenses reasonably incurred in inspection, receipt, transportation and care and custody of goods rightfully rejected, any commercially reasonable charges, expenses or commissions in connection with effecting cover and any other reasonable expense incident to the delay or other breach.

2. Consequential damages resulting from the seller's breach include

a. any loss resulting from general or particular requirements and needs of which the seller at the time of contracting had reason to know and which could not reasonably be prevented by cover or otherwise; and

b. injury to person or property proximately resulting from any breach of warranty.

SECTION 2–716. BUYER'S RIGHT TO SPECIFIC PERFORMANCE OR REPLEVIN

1. Specific performance may be decreed where the goods are unique or in other proper circumstances.

2. The decree for specific performance may include such terms and conditions as to payment of the price, damages, or other relief as the court may deem just.

3. The buyer has a right of replevin for goods identified to the contract if after reasonable effort he is unable to effect cover for such goods or the circumstances reasonably indicate that such effort will be unavailing or if the goods have been shipped under reservation and satisfaction of the security interest in them has been made or tendered.

SECTION 2–717. DEDUCTION OF DAMAGES FROM THE PRICE

The buyer on notifying the seller of his intention to do so may deduct all or any part of the damages resulting from any breach of the contract from any part of the price still due under the same contract.

SECTION 2–718. LIQUIDATION OR LIMITATION OF DAMAGES; DEPOSITS

1. Damages for breach by either party may be liquidated in the agreement but only at an amount which is reasonable in the light of the anticipated or actual harm caused by the breach, the difficulties of proof of loss, and the inconvenience or nonfeasibility of otherwise obtaining an adequate remedy. A term fixing unreasonably large liquidated damages is void as a penalty.

2. Where the seller justifiably withholds delivery of goods because of the buyer's breach, the buyer is entitled to restitution of any amount by which the sum of his payments exceeds

a. the amount to which the seller is entitled by virtue of terms liquidating the seller's damages in accordance with subsection (1), or

b. in the absence of such terms, twenty per cent of the value of the total performance for which the buyer is obligated under the contract or $500, whichever is smaller.

3. The buyer's right to restitution under subsection (2) is subject to offset to the extent that the seller establishes

   a. a right to recover damages under the provisions of this Article other than subsection (1), and

   b. the amount or value of any benefits received by the buyer directly or indirectly by reason of the contract.

4. Where a seller has received payment in goods their reasonable value or the proceeds of their resale shall be treated as payments for the purposes of subsection (2); but if the seller has notice of the buyer's breach before reselling goods received in part performance, his resale is subject to the conditions laid down in this Article on resale by an aggrieved seller (Section 2–706).

SECTION 2–719. CONTRACTUAL MODIFICATION OR LIMITATION OF REMEDY

1. Subject to the provisions of subsections (2) and (3) of this section and of the preceding section on liquidation and limitation of damages,

   a. the agreement may provide for remedies in addition to or in substitution for those provided in this Article and may limit or alter the measure of damages recoverable under this Article, as by limiting the buyer's remedies to return of the goods and repayment of the price or to repair and replacement of non-conforming goods or parts; and

   b. resort to a remedy as provided is optional unless the remedy is expressly agreed to be exclusive, in which case it is the sole remedy.

2. Where circumstances cause an exclusive or limited remedy to fail of its essential purpose, remedy may be had as provided in this Act.

3. Consequential damages may be limited or excluded unless the limitation or exclusion is unconscionable. Limitation of consequential damages for injury to the person in the case of consumer goods is prima facie unconscionable but limitation of damages where the loss is commercial is not.

SECTION 2–720. EFFECT OF "CANCELLATION" OR "RESCISSION" ON CLAIMS FOR ANTECEDENT BREACH

Unless the contrary intention clearly appears, expressions of "cancellation" or "rescission" of the contract or the like shall not be construed as a renunciation or discharge of any claim in damages for an antecedent breach.

SECTION 2–721. REMEDIES FOR FRAUD

Remedies for material misrepresentation or fraud include all remedies available under this Article for non-fraudulent breach. Neither rescission or a claim for rescission of the contract for sale nor rejection or return of the goods shall bar or be deemed inconsistent with a claim for damages or other remedy.

SECTION 2–722. WHO CAN SUE THIRD PARTIES FOR INJURY TO GOODS

Where a third party so deals with goods which have been identified to a contract for sale as to cause actionable injury to a party to that contract

a. a right of action against the third party is in either party to the contract for sale who has title to or a security interest or a special property or an insurable interest in the goods; and if the goods have been destroyed or converted a right of action is also in the party who either bore the risk of loss under the contract for sale or has since the injury assumed that risk as against the other;

b. if at the time of the injury the party plaintiff did not bear the risk of loss as against the other party to the contract for sale and there is no arrangement between them for disposition of the recovery, his suit or settlement is, subject to his own interest, as a fiduciary for the other party to the contract;

c. either party may with the consent of the other sue for the benefit of whom it may concern.

SECTION 2–723. PROOF OF MARKET PRICE: TIME AND PLACE

1. If an action based on anticipatory repudiation comes to trial before the time for performance with respect to some or all of the goods, any damages based on market price (Section 2–708 or Section 2–713) shall be determined according to the price of such goods

prevailing at the time when the aggrieved party learned of the repudiation.

2. If evidence of a price prevailing at the times or places described in this Article is not readily available the price prevailing within any reasonable time before or after the time described or at any other place which in commercial judgment or under usage of trade would serve as a reasonable substitute for the one described may be used, making any proper allowance for the cost of transporting the goods to or from such other place.

3. Evidence of a relevant price prevailing at a time or place other than the one described in this Article offered by one party is not admissible unless and until he has given the other party such notice as the court finds sufficient to prevent unfair surprise.

SECTION 2–724. ADMISSIBILITY OF MARKET QUOTATIONS

Whenever the prevailing price or value of any goods regularly bought and sold in any established commodity market is in issue, reports in official publications or trade journals or in newspapers or periodicals of general circulation published as the reports of such market shall be admissible in evidence. The circumstances of the preparation of such a report may be shown to affect its weight but not its admissibility.

SECTION 2–725. STATUTE OF LIMITATIONS IN CONTRACTS FOR SALE

1. An action for breach of any contract for sale must be commenced within four years after the cause of action has accrued. By the original agreement the parties may reduce the period of limitation to not less than one year but may not extend it.

2. A cause of action accrues when the breach occurs, regardless of the aggrieved party's lack of knowledge of the breach. A breach of warranty occurs when tender of delivery is made, except that where a warranty explicitly extends to future performance of the goods and discovery of the breach must await the time of such performance the cause of action accrues when the breach is or should have been discovered.

3. Where an action commenced within the time limited by subsection (1) is so terminated as to leave available a remedy by another action for the same breach such other action may be commenced after the expiration of the time limited and within six months after the termination of the first action unless the termination resulted from voluntary discontinuance or from dismissal for failure or neglect to prosecute.

4. This section does not alter the law on tolling of the statute of limitations nor does it apply to causes of action which have accrued before this Act becomes effective.

Glossary

A

abandonment   In contract law, the condition that exists when a minor has left home and given up all rights to parental support.

acceptance   An indication made by the offeree that he or she agrees to be bound by the terms of the offer.

accession   The right of an owner of property to any increase in the property.

acid rain   A form of pollution caused by the discharge of sulfur emissions into the atmosphere.

ademption   When a specific bequest of personal property is made, but the personal property is disposed of before the death of the testator.

administrative agency   A governmental body responsible for the control and supervision of a particular activity or area of public interest.

administrative hearing   A trial-like judicial proceeding, without a jury, in which an administrative agency rules on matters of the law that the agency is charged with enforcing.

administrative law   The body of rules, regulations, and decisions created by administrative agencies.

administrator   A personal representative named by the court to perform as the executor would in instances in which the deceased person has not left a will.

advanced directive   A device that documents an individual's expressed wishes regarding his or her health care in the event that the individual is incapacitated without hope of recovery.

adverse possession   When title to land is acquired by a person's exclusive, continuous, open, known, and hostile use of the property over a period of time.

affirmative action plans   Detailed records that demonstrate that an employer's practices are nondiscriminatory.

Age Discrimination in Employment Act of 1967   A federal statute designed to protect individuals from illegal discrimination in employment on the basis of age.

age of majority   The age at which a person is legally recognized as an adult and is bound by the terms of his or her contract.

agency by necessity   An agency that is created when circumstances make such an agency necessary.

agency by operation of law   An agency that is created when a court finds the need for an agency to achieve a desired social policy.

agency by ratification   An agency that results when a principal approves an unauthorized act performed by an agent or approves an act done in the principal's name by an unauthorized person.

agent   A person authorized to act on behalf of another and subject to the other's control in dealing with third parties.

agreement not to compete   An agreement in which the seller of a business agrees not to begin or operate a similar business within a certain geographic area or within a specified period of time.

alternative dispute resolution (ADR)   A system in which contract disputes and other disagreements are resolved by using means other than a lawsuit.

Americans with Disabilities Act (ADA) of 1990   A federal statute designed to protect individuals from illegal discrimination in employment on the basis of disability.

antenuptial or prenuptial agreement   An exchange of promises made by persons planning to marry.

anticipatory breach   When a party to a contract announces his or her intention to break the contract in the future.

apparent authority   The authority that a third party may reasonably assume an agent possesses, despite the fact that the agent does not actually possess such authority.

arbitration   A process for dispute resolution in which a neutral third party decides a case as if he or she were a judge and jury.

arson   The willful or malicious act of causing the burning of another's property.

articles of incorporation   A document that lists the general powers of a corporation.

assignee   The third party to whom rights are transferred in an assignment.

assignment of lease   When a tenant transfers his or her entire interest in the entire premises for the remaining length of the term of the lease.

assignment   The transfer of a contract right to a third party who can receive the benefits of the contract.

assignor   The person who transfers his or her rights in an assignment.

assumption of risk   A defense in a case of negligence in which the defendant demonstrates that the plaintiff voluntarily assumed the risk associated with the dangerous condition caused by the defendant.

attorney in fact   The person appointed as agent when the power of attorney is exercised.

auction sale   A sale in which goods are sold to the highest bidder.

auction with reserve   One that gives the auctioneer the right to withdraw the goods at any time before announcing completion of the sale if reasonable bids are not made.

auction without reserve   One at which the goods must be sold to the highest bidder and may not be withdrawn after bidding has begun.

B

bad check   A check against a bank in which the drawer has insufficient funds on deposit to cover the check or no funds at all.

bailee   The party in a bailment who receives the goods.

bailee's lien   The right of the bailee in a bailment for work and services to hold and, if necessary, sell the property if the bailor does not pay for the services or work done.

bailment   A transaction in which the owner of tangible personal property transfers it (not as a gift) to another party while still retaining ownership.

bailment for the sole benefit of the bailee   A bailment relationship in which only the bailee receives any benefit from the relationship.

bailment for the sole benefit of the bailor   A bailment that exists when the bailor entrusts an article to the bailee for storage or safekeeping without charge, as a favor.

bailor   The party in a bailment who retains ownership and transfers possession of the goods.

bankruptcy   The legal state that occurs when a debtor is insolvent, is in default, and is unable to fulfill his or her obligations to pay back his or her creditors.

Bankruptcy Abuse Prevention and Consumer Protection Act of 2005   A federal law that instituted strict rules and eligibility requirements for debtors filing for bankruptcy.

barren promise   A promise to pay an existing debt or to obey the law, or a similar promise of something already owed.

bearer instrument   An instrument that is payable to anyone who is in possession of it.

beneficiary   An individual who receives gifts of personal or real property by will.

bequest   A gift of personal property by will.

bill of lading   A receipt for goods to be shipped, acknowledging that such goods have been received and indicating agreement that the goods will be transported to the destination specified.

Bill of Rights   The first 10 amendments of the U.S. Constitution.

bill of sale   A written statement that the seller is passing ownership to the buyer.

birthday rule   The modern view that a person attains a given age on the anniversary date of his or her birth.

blank endorsement   An endorsement in which the name of the payee is written by the payee on the back of a negotiable instrument.

blue laws   State statutes and local ordinances that regulate the creation and performance of certain types of contracts on Sundays and legal holidays.

boycott   Citizens' refusal to purchase goods made by a particular business—for example, a business located in another country.

breach of contract   When a party to a contract refuses to perform as required by the contract or performs in an unsatisfactory manner.

bribery   The act of offering, giving, receiving, or soliciting something of value to influence official action or the discharge of a public duty.

burglary   The illegal entering of another person's premises for the purpose of committing a crime.

burning to defraud   A special category of crime providing for the punishment of persons who burn their own property with the aim of collecting insurance money.

bylaws   A document that provides rules for the meetings of a corporation.

C

carrier's lien   A carrier's legal right to hold a shipment until payment is made.

case law   The effects of court decisions that involve the same or similar facts.

cashier's check   A check issued by a cashier or other designated officer of a bank and drawn against bank funds.

certified check   A check that the bank has promised to pay when it is presented for payment.

champerty   An agreement to encourage a lawsuit in which one or more of the parties have no legitimate interest.

Check 21   The term commonly used to refer to the Check Clearing for the 21st Century Act, a federal law revolutionizing the manner in which checks are handled by banks.

check   A written order drawn on a bank by a depositor that requests the bank to pay, on demand and unconditionally, a definite sum of money to the bearer of the check or to the order of a specified person.

churning   A financial planner's unreasonably excessive buying or selling of securities to generate commissions.

Civil Rights Act of 1964   A federal statute designed to protect individuals from illegal discrimination.

Civil Rights Act of 1991   A federal statute that provides additional remedies to an employee who can prove that he or she was a victim of discrimination.

Clean Air Act of 1970   A federal statute that requires all states to develop air quality standards that are at least as rigorous as the federal standards. This statute sets primary and secondary standards and regulates both stationary and mobile pollution.

Clean Water Act of 1972   A federal statute that sets minimum standards for water purity.

code of ethics   A set of rules that a company or other group adopts to express principles of ethical behavior that are expected of its personnel.

codicil   A document, separate from the will, in which a person can make legal changes to his or her will.

collective bargaining agreement   A contract between a union and an employer that covers all terms and conditions of employment.

coming of age rule   In common law, the view that a person's legal birthday is 12:01 a.m. of the day before his or her actual birthday.

comity   A discretionary doctrine that holds that the courts of one country should refrain from deciding cases involving the acts of persons from another country.

commerce clause   A provision of the Constitution that grants Congress the power to regulate trade with foreign nations, and among the several states, and with the Indian tribes.

commercial paper   A number of legally binding and commercially acceptable documents that are used to transfer money from one person to another.

common carrier   An individual or firm in the business of transporting goods between certain points as allowed by the various state commissions that regulate carriers.

common law   The body of recorded decisions that courts refer to and rely upon when making later legal decisions.

community property   Property acquired during marriage that, in some states, belongs to both husband and wife.

comparative negligence   A form of negligence that requires the court to assign damages according to the degree of fault of each party.

competent   Being mentally capable of understanding the terms of a contract.

competent party   A person of legal age and at least normal mentality who is considered by law to be capable of understanding the meaning of a contract and is permitted to enter into a valid contract.

Computer Fraud and Abuse Act (CFAA)   A federal statute that prohibits unlawful access to computers used in national defense, by financial institutions, or by governments.

condemnation   The legal process that occurs when property is taken by the government against the will of the property owner.

conditional sale A sale with contract provisions that specify conditions that must be met by one of the parties.

conditional sales contract A sales contract that includes conditions that must be met either before or after the sale is completed.

conditions precedent Conditions in a sales contract that must be met before title passes.

conditions Restrictions that limit the use of the property.

conditions subsequent Conditions in a sales contract that must be met after title has passed.

consideration The promise to give up something of value that a party to a contract has a legal right to keep, or to do something that the party is not otherwise legally required to do.

consignee The person or party receiving goods in a bailment relationship.

consignor The person or party shipping goods in a bailment relationship.

constructive bailment A bailment in which goods are thrust upon a bailee who does not have any choice about whether he or she wishes to serve as bailee.

Consumer Product Safety Commission (CPSC) The federal agency responsible for the safety of consumer products sold in the United States.

contract A legally enforceable agreement that is created when two or more competent parties agree to perform, or to avoid performing, certain acts that they have a legal right to do and that meet certain legal requirements.

contract for labor and materials A sales contract for goods of special design, construction, or manufacture.

contract for sale A legally enforceable agreement that has as its purpose the immediate transfer of title to personal property in return for consideration.

contract for sale with the right of return A contract for the sale of goods that gives the buyer both title to the goods and the opportunity to return them to the seller at a later time.

contract of adhesion A contract drawn by one party that must be accepted as is on a take-it-or-leave-it basis.

contract of agency An agreement between a principal and an agent by which the agent is vested with authority to represent the principal.

Contracts for the International Sale of Goods (CISG) A treaty created to establish a universal set of legal procedures to be applied to contracts covering international transactions.

contract to sell An agreement to sell future goods.

contractual capacity The ability to make a valid contract.

contributory negligence A legal defense that involves the failure of an injured party to be careful enough to ensure personal safety.

Controlling the Assault of Non-Solicited Pornography and Marketing Act (CAN-SPAM) A federal statute that limits the circumstances under which commercial e-mail may be utilized.

conversion The wrongful exercise of dominion and control over another's personal property.

cookie A file that is embedded on the hard drive of a computer, often without a person's knowledge, that collects and stores information about the user and his or her online behavior, including websites that have been visited.

copyright A valid, government-granted protection given to creators of literary, creative, or artistic works.

corporation A business formed as a separate legal entity.

counterclaim When the maker of a note or other drawer or acceptor of a bill of exchange may deduct from the amount demanded by an immediate party any amounts owed him or her by the payee.

counteroffer A response to an offer in which the terms and conditions of the original offer are changed.

covenant An agreement made by either a landlord or a tenant to do certain things.

cover When the seller fails to deliver the goods, the right of a buyer to buy similar goods elsewhere to substitute for those not delivered by the seller.

creditor An individual or business to which money is owed.

crime An offense against the public at large punishable by the official governing body of a nation or state.

culture The set of shared attitudes, values, goals, and practices that characterize a social, racial, religious, or corporate group.

custom of the marketplace What a warranty usually means in similar transactions.

cybersquatting Registering or using another person's or company's domain name in bad faith for the purpose of earning a profit.

D

debtor An individual or business that owes money.

decedent A deceased person.

deceptive advertising An advertisement that contains a material misrepresentation, omission, or practice likely to mislead a consumer who acts reasonably under the circumstances.

deed The instrument, or document, that conveys an interest in real property between parties.

defamation The harming of a person's reputation and good name by the communication of a false statement.

default The state in which a debtor fails to meet one or more financial obligations to his or her creditors.

defendant The party against whom a lawsuit is brought and from whom recovery is sought.

delegation The appointment of a third party by a party to an existing contract to perform contractual duties that do not involve unique skills, talents, abilities, and so on.

design defect A fault in a product that creates a hazardous condition that causes injury.

design patent A patent awarded to individuals or business firms to protect distinctive patterns, figures, and shapes and to prevent unauthorized copying.

devise A gift of real property by will.

Digital Millennium Copyright Act (DMCA) of 1998 A federal statute that provides that ISPs are not liable for copyright infringements by their subscribers so long as they adhere to certain requirements.

disaffirmance In contract law, to indicate by a statement or act an intent not to live up to the terms of a contract.

disclaimer A denial or repudiation in an express warranty that places specific limitations in the warranty.

dishonored   When a negotiable instrument is not accepted when presented for acceptance, it is not paid when presented for payment at maturity, presentment is excused or waived, or the instrument is past due and unpaid.

divisible contract   An agreement that is made up of two or more parts, each part being independent of the others.

doctrine of preemption   A principle that states that when certain state or local laws are inconsistent with the federal law, the federal law must be followed.

draft   An unconditional written order to a person instructing him or her to pay money to another, third person.

durable power of attorney   An instrument that documents a principal's desire for an agent's authority to remain intact in the event the principal is incapacitated; or to become effective only in the event the principal becomes incompetent.

duress   The act of applying unlawful or improper pressure or influence to a person to gain his or her agreement to a contract.

duty of care   A legal and ethical obligation placed upon a director to act diligently and prudently in conducting the affairs of the corporation.

duty of loyalty   A legal and ethical obligation placed upon a director to administer to the affairs of the corporation with personal integrity, honesty, and candor.

E

easement   A right or interest in land granted to a party to make beneficial use of the land owned by another.

economic espionage act of 1996   A statute that makes the misappropriation or outright theft of trade secrets a federal crime.

Electronic Communications Privacy Act (ECPA)   A federal statute that addresses hacking and other forms of illegal conduct by making it a crime to gain unauthorized access to any communication that is stored on a computer system.

Electronic Funds Transfer Act (EFTA) of 1979   A federal statute that makes it an offense to use any device that is part of an electronic transfer mechanism to steal money, goods, or services or to alter data, interrupt wire transmissions, or use stolen codes or passwords, when the purpose of such activity is to obtain something of value unlawfully; and which established the rights, responsibilities, and liabilities of consumers in dealings with financial institutions.

electronic funds transfer (EFT)   A variety of electronic applications for handling money.

Electronic Signatures in Global and National Commerce Act (ESIGN) of 2000   A federal statute that provides that electronic contracts containing electronic signatures are just as enforceable as those that are printed on paper.

emancipation   In contract law, the condition that exists when minors are no longer under the control of their parents and are responsible for their contracts.

embezzlement   The wrongful taking of money or other property that has been entrusted to a person as a part of his or her job.

eminent domain   When ownership of real property is taken by the government and the previous owner is compensated at the fair market value of the property.

employee handbook   A manual published by an employer that contains the many policies of the firm.

employment at will   A doctrine that states that an employer may terminate an employee's employment at any time for a good reason, a bad reason, or no reason at all.

employment contract   An agreement that specifies that the employer agrees to pay, and the employee agrees to work, for a specified period of time at a specified salary.

endorsee   The person to whom a negotiable instrument is transferred.

endorsement   When the holder of commercial paper signs his or her name, with or without words, on the back of an instrument to transfer ownership to another.

endorser   The person who signs his or her name to a negotiable instrument.

entire contract   An agreement that is made up of two or more parts, in which each part is dependent upon the others.

environmental impact statement (EIS)   An assessment of the environmental consequences of a planned project that must be approved prior to commencement of any project with significant federal involvement (such as federal financing).

Environmental Protection Agency (EPA)   The federal agency that conducts environmental research, assists states and municipalities with grants and technical advice, and administers the federal pollution laws that cover businesses.

Equal Employment Opportunity Commission (EEOC)   A federal agency responsible for administering laws prohibiting discrimination in employment.

Equal Pay Act of 1963 (EPA)   A statute that prohibits any employer from engaging in wage discrimination based on sex.

ergonomics   A developing science that deals with designing workplaces to promote safety and health.

estoppel   A legal bar to using contradictory words or acts in asserting a claim against another.

ethics   The philosophical study of what is right and wrong, good and bad.

European Union (EU)   An entity that established a legal and political relationship among its members that promotes economic growth as well as social and cultural affiliations.

eviction   An action that denies the tenant the use of the premises.

exclusive remedy   A doctrine that states that an employee who sustains a work-related injury or illness can recover damages only through workers' compensation and may not file a lawsuit against his or her employer.

exculpatory clause   A statement in a contract that releases one party from liability resulting from his or her own negligence throughout the performance of a contract.

executed contract   A record of an agreement that has been completed in all respects by all the parties.

executive branch   The branch of a government body that consists of an elected executive, including his or her appointed staff.

executor   A personal representative named in a will to handle matters involving the estate of a deceased person.

executor   A personal representative named in the will.

executory contract   An agreement in which some future act or obligation remains to be performed under its terms.

existing goods   Goods that physically exist and are owned by the seller at the time of sale.

express authority   An agent's authority that the principal voluntarily and specifically sets forth as oral or written instructions in an agency agreement.

express contract   A contract that explicitly states the agreement of the parties, either orally or in writing.

express powers   Those that are specifically stated in the federal Constitution.

express warranty   An explicit, specifically stated promise.

extortion   The act of taking or demanding money or other property from someone by using force, threats of force, or economic harm.

F

failure to warn   The dereliction of a duty to advise purchasers and users of dangers inherent in a product.

fair housing act   A federal law that prohibits discrimination in housing on the basis of race, color, sex, familial status, national origin, religion, or handicap.

Fair Labor Standards Act of 1938 (FLSA)   The FLSA is a law that sets standards for the minimum age an employee can be, the minimum wages an employee can earn, and the rate at which an employee is paid if he or she works more than a certain number of hours in a given workweek.

fair use   Limited copying allowed when the copyrighted material is copied without authorization for use in connection with criticism, news reporting, research, education, or parody.

false pretenses   A broad category of crimes that involve activities intended to deceive others or to obtain goods by making false claims.

Family and Medical Leave Act of 1993 (FMLA)   A federal statute that provides eligible employees with the right to take up to 12 weeks of unpaid leave for personal medical reasons or to care for a child, spouse, or parent.

Federal Trade Commission (FTC)   The federal agency responsible for ensuring that advertising in the United States is truthful.

fee simple   When an owner of a freehold estate holds it absolutely.

felony   A crime punishable by death or imprisonment in a federal or state prison for a term exceeding one year.

fiduciary responsibility   A legal requirement that a person will exercise his or her authority while working under a duty of loyalty and a duty of care.

FOB destination   Title passes from the seller to the buyer when the goods are delivered to the buyer.

FOB shipping point   Title to goods passes from the seller to the buyer when the carrier receives the shipment and it is understood that the buyer will pay the transportation charges.

Food and Drug Administration (FDA)   The federal agency responsible for the safety of food and drugs sold in the United States.

forbearance   The promise to refrain from doing something that a party has a legal right to do.

Foreign Corrupt Practices Act (FCPA)   A federal statute designed to provide executives of American companies with rules and restrictions relating to paying persons in foreign countries to expedite business in these foreign nations.

Foreign Sovereign Immunities Act (FSIA)   A federal law passed in 1976 that established certain exceptions to foreign sovereign immunity.

forged check   A check that is signed by a person other than the drawer.

forgery   The act of fraudulently making or altering a note, check, draft, or some other document, causing the financial loss of another.

forgery   The false making or alteration of a writing with the intent to defraud.

formal contract   A specialty contract that is written and under seal.

franchisee   The independent company in a franchise agreement.

franchisor   The parent firm in a franchise agreement.

fraud   The intentional misstatement or nondisclosure of a material (essential) fact made by one party in an attempt to influence the actions of another party.

fraudulent transfer   A transaction in which the debtor sells property for an amount far below its market value.

freehold estate   An estate in which a person owns the land for life or forever.

frustration of purpose   A doctrine that states that where both parties know the purpose of a contract and, through no fault of either party, the reason for the contract no longer exists, the contract is terminated.

full faith and credit clause   A provision of the Constitution that mandates that each state respect and enforce both the judgments awarded by courts in other states, and the statutes and case law of other states.

full warranty   The promise that a defective product will be repaired without charge and within a reasonable time after a complaint has been made.

fungible goods   Goods that are generally sold by weight or measure.

future goods   Goods that do not exist at the time of the sales transaction but are expected to come into the possession of the seller.

G

gambling agreement   An agreement in which performance by one party depends on the occurrence of an uncertain event.

general agent   A person authorized to assume complete charge of his or her principal's business or who is entrusted with general authority to act for the principal in all business-related matters.

General Agreement on Tariffs and Trade (GATT)   An international agreement that provides a set of rules to ensure that there is no discrimination in trade by its signatories and also spells out a process for resolving international trade disputes.

general release   A written agreement in which an aggrieved party can discharge in whole or in part a claim resulting from an alleged breach of contract.

gift *in causa mortis*   A gift, given by a living person who expects to die from a known cause, that meets all of the legal requirements for a gift.

Good Samaritan laws   Statutes that provide medical professionals who render emergency care or treatment to injured individuals outside the scope of their regular employment immunity from malpractice lawsuits.

government-granted franchise   A legal monopoly in which a state or federal government grants a person or firm a license to conduct a specific business, usually an essential service.

gratuitous agent   One who acts on behalf of a principal without being paid.

gratuitous promise   A promise that does not require some benefit in return.

greenhouse effect   The rising of global temperatures due to the increased burning of fossil fuels that has loaded the atmosphere with heat-trapping carbon dioxide.

guarantor   The party who guarantees the promises assigned.

guaranty   A promise to pay the debts or settle the wrongdoings of another if he or she does not make settlement personally.

H

hacker   A person who gains unauthorized access to computers either for mischief or with criminal intent.

holder in due course   A holder who has taken a negotiable instrument in good faith and for value, before maturity, and without actual or constructive notice of any defects in the instrument.

holographic will   A will that is completely handwritten.

hotelkeeper   A person or firm in the business of offering lodgings or temporary shelter to guests and transients.

I

illusory promise   One that consists of an indefinite, open-ended statement purporting to be an agreement.

implied authority   The authority an agent reasonably assumes he or she has that relates to the express authority granted by the principal.

implied contract   A contract that does not explicitly state the agreement of the parties but in which the terms of the agreement can be inferred from the conduct of the parties, the customs of the trade, or the conditions or circumstances.

implied powers   Those that have arisen as a result of interpretation of the express powers by the courts.

implied warranty   A guarantee suggested or inferred from known facts and circumstances.

implied warranty of fitness for a particular purpose   The law's assumption that goods are fit for their intended use.

implied warranty of merchantability   The law's assumption that goods sold by a merchant/seller are fit to be sold and are adequate for the ordinary purposes for which such goods are sold.

impossibility of performance   When unforeseen circumstances make it impossible to fulfill the terms of a contract; in these cases, the contract is considered void.

incidental beneficiary   A person who will benefit as an indirect consequence of a contract, although that was not the intent of the contracting parties.

incompetent   Being unable to make binding contracts due to having an unsound mind and being unable to safeguard one's own interests and affairs.

independent contractor   One who contracts to do a job and who retains complete control over the methods employed to obtain completion.

infringement   Copying another's literary, creative, or artistic works without permission.

injunction   A permanent court order prohibiting the performance of a certain act.

insider trading   An illegal activity in which a person who has confidential information about a particular company purchases shares of the company's stock with the intention of selling these shares for a higher price when the information is released to the general public.

insolvency   The state that occurs when an individual's or business's liabilities exceed assets.

intellectual property   Personal property that includes knowledge, ways of doing things, and expressions of ideas.

inter vivos gift   A gift between the living that meets all of the legal requirements for a gift.

interest   The charge for using borrowed money, generally expressed as an annual percentage of the amount of the loan (principal).

intermediate scrutiny   A test that measures whether a particular statute is substantially related to an important government objective.

international law   The broad study of the legal systems of major countries, treaties, practices, tariffs and nontariff trade barriers, and import and export quotas.

International Monetary Fund (IMF)   An organization whose purpose is to maintain a stable environment for the economies and the currencies of its members by providing protection against large fluctuations in the value of one currency versus another.

Internet Tax Freedom Act   A federal statute that placed a moratorium on taxing Internet service providers on the services they provide to computer users.

interstate commerce   Trade between two or more states.

intestate   The state in which a person dies without a will.

invitation to trade   An announcement published for the purpose of creating interest and attracting a response by many people. It is not considered a valid offer because it does not contain sufficient words of commitment to sell.

involuntary filing   A form of bankruptcy that occurs when creditors pressure a debtor to file.

irrevocable agency   An agency contract that cannot be terminated by a principal in which the agent has an interest in the subject matter of the agency in addition to the remuneration that he or she receives for services.

J

joint and several liability   Legal exposure such that a person with a claim against a general partnership can elect to sue either all of the partners together or any individual partner whom he or she chooses.

joint tenancy   When two or more persons own equal shares of personal property with right of survivorship.

joint venture   An activity in which individuals become partners for only a short period of time or for only a single project.

judicial branch   The branch of a government body that determines if there have been violations of the law and interprets the law if there are questions about what the law means in particular situations.

judicial review   The process of deciding if a law is contrary to the Constitution.

jurisdiction   The authority of a court, as granted by a constitution or legislative act, to hear and decide cases.

L

landlord   The owner of real property who gives up his or her right of possession.

larceny   The act of taking and carrying away the personal property of another without the right to do so.

lease The document in which the terms of a rental agreement are written.

leasehold estate An estate in which a person has an interest in real property that comes from a lease.

legacy A gift of money by will.

legality of purpose The requirement that the intent of a contract be legal for the contract to be enforceable.

legislative branch The branch of a government body that consists of elected representatives who have the responsibility for passing laws that represent the will of the people.

lemon laws Statutes that provide remedies to consumers for products such as automobiles that repeatedly fail to meet certain standards of quality and performance.

lessee The tenant in a lease agreement.

lessor The landlord in a lease agreement.

liable Being judged legally responsible.

libel The spreading of damaging statements in written form, including pictures, cartoons, and effigies.

life estate A freehold estate in which a person has an ownership interest only for his or her lifetime.

limited liability company A relatively new organizational form available in most states that provides all of the owners with limited liability.

limited liability Legal exposure in which an owner of a business is not personally liable for all of the debts and obligations of the business.

limited partnership A business in which there are one or more general partners and one or more limited partners.

limited warranty A written warranty that does not meet the minimum requirements of a full warranty.

liquidated damages clause A statement wherein damages are explicitly set in the event one of the parties breaches an agreement.

liquidation A process in which assets are sold to obtain cash.

living will A document in which a person directs his or her physician and/or health proxy to forgo certain extraordinary medical procedures in especially dire circumstances.

lockout An action by which an employer does not allow employees to return to work in the event a collective bargaining agreement is not reached.

loss of consortium In a lawsuit by a spouse, a request for damages for loss of companionship.

M

Magnuson-Moss Warranty Act A federal statute that addresses many different kinds of abuses to consumers relating to warranties.

mailbox rule A rule that states that an acceptance sent via the postal system or by courier is effective when sent.

malpractice A professional's improper or immoral conduct in the performance of his or her duties through carelessness or lack of knowledge.

Master Settlement Agreement A contract in which the major cigarette manufacturers in the United States agreed not to engage in certain advertising strategies.

material alteration A deliberate change or alteration of an important element in a written contract that affects the rights or obligations of the parties.

means test A complex formula that measures an individual's income relative to the median income of the people in the state where he or she resides.

mediation A process for dispute resolution in which a neutral third party meets with the disputants in order to have them come to some form of settlement agreement.

memorandum A written contract or agreement.

merchant An individual who deals in goods of the kind being sold in the ordinary course of business, or who presents himself or herself as having the skills or knowledge relating to the goods.

minor A person who has not yet reached the age of majority.

misdemeanor A less serious crime that is generally punishable by a fine and/or a prison sentence of not more than one year.

misrepresentation A misstatement of a material fact that results in inducing another to enter into an agreement to his or her injury.

mistake A belief that is not in accord with the facts.

mitigate The duty of a landlord to make reasonable efforts to reduce his or her losses resulting from a tenant's abandonment.

mitigate The obligation of the injured party to protect the other party from any unnecessary damages.

monopoly power A situation in which one or more people or firms control the market in a particular area or for a particular product.

moral consideration Something that a person is not legally bound to do but that he or she may feel bound to do because of love, friendship, honor, sympathy, conscience, or other reason.

moral law The "law" concerned with the unenforceable obligations that people have to one another.

morals Beliefs about behavior as judged by society.

mutual agreement The state of mind that exists between an offeror and an offeree when a valid offer has been accepted, and the parties know what the terms are and have agreed to be bound by them. Mutual agreement is also known as "a meeting of the minds."

mutual-benefit bailment A bailment in which both the bailee and the bailor derive some benefit, and, as a result, each has rights and duties.

N

National Environmental Policy Act (NEPA) of 1970 A federal statute that requires that any project with significant federal involvement (such as federal financing) must have an approved environmental impact statement prior to the commencement of any work on the project.

National Highway Traffic Safety Administration (NHTSA) The federal agency responsible for the safety of automobiles sold in the United States.

National Labor Relations Board (NLRB) A federal agency responsible for administering laws relating to labor unions.

necessaries Goods and services that are essential to a minor's health and welfare.

negligence *per se* Negligence *per se* occurs when a defendant in a case of negligence has violated a law that was enacted in order to prevent the type of injury that occurred.

negligence The failure to exercise necessary care to protect others from unreasonable risk of harm.

negotiability   The ability to be transferred freely from one person to another and be accepted as readily as cash.

negotiable instrument   An unconditional written promise to pay, or pay to the order of another party, a certain sum of money on demand or at a definite time.

negotiable warehouse receipt   Proof of ownership that can be used to transfer title from one person to another.

nexus   The link or tie that a location must have to a sale in order for the location to collect sales tax.

nonnegotiable warehouse receipt   A receipt for the goods to be stored.

North American Free Trade Agreement (NAFTA)   An economic agreement aimed at promoting and facilitating trade among the United States, Canada, and Mexico.

novation   A situation in which all parties to a contract agree to a significant change to a contract.

nuisance   An unlawful interference with the enjoyment of life or property.

nuncupative will   An oral will.

O

Occupational Safety and Health Act of 1970   A federal statute designed to promote safety and health in the workplace.

Occupational Safety and Health Administration (OSHA)   The federal agency that administers the many provisions of the Occupational Safety and Health Act of 1970.

offer   A proposal made by one party (the offeror) to another person (the offeree) that indicates a willingness to enter into a contract.

offeree   The person to whom a proposal is made.

offeror   The person making a proposal.

option contract   A contract that has a provision to keep an offer open for a certain period of time.

oral contract   An agreement that is not in writing or signed by the parties.

order bill of lading   A receipt for goods to be shipped that is negotiable and is proof of title that can be used to transfer title from one person to another.

order instrument   An item of commercial paper that contains the key words of negotiability, "pay to the order of," or their equivalent.

ordinance   A law that is passed by a local government, such as a city council.

P

parol evidence rule   The rule that any spoken or written words in conflict with what the written contract states cannot be introduced as evidence in a court of law.

particle trespass   The unauthorized entry of pollutants onto another person's land or water.

partnership   A business owned and operated by two or more persons.

past consideration   A promise to repay someone for a benefit after it has been received.

patent   A valid, government-granted protection awarded to inventors that gives the patent holder the exclusive right to manufacture, use, and sell the invention.

periodic tenancy   A possession interest in which the lease continues for successive periods for the same length of time.

perjury   The crime of intentionally giving false oral or written statements under oath in a judicial proceeding after having sworn to tell the truth.

personal defense   A defense against payment of commercial paper that may be used against any party except a holder in due course.

personal property   Tangible and intangible property that is not real property.

personal representative   The person responsible for settling the affairs of the decedent.

personal-service contract   A contract in which services that require a unique skill, talent, ability, and so forth are provided by a specific person.

phishing   The practice of tricking individuals into disclosing personal information via e-mail.

plaintiff   The party who begins a lawsuit by filing a complaint in the appropriate court.

pledge   A promise to donate money to a church, temple, mosque, hospital, college, cultural institution, or other charitable organization.

Ponzi scheme   A type of securities fraud in which large gains are promised to investors, but in reality, newer investments are used to provide a return on older investments.

postdated check   One that is dated later than the date on which the check is written.

power of attorney   An instrument in writing by which one person, as principal, appoints another person as agent and confers the authority to perform certain specified acts on behalf of the principal.

precedent   A model case that a court can follow when facing a similar situation.

preexisting duty   An obligation that a party is already bound to by law or by some other agreement. The party may not use this as consideration in a new contract.

preferential payment   A transfer of funds in which the debtor gives favorable treatment to one creditor over another.

Pregnancy Discrimination Act of 1978   A federal statute designed to protect individuals from illegal discrimination in employment on the basis of pregnancy.

presentment   When the holder of a note tenders it to the maker and demands payment, or shows drafts to the drawer and requests its acceptance or payment, on or after the maturity date at the place stated in the instrument.

primary market   The place where a corporation (an issuer) sells its securities to the public.

principal   A person who authorizes an agent to act on his or her behalf and subject to his or her control.

priority debts   Debts deemed sufficiently important under Chapter 13 of the bankruptcy law that they must be paid in full.

private nuisance   A nuisance that impacts private property.

probable cause   A reasonable belief that a prudent police officer must have that a suspect has committed, is committing, or is about to commit a crime, thereby giving the officer the authority to conduct a search.

probate court   The court responsible for accepting a will that meets all statutory requirements and for supervising the operation of a will.

procedural due process A Constitutional mandate that all persons affected by a legal proceeding receive notice of its subject matter, time, and place and that these proceedings be conducted by a judge who is fair and impartial.

product flaw An abnormality or a condition that was not intended and that makes a product more dangerous than it would have been had it been as intended.

product liability The liability of a manufacturer or seller for injury to purchasers, users, and third parties.

professional A person who does highly specialized work that depends on special abilities, education, experience, and knowledge.

promisee In the making of a contract, the party to whom a promise is made.

promisor In the making of a contract, the party who makes a promise.

promissory note A written note or letter in which one person promises to pay a certain amount of money to another at a definite time.

promissory note A written promise to pay a specified sum of money.

proper form The requirement that the form of a contract be correct for the terms of the contract to be enforceable.

prospectus A document that provides relevant and important information about a company, its businesses, and its prospects to prospective investors.

proxy A legal document that transfers the right to vote in a corporate election to another person.

public figure A well-known person who implicitly allows others to write about him or her in newspapers and magazines and discuss his or her conduct on television and radio.

public nuisance A nuisance that impacts public property.

public offer A general offer to the public at large.

puffing A general expression of opinion, typically in a sales context, that is used to persuade a prospective purchaser to buy. It does not constitute a misrepresentation of material text.

Q

qualified endorsement An endorsement in which the endorser avoids liability for payment even if the maker or drawer defaults on the instrument.

quiet enjoyment The right to use the leased premises without unreasonable interferences from the landlord or third parties.

quorum The minimum number of shares necessary to be present at a corporate meeting in order for action to be taken.

quota systems Restrictions on the numbers and kinds of products that may enter into a nation.

R

raised check A check on which the amount has been raised by the payee or bearer.

ratified An approval of a contract made by a minor after reaching majority.

rational basis A test that measures whether the legislature had a reasonable, and not an arbitrary, basis for enacting a particular statute.

real defense A defense against payment of commercial paper that claims the instrument was void from the beginning.

real property The ground and everything permanently attached to it, including land, buildings, trees, and shrubs; the airspace above and the ground below the land also are included.

reasonable person A completely fictitious individual who is assumed to have the judgment and skill one would expect from a person with the strengths and limitations of the person whose behavior is being judged.

rejection The express or implied refusal by an offeree to accept an offer.

remote party A person with the right to make legitimate sales as a representative of the owner of the goods, although he or she is not a titleholder.

reorganization bankruptcy The name given to a Chapter 13 bankruptcy, in which the debtor agrees to pay back all or a portion of his or her debts over a period of three to five years.

replevin An action to recover possession of specific goods wrongfully taken or detained by another.

request for proposal A request for an offer or an invitation to negotiate that can be accepted or rejected by the person calling for a bid.

respondeat superior A legal doctrine that holds that the acts of an employee committed while performing duties are considered the acts of the employer.

restraining order A court order prohibiting the performance of a certain act. In some states, a restraining order is temporary.

restraint of trade A limitation on the full exercise of doing business with others.

restrictive covenant An agreement in which the employee agrees not to work in similar employment within a certain geographic area or within a specified period of time.

restrictive endorsement An endorsement with a signature to which words have been added restricting further endorsement of the instrument.

revocation The calling back of an offer by the offeror before the offer has been accepted or rejected.

RICO One of the most successful laws used to combat white-collar crime, RICO prohibits an organization's employees from engaging in a pattern of racketeering activity.

robbery The taking of property in the possession of another person against that person's will and under threat of bodily harm.

Robinson-Patman Act A federal statute that makes it unlawful to discriminate, directly or indirectly, in matters involving product pricing, advertising, and promotion.

S

sale on approval A contract for the sale of goods subject to the buyer's approval.

sale or return An agreement whereby the seller will accept the return of goods at the request of the buyer to maintain goodwill, rather than because the seller is legally obliged to accept the returned goods.

Sarbanes-Oxley A federal statute that placed an onus on upper management to monitor closely the financial dealings and disclosures of their firms and that established a board to oversee accounting practices in the United States.

secondary market The place where one member of the public sells securities to another member of the public.

secured debt A loan for which a specific asset is used as collateral.

Securities Act of 1933 The federal law covering the sale of securities (stocks, bonds, and other forms of investment) in the primary market.

Securities and Exchange Commission(SEC) The federal agency responsible for administering the statutes relating to the sale and trading of securities.

Securities Exchange Act of 1934 The federal law covering the trading of securities (stocks, bonds, and other forms of investment) in the secondary market.

securities fraud A fraud that occurs when a person or company provides false information to potential investors to influence their decisions to buy or sell securities.

settlor A person who sets up a trust while still alive.

severalty Ownership of a particular piece of property that is held by one person.

sexual harassment Unwelcome sexual attention, whether verbal or physical, that affects an employee's job condition or creates a hostile working environment.

Sherman Antitrust Act A federal statute that forbids certain agreements that tend to unreasonably inhibit competition, fix prices, allocate territories, or limit production.

simple contract An informal contract made without seal—even though the subject matter of the contract may be extremely complex and may involve huge amounts of money.

slander The spreading of damaging words or ideas about a person, directly or indirectly, in all other forms not considered libel.

slowdown An action wherein employees report to work but intentionally decrease their productivity.

sole proprietorship A business owned and operated by one person.

spam Unsolicited e-mails sent for commercial purposes.

special agent A person delegated to act only in a particular transaction, under definite instructions, and with specific limits on the scope of his or her authority.

special endorsement An endorsement in which the payee specifies the person to whom, or to whose order, it is to be paid.

specific performance A court order directing a person to perform—or not perform—as he or she agreed to do in a contract.

specific performance An order that requires the seller to deliver the goods specified in the contract or face being held in contempt of court.

spoofing A practice in which a legitimate website is reproduced to fool users into thinking that they are connected to a trusted site.

spyware Software that can change a computer's security settings or steal a victim's personal information, such as e-mail addresses, bank account numbers, and credit card numbers.

stakeholders People or groups who may be affected by a firm's actions or decisions.

stale check A check presented more than six months after its date.

stare decisis The practice of relying on previous decisions in which similar disputes arose.

Statute of Frauds A law requiring certain contracts to be in writing to be enforceable.

statute of limitations A legal time limit in which to initiate a lawsuit.

statutory law The field of law involving statutes, which are laws passed by Congress or by state legislatures.

stop-payment order An instruction a depositor gives to his or her bank not to pay a particular check.

stoppage in transit When the buyer is insolvent, the right of an unpaid seller to stop goods in transit and order the carrier to hold them for the seller.

straight bill of lading A nonnegotiable receipt for goods to be shipped, acknowledging that such goods have been received and indicating agreement that the goods will be transported to the destination specified.

straight or liquidation bankruptcy The name given to a Chapter 7 bankruptcy, in which a trustee collects the debtor's nonexempt property, sells it, and dispenses the proceeds.

strict liability The doctrine under which persons may be liable for injuries to others whether or not they have been negligent or committed an intentional tort. This establishes liability without the necessity of proving fault.

strict scrutiny A test that measures whether the legislature had a compelling interest for enacting a particular statute.

subchapter S corporation A corporation that is taxed as a partnership.

subculture An ethnic, economic, regional, religious, or social group with attitudes or behaviors that distinguish it from others within a larger culture.

sublease A transfer of the tenant's interest in part of the term of the lease and/or part of the premises.

subpoena An order requiring the recipient to appear at a legal proceeding to provide testimony.

substantial performance When a party to a contract, in good faith, executes all of the promised terms and conditions of the contract with the exception of minor details that do not affect the real intent of their agreement.

substantial similarity test A test that is used to determine whether an ordinary reasonable observer comparing two works would have to conclude that the work being questioned was copied from the other.

substantive due process A Constitutional mandate that government not unreasonably interfere with an individual's life, liberty, or property rights.

Sunday agreement A contract made on a Sunday; in a small number of jurisdictions, such contracts are invalid unless they are ratified on a weekday.

Superfund A federal statute (also known as the Comprehensive Environmental Response, Compensation, and Liability Act) that regulates the dumping of waste onto land.

supremacy clause A provision of the Constitution that requires state judges to follow federal law in the event of a conflict with state law.

T

tangible personal property   Personal property that can be moved.

tariff   A form of tax, or other restrictions, on imports or exports to attain economic results, such as protecting domestic industries or facilitating the production of certain crops.

tenancy at sufferance   A tenancy that exists only when a tenant wrongfully extends his or her tenancy beyond the term agreed upon.

tenancy at will   A possession interest in which no specific time of lease is agreed upon.

tenancy by the entirety   A form of joint ownership of property by husband and wife in which both have a right to the entire property and the right of survivorship.

tenancy for years   The most common type of possession interest in which the lease is for a specific period of time.

tenancy in common   A form of joint ownership of property by two or more persons in which any owner's interest can be sold, transferred, or inherited.

tenant   The person who agrees to pay for the use of real property.

tender of goods   An offer to provide the goods agreed upon that is considered evidence of a party's willingness to fulfill the terms of a contract.

tender of payment   A money offer of payment of an obligation.

tender of performance   An offer to perform that is considered evidence of a party's willingness to fulfill the terms of a contract.

term insurance   A form of pure life insurance with no savings feature.

termination by lapse of time   When an opportunity to form a contract ends because the offeree fails to accept an offer within the time specified.

testamentary capacity   The requirement that a testator be of sound mind and legal age.

testator   The person who makes a will.

The USA Patriot Act   A federal statute that lowers the standards required for law enforcement officials and government agents to monitor e-mail and personal electronic information, allows increased government cybersurveillance, and makes it easier to charge persons with serious computer-related crimes.

third-party beneficiary   A person who is not a party to a contract but is intended by the contracting parties to benefit as a consequence of a contract.

title insurance   A form of insurance that assures the buyer of real property that there are no other claims to the ownership.

title   Ownership and the right to possess something.

Title VII   The portion of the Civil Rights Act of 1964 that deals with discrimination in employment.

tort   A private wrong that injures another person's physical well-being, property, or reputation.

touting   An activity in which an investor who owns shares of a company's stock posts notices online—in chat rooms, on web pages, on blogs, and elsewhere—that indicate that the value of the stock will increase.

trade dress   A distinctive, nonfunctional feature that distinguishes a merchant's or manufacturer's goods or services from those of another.

trade libel   Defamation that deals with an individual's title to property, or to the quality or conduct of a business.

trade sanctions   Legal restrictions, such as embargoes, placed on trade to achieve desired political results.

trade secret   Specialized knowledge associated with a particular business, including information gained during employment about such matters as manufacturing processes, practices, devices, customer lists, and other confidential information.

trademark   Any word, name, symbol, or device or combination thereof adopted and used by a manufacturer or merchant to identify his or her goods and distinguish them from goods manufactured or sold by others.

transient   A guest whose stay is relatively uncertain.

transnational institutions   Organizations whose purpose is to maintain legal and economic order in trade.

traveler's check   A certified check, useful when traveling in foreign countries, that is issued in denominations of $10 or more by certain banks, travel agencies, and financial services companies.

treason   The levying of war against the United States, or the giving of aid and comfort to the nation's enemies.

trust   A device or mechanism that permits personal or real property to be held by one party, the trustee, for the benefit of another, the beneficiary.

trustee   A person who is entrusted with the management and control of another's property or the rights associated with that property.

U

unconscionable contract   A contract that is so one-sided that it is oppressive and gives unfair advantage to one of the parties.

undue influence   The improper use of excessive pressure by the dominant member of a confidential relationship to convince the weaker party to enter a contract that greatly benefits the dominant party.

unemployment insurance   Unemployment insurance provides financial stability, in the form of unemployment compensation, to eligible employees who lose their jobs.

Uniform Commercial Code (UCC)   A set of laws that govern various commercial transactions and that are designed to bring uniformity to the laws of the states.

unlicensed transaction   An agreement with a person who does not have a required license.

unlimited liability   Legal exposure in which an owner of a business is personally liable for all of the debts and obligations of the business.

use tax   A tax to a consumer who uses goods within a state, as opposed to buying them within the state.

usury   Charging interest higher than the law permits.

V

valid contract   An agreement resulting in an obligation that is legally enforceable.

values   Beliefs or standards considered worthwhile, and from which a society derives its moral rules.

vicarious liability   The concept of laying responsibility or blame upon one person for the actions of another.

vicarious negligence   Charging a negligent act of one person to another.

virus   Instructions hidden in software with the potential to cause significant damage to both hardware and software.

void contract   A contract that is not enforceable from the beginning because it lacks one of the requirements of a valid contract.

voidable contract   An agreement that can be rejected by one of the parties for a legally acceptable reason.

voluntary filing   A form of bankruptcy that occurs when the debtor himself or herself files a bankruptcy petition.

W

warehouse receipt   Much like a bill of lading except that the goods are not being shipped but merely stored.

warehouser   A person or firm that provides storage facilities.

warranty   A guarantee or promise made by the manufacturer or seller that the goods or services offered really are what they claim to be, or that goods or services are what a reasonable person has a right to expect.

warranty of habitability   An implied warranty in which the landlord guarantees that the premises are reasonably fit for occupancy and that there are no defects that would impair the health, safety, or well-being of the occupants.

whistleblower   An employee who discloses to the government, media, or upper management that the company is involved in wrongful or illegal activities.

white-collar crime   A term used to describe various crimes that typically do not involve force or violence committed by and against businesses.

whole life insurance   A relatively costly form of life insurance protection that includes a savings feature.

wildcat strike   A strike without the union's consent.

will   A person's declaration of how he or she wishes property to be distributed upon his or her death.

winding-up period   The time after dissolution of a partnership during which there is an orderly liquidation of the partnership assets.

without recourse   A phrase used to indicate a qualified endorsement.

workers' compensation   A type of insurance that allows employees to recover damages for work-related injuries and illnesses without having to prove negligence on the part of the employer.

World Bank   The popular name given to the International Bank for Reconstruction and Development, an organization that works closely with the International Monetary Fund to ensure that developing countries have access to funds to stimulate their economies.

World Intellectual Property Organization (WIPO)   A specialized agency of the United Nations that administers numerous treaties concerning protection of intellectual property rights.

World Trade Organization (WTO)   An organization with responsibility for overseeing the implementation of all multinational trade agreements negotiated now or in the future.

worm   A type of virus that replicates itself and uses memory but cannot attach itself to other programs.

written contract   An agreement that is reduced to writing on a permanent surface.

wrongful possession   When property, such as stolen goods, is transferred without permission of the owner.

Credits

Part One

Part opening, **page 1:** © Hisham F. Ibrahim/Getty Images/DAL; Chapter 1, **2–3:** © Rubberball/Getty Images/DAL; **4:** © Eyewire (Photodisc)/PunchStock)/DAL; **6:** © Comstock/PunchStock/DAL; **7:** © Jim Sugar/Corbis; **9:** © MC3 Dylan McCord/US Navy/DAL; Chapter 2, **20–21:** © moodboard/Corbis; **23:** © Reuters/Corbis; **24:** © Getty Images/DAL; **28:** © Tom Fox/Dallas Morning News/Corbis; Chapter 3, **36–37:** © Ocean/Corbis: **38:** © Brand X Pictures/DAL; **41:** © Ingram Publishing/DAL; **42:** © 2007 Getty Images, Inc./DAL; **44:** © Adam Crowley/Getty Images/DAL; Chapter 4, **52–53:** © Photographer's Choice/Getty Images/DAL; **55:** © Ingram Publishing/SuperStock/DAL; **58:** © Image Source/PunchStock/DAL; **64:** © Ingram Publishing/DAL; Chapter 5, **72–73:** © Tetra Images/Corbis; **77 top:** © Rob Melnychuk/Getty Images/DAL; **77 bottom:** © The McGraw-Hill Companies, Inc./John Flournoy, photographer/DAL; Chapter 6, **90–91:** © A3463 Rainer Jensen/dpa/Corbis; **93:** © Getty Images/DAL; **95:** © Photodisc/Getty Images/DAL; **97:** © Kitt Cooper-Smith/Alamy/DAL.

Part Two

Part opening, **page 105:** © Stockbyte/Getty Images/DAL; Chapter 7, **106–07:** © John Lund/Drew Kelly/Blend Images LLC/DAL; **110:** © Stockbyte/Getty Images/DAL; **114:** © Royalty-Free/Corbis/DAL; **115:** © Comstock Images/Alamy/DAL; Chapter 8, **124–25:** © Ryan McVay/Getty Images/DAL; **128:** © Royalty-Free/Corbis/DAL; **130:** Photo © by Scott Bauer/USDA/DAL; **132:** © James Hardy/Palo Alto/DAL; Chapter 9, **140–41:** © Jupiterimages/Getty Images/DAL; **143:** © Ryan McVay/Getty Images/DAL; **144:** © Photodisc Collection/Getty Images/DAL; **145:** © Jupiterimages/Brand X Pictures/Alamy/DAL; Chapter 10, **154–55:** © Jim Arbogas/Getty Images/DAL; **159:** © Michael Owen Baker/ZUMA Press/Corbis; **161:** © Ingram Publishing/DAL; Chapter 11, **170–71:** © Imagesource/PictureQuest/DAL; **173:** © LWA/Dann Tardif/Blend Images LLC/DAL; **176:** © Masterfile/DAL; Chapter 12, **184–85:** © Ingram Publishing/DAL; **187:** © Brand X Pictures/DAL; **189:** © Ingram Publishing/DAL; **192 :** © The McGraw-Hill Companies, Inc./Jill Braaten, photographer/DAL; Chapter 13, **200–01:** © Design Pics/PunchStock/DAL; **205:** © Jack Star/PhotoLink/Getty Images/DAL; **206:** © Phillip Spears/Getty Images/DAL; Chapter 14, **216–17:** © Imagesource/Getty Images/DAL; **220:** © Photodisc/Getty Images/DAL; **221:** © Royalty-Free/Corbis/DAL; Chapter 15, **232–233:** © Brand X

Pictures/DAL; **236:** © Stockbyte/Getty Images/DAL; **240:** © Fuse/Getty Images/DAL.

Part Three

Part opening, **page 251:** © Frank and Helena/Cultura/Getty Images/DAL; Chapter 16, **252–53:** © Radius Images/Getty Images/DAL; **256 :** © Alistair Berg/Photodisc/Getty Images/DAL; **259:** © Blend Images/Getty Images/DAL; Chapter 17, **268–69:** © Juice Images/Corbis; **271:** © Royalty-Free/Corbis/DAL; **273:** © Sean Justice/Corbis; **277:** © Comstock Images/Alamy/DAL; Chapter 18, **288–89:** © Getty Images/Photodisc/DAL; **292:** © PhotoLink/Getty Images/DAL; **296:** © Beverley Lu Latter/Alamy/DAL; Chapter 19, **302–03:** © Banana Stock/age fotostock/DAL; **307:** © Ronnie Kaufman/Blend Images LLC/DAL; **310:** © PhotoAlto/Veer/Corbis; Chapter 20, **320–21:** © ColorBlind Images/Blend Images LLC/DAL; **322:** © Ingram Publishing/SuperStock/DAL; **325:** © The McGraw-Hill Companies, Inc./Andrew Resek, photographer/DAL; **326:** © Photodisc/Getty Images/DAL; Chapter 21, **336–37:** © Royalty-Free/Corbis/DAL; **340:** © Stockbyte/Getty Images/DAL; **345:** © Uppercut RF/Getty Images/DAL.

Part Four

Part opening, **page 353:** © Photodisc/Getty Images/DAL; Chapter 22, **354–55:** © Digital Vision/Getty Images/DAL; **362:** © Stockbyte/Getty Images/DAL; **363:** © Janis Christie/Getty Images/DAL; **365:** © Digital Vision/Getty Images/DAL; Chapter 23, **374–75:** © Royalty-Free/Corbis/DAL; **385:** © Photodisc/Getty Images/DAL.

Part Five

Part opening, **page 393:** © Brand X Pictures/DAL; Chapter 24, **394–95:** © M Stock/Alamy/DAL; **397:** © John Lund/Sam Diephuis/Blend Images/DAL; **399:** © T. O'Keefe/PhotoLink/Getty Images/DAL; **404 top:** Brand X Pictures/DAL; **404 bottom:** © Stockbyte/Getty Images/DAL; Chapter 25, **414–415:** © Banana Stock/PunchStock/DAL; **416:** © The McGraw-Hill Companies, Inc./Andrew Resek, photographer/DAL; **419:** © Ingram Publishing/DAL; **421:** © The McGraw-Hill Companies, Inc./Andrew Resek, photographer/DAL; Chapter 26, **430–31:** © Ingram Publishing/DAL; **433:** © Comstock/Jupiterimages/DAL; **437:** © Royalty-Free/Corbis/DAL; **438:** © Image Source/Jupiterimages/DAL; Chapter 27, **448–49:** © Thinkstock/Getty Images/DAL; **451:** © Ingram Publishing/DAL; **453:** © ColorBlind Images/Blend Images LLC/DAL.

Part Six

Part opening, **page 465:** © ColorBlind Images/Blend Images LLC/DAL; Chapter 28, **466–67:** © Photodisc/Getty Images/DAL; **471:** © The McGraw-Hill Companies, Inc./Jill Braaten, photographer/DAL; **474:** © Ingram Publishing/DAL; Chapter 29, **486–87:** © Ryan McVay/Getty Images/DAL; **489:** © Thomas Barwick/Getty Images/DAL; **492:** © Royalty-Free/Corbis/DAL; **495:** © Jupiterimages/Getty Images/DAL; Chapter 30, **504–05:** © Digital Vision/PunchStock/DAL; **507:** © Ryan McVay/Getty Images/DAL; **510:** © The McGraw-Hill Companies, Inc./John Flournoy, photographer/DAL; **513:** © Randy Albritton/Getty Images/DAL.

Part Seven

Part opening, **page 521:** © Ryan McVay/Getty Images/DAL; Chapter 31, **522–23:** © Winston Davidian/Photodisc/DAL; **525:** © Ingram Publishing/DAL; **528:** © Getty Images/DAL; Chapter 32, **536–537:** © Steve Cole/Getty Images/DAL; **539:** © image 100/Corbis/DAL; **540:** © Ingram Publishing/DAL; **542:** © Keith Brofsky/Getty Images/DAL; Chapter 33, **552–53:** © Royalty-Free/Corbis/DAL; **556:** © Studiohio/DAL; **558:** © Image Source/Getty Images/DAL; **560:** © Getty Images/Digital Vision/DAL; Chapter 34, **568–69:** © Tom Grill/Corbis; **571:** © Digital Vision/PunchStock/DAL; **574:** © Ingram Publishing/DAL; **575:** © Kent Knudson/PhotoLink/Getty Images/DAL; Chapter 35, **584–85:** © Banana Stock/DAL; **587:** © Getty Images/DAL; **588:** © Image Source/DAL; **591:** © Charles Gullang/zefa/Corbis/DAL; Chapter 36, **600–01:** © Visions of America/Joe Sohm/Photodisc/Getty Images/DAL; **602:** © Neil Beer/Getty Images/DAL; **604:** © Stockbyte/Punch Stock/Getty Images/DAL; **608:** © Digital Vision/Punch Stock/Getty Images/DAL.

Index

Z